Maryland Deponents

Volume 3

1634-1776

Henry C. Peden, Jr.

HERITAGE BOOKS
2008

HERITAGE BOOKS
AN IMPRINT OF HERITAGE BOOKS, INC.

Books, CDs, and more—Worldwide

For our listing of thousands of titles see our website at
www.HeritageBooks.com

Published 2008 by
HERITAGE BOOKS, INC.
Publishing Division
100 Railroad Ave. #104
Westminster, Maryland 21157

Copyright © 2000 Henry C. Peden, Jr.

All rights reserved. No part of this book may be reproduced or transmitted in any form or by any means, electronic or mechanical, including photocopying, recording or by any information storage and retrieval system without written permission from the author, except for the inclusion of brief quotations in a review.

International Standard Book Numbers
Paperbound: 978-1-58549-612-9
Clothbound: 978-0-7884-7729-4

INTRODUCTION

Deponents are those persons who are called upon by order of the court to give testimony taken upon interrogatories intended to be used upon the trial of a civil action or criminal prosecution. The answers and statements of a deponent, which are taken under oath or affirmation and a written transcript made thereof, is called a deposition. It is essentially a discovery device by which one party asks questions of the other party or of a witness of the other party.

Deponents usually stated their age, or approximate age, and residence, and then would tell the circumstances that surrounded a particular event that they either witnessed or of which they had personal knowledge. Sometimes they would identify family members, friends, and other acquaintances in an attempt to clarify disputes over such things as land boundaries, assaults and batteries, and family affairs and relationships. During the colonial period these disputes were under the jurisdiction of the Provincial Court of Maryland. It should be noted that while European American colonists were deposed and sworn or affirmed under oath, Native Americans (then referred to as Indians) were examined and interrogated, but not sworn; nonetheless, within the scope of this book, all were considered to be deponents.

Depositions are very important sources for genealogical and historical information. In 1991 I compiled my first volume of these records entitled *Maryland Deponents, 1634-1799* and followed it in 1992 with a second volume entitled *More Maryland Deponents, 1716-1799*. The first volume covered the records of the Provincial and Chancery Courts of Maryland and also some of the early county court records. I drew heavily from the work of William F. Creagar and Dr. Christopher Johnston, which also included depositions from the voluminous *Archives of Maryland*. My second volume of deponents was restricted to only those counties that maintained separate record books on land commissions. At that time I did not abstract the depositions contained in the more extensive land records series found in each county.

This third volume primarily contains information gleaned from depositions found in county land records during the colonial period (1634-1776). Depositions abstracted by Robert W. Barnes from selected ejectment papers have also been published with his kind permission. Additionally, this book contains much more material from the *Archives of Maryland* which had been previously overlooked by Creager and Johnston. I have included not only depositions by colonists, but also examinations and interrogations of colonists and Native Americans which they had omitted.

It should be noted that some of the codes used in my first volume were contrived by Creagar and Johnston and some have not been deciphered in spite of a valiant effort by Patricia V. Melville and F. Edward Wright in 1991. However, one mistake that I recently discovered is in source codes P and PL which were reported as being Baltimore County Court (Land Records) 2 and 3. These are actually codes PC and PL which are not the aforesaid land records, but instead refer to Maryland Chancery Court records maintained in bound volumes at the Maryland State Archives.

In addition to the depositions herein, one should also consult *Abstracts of Chancery Court Records of Maryland, 1669-1782* by Debbie Hooper (Family Line Publications, 1996) as well as articles published in the *Maryland Genealogical Society Bulletin* from time to time that mention deponents, especially the work of Robert W. Barnes.

Since every surname has been cross-referenced within the text, there is no need for a separate index to this book. Each entry has been coded as to the source for the information and the volume and/or page number(s) for each source is enclosed in brackets. The codes are as follows:

AALR = Anne Arundel County Land Records
ARMD = *Archives of Maryland* (published)
BALR = Baltimore County Land Records
    (includes present day Harford)
CELR = Cecil County Land Records
CHLR = Charles County Land Records
CMSP = Calendar of Maryland State Papers
DOLR = Dorchester County Land Records
    (includes present day Caroline)
FRLR = Frederick County Land Records
    (includes present day counties of
    Montgomery, Washington, Allegany)
KEEJ = Kent County Ejectment Papers
KELR = Kent County Land Records
PGLR = Prince George's County Land Records
QAEJ = Queen Anne's Ejectment Papers
QALR = Queen Anne's County Land Records
TAEJ = Talbot County Ejectment Papers
TALR = Talbot County Land Records
aet. = *aetatis* (age or approximate age)
dep. = deposed (and/or interrogated)
n.a. = no age given in deposition

prob.= probably
q.v. = *quod vide* ("which see")
ref. = reference

Finally, it is very easy for compilers to unintentionally misspell names and omit pertinent information. My third volume of depositions, although carefully prepared, is no exception. One should always check published information against original records. The records from which this book was compiled are available at the Maryland State Archives, 350 Rowe Blvd., Annapolis, MD 21401.

Henry C. Peden, Jr.
Bel Air, Maryland
August 1, 2000

MARYLAND DEPONENTS, VOLUME 3: 1634-1776

AARON, JOHN, of Dorchester County, aet. about 60, dep. between Aug 12, 1760 and Mar 2, 1761. {DOLR 17 Old 262}

AARON (ARRON), JOHN, of Dorchester County, aet. 45, dep. between Aug 14, 1753 and Nov 16, 1753, mentioned his brother Ambros Arron about 20 years ago. {DOLR 15 Old 11}

ABBOT, THOMAS, of Charles County, n.a., dep. 1664, stated "that upon the seaventeenth day of this present mounth Jan: 1664" Thomas Greenhill, a servant boy of Francis Pope, was accidentally killed by the falling of a tree. {ARMD 53:626} Aet. not given, dep. Dec 7, 1565. {CHLR B:528}

ABBOTT, ESTHER PARRAN, see "Sarah Deaver," q.v.

ABBOTT, MARY PARRAN, see "Sarah Deaver," q.v.

ABBOTT, SAMUELL, of Talbot County, n.a., dep. Sep 21, 1669. {ARMD 54:444}

ABINGTON, JOHN, of Charles County, n.a., dep. 1658, mentioned his master Thomas Cornewaleys. {ARMD 41:242} See "John Tolson," q.v.

ABNEY, NATHANIEL, see "William Depriest," q.v.

ACHILLIS, ELIZABETH, of St. Mary's County, wife of Peter Achillis, n.a., dep. Mar 11, 1661. {ARMD 41:552}

ACHILLIS, PETER, see "Elizabeth Achillis," q.v.

ACTON, HENRY, of Charles County, aet. 61, dep. Jun 5, 1770 and Nov 14, 1770. {CHLR T#3:75, 268} Aet. 62, dep. May 28, 1771. {CHLR T#3:378}

ACTON, HENRY, of Prince George's County, aet. 47, dep. Jun 15, 1731. {PGLR Q:29, 299}

ACTON, HENRY, of Prince George's County, aet. 52, dep. Oct 23, 1770, mentioned Thomas Windsor and James Wheeler about 30 years ago. {PGLR AA#2:497}

ADAMS, BENJAMIN, of Prince George's County, aet. 53, dep. Sep 11, 1733, mentioned Capt. Herbert and Col. Hoskins. {PGLR T:123}

ADAMS, BENJAMIN, of Prince George's County, aet. 30, dep. Sep 14, 1761, mentioned Alexander Halbert about 8 years ago. {PGLR RR:179}

ADAMS, BENJAMIN, of Charles County, aet. 68, dep. Feb 27, 1748/9. {CHLR Z#2:525}

ADAMS, CHARLES, of Charles County, aet. 60, dep. Apr 10, 1732. {CHLR R#2:158}

ADAMS, CHARLES, of Charles County, aet. 39, dep. Jul 6, 1749, mentioned his father Charles Adams. {CHLR Z#2:529}

ADAMS, CHARLES, see "Lodwick Adams," q.v.

ADAMS, FRANCIS, of Prince George's County, aet. 58, dep. Jun 6, 1735. {PGLR T:281}

ADAMS, FRANCIS, of Charles County, aet. 25, dep. 1670. {CHLR D#1:150}

ADAMS, FRANCIS, JR., of Charles County, aet. 28, dep. Sep 8, 1756. {CHLR F#3:652}

ADAMS, FRANCIS, SR., of Charles County, aet. 77, dep. Jan 31, 1756. {CHLR E#3:390} Aet. 82, dep. Aug 1, 1760. {CHLR K#3:6} Aet. 82, dep. Apr 23, 1761. {CHLR K#3:305}

ADAMS, HENRY, see "Henrie Addams" and "Marie Addams" and "George Manners," q.v.

ADAMS, JAMES, of Charles County, aet. 64, dep. Mar 8, 1741. {CHLR O#2:321}

ADAMS, JOHN, of Charles County, aet. 68, dep. Jan 1, 1738/9. {CHLR T#2:535}

ADAMS, JOHN, of Charles County, aet. 24, dep. Jul 23, 1743. {CHLR O#2:614}

ADAMS, JOHN, of Charles County, aet. 23, dep. Oct 30, 1770. {CHLR T#3:140}

ADAMS, JOSIAS, of Charles County, aet. 45, dep. Jul 9, 1770. {CHLR T#3:608}

ADAMS, JOSIAS, JR., of Charles County, aet. 24, dep. May 24, 1771, mentioned his father Lodwick Adams, deceased. {CHLR T#3:604}

ADAMS, LODOWICK, of Charles County, aet. 40, dep. May 29, 1744. {CHLR Y#2:185} Aet. 41, dep. Aug 6, 1745. {CHLR Z#2:397} Aet. 47, dep. Jul 6, 1749, mentioned his father Charles Adams. {CHLR Z#2:529} Aet. 57, dep. Dec 31, 1759. {CHLR I#3:427} Aet. 59, dep. Jul 28, 1761, mentioned his father Charles Adams. {CHLR K#3:301} See "Josias Adams, Jr." and "Rhode Adams," q.v.

ADAMS, MORGAN, of Dorchester County, aet. 60, dep. between Mar 16, 1733/4 and Jun 3, 1734, stated that he was a tenant on *Oscumb's Outlett* about 30 years ago. {DOLR 9 Old 187} Morgan Addams, aet. 60, dep. between Nov 19, 1731 and Feb 23, 1731/2. {DOLR 8 Old 453} See "Walter McDaniel," q.v.

ADAMS, PETER, see "Nehemiah Hubbert," q.v.

ADAMS, RHODE, of Charles County, aet. 26, dep. May 24, 1771, mentioned his father Lodwick Adams, deceased. {CHLR T#3:603}

ADAMS, RICHARD, of Dorchester County, aet. about 56, dep. between Nov 10, 1747 and Apr 26, 1748. {DOLR 14 Old 309}

ADAMS (ADAMES), RICHARD, of Kent County, n.a., dep. Oct 8, 1681. {ARMD 17:62}

ADAMS, SAMUEL, of Charles County, aet. 38, dep. Aug 5, 1745. {CHLR Z#2:398}

ADAMS, THOMAS, of Charles County, aet. 42, dep. Jul 11, 1764. {CHLR M#3:687}

ADAMS, WILLIAM, of Dorchester County, aet. 53, dep. Aug 24, 1745, stated that he was shown the bounded tree of *North Hampton* about 40 years ago by his father William Adams; also mentioned John Dean, now deceased. {DOLR 12 Old 247} William Addams, aet. 58, dep. between Mar 10, 1752 and Mar 10, 1753, stated that he was shown the bounded tree of *Atlantis* about 22 years ago by Col. John Rider, now deceased. {DOLR 14 Old 712}

ADAMS, WILLIAM, see "John Adams," q.v.

ADAMSON, JOHN (captain), of Frederick County, aet. 59, dep. Jun 18, 1764, mentioned Ninian Tannehill, Sr. in 1757; his daughter Rebecca Tannehill, now Rebecca Shaw; William Shaw, Jr., son-in-law of Ninian Tannehill, Jr.; and, Rebecca Adamson, now Rebecca Beall. {FRLR J:435}

ADAMSON, REBECCA, see "John Adamson," q.v.

ADDAMS, ELIZABETH, of Dorchester County, aet. 61, dep. between Aug 10, 1773 and Nov 30, 1773, mentioned Rebeccah North about 33 or 34 years ago. {DOLR 27 Old 354}

ADDAMS (ADDAMES), HENRIE, of Charles County, n.a., dep. Jun 4, 1658. {CHLR A:3} Mr. Henry Addames, n.a., dep. Jul 27, 1663, mentioned Mrs. Margery Brent, deceased. {CHLR B:136}

ADDAMS, JOHN, of Dorchester County, aet. 43, dep. between Aug 10, 1773 and Oct 23, 1773, mentioned his father William Addams about 35 years ago. {DOLR 27 Old 38}

ADDAMS (ADDAMES), MARIE, of Charles County, n.a., wife of Henrie Addames, dep. Jun 4, 1658. {CHLR A:3}

ADDISON, COLONEL, see "Jacob Henderson" and "John Dawson," q.v.

ADDISON, HENRY (reverend), of Prince George's County, aet. 46, dep. Nov 5, 1763, mentioned Humphry Ball about 16 years ago. {PGLR TT:285}

ADDISON, THOMAS, of Prince George's County, aet. 45, dep. Oct 6, 1724. {PGLR I:601} See "John Locker" and "Robert Wade," q.v.

AIREY, THOMAS, see "Henry Ennalls," q.v.

ALEXANDER, JOHN, see "Samuell Carter," q.v.

ALFORD, EDWARD, see "Joseph Alford," q.v.

ALFORD, JOHN, of Dorchester County, aet. about 70, dep. between Mar 15, 1728 and Jun 6, 1729, mentioned his uncle, old John Allford, and young John Alford, son of the afsd. John Alford. {DOLR 8 Old 291} John Allford, aet. about 70, dep. between Aug 16, 1728 and Jan 28, 1728/9, mentioned his uncle John Allford, father of Mathias Allford. {DOLR 8 Old 268} See "James Anderson" and "Mary Jenkins" and "Joseph Alford" and "Isaac Nicolls" and "John Harris" and "Richard Webster," q.v.

ALFORD, JOSEPH, of Dorchester County, aet. 41, dep. Jun 15, 1738, stated that he was shown the bounds of *New Found Land* by Margaret Coxell about 17 years ago when he came to live in the freshes. {DOLR 12 Old 104} Aet. 49, dep. between Jun 11, 1745 and May 23, 1746, mentioned John Alford (deceased, generally called John Alford of Accomack), Benjamin Nicolls (deceased), and Edward Alford (now deceased). {DOLR 14 Old 50} Aet. about 62, dep. between Nov 14, 1758 and Jun 30, 1759, stated that he was shown the bounds of *Mischance*, otherwise known as *Baley's Land*, about 34 years ago by John Fleharty. {DOLR 16 Old 220} Aet. about 64, dep. between Aug 14, 1759 and Mar 11, 1761. {DOLR 17 Old 376} Aet. about 67, dep. between Aug 14, 1764 and Aug 13, 1765. {DOLR 20 Old 237} Aet. about 73, dep. between Nov 14, 1769 and Nov 6, 1770, stated that he was shown the bounds of *Wiltshire* about 30 years ago by Peter Taylor, now deceased. {DOLR 24 Old 308}

ALFORD, MATHIAS, of Dorchester County, n.a., dep. 1721/1722 as noted in deposition of Henry Ennalls in 1729/1730. {DOLR 8 Old 384} See "Isaac Nicolls" and "James Anderson" and "John Nicolls" and "John Alford" and "Henry Ennalls," q.v.

ALIFFE, WILLIAM, of Charles County, n.a., dep. Mar 12, 1660/1. {CHLR A:125}
ALLAN, ROBERT, see "John Kerby," q.v.
ALLANSON, THOMAS, of Charles County, aet. 22, dep. Apr 17, 1660. {CHLR A:86} Thomas Allonson, aet. 24, dep. Mar 4, 1661. {ARMD 53:190}
ALLCOCK, BURTONWOOD, see "Joannah Clark," q.v.
ALLCOCK, THOMAS, of Dorchester County, aet. about 42, dep. between Aug 14, 1764 and Aug 13, 1765, mentioned Joseph Billiter and his father Edward Billiter. {DOLR 20 Old 237}
ALLEN, CAPTAIN, see "Hudson Wathen," q.v.
ALLEN, JOHN, of Charles County, aet. 56, dep. Aug 12, 1719, mentioned his father-in-law John Lambert. {Charles County Land Commissions 1:48}
ALLEN, JOSEPH, of Charles County, aet. 35, dep. Aug 7, 1738. {CHLR T#2:497}
ALLEN, JOSEPH, SR., of Charles County, aet. 64, dep. Apr 7, 1729. {CHLR Q#2:274}
ALLEN (ALLIN), THOMAS, of Prince George's County, aet. 44, dep. Nov 18, 1748. {PGLR BB:699} Thomas Allin, aet. 46, dep. Mar 10, 1752. {PGLR NN:91} See "Samuell Palmer" and "Daniel Gordon," q.v.
ALLEYN, CHARLES, of Talbot's Mannor, Cecil County, n.a., dep. Nov 4, 1722, mentioned the encroachment of Pennsylvanians on his land, particularly Isaac Taylor and son (not named), Elisha Gatchell, William Brown, John Churchman, Richard Brown, and Roger Nerck. {ARMD 25:396}
ALLISON, HENRY, of Prince George's County, aet. 59, dep. Jun 1, 1767, mentioned his father (not named) about 6 or 7 years ago. {PGLR BB#2:114} Henry (Hendry) Allison, aet. 65 or thereabouts, dep. Aug 14, 1772, mentioned his father John Allison, Sr., deceased. {FRLR P:683}
ALLISON, JOHN, see "Henry Allison" and "Ninian Tannehill," q.v.
ALLISON, JOHN, of Prince George's County, aet. 90, dep. Jun 13, 1767, stated that he had known this area for 40 years. {PGLR BB#2:115}
ALLISON, JOHN, of Frederick County, aet. 82 or thereabouts, dep. Jun 6, 1761, stated that he was overseer for Mr. Lee about 17 years ago. {FRLR G:277} John Allison, Sr., aet. 80, dep. Nov 14, 1761. {FRLR G:299}
ALLISON, JOHN, of Prince George's County, aet. 55, dep. Dec 3, 1734. {PGLR T:209} Aet. 77, dep. Aug 10, 1756. {PGLR PP:15, pt. 2}
ALLISON, THOMAS, see "Ninian Tannehill" and "Elizabeth Wicherly" and "Owen Jones," q.v.
ALLMAN, MARGIT, of Cecil County, widow, aet. 46, dep. Jan 29, 1745/6. {CELR 4:478}
ALVEY, POPE, see "John Bissick," q.v.
ALWINKLE (ALLWINCLE), ISAAC, see "William Trego" and "Mary Navey," q.v.
AMBROSE, JOHN, of Kent County, aet. 49, dep. circa 1750. {KEEJ - Isaac and Thomas Crown folder}
AMERY, SAMUEL, of Charles County, aet. 60, dep. Sep 13, 1758. {CHLR K#3:96}

ANNIS, THOMAS, of Charles County, aet. 44, dep. Mar 2, 1730, stated that he had married Elizabeth Mackey, widow of James Mackey. {CHLR Q#2:474} Aet. 45, dep. Apr 10, 1732. {CHLR R#2:158}

ANDERSON, ISAAC, of Dorchester County, aet. 46, dep. between Jun 10, 1755 and Feb 10, 1756, mentioned his father James Anderson about 35 years ago. {DOLR 15 Old 341} See "James Dawson," q.v.

ANDERSON, JAMES, of Talbot County, aet. about 68, dep. between Aug 16, 1728 and Jan 28, 1728/9, mentioned Matthias Allford, son of John Allford, deceased, of Dorchester County. {DOLR 8 Old 268} See "Samuel Wheeler" and "Abraham Gambell" and "Isaac Anderson," q.v.

ANDERSON, JOHN, late master or commander, and John Devereaux and John McKeel, late mates, of the *Dolly and Nancy* of Maryland, burthen about 160 tons, sworn before George Johnston, Notary Public of Charles Town in the Province of South Carolina and Justice for Berkley County in said Province, stated that on May 9, 1763 they sailed from Cork, Ireland with a cargo of beef, pork, and other provisions bound for Havana; on May 27th they met a hard gale of wind; on Jul 4th they arrived at the Island of Anguilla; on Jul 5th they arrived at the Island of Annegada; on Jul 6th they arrived on the north side of St. John de Porto Rico; on Jul 7th they made the east end of Hispaniola; on Jul 11th they made Cape Maize, the east end of Cuba; on Jul 13th they passed Cape Quibinico; on Jul 14th they struck a reef near Cayjo Romano where their vessel was plundered by the Spanish; on Jul 15th they set out in their long boat for Havana where they arrived on Jul 27th; they endeavored to enter a protest but could not since the Spaniards had taken over and no Notaries Publick were there; on Jul 29th they took passage on the ship *Neptune* under John Johnson, master, for Charles Town, South Carolina, where they arrived on Aug 6, 1763 and filed this deposition. {DOLR 18 Old 443}

ANDERSON, JOHN, of Charles County, aet. 68, dep. Mar 2, 1743/4. {CHLR O#2:702} Aet. 70, dep. May 25, 1745. {CHLR Z#2:340}

ANDERSON, JOHN, of Prince George's County, aet. 57, dep. Jun 26, 1734. {PGLR T:126}

ANDERSON, JOHN, see "Benjamin Truman" and "James Collings" and "Sarah Joslin" and "Ann Burnham," q.v.

ANDERSON, MARY, of Prince George's County, n.a., dep. Mar 24, 1706/7, stated that Elizabeth Wallis was taken on Tuesday with fits which caused her to bite her tongue; on Thursday she (deponent) and Sarah Joslin found a child in her bed, black and putrefied; Elizabeth remained ill until the following Tuesday, bloated in her face and swollen in her hands and legs; she had taken some sort of drink from Peter Calico. {CMSP 1:8} See "James Dawson" and "Sarah Joslin," q.v.

ANDERTON, FRANCIS, see "John Anderton" and "Andrew Lord," q.v.

ANDERTON, JOHN, of Dorchester County, aet. 39, between Jun 11, 1732 and Jan 22, 1732/3, stated that he was shown the bounds of *Bath* by his father, Francis

Anderton, about 26 years ago, which land was owned by Charles Rye at that time. {DOLR 9 Old 138} Aet. 55, dep. Mar 8, 1747, stated that he was shown the bounded tree of *Balea* or *Balia* about 20 years ago by John Dyer (now deceased) and about 10 or 12 years ago by Peter Taylor (now deceased), said tract belonging to his cousin Ann Taylor. {DOLR 14 Old 310}

ANDREW, GEORGE, of Dorchester County, aet. about 62, dep. between Nov 14, 1769 and Nov 6, 1770, mentioned Elizabeth Croneen (Cromean), now deceased, and her son John Croneen (Cromean) about 17 or 18 years ago. {DOLR 24 Old 308} Aet. about 63, dep. between Nov 13, 1770 and Aug 2, 1771, mentioned his brother Thomas Andrew about 43 or 44 years ago, now deceased. {DOLR 25 Old 26} See "Jacob Charles," q.v.

ANDREW, GEORGE, JR., of Dorchester County, aet. 54, dep. between Aug 9, 1763 and Mar 31, 1764, stated that he was shown the bounded tree of *Lemster* about 32 years ago by William Layton. {DOLR 19 Old 418} Aet. 58, dep. Mar 25, 1769, stated that about 50 years ago he lived with his father (not named) in Kent County on Delaware near the house of Henry Griffith the Second and he (Andrew) understood that a girl named Sarah Griffith who lived in said house was a daughter of said Henry Griffith and she (Sarah) became the wife of John Needles of Kent County afsd. {DOLR 23 Old 346}

ANDREW, JOHN, of Dorchester County, aet. about 48, dep. between Aug 18, 1733 and Jun 29, 1734, mentioned James Hays, Deputy Surveyor, about 12 or 13 years ago. {DOLR 9 Old 195} Aet. about 50, dep. Jun 2, 1740, mentioned Hezekiah Vickery, later of Dorchester County, about 17 years ago. {DOLR 12 Old 128}

ANDREW, NEHEMIAH, of Dorchester County, aet. about 27, dep. between Nov 11, 1755 and May 20, 1756. {DOLR 16 Old 76} Aet. about 44, dep. between Nov 13, 1770 and Aug 2, 1771. {DOLR 25 Old 26}

ANDREW, SARAH, of Dorchester County, aet. 68, dep. between Mar 14, 1769 and Apr 9, 1770, stated that her father, Samuel Cratcher, once rented land on Fowler's Branch (also known as Rogers' Branch or Bryan's Branch) from the Indians; also mentioned Mary Cratcher, Samuel Cratcher, and Thomas Hackett, all now deceased. {DOLR 24 Old 9}

ANDREW, THOMAS, of Dorchester County, aet. 61, dep. between Nov 10, 1767 and Aug 10, 1768, mentioned John Nicolls (now deceased) about 12 or 13 years ago. {DOLR 23 Old 1} Aet. 62, dep. between Mar 17, 1768 and Aug 9, 1768. {DOLR 22 Old 433} See "John Caulk" and "George Andrew," q.v.

ANDREWS, JOANNA, see "Benjamin Newnam," q.v.

ANDREWS, MARCUS, of Somerset County, n.a., dep. Jul 18, 1722, stated that he owned an Indian boy named James, a customary thing among the inhabitants of Ackamack in Virginia, and he sold Indian James to a gentleman in Philadelphia named Nicholas ---- (he does not remember his surname). {ARMD 25:390-391}

ANDREWS, PATRICK, see "Nathan Wells" and "Sarah Gaither," q.v.

ANDREWS, WILLIAM, of Baltimore County, aet. 65, dep. Aug 15, 1774. {BALR AL#L:355}

ANGE, JOHN, see "Thomas Ange," q.v.

ANGE, THOMAS, of Dorchester County, aet. 40, dep. between Nov 9, 1773 and Nov 9, 1774, mentioned John Ange about 10 or 12 years ago, now deceased. {DOLR 27 Old 359}

ANKETILL, FRANCIS, of St. Mary's County, n.a., dep. Jun 10, 1649. {ARMD 3:187}

ANTHER, PHILIP, see "Mary Greenway," q.v.

APRICE, EDWARD, of St. Mary's County, aet. 72, dep. Jan 11, 1736/7 in Charles County. {CHLR T#2:297} Aet. 77, Oct 3, 1741, stated that he had lived with Capt. Pile about 60 years ago. {CHLR O#2:288}

ARENTON, CORNELIUS, of Dorchester County, aet. 74, dep. Mar 13, 1713. {DOLR 6 Old 223}

AREY, DAVID, see "William Tharp" and "Sarah Kindred" and "David Harrington," q.v.

AREY, ELIZABETH, see "William Tharp" and "Sarah Kindred" and "David Harrington," q.v.

AREY, ESTHER, see "William Tharp" and "Sarah Kindred" and "David Harrington," q.v.

ARMESTRONG, FRANCIS, of St. Mary's County, n.a., dep. Apr 5, 1664. {ARMD 49:193}

ARMSTRONG, FRANCIS, of Kent County, aet. about 30, dep. Mar, 1720. {Chancery Court Records CL:710} Aet. about 42, dep. Dec 29, 1732. {TALR 6:180} Aet. about 49, dep. Sep, 1740; aet. about 55, dep. Aug, 1743. {TAEJ - John Reynolds folders}

ARNETT, JOHN, of Dorchester County, aet. about 66, dep. between Nov 11, 1760 and Apr 4, 1761, stated that Walter Quinton employed him to build a house on *Bunnell's Fields* about 33 years ago. {DOLR 17 Old 329}

ARNOLD, JOHN, prob. of St. Mary's County, n.a., dep. May 17, 1664, mentioned Thomas Thurston, Thomas Meeres, Thomas Turner, Mourice Baker, John Holmewood, Sarah Fuller, Sarah Holmewood, and Sarah Marsh. {ARMD 3:495}

ARRON, AMBROS, see "John Aaron," q.v.

ASH, THOMAS, of Charles County, aet. 44, dep. Jul 26, 1755. {CHLR:49:387}

ASHBROOKE, JOHN, of Charles County, n.a., dep. Jan 26, 1658/9, stated that last Oct 25th Arthur Turner brought a sick child of Lucie Stratton to his house for Roase Ashbrooke to nurse and Arthur thought he was the father of Lucie's child; John also stated that Lucie said the child could belong to William Bowls, but she thought in her conscience it was Arthur's child. {CHLR A:35} Aet. 39, dep. Jan 29, 1661/2. {CHLR A:186}

ASHBROOKE, ROSE (ROASE), of Charles County, aet. 31, dep. Jan 29, 1661/2. {CHLR A:186} See "John Ashbrooke," q.v.

ASHBY, RUDOLPH, of Frederick County, n.a., dep. 1767. {FRLR L:60}

ASHCOMB, JOHN, of Charles County, n.a., dep. 1658. {ARMD 41:73}

ASHCROFT, SUSANNAH (Mrs.), of Talbot County, n.a., dep. Aug 3, 1736, stated that either Edward Elliott (now deceased) or James Hatton gave the 2 acres of land on which the Parish Church of St. Michael's was built. {TALR 14:173}

ASHMAN, GEORGE, of Baltimore County, aet. 52, of Baltimore County, dep. Feb 16, 1767. {BALR B#P:417}

ASHQUASH, ABRAHAM, see "Indian Abraham Ashquash," q.v.

ASHQUASH, JEMMY, see "Indian Jemmy Ashquash," q.v.

ASKINS, GEORGE, of Charles County, aet. 64, dep. Jan 9, 1743/4. {CHLR O#2:700}

ATCHISON (ATCHESON), IGNATIUS, of Prince George's County, aet. 51, dep. Mar 10, 1769, mentioned Edward Cole, Jr. about 30 years ago. {PGLR AA#2:151-152} Ignatius Atcheson, aet. 54, dep. Mar 9, 1772. {PGLR BB#3:79}

ATCHISON (ATCHESON), JAMES, of Prince George's County, aet. 44, dep. 1731. {PGLR Q:373} See "William Atchison," q.v.

ATCHISON, WILLIAM, of Charles County, aet. 23, dep. Oct 8, 1742, mentioned his grandfather Stephen Cawood. {CHLR O#2:468}

ATCHISON (ATCHINSON), WILLIAM, of Prince George's County, aet. 55, dep. Mar 10, 1769, mentioned his father James Atchison about 24 or 25 years ago. {PGLR AA#2:153}

ATHEY, GEORGE, of Prince George's County, aet. 23, dep. Feb 17, 1723/4, mentioned his father George Athey. {PGLR I:542} Aet. 76, dep. Mar 10, 1769. {PGLR AA#2:151} Aet. 82, dep. Nov 14, 1774, stated that Edward Lanham settled on *Stone's Delight* about 48 or 49 years ago when he (deponent) was a chain carrier for William Owen. {PGLR CC#2:58} See "Sarah Athey" and "Thomas Davis," q.v.

ATHEY, SARAH, of Prince George's County, aet. 57, dep. Feb 17, 1723/4, mentioned her his husband George Athey. {PGLR I:543}

ATHEY, THOMAS, of Prince George's County, aet. 60, dep. Aug 5, 1760, stated that he has known of Pomonkey Branch for about 35 years. {PGLR RR:75}

ATKINSON, JOHN, see "James Wilson," q.v.

ATKINSON, RICHARD, of the Inner Temple in London, England, gentleman, n.a., dep. Jun 23, 1770, stated that he did see Thomas Dickenson Richardson in the annexed Letter of Attorney, sign, seal, and deliver it in the presence of his brother Anthony Richardson, of London, merchant; reference is made to the Nov 19, 1740 will of Anthony Richardson, formerly of Talbot County, deceased, in which he left land in Talbot County to his unborn child; Richardson died and left his pregnant wife Elizabeth without altering his will; their second son Thomas Dickenson Richardson was born posthumously on Feb 7, 1741. {TALR 20:316}

ATTERBURN, PETER, of Charles County, aet. 37, dep. Feb 27, 1748/9. {CHLR Z#2:525}

ATTHOW, MARY, see "John Pattison," q.v.

ATTOWAY, THOMAS, of Queen Anne's County, aet. 32, dep. Apr, 1769. {QAEJ - James Hutchens folder}

ATTWOOD, PETER (reverend), of Baltimore County, n.a., dep. Jan 28, 1715 in Annapolis, mentioned a letter written to William Killuck at the Wood Yard in England, dated Dec 21, 1712, concerning the offer of 300 acres of land by James Carroll in Baltimore County "to him or any other Priest of the Romish Communion" willing to settle thereon (deponent and Killuck were Roman Catholic priests). {ARMD 25:332-333}

ATWICKES, ELISABETH, of Charles County, n.a., dep. Nov 14, 1659, stated that Mrs. Hatche thought that Goodie Michel (wife of Thomas Michel) had bewitched her face. {CHLR A:69}

ATWICKES, HUMPHERY, of Charles County, n.a., dep. Jul 28, 1663. {CHLR B:134} Aet. not given, dep. Sep 10, 1663 (name listed as Humphrey Attwicks). {ARMD 49:61} See "Capt. John Price," q.v.

AUSTIN, HENRY, of Baltimore County, aet. 62, dep. Sep 1, 1763. {BALR B#M:90-91} Aet. 64, dep. Nov 12, 1768. {BALR AL#G:443}

AUSTIN, JOHN, of Prince George's County, aet. 40, dep. Aug 25, 1737. {PGLR T:505}

AUSTIN, JOHN, of Prince George's County, aet. 29, dep. several times on Mar 15, 1756, mentioned his father John Austin, deceased. {PGLR NN:433-435} Aet. 35, dep. Oct 6, 1763, mentioned his father (not named) about 20 years ago. {PGLR TT:123}

AVERET, JOHN, see "John Collier," q.v.

AVERY, JOHN, see "John Collier," q.v.

AYRES, THOMAS, of Kent County, aet. about 59, dep. Aug 25, 1746. {KELR JS#25:438} Aet. about 68, dep. Feb 27, 1755. {KELR JS#28:98}

BACKER, PETER, see "George Walters," q.v.

BADEN, ROBERT, of Prince George's County, aet. 50, dep. Jun 7, 1748. {PGLR BB:662} Robert Baden, Jr., aet. 61, dep. May 1, 1755, mentioned John Taylor about 27 years ago, now deceased. {PGLR NN:369} Robert Baden, aet. 69, dep. Nov 15, 1763. {PGLR TT:144}

BAGGOT (BAGETT), JOHN, of Charles County, aet. 44, dep. Apr 29, 1745. {CHLR Z#2:396} Aet. 63, dep. Sep 27, 1764, mentioned his father Samuel Baggot. {CHLR N#3:167}

BAGGOT (BAGGOTT), JOHN, of Charles County, aet. 30, dep. Apr 11, 1755. {CHLR E#3:502}

BAGGOT, SAMUEL, see "John Baggot" and "William Baggot," q.v.

BAGGOT, WILLIAM, of Charles County, aet. 35, dep. Jan 9, 1743/4, mentioned his father Samuel Baggot. {CHLR O#2:701} Aet. 37, dep. Apr 29, 1745. {CHLR Z#2:396}

BAGWELL, JOHN, see "Elizabeth Lamphier," q.v.

BAGWELL, MARY, see "Elizabeth Lamphier," q.v.

BAGWELL, SARAH, see "Elizabeth Lamphier," q.v.

BAILEY, JAMES, of Queen Anne's County, aet. 61, dep. Mar 15, 1760. {QAEJ - Richard Tilghman Earle folder}

BAILEY, JOHN, of Baltimore County, aet. 63, dep. Dec 9, 1776. {BALR WG#B:34}
BAILEY, THOMAS, of Charles County, aet. 51, dep. Jun 3, 1760. {CHLR K#3:10}
BAINBRIDGE, JOHN, see "Henry Chapple," q.v.
BAKER, FRANCIS, see "John Barclay" and "James Dickinson" and "John Gordon" and "Henry Hollyday" and "Nicholas Hyland" and "Robert Lloyd" and "Edward Mitchell" and "Hugh Neill" and "Benjamin Rumsey" and "E. Tilghman" and "Matthew Tilghman," q.v.
BAKER, JEREMIAH, see "Nicholas Hyland" and "Edward Mitchell" and "Benjamin Rumsey," q.v.
BAKER, JOHN, of Charles County, aet. 48, dep. Jun 10, 1725. {CHLR P#2:68} Aet. 50, dep. Feb 15, 1728, stated that he was a former servant of Henry Hawkins. {CHLR Q#2:347} Aet. 53, dep. May 5, 1730 and Nov 9, 1730. {CHLR Q#2:404, 449} See "Thomas Baker" and "John Crain," q.v.
BAKER, MARY, of Charles County, aet. 48, dep. Feb 14, 1728. {CHLR Q#2:347}
BAKER, MORRIS, of Baltimore County, aet. 62, dep. May 12, 1764. {BALR B#O:113}
BAKER, MOURICE (MORRIS), see "Michaell Higgins" and "John Arnold" and "Josias Marsh," q.v.
BAKER, NICHOLAS, see "James Foard," q.v.
BAKER, THEOPHILUS, of Baltimore County, aet. 46, dep. Nov 9, 1767. {BALR B#Q:591} Theophilous Barker, aet. 52, dep. May 20, 1772. {BALR AL#E:278}
BAKER, THOMAS, of Charles County, aet. 40, dep. Sep 8, 1753, mentioned his father John Baker. {CHLR D#3:430} Aet. 43, dep. May 17, 1755. {CHLR E#3:130}
BAKER, THOMAS, of Charles County, n.a., dep. May 1, 1659. {CHLR A:58, ARMD 53:47} Aet. not given, dep. Jul 8, 1662. {CHLR A:225} Aet. not given, dep. Jun 29, 1663, stated that he heard Goodie Nevill say to Mary Dod that she was Capt. Batten's whore. {CHLR B:145} Aet. not given, dep. Nov 11, 1674. {CHLR F#1:32}
BAKER, THOMAS, see "John Crain," q.v.
BAKER, WILLIAM, see "Zebediah Baker," q.v.
BAKER, ZEBEDIAH, of Baltimore County, aet. 66, dep. Jan 15, 1766, mentioned his father William Baker. {BALR B#P:80}
BALCH, JOHN, of St. Mary's County, n.a., dep. Feb 14, 1661. {ARMD 41:527}
BALDWIN, HESTER, of Anne Arundel County, aet. 55, dep. 1684, mentioned her former husband Nicholas Nicholson. {AALR IT#5:29}
BALE, THOMAS, of Baltimore County, aet. 40, dep. between Apr 11, 1704 and Aug 4, 1704, mentioned his "brother" Robert Gibson. {BALR HW#2:368}
BALEY, THOMAS, of Queen Anne's County, aet. 62, dep. Apr, 1750. {QAEJ - William Bishop folder}
BALL, HILLARY (HILLIARY), see "Francis Marbury" and "James Wheeler" and "Ann Scandall," q.v.
BALL, HUMPHRY, see "Henry Addison," q.v.
BALL, RICHARD, see "Richard Baul," q.v.

BALL, THOMAS, of Dorchester County, aet. 32, dep. between Jun 11, 1765 and Aug 15, 1765, mentioned Isaac Covington about 9 years ago, now deceased. {DOLR 20 Old 244} Aet. about 39, dep. between Nov 14, 1769 and Jul 28, 1772. {DOLR 26 Old 100} See "Elizabeth Hodson," q.v.

BALLY (BALLEY), JOHN, of St. Mary's County, n.a., dep. Oct 14, 1665. {ARMD 49:499} Aet. not given, dep. Dec 22, 1673. {ARMD 51:108-109}

BANE, JOHN, of Charles County, aet. 56, dep. May 29, 1773, mentioned his father Richard Bane. {CHLR U#3:271}

BANE, RICHARD, see "John Bane," q.v.

BANKS, JOHN, of Prince George's County, aet. 68, dep. Apr 4, 1746, mentioned Thomas Prather about 35 or 36 years ago. {PGLR BB:306} Aet. 70, dep. Jan 26, 1748/9, stated that he carried the surveyor's chain for James Stoddart about 40 years ago. {PGLR BB:628} Aet. 70, dep. Feb 14, 1748/9, mentioned Francis Swanson about 56 or 57 years ago. {PGLR BB:700} Aet. 76 or thereabouts, dep. May 2, 1754, stated that he has known this area for 40 years. {PGLR NN:256} Aet. 81, dep. Sep 15, 1758, stated that he was appointed a commissioner to prove the bounds of *Friendship* about 30 odd years ago. {PGLR PP:227, pt. 2}

BARBER, CORNELIUS, of Charles County, aet. 56, dep. Oct 1, 1771. {CHLR W#3:77}

BARBER, LUKE, see "Robert Wade," q.v.

BARBER, RICHARD, of Charles County, aet. 50, shipwright, dep. Jun 11, 1726. {CHLR P#2:415}

BARCLAY, JOHN (reverend), of Talbot County, Rector of St. Peter's Parish, n.a., dep. Jun 7, 1769, stated that he has known Francis Baker about seven years. {ARMD 32:327}

BAREBATCH, THOMAS, see "Thomas Brereton," q.v.

BAREFOOT (BARFOOT), NICHOLAS, see "Anne Corse" and "Sutton Quinney," q.v.

BARKER, ELIZABETH, of Frederick County, aet. 48, dep. Apr 1, 1768, mentioned her father Gerah Davis and her former husband John Harding about 20 years ago. {FRLR L:519}

BARKER, JOHN, of Charles County, aet. 61, dep. May 24, 1771, mentioned his father Capt. John Barker and brother William Barker, deceased. {CHLR T#3:603}

BARKER, JOSEPH, of Charles County, aet. 40, dep. Apr 13, 1761. {CHLR K#3:297}

BARKER, THEOPHILOUS, see "Theophilus Baker," q.v.

BARKER, WILLIAM, of Prince George's County, aet. 38, dep. Aug 10, 1756, stated that Thomas Lucas, now deceased, showed him the bounds of *Jamaica Port Royal* about a year ago. {PGLR PP:15, pt. 2} See "John Barker," q.v.

BARKLEY, ISABELLA, see "Peter Johnson," q.v.

BARKLEY, JOHN, of Frederick County, n.a., dep. Dec 2, 1765. {ARMD 32:155-156}

BARKLEY, THOMAS, see "Peter Johnson," q.v.

BARNARD (BERNARD), LUKE, of Prince George's County, aet. 39, dep. Mar 8, 1724. {PGLR I:624} Aet. 44, dep. Sep 22, 1730. {PGLR Q:159} Aet. 55, dep. Nov 26, 1739. {PGLR Y:107} Aet. 69, dep. Mar 16, 1754. {PGLR NN:237}

BARNES, ANNE, see "Thomas Barnes," q.v.

BARNES, FRANCIS, of Queen Anne's County, aet. 68, dep. Apr, 1747, stated that Elizabeth Foreman, an old woman living some years earlier who he knew personally, was said to have been the daughter of one Ellis; she had several children and left the Island. {QAEJ - Samuel Blunt folder}

BARNES, GODSHALL, of Charles County, aet. 64, dep. Jan 31, 1756. {CHLR E#3:391}. Aet. 68, dep. Aug 1, 1760. {CHLR K#3:7} Aet. 68, dep. Feb 20, 1761. {CHLR K#3:154} Aet. 69, dep. Dec 6, 1762, stated that he was shown the bounded tree between *Betty's Delight* and *Planter's Delight* by his mother (not named) and Capt. Theobald about 40 years ago; also mentioned his father Capt. William Barnes. {CHLR M#3:219} Aet. 74, dep. Jun 11, 1766, mentioned Clement Butts, son of John Butts, deceased, and said John Butts had married Christian Goodrick before their son Clement was born; also mentioned Richard Butts, brother of John. {CHLR V#3:453}

BARNES, HANNAH, of Dorchester County, aet. 60, dep. between Apr 6, 1732 and Jun 3, 1732, stated that the bounds of *Armstrong's Hog Pen* were shown to her by old Thomas Pattison about 20 years ago. {DOLR 9 Old 68}

BARNES, HENRY, of Prince George's County, aet. 54, dep. Aug 3, 1730, mentioned his father (not named) and the widow Britt about 20 or 30 years ago. {PGLR Q:68} Aet. 57, dep. Sep 11, 1733. {PGLR T:123}

BARNES, JOHN, of Dorchester County, aet. 40, dep. between Aug 12, 1760 and Mar 2, 1761, mentioned Sarah Murphy and her husband (not named) lived on land called *Oyster Bank Neck*. {DOLR 17 Old 262}

BARNES, JOHN, SR., of Dorchester County, aet. 50, dep. between Aug 12, 1760 and Mar 2, 1761. {DOLR 17 Old 262}

BARNES, MARY, see "Thomas Barnes," q.v.

BARNES, MATTHEW, of Charles County, aet. 55, dep. Sep 8, 1756. {CHLR F#3:653} See "Henry Coffer," q.v.

BARNES, RICHARD, of Charles County, aet. 43, dep. Mar 21, 1769. {CHLR Q#3:410A}

BARNES, SAMUEL, of Charles County, aet. 36, dep. Apr 23, 1761. {CHLR K#3:304}

BARNES, THOMAS, of Queen Anne's County, aet. 60, dep. Sep, 1769, stated that Ralph Distance owned *Isaac's Chance* when he (deponent) was a small boy; Distance died leaving two daughters: Anne married 1st to John Dailey (and had four or five children) and 2nd to Edmund Kelly; and, Mary married 1st to Timothy Matthews and after her father's death she married 2nd to John Gilbert (by whom she had several children). {QAEJ - James Hutchens folder}

BARNES, WILLIAM, of Dorchester County, aet. 27, dep. between Aug 12, 1760 and Mar 2, 1761, mentioned Richard Chapman and his brother John Robson, and Thomas Chapman and his uncle John Robson, about 5 or 6 years ago. {DOLR 17 Old 262} See "Isaac Foxwell" and "Godshall Barnes," q.v.

BARNETT, THOMAS, of Dorchester County, aet. 38, dep. between Jun 14, 1729 and Jul 17, 1729. {DOLR 8 Old 432} See "Benoni Frazier," q.v.

BARNEY, ABSOLOM, of Baltimore County, planter, aet. 48, dep. Feb 26, 1766. {BALR B#P:300} Aet. 50, dep. Sep 1, 1772. {BALR AL#I:210}

BARNEY, BENJAMIN, of Baltimore County, aet. 44, dep. Jun 13, 1772, mentioned his father William Barney. {BALR AL#I:206}

BARNEY, ELINOR, of Dorchester County, aet. 59, dep. between Jan 2, 1741 and Feb 24, 1741, mentioned her master Thomas Mackeel and his wife Cleer. {DOLR 12 Old 154}

BARNEY, ELIZABETH, see "William Barney," q.v.

BARNEY, MOSES, of Baltimore County, aet. 29, dep. Feb 16, 1767. {BALR B#P:420}

BARNEY (BARNAY), WILLIAM, of Baltimore County, n.a., dep. May 12, 1738, stated that a deed for *Morgan's Delight* that was conveyed to him by Morgan Murray in 1716 and a deed for the same land from Mary Stevenson to her daughter Elizabeth Barney were delivered to George Middleton, clerk of Baltimore County. {CMSP 1:57, ARMD 40:157}

BARNEY, WILLIAM, of Baltimore County, aet. 54, dep. May 15, 1772. {BALR AL#I:200} See "Benjamin Barney," q.v.

BARNS, EDMOND, of Dorchester County, aet. 30, dep. between Jun 11, 1765 and Aug 11, 1765. {DOLR 21 Old 45}

BARNS, HENRY, of Prince George's County, aet. 52, dep. Nov 28, 1728. {PGLR M:343}

BARNS, JOHN, of Talbot County, n.a., dep. Mar 15, 1663/4, former servant of Henry Morgan of Isle of Kent, now deceased. {ARMD 54:368}

BARNS, JOHN, of Dorchester County, aet. 48, dep. between Mar 10, 1740 and Jun 4, 1741, stated that he was shown the bounded tree of *Barrel Green* by Daniel Lawrence about 24 years ago. {DOLR 12 Old 138}

BARNS, JOHN, see "Sarah Murfey," q.v.

BARNS, MATT. (captain), of Prince George's County, aet. 64, dep. Jun 6, 1735. {PGLR T:282}

BARON, SAMUEL COOKSEY, of Charles County, aet. 43, dep. Sep 29, 1773. {CHLR U#3:600}

BARRETT, ELIZABETH, of Frederick County, aet. 43 or thereabouts, dep. Jun 18, 1764. {FRLR J:435}

BARRETT, THOMAS, of St. Mary's County, n.a., dep. Jun 2, 1659, stated that he was a member of the company that surprised and overtook a ship called the *St. George* of Amsterdam at Barbadoes upon suspicion of piracy. {ARMD 41:308-309}

BARTHEMEY, JOAN, of Cecil County, n.a., dep. Mar 8, 1706/7. {CMSP 1:7 - The Black Books}

BARTON, NATHAN, see "John Wheeler," q.v.

BARTON, SELIAH, see "Thomas Gibbons," q.v.

BARTON, WILLIAM, see "Barton Smoot" and "Thomas Smoot" and "John Wheeler," q.v.

BASHELS, NATHAN, of Queen Anne's County, aet. 22, dep. Apr, 1765. {QAEJ - William Austin folder}

BASS, CHARLES, of Cecil County, n.a., dep. Sep 5, 1698. {ARMD 23:522}

BASSETT, MARGARETT, of St. Mary's County, wife of Thomas Bassett, n.a., dep. Mar 11, 1661. {ARMD 41:552}

BASSETT, THOMAS, see "Margarett Bassett," q.v.

BATCHELER (BATCHELOR), FRANCIS, of Charles County, aet. 26, dep. Mar 4, 1661/2, stated that he found the will of Joseph Lenton (Lennon) among his papers when he seized the estate in behalf of the Lord Proprietor. (A later entry indicated the will was written on Dec 15, 1660). {CHLR A:195, 205} Francis Batchelor, aet. 26, dep. Nov 5, 1662. {CHLR B:9}

BATEMAN, CHRISTOPHER, of Kent County, aet. 29, dep. 1732. {KELR JS#16:248}

BATEMAN, JOHN, of Charles County, aet. 47, dep. May 22, 1755. {CHLR E#3:135}

BATEMAN, JOHN, of Prince George's County, aet. 56, dep. May 11, 1762. {PGLR RR:267}

BATSON, HENRY, of Charles County, aet. 47, dep. May 30, 1743. {CHLR O#2:567}

BATTHURST, EDWARD, see "John Fichgared," q.v.

BATTIN (BATTEN), CAPTAIN, of Charles County, aet. 43, dep. Apr 22, 1662, mentioned Joseph Lenton and wife (not named). {CHLR A:204} See "Thomas Baker" and "Mary Row" and "Anne Rawser," q.v.

BAUL, HILLERY, see "James Wheeler," q.v.

BAUL, RICHARD, of Prince George's County, aet. 49, dep. Jun 18, 1752. {PGLR NN:34}

BAYARD, WIDOW, see "Johannes Bubenheim" and "John Skuyl" and "Henry Styls," q.v.

BAYLEY, JONAS, of Harford County, aet. 21, dep. Aug 12, 1775, mentioned his father Samuel Bayley. {Land Commission, 1774, Harford County Genealogical Society Newsletter, Jan, 1993, p. 3}

BAYLEY, SAMUEL, of Harford County, aet. 39, dep. Aug 12, 1775, mentioned his father Samuel Bayley about 4 years ago, now deceased. {Land Commission, 1774, Harford County Genealogical Society Newsletter, Jan, 1993, p. 3} See "Jonas Bayley," q.v.

BAYLY, HENRY, of Prince George's County, aet. 28, dep. Feb 26, 1725/6, stated that he attended the funeral of John Tanyhill (Tannyhill) who was buried in Carolina on the first of November last; he believes said Tannyhill was formerly of Calvert County and that Benjamin Short, of Calvert County, was his "brother." {PGLR I:730} See "Thomas Hopkins," q.v.

BAYLY, JOHN, see "Thomas Hopkins," q.v.

BAYLY, RICHARD, see "Thomas Hopkins," q.v.

BAYNARD, JOHN, see "John Lane" and "John Pitt" and "William Clayland" and "John Dixon," q.v.

BAYNARD, THOMAS, see "John Lane" and "John Pitt" and "John Dixon," q.v.

BAYNE, ELSWORTH, of Prince George's County, aet. 50, dep. Aug 29, 1768. {PGLR BB#2:390}

BAYNE, WILLIAM, of Prince George's County, aet. 38, dep. Aug 29, 1768, mentioned his father (not named). {PGLR BB#2:389-390}

BAYNES, JOHN, of Prince George's County, aet. 36, dep. May 17, 1762, mentioned Clement Wheeler about 13 or 14 years ago, now deceased. {PGLR RR:262} Aet. 43, dep. Mar 10, 1769, mentioned James Edelen about 12 years ago, now deceased. {PGLR AA#2:151}

BEACH, ELIAS, see "George Manners," q.v.

BEACHUM, ISAAC, see "Nicholas Benson," q.v.

BEACHUM, ROBERT, see "Nicholas Benson," q.v.

BEADLE, JOHN, prob. of St. Mary's County, n.a., dep. Oct 13, 1665. {ARMD 49:496}

BEALE, THOMAS, of Charles County, aet. 52, dep. Sep 18, 1752. {CHLR B#3:204}

BEALL, ALEXANDER, of Frederick County, aet. 52 and upwards, dep. Sep 25, 1772, mentioned his father (not named) when he (deponent) was a lad. {FRLR P:432}

BEALL, CHARLES, of Prince George's County, aet. 53, dep. Feb 8, 1725/6. {PGLR M:63} Charles Beal, aet. 55, dep. between Aug 12, 1727 and Mar 30, 1728. {PGLR M:269} Charles Beall, aet. 56, dep. Jun 10, 1728, mentioned his father Ninian Beall. {PGLR M:292} Charles Beale, aet. 57, dep. Mar 18, 1728/9, mentioned his father (not named), Nathan Veatch, and Edward Digges, all deceased. {PGLR M:478} Charles Beale (Beall), aet. 57, dep. between Aug 22, 1729 and Jun 23, 1730, mentioned his father Col. Ninian Beale about 18 years ago. {PGLR M:489; PGLR Q:3} Charles Beall, aet. 57, dep. Oct 8, 1731, mentioned his father Ninian Beall about 26 years ago. {PGLR Q:389} Aet. 59, dep. Jun 8, 1732, mentioned his father (not named). {PGLR Y:327} Aet. 60, dep. May 11, 1733 and Sep 25, 1733. {PGLR T:18, 27} Aet. 61, dep. Dec 3, 1734, mentioned John Bradford and Joice his wife. {PGLR T:209}

BEALL, CHARLES, of Prince George's County, aet. 35, dep. Sep 1, 1762. {PGLR RR:229}

BEALL, CHARLES, see "Samuel Magruder 3rd" and "Henry Chapple" and "Thomas Butler" and "John Nicholls," q.v.

BEALL, GEORGE (captain), of Prince George's County, aet. 50, dep. Mar 24, 1745/6. {PGLR BB:10}

BEALL, GEORGE (captain), of Frederick County, aet. 30, dep. Aug 6, 1765. {FRLR K:1348}

BEALL, GEORGE (colonel), of Frederick County, aet. 60, dep. Aug 10, 1757, stated that he was present when Capt. James Edmondston (Edmundson) ran out a tract called *Concord* near the Potomac River opposite Fair Island. {FRLR F:776}

Aet. 65, dep. Jun 3, 1760, mentioned William Black about 33 years ago and stated that about 45 years ago John Powell bought the land tracts of William Manie Farden. {FRLR F:1059} Aet. 65, dep. Nov 19, 1760, mentioned Col. Joseph Belt. {FRLR F:1161} Aet. 67, dep. Sep 26, 1763, mentioned Benjamin Rimmer, a tract called *Flint's Grove*, and the plantation where Charles Coats now dwells. {FRLR H:67} Aet. 70, dep. Aug 5, 1765. {FRLR K:1348} George Beall, Sr., aet. 77, dep. Sep 25, 1772. {FRLR P:433}

BEALL, GEORGE (colonel), of Prince George's County, aet. 60, dep. Dec 10, 1764, mentioned Thomas Evans, son of Walter Evans. {PGLR TT:365-366} Aet. 75, dep. Oct 12, 1770. {PGLR AA#2:206}

BEALL, GEORGE, see "Samuel Magruder 3rd" and "Joseph Chapline" and "John Wight," q.v.

BEALL, JAMES, see "Robert Lashley," q.v.

BEALL, JOHN, see "James Frazer," q.v.

BEALL, JOSHUA, see "Archibald McDonald," q.v.

BEALL, JOSIAH, of Frederick County, aet. 43, dep. Jun 6, 1761. {FRLR G:279}

BEALL, NINIAN (colonel), of Prince George's County, aet. 84, dep. Aug 9, 1725. {PGLR I:676} Aet. 79, dep. Jun 27, 1727, mentioned George Yates of Anne Arundel County and Edward (or Ned) Butler, son of Charles Butler, of Calvert County. {PGLR M:221} See "Charles Beall" and "Archibald Edmonston" and "Samuel Brashears" and "Benjamin Brashears" and "Alexander Magruder" and "Clement Hill" and "Walter Evans" and "Thomas Clagett" and "Francis Sandsbury" and "Humphrey Beckett," q.v.

BEALL, NINIAN, JR., of Prince George's County, aet. 51, dep. between Mar 24, 1745/6 and Mar 26, 1747. {PGLR BB:197}

BEALL, REBECCA, of Frederick County, aet. 27 or thereabouts, dep. Jun 18, 1764, mentioned her father (not named) and Rebecca Tannehill, now Rebecca Shaw, daughter of Ninian Tannehill, Sr. {FRLR J:436} See "John Adamson," q.v.

BEALL, ROBERT, see "Zachariah White," q.v.

BEALL, SAMUEL, of Prince George's County, aet. 48, dep. Nov 8, 1758, mentioned Capt. James Edmonston in 1753. {PGLR PP:228, pt. 2}

BEALL, SAMUEL, of Frederick County, aet. 46, dep. Jul 27, 1762. {FRLR J:67}

BEALL, SAMUEL, JR., of Frederick County, aet. 55, dep. Jul 29, 1762. {FRLR J:68}

BEALL, SAMUEL, SR., of Frederick County, aet. 64 and upwards, dep. Sep 25, 1772. {FRLR P:433} Aet. 65 or thereabouts, dep. Aug 14, 1772, mentioned John Rodgers about 30 or 40 years ago. {FRLR P:684}

BEAN, JOHN, of Prince George's County, aet. 38, dep. Nov 23, 1754. {PGLR NN:308}

BEAN, THOMAS, of Prince George's County, aet. 37, dep. Nov 23, 1754. {PGLR NN:308}

BEANE, ELEANOR, of Charles County, n.a., dep. Sep 24, 1661. {CHLR A:151}

BEANE, WALTER, of Charles County, n.a., dep. Nov 4, 1663. {CHLR B:201}

BEANES, CHARLES, of Prince George's County, aet. 50, dep. Sep 15, 1755. {PGLR NN:410}

BEANES (BEANE), CHRISTOPHER, of Prince George's County, aet. 50, dep. Mar 19, 1753. {PGLR NN:172}

BEANES, CHRISTOPHER, of Prince George's County, aet. 65, dep. Sep 15, 1755, mentioned his father Christopher Beanes; also mentioned William Beanes. {PGLR NN:410}

BEANES, CHRISTOPHER, see "Thomas Bowie" and "Edward Heneberry" and "John Deacons," q.v.

BEANES, RAPHE, see "Thomas Munnes" and "Elkenath Bourne" and "William Mitchell," q.v.

BEANES (BEANS), THOMAS, of Prince George's County, aet. 51, dep. Jul 8, 1769, mentioned his "brother" Ninian Tannihill about 12 or 13 years ago. {PGLR AA#2:11}

BEANES, WILLIAM, of Prince George's County, aet. 53, dep. Dec 24, 1736. {PGLR Y:84} Aet. 59, dep. Jun 28, 1743. {PGLR Y:704}

BEANES, WILLIAM, of Prince George's County, aet. 32, dep. Sep 7, 1761. {PGLR RR:231}

BEANES, WILLIAM, see "Thomas Bowie" and "Christopher Beanes," q.v.

BEARD, RICHARD, of Anne Arundel County, n.a., dep. 1696. {ARMD 20:563}

BEARD, ROBERT, prob. of St. Mary's County, n.a., dep. Oct 13, 1665. {ARMD 49:496}

BEATTY, SUSANNAH, see "Thomas Beatty," q.v.

BEATTY, THOMAS, of Frederick County, aet. 58, dep. Jun 29, 1761, stated that Robert Owen (Owens) had laid out 1,000 acres of *Dulaney's Lot* near Addison's Branch for Susannah Beatty. {FRLR G:73} Aet. 61, dep. Mar 17, 1764, mentioned Rev. Joseph Jennings about 17 or 18 years ago. {FRLR J:224}

BEAVEN, CHARLES, of Charles County, aet. 58, dep. Mar 5, 1743/4. {CHLR O#2:699}

BEAVEN, CHARLES, of Prince George's County, aet. 60, dep. Aug 11, 1757, and aet. 60 odd years, dep. Aug 20, 1757. {PGLR PP:56, 59, pt. 2}

BEAVEN, CHARLES, see "John Boone," q.v.

BEAVEN, EBSWORTH, of Prince George's County, aet. 43, dep. Sep 7, 1761. {PGLR RR:231}

BEAVEN, RICHARD, of Charles County, aet. 45, planter, dep. Jun 6, 1751 in Prince George's County, mentioned his father Richard Beavan, deceased. {PGLR PP:152} Richard Beavain, aet. 46, dep. May 18, 1753, mentioned his father (not named) about 20 years ago. {PGLR NN:135} See "Roger John Sasser" and "Peter Hoggins," q.v.

BECK, ANN, see "Joshua Beck" and "Francis Lamb" and "Rosamond Lamb," q.v.

BECK, ANTHONY, of Prince George's County, aet. 30, dep. May 13, 1769, mentioned his father James Beck about 7 years ago, now deceased. {PGLR AA#2:201-202}

BECK, AQUILLA, see "John Everet," q.v.

BECK, CALEB, of Kent County, aet. about 50, dep. Aug 11, 1750, mentioned his sister Rosamond Lamb, his father (not named), and old Elizabeth Twigg in 1713. {KELR JS#26:370} See "Anne Corse" and "Francis Lamb" and "Rosamond Lamb," q.v.

BECK, EDWARD, see "Joshua Beck" and "Matthew Beck" and "William Beck" and "Anne Corse" and "Francis Lamb" and "Rosamond Lamb" and "Sutton Quinney," q.v.

BECK, ELIJAH, of Baltimore County, aet. 55, dep. May 20, 1772. {BALR AL#E:278}

BECK, JAMES, of Prince George's County, aet. 48, dep. Dec 9, 1754, stated that he was a commissioner to determine the bounds of the tract *Brough* in 1748. {PGLR NN:374} Aet. 52, dep. Aug 11, 1758. {PGLR PP:295, pt. 2} Aet. 56, dep. Oct 10, 1762. {PGLR RR:264} Aet. 59, dep. Jan 31, 1766, mentioned Humphrey Becket, deceased. {PGLR TT:569}

BECK, JAMES, of Prince George's County, aet. 53, dep. Jan 31, 1766. {PGLR TT:568} See "Anthony Beck," q.v.

BECK, JOHN, see "Sarah Emory" and "Joshua Beck" and "Matthew Beck" and "William Beck," q.v.

BECK, JOSHUA, of Kent County, aet. about 41, dep. Oct 20, 1743, mentioned his parents Edward and Anne Beck. {KELR JS#25:97} Aet. about 50, dep. Oct, 1753, stated that his mother Ann Beck was a girl when she came to live on Bacon Bay and she was near age 77 when she died; also stated that old John Beck, aged 50 about 14 years ago, showed him the bounds of *Cornwallis's Choice*. {KELR JS#28:50} Aet. about 52, dep. Jun 19, 1755, mentioned his uncle John Beck. {KELR JS#28:137}

BECK, MATTHEW, of Kent County, aet. about 55, dep. Oct 20, 1743, mentioned his father John Beck and uncle Edward Beck about 30 years ago. {KELR JS#25:196}

BECK, WILLIAM, of Kent County, aet. about 47, dep. Oct 20, 1743, mentioned his father John Beck and uncle Edward Beck about 25 years ago. {KELR JS#25:197}

BECKETT, BENJAMIN, of Prince George's County, aet. 47, dep. Nov 20, 1769, mentioned George Medcalf about 10 years ago, now deceased. {PGLR AA#2:202}

BECKETT (BECKET), HUMPHREY, of Prince George's County, aet. 73, dep. Jan 26, 1748/9, mentioned Col. Ninian Beall about 40 or 50 years ago. {PGLR BB:628} Humphery Becket, aet. 72, dep. Dec 22, 1747. {PGLR BB:665} Humphry Beckett, aet. 80 or thereabouts, dep. Aug 13, 1753. {PGLR NN:177} See "James Beck" and "Philip Pindle," q.v.

BECKWITH, FRANCES, see "Edward Garrett" and "John Lecompte," q.v.

BECKWITH, GEORGE, of Frederick County, aet. 55, dep. Jul 25, 1760. {FRLR G:157}

BECKWITH, HENRY, see "Edward Garrett" and "Abraham Walker," q.v.

BECKWITH, NEHEMIAH, see "Daniel Bruffett," q.v.

BECKWITH, WILLIAM, see "John Swearingen," q.v.

BECRAFT, BENJAMIN, of Prince George's County, aet. 48, dep. Sep 12, 1757. {PGLR PP:60, pt. 2}

BEEVANS, JOHN, see "John Bevans," q.v.

BELL, JAMES, of Talbot County, aet. about 42, dep. between Aug 14, 1764 and Aug 13, 1765, mentioned his father Joseph Bell and old Edward Billiter upwards of 15 years ago. {DOLR 20 Old 237}

BELL, JOSEPH, see "James Bell," q.v.

BELL, WALTER, of Charles County, aet. 45, dep. Jun 5, 1770. {CHLR T#3:607} Aet. 51, dep. May 24, 1771. {CHLR T#3:603}

BELLICAN, CHRISTOPHER, of Kent County, aet. about 42, dep. Jan 4, 1741/2. {KELR JS#24:189} Aet. about 46, dep. Jun 18, 1750. {KELR JS#26:334}

BELT, BENJAMIN, see "Joseph Belt," q.v.

BELT, BENJAMIN, of Prince George's County, aet. 50, dep. Mar 23, 1735. {PGLR T:362} Aet. 66, dep. Nov 17, 1748. {PGLR BB:695} Benjamin Belt, Sr., aet. 73, dep. Aug 19, 1755; name also spelled as "Benia. Belt, Sr." and "Penia. Belt, Sr." {PGLR NN:411}

BELT, BENJAMIN, of Prince George's County, aet. 50, dep. Apr 17, 1740. {PGLR Y:176}

BELT, BENJAMIN, JR., of Prince George's County, aet. 50, dep. Jun 1, 1762, mentioned the land of Alexander Jackson about 24 years ago and John Jackson, of Frederick County, now deceased. {PGLR RR:228} Aet. 60, dep. Sep 22, 1772, mentioned his brother Joseph Belt about 33 years ago and James Pearrie, now deceased. {PGLR BB#3:117}

BELT, JEREMIAH (major), of Prince George's County, aet. 52, dep. Aug 23, 1750. {PGLR:88}

BELT, JOHN, of Prince George's County, aet. 64, dep. Jun 11, 1764, mentioned Nathan Smith about 20 years ago. {PGLR TT:371}

BELT, JOSEPH, of Prince George's County, aet. 18, dep. Mar 23, 1735, mentioned his father Benjamin Belt. {PGLR T:363}

BELT, JOSEPH (colonel), of Prince George's County, aet. 78, dep. Sep 15, 1758, stated that he was appointed a commissioner to prove the bounds of *Friendship* about 30 odd years ago. {PGLR PP:227, pt. 2}

BELT JOSEPH, see "George Beall" and "Benjamin Belt" and "John Moore," q.v.

BENHAM, MATHEW, of St. Mary's County, n.a., dep. Jun 2, 1659, stated that he was a member of the company that surprised and overtook a ship called the *St. George* of Amsterdam at Barbadoes upon suspicion of piracy. {ARMD 41:308-309}

BENNAM, MARGARET, of Charles County, aet. 20, dep. Jul 2, 1661. {CHLR A:143}

BENNETT, EDWARD, of the Parish of St. John's Wapping in the County of Middlesex, England, mariner, n.a., dep. Feb 26, 1734, stated that he knew very well John Fullstone and Anne his wife, both of the parish aforesaid, long since deceased, and he also knew Mary Want the now wife of William Want of the

Parish of Saybridgeworth in the County of Hertford (or Stratford), bricklayer, and the daughter of the said John Fullstone, deceased, and that she was now the only surviving lawful and reputed sister to Richard Fullstone, son of the said John Fullstone, deceased; also stated that Richard Fullstone lately died in Maryland [Kent County] and this deponent knew him well and was intimately acquainted with him in England as they were second cousins; further stated that all of the other children of John Fullstone (Fullston) by his wife Anne are all since dead. {KELR JS#22:295-302}

BENNETT, JOHN, of Queen Anne's County, aet. about 70, dep. Mar, 1746. {QAEJ - Benjamin Tasker folder}

BENNETT, RICHARD, see "Charles Dickinson" and "John Salter," q.v.

BENNETT (BENNITT), THOMAS, of St. Mary's County, aet. 18, dep. Mar 11, 1661. {ARMD 41:552} See "Thomas Joyce" and "Richard Wroth," q.v.

BENNI, JACOB, of Frederick County, aet. 66, dep. 1767. {FRLR L:60}

BENNINGTON, WILLIAM, of Baltimore County, aet. 30, dep. Oct 11, 1763. {BALR B#N:65}

BENNY, JOHN, of Talbot County, aet. 65, dep. Jan 4, 1708/9 to prove the will of William Hadden, deceased. {Will Book 12:345}

BENSON, CATHERINE, see "George Britt," q.v.

BENSON, HENRY, of Dorchester County, aet. 68, dep. between Jun 11, 1751 and Oct 14, 1751. {DOLR 14 Old 552}

BENSON, JAMES, of Talbot County, n.a., dep. Dec 31, 1776. {TALR 20:564}

BENSON, NICHOLAS, of Talbot County, aet. 51, dep. between Mar 11, 1755 and Jul 21, 1755, mentioned Isaac Beachum, son of Robert Beachum. {DOLR 15 Old 282}

BENSON, SARA, of Charles County, aet. 28 or thereabouts, dep. 1658. {ARMD 41:163}

BENSON, STEPHEN, of Charles County, aet. 32 or thereabouts, dep. 1658. {ARMD 41:162-163}

BENSON, WILLIAM, see "George Britt," q.v.

BENTON, VINSON, of Queen Anne's County, aet. 50, dep. Apr, 1765. {QAEJ - William Austin folder}

BERGIN, ROBERT, see "Robert Burgan," q.v.

BERK, RICHARD, of Charles County, aet. 19, dep. Jun 11, 1669. {CHLR D#1:120}

BERNARD, LUKE, see "Luke Barnard," q.v.

BERRY, BENJAMIN, see "Samuel Evans," q.v.

BERRY, ELIZABETH, see "William Silverthorne," q.v.

BERRY, JAMES, see "William Berry" and "William Silverthorne," q.v.

BERRY, JEREMIAH, see "Robert Soper," q.v.

BERRY, SAMUEL, of Charles County, aet. 56, dep. Aug 2, 1774. {CHLR U#3:386}

BERRY, THOMAS, of Prince George's County, aet. 29, dep. Nov 5, 1770, mentioned John Smallwood last spring, now deceased. {PGLR AA#2:498}

BERRY, WILLIAM, of Kent County, aet. about 46, dep. Apr, 1731. {TAEJ - Michael Fletcher folder}

BERRY, WILLIAM of Calvert County, son and heir of James Berry, late of Accomack, but now both of Putuxson in Maryland, n.a., dep. Aug 22, 1657, mentioned a land grant to his father on Maggutty Bay in Northampton (alias Accomack) County, Virginia on Aug 22, 1637. {ARMD 10:518-519}

BESTPITCH, JONATHAN, see "Lucretia Ward," q.v.

BEVAN, CHARLES, of Prince George's County, aet. 42, dep. Mar 1, 1728. {PGLR M:290}

BEVAN, RICHARD, of Prince George's County, aet. 53, dep. Jul 9, 1731. {PGLR Q:521}

BEVANS (BEEVANS), JOHN, of Baltimore County, aet. 65, dep. Jun 6, 1711, stated that he knew Hanah Keon, lawful wife of Lodowick Williams, late of Baltimore County. {BALR TR#A:135}

BEXLEY, NATHANIEL, see "William Bonner," q.v.

BEXLEY, WILLIAM, see "William Bonner," q.v.

BICKERDIKE, RICHARD, of Anne Arundel County, n.a., dep. Mar 30, 1707. {CMSP 1:8}

BIDDISON, JERVIS, of Baltimore County, aet. 48, dep. Sep 1, 1763. {BALR B#M:91}

BIGG, JOHN, of Charles County, aet. 55, dep. May 29, 1752. {CHLR B#3:58}

BIGGER, JOHN, see "Clement Hill" and "Edward Willett," q.v.

BIGGS, GEORGE, of Prince George's County, aet. 47, dep. Aug 29, 1763. {PGLR TT:127}

BILLINGS, JAMES, see "Thomas Williams," q.v.

BILLITER, EDWARD, of Dorchester County, aet. 45, dep. between Jun 14, 1729 and Jul 17, 1729, stated that John Callow showed him the bounds of *Cleland* about 28 years ago. {DOLR 8 Old 432} Edward Billeter, planter, aet. 48, dep. between Nov 10, 1732 and Jan 20, 1732/3, mentioned Emanuell Evans about 20 years ago. {DOLR 9 Old 158} Edward Billiter, n.a., dep. Jun 2, 1740, mentioned land of John Lewellin, of St. Mary's County, called *Hab Nab at a Venture* in Dorchester County. {DOLR 12 Old 128} See "James Bell" and "Thomas Allcock" and "Joseph Billiter," q.v.

BILLITER, JOSEPH, of Dorchester County, aet. about 20, dep. between Aug 14, 1764 and Aug 13, 1765, son of Edward Billitor, now deceased. {DOLR 20 Old 237} Aet. about 27, dep. between Nov 14, 1769 and Nov 6, 1770, stated that he lived at the mouth of Hog Creek with his father Edward Billiter about 18 or 19 years ago when John Hollon, now deceased, came to work for his father; also mentioned old Col. Lowe of Talbot County. {DOLR 24 Old 308} See "Thomas Allcock," q.v.

BIRCH, FRANCIS, of Prince George's County, aet. 35, dep. between Nov 11, 1729 and Mar 26, 1730, stated that his father (not named) was a tenant on John Thompson's part of land called *Air*. {PGLR M:558} Francis Birtch, aet. 30, dep. Feb 17, 1723/4. {PGLR I:542}

BIRCH, OLIVER, of Charles County, aet. 80, dep. Apr 26, 1726. {CHLR P#2:399}

BIRCH, THOMAS, of Charles County, aet. 41, dep. Sep 26, 1726. {CHLR P#2:399}
BIRD, HENRY, prob. of Anne Arundel County, n.a., dep. circa Sep 5, 1692. {ARMD 8:375}
BIRK (BERK), SARAH, of Talbot County, aet. 64 or thereabouts, dep. Feb 27, 1737, stated that her late husband John Worley had lived with Anthony Mayl (Mayle), of Talbot County, about 1689 and was there when Anthony Rumball wrote Mayl's will for him in his wife Mary Mayl's presence; also stated that John Worley has been dead over 4 years. {TALR 14:352}
BISHOP (BISHOPP), HENRY, of Mattapanient, St. Mary's County, planter, n.a., dep. Jan 31, 1637, stated that John Bryant was accidentally killed by the falling of a tree. {ARMD 4:10}
BISHOP, JOSEPH, see "Owen Jones," q.v.
BISHOP, TOM, see "Indian Abraham," q.v.
BISHOP, WILLIAM, see "Frances Shembrooke," q.v.
BISSICK, JOHN, of St. Mary's County, n.a., dep. Jul 5, 1664, mentioned Alice Sandford, servant of Pope Alvey (cooper) at Britton's Bay. {ARMD 51:122}
BLACK, WILLIAM, see "John Hunt" and "George Beall," q.v.
BLACKISTON, EBENEZER (captain), of Kent County, aet. 41, dep. 1726. {KELR JS#X:39} Major Ebenezer Blackiston, aet. 62, dep. 1745. {KELR JS#25:327}
BLACKISTON (BLAKSTONE), EBENEZER, of Kent County, n.a., dep. 1681. {ARMD 17:62}
BLACKISTON, JOHN, see "Prideaux Blackiston," q.v.
BLACKISTON (BLAKISTON), PRIDEAUX, of Kent County, aet. 39, dep. 1735, mentioned his father John Blackiston. {KELR JS#18:124}
BLACKLEACH, BENJAMIN, of Cecil County, n.a., dep. Apr 7, 1707, stated that John Fichgared told William Potts that James Whitaker told him that Edward Batthurst lay with Mary Knowleman, wife of Anthony Knowleman. {CMSP 1:9}
BLACKLEACH (BLACKLEDGE), BENJAMIN, of Kent County, aet. about 44, dep. Oct 1, 1729, mentioned his grandfather William Gallaway and uncles William and James Gallaway about 20 years ago. {KELR JS#X:410} See "Hannah Clove," q.v.
BLACKMAN, JOSEPH, see "Joan Ridgeway," q.v.
BLACKWELL, ELIZABETH, see "John Lane" and "John Pitt" and "William Clayland" and "John Dixon," q.v.
BLACKWELL, JOSEPH, of Dorchester County, aet. 55, dep. between Jun 13, 1728 and Jul 27, 1728, stated that James Kirkman, of Queen Anne's County, showed him the bounds of *Rochester* about 20 years ago. {DOLR 8 Old 379}
BLADEN, JOSEPH, of Prince George's County, aet. 49, dep. Jun 7, 1752. {PGLR NN:64}
BLADEN, WILLIAM, of Prince George's County, aet. 21, dep. May 7, 1752. {PGLR NN:64}
BLAIR, WILLIAM (magistrate), of Frederick County, n.a., dep. Nov 6, 1766. {ARMD 32:191-193}

BLAKWOOD, JOHN, of Charles County, aet. 33, dep. Jun 6, 1660. {CHLR A:94}

BLANCETT, JOHN, of Charles County, aet. 23, dep. May 23, 1761, mentioned his father John Blancett, deceased. {CHLR K#3:224}

BLAND, JOSEPH, of Dorchester County, aet. about 50, dep. between Nov 14, 1769 and Nov 6, 1770. {DOLR 24 Old 308} Aet. 54, dep. between Aug 10, 1773 and Feb 25, 1774, stated that he was shown the bounded tree of *Ryhmohold* about 30 to 40 years ago by William Spencer. {DOLR 27 Old 267}

BLANFORD, JOHN, of Prince George's County, aet. 39, dep. Feb 15. 1749/50. {PGLR PP:126}

BLANFORD, THOMAS, of Prince George's County, planter, aet. 53, dep. Jul 9, 1731. {PGLR Q:521}

BLANFORD, THOMAS, of Charles County, aet. 46, dep. Jun 8, 1772. {CHLR U#3:17}

BLANFORD, THOMAS, see "Thomas King," q.v.

BLANKINSTEIN, WILLIAM, prob. of Baltimore County, aet. 24 or thereabouts, dep. Apr 6, 1684, stated that Jacob Young was too sick to travel and unable to appear before the Maryland Assembly. {ARMD 13:21, 13:80}

BLEW, RICHARD, of Prince George's County, aet. 70 or thereabouts, dep. Oct 23, 1770, mentioned George Hardey and John Wynn about 18 or 19 years ago, now deceased. {PGLR AA#2:497}

BLINCKHORNE, JOHN, of St. Mary's County, n.a., dep. 1664. {ARMD 49:315}

BLUNT, BENJAMIN, of Queen Anne's County, aet. 53, dep. July, 1770. {QAEJ - Henry Carter folder}

BLUNT, MARY, of Queen Anne's County, aet. 65, dep. Mar, 1770. {QAEJ - Henry Carter folder}

BLUNT, RICHARD, of Dorchester County, aet. 68, dep. between Jun 11, 1765 and Mar 9, 1767. {DOLR 21 Old 315}

BOARMAN, BENEDICT LEONARD, of Charles County, aet. 58, dep. May 23, 1745. {CHLR Z#2:342}

BOARMAN, FRANCIS IGNATIUS, of Charles County, aet. 40, dep. Apr 8, 1742. {CHLR O#2:383}

BOARMAN, GERRARD, of Charles County, aet. 45, dep. Sep 29, 1773, also referred to as Ignatius Gerrard Boarman. {CHLR U#3:599} See "Ann McDonald" and "William McPherson," q.v.

BOARMAN, IGNATIUS, see "Ann McDonald" and "William McPherson," q.v.

BOARMAN, JOHN BAPTIST, see "William Simpson, Sr.," q.v.

BOARMAN, MAJOR, of Charles County, aet. 80, dep. Sep 16, 1707. {CHLR C#1:158}

BOARMAN, WILLIAM, of Charles County, aet. 32, dep. Apr 8, 1742. {CHLR O#2:383} Aet. 45, dep. Jul 16, 1755, stated that Mrs. Mudd and Mrs. Green were sisters. {CHLR E#3:389} See "John Jee" and "William McPherson," q.v.

BOAZE, GEORGE, see "George Booz," q.v.

BOAZLEY, WILLIAM, of Dorchester County, aet. 65 or 66, dep. between Aug 14, 1770 and Oct 15, 1770. {DOLR 24 Old 297}

BOBO, GABRIEL, of Charles County, aet. 53, dep. Jul 11, 1772. {CHLR U#3:165}
BOCKNELL, JOHN, of Charles County, aet. 66, dep. Apr 13, 1731. {CHLR R#2:42}
BOGUE, JOHN (lieutenant), of Charles County, n.a., dep. Sep 10, 1663. {ARMD 49:61}
BOIDE, HUGH, see "Hugh Boyd," q.v.
BOLTON, HENRY, of Prince George's County, aet. 70, dep. Jul 29, 1754, mentioned Robert Tyler, father of Robert Tyler, about 20 years ago. {PGLR NN:373}
BOLTON, JAMES, of Charles County, aet. 40, dep. May 25, 1752. {CHLR B#3:121} Aet. 54, dep. Apr 4, 1755. {CHLR E#3:132}
BOLTON, JOHN, see "John Lecompte," q.v.
BOND, JACOB, of Baltimore County, Quaker, aet. 43 or thereabouts, dep. Apr 3, 1769, mentioned his brother John Bond and father Thomas Bond. {BALR AL#A:304}
BOND, JOHN, of Baltimore County, Quaker, aet. 49, dep. Jun 22, 1762. {BALR B#M:136} Aet. 50, dep. Mar 3, 1764. {BALR B#M:372} Aet. 51, dep. Jul 2, 1764. {BALR B#N:308} Aet. 54, dep. Nov 9, 1767. {BALR B#Q:592} Aet. 55 or thereabouts, dep. Nov 22, 1768 and Apr 3, 1769, mentioned his father Thomas Bond and young William Selman about 30 years ago. {BALR AL#A:296, 302} Aet. 54, dep. Nov 15, 1769, mentioned his father Thomas Bond. {BALR AL#C:278} Aet. 56, dep. Apr 15, 1771. {BALR AL#C:610} Aet. 61 or thereabouts, dep. Aug 15, 1774, mentioned his father Thomas Bond. {BALR AL#L:239} See "Thomas Bond" and "Jacob Bond," q.v.
BOND, THOMAS, of Baltimore County, aet. 59, dep. May 12, 1764, stated that he was the second son of Thomas Bond, deceased. {BALR B#O:113} Aet. 65 or thereabouts, dep. Nov 22, 1768, mentioned his brother John Bond and his father Thomas Bond. {BALR AL#A:296} Aet. 66, dep. Jun 14, 1770, mentioned his father Thomas Bond. {BALR AL#C:278} Thomas Bond, Quaker, aet. 70, dep. Aug 15, 1774, mentioned his father Thomas Bond, deceased. {BALR AL#L:239} See "John Bond" and "Jacob Bond" and "James Whitaker" and "John McAdow," q.v.
BOND, THOMAS, JR., of Baltimore County, aet. 38, dep. Apr 15, 1771. {BALR AL#C:610}
BOND, WILLIAM (captain), of Baltimore County, aet. 55, dep. Mar 3, 1764. {BALR B#M:372}
BONIFANT, JAMES, of Prince George's County, aet. 53, dep. Jul 9, 1764. {PGLR TT:283}
BONNER, WILLIAM, of Dorchester County, aet. about 46, dep. between Nov 11, 1755 and May 20, 1756, mentioned William Bexley about 28 years ago, now deceased, and his son Nathaniel Bexley. {DOLR 16 Old 76}
BONNET, JOSEPH, of Prince George's County, aet. 82, dep. Sep 21, 1761, stated that he has known this area for about 50 years. {PGLR RR:227} See "Joseph Punnett (Ponnet)," q.v.
BOOKER, JOHN, see "Francis Meek, Jr.," q.v.

BOONE, FIELDER, aet. 24, dep. Aug 23, 1768. {PGLR BB#2:371}
BOONE, HENRY, of Prince George's County, aet. 42, dep. Mar 22, 1756. {PGLR NN:470} Aet. 54, dep. Feb 20, 1767. {PGLR BB#2:166-167}
BOONE, ISAAC, of Queen Anne's County, aet. 41, dep. Aug, 1752, mentioned his father William Boon(e). {QAEJ - Sarah Starkey folder}
BOONE, JACOB, of Queen Anne's County, aet. 40, dep. Aug, 1752, mentioned his father William Boon(e). {QAEJ - Sarah Starkey folder}
BOONE, JOHN, of Prince George's County, aet. 53, dep. Feb 28, 1731/2. {PGLR Q:431} Aet. 52, dep. Apr 4, 1732. {PGLR Q:573} John Boone, Jr., aet. 55, dep. Mar 19, 1733/4. {PGLR T:152} John Boone, aet. 57, dep. Aug 6, 1735, mentioned James Brooke, brother of Roger Brooke, about 30 years ago. {PGLR T:360} John Boone, aet. 58, dep. Dec 24, 1736. {PGLR Y:85} John Boone, Sr., aet. 72, planter, dep. Jul 31, 1750. {PGLR PP:60} John Boone, aet. 72, planter, dep. Jun 6, 1751, mentioned Charles Beavan about 49 years ago, now deceased. {PGLR PP:152} John Boone, aet. 73, planter, dep. Jun 30, 1752. {PGLR NN:66} Aet. 88, dep. Feb 20, 1767. {PGLR BB#2:167} Aet. 90, dep. Aug 23, 1768, mentioned Roger Brooke and the widow of James Brooke, deceased. {PGLR BB#2:371}
BOONE, JOHN, of Prince George's County, aet. 70 or thereabouts, dep. Mar 22, 1756, mentioned Basil Brooke about 52 years ago. {PGLR NN:470}
BOONE (BOON), WILLIAM, see "John Swift" and "Isaac Boone" and "Jacob Boone," q.v.
BOOZ (BOOZE), GEORGE, of Dorchester County, aet. 39, dep. between Mar 13, 1732 and Aug 22, 1733. {DOLR 9 Old 357} George Boaze, aet. 50, dep. Mar 9, 1741. {DOLR 12 Old 105} George Bozes, aet. 69, dep. between Nov 10, 1761 and Mar 4, 1762. {DOLR 18 Old 83} Aet. 69, dep. between Nov 10, 1761 and Jan 21, 1762. {DOLR 18 Old 87} Aet. 69, dep. between Nov 8, 1763 and Jun 11, 1764, mentioned old Lewis Griffith. {DOLR 19 Old 237} George Booze, aet. 70, dep. between Jun 12, 1764 and Aug 6, 1765, mentioned the late Timothy Macnemara about 50 years ago. {DOLR 20 Old 218}
BOOTS, WILLIAM, of Kent County, aet. about 40, dep. Aug 5, 1745. {KELR JS#25:299}
BOOZMAN, THOMAS, see "Solomon Wright," q.v.
BORDLEY, STEPHEN, of Kent County, aet. about 50, dep. Jul 16, 1762. {KEEJ - John Carville folder}
BORDLEY, STEPHEN, of Baltimore County, aet. 59, dep. Oct 25, 1769. {BALR AL#B:286}
BOREMAN, WILLIAM, of St. Mary's County, aet. about 20, dep. May 28, 1650, mentioned sailing with Andrew Monroe, master of a pinnace on St. Inigoes Creek in 1645. {ARMD 10:12}
BORING, JAMES, see "William Parrish, Jr." and "Nathan Hawkins," q.v.
BOSTICK, RACHEL, of Kent County, Shrewsbury Parish, aet. about 18, dep. Nov, 1732, stated she committed fornication on Jan 10, 1731/2 and had a child (not named) by James Boyer. {Kent Court Records JS#WK:330}

BOSTOCK, NATHANIEL, see "James Sanders," q.v.
BOSWELL, GEORGE, of Charles County, aet. 26, mentioned his father Michael Boswell and brother John Boswell. {CHLR B#3:204}
BOSWELL, JOHN, SR., of Charles County, aet. 38, dep. May 13, 1745. {CHLR 40:337} See "George Boswell," q.v.
BOSWELL, MICHAEL, see "George Boswell," q.v.
BOSWELL, ROBERT, see "Anthony Rawlings," q.v.
BOTELER, CHARLES, of Prince George's County, aet. 34, dep. Aug 25, 1737. {PGLR T:510} Aet. 55, dep. Mar 22, 1756. {PGLR NN:470} Charles Boteler, Sr., aet. 70, dep. Apr 24, 1772. {PGLR BB#3:81}
BOURK, CISLEY, see "Thomas Taylor," q.v.
BOURK, JOHN, see "Thomas Taylor," q.v.
BOURNE, ELKENATH, prob. of St. Mary's County, seaman, n.a., dep. Feb 20, 1649, stated he and Thomas Munnes were employed by Richard Husbands, mariner, about 7 days ago to receive merchantable tobacco from John Jarbo for Raphe Beanes. {ARMD 10:9}
BOWDLE, JOSEPH, of Dorchester County, aet. about 51, dep. between Aug 14, 1759 and Mar 11, 1761, stated that he was shown the bounded tree of *The Gore* about 16 or 17 years ago by Benjamin Nicolls and Edward Hardekin, both now deceased. {DOLR 17 Old 376}
BOWEN, BENJAMIN, see "Josias Bowen," q.v.
BOWEN, JACOB, see "Sarah Deaver," q.v.
BOWEN, JOSIAS, of Baltimore County, aet. 36, dep. Sep 20, 1765. {BALR B#P:173} Aet. 41, dep. Jun 4, 1771, mentioned his brother Benjamin Bowen. {BALR AL#C:597}
BOWEN, NATHAN, of Baltimore County, aet. 44, dep. Sep 20, 1765, mentioned his father's sister Honour Stansbury. {BALR B#P:172}
BOWEN, REES, of Baltimore County, planter, aet. 59, dep. Dec 26, 1767. {BALR B#Q:700}
BOWEN, SOLOMON, of Baltimore County, aet. 40, dep. Sep 20, 1765. {BALR B#P:172} Aet. 43, planter, dep. Dec 26, 1767. {BALR B#Q:699}
BOWERS, JEREMIAH, of Charles County, aet. 37, dep. May 24, 1747. {CHLR Z#2:79}
BOWERS, THOMAS, of Kent County, aet. about 38, dep. 1773. {KEEJ - Samuel Griffith folder}
BOWIE, FIELDER, of Prince George's County, aet. 25, dep. Jun 1, 1770. {PGLR AA#2:142}
BOWIE, JOHN, of Prince George's County, n.a., dep. May 29, 1730. {PGLR Q:153} Aet. 41, dep. Feb 28, 1731. {PGLR Q:431} John Bowie, Sr., aet. 63, dep. Apr 23, 1751. {PGLR PP:132, 155}
BOWIE, THOMAS, of Prince George's County, aet. 31, dep. Dec 9, 1754. {PGLR NN:374} Aet. 32, dep. Mar 12, 1755, mentioned Christopher Beanes and his brother William Beanes. {PGLR NN:412}

BOWIE, WILLIAM, of Prince George's County, aet. 33, dep. Aug 13, 1753, mentioned his father (not named). {PGLR NN:177} Aet. 50, dep. May 22, 1770. {PGLR AA#2:139-140}
BOWLES, ISAAC, see "Mary Davis" and "Robert Meeks," q.v.
BOWLING, JOHN, see "Richard Edelen" and "Ignatius Hagan" and "Mary Routhorn" and "George Thorold," q.v.
BOWLING, JOSEPH, of Charles County, n.a., dep. Feb 25, 1767. {CHLR Q#3:193}
BOWLING, MARY, see "Richard Edelen" and "Ignatius Hagan," q.v.
BOWLING, ROGER, see "Mary Routhorn," q.v.
BOWLING, THOMAS, of Charles County, aet. 60, dep. May 7, 1764. {CHLR M#3:691} Aet. 63, dep. Feb 25, 1767 and Jun 22, 1767. {CHLR Q#3:195, 503} See "Richard Edelen" and "Ignatius Hagan" and "Mary Routhorn" and "George Thorold," q.v.
BOWLING, WILLIAM, of Charles County, aet. 58, dep. May 7, 1765, mentioned William Boarman and his cousin Mary Bowling. {CHLR M#3:589} Aet. 60, dep. Feb 14, 1767. {CHLR Q#3:195}
BOWLS (BOULS), EDWARD, see "Lucie Stratton," q.v.
BOWLS (BOULS), MARGARET, of Charles County, aet. 30, dep. Jun 30, 1663. {CHLR B:166}
BOWLS, WILLIAM, see "John Ashbrooke," q.v.
BOX, THOMAS, see "Charles Walker," q.v.
BOXELL, MARY, of Dorchester County, aet. about 53, dep. between Nov 10, 1747 and Apr 26, 1748, mentioned her mother Caturn Melvill (Melvell), wife of David Melvill, Sr. {DOLR 14 Old 309}
BOY (BOYE), JOHN, of Charles County, aet. 28, dep. Oct 19, 1734. {CHLR R#2:537} Aet. 61, dep. Nov 14, 1766. {CHLR P#3:280}
BOYAD, JOHN, see "Susannah Boyd (Boyad)," q.v.
BOYD, ABRAHAM, see "Thomas Pindle," q.v.
BOYD, BENJAMIN, see "Thomas Boyd," q.v.
BOYD, BENJAMIN, of Prince George's County, aet. 48, dep. Jul 29, 1754, mentioned Robert Tyler, grandfather of Robert Tyler, about 30 years ago. {PGLR NN:372} Aet. not given, dep. Jan 31, 1766. {PGLR TT:568}
BOYD (BOYDE), BENJAMIN, of Prince George's County, aet. near 49, dep. Apr 2, 1748. {PGLR BB:692}
BOYD (BOIDE), HUGH, of Somerset County, n.a., dep. Apr 30, 1696. {ARMD 20:403}
BOYD, JOHN, SR., of Prince George's County, aet. 63, dep. Mar 24, 1742. {PGLR Y:654}
BOYD, THOMAS, of Prince George's County, aet. 31, dep. Jan 31, 1766, mentioned his father Benjamin Boyd, deceased. {PGLR TT:568}
BOYD (BOYAD), SUSANNAH, of Frederick County, aet. 58, dep. Apr 24, 1776, mentioned her husband John Boyad. {FRLR BD#2:374-375}

BOYER, AUGUSTINE, of Kent County, aet. about 50, dep. Aug 26, 1740, mentioned his father William Boyer, Dennis McCarty, and old Elizabeth Hill, relict of Samuel Hill, many years ago. {KELR JS#23:43}

BOYER, JAMES, see "Rachel Bostick," q.v.

BOYER, RICHARD, of Kent County, aet. 49, dep. Apr, 1759. {KEEJ - Thomas Harris folder} Richard Boyer, inspector, aet. about 52, dep. Feb 12, 1761. {KELR JS#X:221}

BOYER, THOMAS, of Kent County, aet. about 36, dep. Apr 17, 1754. {KEEJ - Isaac Freeman folder}

BOYER, WILLIAM, of Kent County, aet. 58, dep. Jun 10, 1725. {KELR JS#W:486} Aet. about 62, dep. May 2, 1728. {KELR JS#X:383} See "Augustine Boyer," q.v.

BRADFORD, COLONEL, see "William Warford" and "Robert White," q.v.

BRADFORD, JOHN, see "John Richard" and "Charles Beall" and "William Magruder Selby," q.v.

BRADFORD, JOICE, see "Charles Beall," q.v.

BRADLEY (BRADLY), BARTHULIA, of Dorchester County, aet. 35, dep. between Aug 12, 1760 and Jun 11, 1761, mentioned her father Andrew Ramsey about 22 years ago. {DOLR 17 Old 354}

BRADLEY (BRADLY), CHARLES, of Dorchester County, aet. 70, dep. between Jun 13, 1728 and Jul 27, 1728. {DOLR 8 Old 379}

BRADLEY, ROBERT, of Prince George's County, aet. 56, dep. Mar 1, 1756. {PGLR NN:469} Aet. 64, dep. Jul 21, 1764. {PGLR BB#2:165}

BRADLEY, WILLIAM, see "Charles Thompson," q.v.

BRADNOX, THOMAS, of St. Mary's County, aet. 40 or thereabouts, dep. Sep 11, 1647, mentioned Nathaniel Pope. {ARMD 3:192}

BRADSHAW, ELIZABETH, see "Elizabeth Lamphier," q.v.

BRADSHAW, GEORGE, of Charles County, n.a., dep. Jan 5, 1663/4, mentioned John alias Jacob Lumbroso. {CHLR B:214}

BRAMBLE, JOHN, of Dorchester County, aet. 70, dep. between May 6, 1726 and Aug 14, 1727. {DOLR 8 Old 227} See "George Stapleford," q.v.

BRAMBLE, THOMAS, of Dorchester County, aet. 49, dep. Mar 9, 1741. {DOLR 12 Old 105}

BRANDT, RANDOLPH, of Charles County, aet. 39, dep. Jul 24, 1742. {CHLR O#2:425}

BRANNOCK, EDMOND, of Dorchester County, aet. 52, dep. between Mar 8, 1763 and Nov 2, 1763, mentioned his father Thomas Brannock. {DOLR 19 Old 84} Edmund Brannock, aet. 62, dep. between Nov 10, 1772 and Mar 28, 1774, mentioned his brother Thomas Brannock and his uncle John Brannock about 40 years ago; also mentioned a quarrel between Thomas Soward and Frank Soward. {DOLR 27 Old 356} See "Henry Brannock" and "John King, Sr.," q.v.

BRANNOCK, HENRY, of Dorchester County, aet. 56, dep. between Aug 11, 1772 and Jul 29, 1773, mentioned his father Thomas Brannock about 30 years ago, and the plantation where the present Edmond Brannock, Sr. now lives. {DOLR 27 Old 31} See "John King, Sr.," q.v.

BRANNOCK, JOHN, SR., of Dorchester County, n.a., dep. between Nov 19, 1731 and Jan 26, 1731/2. {DOLR 8 Old 454} See "Thomas Brannock" and "Edmond Brannock," q.v.

BRANNOCK, THOMAS, see "Edmond Brannock" and "Henry Brannock," q.v.

BRANNOCK, THOMAS, of Dorchester County, aet. 64, dep. between Aug 8, 1738 and Mar 9, 1738/9. {DOLR 11 Old 244} Thomas Brannock, Sr., aet. 65, dep. between Mar 13, 1738/9 and Nov 12, 1739. {DOLR 12 Old 119}

BRANNOCK, THOMAS, SR., of Dorchester County, aet. 60, dep. between Nov 13, 1739 and Apr 4, 1740, stated that "he was at Benjamin Woodwards and Benjamin Woodward, desieced" about 14 years ago regarding *Woodward's Content* and a survey to be run by Thomas Pearson. {DOLR 12 Old 109} Aet. 68, dep. between Nov 8, 1743 and Dec 17, 1743, mentioned his brother John Brannock. {DOLR 12 Old 136}

BRANSON, ANNE (ANE), of Charles County, aet. 20, dep. Jul 8, 1662. {CHLR A:219}

BRANTWELL, WILLIAM, see "Robert Clarke," q.v.

BRASHARE, JOHN, of Prince George's County, aet. 61, dep. Jun 16, 1763. {PGLR TT:83}

BRASHEARS, BENJAMIN, see "Samuel Henness," q.v.

BRASHEARS (BRASHEIR), BENJAMIN, JR., of Prince George's County, aet. 37, dep. Mar 23, 1735. {PGLR T:363}

BRASHEARS (BRESHEARS, BRAUSSUER), BENJAMIN, SR., of Prince George's County, aet. 64, dep. Sep 22, 1730. {PGLR Q:158} Aet. 66, dep. Jun 20, 1729, mentioned Col. Ninian Beall about 40 years ago. {PGLR M:438} Benjamin Brasheir, aet. 73, dep. Mar 23, 1735. {PGLR T:362} Benjamin Breshears, aet. 80, dep. Aug 23, 1738. {PGLR T:636} Benjamin Braussuer, aet. 80, dep. Nov 26, 1739, mentioned his brother Samuel Braussuer. {PGLR Y:107}

BRASHEARS, OTHO, of Prince George's County, aet. 31, dep. Dec 5, 1748, mentioned Elizabeth Plummer about 18 or 20 years ago. {PGLR BB:700}

BRASHEARS (BRASHEIR), ROBERT, of Prince George's County, aet. 48, dep. Mar 23, 1735. {PGLR T:362} Robert Brashears, aet. between 60 and 70, dep. between Mar 24, 1745/6 and Mar 26, 1747. {PGLR BB:197} Robert Brashears, Sr., aet. near 73, dep. May 19, 1748, mentioned Robert Tyler, Sr. about 21 years ago, now deceased, and his son Robert Tyler. {PGLR BB:693} See "Samuel Brashears," q.v.

BRASHEARS (BRESHEARS), SAMUEL, of Prince George's County, planter, aet. 51, dep. Oct 2, 1724. {PGLR I:596} Samuel Breshears, aet. 56, dep. Jun 20, 1729, mentioned his father Robert Breshears. {PGLR M:438} Samuel Breshear, aet. 61, dep. Mar 10, 1735/6, mentioned his father-in-law Col. Ninian Beall. {PGLR T:279} Samuel Brashers, aet. 60, dep. Nov 29, 1734. {PGLR T:203} Samuel

Brashear, aet. 66, dep. Apr 17, 1740, mentioned John Darnall and his father-in-law James Williams. {PGLR Y:176}
BRASHEARS, SAMUEL, of Prince George's County, aet. 55, dep. Nov 18, 1748 and since deceased. {PGLR BB:696-697}
BRASHEARS, SAMUEL, of Prince George's County, aet. 51, dep. Dec 5, 1748. {PGLR BB:700}
BRASHEARS, THOMAS, of Prince George's County, n.a., dep. Apr 22, 1755. {PGLR NN:371}
BRASHEARS, THOMAS, SR., of Prince George's County, aet. 47, dep. Apr 2, 1755. {PGLR NN:374}
BRASHEARS, WILLIAM, SR., of Prince George's County, aet. 43, dep. Mar 21, 1748/9. {PGLR BB:701} Aet. 48, dep. Dec 9, 1754. {PGLR NN:374} Aet. 50, dep. Nov 16, 1758. {PGLR PP:275, pt. 2}
BRATON (BRADON), JOSEPH, see "John Carmack," q.v.
BRAUSSUER, SAMUEL, see "Benjamin Brashears," q.v.
BRAWHAUN, PATRICK, see "John Kirke," q.v.
BRAWHAWN, JEAN, of Dorchester County, aet. 15, dep. between Nov 13, 1764 and May 4, 1765. {DOLR 20 Old 173}
BRAWHAWN, WIDOW, see "Thomas Soward," q.v.
BRAWNER, EDWARD, of Charles County, aet. 75, dep. Mar 27, 1758, stated that John Woodward, Jr. died in his minority and his father John Woodward married the widow Newton who was deemed to be the daughter of Garrard Brown; Dr. John Cornish, then between 60 and 70 years of age, married the widow of Garrard Brown and lived on *Simpson's Supply*; Richard Marshall married Mary Brown, the youngest daughter of Garrard Brown, about 60 years ago and lived at the same place; Richard Marshall had a son Garrard Marshall and when said Richard died his widow married Richard Wise and lived at the same place; and, when Richard Wise died his widow married a Dunaway (first name not given). {CHLR B#3:424, 581} Aet. 77, dep. Aug 11, 1760. {CHLR K#3:5}
BRAWNER, EDWARD, of Prince George's County, aet. 77, dep. Aug 5, 1760, mentioned Capt. Robert Wade, Sr., about 50 years ago. {PGLR RR:74}
BRAWNER, EDWARD, see "John Brawner," q.v.
BRAWNER, HENRY, of Charles County, aet. 23, dep. Apr 6, 1733. {CHLR R#2:332}
BRAWNER, JOHN, of Charles County, aet. 46, dep. May 18, 1769, mentioned his father Edward Brawner. {CHLR Q#3:442}
BRAWNER, WILLIAM, of Charles County, aet. 50, dep. May 18, 1769. {CHLR Q#3:442}
BRENT, ----, see "John Rowles," q.v.
BRENT, GILES, see "Margaret Brent" and "William Hambleton," q.v.
BRENT, MARGARET, of Charles County, aet. 20, dep. Mar 10, 1658/9, mentioned her master William Marshall. {CHLR A:44}

BRENT, MARGARETT (Mrs.), of St. Mary's County, n.a., dep. Jun 10, 1647, stated "that the late Governor Leonard Calvert, Esq., being lying upon his death bed, did by word of mouth on the ninth of this month, nominate Thomas Greene, Esq., Governor of the Province of Maryland." {ARMD 3:187} Mrs. Margaret Brent mentioned her brother Capt. Giles Brent in 1649. {ARMD 4:541} See "Thomas Hamper" and "Henrie Addams," q.v.

BRENT, MARY (Mrs.), of St. Mary's County, n.a., dep. Jun 10, 1649. {ARMD 3:187}

BRERETON, THOMAS, of Anne Arundel County, n.a., dep. Apr 7, 1707, mentioned being at the Bay Side in Fluits Pound and a trip to Somerset County, his cousin John Shipley, his uncle Samuel Smith, his uncle ---- Shapley, his brother William Brereton, skipper John Spry, "saylor" Thomas Barebatch, and Mr. Thomas Plumer at New Point Comfort. {ARMD 27:115-117}

BRERETON, WILLIAM, see "Thomas Brereton," q.v.

BRETT, GEORGE, of Charles County, aet. 43, dep. Aug 4, 1761, mentioned his brother Richard Brett and uncle George Brett who owned *Brett's Good Chance* about 27 years ago. {CHLR K#3:300}

BRETT, RICHARD, see "George Brett," q.v.

BRETTON, WILLIAM, of St. Mary's County, n.a., dep. 1659. {ARMD 41:346}

BREWER, JAMES, of Kent County, aet. about 30, dep. Mar 24, 1774, mentioned his uncle James Brewer. {KEEJ - John Comegys folder}

BRICE, SAMUEL, of New Connaught, Cecil County, n.a., dep. Nov 4, 1722, mentioned the encroachment of Pennsylvanians on his land, particularly Isaac Taylor and son (not named), Elisha Gatchell, William Brown, John Churchman, Richard Brown, and Roger Nerck. {ARMD 25:396}

BRIDGES, CAPTAIN, see "Indian Chotike," q.v.

BRIGHT, FRANCIS, of Queen Anne's County, aet. about 53, dep. Mar, 1759. {QAEJ - Henry Carter folder}

BRIGHT, THOMAS, see "Elesabeth Lockett," q.v.

BRIGHT, WILLIAM, of Prince George's County, aet. 52, dep. Oct 6, 1763, mentioned George Jones the second and Thomas Swan about 10 years ago, both deceased. {PGLR TT:122} Aet. 58, dep. Mar 27, 1770, mentioned James Naylor, Sr. in 1765. {PGLR AA#2:194} William Bright, Sr., aet. 59, dep. Aug 20, 1771. {PGLR AA#2:277-278}

BRIGHTWELL, ANN, of Prince George's County, n.a., dep. Mar 17, 1768, stated that John Brightwell, Jr., son of Peter Brightwell, was born in Jan, 1738. {PGLR AA#2:206}

BRIGHTWELL, JOHN, of Prince George's County, aet. 52, dep. Jan 9, 1748/9, mentioned William Watson, deceased. {PGLR BB:626} Aet. not given, dep. Mar 17, 1768, stated that John Brightwell, Jr., son of Peter Brightwell, was born in Jan, 1738. {PGLR AA#2:206} John Brightwell, Sr., aet. 73, dep. Jul 7, 1772. {PGLR BB#3:77} See "Richard Brightwell" and "Ann Brightwell," q.v.

BRIGHTWELL, PETER, of Prince George's County, aet. 46, dep. Aug 25, 1737. {PGLR T:504} Aet. 47, dep. Jul 1, 1739. {PGLR T:607} Aet. 53, dep. Aug 24, 1741. {PGLR Y:361} Aet. not given, dep. Mar 16, 1745/6, mentioned John Nicholls and wife (not named), a woman named ---- [blank] Mitchell, and Arnold Livers at Monocacy. {ARMD 44:692, CMSP 1:75} See "John Brightwell," q.v.

BRIGHTWELL, RICHARD, of Prince George's County, aet. 51, dep. Jul 1, 1738. {PGLR T:609} Aet. 60, dep. Mar 15, 1747/8, mentioned John Brightwell and William Watson about 32 or 33 years ago. {PGLR BB:492-493} Aet. 63, dep. Apr 9, 1753, mentioned Rose Warring and Samuel Warring. {PGLR NN:282}

BRIGHTWELL, RICHARD, SR., of Prince George's County, aet. 66, dep. Nov 23, 1754, mentioned William Watson, Sr., deceased. {PGLR NN:308} Aet. 70, dep. Aug 29, 1763. {PGLR TT:128} Aet. 82, dep. Jun 2, 1770. {PGLR BB#3:77} Aet. 88, dep. Jul 7, 1772. {PGLR BB#3:75}

BRISBANE, ELEANOR, of Queen Anne's County, aet. 53, dep. Sep, 1761, mentioned her sister Mary Towers. {QAEJ - William Webb folder}

BRISCOE, HEZEKIAH, of Charles County, aet. 25, dep. Jan 23, 1755, mentioned his father John Briscoe. {CHLR E#3:137}

BRISCOE, JOHN, see "Hezekiah Briscoe" and "Philip Briscoe," q.v.

BRISCOE, PHILIP, of Charles County, aet. 36, dep. Jan 23, 1755, mentioned his father John Briscoe, deceased. {CHLR E#3:137}

BRISPO, ANTHONY, of Anne Arundel County, aet. 20 or thereabouts, dep. Oct 11, 1665, stated that he saw Negro Jacob stab Mrs. Mary Utie with a knife last Sep 30 about 10 o'clock on Saturday night (two wounds in the right arm, one of which was four fingers wide) and she died the following Wednesday, having bled to death. {ARMD 49:490}

BRITT, GEORGE, of Prince George's County, aet. 43, dep. between Nov 11, 1729 and Mar 26, 1730, mentioned Catherine Benson, wife of William Benson, and Henry Ward in 1704. {PGLR M:567} Aet. 48, dep. Apr 26, 1735. {PGLR T:253}

BRITT, WIDOW, see "Henry Barnes," q.v.

BRITTON, LIONE, of Charles County, n.a., dep. Jul 30, 1663. {CHLR B:144}

BROADAWAY, AMBROSE, of Queen Anne's County, aet. about 30, dep. Sep, 1761. {QAEJ - William Webb folder}

BROADAX, RALPH, see "Robert Graves," q.v.

BROADNOX, THOMAS, see "Robert Clarke," q.v.

BROCK, EDWARD, see "Thomas Drane," q.v.

BROOKE, BAKER, of Charles County, aet. 45, dep. Aug 17, 1769. {CHLR T#3:77}

BROOKE, BASIL, see "John Boone," q.v.

BROOKE, CLEMENT, see "Thomas Clagett" and "Thomas Sansbery" and "Henry Hill," q.v.

BROOKE, DANIEL, of Baltimore County, aet. 70, dep. Apr 15, 1771. {BALR AL#C:610}

BROOKE, ISAAC, of Prince George's County, aet. 27, dep. Feb 15, 1749/50. {PGLR PP:126}

BROOKE, JAMES, of Frederick County, aet. 53, Quaker, dep. Sep 23, 1758 in Prince George's County, mentioned his father (not named) and uncle John Brooke. {PGLR PP:225, pt. 2} See "John Boone" and "John Miller" and "Thomas King," q.v.
BROOKE, JANE, see "Thomas Clagett," q.v.
BROOKE, JOHN, see "James Brooke," q.v.
BROOKE (BROOKS), JOHN, of Charles County, aet. 36, dep. Nov 11, 1745. {CHLR Z#2:468} John Brooks, aet. 46, dep. Oct 1, 1754. {CHLR E#3:91} Aet. 53, dep. Jan 6, 1762 and Jul 5, 1762. {CHLR K#3:480, 56:216}
BROOKE (BROOKES), JOHN, JR., of Charles County, aet. 30, dep. Sep 7, 1738. {CHLR T#2:518}
BROOKE, JOSEPH, see "Thomas King," q.v.
BROOKE (BROOK), LEONARD, of Prince George's County, aet. 29, dep. Mar 15, 1757. {PGLR PP:16, pt. 2}
BROOKE, ROGER, see "John Miller" and "John Boone," q.v.
BROOKE, THOMAS, of Prince George's County, aet. 47, dep. Jun 2, 1732. {PGLR Q:524} Aet. 53, dep. Dec 24, 1736, mentioned Mrs. Elizabeth Major and her son (not named). {PGLR Y:84}
BROOKE, THOMAS, of Prince George's County, aet. 36, dep. Mar 14, 1754, mentioned Capt. John Howard about 20 years ago. {PGLR NN:238}
BROOKE, THOMAS, see "Thomas Wall" and "Walter Evans" and "Thomas Hodgkin," q.v.
BROOKE, WIDOW, see "John Boone," q.v.
BROOKE, WILLIAM, of St. Mary's County, n.a., dep. Sep 9, 1663, stated that there was a falling out between Elizabeth Greene and John Williams and she called John's daughter Olive a whore. {ARMD 49:52} See "Thomas King," q.v.
BROOKS, CHRISTOPHER, see "Rebecca Brooks," q.v.
BROOKS, FRANCIS, see "William Samford," q.v.
BROOKS, JOHN, see "John Brooke," q.v.
BROOKS, REBECCA, of Queen Anne's County, aet. about 33, wife of Christopher Brooks, dep. Aug, 1743, mentioned James Wyat about 13 years ago (now deceased) and Nathaniel Chaires (who married Elizabeth Sweatnam). {QAEJ - Sweatnam Burn folder}
BROOKS (BROOKES), ROBERT, see "Lewis Froman," q.v.
BROWN, ANN, see "William Wilson," q.v.
BROWN, BASIL, of Prince George's County, aet. 36, dep. Apr 8, 1769, mentioned his father (not named) about 25 years ago. {PGLR AA#2:201}
BROWN, CHARLES, of Dorchester County, aet. 30, dep. Aug 9, 1742. {DOLR 12 Old 260}
BROWN, FRANCIS, of Charles County, aet. 39, dep. Jun 6, 1732. {CHLR R#2:155}
BROWN, GARRARD (GERRARD), see "Edward Brawner" and "John Franklin" and "James Johnson" and "Henry Woodward," q.v.

BROWN, GUSTAVUS (doctor), of Charles County, aet. 57, dep. Apr 2, 1747. {CHLR Z#2:81}
BROWN, HANNAH, of Prince George's County, aet. 60, dep. Jul 1, 1738. {PGLR T:608}
BROWN, ISAAC, of Dorchester County, aet. 45, dep. between Nov 9, 1756 and Nov 7, 1760, mentioned his father John Brown about 2 years ago, now deceased. {DOLR 17 Old 213}
BROWN, JACOB, see "William Wilson," q.v.
BROWN, JAMES, of Dorchester County, aet. 80 or upwards, dep. between Mar 17, 1768 and Aug 9, 1768, mentioned John Carter, late of Somerset County, deceased, and Charles Thompson, late of Dorchester County, deceased. {DOLR 22 Old 433}
BROWN, JAMES, of Baltimore County, aet. 56, dep. Apr 8, 1772, mentioned his father (not named) and John Jackson about 24 years ago. {BALR AL#E:402}
BROWN, JAMES (captain), of Queen Anne's County, aet. 60, dep. Mar, 1755. {QAEJ - Matthew Dockery folder}
BROWN, JAMES, see "Elizabeth Flowers," q.v.
BROWN, JOHN, see "Richard Webster" and "Owen Ellis" and "Isaac Brown," q.v.
BROWN, JOHN, of Prince George's County, aet. 52, dep. Oct 10, 1761, mentioned old James Mullikin and old Charles Walker about 34 years ago, both now deceased. {PGLR RR:181}
BROWN, JOHN, of Baltimore County, aet. 40, dep. May 8, 1770. {BALR AL#B:288}
BROWN, JOHN, of Charles County, aet. 50, dep. Jul 24, 1742. {CHLR O#2:424}
BROWN, JOHN, of Dorchester County, aet. 36, dep. Aug 28, 1742. {DOLR 12 Old 125}
BROWN, JOHN, of Dorchester County, aet. 53, dep. between Mar 10, 1752 and Mar 10, 1753, stated that he was shown the bounded tree of *Atlantis* about 17 years ago by Daniel Hubbert, now deceased, located at the southern end of Nehemiah Hubbert's now dwelling plantation. {DOLR 14 Old 712}
BROWN, JOHN, of Queen Anne's County,
BROWN, JOHN (captain), of Queen Anne's County, aet. about 27, dep. Apr, 1755. {QAEJ - Matthew Dockery folder} Aet. about 30, dep. Jun 22, 1759. {KELR JS#29:119} Aet. about 33, dep. Aug 11, 1760, mentioned Charles Gafford in 1754 (now deceased) and Gafford's three sons Richard, Charles, and John. {QAEJ - John Gafford folder} Aet. about 44, dep. Feb, 1769. {QAEJ - John Moore folder}
BROWN, JOHN, SR., of Dorchester County, aet. 67, dep. between Nov 9, 1742 and Nov 5, 1743. {DOLR 12 Old 157}
BROWN, JONAS, of Frederick County, n.a., dep. between Dec 3, 1764 and Mar 11, 1765. {FRLR K:427}
BROWN, JOSEPH, of Prince George's County, planter, aet. 64, dep. Mar 18, 1728/9. {PGLR M:480} Aet. 73, dep. Mar 23, 1735. {PGLR T:362}
BROWN, JOSEPH, of Prince George's County, aet. 56, dep. May 20, 1725. {PGLR I:675}

BROWN, JOSEPH, of Prince George's County, aet. 33, dep. Jun 5, 1740, mentioned Major Edward Sprigg. {PGLR Y:185}
BROWN, JOSEPH, see "Henry Darnall," q.v.
BROWN, MARK, of Prince George's County, aet. 57, dep. Mar 24, 1742. {PGLR Y:654} See "Richard Lansdale," q.v.
BROWN, MARY, see "James Hopkins" and "Edward Brawner," q.v.
BROWN, RICHARD, see "Samuel Brice" and "Charles Alleyn" and "Edward Lang" and "Daniel Smith," q.v.
BROWN, THOMAS, of Dorchester County, aet. 41, dep. between Nov 9, 1742 and Nov 5, 1743. {DOLR 12 Old 157}
BROWN, WIDOW, see "John Kenslaugh," q.v.
BROWN, WILLIAM, see "Samuel Brice" and "Charles Alleyn" and "Edward Lang" and "Daniel Smith," q.v.
BROWNE, JOHN, of Charles County, aet. 26, dep. Jun 29, 1663, stated that Dr. Lumbroso had laid with his maid Elisabeth Wild and she was with child, so the doctor gave her physic to destroy it. {CHLR B:163}
BROWNE, ELIZABETH, of Cecil County, widow, aet. between 40 and 50, dep. Jun 30, 1702 in Kent County. {TALR 9:382} See "Richard Goostree," q.v.
BROWNE, GEORGE, see "Francis Posey," q.v.
BROWNE, LITTLE, see "Edmond Linsey," q.v.
BROWNE, RICHARD, see "Francis Posey," q.v.
BROWNE, THOMAS, of Craven County, North Carolina, planter, aet. 50, dep. Nov 30, 1744, stated that he was the executor of the will of Robert Miller, deceased, who lived near Dividing Creek in Great Choptank in Maryland, and the said Robert Miller left one son William Miller unto his care and that son is now about 28 years old and lives in Craven County. {TALR 16:145} See "Richard Goostree," q.v.
BROWNING, JULIANA, of Queen Anne's County, aet. 53, dep. Aug 13, 1760, mentioned her former husband John Woodall about 21 years ago. {QAEJ - John Gafford}
BROXAM, THOMAS, of Calvert County, n.a., servant to Richard Preston, Sr., dep. Mar 31, 1663. {ARMD 49:9-10}
BRUFF, REBECCA, see "James Means" and "Frances Gibson" and "Jonathan Gibson," q.v.
BRUFF, RICHARD, see "James Means" and "Frances Gibson" and "Jonathan Gibson," q.v.
BRUFFETT, DANIEL, of Dorchester County, aet. about 27, dep. between Apr 6, 1732 and Jun 3, 1732. {DOLR 9 Old 58} Aet. about 38, dep. between Nov 10, 1741 and Mar 11, 1741/2. {DOLR 12 Old 154} Daniel Bruffit, aet. about 45, dep. between Mar 14, 1748 and Jun 10, 1749. {DOLR 14 Old 465} Aet. about 59, dep. between Jun 10, 1760 and Jul 16, 1762. {DOLR 19 Old 65} Daniel Bruffitt, aet. about 59, dep. between Jun 9, 1761 and Oct 31, 1761. {DOLR 18 Old 128} Daniel Bruffit, aet. about 60, dep. between Nov 9, 1762 and Jun 18, 1763, stated that

he was shown the bounds of *Lecompte's Pasture* about 30 years ago by Abraham Walker who had been shown the bounds by his young master Nehemiah Beckwith. {DOLR 18 Old 437}

BRUFFETT, MARY, see "Charles Thompson" and "Elizabeth Ellis," q.v.

BRUMWELL, JOHN, see "Solomon Wright" and "William Payne," q.v.

BRUMWELL, ROBERT, see "Solomon Wright," q.v.

BRUSBANKS, ABRAHAM, of Baltimore County, aet. 54, dep. Apr 8, 1772. {BALR AL#E:402}

BRYAN, CHARLES, of Charles County, aet. 55, dep. Oct 20, 1741. {CHLR O#2:285}

BRYAN, DARBY, see "Robert Meeks," q.v.

BRYAN, DINAH, of Queen Anne's County, aet. about 40, dep. Feb, 1737. {QAEJ - Alexander Toulson folder}

BRYAN (BRYANT), JAMES, of Charles County, aet. 48, dep. Oct 18, 1763. {CHLR M#3:357, 592} Aet. 62, dep. Oct 3, 1774, mentioned his father John Bryan and stated that Mary Hagan was the mother of William, James, Thomas, and Ignatius Hagan. {CHLR W#3:485}

BRYAN, JOHN, see "James Bryan," q.v.

BRYAN, MARY, see "Elizabeth Southerland," q.v.

BRYAN, PHILIP, of Charles County, aet. 47, dep. Oct 1, 1771. {CHLR T#3:617}

BRYAN, PHILIP, of Prince George's County, aet. 48, dep. Mar 9, 1772, mentioned Oliver Harris about 5 years ago, now deceased. {PGLR BB#3:79}

BRYAN, RICHARD, of Prince George's County, aet. 38, dep. Mar 10, 1769. {PGLR AA#2:150}

BRYAN, SARAH, of Dorchester County, aet. 55, dep. between Mar 14, 1769 and Apr 9, 1770, mentioned her father Moses Lord. {DOLR 24 Old 9}

BRYAN, SOLOMON, of Dorchester County, aet. 78, dep. between Mar 13, 1770 and Jul 21, 1770. {DOLR 24 Old 303}

BRYAN, SUSANNA, of Dorchester County, aet. 37, dep. between Mar 15, 1731 and Apr 13, 1732, stated that the bounds of Edward Pritchett's land were shown to her by Mary Lake. {DOLR 9 Old 63}

BRYAN, TERRENCE, of Charles County, aet. 64, dep. Mar 30, 1741. {CHLR O#2:243}

BRYAN, THOMAS, of Dorchester County, aet. 42, dep. between Mar 10, 1761 and Jun 11, 1761, stated that he was shown the bounds of *Addition to Charleton* about 21 years ago by David Melvill, now deceased. {DOLR 17 Old 352} Aet. 43, planter, dep. between Aug 12, 1760 and Jun 11, 1761, stated that he was shown the bounds of *Charleton* about 14 or 15 years ago by David McCollister, now deceased. {DOLR 17 Old 354} Aet. 46, dep. between Nov 9, 1762 and Aug 13, 1764, stated that he was shown the bounded hickory tree of *Canawhy* about 25 years ago by David McCallister, now deceased. {DOLR 19 Old 293} See "Elizabeth Southerland" and "Francis Ware," q.v.

BRYAN, TORRENCE, of Prince George's County, aet. 66, dep. Mar 25, 1743. {PGLR Y:657}

BRYAN, WILLIAM, of Prince George's County, aet. 57, dep. Mar 10, 1769, mentioned Edward Cole, grandfather of the present James Cole, about 43 or 44 years ago. {PGLR AA#2:150}

BRYAN, WILLIAM, of Charles County, aet. 33, dep. Aug 4, 1772. {CHLR U#3:166}

BRYAN (BRYON), WILLIAM, of Charles County, aet. 23, dep. Mar 3, 1736/7. {CHLR T#2:299}

BRYANT, JOHN, see "Henry Bishop" and "Joseph Edlow," q.v.

BUBENHEIM, JOHANNES, of Cecil County, n.a., dep. Jul 8, 1723, stated that John Crowman, tailor, of Cecil County, died about 2 o'clock last Saturday afternoon at the home of the widow Bayard; on Jul 5th Crowman stated he wanted Adam Lytner to have his clothes; he died and was buried on Bayard's plantation on Jul 7th. {CELR 4:20}

BUCHANAN, GEORGE, of Charles County, aet. 60, dep. Jul 9, 1770. {CHLR T#3:609}.

BUCHER (BUCKER), BARTHOLOMEW, of Frederick County, aet. 47, dep. 1767. {FRLR L:60}

BUD, KATHERINE (CATHERINE), of Charles County, n.a., dep. Dec 16, 1662. {CHLR B:37} See "Robert Landen" and "Joseph Harrison," q.v.

BUENCE, MARY, of London, England, widow, aet. 52, dep. Jun 21, 1699 at His Majesty's Court held in the Chamber of the Guildhall, stated that Richard Owens married her mother Mary Ann Potter and died about 23 years ago without children; also stated that she knew Henry Jones and his wife Ellinor, both deceased, and all of their children except son William Jones, now living in Maryland, and that Richard Owens and Ellinor Jones were brother and sister; further stated that she knew Col. John Owens who died in England about 17 years ago and whose children are all deceased, and she believes Col. John Owens was the son of Richard Owen and was Ellinor's father's brother; and, after her (deponent's) mother married Richard Owens she became familiar with the friends and relatives of Richard Owens, particularly Henry Jones, his wife Ellinor, and their son William. {AALR PK:221-226} See "Owen Hughes," q.v.

BULLOCK, FRANCIS, see "Charles Standford," q.v.

BULLRAM (BURHAM), AARON, of Baltimore County, aet. 60 odd years, dep. Mar 4, 1763. {BALR B#M:156}

BULMAN, THOMAS, of Charles County, aet. 24, dep. Nov 14, 1766. {CHLR P#3:281}

BUNNELL, FRANCIS, of Prince George's County, aet. 46, dep. Jun 8, 1725. {PGLR I:647}

BUNT, JOHN, of Prince George's County, aet. 56, dep. Feb 23, 1724/5. {PGLR I:625}

BUNTEN, ELIZABETH, of Kent County, aet. 14, dep. Oct 8, 1684, mentioned her mother Mrs. [Anne] Tovey. {ARMD 17:292}

BUR, MARY, see "Charles Thompson," q.v.

BURCH, BARBARA, see "Thomas Burch, Sr.," q.v.

BURCH, BENJAMIN, of Charles County, aet. 41, dep. Feb 24, 1743/4. {CHLR O#2:704}
BURCH, EDWARD, of Charles County, aet. 45, dep. Jun 10, 1745. {CHLR Z#2:339} See "Jesse Burch," q.v.
BURCH, FRANCIS, of Prince George's County, aet. 63, dep. Aug 22, 1753 (1757?), mentioned his father John Burch, deceased. {PGLR PP:64, pt. 2}
BURCH, JESSE, of Charles County, aet. 43, dep. Oct 1, 1771, mentioned his father Edward Burch. {CHLR U#3:17}
BURCH, JOHN, of Charles County, aet. 40, dep. Sep 24, 1764. {CHLR N#3:63} See "Francis Burch," q.v.
BURCH, JUSTINIAN, of Charles County, aet. 50, dep. Jun 14, 1732. {CHLR R#2:157} Aet. 71 or 72, dep. May 29, 1752. {CHLR B#3:59} Justinian Burch, Sr., aet. 75, dep. Jul 26, 1755. {CHLR E#3:389}
BURCH, JUSTINIAN, of Charles County, aet. 53, dep. Jun 22, 1767. {CHLR P#3:504}
BURCH, OLIVER, of Charles County, aet. 62, dep. Mar 25, 1775. {CHLR X#3:11} See "Thomas Burch, Sr.," q.v.
BURCH, THOMAS, SR., of Charles County, aet. 48, dep. Sep 28, 1734. {CHLR R#2:536} Aet. 49, dep. Jul 19, 1737, mentioned his mother Barbara Burch. {CHLR T#2:371} Aet. 55, dep. Oct 3, 1741. {CHLR O#2:289} Aet. 68, dep. Dec 30, 1752. {CHLR B#3:235} Aet. 71, dep. Jul 26, 1755, mentioned his father Oliver Burch. {CHLR E#3:387}. Aet. 78, dep. Oct 20, 1763, mentioned his uncle John Scott and old Thomas Simson about 40 years ago. {CHLR M#3:354}
BURCHFIELD, ADAM, of Baltimore County, aet. 80, dep. Jan 4, 1763. {BALR B#L:497}
BURCHFIELD, ADAM, JR., of Baltimore County, aet. 30, dep. Jan 4, 1763. {BALR B#L:498}
BURCHFIELD, MARY, of Baltimore County, aet. 78, wife of Adam Burchfield, Sr., dep. Jan 4, 1763. {BALR B#L:497}
BURCHFIELD, ROBERT, of Baltimore County, aet. 60, dep. Oct 21, 1771. {BALR AL#D:276}
BURDETT, JOHN, of St. Mary's County, n.a., dep. Mar 7 and Mar 8, 1678, mentioned John Llewellin, Anthony Evans, Christopher Rousby, and Henry Exon. {ARMD 15:227, 230} See "John Llewellin," q.v.
BURDIT (BURDETT), THOMAS, of Charles County, aet. 27, dep. Jul 24, 1663. {CHLR B:133, ARMD 53:369} See "Ann Doughty," q.v.
BURGAN (BERGIN), ROBERT, of Baltimore County, aet. 44, dep. Sep 1, 1763. {BALR B#M:92}
BURGEE, EZEKIEL, of Prince George's County, aet. near 60, dep. Sep 10, 1763, mentioned John Prigg, surveyor, about 6 years ago. {PGLR TT:606}
BURGESS, BENJAMIN, see "John Burgess" and "Samuel Burgess," q.v.
BURGESS, GEORGE, see "Walter Evans," q.v.
BURGESS, HENRY, see "Elizabeth Lamphier," q.v.

BURGESS, JAMES, of Prince George's County, aet. 60, dep. Aug 6, 1735. {PGLR T:359}

BURGESS, JOHN, of Charles County, aet. 23, dep. Jul 6, 1742, mentioned his father Benjamin Burgess. {CHLR O#2:423} See "Elizabeth Lamphier," q.v.

BURGESS, JOHN (magistrate), of Elk Ridge, Anne Arundel County, n.a., dep. Dec 10, 1765. {ARMD 32:111}

BURGESS, RICHARD, of Prince George's County, aet. 40, Quaker, dep. Apr 24, 1759. {PGLR PP:315, pt. 2}

BURGESS, SAMUEL, of Charles County, aet. 36, dep. Jul 6, 1742, mentioned his father Benjamin Burgess. {CHLR O#2:423}

BURHAM, AARON, see "Aaron Bullram," q.v.

BURIDGE, JOHN, of Charles County, n.a., dep. 1658, mentioned Capt. William Fuller. {ARMD 41:163}

BURK, JOHN, see "John Wood," q.v.

BURN, ANN, see "John Franklin," q.v.

BURN, JAMES, of St. Mary's County, n.a., dep. Apr 24, 1749. {ARMD 28:509}

BURN, ROBERT, prob. of Anne Arundel County, n.a., dep. Apr 13, 1774. {CMSP 1:212}

BURNHAM, ANN (Mrs.), of Prince George's County, n.a., dep. Mar 24, 1706/7, stated that October last John Anderson came to the house of Gabriel Burnham to borrow a pint of rum, saying his sister-in-law (not named) was very ill; she (deponent) and her daughter (not named) went to see her the next day and Anderson and his wife told them they had found a dead child in the bed with the sister; and, she had taken several decoctions of herbs from Peter Calico. {CMSP 1:8} See "Sarah Joslin" and "Mary Anderson," q.v.

BURNHAM, GABRIEL, see "Ann Burnham" and "Owen Ellis," q.v.

BURNHAM, WILLIAM, see "James Johnson," q.v.

BURNOYE, CORNELIUS, see "William Hickman," q.v.

BURNS, JAMES, of Prince George's County, aet. 36, dep. Nov 15, 1756, mentioned Thomas Lucas, Sr. about 8 months ago. {PGLR PP:16, pt. 2}

BURROUGHS, JOHN, of Charles County, n.a., dep. Aug 17, 1678, stated that Daniel Cunningham and some of his family were murdered by four Pascattoway Indians; Mrs. Cunningham was wounded, but survived; her mother, Mrs. Edwards, believed they were attacked by the rogue Indian Wassetass. {ARMD 15:179}

BURROUGHS, JOHN, of Charles County, aet. 50, dep. Sep 24, 1764, mentioned his father Richard Burroughs and stated that he was with Capt. John Sothoron and Mr. John Lawson about 27 years ago, both now deceased. {CHLR N#3:63}

BURROUGHS, RICHARD, see "John Burroughs," q.v.

BURTON, THOMAS, of Queen Anne's County, aet. about 25, dep. Sep, 1761. {QAEJ - William Webb folder}

BUSH, GEORGE, of Queen Anne's County, aet. 64, dep. Apr 1, 1772. {QAEJ - John and Sophia Downes folder}

BUSICK, JAMES, SR., of Dorchester County, aet. 50, dep. between Mar 12, 1771 and Apr 22, 1771. {DOLR 26 Old 42} Aet. 51, dep. between Aug 11, 1772 and Jul 29, 1773, mentioned his father (not named) and his uncle Richard Busick. {DOLR 27 Old 31} See "Roger Woolford," q.v.

BUSICK, JOSHUA, of Dorchester County, aet. 34, dep. between Aug 11, 1772 and Jul 29, 1773, mentioned old Thomas Mace about 5 years ago. {DOLR 27 Old 31}

BUSICK, RICHARD, see "James Busick, Sr.," q.v.

BUSSARD, SAMUEL, of Frederick County, aet. 41, dep. 1767. {FRLR L:60}

BUSSEY (BUSSEE), HEZEKIAH, of Prince George's County, aet. 48, dep. Feb 25, 1725/6, stated that John Tannyhill was buried in Carolina on the first of November last. {PGLR I:730}

BUSSEY, GEORGE, of Prince George's County, aet. 54, dep. May 20, 1725. {PGLR I:675}

BUTLER, CHARLES, see "Ninian Beall," q.v.

BUTLER, EDWARD, see "Ninian Beall," q.v.

BUTLER, PETER, of Baltimore County, aet. 49, dep. May 7, 1764. {BALR B#N:139}

BUTLER, THOMAS, of Frederick County, aet. 53 or thereabouts, dep. Jun 6, 1761, mentioned Charles Beall and Joseph Spark in 1726. {FRLR G:278} See "John Wight," q.v.

BUTT, SAMUEL, of Prince George's County, aet. 58 or thereabouts, dep. Mar 21, 1769, mentioned Henry Odel about 40 years ago, now deceased. {PGLR AA#2:200}

BUTTON, JOHN, see "Mary Drury," q.v.

BUTTON, MARY, of Dorchester County, aet. 60, dep. between Jun 16, 1727 and Mar 17, 1727/8. {DOLR 8 Old 200}

BUTTON, NATHANIELL, see "James Johnson," q.v.

BUTTS, CHRISTIAN, see "Thomas Reeves," q.v.

BUTTS, CLEMENT, see "Godshall Barnes" and "Thomas Reeves," q.v.

BUTTS, JOHN, of Charles County, aet. 66, dep. Nov 11, 1745. {CHLR Z#2:469} See "Godshall Barnes" and "Thomas Reeves," q.v.

BUTTS, RICHARD, see "Godshall Barnes" and "Thomas Reeves," q.v.

BYRN, CHARLES, of Charles County, aet. 48, dep. Aug 18, 1735. {CHLR T#2:100}. Aet. 56, dep. Jul 6, 1742, stated that he was a servant to Col. Robert Hanson about 35 years ago. {CHLR O#2:422}

BYRN, JOHN, of Dorchester County, aet. 37, dep. between Mar 12, 1771 and May 4, 1771. {DOLR 25 Old 6}

BYUS, WILLIAM, of Dorchester County, aet. 67, dep. between Nov 10, 1772 and Mar 30 1773. {DOLR 26 Old 399} Aet. 67, dep. between Aug 10, 1773 and Oct 23, 1773. {DOLR 27 Old 38} Aet. 67, dep. between Aug 11, 1772 and Mar 30, 1773, mentioned John Soward some 20 odd years ago. {DOLR 27 Old 348} Aet. near 70, dep. Mar 1, 1775, mentioned old John Pollard and old William Trego about 30 years ago. {DOLR 28 Old 174} See "John Mitchel," q.v.

CABLE, JOHN, of Charles County, aet. 24, dep. Oct 23, 1660. {CHLR A:108}

CADELL, EDWARD, of Charles County, aet. 53, dep. Sep 29, 1773. {CHLR U#3:600} Aet. 56, dep. Mar 25, 1775, stated that Abraham Lemaster gave parts of *Betty's Delight* to his daughter and granddaughter (not named). {CHLR X#3:11} See "Edward Caudle," q.v.

CADELL, ROBERT, of Charles County, aet. 34, dep. Nov 21, 1758. {CHLR B#3:584}

CADWELL, JOHN, JR., see "John Davis," q.v.

CAFFEY, JOHN, of Dorchester County, aet. about 39, dep. between Mar 13, 1764 and Jun 4, 1767, stated that he lived about 13 or 14 years ago on land of Rosannah Hodson, widow of John Hodson; also mentioned John Littleton, now deceased, son of John Littleton. {DOLR 21 Old 382}

CAFFEY, MICHAEL, see "David Poole," q.v.

CAGE, ANN (Mrs.), of Charles County, n.a., dep. Sep 24, 1661. {CHLR A:151}

CAGE, WILLIAM, of Charles County, aet. 46, dep. Apr 30, 1744. {CHLR Y#2:11} Aet. 53, dep. Feb 19, 1750/1, mentioned Jane Penn, wife of John Penn, and formerly the wife of Thomas Warren, about 20 to 30 years ago. {CHLR Z#2:143}

CAIN, CAPEWELL, of Dorchester County, aet. 31, dep. between Aug 12, 1760 and Mar 2, 1761. {DOLR 17 Old 262}

CAIN (CAINE), JOHN, of Charles County, aet. 40, dep. Sep 4, 1660, mentioned Hennery Grace, former servant of John Cherman. {CHLR A:100}

CALICO, PETER, see "Mary Anderson" and "Ann Burnham," q.v.

CALLAGHAN, FERDINANDO, of Kent County, aet. about 84, dep. Aug, 1755. {TAEJ - George Maxwell folder}

CALLAGHAN, JAMES, of Kent County, aet. about 45, dep. Apr, 1761. {TAEJ - William Elbert folder}

CALVERT, ELIZABETH, see "Ann Doughty," q.v.

CALVERT, LEONARD, see "Joseph Edlow" and "Margaret Brent," q.v.

CALVERT, PHILIP, see "Gerrard Slye," q.v.

CALVERT, ROBERT, of Charles County, aet. 45, dep. Apr 8, 1736. {CHLR T#2:200}

CAMBLE, JOHN, see "Thomas Webb," q.v.

CAMEY, WALTER, of Dorchester County, aet. 70, dep. between Aug 20, 1734 and Aug 25, 1735. {DOLR 9 Old 337}

CAMPBELL, DANIEL, see "Barton Colins," q.v.

CAMPBELL, WALTER, of Dorchester County, aet. 47, dep. Aug 16, 1712. {DOLR 6 Old 217} Aet. about 65, dep. between Mar 13, 1732 and Nov 14, 1733. {DOLR 9 Old 135}

CAMPERSON, STEPHEN, see "Stephen Kemperson" and "William Rabbitt," q.v.

CANNON, ELIZABETH, of Dorchester County, aet. about 34, dep. between Aug 14, 1764 and Jan 4, 1768. {DOLR 22 Old 418} See "Mary Mitchel," q.v.

CANNON, HENRY, of Dorchester County, aet. 64, dep. between Nov 10, 1767 and Jan 11, 1768. {DOLR 22 Old 415} See "Thomas Cannon," q.v.

CANNON, JAMES, of Dorchester County, aet. 58, dep. Sep 17, 1744. {DOLR 12 Old 107} Aet. 61, dep. between Nov 11, 1746 and Apr 14, 1748, stated that he was shown the bounds of *Joseph's Forest* or *Forest of Joseph* about 40 years ago by William Nutter, late of Dorchester County, deceased. {DOLR 14 Old 231} Aet. 64, dep. between Aug 14, 1750 and Dec 20, 1750, mentioned Thomas Gordon and John Lyons about 50 years ago. {DOLR 14 Old 497} See "Elizabeth Flowers," q.v.

CANNON, JAMES, SR., of Dorchester County, aet. 55, dep. between Nov 9, 1742 and Nov 5, 1743, stated that Henry Smith and Thomas Smith showed him the bounds of *Dublin* about 35 years ago. {DOLR 12 Old 157}

CANNON, JOHN, of Dorchester County, aet. 46, dep. between Nov 10, 1767 and Jan 11, 1768, mentioned his father John Cannon. {DOLR 22 Old 415}

CANNON, JOHN, of Dorchester County, aet. 46, dep. Aug 28, 1742. {DOLR 12 Old 125}

CANNON, JOHN, see "Thomas Cannon," q.v.

CANNON, JOSHUA, see "Thomas Cannon," q.v.

CANNON, THOMAS, of Dorchester County, n.a., dep. Feb 28, 1770, mentioned division posts of lands of John Cannon, Henry Cannon, and Joshua Cannon set about 25 years ago {DOLR 25 Old 5}

CANNON, WILLIAM, of Dorchester County, aet. 44, dep. between Jun 11, 1765 and Aug 15, 1765, mentioned his mother (not named) about 30 years ago. {DOLR 20 Old 244} Aet. about 47, dep. between Aug 14, 1764 and Jan 4, 1768, mentioned William Robinson, son of William Robinson, about 21 or 22 years ago. {DOLR 22 Old 418}

CANNON, WILLIAM, SR., of Dorchester County, aet. 52, dep. between Mar 12, 1771 and May 4, 1771. {DOLR 25 Old 6}

CAPLE, ALSE, of Baltimore County, n.a., dep. Jan 11, 1767, mentioned her father William Cole. {BALR B#P:459}

CARBENY (CARBERRY?), JOHN BAPTISTA, of St. Mary's or Charles County, n.a., dep. Jun 29, 1698 in Annapolis. {ARMD 23:435}

CARBERRY, JOHN BAPTIST, of Charles County, aet. 67, dep. Jun 20, 1769. {CHLR U#3:11}

CARMACK, JOHN, of Frederick County, aet. 40 or thereabouts, dep. Mar 17, 1764, stated that he was shown the bounded tree of *Bradon's Lot* about 12 years ago by Joseph Braton (Bradon). {FRLR J:224}

CARMAN, THOMAS, of Talbot County, n.a., dep. Sep 19, 1671. {ARMD 54:510}

CARMAN, WILLIAM, of Queen Anne's County, aet. about 53, dep. Mar 29, 1760. {QAEJ - Earle: oversize folder}

CARNOLE, SAMUEL, of Frederick County, aet. 52, dep. Jun 5, 1764. {FRLR J:941}

CARPENTER, BENJAMIN, of Charles County, aet. 26, dep. Mar 30, 1758, stated that Benjamin Clements married the daughter of John Saunders. {CHLR H#3:431}

CARR, FRANCIS, of Dorchester County, aet. 53, dep. between Nov 10, 1761 and Nov 19, 1762. {DOLR 19 Old 34}

CARR, JOHN, see "Thomas Garton," q.v.

43

CARR (CARRE), NICHOLAS, prob. of St. Mary's or Calvert County, n.a., dep. Feb 12, 1661 and May 31, 1664. {ARMD 41:520, 49:218}

CARR, PETER, of Charles County, aet. 34, dep. Mar 10, 1658/9. {CHLR A:44}

CARRAWAY, MARY, of Dorchester County, aet. 45, dep. between Mar 18, 1726 and Jul 18, 1727. {DOLR 8 Old 201}

CARRICK, JOHN, of Prince George's County, aet. 54, dep. Nov 5, 1763, mentioned his father (not named). {PGLR TT:572} Aet. 60, dep. May 14, 1765, mentioned Pharoah Ryley about 26 years ago, now deceased. {PGLR TT:455}

CARRICOE, JAMES, of Charles County, aet. 70, dep. Sep 28, 1767, mentioned his father Peter Carricoe. {CHLR P#3:614}

CARRICOE, MARGARET, of Charles County, aet. 52, dep. Sep 28, 1767, mentioned her husband Peter Carricoe. {CHLR P#3:614}

CARRICOE, PETER, see "James Carricoe" and "Margaret Carricoe," q.v.

CARRINGTON, JOHN, of Charles County, aet. 35, dep. Jul 5, 1762. {CHLR M#3:215} Aet. 40, dep. Jun 4, 1771, mentioned his father Timothy Carrington. {CHLR T#3:600}

CARRINGTON, TIMOTHY, of Charles County, aet. 38, dep. Jul 5, 1762. {CHLR M#3:216} Aet. 48, dep. Jun 4, 1771, mentioned his father Timothy Carrington. {CHLR T#3:599}

CARRINGTON, TIMOTHY, of Charles County, aet. 40, dep. Jun 6, 1726. {CHLR P#2:293} Aet. 67, Nov 11, 1745. {CHLR Z#2:469}

CARRINGTON, TIMOTHY, see "John Carrington," q.v.

CARROLL, CHARLES, see "George Turnball" and "Uncle Unckles" and "James Goare" and "James Carroll," q.v.

CARROLL, CHRISTOPHER, of Charles County, aet. 27, dep. Oct 19, 1741. {CHLR O#2:281} Aet. 59, dep. Apr 28, 1772, mentioned Richard Woodward, son of Richard Woodward, deceased. {CHLR T#3:602}

CARROLL, JAMES, of Prince George's County, aet. 48, dep. Jun 27, 1727, mentioned Charles Carroll, deceased, and Col. Henry Ridgely. {PGLR M:220}

CARROLL, JAMES, of Charles County, aet. 59, dep. Jul 22, 1756. {CHLR F#3:422} James Carrole, aet. 60, dep. Sep 8, 1756. {CHLR F#3:652}

CARROLL, JAMES, of Baltimore County, n.a., dep. Jan 28, 1715, stated that he had offered some land about 3 years ago to any Roman Catholics willing to settle thereon. {ARMD 25:333-334}

CARROLL, JAMES, see "Peter Attwood," q.v.

CARROLL, JOSEPH, of Prince George's County, aet. 26, dep. Jan 12, 1748/9, mentioned John Wilburn, now living. {PGLR BB:663} See "Thomas Wall," q.v.

CARROWAN, PATRICK, of Dorchester County, aet. 63, dep. between Aug 20, 1735 and Feb 17, 1735/6, mentioned Josias Mace about 9 years ago. {DOLR 9 Old 391}

CARTER, HENRY, see "Jacob Carter," q.v.

CARTER, JACOB, of Queen Anne's County, aet. 50, dep. Mar, 1770, mentioned his brother Henry Carter. {QAEJ - Henry Carter folder}

CARTER, JOHN, of Somerset County, aet. 73, dep. between Jun 16, 1733 and Feb 25, 1733/4 in Dorchester County, mentioned Samuel Cooper, Surveyor of Somerset County, Edward Wright, and Thomas Gordin about 50 years ago. {DOLR 9 Old 149} Aet. 74, dep. between Aug 20, 1734 and Aug 25, 1735, mentioned John Gladstone and John Claibun about 37 years ago. {DOLR 9 Old 337} See "James Brown," q.v.

CARTER, MARY, of Charles County, aet. 64, midwife, dep. Feb 22, 1772. {CHLR S#3:244}

CARTER, SAMUELL, of Talbot County, aet. about 26, dep. 1705, stated that a servant boy named Thomas Hughes, who was bound to Nathaniel Hughes of Liverpool, England for a term of 5 years, was sold to John Alexander and after their arrival in Maryland some time in 1704 he (Carter) indentured Thomas Hughes for 5 years and delivered him to John Alexander. {TALR 9:348}

CARTER, WILLIAM, of Baltimore County, aet. 52, dep. May 11, 1768, mentioned Ann Grant and Mary Ford (wife of Lloyd Ford), heirs of Alexander Grant, deceased. {BALR AL#B:594}

CARTER, WILLIAM, of Charles County, aet. 60, dep. Nov 18, 1719, stated that he has lived in these parts for 40 years. {CHLR M#2:72} Aet. 66, dep. Feb 28, 1726/7. {CHLR P#2:419} Aet. 78, dep. Jun 16, 1738. {CHLR T#2:496} Aet. 78, dep. Jan 1, 1738/9, stated that he has been in the county for 63 years. {CHLR T#2:585} Aet. 79, dep. Apr 13, 1728. {CHLR T#2:466} Aet. 82, dep. Nov 2, 1742. {CHLR O#2:465} Aet. 84, dep. Feb 28, 1742. {CHLR O#2:504} Aet. 84, dep. Jul 16, 1743. {CHLR O#2:614}

CARTER, WILLIAM, SR., of Prince George's County, aet. 74, dep. Jun 26, 1734. {PGLR T:125}

CARTWRIGHT, PETER, of Charles County, aet. 50, dep. Jul 19, 1737. {CHLR T#2:371}

CARVER, JOHN, of Charles County, aet. 40, dep. Feb 19, 1750/1. {CHLR Z#2:144}

CARVILLE, JOHN (captain), of Kent County, aet. about 50, dep. Oct 4, 1756. {KELR JS#28:294} John Carvill, aet. 56, dep. Aug 30, 1763. {KEEJ - Isabella Barclay folder}

CARWIN, JOHN, of Dorchester County, aet. 23, dep. between Aug 10, 1762 and Mar 8, 1763. {DOLR 18 Old 333}

CASTLETON, ROBERT, of Charles County, aet. 19 or 20, dep. Sep 13, 1681. {CHLR I#1:169}

CATEN, JOHN, of Charles County, aet. 49, dep. Oct 1, 1754. {CHLR E#3:91}

CAUDLE, JOHN, of Charles County, aet. 69, dep. Jun 14, 1732. {CHLR R#2:157} See "Edward Caudle," q.v.

CAUDLE, EDWARD, of Charles County, aet. 53, dep. Feb 6, 1775, mentioned his father John Caudle. {CHLR X#3:483}

CAULK, ISAAC, see "William True," q.v.

CAULK, JACOB, of Kent County, aet. about 34, dep. Aug 14, 1736. {KELR JS#18:308}

CAULK, JOHN, of Kent County, aet. about 39, dep. Apr, 1759. {KEEJ - Thomas Harris folder}
CAULK, JOHN, of Dorchester County, aet. 21, dep. between Aug 9, 1768 and Oct 10, 1768, stated that he was shown the bounds of *Ring's End* last spring by Thomas Andrew, now deceased. {DOLR 23 Old 129}
CAULK, MARY, see "William True," q.v.
CAVENAUGH, HUGH, of Charles County, aet. 21 or 22, dep. Jun 9, 1668. {CHLR C#1:69}
CAWOOD, JOHN, of Charles County, aet. 52, dep. Apr 30, 1745. {CHLR Z#2:336} See "John Harris," q.v.
CAWOOD, STEPHEN, of Charles County, aet. 42, dep. Oct 8, 1742, mentioned his father Stephen Cawood, deceased. {CHLR O#2:469} See "Peter Atterburn," q.v.
CAYHAILE, EDWARD, of Queen Anne's County, aet. about 48, dep. between Aug 14, 1764 and Aug 13, 1765, mentioned his brother-in-law John Leynord, of Queen Anne's County, son of John Leynord the Elder. {DOLR 20 Old 237}
CECILL, JOSHUA, see "John Dewitt," q.v.
CETCHMEY, ----, see "Ann Johnson," q.v.
CHAD, SARAH, of Charles County, n.a., dep. Nov 4, 1663, mentioned her master James Lee. {CHLR B:203}
CHAIRES, NATHANIEL, see "Rebecca Brooks," q.v.
CHAMBERLAIN, ANN, see "Daniel Peck," q.v.
CHAMBERLAIN, SAMUEL, see "Daniel Peck," q.v.
CHAMBERS, CHARLES, of Queen Anne's County, aet. about 23, dep. Apr, 1769. {QAEJ - James Hutchens folder}
CHANDLER, JOHN, of Charles County, aet. 35, dep. Mar 14, 1748. {CHLR Z#2:348} Aet. 51, dep. May 10, 1765 and Aug 16, 1765. {CHLR N#3:380, 790} Aet. 56, dep. Dec 5, 1769. {CHLR Q#3:570}
CHANDLER, STEPHEN, of Charles County, aet. 27, dep. Apr 3, 1747. {CHLR Z#2:82} Aet. 56, Sep 29, 1775. {CHLR X#3:543}
CHANDLER, WILLIAM, of Charles County, aet. 48, dep. Nov 30, 1725. {CHLR P#2:143} Aet. 49, dep. Mar 15, 1726/7. {CHLR P#2:298} See "William Combs, Sr." and "Winifred Combs," q.v.
CHANEY, CHARLES, SR., of Frederick County, aet. 74, dep. Feb 6, 1775, mentioned his brother Greenbury Chaney. {FRLR BD#1:206}
CHANEY, GREENBORNE (GREENBUNE), JR., see "Thomas Walling" and "James Walling" and "Edmund Rutter," q.v.
CHANEY, GREENBURY, see "Charles Chaney," q.v.
CHAPLINE, JOSEPH, of Frederick County, aet. 53, dep. Mar 13, 1761. {FRLR G:159} Aet. 55, dep. Oct 22, 1762, mentioned Capt. Jonathan Hager and Col. George Beall about 20 years ago. {FRLR H:192} Aet. 57, dep. Jul 26, 1764, stated that about 20 or 21 years ago he surveyed *Pell Mell* for John VanMeter. {FRLR J:939} Aet. 58, dep. Oct 10, 1765, stated that he surveyed *Williams Project* for

Rev. William Williams in Aug, 1739, at the request of Peter Dent, then surveyor for Prince George's County. {FRLR K:427} Joseph Chapline, Sr., n.a., dep. Nov 11, 1765. {FRLR K:553} Aet. 60, dep. 1767. {FRLR L:60} See "Thomas Tomkins" and "Evan Shelby," q.v.

CHAPLINE, MOSES, of Frederick County, n.a., dep. Aug 8, 1755, stated that about 20 years ago the bounds of *Fell Foot* were laid out by the side of Little Antietam Creek and within ten perches of the Old Wagon Road that goes to Monocacy. {FRLR E:906}

CHAPMAN, JAMES, of Dorchester County, aet. 32, dep. between Nov 14, 1732 and Aug 1, 1733. {DOLR 9 Old 355}

CHAPMAN, JOHN, of Charles County, aet. 49, dep. Nov 8, 1774. {CHLR W#3:609}

CHAPMAN, RICHARD, see "Richard Patterson" and "William Barnes" and "Isaac Foxwell," q.v.

CHAPMAN, RICHARD, of Charles County, aet. 52, dep. Oct 28, 1726. {CHLR P#2:405} Aet. 54, dep. Jul 23, 1728. {CHLR Q#2:165} Aet. 59, dep. Mar 2, 1729/30. {CHLR Q#2:476}

CHAPMAN, RICHARD, of Dorchester County, aet. 47 or 48, dep. between Nov 13, 1764 and Dec 22, 1764. {DOLR 20 Old 11}

CHAPMAN, RICHARD, of Dorchester County, aet. 53, dep. Apr 2, 1740. {DOLR 12 Old 127}

CHAPMAN, ROBERT, of Baltimore County, aet. 68, dep. Dec 9, 1776. {BALR WG#B:33}

CHAPMAN, ROBERT, SR., of Baltimore County, aet. 48, dep. Jun 29, 1767. {BALR B#P:84}

CHAPMAN, THOMAS, of Charles County, aet. 21, dep. Feb 10, 1662/3, stated that he had been hired in Virginia by Richard Pinner to serve at Portobacco with Edmond Linsey; also mentioned his mate Ralph Wormly would be sent for. {CHLR B:71} See "William Barnes" and "Isaac Foxwell," q.v.

CHAPPLE, HENRY, of Frederick County, aet. 59, dep. Jun 20, 1760, mentioned John Flint and Capt. Charles Beall about 14 or 15 years ago and the tract *Addition to the Rock of Dunbarton*; also stated that he (Chapple) and John Bainbridge carried the chain for Nathaniel Wickham, surveyor. {FRLR F:1059}

CHARLES, JACOB, of Dorchester County, aet. 56, dep. between Aug 9, 1763 and Mar 31, 1764, mentioned George Andrew, deceased, and Thomas Williams, father of Meredith Williams, deceased. {DOLR 19 Old 418}

CHARTER, THOMAS, of Prince George's County, aet. 47, dep. Sep 25, 1733. {PGLR T:17} Thomas Charters (Chartor), aet. 62, dep. Jun 22, 1752, mentioned Solomon Stimson about 29 years ago, now deceased. {PGLR NN:37}

CHENEY, CHARLES, of Prince George's County, aet. 50, dep. Jul 17, 1724, stated that he was shown the bounds of *Cheney's Adventure* by Richard Cheney in 1696. {PGLR I:580}

CHENEY, CHARLES, of Prince George's County, aet. near 61, dep. Nov 5, 1763, mentioned his father (not named). {PGLR TT:571}

CHENRY, CHARLES, see "Charles Chaney" and "Samuel Evans" and "Joseph Peach," q.v.
CHENEY, CLARK, see "Joseph Jacob," q.v.
CHENEY, RICHARD, see "Charles Cheney," q.v.
CHERMAN, ELISABETH, of Charles County, aet. 32, dep. Jun 29, 1663. {CHLR B:164}
CHERMAN, JOHN, of Charles County, n.a., dep. Dec 16, 1662 and Dec 18, 1662. {CHLR B:33, 51} Aet. not given, dep. Nov 4, 1663, mentioned his wife (not named). {CHLR B:202} See "John Caine" and "John Kirby," q.v.
CHESELDYN, KENELM, of St. Mary's County, n.a., dep. Dec 12, 1696, stated that he has been Commissary General under Gov. [Francis] Nicholson for about 3 years, and also one of the Masters in Chancery for some time and one of his Majesty's Justices for St. Mary's County; Aet. not given, dep. Jun 29, 1698 in Annapolis. {ARMD 20:576, 23:435}
CHESUM, WILLIAM, of Dorchester County, aet. 49, dep. between Nov 14, 1729 and Nov 14, 1730. {DOLR 8 Old 384}
CHEW, JOSEPH, of Prince George's County, aet. 40, dep. Jun 16, 1730. {PGLR Q:13} See "William Diggs," q.v.
CHEW, SAMUEL, see "Indian Tequassino," q.v.
CHILCOAT (CHILCOTT), ROBINSON, of Baltimore County, n.a., dep. Jan 11, 1767, mentioned his father John Chilcoat (Chilcott). {BALR B#P:460}
CHILCOAT (CHILCOTT), JOHN, see "Robinson Chilcoat," q.v.
CHILCUT, ANTHONY, of Dorchester County, aet. 55, dep. Sep 7, 1711. {DOLR 6 Old 180} Anthony Chilcutt, aet. 81, dep. between Aug 15, 1734 and Sep 12, 1734, stated that he was shown the bounds of *Grantham* by Thomas Nurkeum about 40 years ago. {DOLR 9 Old 267} Aet. 80, dep. between Jun 15, 1737 and Apr 8, 1738. {DOLR 9 Old 507}
CHILCUTT, ANTHONY, of Dorchester County, aet. 40, dep. between Nov 12, 1745 and Nov 11, 1747, stated that he was shown the bounded tree of *Paradice* by George Chilcutt (now deceased) about 12 or 13 years ago. {DOLR 14 Old 173} Anthony Chillcutt (Chilcut), aet. 55, dep. between Nov 10, 1761 and Feb 24, 1762, mentioned his father (not named) about 37 or 38 years ago. {DOLR 18 Old 72} Aet. 55, between Nov 9, 1762 and May 9, 1763, mentioned his father (not named) about 45 years ago. {DOLR 19 Old 425} Anthony Chilcut, aet. 60, dep. between Mar 17, 1768 and Aug 9, 1768, mentioned his father Anthony Chilcut (now deceased) about 44 or 45 years ago. {DOLR 22 Old 433} Aet. 60, dep. between Nov 8, 1768 and Oct 10, 1768, stated that he was shown the bounded tree of *Ring's End* about 30 or 40 years ago by John Griffith (now deceased), son of Henry Griffith, deceased, who took up said tract. {DOLR 23 Old 129} See "Richard Webster," q.v.
CHILCUTT, GEORGE, see "Anthony Chilcutt" and "Richard Webster," q.v.
CHILCUTT, JOHN, see "Edward Poole" and "Richard Webster," q.v.

CHITTLE, WILLIAM, of Dorchester County, n.a., dep. between Jun 13, 1728 and Jul 27, 1728 {DOLR 8 Old 379}. Aet. 78, dep. between Jun 13, 1730 and Nov 11, 1730. {DOLR 8 Old 392} See "William Harper, Sr.," q.v.

CHRISTIAN, ADAM, of St. Mary's County, aet. 28, dep. Jan 20, 1658, stated that he was once a servant to Symon Overzee. {ARMD 41:240}

CHRISTIAN, JOHN, see "Jonathan Jones," q.v.

CHUNN, BENJAMIN, of Charles County, aet. 45, dep. Sep 23, 1741. {CHLR O#2:288} Aet. 47, dep. May 30, 1743. {CHLR O#2:567} See "Lancelot Chunn," q.v.

CHUNN, LANCELOT, of Charles County, aet. 39, dep. Nov 23, 1761, mentioned his father Benjamin Chunn, deceased. {CHLR K#3:407}

CHURCH, THOMAS, of Cecil County, n.a., dep. Sep 5, 1698, mentioned John Willis and wife (not named). {ARMD 23:522}

CHURCHMAN, JOHN, see "Samuel Brice" and "Charles Alleyn" and "Edward Lang" and "Daniel Smith," q.v.

CHURNELL, JOSEPH, see "George Elbridge," q.v.

CISSELL, JOHN, of St. Mary's County, n.a., dep. Mar 11, 1661. {ARMD 41:553}

CLAGETT, EDWARD, of Prince George's County, aet. 42, dep. Mar 12, 1755. {PGLR NN:412}

CLAGETT, JOHN, of Frederick County, aet. 48, commissioner, dep. Jun 6, 1761, stated that he was employed as a surveyor by John Flint about 19 years ago. {FRLR G:279}

CLAGETT, JOHN, of Prince George's County, aet. 72, dep. Sep 15, 1755, mentioned Capt. Thomas Clagett and Capt. Richard Reed. {PGLR NN:410} John Cleagett, aet. 80, dep. Jul 21, 1764. {PGLR BB#2:164}

CLAGETT, RICHARD, of Prince George's County, aet. 62, dep. Jun 28, 1743. {PGLR Y:703}

CLAGETT, THOMAS, of Frederick County, aet. 48, dep. Jun 6, 1761, mentioned Mrs. Jane Brooke, widow of Clement Brooke, about 19 years ago. {FRLR G:279}

CLAGETT, THOMAS (captain), of Prince George's County, gentleman, aet. 49, dep. Mar 1, 1728. {PGLR M:290} Aet. 50, dep. Mar 18, 1728/9, mentioned his father (not named) about 15 years ago, and Capt. Richard Smith, Capt. Henry Darnall, Col. Ninian Beale (Beall), and Charles Ridgely, all deceased. {PGLR M:479, 484} Aet. 50, dep. Feb 24, 1729/30. {PGLR Q;234}

CLAGGETT, THOMAS, see "Mareen Duvall" and "John Clagett" and "Mareen Duvall," q.v.

CLAHAY, ARTHURE, of Charles County, n.a., dep. 1658, mentioned Agnes Ware, widow of Richard Ware. {ARMD 41:53-54}

CLAIBUN, JOHN, see "John Carter," q.v.

CLARAGE, JOHN, see "Thomas North, Jr.," q.v.

CLARAGE, MARY, of Dorchester County, aet. 70, widow of John Clarage, dep. between Apr 20, 1768 and May 27, 1768. {DOLR 22 Old 423}

CLARBOE, FRANCIS, see "Francis Marbury," q.v.

CLARK, ABRAHAM, of Dorchester County, aet. about 63, dep. between Nov 11, 1760 and May 20, 1761, mentioned his father Richard Clark about 50 years ago. {DOLR 17 Old 324} Aet. about 77, dep. between Nov 14, 1769 and Nov 6, 1770. {DOLR 24 Old 308}

CLARK, BENJAMIN, of Prince George's County, aet. 39, dep. Mar 1, 1756. {PGLR NN:469} See "William Lock Weems," q.v.

CLARK, DANIEL, see "Edward Willoughby," q.v.

CLARK, GEORGE, of Prince George's County, aet. 40, dep. Dec 3, 1763, mentioned Thomas Richardson, son of Mark, about 24 years ago. {PGLR TT:191-192}

CLARK, GILBERT, of Charles County, n.a., dep. Jun 29, 1698 in Annapolis. {ARMD 23:435, 23:441}

CLARK, JAMES, of Dorchester County, aet. about 40, dep. between Nov 11, 1760 and May 20, 1761, stated that his father Thomas Clark, now deceased, showed him the bounds of *Retaliation* about 30 years ago. {DOLR 17 Old 324}

CLARK, JOANNAH, of Kent County on Delaware, aet. about 56, dep. between Nov 14, 1758 and Jun 30, 1759, mentioned her former husband Burtonwood Allcock. {DOLR 16 Old 220}

CLARK, JOHN, of Dorchester County, aet. 23, son of Richard Clark, dep. between Jun 14, 1729 and Jul 17, 1729. {DOLR 8 Old 432}

CLARK, JOHN, of Prince George's County, aet. 52, dep. Jun 19, 1755. {PGLR NN:392}

CLARK, NEAL, of Anne Arundel County, planter, aet. 63, dep. Jul 1, 1726 in Prince George's County land case. {PGLR M:32}

CLARK, PHILIP, of St. Mary's County, n.a., dep. between Apr 14, 1698 and Jul 1, 1698 in Annapolis. {ARMD 23:412, 413, 442}

CLARK, RICHARD, see "Edward Coxell" and "John Clark" and "Abraham Clark" and "Silvester Welch," q.v.

CLARK, ROBERT, of Prince George's County, aet. 50, dep. Nov 24, 1740. {PGLR Y:237} See "Mary Greenway," q.v.

CLARK, SARAH, of Talbot County, n.a., dep. Aug 11, 1744, wife of Thomas Clark, innholder, stated that her late husband John Guy Williams directed that the birth of his son John be recorded one year later than it ought to have been and that the son John is at this time 21 years of age. {TALR 16:105}

CLARK, THOMAS, of Anne Arundel County, aet. 36, dep. Jul 25, 1724 in Prince George's County land case. {PGLR I:591}

CLARK, THOMAS, of Dorchester County, aet. 37, dep. between Jun 14, 1729 and Jul 17, 1729. {DOLR 8 Old 432}

CLARK, THOMAS, see "James Clark" and "Sarah Clark," q.v.

CLARK, WILLIAM, see "John Wilson," q.v.

CLARKE, DANIELL, of Dorchester County, aet. 77, dep. Nov 12, 1700, stated that the road from Indian Town to Jordan's Point was the Indian path about 37 years ago. {DOLR 5 Old 178} See "John Hodson, Sr.," q.v.

CLARKE, EDWARD, of St. Mary's County, n.a., dep. Feb 11, 1663. {ARMD 49:145}
CLARKE, JANE (Mrs.), of Charles County, n.a., dep. Jun 4, 1658. {CHLR A:3}
CLARKE, JOHN, of Prince George's County, aet. 52, dep. May 23, 1754. {PGLR NN:254}
CLARKE, NEAL, of Anne Arundel County, aet. 60, dep. Jul 25, 1724 in Prince George's County land case. {PGLR I:590}
CLARKE, RICHARD, of Anne Arundel County, n.a., dep. Mar 27, 1708, offered no worthy confession regarding his alleged outlawry, so he "was committed to Her Majesty's Goall" [county jail]. {ARMD 25:238} See "Silvester Welch" and "John Spry," q.v.
CLARKE, ROBERT, of Kent County, n.a., dep. Feb 2, 1652, stated that as Surveyor General of this Province in 1640 he laid out 1400 acres on the northernmost part of the Isle of Kent for William Brantwell, gentleman, and Thomas Broadnox, planter, to invite inhabitants to seat the said island. {ARMD 54:11}
CLARKE, WILLIAM, of Prince George's County, aet. 61, dep. Jan 26, 1748/9, mentioned Charles Walker about 38 or 40 years ago and John Prather, now deceased. {PGLR BB:628}
CLARKSON, WILLIAM, see "Elizabeth Flowers," q.v.
CLARRIDGE, MARGARET, see "Benjamin Granger," q.v.
CLARVO (CLARVOE), JOHN, see "Francis Wheeler," q.v.
CLAYBURN, JOHN, see "Ellinor Lewis," q.v.
CLAYLAND, JAMES, see "John Lane" and "William Clayland" and "John Dixon," q.v.
CLAYLAND, JOHN, of Queen Anne's County, aet. 72, dep. Sep, 1766. {QAEJ - John and Sophia Downes folder}
CLAYLAND, WILLIAM, of Queen Anne's County, n.a., stated that his father, Rev. James Clayland, kept a book of accounts which noted that he had charged John Baynard and Elizabeth Blackwell 400 pounds of tobacco for their marriage. {QALR ET#A:62}
CLAYTON, JOHN, see "Henry Smith," q.v.
CLAYTON, SOLOMON, of Queen Anne's County, aet. about 38, dep. Apr, 1723. {QAEJ - William Bishop folder}
CLEAVER, JOHN, JR., of Kent County, aet. about 50, dep. May 19, 1752. {KELR JS#27:147} Aet. about 51, dep. Jun 12, 1753. {KELR JS#27:287} Aet. about 52, dep. Feb 27, 1755. {KELR JS#28:97}
CLEMENS, CALEB, of Queen Anne's County, aet. 40, dep. Oct 5, 1768. {QAEJ - Gideon Emory folder}
CLEMENS, EDWARD, of Prince George's County, aet. 54, dep. Mar 10, 1735/6. {PGLR T:283}
CLEMENS, JOHN, of Prince George's County, aet. 49, dep. Nov 28, 1728. {PGLR M:343} Aet. 50, dep. Aug 3, 1730, stated that he built the first house on John Edgar's land called *Horsepenn*. {PGLR Q:67} Aet. 53, dep. Sep 11, 1733. {PGLR T:123}

CLEMENT, FRANCIS, of Prince George's County, aet. 30 or thereabouts, dep. Oct 15, 1776. {PGLR CC#2:311-312}
CLEMENTS, BENJAMIN, see "Benjamin Carpenter," q.v.
CLEMENTS, BENJAMIN NOTLEY, of Charles County, aet. 55, dep. Mar 26, 1772. {CHLR T#3:611}
CLEMENTS, CHARLES, of Charles County, aet. 26, dep. Jul 31, 1765. {CHLR N#3:721}
CLEMENTS, EDWARD, see "William Clements," q.v.
CLEMENTS, GEORGE, of Charles County, aet. 32, dep. Aug 6, 1762. {CHLR M#3:5} Aet. 33, dep. Aug 18, 1763. {CHLR M#3:508} Aet. 44, dep. May 26, 1770. {CHLR T#3:606}
CLEMENTS, JACOB, of Charles County, aet. 31, dep. Jul 31, 1765. {CHLR N#3:721}
CLEMENTS, JACOB, of Charles County, aet. 30, dep. Sep 18, 1752, mentioned his father William Clements. {CHLR B#3:205}
CLEMENTS, JOHN, of Charles County, aet. 25, dep. Aug 2, 1774. {CHLR U#3:382}
CLEMENTS, JOHN, of Charles County, aet. 78, Jun 6, 1726. {CHLR P#2:389}
CLEMENTS, JOSEPH, of Charles County, aet. 60, dep. Jan 1, 1754. {CHLR D#3:236} Aet. 66, dep. Jun 8, 1759. {CHLR I#3:261}
CLEMENTS, LEONARD, of Charles County, aet. 42, dep. Nov 1, 1762. {CHLR M#3:62} Aet. 56, dep. Nov 17, 1775. {CHLR X#3:545}
CLEMENTS, RALPH, of Charles County, aet. 20, dep. Aug 2, 1774. {CHLR W#3:388}
CLEMENTS, WILLIAM, of Charles County, aet. 56, dep. Jul 31, 1765. {CHLR N#3:720} Aet. 64, dep. Aug 24, 1773, mentioned his father Edward Clements. {CHLR U#3:601} See "Jacob Clements," q.v.
CLIFFORD, JOHN, of Prince George's County, aet. 35, dep. Oct 30, 1769. {PGLR AA#2:186}
CLIFTON, MARY, of Dorchester County, aet. about 70, dep. between Mar 12, 1744 and Aug 11, 1745, mentioned her son Daniel Morris and her husband Mauris Morris, now deceased, and that she and her husband lived on *Piney Ridge* before her on was born; also stated that if she had her sight she could show where the bounded tree stood, but is now blind. {DOLR 12 Old 250}
CLINKSALES, ADAM, of Charles County, aet. 43, dep. Apr 16, 1772, mentioned James Gow, son of James Gow. {CHLR T#3:612}
CLIPSHAM, ROBERT, of St. Mary's County, merchant, n.a., dep. Jul 16, 1654, mentioned William Wright of Poplar Hill, Maryland. {ARMD 10:396-397}
CLOAK, MORRIS, of Kent County, aet. 63, dep. Mar, 1746. {QAEJ - Benjamin Tasker folder}
CLOCKER, MARY, of St. Mary's County, n.a., dep. Jan 29, 1650, mentioned Blanch Oliver in 1646. {ARMD 10:96}
CLOVE, HANNAH (Mrs.), of Kent County, aet. about 56, dep. Nov 21, 1727. {KELR JS#X:207} Aet. about 57, dep. Oct 1, 1729, stated that she lived with her former husband Benjamin Blackledge about 40 years ago on the plantation

where Richard West now lives; mentioned her mother Lucy Gallaway, her father William Gallaway, and her brothers James and William Gallaway; also mentioned Robert Garman, son-in-law of William Gallaway. {KELR JS#X:409, 416}

CLOUDS, RICHARD (captain), of St. Mary's or Charles County, n.a., dep. between Jun 29, 1698 and Jul 1, 1698 in Annapolis. {ARMD 23:442}

CLOYD, ROBERT, of Prince George's County, aet. 50, dep. 1731, stated that he was a servant to William Hutchison about 28 years ago. {PGLR Q:372}

COAFFER, JOHN, JR., of Prince George's County, aet. 34, dep. Nov 28, 1728. {PGLR M:344}

COAFFER, JOHN, of Prince George's County, aet. 63, dep. Nov 28, 1728. {PGLR M:343}

COATS, CHARLES, see "George Beall," q.v.

COCKERELL, ROBERT, of Charles County, n.a., dep. Jul 30, 1663. {CHLR B:146}

COCKEY, EDWARD, see "Mary Cockey," q.v.

COCKEY, MARY, of Queen Anne's County, aet. about 50, wife of Edward Cockey, dep. Mar, 1759; aet. 60, dep. Mar, 1770. {QAEJ - Henry Carter folder}

COCKRELL, ANDREW, of Queen Anne's County, aet. about 56, dep. Oct 5, 1768. {QAEJ - Gideon Emory folder}

COCKRELL, WILLIAM, of Queen Anne's County, aet. Oct 5, 1768. {QAEJ - Gideon Emory folder}

COCKS, JOHN, of Charles County, aet. 52, dep. Jun 7, 1731, mentioned his father John Cocks. {CHLR Q#2:517}

COCKSHOOTE, JANE (Mrs.), of Charles County, n.a., dep. Jun 4, 1658. {CHLR A:3}

CODWELL, WILLIAM, of Charles County, aet. 23, dep. Jan 28, 1661/2. {CHLR A:178}

COE, JOHN, of Charles County, aet. 36, dep. Sep 18, 1752. {CHLR B#3:204}

COEN, JOHN, see "William Coen," q.v.

COEN, WILLIAM, of Harford County, aet. 57, dep. May 25, 1775, mentioned his father John Coen, deceased. {Land Commission, 1774, Harford County Genealogical Society Newsletter, Jan, 1993, p. 3}

COFFER, HENRY, of Charles County, aet. 37, dep. Oct 15, 1741, mentioned his father John Coffer. {CHLR O#2:283} Age 61, dep. Nov 1, 1762. {CHLR M#3:62} Aet. 62, dep. Sep 3, 1762, mentioned his father John Coffer, his brother Matthew Coffer, and his uncle Matthew Barnes. {CHLR N#3:165} Henry Copher, aet. 54, dep. Jun 13, 1758. {CHLR H#3:328}

COFFER, HENRY, of Charles County, aet. 40, dep. Feb 23, 1774, mentioned his father Henry Coffer. {CHLR W#3:82}

COFFER, JOHN, see "Henry Coffer," q.v.

COFFER, MATTHEW, of Charles County, aet. 60, dep. Nov 1, 1762. {CHLR M#3:62}

COGHAN, DARBY, see "Edward Elliott," q.v.

COGHILL, SMALLWOOD, see "John Fraser," q.v.

COHOE, JAMES, of Charles County, aet. 78, dep. Jan 9, 1743/4. {CHLR O#2:700}
COHONK, JAMES, see "Indian Jemmey Cohonk," q.v.
COKE, JOHN, see "Bartholomew Hendrickson" and "Andrew Peterson" and "Alexander Shresse," q.v.
COLE, EDWARD, see "William Bryan" and "Ignatius Atchison," q.v.
COLE, JAMES, see "William Bryan," q.v.
COLE, JOHN, see "Peter Cole" and "Charles Paul" and "George Wilson," q.v.
COLE, OLD, see "Philip Evans," q.v.
COLE, PETER, of Kent County, aet. about 28, dep. May 2, 1728, stated that his father John Cole showed him the bounds of *Adventure* about 15 years ago. {KELR JS#X:383} Aet. about 50, dep. Oct 24, 1749. {KELR JS#26:269} Aet. about 57, dep. Apr 3, 1759. {KEEJ - Thomas Harris folder} See "George Wilson," q.v.
COLE, PETER, JR., of Kent County, aet. about 31, dep. Aug 11, 1757. {KELR JS#28:370}
COLE, WILLIAM, of Baltimore County, n.a., dep. Jan 11, 1767. {BALR B#P:460} See "Alse Caple," q.v.
COLEBORNE, WILLIAM, see "William Keene," q.v.
COLEGATE, BENJAMIN, see "John Colegate," q.v.
COLEGATE, JOHN, of Baltimore County, aet. 49, dep. Aug 29, 1763, mentioned his brother Benjamin Colegate and Charles Green (deceased). {BALR B#N:136}
COLEMAN, DOCTOR, see "Thomas Hamilton," q.v.
COLEMAN, MORDICA, see "Benjamin Harris," q.v.
COLEMAN, THOMAS, of Charles County, aet. 58, dep. Nov 17, 1719. {CHLR M#2:71} Aet. 65, dep. Sep 13, 1729. {CHLR Q#2:345}
COLEMAN, THOMAS, of Prince George's County, aet. 65, dep. Sep 13, 1729, mentioned Clark Skinner about 31 years ago. {PGLR M:519}
COLEMAN, THOMAS, see "Benjamin Harris," q.v.
COLIS, THOMAS, of Charles County, aet. 46, dep. Dec 30, 1743. {CHLR O#2:699}
COLLARD, HELENA, of Prince George's County, aet. 50, dep. Sep 12, 1757, mentioned her husband Arnold Livers, deceased. {PGLR PP:59-60, pt. 2}
COLLIER, JOHN (captain), of Anne Arundel County, aet. 33, dep. Nov 11, 1661, mentioned John Averet and John Avery. {ARMD 3:456}
COLLIER, SARAH, of Queen Anne's County, aet. about 61, dep. Mar, 1764. {QAEJ - Robert Small folder}
COLLIER, WIDOW, see "John Franklin," q.v.
COLLINGS, JAMES, of Prince George's County, aet. 32, dep. Nov 24, 1753. {PGLR NN:283} Aet. 34, dep. Jun 23, 1757. {PGLR PP:13, pt. 2} Aet. 42, dep. Aug 29, 1763. {PGLR TT:127} Aet. 45, dep. Feb 1, 1768, mentioned John Anderson about 25 or 26 years ago. {PGLR BB#2:291}
COLLINGS, JAMES, of Frederick County, aet. 59, dep. Sep 25, 1772. {FRLR P:432}
COLLINS, ANN, of Kent County, Quaker, aet. about 52, dep. Feb 21, 1743, mentioned her late husband Roger Hales (Hails) and John Gale the Elder, both deceased. {KELR JS#29:183}

COLLINS (COLINS), BARTON, of Queen Anne's County, n.a., sergeant in Capt. Daniel Campbell's Company, dep. Sep 3, 1746, mentioned the enlistment of Abell Bell on Aug 27, 1746; also mentioned magistrates Joseph Sadler and Robert Norrest Wright. {ARMD 28:367}

COLLINS, MARTHA, of Queen Anne's County, aet. 41, dep. Apr, 1723. {QAEJ - William Bishop folder}

COMBS, BENNETT, of Charles County, aet. 39, dep. Aug 18, 1763. {CHLR M#3:508}

COMBS, JOHN ANTHONY, of Charles County, aet. 32, dep. May 15, 1760. {CHLR I#3:544}

COMBS, RICHARD, of Charles County, aet. 75, dep. Apr 24, 1729. {CHLR Q#2:275} Aet. 89, dep. Mar 17, 1741/2. {CHLR O#2:323}

COMBS, THOMAS WHARTON, of Charles County, aet. 35, dep. Aug 18, 1763. {CHLR M#3:509}

COMBS (COOMS), WILLIAM, SR., of Charles County, aet. 62, dep. Aug 6, 1762, stated that he was shown the bounded tree of *Green Springs* by William Chandler about 37 or 38 years ago. {CHLR M#3:4} William Combs, aet. 63, dep. Aug 18, 1763. {CHLR M#3:508} William Cooms, aet. 57, dep. Apr 21, 1757, stated that he has known since 1714 where this path was. {CHLR F#3:486} William Coomes, aet. 72, dep. Nov 21, 1771. {CHLR U#3:25}

COMBS, WINIFRED, of Charles County, aet. 54, dep. Aug 6, 1762, stated that she had lived on the land of William Chandler from her infancy until she was married. {CHLR M#3:5} Aet. 54, dep. Aug 18, 1763. {CHLR M#3:507}

COMEGYS, CORNELIUS, of Kent County, aet. 51, dep. 1755. {KELR JS#28:140}

COMEGYS, CORNELIUS, of Cecil County, n.a., dep. May 11, 1696, stated that he and his wife and children (no names given) live on a frontier plantation exposed to the enemy. {ARMD 20:415}

COMEGYS, CORNELIUS, SR., of Kent County, aet. 60, dep. 1698. {KELR M:78} See "Arthur Foreman," q.v.

COMEGYS, EDWARD, of Kent County, aet. 50, dep. Mar 22,1739. {KELR JS#22:523}

COMEGYS, JOHN, of Queen Anne's County, aet. about 51, dep. July, 1758; aet. about 53, dep. Mar, 1762. {QAEJ - Henry Callister folders}

COMEGYS, MAJOR, see "Arthur Foreman," q.v.

COMEGYS, WILLIAM, SR., of Kent County, aet. about 62, dep. Jun 21, 1727. {KELR JS#X:93} Aet. about 65, dep. Dec 26, 1729. {KELR JS#X:440} Aet. 66, dep. 1730. {KELR JS#16:58} Aet. 68, dep. Jun 6, 1732, stated that he married James Stavely's mother some years ago. {KELR JS#16:225} Aet. 70, dep. 1734. {KELR JS#18:41}

COMPTON, JAMES, of Charles County, aet. 31, dep. Aug 7, 1738, mentioned his grandfather John Compton. {CHLR T#2:497}

COMPTON, JOHN, see "James Compton" and "Matthew Compton" and "Thomas Douglas," q.v.

COMPTON, MATTHEW, of Charles County, aet. 67, dep. Aug 7, 1738, mentioned his father John Compton. {CHLR T#2:497} Aet. 71, dep. Jan 8, 1742. {CHLR O#2:508} Aet. 72, dep. May 30, 1743, mentioned his father John Compton. {CHLR O#2:567, 568} Aet. 72, dep. Apr 30, 1744. {CHLR Y#2:12}

COMPTON, MATTHEW, JR., of Charles County, aet. 34, dep. May 30, 1743. {CHLR O#2:568} Aet. 46, mentioned his father Matthew Compton. {CHLR E#3:135}

COMPTON, WILLIAM, of Charles County, aet. 22, dep. Jan 23, 1755, mentioned his grandfather Matthew Compton. {CHLR E#3:136}

COMPTON, WILLIAM, of Charles County, aet. 46, dep. May 30, 1743. {CHLR O#2:568}

CONALLY, JOHN, of St. Mary's County, n.a., dep. Feb 28, 1749. {ARMD 28:510}

CONDEMAN, WILLIAM, see "William Holmes," q.v.

CONN, HUGH, see "John Nicholls," q.v.

CONNANT, ROBERT, see "Thomas Walker," q.v.

CONNELL, WILLIAM, of Charles County, aet. 47, dep. Aug 2, 1737. {CHLR T#2:370}

CONNER, CHARLES, of Queen Anne's County, aet. about 50, dep. Apr, 1769. {QAEJ - James Hutchings folder}

CONNER, ELIZABETH, see "Elizabeth Woodward" and "Mary Mitchel," q.v.

CONNER, JOSEPH, see "Thomas Pollet," q.v.

CONNERLY, PATRICK, of Dorchester County, aet. 43, dep. between Aug 9, 1763 and Mar 31, 1764, mentioned Nicols Layton, deceased. {DOLR 19 Old 418}

CONTEE, JOHN, see "John Courts," q.v.

CONTEE, MARY, see "John Courts," q.v.

CONTEE, THOMAS, of Charles County, aet. 46, dep. Jan 31, 1776. {CHLR X#3:536}

COOD, JOHN, SR., see "William Taylard," q.v.

COOK, EDWARD, of Dorchester County, aet. 66, dep. between Mar 8, 1742 and May 7, 1743. {DOLR 12 Old 166} See "Edward Willibee," q.v.

COOK, ELIZABETH, see "Sarah Kindred," q.v.

COOK, GEORGE, of Prince George's County, aet. 63, dep. Jul 2, 1764. {PGLR TT:372}

COOK, THOMAS, of Dorchester County, aet. 55, dep. between Aug 10, 1762 and Oct 27, 1762. {DOLR 19 Old 88} Aet. 56, dep. between Aug 13, 1765 and Dec 21, 1765, mentioned old Jane Thomas about 24 or 25 years ago. {DOLR 21 Old 447} Aet. 60, dep. between Mar 8, 1768 and Jul 23, 1768, mentioned Jane Thomas and her father Humphrey Hubbert about 20 years ago. {DOLR 23 Old 5} Aet. 65, dep. between Aug 11, 1772 and Dec 11, 1772, mentioned John Seward about 20 odd years ago. {DOLR 27 Old 348} See "Edward Stephens," q.v.

COOK, THOMAS, JR., of Dorchester County, aet. 31, dep. between Mar 8, 1768 and Jul 23, 1768, mentioned his father (not named) and John Thomas (now deceased), son of the present John Thomas, about 15 years ago. {DOLR 23 Old 5}

COOKE, ANDREW, of Calvert County, n.a., dep. Oct 25, 1664. {ARMD 49:293}

COOKE, EDWARD, of Dorchester County, aet. 50, dep. between Nov 16, 1731 and Sep 4, 1732, mentioned his father Edward Cooke. {DOLR 9 Old 71}

COOKE, JOHN, of Prince George's County, aet. near 45, dep. Mar 21, 1761, mentioned Col. Edward Sprigg and Mr. Osborn Sprigg about 18 years ago. {PGLR RR:233}

COOKE, WILLIAM, prob. of St. Mary's County, n.a., dep. Oct 13, 1665. {ARMD 49:496}

COOKSEY, JUSTINIAN, SR., of Charles County, aet. 56, dep. Aug 29, 1758. {CHLR B#3:576}

COOKSEY, WILLIAM, of Charles County, aet. 55, dep. Mar 1, 1759. {CHLR I#3:26} Aet. 65, dep. Oct 3, 1767, stated that he married the sister (not named) of Clebourn Simes, son of John Simes. {CHLR P#3:666}

COOLEY, GEORGE, see "Amos Cottrel," q.v.

COOMBES, RICHARD, of Charles County, aet. 63, dep. Nov 4, 1719, mentioned Thomas Wicherly who married the relict of Edward Ford. {Charles County Land Commissions 1:66-67}

COOMES (COOMS), WILLIAM, see "William Combs," q.v.

COOPER, JOHN, of Charles County, aet. 48, dep. Sep 27, 1734. {CHLR R#2:539}

COOPER, JOHN, of Queen Anne's County, aet. 85, Quaker, dep. Sep, 1761, affirmed that two years earlier Thomas Towers was his servant. {QAEJ - William Webb folder}

COOPER, RICHARD, see "Obed Dixon" and "Richard Sullivant," q.v.

COOPER, SAMUEL, see "John Carter," q.v.

COOPER, WILLIAM, of Charles County, aet. 43, dep. Jul 3, 1745. {CHLR Z#2:406}

COPHER, HENRY, see "Henry Coffer," q.v.

COPLEN (COEPLEN), SAMUEL, of Calvert County, n.a., servant to Richard Preston, Sr., dep. Mar 31, 1663. {ARMD 49:9-10}

COPPAGE, JOHN, of Queen Anne's County, aet. 36, dep. July, 1770. {QAEJ - James Hutchings folder} Aet. 37, dep. Sep, 1771, mentioned his father Philip Coppage when he (deponent) was 15 or 17 years old. {QAEJ - Henry Carter folder}

COPPAGE, PHILIP, see "John Coppage," q.v.

COPPER, GEORGE, of Kent County, aet. about 56, dep. Mar 3, 1725/6, mentioned his master Col. Hance Hanson and Capt. John Derricutt. {KELR JS#W:543} Aet. about 78, dep. Feb 26, 1746. {KELR JS#26:32} George Copper, Sr., aet. about 77, dep. Aug 25, 1746. {KELR JS#25:438} George Copper, aet. 87, dep. Jul 31, 1753. {KEEJ - Matthias Harris folder}

CORD, THOMAS, of Baltimore County, aet. 61, dep. Nov 11, 1764. {BALR B#N:375}

CORNELIUS, JOHN, see "William Eddey," q.v.

CORNISH, JOHN, of Charles County, aet. 35, dep. Jan 20, 1726/7. {CHLR P#2:491} See "Edward Brawner" and "Henry Woodward," q.v.

CORNISH, ROBERT, of St. Mary's County, n.a., dep. 1659. {ARMD 41:364}

CORNISH, WIDOW, see "John Franklin," q.v.

CORNWALLIES (CORNEWALEYS), THOMAS, see "John Abington" and "John Wheatley," q.v.

CORSE (COURSE), ANNE, of Kent County, Quaker, aet. about 50, dep. affirmed Oct 3, 1743, mentioned her brother Caleb Beck and Nicholas Barefoot, servant of Edward Beck. {KELR JS#25:192} Ann Corse, aet. about 60, dep. Oct, 1753. {KELR JS#28:48} Ann Course, Quaker, aet. about 59, dep. affirmed Mar 13, 1753, mentioned her husband James Course, deceased. {KELR JS#27:254}

CORSE (COURSE), JAMES, of Kent County, Quaker, aet. about 45, dep. affirmed Sep 10, 1735. {Re: KELR JS#18:195} Aet. about 55, dep. affirmed Feb 21, 1743. {KELR JS#25:33} See "Anne Corse" and "Rachel Vansant" and "Elizabeth Redgrave," q.v.

CORSE, JENNETT, see "Rachel Vansant," q.v.

COST, FRANCIS, of Frederick County, aet. 36, dep. Aug 21, 1776, mentioned William Thomas about 14 or 15 years ago, now deceased. {FRLR BD#2:333-334}

COSTIN, HENRY, JR., of Queen Anne's County, n.a., dep. Sep 18, 1730. {QALR IK#C:19}

COTTEN, EDWARD, see "Walter Pakes," q.v.

COTTREL, AMOS, of Dorchester County, aet. 59, dep. between Nov 17, 1726 and Jul 21, 1729, stated that the bounds of *Hogg Island* were shown to him by George Cooley about 15 or 16 years ago. {DOLR 8 Old 293}

COTTRELL, JAMES, of Charles County, aet. 60, dep. Aug 16, 1765. {CHLR N#3:788}

COTTRELL, THOMAS, of Charles County, aet. 43, dep. Mar 14, 1748/9. {CHLR Z#2:348}

COURTMANN, CAPTAIN, see "Peter Janson," q.v.

COURSE, JAMES, see "Anne Corse" and "James Corse" and "Elizabeth Redgrave," q.v.

COURSEY, DIXON, see "Indian Jemmey Cohonk," q.v.

COURSEY, THOMAS, see "Thomas Willson," q.v.

COURSEY, WILLIAM, of Anne Arundel County, n.a., dep. 1659, stated he was a surveyor and mentioned his brother Henry Coursey. {ARMD 41:322}

COURSEY, WILLIAM, of Queen Anne's County, aet. 64, dep. Oct 2, 1767. {QAEJ - Downe: oversize folder}

COURTNEY, THOMAS, see "Emanuel Ratcliffe," q.v.

COURTS, GOODMAN, see "Daniell Johnson" and "John Piper," q.v.

COURTS (COURT), JOHN, of Charles County, gentleman, aet. 17, dep. Aug 21, 1708 to prove the will of Col. John Contee, deceased. {Will Book 12:276} Aet. not given, dep. Nov 6, 1712, mentioned "arms and ammunition in his father Col. John Court's house which came to the hands of Col. John Contee and his executor and by her sold and embezilled." {ARMD 29:96} Aet. not given, dep. Nov 6, 1714, mentioned county arms, ammunition, and Philemon Hemsley and Mary his wife, lately called Mary Contee. {ARMD 29:403-404} Aet. 46, dep. Oct 10, 1738. {CHLR T#2:513}

COUSANS, EDWARD, of Kent County, aet. about 40, dep. Mar 21, 1750. {KELR JS#27:27}
COVERT, ROBERT, of Charles County, aet. 44, dep. Aug 23, 1736. {CHLR T#2:294} Aet. 46, dep. Aug 15, 1738. {CHLR T#2:519} Aet. 55, dep. May 24, 1744. {CHLR Y#2:185}
COVILL, JEREMIAH, of Frederick County, aet. 51, dep. Nov 28, 1760, mentioned Thomas Manyard (now deceased). {FRLR G:70}
COVINGTON, ABRAHAM, of Dorchester County, aet. 50, dep. between Apr 6, 1732 and Apr 23, 1733, mentioned a survey made for Solomon Turpin abut 15 years ago. {DOLR 9 Old 100} Aet. 67, dep. between Aug 14, 1750 and Dec 20, 1750, mentioned Solomon Turpin, Sr. and old Thomas Gordon. {DOLR 14 Old 497} Abraham Coventon, aet. 69, dep. between Jun 11, 1751 and Oct 14, 1751. {DOLR 14 Old 552} See "Mary Walter," q.v.
COVINGTON, ISAAC, of Dorchester County, aet. 21, dep. between Aug 10, 1762 and Jan 1, 1763. {DOLR 18 Old 341} See "Thomas Ball," q.v.
COVINGTON, LEVIN, of Dorchester County, aet. 24, dep. between Aug 10, 1762 and Jan 1, 1763. {DOLR 18 Old 341}
COWSEY, WILLIAM, see "John Salter," q.v.
COX, ABRAHAM, of Prince George's County, n.a., dep. Sep 27, 1751. {PGLR PP:139}
COX, ANN, of Dorchester County, aet. 40, dep. between Mar 10, 1740 and Jan 23, 1741, mentioned her deceased husband Charles Manship. {DOLR 12 Old 89}
COX, JACOB, of Baltimore County, aet. 41, dep. May 28, 1764. {BALR B#N:141} See "William Cox," q.v.
COX, JAMES, of Charles County, aet. 31, dep. Nov 11, 1674. {CHLR F#1:32}
COX, JOHN, of Charles County, aet. 49, dep. Sep 28, 1775. {CHLR X#3:540}
COX, JOHN, of Charles County, aet. 60, dep. Apr 28, 1737. {CHLR T#2:568}
COX, JOHN, see "William Depriest," q.v.
COX, WILLIAM, of Baltimore County, aet. 31, dep. May 31, 1764, mentioned his brother Jacob Cox. {BALR B#N:140}
COXELL (COXCELL), EDWARD, of Dorchester County, aet. about 31, dep. between Jun 14, 1729 and Jul 17, 1729. {DOLR 8 Old 432} Aet. about 35, dep. between Mar 16, 1733 and May 11, 1734, stated that his mother Margaret Coxcell showed him the bounds of Richard Clark's land about 18 or 19 years ago. {DOLR 9 Old 238} See "Robert Sherwin," q.v.
COXELL, MARGARET, see "Edward Coxell" and "Joseph Alford," q.v.
CRABB, JEREMIAH, of Prince George's County, aet. 32, dep. Jun 16, 1760, mentioned Robert Tyler's grandfather (not named) about 23 or 24 years ago; also mentioned Priscilla Crabb. {PGLR RR:106-107}
CRABB, PRISCILLA, see "Jeremiah Crabb," q.v.
CRABB, THOMAS, see "Philip Pindle," q.v.
CRABTREE, JOHN, see "Phillip Morgan," q.v.

CRAIN (CRAEN), JOHN, of Charles County, aet. 51, dep. May 17, 1725. {CHLR P#2:36}
CRAIN (CRAINE), JOHN, of Charles County, aet. 40, dep. Sep 8, 1753. {CHLR D#3:430} Aet. 42, dep. May 17, 1755, stated that Thomas Baker was the son of John Baker. {CHLR E#3:130}
CRACKSON (CRAKSON), THOMAS, of Charles County, aet. 22 or thereabouts, dep. Sep 24, 1661 and Nov 19, 1661. {CHLR A:156, 168; ARMD 53:159} Aet. not given, dep. Jan 12, 1664/5. {CHLR B:424}
CRAMER, RENDALL, of Charles County, n.a., dep. Oct 1, 1662. {CHLR A:247}
CRANE, EDWARD, of Calvert or St. Mary's County, n.a., dep. Apr 23, 1691. {ARMD 8:247}
CRANLY, ANNE, of Calvert County, n.a., dep. 1659. {ARMD 41:276}
CRANLY, MICHAEL, of Calvert County, n.a., dep. 1659. {ARMD 41:276}
CRATCHER, MARY, see "Sarah Andrew" and "Walter Kimmey" and "John King" and "Spencer Martrum Waters" and "Danair Sulivane" and "Mary Snow" and "Jemima Stainton" and "Solomon Wright," q.v.
CRATCHER, SAMUEL, see "Sarah Andrew" and "Danair Sulivane," q.v.
CRAWFORD, QUINTON, of Charles County, aet. 27, dep. Dec 31, 1759. {CHLR I#3:429}
CRAYCROFT, CHARLES, of Charles County, aet. 38, dep. Apr 13, 1739. {CHLR T#2:465}
CRAYCROFT, JOHN, of Charles County, aet. 37, dep. Feb 28, 1742. {CHLR O#2:504}
CRAYCROFT, NICHOLAS, of Charles County, aet. about 38, dep. between Nov 8, 1774 and Feb 7, 1775. {CHLR W#3:607}
CREAGER, LARRANCE, of Frederick County, aet. 57, dep. Apr 6, 1772, stated that he was a member of the church known by the name of the United Brethern. {FRLR P:169}
CREEK, JOHN, see "James Langrall," q.v.
CRESAP, THOMAS, see "Thomas Prather" and "Ewen McDonall," q.v.
CRESSY, SAMUEL, of Charles County, aet. 21, dep. Mar 10, 1670/1. {CHLR E#1:42}
CRESWELL, WILLIAM, of Harford County, aet. 58, dep. June 17, 1775. {Land Commission, 1774, Harford County Genealogical Society Newsletter, Jan, 1993, p. 3}
CRIFFWELL, JOHN, of Charles County, aet. 72, dep. Nov 14, 1770. {CHLR U#3:268}
CROMEAN, ELIZABETH, see "George Andrew," q.v.
CROMEAN, JOHN, see "George Andrew," q.v.
CROMEY, JAMES, of Baltimore County, aet. 61, dep. Oct 11, 1763. {BALR B#N:64}
CRONEENE, DANIEL, of Dorchester County, aet. 36 or 37, dep. between Nov 11, 1755 and May 20, 1756, mentioned his father-in-law Moses Nicolls about 26 years ago. {DOLR 16 Old 76}
CROSS, JOHN, of Baltimore County, aet. 63, dep. Oct 31, 1763. {BALR B#N:184}

CROSSON, MARY, of Charles County, aet. 53, dep. May 14, 1752, mentioned her mother Elizabeth Keeth. {CHLR B#3:354}
CROUCH, JOSIAH, of Cecil County, n.a., dep. Mar 8, 1706/7. {CMSP 1:7 - The Black Books}
CROUCH, RALPH, of St. Mary's County, n.a., dep. 1650/1, stated that he had sailed with Capt. Richard Ingle aboard the ship *Reformation* on the Thames River in London about Oct, 1644. {ARMD 10:102-103}
CROUCH, RICHARD, of Kent County, aet. about 53, dep. Feb 26, 1746, mentioned John Huff about 30 or 40 years ago and his (Huff's) father-in-law Henry Morgan. {KELR JS#26:32} Aet. about 67, dep. Oct 9, 1761, mentioned Wedge Crouch was the brother *[sic]* of Mr. Ringgold. {KELR DD#1:618}
CROUCH, RICHARD, JR., of Kent County, aet. 42 or 43, dep. Jun 20, 1757. {KELR JS#28:426}
CROUCH, WEDGE, of Kent County, n.a., dep. Feb 26, 1746. {KELR JS#26:32} See "Richard Crouch," q.v.
CROUPER, RICHARD, see "Thomas Davis," q.v.
CROW, ISAAC (ISSIAC), of Kent County, aet. 47, dep. 1752. {KELR JS#27:147} Aet. about 55, dep. Sep 29, 1762, mentioned his father William Crow about 40 years ago, now deceased. {KELR DD#1:310}
CROW, THOMAS, of Kent County, aet. 41, dep. 1749. {KELR JS#26:302} Aet. 60, dep. 1769, stated he married the widow Skirven. {KELR DD#3:197}
CROWE, WILLIAM, of Kent County, aet. 51, dep. 1726. {KELR JS#X:39} See "Isaac Crow," q.v.
CROWMAN, JOHN, see "Johannes Bubenheim" and "John Skuyl" and "Henry Styls," q.v.
CRUMP, FRANCES, of Queen Anne's County, n.a., dep. Apr 2, 1715. {QALR IK#A:64}
CRUMPTON, THOMAS, of Dorchester County, now dwelling on Hunting Creek, aet. 47, dep. Aug 25, 1696. {DOLR 5 Old 75}
CRUTHER, MARY, of Dorchester County, aet. about 63, dep. between Nov 12, 1745 and Mar 8, 1745, mentioned her husband Samuel Cruther. {DOLR 14 Old 48}
CRUTHER, SAMUEL, see "Mary Cruther," q.v.
CUBBAGE, PHILEMON, of Dorchester County, aet. about 52, dep. between Jun 9, 1747 and Mar 5, 1753. {DOLR 14 Old 688}
CUDGINS, JOHN, see "John Gudgins," q.v.
CULLEN, JAMES, of Dorchester County, aet. about 40, dep. between Nov 10, 1761 and Feb 26, 1762, mentioned John Lecompte and his son Anthony Lecompte about 12 years ago. {DOLR 18 Old 130}
CULLEN, JOHN, of Dorchester County, aet. about 44, dep. between Nov 19, 1731 and Jan 26, 1731/2. {DOLR 8 Old 454}
CULVER, HENRY, see "Francis Sausberg," q.v.
CUMBERLAND, JAMES, see "John Fraser," q.v.

CUMBERLAND, JOHN, see "John Fraser," q.v.
CUMBERLAND, LEVIN, see "John Fraser," q.v.
CUMMIN, HUGH, of Somerset County, n.a., dep. Apr 30, 1696. {ARMD 20:403}
CUMMINGS, WILLIAM, JR., of Frederick County, n.a., dep. May 28, 1763, stated that he purchased *Drummine* on Sep 13, 1762, the property of William Cummings, deceased, for whose debt the sale was made by the sheriff of this county to William Cummings, Jr. {FRLR H:527}
CUNNINGHAM, DANIEL, see "John Burroughs," q.v.
CUZ, ----, see "Ann Johnson," q.v.
DAGER, ELISABETH, of Charles County, n.a., dep. Oct 1, 1662 and Jul 30, 1663. {CHLR A:247, CHLR B:169}
DAGG, CATHERINE, see "Nehemiah Hubbert," q.v.
DAGG, JOHN, see "William Littleton," q.v.
DAILEY, ANN, see "Benjamin Kirby," q.v.
DAILEY, JOHN, see "Thomas Barnes," q.v.
DAILEY, WILLIAM, of Charles County, aet. 77, dep. Oct 17, 1771. {CHLR W#3:79}
DALY, BRYANT, of Charles County, n.a., dep. 1658. {ARMD 41:218}
DALZEEL (DALSELL), ANNA, see "James Hopkins," q.v.
DALZEEL (DALSELL), JAMES, see "James Hopkins," q.v.
DANDY, JOHN, see "Thomas Maidwell" and "John Russell," q.v.
DANIEL, THOMAS, see "William Rawley," q.v.
DANIELSON, DANIEL, of Prince George's County, aet. 67, dep. Feb 6, 1717/8. {PGLR I:595}
DANSON, JOHN, of Prince George's County, aet. 55, dep. Mar 5, 1763. {PGLR TT:13}
DARBY, WALTER, see "Walter Derby," q.v.
DARNALL, HENRY, see "Walter Evans" and "Thomas Clagett," q.v.
DARNALL, HENRY, of Dorchester County, n.a., dep. Jun 26, 1722, stated that Joseph Brown had a lease granted to him by Henry Darnall (deponent's father) as Lord Baltimore's Agent, but said Brown being imprisoned for debt and fearing he and his wife and children (not named) might be deprived of this lease, confided in his brother-in-law Charles Walker to have said Brown's lease right transferred to him (Walker) while he was in confinement. {PGLR I:302}
DARNALL, HENRY (esquire), of Prince George's County, aet. 53, dep. Aug 16, 1757, mentioned his father Henry Darnall, deceased. {PGLR PP:58, pt. 2}
DARNALL, HENRY, JR., of Prince George's County, aet. 41, dep. Jul 9, 1764. {PGLR TT:283}
DARNALL, JOHN, see "Samuel Breshears," q.v.
DARSON (DORSON), EDWARD, SR., of Prince George's County, aet. 81, dep. Jun 26, 1728. {PGLR M:290}
DARSON (DORSON), EDWARD, JR., of Prince George's County, aet. 45, dep. Jun 26, 1728. {PGLR M:290}

DAUGHERTY, GEORGE, of Baltimore County, aet. 36, dep. May 11, 1770. {BALR AL#B:415}
DAVIDSON, JOHN, of Frederick County, n.a., dep. Jul 27, 1762. {FRLR J:66}
DAVIS, ABIGAIL, see "John Lecompte," q.v.
DAVIS, ALICE, of Dorchester County, n.a., dep. Jun 3, 1681, mentioned William Keed (Keede). {ARMD 15:361}
DAVIS, ANN, of Charles County, aet. 47, dep. Sep 24, 1764. {CHLR N#3:64}
DAVIS, DAVID, of Charles County, aet. 61, dep. May 29, 1773. {CHLR U#3:272}
DAVIS, DAVID, of Charles County, aet. 77, dep. Oct 10, 1767. {CHLR Q#3:312} Aet. 77, dep. Oct 10, 1768, mentioned Henry Norris and William Stone about 55 or 56 years ago. {CHLR Q#3:506}
DAVIS, DAVID, of Prince George's County, aet. 61, dep. Oct 2, 1769, mentioned his brother Henry Davis. {PGLR AA#2:185-186} David Davis, Sr., aet. 60, dep. Apr 24, 1772, mentioned his uncle John Davis and wife (not named). {PGLR BB#3:81}
DAVIS, EDWARD, of Charles County, aet. 57, dep. Sep 30, 1745. {CHLR Z#2:466}
DAVIS, EDWARD, of Charles County, aet. 71, dep. Dec 27, 1731. {CHLR R#2:408}
DAVIS, EDWARD, see "Richard Davis," q.v.
DAVIS, GARA (GERAH), of Frederick County, aet. 59, dep. Apr 16, 1754, stated that he was shown the bounds of *Hope* on the east side of Monocacy Creek, near Bennett's Creek, about 16 or 17 years ago by Bald. Edmonston and Thomas Gittings (now deceased). {FRLR E:781} See "Elizabeth Barker," q.v.
DAVIS, HENRY, of Charles County, aet. 59, dep. Sep 30, 1745. {CHLR Z#2:466}
DAVIS, HENRY, of Charles County, aet. 33, dep. Dec 13, 1757. {CHLR H#3:122} Aet. 46, dep. Jul 9, 1770. {CHLR T#3:609} Aet. 48, dep. Jun 22, 1772. {CHLR U#3:163}
DAVIS, HENRY, of Dorchester County, aet. 65, dep. between Jun 9, 1736 and Jul 13, 1736. {DOLR 9 Old 386}
DAVIS, HENRY, see "Ebenezar Vaux" and "Edward Willoughby" and "David Davis," q.v.
DAVIS, JOHN, of Prince George's County, aet. 51, dep. Jul 1, 1738. {PGLR T:604} John Daviss, aet. 65, dep. May 7, 1752. {PGLR NN:64}
DAVIS, JOHN, of Baltimore County, aet. 35, dep. Jul 28, 1770, stated that James Denton, son of William Denton, died of smallpox ten years ago while serving as a soldier under General Holson at Halifax, Nova Scotia. {BALR B#G}
DAVIS, JOHN, prob. of Calvert County, aet. 41, dep. affirmed Sep 25, 1657 at Patuxent. {ARMD 10:530-531}
DAVIS, JOHN, of Somerset County, n.a., dep. Apr 2, 1715, stated that last October he was employed by John Cadwell, Jr. {ARMD 30:135}
DAVIS, JOHN, of Kent County, aet. about 59, dep. Apr 2, 1745. {KELR JS#25:277}
DAVIS, JOHN, see "David Davis," q.v.
DAVIS, JONATHAN, JR., of Charles County, aet. 34, dep. Apr 13, 1738. {CHLR T#2:465}

DAVIS, MARY, of Kent County, aet. about 57, dep. Aug 19, 1746, stated that around 1704 she was the wife of Isaac Bowles, Jr. and she often heard him talk to his father about the land. {KELR JS#25:430}

DAVIS, MEREDITH, see "Daniel Pearl," q.v.

DAVIS, NICHOLAS, of Prince George's County, aet. 40, dep. Jul 9, 1731, mentioned his father (not named) about 20 years ago. {PGLR Q:522}

DAVIS, PHILIP, of Kent County, aet. about 34, dep. Jan 4, 1741. {KELR JS#24:190}

DAVIS, PHILIP, of Kent County, aet. about 22, dep. Feb 27, 1755, mentioned Morgan Hurt and his cousin Vincent Hatchinson about 17 years ago. {KELR JS#28:99}

DAVIS, PRISCILLA, of Charles County, aet. 60, dep. Feb 14, 1738. {CHLR T#2:538}

DAVIS, RICHARD, of Charles County, aet. 64, dep. Oct 10, 1768, mentioned his father Edward Davis. {CHLR Q#3:509} Aet. 66, dep. May 1, 1769, mentioned his father Edward Davis. {CHLR Q#3:498}

DAVIS, RICHARD, of Charles County, aet. 42, dep. Sep 30, 1745. {CHLR Z#2:466} Aet. 63, dep. Nov 14, 1766, mentioned his father William Davis. {CHLR P#3:281} Aet. 64, dep. Oct 10, 1768. {CHLR Q#3:407} Richard Davis, Sr., aet. 67, dep. Nov 5, 1770. {CHLR T#3:144}

DAVIS, RICHARD, of Kent County, aet. about 53, dep. May 22, 1732, mentioned Robert Foreman, deceased. {KELR JS#16:251}

DAVIS, RICHARD, see "John Lecompte," q.v.

DAVIS, SAMUEL, of Kent County, aet. about 34, dep. Sep 2, 1751. {KEEJ - John Davis, Jr. folder} Aet. about 38, dep. Sep 4, 1753. {KELR JS#27:350}

DAVIS, SOLLOMAN, of Dorchester County, cooper, aet. about 69, dep. between Nov 9, 1756 and Jun 15, 1757. {DOLR 15 Old 522} Solomon Davice, aet. about 65, dep. between Nov 14, 1752 and Jun 13, 1753. {DOLR 14 Old 709}

DAVIS, THOMAS, of Charles County, aet. 38, dep. Jun 2, 1738, stated that Richard Crouper married the relict of Humphrey Pose. {CHLR T#2:464} Aet. 44, dep. May 29, 1744. {CHLR Y#2:185} Aet. 48, dep. Aug 1, 1748, stated that William Dent showed him the bounds of *Athey's Hopewell* about 34 years ago; also mentioned Capt. George Athey. {PGLR BB:490}

DAVIS, THOMAS, of Prince George's County, aet. 42, dep. Jun 28, 1743, mentioned his father William Davis, deceased. {PGLR Y:705}

DAVIS, THOMAS, of Prince George's County, aet. 70 or thereabouts, dep. Mar 13, 1756, mentioned Marsh Mareen Duvall about 40 years ago, now deceased. {PGLR NN:437}

DAVIS, THOMAS, see "Philip Tennally" and "Philip White," q.v.

DAVIS, WILLIAM, of Charles County, aet. 70, dep. Feb 14, 1738. {CHLR T#2:538}

DAVID, WILLIAM, of Prince George's County, aet. 60, dep. May 11, 1754, mentioned his uncle Thomas Roper about 30 years ago. {PGLR NN:281} Aet. 65, dep. Nov 16, 1759, mentioned Capt. John Welsh, of Anne Arundel County, about 30 or 40 years ago. {PGLR RR:17}

DAVIS, WILLIAM, of Talbot County, n.a., dep. Jun 21, 1670, mentioned William Ladd's wife (not named). {ARMD 54:466}
DAVIS, WILLIAM, see "Thomas Davis" and "Richard Davis," q.v.
DAWNEY, JAMES, of Baltimore County, aet. 47, dep. Nov 3, 1766. {BALR B#P:307}
DAWNEY, JOHN, of Baltimore County, aet. 60, dep. Sep 15, 1750. {BALR TR#E:9}
DAWNEY, THOMAS, of Baltimore County, aet. 66, dep. Oct 25, 1769, stated that he has been in this country at least 40 years. {BALR AL#B:284}
DAWSON, ----, see "James Wilson," q.v.
DAWSON, ANTHO:, of Talbot County, n.a., dep. Sep 21, 1669. {ARMD 54:444}
DAWSON, EDWARD, of Prince George's County, aet. 45, dep. Jun 6, 1735. {PGLR T:285} See "James Drane," q.v.
DAWSON, JAMES, of Dorchester County, aet. about 47, dep. between Nov 13, 1770 and Aug 2, 1771, mentioned Mary Anderson, wife of Isaac Anderson and daughter of old Benjamin Edgell (Edgill). {DOLR 25 Old 26} Aet. 48, dep. Nov 12, 1771. {DOLR 26 Old 23}
DAWSON, JOHN, of Dorchester County, aet. about 40, dep. between Nov 14, 1758 and Jun 30, 1759, mentioned his father Jonas Dawson. {DOLR 16 Old 220}
DAWSON, JOHN, of Prince George's County, aet. 40, dep. Mar 19, 1746/7, mentioned Col. Thomas Addison about 27 or 28 years ago. {PGLR BB:199}
DAWSON, JOHN, see "Indian Abraham," q.v.
DAWSON, JONAS, see "John Tomlinson" and "Robert Sherwin" and "John Dawson," q.v.
DAWSON, OBEDIAH, of Dorchester County, aet. 42, dep. between Jun 22, 1741 and Jul 13, 1741. {DOLR 12 Old 122} Aet. about 46, dep. between Mar 12, 1744 and Nov 8, 1748. {DOLR 14 Old 317}
DAWSON, RICHARD, of Dorchester County, aet. about 60, dep. between Mar 17, 1768 and Aug 9, 1768. {DOLR 22 Old 433}
DAWSON, SAMUEL, of Cecil County, aet. 44, dep. Oct 22, 1748, stated that about 30 years ago a Dutchman (not named) settled on the place where Mary McFadien now lives. {ARMD 28:442}
DAWSON, SARAH, of Kent County, aet. about 80, dep. Aug, 1772. {TAEJ - Matthew Tilghman folder}
DAY, EDWARD, see "John Day," q.v.
DAY, JOHN, of Baltimore County, aet. 40, dep. Mar 3, 1764, mentioned his father Edward Day. {BALR B#M:370} Aet. 41, dep. Nov 11, 1764, mentioned his father Edward Day. {BALR B#N:461}
DAY, MATHEW, of Prince George's County, aet. 43, dep. May 1, 1755. {PGLR NN:369}
DEACONS, JOHN, of Prince George's County, aet. 57, dep. Jun 11, 1727, mentioned Christopher Beane (Beans), deceased. {PGLR Q:468}
DEAKINS, JOHN, of Prince George's County, aet. 62, dep. May 11, 1733. {PGLR T:28}

DEAKINS, WILLIAM, of Prince George's County, aet. aet. 38, dep. Aug 11, 1757, mentioned Thomas Hodgkin about 4 years ago, now deceased. {PGLR PP:28, pt. 2} Aet. 50, dep. May 22, 1770. {PGLR AA#2:139}
DEAN, CHARLES, see "Henry Windows," q.v.
DEAN (DEANE), EDWARD, of Charles County, aet. 43, dep. Jul 12, 1664, mentioned Thomas Stone and his brother John Stone. {CHLR B:327}
DEAN, EDWARD, of Dorchester County, aet. about 50, dep. between Aug 9, 1757 and Aug 9, 1758, mentioned Thomas Williams and William Spencer, both deceased. {DOLR 16 Old 80} Aet. about 65, dep. between Nov 13, 1770 and Aug 2, 1771. {DOLR 25 Old 26} Aet. 65, dep. between Mar 12, 1771 and Jul 22, 1771, mentioned old Robert Watson about 46 or 47 years ago, now deceased. {DOLR 25 Old 73}
DEAN, FRANCIS, of Dorchester County, aet. near 50, dep. between Nov 10, 1761 and Feb 24, 1762, stated that William Spencer, now deceased, told him about 37 or 38 years ago that *Smithson's Endeavour* was given by Thomas Smithson to Jenny Taylor who married a Tate and built a house on said land. {DOLR 18 Old 72}
DEAN (DEANE), HENRY, of Dorchester County, aet. about 30, dep. between Mar 18, 1726/7 and Jun 3, 1727. {DOLR 8 Old 215} Aet. about 38, dep. between Nov 24, 1732 and Jan 31, 1732/3. {DOLR 9 Old 97, 98}
DEAN, JOHN, of Dorchester County, aet. about 52, dep. between Nov 11, 1755 and May 20, 1756. {DOLR 16 Old 76} Aet. about 58, dep. between Nov 10, 1761 and Feb 24, 1762. {DOLR 18 Old 72} See "Morgan Addams," q.v.
DEAN, MATHEW, see "William Gray," q.v.
DEAN, RICHARD, of Frederick County, aet. 60, dep. Mar 16, 1761. {FRLR G:158}
DEAN, WILLIAM, of Dorchester County, aet. about 54, dep. between Aug 14, 1764 and Jan 4, 1768. {DOLR 22 Old 418}
DEAN, WILLIAM, of Dorchester County, aet. 52, dep. between Jun 17, 1734 and Sep 19, 1734, stated that the bounds of *Safford* were identified by Michael Todd and Benjamin Todd about 27 years ago. {DOLR 9 Old 249} Aet. 63, dep. Aug 24, 1745. {DOLR 12 Old 247}
DEATH, JAMES, of Harford County, n.a., dep. June, 1775. {Land Commission, 1774, Harford County Genealogical Society Newsletter, Jan, 1993, p. 3}
DEAVER, JOHN, of Baltimore County, aet. 43, dep. Aug 15, 1774, stated that he was shown the bounds of *Elbert's Field* by his father Antill Deaver in 1752; also mentioned Thomas Thurston, son of Colla Thurston. {BALR AL#L:236}
DEAVER, SARAH, of Baltimore County, aet. 63, dep. Jul 25, 1760, stated that John Parran had conveyed his land to his natural daughters Esther Parran Abbott and Mary Parran Abbott and after their deaths to his brother Moses Parran (now deceased); John died in 1733; his widow (not named) has since married twice to James Duke and John Gray, both deceased; Young Parran, his eldest brother, is still living; and, Mary Parran Abbott married Jacob Bowen of Calvert County, Maryland. {BALR B#O:110}

DEBRULAR, BENJAMIN, of Baltimore County, aet. 34, dep. Nov 3, 1766. {BALR B#P:307}
DELAHAY, JANE, of Charles County, aet. 30, dep. May 1, 1659. {CHLR A:57, ARMD 53:46} Aet. 33, dep. Apr 22, 1662. {CHLR A:205, ARMD 53:208}
DELAHAY, JOHN (JHOANNIS), of Charles County, aet. 36, dep. May 1, 1659. {CHLR A:57, ARMD 53:46}
DELASHMET (DELASHMUT), ELIAS, of Frederick County, aet. 51, dep. Nov 5, 1772, mentioned John Nelson about 39 years ago. {FRLR P:430} See "James Hook," q.v.
DELL, THOMAS, see "Lucretia Ward," q.v.
DELL, WILLIAM, of Talbot or Dorchester County, n.a., dep. Dec 17, 1670. {ARMD 51:348}
DELOZIER, GEORGE, of Charles County, aet. 44, dep. May 22, 1755. {CHLR E#3:135} Aet. 56, dep. Nov 20, 1766. {CHLR P#3:286}
DELOZIER, JOHN, of Charles County, aet. 57, dep. Nov 20, 1766. {CHLR P#3:286} Aet. 60, dep. Apr 21, 1769. {CHLR Q#3:442}
DEMALL, JOHN, of Prince George's County, aet. 70, dep. Mar 24, 1726/7, mentioned James Williams and his son James Williams, deceased, and Richard Hartrup, son of Richard and Elizabeth Hartrup; also mentioned Elizabeth Hartrup was a sister to James Mullikin, deceased, father of James Mullikin, and Elizabeth Hartrup and James Mullikin were children of James and Mary Mullikin. {PGLR M:222} See "Joseph Ray" and "Thomas Drane," q.v.
DEMALL, MARY, of Prince George's County, aet. 61, dep. Feb 2, 1734/5. {PGLR T:286} See "Thomas Drane," q.v.
DEMENT, CHARLES, of Charles County, aet. 27, dep. Oct 30, 1770. {CHLR T#3:141}
DEMENT, JOHN, of Charles County, aet. 53, dep. Sep 24, 1766. {CHLR N#3:64}
DEMPSEY, JOHN, of Charles County, aet. 67, dep. Aug 2, 1737. {CHLR T#2:370}
DEMPSEY, MARY, of Charles County, aet. 58, dep. Apr 6, 1733. {CHLR R#2:332} Aet. 60, dep. Aug 2, 1737, mentioned her former husband Stephen Nowland. {CHLR T#2:370}
DENNIS, JOHN, see "Thomas Jameson," q.v.
DENNY, CHRISTOPHER, of Queen Anne's County, aet. about 75, dep. May 6, 1728. {QAEJ - Christopher Wilkinson folder}
DENT, GEORGE (colonel), of Charles County, aet. 45, dep. Nov 20, 1735. {CHLR T#2:201} Aet. 46, dep. Apr 28, 1737. {CHLR T#2:368}
DENT, HATCH, of Charles County, aet. 61, dep. Oct 10, 1768, mentioned his father John Dent. {CHLR Q#3:407}
DENT, JOHN, SR., of Charles County, aet. 53, dep. May 2, 1727. {CHLR P#2:488} See "Hatch Dent" and "Michael Dent," q.v.
DENT, MAJOR, see "Terence O'Brian," q.v.
DENT, MICHAEL, of Charles County, aet. 55, dep. Oct 10, 1768, mentioned his father John Dent. {CHLR Q#3:409}

DENT, PETER, of Charles County, aet. 34, dep. Jun 5, 1752 and Dec 30, 1752. {CHLR B#3:59, 344} Aet. 37, dep. Jul 26, 1755. {CHLR E#3:387} Aet. 44, dep. Nov 23, 1761. {CHLR K#3:407} Aet. 46, dep. Oct 11, 1763. {CHLR M#3:354}
DENT, PETER, of Charles County, aet. 41, dep. Oct 1, 1771, mentioned his father Peter Dent. {CHLR T#3:618}
DENT, PETER, see "Joseph Chapline" and "Van Swearingen" and "Thomas Waller" and "John Harris," q.v.
DENT, THOMAS, of Charles County, aet. 39, dep. Nov 12, 1725. {CHLR P#3:139}
DENT, WILLIAM, of Prince George's County, aet. 27, dep. Sep 15, 1757 (1758?). {PGLR PP:237, pt. 2}
DENT, WILLIAM, of Prince George's County, aet. 57, dep. Feb 17, 1723/4. {PGLR I:542}
DENT, WILLIAM, of Frederick County, aet. 34, dep. Jun 5, 1764, stated that he was Deputy Surveyor in 1757. {FRLR J:942}
DENT, WILLIAM, see "Thomas Davis," q.v.
DENTON, HENRY, of Anne Arundel County, n.a., dep. Dec 12, 1696, stated that he has served as Clerk of the Maryland Council and in the Assembly, and Register of the Court of Vice Admiralty on the Western Shore, and Naval Office of the Port of Annapolis under Gov. Francis Nicholson. {ARMD 20:576} See "William Taylard," q.v.
DENTON, JAMES, see "John Davis," q.v.
DENTON, WILLIAM, see "John Davis," q.v.
DENUNE, DOCTOR, see "Benjamin White" and "John Fowler," q.v.
DEPRIEST, WILLIAM, alias William Williams, of Marrowbone Creek, Smiths River, Pittsylvania County, Virginia, n.a., dep. Sep 25, 1767 (confession) in Frederick County, Maryland, mentioned a counterfeit ring involving Joseph Wilcox and John Cox of Frederick County, and Nathaniel Abney, David Lyles, and Michael Hill Rogers of Pittsylvania County, and William Redman and John Ethrington of Loudon County. {ARMD 32:216}
DERBY, WALTER, of Somerset County, aet. about 36, dep. between Mar 15, 1735 and Nov 9, 1737. {DOLR 9 Old 493}
DERRICUTT, JOHN, see "George Copper," q.v.
DE SOUSA, MATHIAS, of St. Mary's County, n.a., dep. 1642, stated that he owned a pinnace which he hired out to Mr. Pulton (skipper) and John Prettiman (sailor) to trade with the Sesquihanoughs. {ARMD 4:138}
DEVEREAUX, JOHN, see "John Anderson," q.v.
DEWERTY, JOAN, of Cecil County, n.a., dep. Mar 8, 1706/7, stated that Mary Knoleman called Capt. William Potts a chimney corner justice. {CMSP 1:7 - The Black Books}
DEWIT, JOHN, of Charles County, aet. 76, dep. Nov 2, 1742. {CHLR O#2:465}
DEWITT, JOHN, of Prince George's County, aet. 62, dep. May 31, 1731, stated that he was overseer for Joshua Cecill at *Mansfield* about 28 years ago. {PGLR Q:604}

DICKASON, WALTER, see "Daniel Rutty" and "Henry Potts," q.v.
DICKERSON, JOHN, see "John Rawlings," q.v.
DICKESON, HENRY, of Prince George's County, aet. 54, dep. Jun 27, 1743. {PGLR Y:701}
DICKESON, JOHN, SR., of Prince George's County, aet. 66 dep. Jun 27, 1743. {PGLR Y:702} See "Thomas Wilcoxon," q.v.
DICKINSON, CHARLES, of Dorchester County, aet. about 40, dep. between Jun 11, 1745 and May 23, 1746. {DOLR 14 Old 50} Aet. about 50, dep. between Nov 11, 1755 and May 20, 1756. {DOLR 16 Old 76} Aet. 62, dep. between Nov 8, 1768 and Dec 10, 1768. {DOLR 23 Old 133} Aet. about 65, dep. between Nov 13, 1770 and Aug 2, 1771, mentioned Richard Bennett, Esq., Thomas Nevett, and John Kirk around 1730. {DOLR 25 Old 26} Aet. in his 65th year, dep. between Mar 12, 1771 and Jul 22, 1771. {DOLR 25 Old 73}
DICKINSON, JAMES, of Talbot County, n.a., dep. Jun 7, 1769, stated that he has known Francis Baker several years. {ARMD 32:326}
DICKINSON, JOHN, see "Thomas Shearwood," q.v.
DICKINSON, SAMUEL, see "Peter Edmondson," q.v.
DICKISON, THOMAS, of Prince George's County, aet. 76, dep. Nov 17, 1724, mentioned Mary Wheeler, wife of John Wheeler. {PGLR I:646}
DICKSON, GEORGE, of Prince George's County, aet. 51, dep. Aug 17, 1732. {PGLR Q:528}
DIGGES, EDWARD, see "Charles Beall," q.v.
DIGGES, WILLIAM, of Prince George's County, aet. 31, dep. Mar 25, 1743. {PGLR Y:657} Aet. 65 or thereabouts, dep. Oct 15, 1776. {PGLR CC#2:311}
DIGGS, WILLIAM, of Prince George's County, aet. 40, dep. Mar 6, 1759. {PGLR PP:279, pt. 2} William Diggs, Esq., aet. 56, dep. Apr 21, 1767, mentioned Joseph Chew about 16 years ago. {PGLR BB#2:120-121}
DIKE, MATHEW, see "Henry Tanner," q.v.
DILLION, THOMAS, of St. Mary's or Charles County, n.a., dep. Jun 29, 1698 in Annapolis. {ARMD 23:435}
DILLON, JAMES, of Baltimore County, aet. 39, dep. Oct 21, 1771. {BALR AL#D:276}
DIMPSY, JOHN, of Prince George's County, aet. about 52, dep. between Nov 11, 1729 and Mar 26, 1730, mentioned John Ward and his brother Henry Ward about 3 years ago. {PGLR M:568}
DISTANCE, RALPH, see "Thomas Barnes," q.v.
DIXON, FRANCIS, of Charles County, aet. 34, dep. Jan 31, 1776, mentioned his father Jacob Dixon. {CHLR X#3:536}
DIXON, GEORGE, see "Giles Virmillion," q.v.
DIXON, JACOB, of Charles County, aet. 58, dep. Jul 21, 1767. {CHLR P#3:661} Aet. 59, dep. Jul 18, 1767. {CHLR P#3:663} Aet. 62, dep. Jun 13, 1771. {CHLR T#3:242} See "Francis Dixon," q.v.

DIXON, JOHN, of Queen Anne's County, aet. 46, planter, dep. Aug 23, 1710, stated that he saw Rev. James Clayland, minister of Talbot County, marry John Baynard and Elizabeth Blackwell in the house of Richard Dudley about 33 years ago and their son Thomas Baynard was born in wedlock. {QALR ET#A:62}
DIXON, JOHN, of Kent County, aet. about 61, dep. Jun 18, 1750. {KELR JS#26:334}
DIXON, OBED, of Dorchester County, aet. about 56, dep. between Jun 11, 1765 and Mar 9, 1767, mentioned Richard Cooper about 8 or 9 years ago, now deceased. {DOLR 21 Old 315}
DIXON, WILLIAM, see "John Pitts" and "Joseph Rodgers" and "John Harnam," q.v.
DOBSON, SAMUEL, of Charles County, aet. 34, dep. Jul 10, 1662. {CHLR A:235}
DOCKERY, MATHEW, of Queen Anne's County, aet. 52, dep. Mar 15, 1760, mentioned John Meredith, father of Thomas and John Meredith, in 1732, and Thomas Wilkinson and son John Wilkinson in 1755. {QAEJ - Richard Tilghman Earle folder} Aet. near 52, dep. Feb 29, 1760. {QAEJ - Earle: oversize folder} Aet. near 53, dep. Aug 13, 1760. {QAEJ - John Gafford folder}
DOCKERY, THOMAS, of Queen Anne's County, aet. 41, dep. Mar 15, 1760. {QAEJ - Richard Tilghman Earle folder}
DOD (DODE), MARY, of Charles County, aet. 26, dep. Jul 9, 1662. {ARMD 53:233} Marie Dode, aet. 21, dep. Jan 26, 1658/9, mentioned her husband Richard Dode. {CHLR A:38} See "Thomas Baker," q.v.
DOD (DODE), RICHARD, of Charles County, aet. 25, dep. Jan 26, 1658/9. {CHLR A:38} Richard Dod, n.a., dep. Jul 9, 1662. {CHLR A:233, ARMD 53:233} See "Mary Dod," q.v.
DODD, THOMAS, prob. of Anne Arundel County, n.a., dep. circa Sep 5, 1692. {ARMD 8:375}
DODGIN, DANIEL, see "Daniel Haskins," q.v.
DOLTON, ANN, of Charles County, aet. 70, dep. Oct 10, 1759, stated she had formerly lived with Mrs. Lynch in Liverpool, County Lancaster, England, who had a daughter Ann Jameson whom she had sent to Thomas Jameson who had been in Maryland for some years; further stated that she (Dolton) had met Ann Jameson about 3½ years after her (Jameson) arrival, Sep 6, 1751. {CHLR G#3:370}
DONALD, MICHAEL, of Charles County, aet. 64, dep. Jul 26, 1755. {CHLR E#3:388}
DONALDSON, MOSES, of Prince George's County, aet. 32, dep. Nov 5, 1763. {PGLR TT:571}
DOOLEY, JOHN, of Charles County, aet. 34, dep. Feb 13, 1776. {CHLR Y#3:379}
DOPSON, ----, see "George Wilson," q.v.
DORRINGTON, ----, see "Robert Parkinson," q.v.
DORROSELL, JOSEPH, of Charles County, aet. 40, dep. May 12, 1663, mentioned John Goold and wife Margerie Goold. {CHLR B:115} Aet. 40, dep. Jul 30, 1663, stated that Dr. John Lumbroso did lie with his maid (not named) and

she was with child; the doctor administered a strong purge to take away the swelling and kill the child. {CHLR B:161} Aet. not given, dep. Jan 5, 1663/4. {CHLR B:213}

DORSETT, JOHN, of Prince George's County, aet. 28, dep. Jul 26, 1751. {PGLR PP:132}

DORSETT, THOMAS, of Prince George's County, aet. 60, planter, dep. Jul 1, 1751. {PGLR PP:155}

DORSETT, WILLIAM, of Prince George's County, aet. 36, dep. May 9, 1768. {PGLR BB#2:371}

DOSSEY, MARY, of Queen Anne's County, aet. 54, dep. Mar, 1759. {QAEJ - Henry Carter folder}

DOUGHTY, ANN (ANE), of Charles County, aet. 42, dep. Nov 5, 1662, stated that she had 7 silver spoons and arranged for 6 new silver spoons to be delivered by Richard Rich on his next return from England for "her son Burdit's use" [son-in-law Thomas Burditt] and inscribed "EB" which were the initials of her daughter's child's name; also mentioned her cousin Elisabeth Calvert. {CHLR B:10}

DOUGHTY, ENOCK, of Charles County, aet. 22, dep. Sep 25, 1661, mentioned his father Francis Doughty and also Richard Watson, a blind man. {CHLR A:157}

DOUGHTY, FRANCIS, see "Enock Doughty," q.v.

DOUGLAS, BENJAMIN, of Charles County, aet. 39, dep. 1762, mentioned Benjamin Douglas and John Wakefield about 16 years ago, both now deceased. {CHLR K#3:478}

DOUGLAS, BENJAMIN, of Charles County, aet. 50, dep. Dec 20, 1737. {CHLR T#2:430}

DOUGLAS, BENJAMIN, see "Thomas Douglas," q.v.

DOUGLAS, CHARLES, of Charles County, aet. 53, dep. Jul 18, 1767. {CHLR P#3:663}

DOUGLAS, ELIZABETH, of Charles County, aet. 48, dep. May 19, 1744. {CHLR Y#2:623}

DOUGLAS, JOHN, of Charles County, aet. 45, dep. Apr 29, 1754. {CHLR D#3:323}

DOUGLAS, JOHN, of Charles County, aet. 25 or thereabouts, dep. Sep 25, 1661 and Nov 19, 1661. {CHLR A:169, ARMD 53:160}

DOUGLAS, JOSEPH (captain), of Charles County, aet. 65, dep. Nov 1, 1736. {CHLR T#2:267} Aet. 63, dep. Dec 20, 1737. {CHLR T#2:430} Aet. 66, dep. Dec 15, 1742. {CHLR O#2:503}

DOUGLAS, THOMAS, of Charles County, aet. 45, dep. Oct 17, 1775. {CHLR X#3:544}

DOUGLAS, THOMAS, of Charles County, aet. 52, dep. May 7, 1744, stated that about 30 years ago he lived with his guardian John Compton at *Blythwood*, now owned by Benjamin Douglas. {CHLR Z#2:17}

DOULL, JAMES, see "John Locker," q.v.

DOULTON, WILLIAM, of Charles County, aet. 73, dep. Sep 26, 1747. {CHLR Z#2:188}

DOWDALL, MAJOR, see "Ephraim Gilbert," q.v.

DOWDEN, JOHN, of Frederick County, aet. 59 or thereabouts, dep. Jul 27, 1762. {FRLR J:66} John Dowden, Sr., aet. 64, dep. Aug 5, 1765. {FRLR K:1350}
DOWING, DENNIS, of Charles County, aet. 66, dep. Oct 11, 1772. {CHLR U#3:263} See "William Dowing," q.v.
DOWING, JOHN, of Charles County, aet. 39, dep. Oct 11, 1772. {CHLR U#3:263}
DOWING, WILLIAM, of Charles County, aet. 33, dep. Apr 11, 1769, mentioned his father Dennis Dowing. {CHLR Q#3:440}
DOWNES, FRANCIS, see "Joseph Tilly," q.v.
DOWNES, JOHN, see "Edward Tilghman" and "Sarah Emory," q.v.
DOWNES, SOPHIA, see "Edward Tilghman" and "Sarah Emory," q.v.
DOWNES, SUSANNAH, of Dorchester County, aet. 36, dep. Sep 8, 1705. {DOLR 6 Old 74}
DOWNEY, VALENTINE, of Queen Anne's County, aet. about 37, dep. Apr, 1769, stated that he had married the heiress (no name given) of the land in dispute (*Isaac's Chance*) and several persons told him that he had a right to the whole land. {QAEJ - James Hutchens folder}
DOWNEY, WILLIAM, of Frederick County, aet. 33, dep. Mar 13, 1761. {FRLR G:160}
DOWNS, ELEANOR, of Charles County, aet. 23, dep. Oct 1, 1771, mentioned her father William Downs. {CHLR T#3:617}
DOWNS, ROBERT, of Charles County, n.a., dep. Oct 2, 1662. {CHLR A:248}
DOWNS, WILLIAM, of Charles County, aet. 47, dep. May 25, 1752. {CHLR B#3:121} Aet. 62, dep. Aug 26, 1767. {CHLR P#3:654} See "Eleanor Downs," q.v.
DOYNE, IGNATIUS, see "Benjamin Jameson," q.v.
DOYNE, JEAN (Mrs.), of Charles County, aet. 64, dep. Nov 8, 1774. {CHLR W#3:609} See "Jane Wharton," q.v.
DRAIN, ELIZABETH, of Prince George's County, aet. 66, dep. Feb 2, 1734/5. {PGLR T:285}
DRANE, JAMES, of Prince George's County, aet. 39, dep. May 8, 1753. {PGLR NN:138} James Draine, aet. 41, dep. Mar 12, 1755. {PGLR NN:436} James Drane, aet. 47, dep. Sep 13, 1760, mentioned Thomas Drane, John Perry, Sr., and Edward Dawson about 30 odd years ago. {PGLR RR:125}
DRANE, THOMAS, of Prince George's County, aet. 60, dep. May 8, 1753. {PGLR NN:137} Aet. 68, dep. Sep 13, 1760, mentioned James Drane, Nathaniel Wickham, Sr., Brock Mockbee, and James Plummer about 20 years ago. {PGLR RR:125} Aet. 72, dep. Jun 11, 1764, mentioned Mrs. Dumall and her father-in-law Capt. Edward Brock and her husband John Dumall; also mentioned William Offutt about 30 years ago. {PGLR TT:371-372} See "James Drane," q.v.
DRIVER, MARTIN, see "Mary Lecompte," q.v.
DRURY, CHARLES, of Prince George's County, aet. 60, dep. Dec 24, 1736. {PGLR Y:84} Aet. 64, dep. Aug 25, 1737. {PGLR T:509}
DRURY, MARY, of Dorchester County, aet. about 60, formerly the wife of John Button, dep. between Nov 19, 1732 and May 10, 1732. {DOLR 9 Old 64}

DUCKER, WILLIAM, of Prince George's County, aet. 37, dep. Oct 10, 1762. {PGLR RR:263}
DUCKETT, RICHARD, of Prince George's County, aet. near 40, dep. Jan 6, 1747/8, mentioned his father (not named). {PGLR BB:691} Aet. 61, dep. Jan 31, 1766, mentioned his father (not named). {PGLR TT:569} See "Benjamin Jacob," q.v.
DUDLEY, RICHARD, see "John Lane" and "John Pitt" and "John Dixon," q.v.
DUKE, JAMES, see "Sarah Deaver," q.v.
DUKE, THOMAS, SR., of Dorchester County, aet. about 63, dep. between Nov 9, 1762 and May 9, 1763, mentioned Cornelius Johnson about 30 years ago, now deceased. {DOLR 19 Old 425}
DULANY, DANIEL, see "Thomas Lawson," q.v.
DULY, MATHEW, see "Thomas Shearwood," q.v.
DUMALL, JOHN, see "Thomas Drane," q.v.
DUNAWAY, ----, see "Edward Brawner," q.v.
DUNAWAY, TIMOTHY, see "William Nelson," q.v.
DUNCAN, WILLIAM, of Kent County, aet. about 58, dep. circa 1773, mentioned Robert Peacock, son of Richard. {KEEJ - Samuel Griffith folder}
DUNN, JAMES, of Kent County, aet. about 28, dep. Jun 20, 1757. {KELR JS#28:427} Aet. about 33, dep. Dec 18, 1761. {KELR DD#1:100} See "John Rowles," q.v.
DUNN, JOHN, of Prince George's County, aet. 55, dep. Jan 21, 1760, stated that he lived with John Wood about 33 years ago. {PGLR RR:39} Aet. 68, dep. Mar 15, 1774. {PGLR BB#3:400}
DUNN, JOHN, of Charles County, aet. 65, dep. Oct 30, 1770. {CHLR T#3:140}
DUNN, ROBERT, of Kent County, aet. about 52, dep. Aug, 1726. {KELR JS#X:40} See "Thomas Hynson" and "George Geves," q.v.
DUNN (DUN), ROBERT, of Kent County, aet. about 39, dep. Aug 14, 1732, mentioned his father Robert Dun. {KELR JS#16:255}
DUNN, WILLIAM, of Kent County, aet. about 35, dep. circa 1761. {KEEJ - James Dunn folder}
DUNNING, JAMES, of Prince George's County, aet. 51 or 52, dep. Jul 3, 1775, mentioned James Wood about 10 or 12 years ago, now deceased. {PGLR CC#2:179}
DUNNINGTON, FRANCIS, of Charles County, aet. 45, dep. Feb 25, 1745/6. {CHLR Z#2:518} Aet. 61, dep. Aug 4, 1761. {CHLR K#3:300} Aet. 73, dep. Aug 30, 1773. {CHLR W#3:91} Aet. 74, dep. Feb 23, 1774. {CHLR W#3:82}
DURDIN, JOSEPH, of Kent County, Quaker, aet. about 42, dep. affirmed Aug 17, 1743. {TAEJ - Isaac Cox(?) folder}
DURDING, WILLIAM, of Queen Anne's County, aet. 33, dep. Oct 5, 1768. {QAEJ - Gideon Emory folder}
DURHAM, ABRAHAM, of Baltimore County, aet. 39 in Dec, 1753, dep. recorded in land records in Oct, 1778. {BALR WG#G:206}

DURHAM, STALEY, of Baltimore County, aet. 49 in Dec, 1753, dep. recorded in land records in Oct, 1778, mentioned John Leakins, father of Thomas Leakins, about 30 or 35 years ago. {BALR WG#G:206}

DURIGS, WILLIAM, see "Torrence O'Brian," q.v.

DUTTON, GERRARD, see "John Penn," q.v.

DUTTON, NOTLEY, see "John Penn," q.v.

DUTTON, ROBERT, of Baltimore County, aet. 57, dep. May 8, 1770. {BALR AL#B:289}

DUTTON, THOMAS, see "John Penn," q.v.

DUVAL, ALEXANDER, of Frederick County, aet. 58, dep. Apr 1, 1768, mentioned Thomas Giddins about 28 years ago. {FRLR L:519}

DUVALL, ALEXANDER, of Prince George's County, aet. 23, dep. Oct 10, 1762, mentioned his uncle Mareen Duvall. {PGLR RR:264}

DUVALL, BENJAMIN, JR., see "Mash Benjamin Duvall," q.v.

DUVALL (DEVALL), BENJAMIN, 3RD, of Prince George's County, aet. 52, dep. Oct 30, 1769, mentioned Samuel Duvall and his grandfather (not named). {PGLR AA#2:187}

DUVALL, CORNELIUS, of Prince George's County, aet. 27, dep. Oct 10, 1762. {PGLR RR:264}

DUVALL, EPHRAIM, of Prince George's County, aet. 21, dep. Oct 10, 1762. {PGLR RR:264}

DUVALL, JAMES, of Prince George's County, aet. 28, dep. Oct 10, 1761, mentioned his uncle James Mullikin. {PGLR RR:182}

DUVALL, JOHN, of Prince George's County, aet. 49, dep. May 11, 1762. {PGLR RR:265-266} Aet. 53, dep. Apr 14, 1766. {PGLR TT:569} See "Mareen Duvall" and "Samuel Duvall," q.v.

DUVALL, MAREEN, see "Alexander Duvall" and "Marsh Benjamin Duvall" and "Thomas Davis" and "Samuel Duvall" and "Samuel Duvall, 3rd," q.v.

DUVALL, MAREEN, of the Great Marsh, Prince George's County, aet. 46, dep. Oct 4, 1726, mentioned his brothers John, Mareen, and Samuel Duvall. {PGLR M:216} Aet. 59, dep. Jul 31, 1746, mentioned his father Mareen Duvall, Sr. {PGLR BB:59-60}

DUVALL, MAREEN, JR., of Prince George's County, aet. 32, dep. Jul 31, 1746, mentioned his grandfather Mareen Duvall, Sr., deceased. {PGLR BB:58-59} Mareen Duvall, aet. 45, dep. Nov 9, 1759, mentioned his father (not named) and grandfather (not named) about 35 years ago; also mentioned Dr. Richard Pile, Thomas Clagett, and Thomas Clagett, Jr. {PGLR RR:81} Mareen Devall, aet. 55, dep. Oct 30, 1769, mentioned his father (not named). {PGLR AA#2:194}

DUVALL, MAREEN, SR., of Prince George's County, aet. 55, dep. Dec 15, 1718, stated that he was shown the bounded tree (now a dead red oak) of *Wilson's Plain* by his father (not named); deponent's name listed as Mareen Duvall the Elder. {PGLR I:125} Maureen Duvall, Sr., aet. 65, planter, dep. Oct 4, 1726, mentioned his father (not named). {PGLR M:215} Mareen Duvall, Sr., aet. 66, dep. Jun 27, 1727, mentioned Samuel Magruder, deceased. {PGLR M:202} Maren Duvall, aet. 67, planter, dep. Oct 9, 1728, mentioned Philip Gittings, Sr., about 27 or 28 years ago, now deceased. {PGLR M:402}

DUVALL, MARSH MAREEN, see "Thomas Davis," q.v.

DUVALL, MASH (MARSH) BENJAMIN, of Prince George's County, aet. near 36, dep. Feb 3, 1747/8, also gave deposition as Benjamin Duvall, Jr. {PGLR BB:692} Benjamin Duvall (Marsh), aet. 50, dep. May 11, 1762, stated that he was overseer for Jacob Henderson about 26 years ago. {PGLR RR:266} See "David Evans," q.v.

DUVALL, SAMUEL, see "Maureen Duvall" and "William Mullikin" and "John Wilson" and "Benjamin Duvall 3rd," q.v.

DUVALL, SAMUEL, of Prince George's County, aet. 51, dep. Dec 15, 1718, mentioned his brother John Duvall. {PGLR I:125} Aet. 58, dep. Oct 4, 1726, mentioned his father (not named). {PGLR M:216}

DUVALL, SAMUEL, of Prince George's County, aet. 56, dep. Oct 10, 1762, mentioned his uncle Mareen Duvall and grandfather Mareen Duvall. {PGLR RR:263-264} Aet. 57, dep. Nov 5, 1763. {PGLR TT:573}

DUVALL, SAMUEL, 3RD, of Prince George's County, aet. 32, dep. Jul 31, 1746, mentioned his grandfather Mareen Duvall, Sr., deceased. {PGLR BB:59-60}

DYAR (DYER), JOHN, of Dorchester County, aet. 56, dep. Nov 21, 1711. {DOLR 6 Old 191} See "George Pounce" and "John Anderton," q.v.

DYER, EDWARD, of Kent County, aet. about 39, dep. circa 1750. {KEEJ - Isaac and Thomas Crown folder} Aet. about 40, dep. Jun 11, 1750. {KELR JS#26:414}

DYER, THOMAS, of Prince George's County, aet. 43, dep. Jan 21, 1760. {PGLR RR:39}

DYSON, GEORGE, of Charles County, aet. 52, dep. Oct 10, 1767 and Oct 10, 1768, mentioned his father Thomas Dyson. {CHLR Q#3:312, 408}

DYSON, JOHN, of Charles County, aet. 61, dep. Jul 20, 1743. {CHLR O#2:621} Aet. 63, dep. Sep 30, 1745, mentioned his father Thomas Dyson, deceased. {CHLR Z#2:466} John Dyson, Sr., aet. 71, dep. Dec 29, 1753. {CHLR D#3:235}

DYSON, THOMAS, of Charles County, aet. 50, dep. Apr 7, 1729. {CHLR Q#2:274} Aet. 66, dep. Sep 30, 1745, mentioned his father Thomas Dyson, deceased. {CHLR Z#2:466} See "George Dyson" and "John Dyson," q.v.

EAGLE, MARY, of Anne Arundel County, n.a., dep. 1680, stated that she knew the brothers John, Hugh, and Joshua Merekin quite well; John lived on *New Scotland* and after his death the two surviving brothers, Hugh and Joshua, lived together for 4 or 5 years and then married and parted; they lived on opposite sides of the creek from one another until Hugh went to England; after Hugh died, Joshua Merekin, uncle of the present Joshua Merekin, took possession and remained there until his death; and, John Merekin, son of the said Joshua, now lives there. {AALR IT#5:46-47} See "David Rablin," q.v.

EAGLE, ROBERT, of Anne Arundel County, aet. 71, dep. 1680, stated that about 40 years ago he heard that John Merekin, uncle to the present Joshua Merekin, lived on *New Scotland* and said tract was owned by his father Hugh Merekin. {AALR IT#5:45}

EARICKSON, ELIZABETH, of Queen Anne's County, aet. over 50, dep. Mar, 1770. {QAEJ - Henry Carter folder}

EARL, BETTY, see "Mary Moore," q.v.

EARL, JAMES, see "James Earle," q.v.

EARL, MARY, see "Elizabeth Woodward" and "Mary Moore" and "Mary Mitchel," q.v.

EARL, THOMAS, see "Mary Mitchel," q.v.

EARLE, JAMES, of Queen Anne's County, aet. about 50, dep. Apr 29, 1728, stated that about 38 years ago he lived on the land where Capt. James Earl now lives. {QAEJ - Christopher Wilkinson folder}

EARLE, MICHAEL, see "John Salter," q.v.

EARLY, JOHN, see "Daniel Foxwell" and "Zebulon Pritchett," q.v.

EARLY, WILLIAM, of Prince George's County, aet. 26, dep. Mar 1, 1756. {PGLR NN:468} Aet. 45, dep. Nov 7, 1767. {PGLR BB#2:162}

EATON, HENRY HOW, of Charles County, aet. 54, dep. Nov 5, 1770. {CHLR T#3:144}

EATON, JOHN, of Charles County, aet. 63, dep. Dec 24, 1731. {CHLR R#2:408} See "William Eaton," q.v.

EBURNATHY, ANN, see "Francis Ware," q.v.

EATON, WILLIAM, of Charles County, aet. 44, dep. May 1, 1769, mentioned his father John Eaton, deceased. {CHLR Q#3:498}

ECCLESTON, HUGH, see "Charles Thompson," q.v.

ECCLESTON, JOHN, of Dorchester County, aet. 51, dep. Jul 12, 1748. {DOLR 14 Old 312}

ECCLESTON, WILLIAM, of Dorchester County, aet. about 36, dep. between Nov 12, 1771 and Apr 17, 1772, mentioned Solomon Wright about 2 years ago, now deceased. {DOLR 26 Old 50}

EDDEY, WILLIAM, of St. Mary's County, n.a., dep. Jan 22, 1652, mentioned the exchange of two servants (not named) between George Mee and John Cornelius about 6 months ago. {ARMD 10:224-225}

EDELEN (EDELIN), CHRISTOPHER, SR., of Prince George's County, aet. 66, dep. Apr 8, 1749, mentioned his brother Edward Edelin. {PGLR PP:16} Christopher Edelen, aet. 76, dep. Jan 21, 1760. {PGLR RR:39} Christopher Edlen, aet. 78, dep. Sep 21, 1761, stated that he has known this area for about 50 to 60 years. {PGLR RR:227} See "Richard Edelen" and "James Rudd" and "Thomas Middleton," q.v.

EDELEN (EDELIN), EDWARD, of Prince George's County, aet. 67, dep. Mar 25, 1743. {PGLR Y:657}

EDELEN, EDWARD, of Charles County, aet. 55, dep. Aug 4, 1772, mentioned his father Edward Edelen. {CHLR U#3:166}

EDELEN, EDWARD, see "Christopher Edelen" and "Richard Edelen" and "Thomas Middleton," q.v.
EDELEN (EDELIN), JAMES, of Prince George's County, aet. 50, dep. Sep 12, 1761. {PGLR RR:180} See "John Baynes," q.v.
EDELEN, RICHARD, of Charles County, aet. 31, dep. Mar 10, 1670/1, mentioned he was a Deputy Surveyor. {CHLR E#1:42}
EDELEN, RICHARD, of Charles County, aet. 56, dep. Sep 29, 1726. {CHLR P#2:34} Aet. 57, dep. Jul 16, 1728. {CHLR Q#2:167} Aet. 58, dep. Feb 14, 1728/9. {CHLR Q#2:347} Aet. 63, dep. Aug 13, 1734, stated that John Bowling came to Maryland from Lancashire, England, and Thomas Bowling was the eldest son of said John Bowling and Mary his wife. {CHLR R#2:528} Aet. 70, dep. Oct 3, 1741. {CHLR O#2:289} Aet. 74, dep. May 23, 1745. {CHLR Z#2:342} Aet. 82, dep. Oct 6, 1752. {CHLR B#3:356} Aet. 82, dep. Aug 20, 1753. {CHLR D#3:152} Aet. 87, dep. Jul 24, 1758, stated that his father (not named) was County Surveyor about 70 years ago. {CHLR H#3:570}
EDELEN, RICHARD, of Prince George's County, aet. 60 or thereabouts, dep. Apr 10, 1775, stated that John Pritchet showed him the bounds of *Rozier's Gift* about 30 years ago. {PGLR CC#2:186} Aet. 61, dep. Oct 15, 1776, mentioned his father Christopher Edelen and uncle Edward Edelen. {PGLR CC#2:310}
EDELEN, RICHARD, of Prince George's County, aet. 70 or thereabouts, dep. Apr 10, 1775, stated that John Pritchet showed him the bounds of *Rozier's Gift* about 30 years ago. {PGLR CC#2:186}
EDELEN (EDELIN), THOMAS, of Prince George's County, aet. 56, dep. Nov 28, 1728. {PGLR M:346} Aet. about 57, dep. between Jun 11, 1729 and Nov 26, 1729. {PGLR M:522} Thomas Edelin, Sr., aet. 57, dep. between Nov 11, 1729 and Mar 26, 1730, mentioned old Thomas Frederick about 25 years ago. {PGLR M:558, 561}
EDELEN, WILLIAM, of Prince George's County, aet. 50, dep. Jun 5, 1769. {PGLR BB#2:437}
EDGAR, JOHN, see "John Clemens," q.v.
EDGAR, WILLIAM, of Dorchester County, aet. about 30, dep. between Mar 13, 1770 and Oct 20, 1770. {DOLR 26 Old 396}
EDGELL, BENJAMIN, of Dorchester County, aet. 31, dep. between Aug 10, 1773 and Feb 25, 1774, mentioned he was with his father John Edgell about 15 or 18 months ago on Hunting Creek. {DOLR 27 Old 267} See "James Edgell" and "James Dawson," q.v.
EDGELL, JAMES, of Dorchester County, aet. about 55, dep. between Nov 14, 1769 and Nov 6, 1770, mentioned his father Benjamin Edgell (Edgill) who lived about 46 years ago where Walter Stevens now lives; also mentioned William Perry and Andrew Gray about 20 years ago, both now deceased. {DOLR 24 Old 308} See "Sarah Kennerly," q.v.
EDGELL, JOHN, of Dorchester County, aet. 54, dep. Nov 12, 1771. {DOLR 26 Old 23} See "Benjamin Edgell," q.v.

EDGER, SUSANNAH, of Dorchester County, aet. about 60, daughter Richard Kendall, dep. between Nov 19, 1731 and Feb 23, 1731/2. {DOLR 8 Old 453} Aet. about 70, dep. between Nov 28, 1734 and Jul 31, 1735, mentioned her father, Richard Kindal, about 40 years ago. {DOLR 9 Old 312}

EDLER, JOSEPH, of Calvert or St. Mary's County, n.a., dep. Apr 23, 1691. {ARMD 8:247}

EDLOW, JOSEPH, of Mattapanient, St. Mary's County, planter, n.a., dep. Jan 31, 1637, stated that John Bryant was accidentally killed by the falling of a tree. {ARMD 4:10} Joseph Edlo, n.a., dep. 1647, mentioned Blanch Oliver, late wife of Roger Oliver, and Leonard Calvert, Esq., deceased. {ARMD 4:334}

EDMONDS, JOSEPH, see "Patrick Humes," q.v.

EDMONDSON (EDMONSTON), ARCHIBALD (captain), of Prince George's County, aet. 60, dep. Mar 19, 1728/9 and Jun 16, 1730 (no age given). {PGLR M:479; PGLR Q:15} Aet. 60 odd years, dep. May 31, 1731. {PGLR Q:608} Aet. 60 and upwards, dep. Sep 29, 1731. {PGLR Q:396} Aet. 60 odd years, dep. Nov 29, 1734, mentioned Col. Ninian Beall, deceased. {PGLR T:202} See "Edward Wilson" and "Archibald Edmonston," q.v.

EDMONDSON (EDMONSTON), JAMES (captain), of Prince George's County, aet. 34, dep. Nov 29, 1734, mentioned his father (not named) and the widow Wells about 23 years ago. {PGLR T:202} Capt. James Edmondston, aet. 50, dep. Dec 5, 1748. {PGLR BB:700} Capt. James Edmonston, aet. 53, dep. Mar 23, 1752. {PGLR NN:91} See "George Beall" and "Samuel Beall" and "John Moore," q.v.

EDMONDSON, JOHN, of Dorchester County, aet. 45, dep. Aug 22, 1744. {DOLR 12 Old 113} John Edmondson, Quaker, aet. about 56, dep. between Nov 11, 1755 and May 20, 1756, stated that he built a house for John Willis about 28 or 29 years ago. {DOLR 16 Old 76} See "Mary Perry" and "Peter Edmondson" and "Isaac Nicolls," q.v.

EDMONDSON, PETER, of Dorchester County, aet. about 45, dep. between Jun 13, 1749 and Jan 8, 1749/50. {DOLR 14 Old 394} Aet. about 54, dep. between Aug 9, 1757 and Aug 9, 1758. {DOLR 16 Old 80} Aet. about 58, dep. between Aug 14, 1759 and Mar 11, 1761. {DOLR 17 Old 376} Aet. about 59, dep. between Jun 10, 1760 and Jul 16, 1762, stated that he was shown the bounded tree of *Fox Hill* and *The Gore* about 40 years ago by Samuel Dickinson and William Edmondson, both late of Talbot County, deceased. {DOLR 19 Old 65} Aet. about 65, dep. between Nov 10, 1767 and Aug 10, 1768, mentioned Edward Hardekin (now deceased) about 20 years ago. {DOLR 23 Old 1} Aet. about 70, dep. between Nov 13, 1770 and Aug 2, 1771, mentioned his brother John Edmondson. {DOLR 25 Old 26}

EDMONDSON, PETER SHARPE, of Dorchester County, aet. about 63, dep. between Mar 13, 1764 and Oct 21, 1765, stated that he was shown the bounds of *Willonborough* about 40 years ago by William Perry and Mary Perry, both now deceased; also mentioned Thomas Skillington, late of Talbot County, deceased. {DOLR 20 Old 429}

EDMONDSON, POLLARD, of Dorchester County, aet. 57, dep. Nov 25, 1774, mentioned Major Tobias Pollard, Pason Lake, and John Pollard, Sr. about 35 or 36 years ago. {DOLR 28 Old 172}

EDMONDSON, SAMUEL, of Dorchester County, aet. 23, dep. May 25, 1762, stated that Alexander Frazier, gentleman, and Sarah Perry were married according to the Liturgy of the Church of England "by Rd. Reynolds Clerk Curate of Dorchester Parish in the Province of Maryland" on May 24, 1762. {DOLR 19 Old 196}

EDMONDSON, THOMAS, see "Mary Perry," q.v.

EDMONDSON, WILLIAM, of Dorchester County, aet. about 50, dep. between Mar 12, 1744 and Aug 5, 1745, stated that Peter Sharp, of Talbot County, was his guardian in 1712. {DOLR 12 Old 215} See "Isaac Nicolls" and "Peter Edmondson" and "John Sulivane" and "John Sherwood" and "Robert Sherwin," q.v.

EDMONSTON, ARCHIBALD, of Prince George's County, aet. 51, dep. Aug 16, 1758. {PGLR PP:230, pt. 2}

EDMONSTON, ALEXANDER, see "George Wells," q.v.

EDMONSTON, BALD., see "Gara Davis," q.v.

EDMONSTON, JAMES, of Prince George's County, aet. 28, dep. Dec 5, 1763. {PGLR TT:189} See "George Wells," q.v.

EDWARDS, ELEANOR, of Charles County, aet. 25, dep. Dec 27, 1731. {CHLR R#2:408}

EDWARDS, MRS., see "Daniel Cunningham," q.v.

EDWINE, MARY, of St. Mary's County, n.a., wife of William Edwine, dep. Jan 20, 1652. {ARMD 10:224}

EDWINE, WILLIAM, see "Mary Edwine," q.v.

EGERTON, JAMES, of St. Mary's County, n.a., dep. Apr 24, 1749. {ARMD 28:509}

EILBECK, WILLIAM, of Charles County, aet. 57, dep. Sep 17, 1753. {CHLR D#3:309}

ELBERT, FRANCES, of Talbot County, n.a., wife of William Elbert, dep. Mar 31, 1725, mentioned her serving man David Pritchard and her husband's servant William Pepper whose ear was bitten off by a horse. {TALR 13:176}

ELBERT, WILLIAM, of Queen Anne's County, n.a., dep. Sep 18, 1730. {QALR IK#C:19} See "Frances Elbert," q.v.

ELBOROUGH, JOHN, of Prince George's County, aet. 29, dep. between Nov 11, 1729 and Mar 26, 1730. {PGLR M:567}

ELBRIDGE, GEORGE, of Westmoreland County, Virginia, gentleman, n.a., dep. Apr 30, 1698 (recorded in Queen Anne's County records on Jan 28, 1717), stated under oath before Samuel Young, a Justice of the Peace of the Province of Maryland, that he was present on Apr 4, 1698 at the making of the will of Joseph Churnell, planter, of Yocomocoe Neck in Westmoreland County; further stated that Churnell died soon thereafter and William Pickrell was the eldest son of Henry Pickrell, an heir at law named in the aforesaid will. {QALR IK#A:163}

ELDESLEY, HENRY, see "Joan Ridgeway," q.v.
ELGIN, JOHN, of Charles County, aet. 52, dep. Aug 4, 1761. {CHLR K#3:300} Aet. 61, dep. Jun 5, 1770. {CHLR T#3:606} Aet. 64, dep. Aug 30, 1773. {CHLR W#3:91}
ELLIOT, CHARLES, of Dorchester County, aet. 45, dep. between Jun 8, 1758 and Dec 15, 1759, mentioned his father (not named) some time ago showed him the bounded tree of Capt. Henry Trippe's land. {DOLR 16 Old 212}
ELLIOT, EDWARD, of Dorchester County, aet. about 38, dep. between Nov 28, 1734 and Jul 31, 1735. {DOLR 9 Old 312}
ELLIOT, JOHN, of Dorchester County, shipwright, n.a., dep. between Aug 12, 1755 and Aug 10, 1757, mentioned his father Edward Elliot and Roger Hurley, father of the present old Roger Hurley. {DOLR 15 Old 512}
ELLIOTT, EDWARD, of Talbot County, n.a., dep. Aug 3, 1736, stated that the Parish Church of St. Michael's was built by his father (not named) and Darby Coghan (no date given); several years later a dispute arose between his father and James Hatton over whose 2 acres the church was built on. {TALR 14:173}
ELLIOTT, EDWARD, see "Mary Walter" and "Susanna Ashcroft" and "John Elliot" and "Edward Elliot," q.v.
ELLIOTT, JAMES, of Baltimore County, aet. 57, dep. May 10, 1771. {BALR AL#C:604}
ELLIOTT, JANE, see "Arthur Smith," q.v.
ELLIOTT, JOHN, of Dorchester County, aet. about 42, dep. between Mar 18, 1726 and Jul 18, 1727. {DOLR 8 Old 201}
ELLIOTT, JOHN, of Queen Anne's County, aet. about 36, dep. Mar, 1770; aet. about 38, dep. July, 1770. {QAEJ - Henry Carter folder}
ELLIOTT, JOHN, see "Andrew Robinson" and "Michael Todd" and "John Elliot" and "James Hutchings," q.v.
ELLIOTT, THOMAS, of Queen Anne's County, aet. about 31, dep. Mar, 1770. {QAEJ - Henry Carter folder}
ELLIS, ----, see "Francis Barnes," q.v.
ELLIS, ELIZABETH, of Dorchester County, aet. 56, dep. between Aug 14, 1744 and Sep 22, 1744, stated that her master was James Moasley and a bounder of *Whiteley's Choice* was still standing the second time she came to see her master after the death of his first wife (not named). {DOLR 12 Old 92}
ELLIS, ELIZABETH, of Dorchester County, aet. 64, dep. between Nov 8, 1743 and Jan 9, 1743/4, stated that about 18 or 19 years ago she was a tenant to Mary Warner (Worner), formerly called Mary Bruffett. {DOLR 12 Old 143}
ELLIS, JONATHAN, of Prince George's County, aet. 46, dep. Aug 29, 1763. {PGLR TT:127}
ELLIS, OWEN, of Charles County, aet. 51, dep. Sep 13, 1729. {CHLR Q#2:345}
ELLIS, OWEN, of Prince George's County, aet. 54, dep. Jun 26, 1734. {PGLR T:125} Aet. 55, dep. Jul 16, 1734, mentioned Gabriel Burnham and John Brown, shipwright, about 35 years ago. {PGLR T:155}

ELLIS, SAMUEL, of Frederick County, aet. 51, dep. Apr 1, 1768, mentioned John Hughson about 20 or 21 years ago. {FRLR L:519}
ELTING, CORNELIUS, see "William Hickman," q.v.
ELTONHEAD, WILLIAM, of St. Mary's County, gentleman, n.a., dep. Jun 25, 1650. {ARMD 10:25}
ELWES, THOMAS, of St. Mary's County, n.a., dep. Apr 7, 1665. {ARMD 49:479}
EMERSON, JOHN, of Charles County, aet. 51, dep. May 25, 1752. {CHLR B#3:123}
EMERSON, JOHN, of Prince George's County, n.a., dep. Aug 5, 1760, mentioned Peter Dent about 27 or 28 years ago, now deceased. {PGLR RR:74}
EMORY, ARTHUR, of Queen Anne's County, aet. 32, dep. Apr, 1765, mentioned his father (not named) in 1760. {QAEJ - William Austin folder} Aet. 33, dep. Sep, 1766. {QAEJ - John and Sophia Downes folder} Aet. 36, dep. Oct 5, 1768, mentioned his brothers James and Charles Emory. {QAEJ - Gideon Emory folder} See "Sarah Emory" and "James Walters," q.v.
EMORY, CHARLES, see "Arthur Emory," q.v.
EMORY, JAMES, see "Arthur Emory," q.v.
EMORY, JOHN, of Queen Anne's County, aet. 42, dep. Apr, 1730. {QAEJ - Ernault Hawkins folder} Aet. 77, dep. Mar, 1762. {QAEJ - Henry Callister folder} See "Sarah Emory" and "William Emory" and "Mary Moore," q.v.
EMORY, SARAH, of Queen Anne's County, aet. about 64, dep. Oct 5, 1768, mentioned her husband William Emory (deceased), her son John Emory, and her husband's brother John Emory (surveyor). {QAEJ - Gideon Emory folder} Aet. 69, dep. Mar 31, 1772, stated that she was not yet 10 years old when her father, John King, died; her mother lived a widow for about 5 years and died in the house where her father died (the house where John Downes now lives); a year after her mother died she (deponent) and her sister Sophia Downes (wife of John Downes, plaintiff) were boarded at Major William Turbitt's under the care of Arthur Emory, the brother of her father *[sic]*; John Beck married her sister; also mentioned Richard Walters, eldest son of Robert Walters; after Richard died his brother John Walters inherited the land; also mentioned John King's eldest brother Robert King; John (or Robert) King was proved heir at law of his grandfather Robert Smith. {QAEJ - John and Sophia Downes folder}
EMORY, WILLIAM, of Queen Anne's County, aet. 31, dep. Oct 5, 1768, mentioned his brother John Emory and his uncle John Emory. {QAEJ - Gideon Emory folder} See "Sarah Emory" and "Sophia Lloyd" and "Edward Tilghman," q.v.
EMPSON, ELINOR, see "Thomas Hussey" and "Anne Ges," q.v.
EMPSON, WILLIAM, of Charles County, aet. 28, dep. Nov 23, 1658. {CHLR A:31} See "Daniell Johnson" and "John Piper" and "John Wood" and "George Newman," q.v.
ENGLISH, GEORGE, of Charles County, n.a., dep. Jun 13, 1665. {ARMD 53:586}

ENNALLS, BARTHO., of Dorchester County, aet. about 50, dep. Mar 8, 1747. {DOLR 14 Old 310} Aet. about 63, dep. between Nov 10, 1761 and Nov 19, 1762, stated that he was shown the bounded tree of *Smart's Folly* about 30 years ago by Capt. Richard Smart. {DOLR 19 Old 34}

ENNALLS, BARTHOL, of Dorchester County, n.a., dep. May 22, 1681, mentioned John Kirk. {ARMD 15:359-360}

ENNALLS, HENRY, see "William McCollister" and "William Murray" and "Henry Travers" and "William Wilson," q.v.

ENNALLS, HENRY (major), of Dorchester County, aet. 54, dep. between Aug 16, 1728 and Nov 3, 1728. {DOLR 8 Old 247}

ENNALLS, HENRY, of Dorchester County, aet. 55, dep. Nov 14, 1729 and Nov 14, 1730, mentioned the deposition of Mathias Alford regarding the bounds of *Skillington's Right* and *Richardson's Folly* about 8 years ago. {DOLR 8 Old 384}

ENNALLS, HENRY, of Dorchester County, aet. 47, dep. between Aug 8, 1749 and Nov 10, 1749. {DOLR 14 Old 392} Aet. 49, dep. between Nov 12, 1751 and May 13, 1752. {DOLR 14 Old 604} Aet. about 59, dep. between Jun 10, 1761 and Sep 8, 1761, stated that he was a vestryman of Great Choptank Parish about 14 or 15 years ago when the vestry and Thomas Airey (rector) employed John Stewart to pail in the church yard anew. {DOLR 18 Old 14} Aet. about 59, dep. between Jun 9, 1761 and Mar 9, 1762, stated that he was shown the bounded tree of *Ennalls' Outrange* about 20 years ago by John Stewart, now deceased. {DOLR 18 Old 75} Aet. about 59, dep. between Jun 10, 1760 and Jul 16, 1762, formerly surveyor of Dorchester County. {DOLR 19 Old 65} Aet. about 61, dep. between Nov 8, 1763 and Apr 7, 1764. {DOLR 19 Old 233}

ENNALLS, HENRY, JR., of Dorchester County, aet. about 31, dep. between Mar 13, 1732 and Nov 14, 1733. {DOLR 9 Old 135}

ENNALLS, HENRY, JR., of Dorchester County, aet. about 34, dep. between Nov 9, 1756 and Nov 7, 1760. {DOLR 17 Old 213}

ENNALLS, JOHN, see "Capt. John Hodson," q.v.

ENNALLS, JOSEPH, see "William Murray," q.v.

ENNALLS, JOSEPH, JR., of Dorchester County, residing at Transquaking, aet. about 22, dep. between Mar 13, 1764 and Jun 4, 1767. {DOLR 21 Old 382}

ENNALLS, THOMAS, of Dorchester County, aet. about 34, dep. between Nov 16, 1734 and Apr 10, 1735, mentioned his father (not named). {DOLR 9 Old 436} See "Mary Pitts" and "William Murray" and "Capt. John Hodson," q.v.

ENNALLS, WILLIAM, see "David Poole" and "Philemon Lecompte," q.v.

ENSEY, JOHN, of Charles County, aet. 48, dep. Aug 6, 1762. {CHLR M#3:5} Aet. 49, dep. Aug 18, 1763, mentioned his brother William Ensey and his father John Ensey. {CHLR M#3:507} Aet. 51, dep. Jul 31, 1765. {CHLR N#3:721} See "Barbry McPherson," q.v.

ENSEY, WILLIAM, see "John Ensey," q.v.

ENSLEY, ANDREW, see "Phillip Wingate," q.v.

ENSLEY, JAMES, see "Ruth Robinson" and "Phillip Wingate" and "James Insley," q.v.

ENSLEY, WILLIAM, see "Ruth Robinson" and "Phillip Wingate," q.v.

ENSOR, JOHN, SR., of Baltimore County, aet. 70, dep. Jul 2, 1764, mentioned his father John Ensor. {BALR B#N:308} Aet. 73, dep. May 11, 1768. {BALR AL#B:595} John Ensor, aet. 79, dep. Jun 10, 1772. {BALR AL#E:285}

ENSOR, THOMAS, of Baltimore County, aet. 50, dep. May 8, 1770. {BALR AL#B:290}

ERICKSON, GUNDER, see "Capt. John Smith," q.v.

ESHLEMAN, BENEDICT, of Pennsylvania, aet. 54, a native of Germany, dep. Aug 17, 1767 in Frederick County, Maryland, stating he was of the Society of the Mennonites and lived about 9 miles from Lancaster. {FRLR L:58}

ESTEP, JOHN, of Charles County, aet. 43, dep. May 22, 1744. {CHLR Y#2:19}

ETHRINGTON, JOHN, see "William Depriest," q.v.

EVANS, ----, see "David Rogers" and "John Rumbly, Sr.," q.v.

EVANS, ANTHONY, of St. Mary's County, n.a., dep. Mar 8, 1678, mentioned Thomas Smith and Christopher Rousby. {ARMD 15:229-230} See "John Burdett," q.v.

EVANS, DAVID, of Prince George's County, aet. 63, dep. Oct 10, 1762, mentioned Mareen Duvall, son of Marsh Duvall, about 14 years ago. {PGLR RR:264}

EVANS, EDWARD, see "John Long, Jr.," q.v.

EVANS, EMANUELL, see "Edward Billiter," q.v.

EVANS, FRANCIS, of Charles County, aet. 43, dep. Jun 5, 1770. {CHLR T#3:604}

EVANS, JOB, of Baltimore County, aet. 66, dep. May 15, 1772. {BALR AL#I:201}

EVANS, JOHN, of Charles County, aet. 69, dep. May 26, 1770. {CHLR T#3:606}

EVANS, JOHN, of Charles County, aet. 37, dep. May 27, 1772. {CHLR U#3:21}

EVANS, JOHN, of Prince George's County, aet. 53, dep. 1731, mentioned the widow Wells. {PGLR Q:237}

EVANS, JOHN, of Prince George's County, aet. 47, dep. Nov 17, 1748, mentioned his father (not named) about 25 years ago. {PGLR BB:694-695} John Evens, aet. 52, dep. Mar 23, 1752. {PGLR NN:91} John Evans, aet. 53, dep. Sep 10, 1754, mentioned his father (not named). {PGLR NN:309}

EVANS, JOHN, JR., of Charles County, aet. 35, dep. May 26, 1770. {CHLR T#3:604}

EVANS, JOSEPH, of Prince George's County, aet. 39, dep. Aug 22, 1753 (1757?). {PGLR PP:66, pt. 2}

EVANS, PENELOPE, of Talbot or Dorchester County, n.a., dep. Dec 17, 1670. {ARMD 51:348}

EVANS, PHILIP, of Prince George's County, aet. 59, dep. May 22, 1754, mentioned his father Walter Evans about 27 years ago and Thomas Evans about 20 years ago. {PGLR NN:258} Aet. 64, dep. Feb 15, 1759. {PGLR PP:281, pt. 2} Aet. 65, dep. Jul 19, 1760, mentioned his brother Thomas Evans and a dispute about

40 years ago between "Old Cole" and his father Walter Evans, now deceased. {PGLR RR:121} Aet. 57, dep. Jan 22, 1761, mentioned his father Walter Evans. {PGLR RR:202} Aet. 60, dep. Sep 1, 1762, mentioned his father Walter Evans. {PGLR RR:230}

EVANS, PHILIP, JR., of Prince George's County, aet. 38, dep. Nov 9, 1761. {PGLR RR:178}

EVANS, SAMUEL, of Prince George's County, aet. near 66, dep. Aug 22, 1760, mentioned Benjamin Berry, surveyor, about 46 years ago. {PGLR RR:105} Aet. near 69, dep. Jul 17, 1763 and Nov 5, 1763, mentioned Charles Cheney, son of Charles Cheney (deceased), about 30 years ago. {PGLR TT:571, 606}

EVANS, SARAH, of Dorchester County, aet. 65, dep. between Jun 16, 1727 and Mar 17, 1727/8. {DOLR 8 Old 200}

EVANS, STEPHEN, of Charles County, aet. 52, dep. May 16, 1729. {CHLR Q#2:277}

EVANS, THOMAS, of Prince George's County, aet. 52, dep. Nov 7, 1726. {PGLR M:152} Aet. 44, planter, dep. May 1, 1729, mentioned his father (not named) about 34 years ago. {PGLR M:443} See "Philip Evans" and "Walter Evans" and "Col. George Beall" and "Thomas Hamilton," q.v.

EVANS, WALTER, of Prince George's County, aet. 78, dep. May 20, 1725. {PGLR I:675} Aet. 79, dep. Nov 7, 1726. {PGLR M:154} Aet. 81, planter, dep. Oct 9, 1728, mentioned Col. Thomas Brookes, Col. Henry Darnall, and Col. Ninian Beale (Beall). {PGLR M:401} Aet. 81, dep. May 1, 1729, mentioned George Burgis (Burgess) about 34 years ago. {PGLR M:443} Aet. about 80, dep. between Jul 15, 1729 and Jun 23, 1730. {PGLR M:487, PGLR Q:2}

EVANS, WALTER, of Prince George's County, aet. 44, dep. Dec 10, 1764, mentioned Thomas Evans, son of Walter Evans. {PGLR TT:366} Aet. not given, dep. Sep 20, 1771. {PGLR AA#2:431}

EVANS, WALTER, see "Philip Evans" and "Col. George Beall," q.v.

EVANS, WILLIAM (captain), of St. Mary's County, n.a., dep. 1659. {ARMD 41:347}

EVERARD, LAWRENCE, of Queen Anne's County, aet. about 40, dep. Feb, 1737. {QAEJ - Alexander Toulson folder}

EVERET, JOHN, of Kent County, aet. about 19, dep. Oct 20, 1743, mentioned Aquilla Beck. {KELR JS#25:194}

EVERITT, LAWRENCE, of Queen Anne's County, aet. about 65, dep. Mar, 1759. {QAEJ - Henry Carter folder}

EVERLY (EVERALLY), JOHN, of Frederick County, aet. 53, dep. 1767. {FRLR L:60}

EVERLY, MICHAEL, of Frederick County, aet. 54, dep. 1767. {FRLR L:60}

EVERSFIELD, ELEANOR (Mrs.), see "Rev. John Eversfield" and "Thomas Hodgkin," q.v.

EVERSFIELD, JOHN (reverend), of Prince George's County, aet. 68, dep. several times on May 22, 1770, mentioned Mrs. Eleanor Eversfield. {PGLR AA#2:138-143}

EVERSFIELD, MATTHEW, of Prince George's County, aet. upwards of 27 years, dep. May 22, 1770. {PGLR AA#2:137-138}

EVERSFIELD, WILLIAM, of Prince George's County, aet. 40, dep. Jun 1, 1762, mentioned Philip Jackson and John Jackson, deceased, some years ago. {PGLR RR:228}

EVINS, ROBERT, of Frederick County, aet. 73, dep. 1767. {FRLR L:60}

EVITTS, NATHANIELL, of Talbot County, n.a., dep. Jan 18, 1669/70. {ARMD 54:456}

EXON, HENRY, of St. Mary's County, innholder, aet. 49, dep. Dec 2, 1684. {ARMD 17:322} See "John Burdett," q.v.

FAGG, JOHN, of Charles County, aet. 58, dep. Jun 5, 1770. {CHLR T#3:604}

FANNING, BENONI, see "Hannah Phillips," q.v.

FARDEN, WILLIAM MANIE, see "George Beall," q.v.

FARDINANDO, PETER, of Charles County, aet. 71, dep. Sep 29, 1726. {CHLR P#2:39}

FARMER, GEORGE, of Prince George's County, aet. 30, dep. Feb 26, 1725/6, stated that John Tanyhill (Tannyhill) of Nuce River in North Carolina, formerly of Calvert County, Maryland, is dead and he believes said Tanyhill had been on board the vessel he sailed in to inquire after his wife and child (not named) whom he left here, but in a letter from James Sowell, of Calvert County, he understood his wife was dead and he (Tanyhill) desired that his son (not named) be brought to Carolina; however, Tanyhill took ill and died before this could be accomplished. {PGLR I:730} See "Henry Bayly," q.v.

FARNANDIS, PETER, of Charles County, aet. 35, dep. Nov 17, 1775. {CHLR X#3:546} Peter Fernandis, aet. 43, dep. Oct 22, 1743. {CHLR Z#2:191} Aet. 46, dep. Feb 27, 1748/9. {CHLR Z#2:526} Peter Fernandes, aet. 58, dep. Jun 8, 1759. {CHLR I#3:262} Aet. 57, dep. May 10, 1761. {CHLR K#3:226}

FARQUHAR (FARQUAR), ALLAN, of Frederick County, n.a., Quaker, dep. Dec 5, 1764. {FRLR K:431}

FARQUHAR (FARQUAR), WILLIAM, of Frederick County, n.a., Quaker, dep. Dec 5, 1764, mentioned Dr. Samuel Stringer and Alexander Warfield about 25 or 26 years ago. {FRLR K:430}

FARRELL, JAMES, of Prince George's County, aet. 45, dep. Feb 2, 1761, mentioned his brother Charles Farrell. {PGLR RR:236}

FARRELL, CHARLES, see "James Farrell," q.v.

FARTHING, JOHN, of Charles County, aet. 60, dep. May 24, 1747. {CHLR Z#2:80}

FEARSON, ATTWICKS (ATTWIX), of Charles County, aet. 32, dep. Jul 24, 1742, mentioned his father Samuel Fearson. {CHLR O#2:425} Atwix Fearson, aet. 56, dep. Sep 6, 1760. {CHLR K#3:98} Attwix Pherson, aet. 66, dep. Oct 29, 1774. {CHLR W#3:685}

FEARSON, ELEANOR, of Charles County, aet. 51, dep. Sep 13, 1758, mentioned her mother Sarah Woodman and her aunt Elizabeth Williams. {CHLR K#3:97} Eleanor Pherson, aet. 63, dep. Oct 29, 1774, mentioned her grandfather George

Newman, her aunt Mary Newman and her (Newman's) son-in-law Samuel Pherson (Phearson). {CHLR W#3:603}

FEARSON, PEARSEY, of Charles County, aet. 50, dep. Sep 13, 1758. {CHLR K#3:98}

FEARSON, SAMUEL, see "Attwicks Fearson" and "Walter Fearson" and "Attwicks Fearson," q.v.

FEARSON, WALTER, of Charles County, aet. 24, dep. Jun 6, 1732, mentioned his father Samuel Fearson. {CHLR R#2:158} Aet. 36, dep. Sep 21, 1742. {CHLR O#2:462} Aet. 37, dep. Sep 10, 1743, stated that he married Eleanor Newman, daughter of George Newman. {CHLR O#2:665}

FELKS, EDWARD, prob. of Anne Arundel County, n.a., dep. Oct 1, 1692. {ARMD 8:375}

FENDALL, CAPTAIN, see "Indian Sachennaws," q.v.

FENDALL, JOHN, of Charles County, aet. 31, dep. Jul 11, 1762. {CHLR M#3:223}

FENDALL, JOHN (captain), of Charles County, aet. 46, dep. Aug 12, 1719, mentioned Philemon Hemsley and wife Mary Hemsley. {Charles County Land Commissions 1:53} Aet. 56, dep. May 5, 1730. {CHLR Q#2:403}

FENDALL, JOHN, see "Edward Stephens" and "Thomas Lomax," q.v.

FENERLY (FENNELY), PHILIP, of Prince George's County, aet. 76, dep. Sep 7, 1761. {PGLR RR:230-231} Philip Fennely, aet. 81, dep. Mar 5, 1763. {PGLR TT:13} See "Philip Tennally," q.v.

FENLEY, JOHN, of Prince George's County, aet. 34, dep. Sep 14, 1761. {PGLR RR:179}

FENWICK, CUTHBERT, of Charles County, n.a., dep. Sep 10, 1663, mentioned his mother (not named). {ARMD 49:61} See "Charles Rawlinson," q.v.

FENWICK, IGNATIUS, of Prince George's County, aet. 28, dep. Mar 10, 1769, stated that he came to live on *St. Anthony's* in 1763; also mentioned Edward Lanham, now deceased. {PGLR AA#2:151}

FENWICK, JANE (Mrs.), of Charles County, n.a., dep. 1658, mentioned her husband (not named). {ARMD 41:142}

FERGUSON, ALEXANDER, see "James Ferguson," q.v.

FERGUSON, GEORGE, see "John Lewis," q.v.

FERGUSON, JAMES, of Dorchester County, aet. 51, dep. between Mar 10, 1761 and Jun 6, 1761, mentioned his mother (not named) about 32 years ago, and his brother Alexander Ferguson. {DOLR 17 Old 318}

FERNALY, FRANCIS, of Charles County, aet. 30, dep. Sep 9, 1667. {CHLR C#1:239}

FERNANDIS, PETER, see "Peter Farnandis," q.v.

FERRALL, ROSAMOND, of Charles County, aet. 55, dep. May 13, 1745, mentioned her father Patrick McAtee, deceased. {CHLR Z#2:338}

FERRILL, DANIEL, of Kent County, aet. about 43, dep. Mar 3, 1725/6. {KELR JS#W:542} Aet. about 44, dep. Sep 15, 1726. {KELR JS#X:46} Aet. about 50, dep. Aug 14, 1732. {KELR JS#16:254}

FICHGARED, JOHN, see "Benjamin Blackleach" and "Mary Knoleman," q.v.
FIELD, EDWARD, of Charles County, aet. 59, dep. Apr 30, 1745. {CHLR Z#2:12}
FIELDS, EDWARD, of St. Mary's or Charles County, n.a., dep. Jun 29, 1698 in Annapolis. {ARMD 23:435}
FIELDS, BARTHOLOMEW, of Prince George's County, aet. 44, dep. Sep 4, 1758, mentioned Murphy Ward about 20 years ago, now deceased. {PGLR PP:279, pt. 2}
FIFE, JAMES, of Frederick County, aet. 63, dep. Sep 25, 1772. {FRLR P:432}
FINCH, FRANCIS, see "William True," q.v.
FINCH, PETER, of Frederick County, aet. 32, dep. 1767. {FRLR L:60}
FINCH, THOMAS, of Prince George's County, aet. 42, dep. May 1, 1755. {PGLR NN:369}
FINK, PHILIP, of Frederick County, n.a., dep. 1767. {FRLR L:60}
FINNEY, WILLIAM, of Talbot County, n.a., dep. Oct 1, 1692. {ARMD 8:372-373}
FISHER, EDWARD, see "Benjamin Palmes," q.v.
FISHER, FRANCES, see "Richard Willis" and "William Rawley," q.v.
FISHER, HENRY, of Dorchester County, aet. 61, dep. between Nov 24, 1732 and Jan 20, 1732/3, mentioned Robert Lake, former owner of *Boarn's Landing*. {DOLR 9 Old 97}
FISHER, JOSEPH, see "Thomas Savage," q.v.
FISHER, MARY, of Dorchester County, aet. about 48, dep. between Mar 15, 1731 and Apr 13, 1732, mentioned Edward Pritchett's land. {DOLR 9 Old 63} Aet. about 60, dep. between Jun 14, 1743 and Aug 1, 1743, mentioned her father John Pritchett. {DOLR 12 Old 167} Aet. about 62, dep. Aug 24, 1745, mentioned her father John Pritchett, deceased, who showed her the bounds of *North Hampton* about 49 years ago. {DOLR 12 Old 247}
FISHER, MARY, of the Parish of St. John's Wapping in the County of Middlesex, England, widow, n.a., dep. Feb 26, 1734, stated that she knew Mary Want very well to be the only surviving lawful and reputed sister to Richard Fullstone [late of Kent County, Maryland]. {KELR JS#22:295-302}
FITCH, WILLIAM, of Baltimore County, aet. 59 or thereabouts, dep. Sep 20, 1767, mentioned Thomas Sutton, father of Christopher Sutton. {BALR AL#A:122} See "James Robinson," q.v.
FITCHEW, THOMAS, of Dorchester County, aet. 53, dep. between Mar 12, 1771 and Apr 22, 1771. {DOLR 26 Old 42}
FITCHEW, WALTER, of Dorchester County, aet. 65, dep. between Aug 8, 1749 and Nov 10, 1749. {DOLR 14 Old 392}
FITZGERALD, JOHN, see "John Fichgared," q.v.
FITZHERBERT, MR., see "Richard Smith," q.v.
FLAHARTY, JOHN, of Dorchester County, aet. 30, dep. Aug 25, 1696. {DOLR 5 Old 75}
FLEETE, EDWARD, see "Simon Richardson," q.v.

FLEGOR, ARCHIBALD, of Frederick County, n.a., dep. Dec 2, 1765. {ARMD 32:156-157}
FLEHARTY, JOHN, of Dorchester County, aet. 90, dep. between Jun 13, 1728 and Jul 27, 1728, stated that the bounds of *Marshey Point* were formerly identified to him by Thomas Flowers and the bounds of *Indian Quarter* were described to him by Robert More about 30 years ago. {DOLR 8 Old 248, 379} John Freharty, aet. 91, dep. between Jun 14, 1729 and Jul 17, 1729, stated that he was shown the bounded tree of Billin's land by Thomas Flowers about 40 year ago. {DOLR 8 Old 432} See "Robert Sherwin" and "Joseph Alford," q.v.
FLEHARTY, STEPHEN, of Dorchester County, aet. about 75, dep. between Nov 11, 1760 and May 20, 1761. {DOLR 17 Old 324}
FLETCHALL, THOMAS, see "William Warford," q.v.
FLETCHER, CURTIS, of St. Mary's County, aet. 23, dep. Apr 29, 1664. {ARMD 49:210}
FLINN, BRYAN, of Charles County, aet. 81, dep. Jun 13, 1771. {CHLR T#3:241}
FLINN, DANIEL, of Kent County, aet. about 43, dep. Oct 30, 1750. {KELR JS#26:416}
FLINT, JOHN, of Prince George's County, aet. 38, dep. Jun 16, 1730. {PGLR Q:14} Aet. 40, dep. May 11, 1733. {PGLR T:27} Aet. 40, planter, dep. Jul 16, 1734. {PGLR T:154} Aet. 54, dep. Mar 24, 1745/6. {PGLR BB:10} Aet. 66, dep. Jun 21, 1756. {PGLR PP:15, pt. 2} Aet. 68, dep. Apr 25, 1758. {PGLR PP:233, pt. 2}
FLINT, JOHN, of Prince George's County, aet. 43, dep. Oct 12, 1770, mentioned his father John Flint about 15 years ago. {PGLR AA#2:206}
FLINT, JOHN, see "John Clagett" and "Henry Chapple" and "John Richard," q.v.
FLINT, JOSEPH, see "Evan Shelby," q.v.
FLINTHAM, WILLIAM, of Frederick County, aet. 65, dep. Feb 6, 1775. {FRLR BD#1:206}
FLOWERS, ELIZABETH, of Dorchester County, aet. 59, dep. between Mar 17, 1768 and Aug 9, 1768, mentioned James Brown, James Cannon, and William Clarkson, commissioners, about 33 years ago. {DOLR 22 Old 433}
FLOWERS, LAMEROCK, see "Edward Southwell," q.v.
FLOWERS, THOMAS, see "John Fleharty," q.v.
FOARD, JAMES, of Frederick County, aet. 47, dep. Apr 11, 1767, mentioned Nicholas Baker about 13 years ago. {FRLR K:1346}
FOARD, WILLIAM, of Charles County, aet. 39, dep. May 23, 1761. {CHLR K#3:224}
FOLK, WILLIAM, see "William Murray," q.v.
FOLLEN, FRANCES, of Dorchester County, aet. 61, dep. between Nov 20, 1738 and Dec 2, 1738, mentioned her husband Redman Follen about 30 years ago. {DOLR 12 Old 111}
FOLLEN, REDMAN, see "Frances Follen," q.v.
FOLLING, DANIEL, of Dorchester County, aet. 36, dep. between Nov 24, 1732 and Jan 20, 1732/3. {DOLR 9 Old 97}

FORD, CHARLES ALLISON, of Charles County, aet. 30, dep. Apr 30, 1744. {CHLR Y#2:10} Aet. 58, dep. Dec 6, 1770. {CHLR T#3:245}
FORD, EDWARD, of Charles County, aet. 49, dep. Mar 11, 1737. {CHLR T#2:423} Aet. 55, dep. May 7, 1744. {CHLR Y#2:16} Aet. 56, dep. Sep 24, 1744. {CHLR Y#2:187} Aet. 62, dep. Feb 19, 1750/1. {CHLR Z#2:144} Aet. 63, dep. Apr 28, 1753. {CHLR D#3:78} Aet. 66, dep. Feb 15, 1755. {CHLR E#3:216} Aet. 70, dep. Sep 13, 1758. {CHLR K#3:96} Aet. 73, dep. Jul 28, 1761. {CHLR K#3:307} Aet. 74, dep. Jul 11, 1762. {CHLR M#3:224} See "Richard Coombes," q.v.
FORD, JACOB, of Queen Anne's County, aet. about 42, dep. Oct 20, 1735. {QAEJ - John Coursey folder} Aet. about 62, dep. Aug 12, 1760. {QAEJ - John Gafford folder} Aet. about 70, dep. Apr, 1765. {QAEJ - William Austin folder} Aet. 77, dep. Feb, 1769, mentioned Thomas Mountsier about 50 years ago, grandfather of the present Thomas Mountsier. {QAEJ - John Moore folder}
FORD, LLOYD, see "William Carter," q.v.
FORD, MARY, see "William Carter," q.v.
FORD, NOTLEY, of Charles County, aet. 39, dep. Dec 6, 1770. {CHLR T#3:246}
FORD, ROBERT, of Kent County, aet. about 42, dep. Aug 7, 1764. {KELR DD#1:572}
FORD, THOMAS, of Charles County, aet. 51, dep. Jan 20, 1726/7. {CHLR P#2:491} Aet. 64, dep. Oct 5, 1732. {CHLR R#2:240}
FORD, THOMAS, of Prince George's County, aet. 48, dep. Apr 26, 1735. {PGLR T:253}
FORD, WILLIAM, of Charles County, aet. 38, dep. Aug 11, 1760. {CHLR K#3:4} Aet. 46, dep. Aug 5, 1768. {CHLR Q#3:258}
FOREMAN, ARTHUR, of Kent County, aet. about 53, dep. May 22, 1732, mentioned his father (not named), Major Comegys, and Cornelius Comegys (the major's son). {KELR JS#16:248} Aet. about 58, dep. Nov 13, 1738. {KELR JS#22:289} Aet. about 64, dep. June, 1743. {KELR JS#24:407} Aet. about 66, dep. Aug 19, 1746, mentioned Mr. Pollard and John Wright about 16 or 17 years ago. {KELR JS#25:429}
FOREMAN, DEBORAH, of Kent County, aet. about 36, dep. Aug 19, 1755. {KELR JS#28:166}
FOREMAN, DEBORAH (Mrs.), of Kent County, aet. 55 or 56, dep. Oct, 1753, stated that soon after Dr. Thomas Williams was married to Mrs. Mary Hopkins there was a dispute between him and William Powell, this deponent's husband. {KELR JS#26:46}
FOREMAN, ELIZABETH, see "Francis Barnes," q.v.
FOREMAN, MARGARETT, of Kent County, aet. about 60, dep. Jan 4, 1741, mentioned her husband Robert Foreman. {KELR JS#24:296}
FOREMAN, ROBERT, of Kent County, aet. about 56, dep. Jul 19, 1748. {KELR JS#26:142} Aet. about 64, dep. Mar 1, 1757. {KELR JS#28:323} See "Margarett Foreman" and "Richard Davis," q.v.

FOREST, WILLIAM, of Prince George's County, aet. 77, dep. Apr 8, 1769, mentioned Rignel Odel about 25 years ago, now deceased. {PGLR AA#2:201}
FORSTER, RICHARD, of St. Mary's County, aet. 40 or thereabouts, dep. Aug 10, 1661. {ARMD 41:484}
FOSTER, JOHN, see "Mary Pitts" and "William Murray," q.v.
FOSTER, MARY, see "Mary Pitts," q.v.
FOSTER, REBECCAH, of Dorchester County, aet. 45, dep. between Aug 10, 1773 and Feb 25, 1774, mentioned Richard Willis and his father John Willis about 22 or 23 years ago. {DOLR 27 Old 267}
FOSTER, RICHARD, see "James Willson," q.v.
FOUNTAIN, MARSY, see "David Melvell," q.v.
FOUNTAIN, SAMUEL, of Dorchester County, aet. about 37, dep. between Nov 10, 1741 and Feb 16, 1742. {DOLR 14 Old 54}
FOUNTAIN, WILLIAM, see "David Melvell," q.v.
FOWKE (FFOWKE), GEORGE, of Charles County, gentleman, aet. 21 or thereabouts, dep. Nov 11, 1679; however, the name of Roger Fowke, not George Fowke, appears at the end of the deposition. {ARMD 51:312}
FOWKE, GERARD, of Charles County, aet. 63, dep. Nov 12, 1725. {CHLR P#2:138} Aet. 64, dep. Jun 6, 1726. {CHLR P#2:388}
FOWLER, JEREMIAH, of Prince George's County, aet. 47, dep. Aug 11, 1758. {PGLR PP:295, pt. 2}
FOWLER, JOHN, of Prince George's County, aet. 50, dep. Mar 13, 1756, mentioned William Fowler and Dr. William Denune. {PGLR NN:473-438}
FOWLER (FOULER), JOHN, of Queen Anne's County, n.a., dep. Apr 2, 1715. {QALR IK#A:64} Aet. 56, dep. Apr, 1723. {QAEJ - William Bishop folder}
FOWLER, ROGER, see "Thomas Hackett," q.v.
FOWLER, WILLIAM, of Prince George's County, aet. 44, dep. Mar 24, 1742. {PGLR Y:654} See "John Fowler," q.v.
FOX, JAMES, of Charles County, n.a., dep. Mar 12, 1660/1. {CHLR A:126} Aet. not given, dep. Jul 9, 1662, mentioned John Nevil and wife (not named). {ARMD 53:233}
FOXON, JAMES, see "Richard Peirson," q.v.
FOXWELL, DANIEL, of Dorchester County, aet. about 41, dep. between Mar 15, 1731 and Apr 13, 1732, stated that the bounds of Edward Pritchett's land were shown to him by old Henry Lake and John Early. {DOLR 9 Old 63} Aet. about 46, dep. between Mar 16, 1733/4 and Jul 6, 1734, mentioned bounds of *Meredith's Chance* set about 11 years ago by Thomas Rotton, deceased, by order of John Robson (justice), deceased. {DOLR 90 Old 193} Aet. 56, dep. between Jun 14, 1743 and Aug 1, 1743, stated that he was shown the bounds of *Edenburrough* by John Early about 35 or 40 years ago. {DOLR 12 Old 167} Aet. 57, dep. Aug 24, 1745. {DOLR 12 Old 247} Aet. about 67, dep. between Mar 11, 1755 and Jul 23, 1755. {DOLR 15 Old 452} Aet. about 75, dep. between Nov 10, 1761 and Jan 21, 1762. {DOLR 18 Old 87} Aet. about 75, dep. between Nov 10, 1761 and Feb 20,

1762, mentioned his uncle Richard Pearson, his aunt Susanna Shorter, and her father Kendel. {DOLR 18 Old 90} {DOLR 19 Old 99} Aet. about 76, dep. between Aug 10, 1762 and Mar 8, 1763, mentioned Richard Person the Elder. {DOLR 18 Old 333} See "Richard Willis," q.v.

FOXWELL, ISAAC, of Dorchester County, aet. about 23, dep. between Aug 12, 1760 and Mar 2, 1761, mentioned old William Murphy, Richard Chapman, Thomas Chapman, and John Robson, uncle of Thomas Chapman, about 8 or 9 years ago. {DOLR 17 Old 262}

FOXWELL, RICHARD KENDALL, of Dorchester County, aet. about 67, dep. between Aug 10, 1762 and Mar 8, 1763, mentioned his mother (not named) and uncle Richard Person. {DOLR 18 Old 333} Aet. about 68, dep. between Aug 13, 1765 and Dec 28, 1765. {DOLR 21 Old 42}

FRAILE, DAVID, of Prince George's County, aet. 55, dep. May 11, 1733. {PGLR T:28}

FRAME, MAJOR, see "George Middleton," q.v.

FRANKLIN, JOHN, of Charles County, aet. 55, dep. Jan 20, 1726/7. {CHLR P#2:492} Aet. 58, dep. Apr 29, 1729. {CHLR Q#2:275} Aet. 63, dep. Apr 6, 1733. {CHLR R#2:332} Aet. 65, dep. Apr 7, 1736. {CHLR T#3:198} Aet. 88, dep. Mar 11, 1758, stated that he was shown the bounds of William Collier's part of *Simpson's Supply* by the widow Cornish about 40 years ago; also stated that Mary Wise and Jane Woodward were daughters of the widow Cornish by her husband Garrard Brown; also mentioned John Woodward and Ann Burn about 43 years ago. {CHLR H#3:425} Aet. 90, dep. Aug 11, 1760. {CHLR K#3:4}

FRANKLIN, JOHN, of Prince George's County, aet. 59, dep. Aug 3, 1730. {PGLR Q:67} Aet. 64, dep. Apr 26, 1735. {PGLR T:254}

FRANKLIN, RICHARD, see "Elizabeth Lamphier," q.v.

FRANKLIN, THOMAS (major), of Baltimore County, aet. 58, dep. Dec 10, 1762. {BALR B#L:192} Aet. 58, dep. Aug 29, 1763. {BALR B#N:135} Aet. 63 or thereabouts, dep. Oct 2, 1767, stated that John Merryman showed him the bounds of *Chive Chase* about 20 years ago. {BALR AL#A:120-121} Aet. 70 or thereabouts, dep. Apr 15, 1771. {BALR AL#C:608}

FRANKLIN, WILLIAM, of Charles County, aet. 43, dep. Apr 13, 1761. {CHLR K#3:298}

FRANKS, JOHN, see "Andrew Lord," q.v.

FRASER, JOHN, of Prince George's County, aet. 55, dep. May 9, 1774, mentioned James Cumberland, Levin Cumberland, John Cumberland, and their mother (not named), and Smallwood Coghill, about 37 or 38 years ago. {PGLR CC#2:56}

FRASHER, DANIEL, of Dorchester County, aet. about 59, dep. between Aug 14, 1764 and Jan 8, 1765, mentioned old Edward Willoughby some years ago. {DOLR 19 Old 440}

FRASHER, JOHN, see "Job Garrettson," q.v.

FRAYLE, DAVID, of Prince George's County, aet. 53, dep. Jun 16, 1730. {PGLR Q:12}

FRAZER, JAMES, of Prince George's County, aet. 60, dep. Jul 10, 1759, stated that he was overseer for John Beall, now deceased, about 22 years ago. {PGLR RR:78}

FRAZIER, ALEXANDER, of Dorchester County, aet. 15, dep. Nov 18, 1774. {DOLR 27 Old 372} See "Samuel Edmondson' and "Mary Perry," q.v.

FRAZIER, BENONI, of Dorchester County, aet. in his 78th year, dep. between Nov 12, 1771 and Dec 17, 1771, mentioned Thomas Barnett about 47 years ago. {DOLR 26 Old 34} Benonie Frazier, aet. about 77, dep. between Nov 13, 1770 and Aug 2, 1771. {DOLR 25 Old 26}

FRAZIER, DANIEL, of Dorchester County, aet. 60, dep. between Aug 11, 1772 and Dec 11, 1772, mentioned Edward Willoby when he (Frazier) was a boy. {DOLR 27 Old 348} See "Daniel Frasher," q.v.

FRAZIER, JOHN, of Dorchester County, aet. 58, dep. between Mar 13, 1770 and Jul 21, 1770. {DOLR 24 Old 303}

FRAZIER, JOHN, of Baltimore County, aet. 50, dep. Aug 29, 1763, stated that he married the widow (not named) of James Boring (deceased) about 24 years ago and the grave of said James was located at the end of Bladen's line. {BALR B#N:134}

FRAZIER, THOMAS, of Queen Anne's County, aet. about 70, dep. Mar 29, 1760. {QAEJ - Earle: oversize folder}

FREDERICK, THOMAS, see "Thomas Edelin," q.v.

FREEMAN, ABRAHAM, of Kent County, aet. about 29, dep. Mar, 1759, mentioned his deceased father (not named). {KEEJ - Thomas Harris folder}

FREEMAN, ISAAC, of Kent County, aet. 51, dep. Oct 24, 1759. {KELR JS#26:269}

FREEMAN, JAMES, of Charles County, aet. 40, dep. Jul 12, 1743. {CHLR O#2:662}

FREEMAN, JOHN, of Anne Arundel County, n.a., dep. Dec 12, 1696, stated that he has served as Register of the High Court of Chancery in Maryland for the past 2 years and almost 3 months. {ARMD 20:577}

FREEMAN, NATHANIEL, of Charles County, aet. 42, dep. Sep 28, 1775. {CHLR X#3:540}

FREHARTY, JOHN, see "John Fleharty," q.v.

FRENCH, COLONEL, see "Nathaniel Hynson," q.v.

FRENCH, FRANCIS, of London, England, chirurgion aboard the ship *Globe* commanded by Bartholomew Watts, dep. May 8, 1682 in St. Mary's County. {ARMD 7:281}

FREY, JAMES, of Prince George's County, aet. 40, dep. Jan 11, 1759, mentioned his father Joseph Frey about 30 years ago. {PGLR PP:277, pt. 2}

FREY, JOSEPH, see "James Frey," q.v.

FRISBY, JAMES, of Kent County, n.a., dep. Oct 8, 1681. {ARMD 17:63} See "Michael Miller," q.v.

FRISELL, JAMES, of Baltimore County, n.a., dep. Aug 16, 1692, mentioned Jacob Looton and wife (not named). {ARMD 8:347-348}

FRITH, HENRY, see "Samuel Guitchard," q.v.

FRIZEL, JASON, of Frederick County, aet. 40, dep. Dec 7, 1764, stated that he was shown the bounded tree of *Long Bottom* by John Howard (surveyor), son of Gideon Howard, about 13 years ago. {FRLR J:1212}

FROMAN, LEWIS, prob. of St. Mary's or Calvert County, aet. 29, dep. Aug 8, 1653, stated that he was a servant to Robert Brookes (who was seated on Patuxent River) and was also employed as an interpreter by him to the Indians; also mentioned Brookes' sons (not named). {ARMD 10:353}

FRY, JOSEPH, see "Paul Rawlings," q.v.

FULLER, SARAH, see "John Arnold," q.v.

FULLER, WILLIAM, see "John Buridge" and "Michaell Higgins," q.v.

FULLSTONE, ANNE, see "Edward Bennett," q.v.

FULLSTONE, JOHN, see "Edward Bennett" and "Mary Fisher," q.v.

FULLSTONE, MARY, see "Mary Fisher," q.v.

FULLSTONE, RICHARD, see "Edward Bennett" and "Mary Fisher," q.v.

FUNKYN, THOMAS, of Charles County, aet. 27, dep. Mar 5, 1682/3. {CHLR K#1:126}

FURGUSON, JOHN, see "Mary Trundle," q.v.

FURLONG, EDWARD, see "John Hepworth" and "Esther Hepworth," q.v.

GABRIELL, BARTHOLOME, of Charles County, aet. 28 or thereabouts, dep. May 1, 1659 (name listed once as Bartholomi Gabrielis). {CHLR A:56; ARMD 53:46}

GADD (GAD), MATTHEW, of Dorchester County, aet. about 60, dep. between Apr 6, 1732 and Jun 3, 1732, stated that the bounds of *Armstrong's Hog Pen* were shown to him by old Thomas Pattison about 30 years ago. {DOLR 9 Old 68} See "Richard Gadd," q.v.

GADD (GAD), RICHARD, of Dorchester County, aet. about 36, dep. between Aug 13, 1747 and Sep 18, 1749, mentioned his father Matthew Gadd about 20 years ago. {DOLR 14 Old 463} Aet. about 52, dep. between Jun 11, 1765 and Aug 11, 1765. {DOLR 21 Old 45}

GAFFORD, CHARLES, see "John Gafford" and "John Brown," q.v.

GAFFORD, JOHN, of Queen Anne's County, aet. 43, dep. Apr, 1765, mentioned his father Charles Gafford about 20 years ago. {QAEJ - John Moore folder} See "John Brown," q.v.

GAFFORD, RICHARD, of Queen Anne's County, aet. 33, dep. Mar, 1753. {QAEJ - Peter Johnson folder} Aet. about 50, dep. Feb, 1769. {QAEJ - John Moore folder} See "John Brown," q.v.

GAITHER, SARAH (Mrs.), of Prince George's County, n.a., dep. Jul 31, 1764, stated that about 50 odd years ago John Ouchterlony came into this province a youth under the direction of Patrick Andrews, merchant, with whom he lived as storekeeper; said John married Frances Wells and had 2 daughters, Mary (married James Plummer) and Elizabeth; said John also became a merchant after Patrick Andrews declined the business. {PGLR AA#2:121}

GALE, JOHN, of Kent County, aet. about 36, dep. Mar 18, 1740. {KELR JS#23:188} John Gale, Sr., Quaker, aet. about 49, dep. affirmed Mar 13, 1753. {KELR JS#27:255, 319} John Gale, Quaker, aet. 52, dep. affirmed Sep, 1755. {KEEJ - Thomas Chandler folder} See "Ann Collins," q.v.
GALLAWAY, JAMES, see "Elizabeth Meekins" and "Benjamin Blackleach" and "Hannah Clove" and "Hannah Inch," q.v.
GALLAWAY, LUCY, see "Hannah Clove," q.v.
GALLAWAY, WILLIAM, see "Elizabeth Meekins" and "Benjamin Blackleach" and "Hannah Clove," q.v.
GALLION, JAMES, SR., of Baltimore County, aet. 58, dep. May 12, 1764, mentioned his father John Gallion. {BALR B#O:109}
GALLION, JOHN, see "James Gallion, Sr.," q.v.
GALLOWAY, SAMUELL, see "William Smith," q.v.
GALWITH, JOHN, SR., of Charles County, aet. 61, dep. Mar 26, 1744. {CHLR Y#2:9}
GAMBALL, JOHN, of Kent County, aet. 61, dep. Oct, 1753, mentioned Nathaniel Griffith, son of Benjamin, about 14 years ago. {KELR JS#28:43} Aet. about 64, dep. Aug 19, 1755. {KELR JS#28:162}
GAMBELL, ABRAHAM, of Dorchester County, aet. 51, dep. between Aug 12, 1746 and May 2, 1747, stated that he was shown the bounded tree of *Squire's Chance* by Joseph Nicolls (deceased) about 36 years ago. {DOLR 14 Old 237} Abraham Gamble, aet. about 60, dep. between Jun 10, 1755 and Feb 10, 1756, mentioned James Anderson and John Harris about 35 years ago, both now deceased. {DOLR 15 Old 341}
GAMBELL, GIDEON, of Dorchester County, under sheriff, aet. about 39, dep. between Mar 13, 1764 and Jun 4, 1767, mentioned Joseph Thompson, lately deceased. {DOLR 21 Old 382}
GAMBLE, JOHN, see "William Pearce," q.v.
GAMBOL, AUGUSTINE, see "Richard Warfield," q.v.
GANDIE, WILLIAM, of Charles County, n.a., dep. Mar 14, 1664/5, stated that Mary Grub (expecting a child) said that no man in the world had anything to do with her but John Grub and her former husband in England. {CHLR B:445}
GANTT, THOMAS, of Prince George's County, gentleman, aet. 66, dep. Jun 7, 1752. {PGLR NN:64} Aet. 70 or thereabouts, dep. Mar 18, 1757. {PGLR NN:516}
GARDINER, BENJAMIN, of Charles County, aet. 70, dep. Apr 25, 1774, mentioned his brother John Gardiner about 30 or 40 years ago. {CHLR W#3:81} Benjamin Gardner, aet. 38, dep. Oct 26, 1741. {CHLR O#2:284}
GARDINER, JOHN, of Prince George's County, aet. 76, dep. Nov 28, 1728. {PGLR M:343} Aet. 78, dep. Aug 3, 1730. {PGLR Q:68} Aet. 80, dep. Apr 26, 1735, mentioned Col. George Mason about 50 years ago. {PGLR T:253, 280}
GARDINER, JOHN, of Charles County, aet. 45, dep. Apr 25, 1774, mentioned his father Joseph Gardiner. {CHLR W#3:80} Aet. 46, dep. Feb 23, 1774/5. {CHLR W#3:82}

GARDINER, JOHN, see "Benjamin Gardiner," q.v.
GARDINER, JOSEPH, of Charles County, aet. 50, dep. Feb 27, 1748/9, mentioned his father John Gardiner. {CHLR Z#2:526} Aet. 63, dep. May 18, 1763. {CHLR Q#3:441}
GARDNER, JAMES, of Baltimore County, aet. 61, dep. Jan 11, 1766. {BALR B#P:81}
GARDNER, JOHN, of Queen Anne's County, aet. 33, dep. Oct 2, 1767, mentioned Mrs. Ann Walters and her son James. {QAEJ - Downe: oversize folder}
GARLAND, HENRY, of Baltimore County, aet. 51, dep. Jan 4, 1763. {BALR B#L:500}
GARNER, BENJAMIN, of Charles County, aet. 41, dep. Oct 22, 1740, mentioned his father John Garner. {CHLR Z#2:192}
GARNER, JAMES, of Charles County, aet. 61, dep. Jun 13, 1759. {CHLR H#3:329}
GARNER, JOHN, of Charles County, aet. 80, dep. Apr 6, 1733. {CHLR R#2:332} See "Benjamin Garner," q.v.
GARNER, JOHN, JR., of Charles County, aet. 49, dep. Oct 15, 1741. {CHLR O#2:283} Aet. 67, dep. Jun 13, 1758. {CHLR H#3:329} Aet. 70, dep. Aug 3, 1761. {CHLR K#3:309} Aet. 75, dep. Jul 24, 1764. {CHLR M#3:688}
GARNETT, GEORGE, of Kent County, aet. about 33, dep. Jun 25, 1743. {KELR JS#24:440} Aet. about 34, dep. Feb 21, 1743/4. {KELR JS#25:37} Aet. about 35, dep. Aug 5, 1745. {KELR JS#25:298}
GARRARD, THOMAS, see "Samuel Love," q.v.
GARRATT, NATHANIELL, of Kent County, n.a., dep. Oct 8, 1681. {ARMD 17:63}
GARRETT, EDWARD, of Dorchester County, aet. 77, dep. on Apr 6, 1732 and Jun 3, 1732, stated that he was a servant of old Henry Beckwith about 34 years ago. {DOLR 9 Old 58} Aet. 77, dep. Jan 13, 1732/3, mentioned Mrs. Frances Beckwith. {DOLR 8 Old 471}
GARRETT, SETH, of Talbot County, aet. 40 and upwards, dep. Mar 10, 1704 (recorded in Queen Anne's County records on Jun 29, 1716 for Rebeckah Kenton), stated that he was a chain carrier on *Upland* (date not stated), formerly Emanuel Jenkinson's land, which bounded *Poplar Ridge Addition* that was laid out for Loveless Gossage. {QALR IK#A:81}
GARRETTSON, EDWARD, of Baltimore County, aet. 44, dep. Jun 18, 1770. {BALR AL#B:414}
GARRETTSON, JOB, of Baltimore County, aet. 32, dep. Jun 10, 1772, mentioned his uncle John Frasher about 19 or 20 years ago. {BALR AL#E:287}
GARRETTSON, JOHN, of Baltimore County, aet. 64, dep. Dec 19, 1769. {BALR AL#A:736}
GARRETTSON, JOHN, of Baltimore County, aet. 51, dep. Jan 4, 1763. {BALR B#L:499}
GARRETTSON, JOHN, of Baltimore County, aet. 56, dep. Mar 4, 1763. {BALR B#L:206}
GARTHERELL, BARTHOLME, of Charles County, aet. 27, dep. Jul 10, 1662. {CHLR A:236}

GARTON, THOMAS, of Prince George's County, aet. 57, dep. Apr 14, 1759, stated that Lewis Wilcoxon and John Carr built a schoolhouse about 20 years ago. {PGLR PP:314, pt. 2}

GARY, JOHN, see "Elizabeth Greene," q.v.

GARY, STEPHEN, see "John White," q.v.

GARY, WILLIAM, of Talbot County, n.a., dep. Sep 21, 1669, mentioned Anthony Pecheco, servant to John Kinemant. {ARMD 54:443}

GATCHELL, ELISHA, see "Samuel Brice" and "Charles Alleyn" and "Edward Lang" and "Daniel Smith," q.v.

GATES, CHARLES, of Charles County, aet. 51, dep. Mar 26, 1772. {CHLR T#3:611}

GATES, JOHN, of Charles County, aet. 63, dep. Jun 29, 1744. {CHLR Y#2:86}

GATES, JOHN, of Charles County, aet. 32, dep. Oct 18, 1763, mentioned his father John Gates. {CHLR M#3:357}

GATES, ROBERT, of Charles County, aet. 64, dep. Mar 9, 1775. {CHLR X#3:9}

GENTLE, GEORGE, of Prince George's County, aet. 58, dep. Jul 1, 1738. {PGLR T:604}

GENTLE, GEORGE, of Charles County, aet. 62, dep. Nov 2, 1742. {CHLR O#2:465}

GEOGHEGAN, WILLIAM, of Dorchester County, aet. 49, dep. between Mar 13, 1753 and Jun 2, 1753. {DOLR 15 Old 134}

GEORGE, JOHN, of Prince George's County, aet. 64, dep. Jun 26, 1734. {PGLR T:124} See "Paul Rawlings" and "William Read, Jr.," q.v.

GEORGE, JOSEPH, of Kent County, Quaker, aet. about 40, dep. Mar 25, 1749. {KELR JS#26:243}

GERARD (GERRARD), JOHN, see "Thomas Lancaster," q.v.

GERARD, JUSTINIAN, of St. Mary's County, n.a., dep. Oct, 13, 1665, mentioned his father Thomas Gerard. {ARMD 49:496}

GERARD, THOMAS, see "Justinian Gerard," q.v.

GERMAN, STEPHEN, of Prince George's County, aet. between 60 and 70, dep. between Nov 11, 1729 and Mar 26, 1730. {PGLR M:561}

GES, ANNE, of Charles County, aet. 26, dep. Jan 28, 1661/2. {CHLR A:178} Ane Ges, aet. 26, dep. Mar 4, 1661/2, mentioned Elinor Morris, formerly Elinor Empson. {CHLR A:195}

GES, WALTER, of Charles County, n.a., dep. Jan 26, 1658/9, stated that Lucie Stratton said that her child could belong to William Bowls, but she thought in her conscience that it was Arthur Turner's child. {CHLR A:35}

GEVES, GEORGE, of Kent County, aet. about 24, dep. Sep 24, 1678, mentioned Robert Dunn, sheriff (deceased) and his son-in-law Robert Hood about 4 years ago. {KELR A:464}

GEY, ANNE, of Charles County, aet. 50, dep. Jan 26, 1658/9, stated that Arthur Turner came to her house the Saturday after Lucie Stratton had given birth and asked her (Lucie) to marry him, but she said she did not love him and would not marry him. {CHLR A:35}

GIBBONS, GEORGE, see "Thomas Gibbons," q.v.

GIBBONS, THOMAS, of Prince George's County, aet. 27, dep. Jul 1, 1738. {PGLR T:606}
GIBBONS, THOMAS, of Charles County, aet. 46, dep. May 29, 1773, mentioned his father George Gibbons. {CHLR U#3:272}
GIBBONS, THOMAS, of Baltimore County, aet. 68, dep. Oct 22, 1767, mentioned Seliah Barton about 20 years ago. {BALR B#Q:588}
GIBBONS, TURNER, of Prince George's County, aet. 28, dep. Jul 1, 1738. {PGLR T:606}
GIBBS, ANDREW, of Charles County, aet. 50, dep. Aug 26, 1767. {CHLR P#3:655} Aet. 52, dep. Oct 30, 1770. {CHLR T#3:141}
GIBBS, BARTHOLOMEW (BARTHOLOMON), of Dorchester County, aet. 30, dep. between Jun 14, 1743 and Aug 4, 1743, mentioned his father-in-law John Spicer. {DOLR 12 Old 164}
GIBBS, RICHARD, of Calvert County, n.a., servant to Richard Preston, Sr., dep. Mar 31, 1663. {ARMD 49:9-10}
GIBSON, FRANCES, of Talbot County, n.a., dep. Mar 15, 1760, stated that Rebecca Bruff, daughter of Richard, was given negro Jacob and another child born of the same woman. {TALR 19:185} See "James Means," q.v.
GIBSON, JONATHAN, of Talbot County, n.a., dep. Mar 15, 1760, stated that Rebecca Bruff, daughter of Richard, was given "two negro children born of a negro woman, he had by his wife." {TALR 19:185} See "James Means," q.v.
GIBSON, ROBERT, see "Thomas Bale," q.v.
GIBSON, WILLIAM, of Charles County, aet. 47, dep. Aug 20, 1753. {CHLR D#3:153}
GIBSON, WOOLMAN, of Kent County, aet. about 45, dep. Sep, 1740. {TAEJ - Robert Newcomb folder}
GIDDINS, THOMAS, see "Alexander Duval," q.v.
GILBERT, EPHRAIM, of Kent County, aet. about 32, dep. Aug 17, 1737, stated that he was overseer to Major Dowdall who showed him the bounds of *Hopewell* about 9 or 10 years ago. {KELR JS#22:19}
GILBERT, JOHN, of Queen Anne's County, aet. 55, dep. Apr, 1747. {QAEJ - Samuel Blunt folder} See "Thomas Barnes," q.v.
GILBERT, MICHAEL, of Harford County, aet. 68, dep. May 25, 1775. {Land Commission, 1774, Harford County Genealogical Society Newsletter, Jan, 1993, p. 3}
GILDERT, JAMES, see "Sarah Kennerly," q.v.
GILES, JACOB, of Baltimore County, Quaker, aet. 70, dep. Aug 15, 1774, mentioned ---- Larcan about 50 years ago. {BALR AL#L:241}
GILES, PETER, of Charles County, aet. 25 or 26, dep. Mar 6, 1680/1. {CHLR I#1:114}
GILLINS (GILLANS, JELLINGS, JINNIGS), EDWARD, of Charles County, aet. 37, dep. Mar 1, 1737/8. {CHLR T#2:627} Edward Jellings, aet. 33, dep. May 17, 1733. {CHLR R#3:335} Edward Gillins, aet. 38, dep. Sep 5, 1738. {CHLR T#2:516} Edward Gillans, aet. 43, dep. Dec 29, 1744. {CHLR Y#2:335} Edward Jinnig (or Gillans), aet. 43, dep. Dec 29, 1744. {CHLR Y#2:335}

GILPIN, FRANCIS, of Charles County, aet. 29, dep. Jan 31, 1776, mentioned his father Thomas Gilpin. {CHLR X#3:536}
GILPIN, ISAAC, of Charles County, aet. 51, dep. Oct 11, 1727. {CHLR P#2:403}
GILPIN, ISAAC, of Charles County, aet. 27, dep. Jul 18, 1767 and Jul 21, 1767, mentioned his father William Gilpin. {CHLR P#3:660, 664}
GILPIN, NOTLEY, of Charles County, aet. 17, dep. Jul 21, 1767, mentioned his father William Gilpin. {CHLR P#3:661}
GILPIN, THOMAS, see "Francis Gilpin," q.v.
GILPIN, WILLIAM, see "Isaac Gilpin" and "Notley Gilpin," q.v.
GITTINGS, PHILIP, see "Maureen Duvall" and "Edward Sprigg," q.v.
GITTINGS, THOMAS, of Prince George's County, gentleman, aet. 29, dep. Oct 9, 1728. {PGLR M:401} See "Gara Davis," q.v.
GLADING, ROBERT, of Charles County, aet. 45, dep. Sep 16, 1758. {CHLR H#3:486}
GLADSTONE, JOHN, see "John Carter," q.v.
GLANVILL, STEPHEN, of Kent County, aet. 36 or 37, dep. 1773. {KELR DD#4:249}
GLASS, FRANCIS, of Charles County, aet. 58, dep. Mar 4, 1731/2. {CHLR R#2:83} Aet. 60, dep. Dec 20, 1737. {CHLR T#2:430} Aet. 65, dep. May 7, 1744. {CHLR Y#2:17} Aet. 64, dep. Sep 24, 1744. {CHLR Y#2:187} Aet. 71, dep. Feb 19, 1750/1. {CHLR Z#2:143} Aet. 87, dep. Apr 28, 1753. {CHLR D#3:78}
GLAZE, JOHN, of Charles County, aet. 50, dep. Jan 9, 1726/7. {CHLR P#2:421} Aet. 60, dep. Dec 29, 1736 and Jan 10, 1736/7. {CHLR T#2:292, 296} See "John Jee," q.v.
GLEN, NICHOLAS, of Talbot County, aet. 23 or thereabout, dep. Nov 5, 1734, stated that George Johnings and John Kelld got into a fight last October and Kelld's right ear was badly bitten. {TALR 14:46}
GLENN, ANN, se "Robert Meeks," q.v.
GLENTWORTH, JOSEPH, of Dorchester County, n.a., dep. between Mar 12, 1744 and Aug 5, 1745. {DOLR 12 Old 215}
GLOVER, ELIZABETH, see "Richard Trew" and "Henry Tanner," q.v.
GLOVER, GILES (GILS), see "Richard Trew" and "Henry Tanner," q.v.
GLOVER, WILLIAM, see "Henry Tanner," q.v.
GOADY, WILLIAM, of Charles County, aet. 57, dep. May 19, 1725. {CHLR P#2:40}
GOADY, WILLIAM, of Charles County, aet. 71, dep. Dec 21, 1723. {CHLR P#2:141}
GOARE, JAMES, of Frederick County, aet. 53 or thereabouts, dep. Jul 27, 1762, stated that Hugh Tomlinson was a tenant to Mr. Charles Carroll on the tract *Girl's Portion*. {FRLR J:67}
GODDING, SUSANNA, see "Elizabeth Lamphier," q.v.
GODFREY, FRANCIS, see "Catharine Milstead," q.v.
GODFREY, WILLIAM, of Charles County, aet. 57, dep. Apr 7, 1736. {CHLR R#2:198} Aet. 65, dep. Oct 22, 1744. {CHLR Y#2:191} See "William Speake," q.v.

GOING, ROBERT (family), see "Elizabeth Lamphier," q.v.
GOLD, JAMES, of Queen Anne's County, aet. about 50, dep. Oct 20, 1735. {QAEJ - John Coursey folder}
GOLDING, WILLIAM, of Charles County, aet. 60, dep. Dec 31, 1759. {CHLR I#3:429}
GOODMAN, JOHN, of Prince George's County, aet. 54, dep. Jun 5, 1769, mentioned Thomas James about 16 or 20 years ago. {PGLR BB#2:438}
GOODMAN, RICHARD, of Queen Anne's County, aet. about 52, dep. Mar, 1759. {QAEJ - Henry Carter folder}
GOODRICK, CHRISTIAN, see "Godshall Barnes," q.v.
GOODRICK, EDWARD, of Charles County, aet. 23, dep. Jan 6, 1748/9, mentioned his father Francis Goodrick. {CHLR Z#2:34}
GOODRICK, FRANCIS, of Charles County, aet. 79, dep. Jun 6, 1726. {CHLR P#2:387} See "Edward Goodrick" and "George Goodrick," q.v.
GOODRICK, GEORGE, of Charles County, aet. 32, dep. Jul 5, 1762, mentioned his father Francis Goodrick. {CHLR M#3:215} See "William Goodrick" and "Francis Ware," q.v.
GOODRICK, ROBERT, see "Mary Speake" and "Juliana Sympson" and "Francis Ware," q.v.
GOODRICK (GOODERICK), URSULA (Mrs.), of Charles County, n.a., dep. Jun 4, 1658. {CHLR A:3}
GOODRICK, WILLIAM, of Charles County, aet. 44, dep. Nov 11, 1745, mentioned his father George Goodrick. {CHLR Z#2:468}
GOOFF, BARTHOLOMNE, see "Caleb Norris," q.v.
GOOLD, JOHN, see "Joseph Dorrosell," q.v.
GOOLD, MARGERIE, see "Joseph Dorrosell," q.v.
GOOSTREE, RICHARD, of Dorchester County, aet. about 60, dep. Jun 10, 1721, stated that he was a former servant of Thomas Browne and his wife Eliza. {DOLR 8 Old 9} Aet. about 60, dep. between Mar 18, 1726/7 and Jun 3, 1727. {DOLR 8 Old 215}
GOOTEE, ELIZABETH, of Dorchester County, aet. about 45, dep. between Aug 14, 1764 and Jan 4, 1768, mentioned her grandfather ---- Robinson when she was a girl. {DOLR 22 Old 418}
GOOTEE, JOHN, of Dorchester County, aet. about 57, dep. between Aug 14, 1764 and Jan 4, 1768, mentioned Ruth Robinson, wife of old William Robinson, about 4 years ago. {DOLR 22 Old 418} John Gotee, aet. 54 or upwards, dep. between Jun 12, 1764 and Aug 6, 1765. {DOLR 20 Old 218}
GORDON (GORDIAN), DANIEL, of Charles County, aet. 34, dep. Apr 17, 1660. {CHLR A:86} Daniell Gordian, n.a., dep. Feb 12, 1660/1 and Mar 12, 1660/1, regarding a disturbance of the peace with mutinous and reproachful words, stated that he heard that many men were to be hanged, including Lt. Robert Troope and Thomas Allen. {CHLR A:121, 125} Daniel Gordon, n.a., dep. May 12,

1663. {CHLR B:122} Daniell Gourden, n.a., dep. Apr 24, 1655 at Patuxent. {ARMD 10:416}

GORDON, GEORGE, of Prince George's County, aet. 45, dep. Mar 24, 1745/6. {PGLR BB:10}

GORDON, JAMES, see "Robert Gordon," q.v.

GORDON, JOHN, of Prince George's County, aet. 53, dep. Mar 21, 1761, mentioned his brother Thomas Gordon. {PGLR RR:233}

GORDON, JOHN (reverend), of Talbot County, Rector of St. Michael's Parish, n.a., dep. Jun 7, 1769, stated that he has known Francis Baker to be an honest man these 9 or 10 years as he has lived on the borders of my parish. {ARMD 32:327}

GORDON, PATRICK, of Queen Anne's County, aet. 54, dep. about Sep, 1730, stated that he was born on the plantation where Robert Small now lives. {QAEJ - William Stavely folder}

GORDON, ROBERT, of Charles County, aet. 49, dep. Oct 1, 1771, mentioned his brother James Gordon and father Robert Gordon. {CHLR T#3:616}

GORDON, ROBERT, of Charles County, aet. 59, dep. May 25, 1752. {CHLR B#3:121}

GORDON, THOMAS, of Dorchester County, aet. 59, dep. between Jun 11, 1751 and Oct 14, 1751, mentioned his father Thomas Gordon about 40 years ago. {DOLR 14 Old 552} See "James Cannon" and "Abraham Covington" and "John Carter" and "John Gordon," q.v.

GORSLETT, HENRY, of Calvert County, n.a., servant to Richard Preston, Sr., dep. Mar 31, 1663. {ARMD 49:9-10}

GORSUCH, AQUILA, of Baltimore County, aet. 42, dep. Nov 11, 1768. {BALR AL#G:443}

GORSUCH, DAVID, of Baltimore County, aet. 29, dep. Jul 2, 1764. {BALR B#N:308}

GORSUCH, JOSEPH, of Frederick County, aet. 35, dep. between Nov 25, 1760 and Apr 13, 1761 in Baltimore County. {BALR B#L:198}

GORSUCH, THOMAS, SR., of Baltimore County, aet. 90 or thereabouts, dep. May 11, 1768. {BALR AL#B:595} Thomas Gorsuch, aet. 90 or 91, dep. Jun 10, 1772, mentioned Col. William Hammond. {BALR AL#E:286}

GOSSAGE, LOVELESS, see "Seth Garrett," q.v.

GOULSON, SARAH, see "Ann Johnson," q.v.

GOUTEE, ANDREW, of Dorchester County, aet. 52, dep. between Nov 13, 1750 and Feb 16, 1750, stated that he was shown the bounds of *Foxton Is Defeated* and *The Old Baily* about 32 or 33 years ago by old George Slaycomb; also mentioned William Hooper and wife Grace Hooper about 35 years ago. {DOLR 14 Old 527}

GOVANE, WILLIAM, of Baltimore County, aet. 49, dep. Feb 26, 1766. {BALR B#P:301}

GOVER, EPHRAIM, of Prince George's County, aet. 73, Quaker, dep. Mar 12, 1755. {PGLR NN:412}

GOVER, EPHRAIM, JR., of Prince George's County, aet. 30, Quaker, dep. Mar 1, 1756. {PGLR NN:469} See "Thomas King," q.v.

GRACE, HENNERY, see "John Caine," q.v.

GRAFTON, WILLIAM, of Baltimore County, aet. 79, dep. May 12, 1764. {BALR B#O:112}

GRAHAM, HABELL, of Dorchester County, aet. about 50, daughter of Peter Stoaks, dep. between Jun 16, 1727 and Mar 17, 1727/8. {DOLR 8 Old 200}

GRAHAM, JOHN, of Kent County, aet. about 38, dep. Jul 25, 1757. {KELR JS#28:367} See "James Hopkins," q.v.

GRAINGER, JOHN, of Dorchester County, aet. 64, dep. between Apr 6, 1732 and Jun 3, 1732. {DOLR 9 Old 68}

GRANGER, BENJAMIN, of Dorchester County, aet. 39, dep. Aug 10, 1742. {DOLR 12 Old 98}

GRANGER, BENJAMIN, of Dorchester County, aet. 80 or upwards, dep. between Aug 10, 1762 and Oct 27, 1762. {DOLR 19 Old 88} Benjamin Grainger, aet. about 80, dep. between Jun 14, 1763 and Aug 16, 1763, stated that he was shown the bounded tree of *Tenches Hope* about 40 years ago by Margaret Clarridge. {DOLR 19 Old 279}

GRANGER, ELIZA (Mrs.), of Queen Anne's County, aet. about 56, dep. Sep, 1733, mentioned her father, old Col. William Lawrence, living 30 years ago. {QAEJ - James Hutchens folder}

GRANGER, RICHARD, see "Richard Greynger," q.v.

GRANT, ALEXANDER, see "William Carter" and "Elizabeth Grant," q.v.

GRANT, ANN, see "William Carter," q.v.

GRANT, ELIZABETH, of Baltimore County, aet. 68, dep. May 11, 1768, mentioned her husband Alexander Grant. {BALR AL#B:594}

GRANTHAM, WILLIAM, of Dorchester County, aet. about 47, dep. between Nov 13, 1744 and Nov 10, 1748. {DOLR 14 Old 315}

GRASHIRE, ELIZABETH, see "Edward Needles," q.v.

GRAVES, ROBERT, of Baltimore County, aet. 54 or thereabouts, dep. Sep 20, 1767, mentioned Joseph Thomas about 23 years ago; also mentioned Ralph Broadax's eldest son (not named). {BALR AL#A:121}

GRAVES, SARAH (Mrs.), of Kent County, aet. 32, dep. Oct, 1753, mentioned her husband William Graves. {KELR JS#28:52}

GRAVES, WILLIAM, of St. Mary's County, n.a., dep. Aug 13, 1661. {ARMD 41:481}

GRAVES, WILLIAM, of Kent County, aet. about 31, dep. Sep 22, 1747. {KELR JS#26:101}

GRAY, ANDREW, of Dorchester County, aet. 43, dep. Mar 10, 1743, stated that he was shown the first bounded tree of Dr. Jacob Loockerman's land about 27 or 28 years ago by Robert Watson who had been shown the tree by Henry Trippe, deceased. {DOLR 12 Old 137} Aet. 45, dep. between Aug 13, 1745 and Jun 4, 1746. {DOLR 14 Old 59} Aet. 45, dep. between Nov 12, 1745 and Nov 11, 1747, mentioned Thomas Turner, deceased. {DOLR 14 Old 173} Aet. 46, dep.

between Aug 12, 1746 and May 2, 1747, mentioned William Spencer, deceased. {DOLR 14 Old 237} See "Thomas Gray" and "James Edgell," q.v.

GRAY, EDWARD, of Charles County, aet. 41, dep. Mar 15, 1725, mentioned his father John Gray and grandfather John Ward. {CHLR P#2:299} Aet. 84, dep. Aug 27, 1764. {CHLR N#3:61} Edward Grey, aet. 55, dep. Jun 2, 1738, mentioned his brother James Grey, his father John Grey, and Benjamin Posey, son of Humphrey Posey, who now lives in Virginia. {CHLR T#2:464}

GRAY, FRANCIS, see "Edward Thomson," q.v.

GRAY, HENRY, of Charles County, aet. 47, dep. Aug 27, 1764. {CHLR N#3:61} Aet. 54, dep. May 20, 1772. {CHLR T#3:619}

GRAY, HENRY, of Charles County, aet. 46, dep. May 23, 1751. {CHLR K#3:224}

GRAY, ISABEL, of Dorchester County, aet. 36, dep. between Sep 1, 1732 and Dec 9, 1732. {DOLR 9 Old 57}

GRAY, JACOB, see "Thomas Whitely," q.v.

GRAY, JAMES, see "William Gray" and "Edward Gray," q.v.

GRAY, JOHN, of Charles County, aet. 61, dep. May 20, 1772. {CHLR T#3:619} See "Edward Willoby" and "Edward Gray" and "Sarah Deaver," q.v.

GRAY, PRISCILLA, of Charles County, aet. 26, dep. Apr 13, 1761, mentioned her father Richard Gray. {CHLR K#3:296}

GRAY, RICHARD, see "Priscilla Gray," q.v.

GRAY, SAMUEL, of Charles County, aet. 56, dep. Dec 31, 1759. {CHLR I#3:429} Aet. 60, dep. Aug 27, 1764. {CHLR N#3:61}

GRAY, THOMAS, of Dorchester County, aet. about 35, dep. between Aug 12, 1746 and May 2, 1747. {DOLR 14 Old 237} Aet. about 52, dep. between Nov 10, 1761 and Feb 24, 1762, mentioned Andrew Gray, now deceased. {DOLR 18 Old 72} Aet. 58, dep. between Nov 8, 1768 and Dec 10, 1768. {DOLR 23 Old 133} Aet. about 60, dep. between Nov 13, 1770 and Aug 2, 1771, mentioned his brother Andrew Gray about 30 years ago, now deceased. {DOLR 25 Old 26, 73}

GRAY, WILLIAM, of Dorchester County, n.a., dep. Sep 6, 1746, stated that he wrote the will for Daniel Hubbart about 3 years before he died, providing his land equally to sons Humphrey and Nehemiah Hubbart. {DOLR 14 Old 74} Aet. near 32, dep. between Nov 11, 1755 and May 20, 1756, mentioned Mathew Dean, deceased. {DOLR 16 Old 76} Aet. 53, dep. between Aug 10, 1773 and Feb 25, 1774. {DOLR 27 Old 267}

GRAY, WILLIAM, of Charles County, aet. 31, dep. Sep 24, 1775, mentioned his father James Gray. {CHLR X#3:16}

GRAYHAM, ALEXANDER, of Charles County, aet. 33, dep. Sep 24, 1764, mentioned his brother George Grayham, deceased. {CHLR N#3:63}

GRAYHAM, GEORGE, see "Alexander Grayham," q.v.

GRAYHAM, WILLIAM, of Charles County, aet. 43, dep. Nov 5, 1770. {CHLR T#3:145}

GRAYLIS, TIMOTHY, see "Rosanna Murrain," q.v.

GREAVES, MATTHEW, of Queen Anne's County, aet. about 50, dep. Apr, 1755. {QAEJ - Matthew Dockery folder}
GREEN, ABRAHAM, of Baltimore County, aet. 46, dep. Feb 22, 1773. {BALR AL#G:447}
GREEN, BENJAMIN, of Kent County, aet. about 30, dep. Aug 26, 1737. {KELR JS#22:14}
GREEN, CHARLES, see "George Green," q.v.
GREEN, FRANCIS, of Charles County, aet. 47, dep. Aug 6, 1762. {CHLR M#3:4}
GREEN, FRANCIS, of Charles County, aet. 47, dep. Apr 22, 1742. {CHLR O#2:379}
GREEN, FRANCIS, see "Patrick Hamilton" and "John Wynn," q.v.
GREEN, GEORGE, of Baltimore County, aet. 43, dep. May 7, 1764, mentioned his father Charles Green. {BALR B#N:137}
GREEN, GILES, of Charles County, aet. 64, dep. Jul 5, 1762. {CHLR M#3:214}
GREEN, HENRY, of Baltimore County, aet. 31, dep. between Apr 13, 1762 and Nov 22, 1762, mentioned his father William Green. {BALR B#L:200}
GREEN, JAMES, of Charles County, aet. 40, dep. Nov 11, 1745, mentioned his father James Green. {CHLR Z#2:468}
GREEN, JAMES, of Prince George's County, aet. 73, dep. between Nov 11, 1729 and Mar 26, 1730, mentioned John Thompson and William Hutchison about 40 years ago. {PGLR M:558}
GREEN, JAMES, of Prince George's County, aet. 64, dep. Mar 10, 1769, mentioned John Hawkins, Jr. about 15 or 16 years ago, now deceased. {PGLR AA#2:150} Aet. 66, dep. Mar 12, 1772. {PGLR AA#2:498} Aet. 70, dep. Nov 14, 1774, stated that he saw the bounds of *Stone's Delight* about 53 or 54 years ago. {PGLR CC#2:58}
GREEN, JAMES, see "Giles Virmillion," q.v.
GREEN, JOHN, SR., of Baltimore County, aet. 62, dep. May 28, 1764. {BALR B#N:141}
GREEN, LEONARD, of Charles County, aet. 50, dep. Aug 18, 1763. {CHLR M#3:508}
GREEN, MICHAEL, of Queen Anne's County, aet. about 40, dep. Apr, 1755. {QAEJ - William Bishop folder} Aet. 60, dep. Oct 5, 1768. {QAEJ - Gideon Emory folder}
GREEN, MRS., see "William Boarman" and "John Marten" and "William Nally," q.v.
GREEN, PETER, of Queen Anne's County, n.a., dep. Apr 2, 1715, mentioned his father (not named). {QALR IK#A:64}
GREEN, ROBERT, of Baltimore County, aet. 78, dep. Nov 12, 1768. {BALR AL#G:443} See "Thomas Green," q.v.
GREEN, THOMAS, of Charles County, aet. 60, dep. Aug 1, 1743, mentioned his father Robert Green, deceased. {CHLR O#2:619}
GREEN, WILLIAM, of Dorchester County, aet. 44, dep. between Jun 10, 1755 and Feb 10, 1756, mentioned Peter Taylor, now deceased. {DOLR 15 Old 341}
GREEN, WILLIAM, of Baltimore County, aet. about 70, dep. between Nov 25, 1760 and Apr 13, 1761. {BALR B#L:196}

GREEN, WILLIAM, see "Henry Green" and "William Hambleton," q.v.
GREENE, ELIZABETH, of St. Mary's or Calvert County, n.a., dep. Sep 9, 1663, mentioned her servant boy Richard Joanes and "her husband Potters papers" (which included a receipt for Henry Potter that was signed by Teagar Winn on Mar 3, 1659). {ARMD 49:53, 217} Aet. not given, dep. Jul 5, 1664 in Calvert County, stated she was born 5 miles from Norwich, last lived with John Gary, and had a bastard child (father not named), but did not murder it. {ARMD 49:232} See "William Brooke," q.v.
GREENE, GEORGE, see "James Ringgold," q.v.
GREENE, JAMES, of Charles County, aet. 69, dep. Jun 6, 1726, stated that he came to this country about 54 years ago. {CHLR P#2:358}
GREENE, JOSEPH, see "John Salter," q.v.
GREENE, THOMAS, see "Margaret Brent," q.v.
GREENESTEAD, WILLIAM, see "John Malham," q.v.
GREENEWOOD, JONAS, of Kent County, aet. 34, dep. Oct 8, 1684, mentioned Samuel Tovey, deceased, and his children in England. {ARMD 17:290-291}
GREENFIELD, JAMES (captain), of Prince George's County, aet. 46, dep. Jul 7, 1731. {PGLR Q:525} See "James Edmondson," q.v.
GREENFIELD, THOMAS, see "Alexander Magruder" and "Francis Waring," q.v.
GREENFIELD, THOMAS TRUMAN (colonel), of Prince George's County, aet. 47, dep. Sep 13, 1729. {PGLR M:520; CHLR Q#2:345} Aet. 49, dep. Jul 7, 1731 and Jul 9, 1731, mentioned Capt. Richard Reed and Capt. George Harris. {PGLR Q:521, 526} See "Phillip Willocy," q.v.
GREENHALGH, EDWARD, of Calvert of St. Mary's County, n.a., dep. Apr 23, 1691. {ARMD 8:247}
GREENHILL, THOMAS, see "Thomas Abbot," q.v.
GREENUP, JOHN, of Prince George's County, aet. 54, dep. Mar 21, 1761, mentioned a dispute about 20 years ago with Elizabeth Johnston. {PGLR RR:233}
GREENWAY, JOHN, see "Mary Greenway," q.v.
GREENWAY, MARY, of St. Mary's County, n.a., dep. Mar 20, 1651, wife of John Greenway, mentioned James Langworth and the accidental shooting death of Philip Anther last Feb 17th at the house of Robert Clark in Newtown where she and John Greenway then lived. {ARMD 10:142-143}
GREENWOOD, JAMES, of Kent County, aet. 49, dep. Apr 7, 1762. {KEEJ - Peregrine Brown folder}
GREENWOOD, JOHN, SR., of Kent County, planter, aet. about 64, dep. Aug 10, 1725. {KELR JS#W:97} Aet. about 73, dep. Jun 6, 1732, mentioned John Stavely, son of James Stavely (deceased). {KELR JS#16:225} See "Joseph Greenwood," q.v.
GREENWOOD, JOSEPH, of Kent County, aet. about 58, dep. Mar 31, 1757, mentioned his father John Greenwood, deceased. {KELR JS#28:377}
GREENWOOD, JOSEPH, of Kent County, aet. about 23, dep. Aug 11, 1757, mentioned his father Joseph Greenwood, deceased. {KELR JS#28:380}

GREER, ANNANIAS, of Prince George's County, aet. 41, dep. Apr 9, 1753. {PGLR NN:282}
GREY, EDWARD, see "Edward Gray," q.v.
GREYNGER, RICHARD, see "Edmond Linsey," q.v.
GRIFFEN, JAMES, of Prince George's County, aet. 67, dep. Aug 5, 1760. {PGLR RR:75}
GRIFFEN, JOHN, of Dorchester County, aet. 55, dep. between Jun 12, 1728 and Jul 16, 1728. {DOLR 8 Old 245}
GRIFFIN, ALICE, see "Ann Johnson," q.v.
GRIFFIN, ANN, of Dorchester County, aet. 48, dep. between Jun 9, 1761 and Oct 31, 1761, mentioned John Lecompte, deceased. {DOLR 18 Old 128}
GRIFFIN, BENJAMIN, of Kent County, aet. about 51, dep. Aug 28, 1734. {KELR JS#18:81}
GRIFFIN, HANNAH, of Dorchester County, n.a., dep. between May 6, 1726 and Aug 14, 1727. {DOLR 8 Old 227}
GRIFFIN, JAMES, of Charles County, aet. 51, dep. Apr 30, 1745, mentioned his father-in-law James Smallwood. {CHLR Z#2:336} James Griffith, aet. 51, dep. Oct 8, 1742, mentioned his father-in-law James Smallwood. {CHLR O#2:469}
GRIFFIN, JOHN, of Dorchester County, n.a., dep. between May 6, 1726 and Aug 14, 1727. {DOLR 8 Old 227}
GRIFFIN, LEWIS, of Dorchester County, aet. 53, dep. between Jun 12, 1728 and Jul 16, 1728. {DOLR 8 Old 245, 430} Lewis Griffen, aet. 57, dep. between Sep 1, 1732 and May 10, 1732/3, mentioned Samuel Millington and John Lun, now deceased. {DOLR 9 Old 57, 64} Lewis Griffin, aet. 67, dep. between Jun 14, 1743 and Aug 1, 1743. {DOLR 12 Old 167}
GRIFFIN, MARY, of Dorchester County, aet. 57, dep. Mar 1, 1775, mentioned old John Pollard about 40 years ago. {DOLR 28 Old 174}
GRIFFIN, NICHOLAS, of Queen Anne's County, aet. about 50, dep. July, 1756(?). {QAEJ - Thomas Wilson folder}
GRIFFIN, SAMUEL, of Dorchester County, aet. 48, dep. between Nov 9, 1742 and Nov 5, 1743, stated that he was shown the bounds of *Dublin* by Thomas Smith about 18 years ago. {DOLR 12 Old 157}
GRIFFITH, BENJAMIN, of Kent County, aet. about 43, dep. Dec 10, 1724. {KELR JS#W:404} Aet. about 51, dep. Oct 22, 1735. {KELR JS#18:192} See "John Gamball," q.v.
GRIFFITH, DANIEL, of Queen Anne's County, aet. 64, dep. Oct 2, 1767. {QAEJ - Downe: oversize folder}
GRIFFITH, ELIZABETH, of Dorchester County, aet. about 50, dep. between Mar 16, 1733/4 and Jul 6, 1734. {DOLR 9 Old 193}
GRIFFITH, GEORGE, of Kent County, aet. about 60, dep. May 22, 1755. {KELR JS#28:134} See "Richard Wallace," q.v.
GRIFFITH, HANNAH C., of Dorchester County, aet. about 65, dep. between Mar 14, 1748 and Apr 22, 1749. {DOLR 14 Old 374} See "Richard Wallace," q.v.

GRIFFITH, HENRY, see "Anthony Chilcutt" and "George Andrew, Jr.," q.v.
GRIFFITH, JAMES, see "James Griffin," q.v.
GRIFFITH, JOHN, of Dorchester County, aet. 38, dep. between Mar 9, 1773 and Feb 5, 1774. {DOLR 27 Old 115} See "Thomas Griffith" and "Edward Poole" and "Noah Pearson" and "Richard Webster" and "Charles Paul" and "Anthony Chilcutt" and "Henry Kimmey" and "Thomas Pindle" and "Compton Guyther," q.v.
GRIFFITH, JOSEPH, see "James Hodson," q.v.
GRIFFITH, LEWIS, of Dorchester County, aet. 54, dep. Aug 22, 1753, mentioned his father (not named). {DOLR 15 Old 74}
GRIFFITH, LEWIS, of Dorchester County, aet. about 60, dep. between Aug 18, 1733 and Mar 15, 1733/4. {DOLR 9 Old 155} Aet. about 60, dep. between Mar 16, 1733/4 and Jul 6, 1734, mentioned William Meredith (deceased), George Hooper, and Sarah Meredith, wife of John Meredith (deceased), when he (Griffith) was a boy. {DOLR 9 Old 193} Lewis Griffith, Sr., n.a., dep. between Nov 28, 1734 and Jul 31, 1735. {DOLR 9 Old 312} Aet. about 66, dep. Aug 24, 1741, mentioned bounds of Howell Powell's land on a point near Cabin Branch about 40 years ago and John Snelson, kinsman to John Snelson, some time later. {DOLR 12 Old 133}
GRIFFITH, LEWIS, see "Noah Pearson" and "George Bozes" and "Thomas Wroughton" and "Robert Griffith," q.v.
GRIFFITH, NATHANIEL, see "John Gamball," q.v.
GRIFFITH, ROBERT, of Dorchester County, aet. 39, dep. between Nov 10, 1761 and Mar 4, 1762, mentioned his brother Lewis Griffith. {DOLR 18 Old 83}
GRIFFITH, SAMUEL, see "Henry Kimmey," q.v.
GRIFFITH, SARAH, see "George Andrew, Jr.," q.v.
GRIFFITH, THOMAS, of Dorchester County, aet. about 63, dep. between Nov 12, 1745 and Nov 11, 1747, stated that he was shown the bounded tree of *Paradice* by John Griffith (now deceased) about 7 or 8 years ago. {DOLR 14 Old 173}
GRINDINGSTONE, CAPTAIN, see "Robert Troope" and "Edmond Linsey," q.v.
GRIPE, JACOB, JR., of Frederick County, aet. 31, dep. affirmed Aug 7, 1772. {FRLR P:309}
GROOM, ELIZABETH, of Queen Anne's County, aet. about 25, dep. Apr, 1769, stated that she had been a servant for James Hutchings. {QAEJ - James Hutchings folder}
GROOM, ROBERT, of Baltimore County, aet. 78, dep. Nov 11, 1768. {BALR AL#G:443}
GROOME, RICHARD, see "Thomas King," q.v.
GROOME, SAMUEL, of Kent County, aet. 63, dep. 1755. {KELR JS#28:137} Aet. 65, dep. 1756. {KELR JS#28:293}
GROOME, SAMUELL, see "Jane Slye," q.v.
GROOME, WILLIAM, see "Aaron Orme," q.v.

GROVES, JOHN, of Charles County, aet. 47, dep. Feb 17, 1742/3. {CHLR O#2:507} Aet. 47, dep. Apr 30, 1744. {CHLR Y#2:12}
GROVES, WILLIAM, of Charles County, aet. 88, dep. May 18, 1763. {CHLR M#3:221}
GRUB, JOHN, see "William Gandie" and "Amy Lambert" and "Brigit Philpot," q.v.
GRUB, MARY, see "William Gandie" and "Amy Lambert" and "Brigit Philpot," q.v.
GUDGINS, JOHN, of Baltimore County, aet. 30, dep. between Apr 11, 1704 and Aug 4, 1704. {BALR HW#2:367}
GUIBERT, JOSHUA, of St. Mary's County, n.a., dep. Jun 29, 1698 in Annapolis. See "John Jee," q.v. {ARMD 23:435, 442, 475}
GUITCHARD, SAMUEL, of Anne Arundel County, aet. 51, dep. May 23, 1715, mentioned Henry Stith (Frith?), blacksmith. {Chancery Court Records PL#3:267-268}
GUN, CHRISTIAN, see "Samuel Magruder 3rd," q.v.
GUNERY, SPRY GODFERY, of Baltimore County, aet. 71, dep. Sep 15, 1750. {BALR TR#E:10}
GUTRIGE, HENRY, see "George Stapleford," q.v.
GUY, WILLIAM, see "John Long, Jr.," q.v.
GUYTHER, COMPTON, of St. Mary's or Charles County, aet. 21, dep. 1668, stated that in the year 1666 he transported into this province a servant, John Griffith, for 4 years service, and the indenture was signed in Wales. {Chancery Court Records CD:2}
GWINN, BENJAMIN, of Charles County, aet. 35, dep. Apr 30, 1744. {CHLR Y#2:11} Aet. 46, dep. Apr 28, 1753. {CHLR D#3:79}
GWINN, JOSEPH, of Charles County, aet. 55, dep. Apr 29, 1754. {CHLR D#3:323}
GWINN, RALPH, of Charles County, aet. 42, dep. Oct 1, 1754. {CHLR E#3:91}
GWITHER, MARY, of St. Mary's or Charles County, n.a., wife of Nicholas Gwither, dep. Oct 17, 1650. {ARMD 10:32}
GWY, ANNE, of Charles County, aet. 50 or thereabouts, dep. Mar 10, 1658. {ARMD 41:293}
GWYNN, RALPH, see "Alexander McPherson," q.v.
GWYTHER, NICHOLAS (captain), of St. Mary's or Charles County, n.a., dep. 1658. {ARMD 41:142, 242} See "Mary Gwither," q.v.
HACK, SEPHARINAH (SEPHARINA), of St. Mary's or Calvert County, aet. 21, dep. affirmed Sep 25, 1657 at Patuxent. {ARMD 10:531}
HACKER, CHARLES, of Dorchester County, aet. about 40, dep. between Mar 15, 1735 and Nov 9, 1737, mentioned his father Richard Hacker (Haker) about 10 years ago. {DOLR 9 Old 493}
HACKETT, FRANCES, see "Jemima Stainton," q.v.
HACKETT, MICHAEL, see "Francis Meeks," q.v.
HACKETT, NICHOLAS, of Dorchester County, aet. 44, dep. Jun 3, 1686. {DOLR 5 Old 36}

HACKETT, OLIVER, of Dorchester County, aet. 51 or 52, dep. between Mar 14, 1771 and Nov 13, 1771, mentioned his father Thomas Hackett upwards of 30 years ago, now deceased. {DOLR 25 Old 238} See "John King" and "Theophilus Hackett" and "Jemima Stainton" and "Roseanna Williams," q.v.

HACKETT, REBECCA, of Dorchester County, aet. about 70, dep. between Mar 14, 1769 and Apr 9, 1770. {DOLR 24 Old 9} Aet. about 70, dep. between Mar 14, 1771 and Nov 13, 1771, mentioned her husband Thomas Hackett, deceased. {DOLR 25 Old 238}

HACKETT, THEOPHILUS, of Dorchester County, aet. 57, dep. between Mar 14, 1769 and Apr 9, 1770, mentioned his father Oliver Hackett (Hacket), deceased. {DOLR 24 Old 9} Aet. 59 or 60, dep. between Nov 12, 1771 and Apr 12, 1772, mentioned his father, mother (deceased), and grandfather (no names given), and his uncle Thomas Hackett. {DOLR 26 Old 50}

HACKETT, THOMAS, of Dorchester County, aet. about 55, dep. between Mar 12, 1744 and Aug 11, 1745. {DOLR 12 Old 250} Aet. about 57, dep. between Mar 11, 1745 and Sep 27, 1746, mentioned Roger Fowler about 40 years who dwelled in a house about 200 yards from the last bounded white oak of *Traverse Purchase* owned by Matthew Travers on Bryan's Branch near land of the Nanticoke Indians. {DOLR 14 Old 102} See "Sarah Andrew" and "Oliver Hackett" and "Rebecca Hackett" and "Theophilus Hackett" and "Billinder Stevens" and "William Hutton" and "Roseanna Williams" and "Solomon Wright," q.v.

HADDEN, WILLIAM, see "John Benny," q.v.

HADDOCK, JAMES, see "Phillip Willocy," q.v.

HAGAN, IGNATIUS, of Charles County, aet. 48, dep. Aug 13, 1734, stated that Thomas Bowling was the eldest son of John and Mary Bowling. {CHLR R#2:528} Aet. 78, dep. Dec 5, 1764. {CHLR P#3:272} See "James Bryan," q.v.

HAGAN, JAMES, of Charles County, aet. 66, dep. Jan 10, 1736/7 and Mar 16, 1737. {CHLR T#2:292, 428} Aet. 74, dep. Jan 9, 1743/4. {CHLR O#2:701}

HAGAN, JAMES, of Prince George's County, aet. 37, dep. Feb 20, 1767. {PGLR BB#2:169}

HAGAN, JAMES, see "James Bryan" and "Thomas Hagan," q.v.

HAGAN, JOHN, of Charles County, aet. 26, dep. Jan 16, 1753. {CHLR B#3:349}

HAGAN, MARY, of Charles County, aet. 50, dep. Dec 27, 1766, mentioned William Simpson, his wife (not named) and his daughter Elizabeth Simpson. {CHLR O#3:143} See "James Bryan," q.v.

HAGAN, THOMAS, see "James Bryan" and "William Hagan," q.v.

HAGAN, THOMAS, of Charles County, aet. 53, dep. Mar 16, 1737/8, mentioned his father Thomas Hagan. {CHLR T#2:429} Aet. 54, dep. Jun 16, 1738. {CHLR T#2:495}

HAGAN, THOMAS, of Charles County, aet. 32, dep. Aug 11, 1755, mentioned his uncle James Hagan, deceased. {CHLR E#3:501}

HAGAN, THOMAS, SR., of Prince George's County, aet. 27, dep. May 31, 1750. {PGLR NN:59}

HAGAN, WILLIAM, of Charles County, aet. 71, dep. Feb 25, 1767, mentioned his brother Thomas Hagan. {CHLR Q#3:195} See "James Bryan," q.v.
HAGER, JONATHAN, of Frederick County, aet. 53, dep. 1767. {FRLR L:60}
HAGER, JONATHAN (captain), of Frederick County, aet. 40, dep. Oct 21, 1762. {FRLR H:196}
HAGER, JONATHAN, see "Joseph Chapline," q.v.
HAGGATE, HUMPHERIE, of Charles County, aet. 33 or thereabouts, dep. Apr 22, 1662, stated that Ursula Lenton was the widow of Joseph Lenton who was newly dead and left a will. A later entry stated that the widow and two children (not named) also died suddenly. {CHLR A:204, 205; ARMD 53:208} Humphery Haggat (Humphery Haggate), n.a., dep. Dec 18, 1662. {CHLR B:53, ARMD 53:313}
HAGGATY, JOHN, of Prince George's County, aet. 45, dep. Aug 29, 1763, mentioned his father (not named). {PGLR TT:127}
HAIL, MATTHEW, of Baltimore County, n.a., dep. Jan 11, 1767. {BALR B#P:459}
HAILS, ROGER, see "Ann Collins," q.v.
HAISLIP, HENRY, of Charles County, aet. 42, dep. Oct 17, 1749. {CHLR Z#2:523} Henry Hazlip, aet. 50, dep. Sep 8, 1756. {CHLR F#3:223} Henry Hayslip, aet. 54, dep. May 23, 1761. {CHLR K#3:223} Henry Haislip, aet. 65, dep. May 20, 1772. {CHLR T#3:619}
HAISLIP, ROBERT, of Charles County, aet. 54, dep. Jun 3, 1760. {CHLR K#3:9} Aet. 57, dep. Nov 8, 1762. {CHLR M#3:122} Robert Hayslip, aet. 59, dep. May 23, 1761. {CHLR K#3:223} Robert Hazlip, aet. 48, dep. Sep 8, 1756. {CHLR F#3:654}
HAISLOPER, MARY, of Charles County, aet. 33, dep. Oct 11, 1772. {CHLR U#3:263}
HALBERT, ALEXANDER, see "Benjamin Adams," q.v.
HALES, ROGER, see "Ann Collins," q.v.
HALFHEAD, JOHN, of St. Mary's County, n.a., dep. Oct 11, 1650, mentioned Mr. Hebden, deceased. {ARMD 10:37}
HALL, BENJAMIN, see "Thomas Mullikin," q.v.
HALL, COLONEL, see "Benjamin Rumsey," q.v.
HALL, ELIZABETH, of Charles County, aet. 27, dep. Feb 20, 1738. {CHLR T#2:536}
HALL, IGNATIUS, of Charles County, aet. 50, dep. Sep 28, 1767. {CHLR P#3:614}
HALL, JOHN, of Kent County, aet. about 62, dep. Oct, 1771. {TAEJ - Matthew Tilghman folder}
HALL, JOHN, of Kent County, aet. about 50, dep. Aug, 1772. {TAEJ - Matthew Tilghman folder}
HALL, JOHN (captain), of Baltimore County, aet. 43, dep. Jan 4, 1763. {BALR B#L:500} John Hall, of Cranberry, aet. 44, dep. Nov 11, 1764. {BALR B#N:460}
HALL, MARY, of Dorchester County, aet. about 35, dep. between Nov 11, 1746 and Apr 14, 1748, mentioned her mother Ellinor Smith, widow of James Smith, about 23 or 24 years ago; also mentioned Henry Smith (deceased) and that

Ellinor Smith was sister of said Henry Smith. {DOLR 14 Old 231} See "Ellinor Lewis," q.v.

HALL, ROBERT CLARK, of Charles County, aet. 52, dep. Jun 6, 1772. {CHLR U#3:23}

HALL, VERLINDA, see "Mary Trundle," q.v.

HALLEY, NATHANIEL, of Prince George's County, aet. 44, dep. Mar 15, 1774, mentioned Malcom McBean about 20 years ago. {PGLR BB#3:399}

HALLOWELL, BENJAMIN, of North Carolina, n.a., dep. Aug 14, 1723 in Queen Anne's County, stated that he has been acquainted with John Jordan, Sr. and wife Charity for the past 12 years and they did acknowledge that John Jordan, Jr. (who has been almost blind for some time) was their lawful son; also stated that John Jordan, Sr. has been dead about 3 years. {QALR IK#B:209}

HALLY, JOHN, of Charles County, aet. 59, dep. Aug 23, 1745. {CHLR Z#2:464}

HALPENNY, ELIZABETH, see "John Harris" and "Thomas Taylor" and "Robert Jones," q.v.

HALPENNY, JOHN, see "Robert Jones," q.v.

HALSAY, JOHN, of Prince George's County, n.a., dep. Nov 21, 1763. {PGLR TT:196}

HALSELL, JOHN, of Prince George's County, aet. 54, dep. Apr 21, 1767. {PGLR BB#2:121}

HAMBLETON, JOANNA, of Queen Anne's County, aet. 50, wife of John Hawkins Hambleton, dep. Aug, 1743. {QAEJ - Sweatnam Burn folder}

HAMBLETON, JOHN, of St. Mary's County, n.a., dep. Jun 8, 1653. {ARMD 10:274}

HAMBLETON, JOHN HAWKINS, of Queen Anne's County, aet. about 46, dep. Aug, 1743. {QAEJ - Sweatnam Burn folder} See "Joanna Hambleton," q.v.

HAMBLETON, THOMAS, of Charles County, aet. 40, dep. Nov 15, 1756. {CHLR F#3:300}

HAMBLETON, WILLIAM,, of Charles County, aet. 33 or thereabouts, dep. Dec 22, 1669, stated that about 1657 he lived at Capt. Giles Brent's on the Potomac River for 9 or 10 months, and William Green (carpenter) and wife (not named) also lived there. {ARMD 51:18}

HAMBROOK, JOHN, see "James Wallace," q.v.

HAMIL (HAMILL), JOHN, of Charles County, aet. 37, dep. Feb 14, 1728. {CHLR Q#2:347} Aet. 38, dep. May 5, 1730. {CHLR Q#2:403} Aet. 42, Aug 18, 1735. {CHLR T#2:99} Aet. 42, dep. Oct 21, 1736. {CHLR T#2:268} Aet. 46, dep. Feb 13, 1738/9. {CHLR T#2:537} Aet. 52, dep. Feb 12, 1744/5. {CHLR Z#2:252} Aet. 54, dep. Apr 3, 1747. {CHLR Z#2:82} Aet. 56, dep. Mar 14, 1747/8. {CHLR Z#2:348} Aet. 59, dep. Sep 18, 1752. {CHLR R#3:204} Aet. 60, dep. Aug 20, 1753. {CHLR D#3:154} Aet. 61, dep. Apr 29, 1754. {CHLR D#3:323} Aet. 69, dep. Mar 4, 1762. {CHLR K#3:475} Aet. 70, dep. Dec 6, 1763. {CHLR M#3:502}

HAMIL (HAMILL), JOHN, of Charles County, aet. 29, dep. Sep 18, 1731. {CHLR R#2:46}

HAMIL (HAMILL), JOHN, of Charles County, aet. 60, dep. Oct 10, 1738. {CHLR T#2:514}

HAMILTON, ANDREW, of Prince George's County, aet. 46, dep. Sep 1, 1762. {PGLR RR:229} Aet. 56, dep. Sep 20, 1771. {PGLR AA#2:431}
HAMILTON, JOHN, of Charles County, aet. 52, dep. Jul 5, 1762 and Aug 6, 1762. {CHLR M#3:4, 213}
HAMILTON, PATRICK, of Charles County, aet. 45, dep. Aug 6, 1762, mentioned Francis Green about 5 or 6 years ago, now deceased. {CHLR M#3:4}
HAMILTON, THOMAS, of Prince George's County, aet. 55 years and some months, dep. Sep 2, 1765. {PGLR BB#2:18} Aet. 59, dep. Jul 8, 1769, mentioned his father-in-law Thomas Evans. {PGLR AA#2:11} Aet. 60, dep. Mar 23, 1771, stated that he has known this area for 50 years; also mentioned Dr. Coleman. {PGLR AA#2:430}
HAMMON, BENJAMIN, see "Thomas James," q.v.
HAMMOND, WILLIAM, see "Thomas Gorsuch," q.v.
HAMPER, THOMAS, of St. Mary's County, n.a., dep. 1649, mentioned George Manners and Mrs. Margaret Brent. {ARMD 4:482}
HAMPTON, THOMAS, of Queen Anne's County, aet. about 60, dep. Sep, 1733, stated that he has lived on *Long Point* for the last 23 years and has been a resident of Queen Anne's County for nearly 30 years. {QAEJ - James Hutchens folder}
HANDY, JOHN (captain), of Dorchester County, aet. about 49, dep. between Nov 9, 1742 and Nov 5, 1743, mentioned Charles Nutter and his brother William Nutter about 19 or 20 years ago. {DOLR 12 Old 157}
HANLEY, ROBERT, of Charles County, aet. 46, dep. May 17, 1733. {CHLR R#2:335}
HANSON, GUSTAVUS, of Kent County, aet. 44, dep. 1769. {KELR DD#3:205} Aet. 49, dep. 1775. {KELR DD#4:59}
HANSON, HANS (HANCE), of Kent County, aet. 40, dep. Dec 5, 1752, mentioned Edward Skidmore about 10 years ago who was the son of Edward Skidmore (both deceased); also mentioned Michael Skidmore, brother of Edward Skidmore (the father) aforesaid. {KELR JS#27:247} See "Margaret Hanson" and "George Copper," q.v.
HANSON, JOHN, of Charles County, aet. 66, dep. Sep 9, 1747. {CHLR Z#2:186}
HANSON, JOHN, of Prince George's County, aet. 49, dep. Mar 6, 1759. {PGLR PP:279, pt. 2}
HANSON, JOHN, see "Joseph Pulluffus," q.v.
HANSON, JONATHAN, of Baltimore County, aet. about 58, dep. between Oct 11, 1768 and Mar 11, 1772. {BALR AL#D:438}
HANSON, MARGARET, of Kent County, aet. 42, dep. circa 1750, mentioned her husband Hans Hanson. {KEEJ - Isaac and Thomas Crown folder}
HANSON, ROBERT, of Charles County, aet. 45, dep. Jun 10, 1725. {CHLR P#2:67} Aet. 56, dep. Jul 6, 1736, mentioned George Goodrick, son of Robert Goodrick. {CHLR T#2:225} Aet. 58, dep. Apr 13, 1738. {CHLR T#2:225} Aet. 61, dep. Mar 25, 1740. {CHLR O#2:242} Aet. 62, dep. Mar 8, 1741/2. {CHLR O#2:321} Aet. 63, dep.

Jan 9, 1743/4. {CHLR O#2:700} Aet. 64, dep. Oct 1, 1744, mentioned Juliana Price (widow), Thomas Hussey Luckett and wife Elizabeth Luckett, and Mary Price, deceased. {CHLR Z#2:189} Col. Robert Hanson, aet. 65, dep. Jul 23, 1745. {CHLR Z#2:394}

HANSON, ROBERT, of Charles County, aet. 57, dep. Sep 1, 1727. {CHLR T#2:391} Aet. 58, dep. May 5, 1730. {CHLR Q#2:449}

HANSON, ROBERT, see "Charles Byrn" and "Samuel Hanson" and "William Hanson" and "Joseph Pulluffus," q.v.

HANSON, SAMUEL, of Charles County, aet. 39, dep. Oct 1, 1744, mentioned his parents Robert and Benedict (Hoskins) Hanson. {CHLR Z#2:189}

HANSON, THEOPHILUS, of Charles County, aet. 27, dep. Nov 20, 1770, mentioned his father William Hanson. {CHLR T#3:242}

HANSON, THOMAS, of Charles County, aet. 39, dep. Jan 31, 1776 and Feb 14, 1776, mentioned his father William Hanson. {CHLR X#3:537, Y#3:380}

HANSON, WILLIAM, of Charles County, aet. 50, dep. Dec 15, 1760. {CHLR K#3:149} Aet. 52, dep. Aug 6, 1762. {CHLR M#3:4} Aet. 54, dep. Sep 3, 1764. {CHLR N#3:166} Aet. 55, dep. Nov 13, 1765, mentioned his father Robert Hanson about 36 years ago. {CHLR N#3:789} See "Theophilus Hanson" and "William Marlow," q.v.

HARBERT, ALEXANDER, of Prince George's County, aet. 60, dep. Sep 25, 1733. {PGLR T:17}

HARBIN, EDWARD VILLERS, see "Edward Willett" and "William Tuell," q.v.

HARBIN, ELISHA, of Charles County, aet. 46, dep. Oct 1, 1771. {CHLR U#3:18}

HARBIN, FRANCIS (captain), of St. Mary's or Charles County, n.a., dep. Jun 29, 1698 in Annapolis. {ARMD 23:435}

HARBIN, JOHN, see "Edward Willett," q.v.

HARBIN, LYDIA, of Prince George's County, aet. 44, dep. Jun 1, 1767, mentioned Thomas Lucas about 15 years ago. {PGLR BB#2:114}

HARBIN, WILLIAM, see "William Tuell," q.v.

HARDEKIN, EDWARD, see "Joseph Bowdle" and "Peter Edmondson," q.v.

HARDESTY, SAMUEL, of Baltimore County, aet. 43, dep. Apr 6, 1773. {BALR AL#G:448}

HARDING, JOHN, see "Elizabeth Barker," q.v.

HARDMAN, THOMAS, of Charles County, aet. 54, dep. Oct 3, 1767. {CHLR P#3:667}

HARDY, GEORGE, see "Richard Blew," q.v.

HARDY, JAMES, of Dorchester County, aet. 49, dep. between Mar 14, 1769 and Apr 9, 1770, mentioned Capt. Thomas Hicks, now deceased, about 17 years ago, and John Thompson, son of Joseph, late of Dorchester County, deceased, about 10 or 11 years ago showed him a bounded tree. {DOLR 24 Old 9}

HARE, HENRY, of Talbot County, n.a., dep. Mar 15, 1663/4, servant of Henry Morgan of Isle of Kent, now deceased. {ARMD 54:368}

HARE, JAMES, of Charles County, aet. 30, dep. Nov 23, 1658. {CHLR A:27}

HARGETON, EDWARD, of Dorchester County, aet. 49, dep. Aug 22, 1744. {DOLR 12 Old 113} Edward Hargaton, aet. 50, dep. between Jun 11, 1745 and May 23, 1746. {DOLR 14 Old 50}

HARGRAVE, RICHARD, SR., of Dorchester County, aet. 60, dep. Apr 16, 1672, stated that Ann Mason, wife of Col. Lemuel Mason and daughter of Henry Sewell, merchant, was born "about seaven or eight and thirty years since." {DOLR 4 Old 6}

HARNAM (HAVNAM?), JOHN, of Talbot County, aet. 66, dep. Feb 16, 1708/9 to prove the will of William Dixon, deceased. {Will Book 12:17, pt. 2}

HARPAM, WILLIAM, of St. Mary's County, clerk of the Mayor's Court in St. Mary's City, n.a., dep. Apr 15, 1698 in Annapolis. {ARMD 23:420}

HARPER, DAVID, of Dorchester County, aet. about 38, dep. between Mar 14, 1769 and Apr 9, 1770. {DOLR 24 Old 9}

HARPER, EDWARD, of Dorchester County, aet. about 60, dep. between Aug 14, 1750 and Dec 20, 1750. {DOLR 14 Old 497}

HARPER, FRANCIS, of Dorchester County, aet. about 55, dep. between Mar 12, 1750 and Jun 10, 1751, mentioned his father (not named). {DOLR 14 Old 525} See "Anne Shenton," q.v.

HARPER, JAMES, of Dorchester County, aet. about 57, dep. between Nov 11, 1760 and Apr 4, 1761. {DOLR 17 Old 329}

HARPER, JOHN, of Dorchester County, aet. 63, dep. between Jun 12, 1764 and Aug 6, 1765, stated that he was shown the bounds of *Calis* about 42 years ago by Richard Hart, lately deceased. {DOLR 20 Old 218} Aet. about 64, cooper, dep. between Mar 13, 1764 and Jun 4, 1767, mentioned John Littleton about 20 years ago, now generally reported to be dead. {DOLR 21 Old 382} Aet. 70 odd years, dep. between Nov 12, 1771 and Apr 17, 1772, mentioned Thomas Williams about 30 years ago, now deceased. {DOLR 26 Old 50} See "William Harper" and "Edward Rumsey," q.v.

HARPER, JOHN, SR., of Dorchester County, cooper, aet. 64, dep. between Jun 11, 1765 and Aug 15, 1765, mentioned Arthur Hart and his son Richard Hart about 50 years ago. {DOLR 20 Old 244}

HARPER, JOSEPH, of Dorchester County, aet. 43, dep. between Mar 12, 1750 and Jun 10, 1751. {DOLR 14 Old 525} Aet. 55, dep. between Nov 10, 1761 and Jan 21, 1762. {DOLR 18 Old 87}

HARPER, MARY, of Dorchester County, aet. 60, dep. between May 6, 1726 and Aug 14, 1727. {DOLR 8 Old 227}

HARPER, SAMUEL, of Dorchester County, aet. 66, dep. between May 6, 1726 and Aug 14, 1727, mentioned Charles Stapleford, brother of George Stapleford. {DOLR 8 Old 227}

HARPER, SAMUEL, of Dorchester County, aet. 66, dep. between Jun 16, 1735 and Dec 16, 1735, mentioned Samuel Millington when he (Harper) was about 10 years old. {DOLR 9 Old 335}

HARPER, SAMUEL, see "Richard Willis," q.v.

HARPER, SARAH, of Dorchester County, aet. 60, dep. between Mar 14, 1748 and Apr 22, 1749. {DOLR 14 Old 374}
HARPER, THOMAS, see "Edward Rumsey," q.v.
HARPER, WILLIAM, of Dorchester County, aet. 37, dep. between Mar 11, 1755 and Jul 23, 1755, mentioned old William Rotten about 27 or 28 years ago. {DOLR 15 Old 452} Aet. about 43, cooper, son of John Harper, dep. between Mar 13, 1764 and Jun 4, 1764. {DOLR 21 Old 382} Aet. about 47, dep. between Aug 13, 1765 and Dec 28, 1765, mentioned his father (not named). {DOLR 21 Old 42} See "Richard Willis," q.v.
HARPER, WILLIAM, SR., of Dorchester County, aet. 61, dep. Aug 30, 1738, stated that he was shown the bounds of *Hall's Fortune* by William Chettel (Chittle) about 42 years ago. {DOLR 12 Old 102}
HARPIN, THOMAS, see "Benjamin Palmes," q.v.
HARRICE, JOHN, of St. Mary's County, aet. 22, dep. Mar 2, 1664/5. {ARMD 49:458}
HARRINGTON, DAVID, of Queen Anne's County, planter, aet. 47, dep. Aug 18, 1747, stated that some time this fall it will be 37 years since he went to live with David Arey, of Talbot County, and at that time Esther Arey, daughter of David and wife Elizabeth, was not more than 5 or 6 months of age. {TALR 17:117}
HARRINGTON, JOHN, of Dorchester County, aet. 62, dep. between Jun 14, 1768 and Sep 3, 1768, mentioned his father John Harrington and mother Mary Harrington about 50 years ago; also mentioned William Ross, son of John Ross. {DOLR 23 Old 271} See "Peter Harrington," q.v.
HARRINGTON, JOSEPH, see "Peter Harrington," q.v.
HARRINGTON, MARY, see "John Harrington," q.v.
HARRINGTON, PETER, of Dorchester County, aet. 50, dep. between Apr 20, 1768 and May 27, 1768, mentioned his father John Harrington and his brother Joseph Harrington. {DOLR 22 Old 423} Aet. 57 or 58, dep. between Aug 10, 1773 and Nov 30, 1773, mentioned his brother John Harrington about 13 years ago. {DOLR 27 Old 354}
HARRINGTON, RICHARD, of Talbot County, n.a., dep. Aug 3, 1736. {TALR 14:173}
HARRIS, ALES, of Charles County, aet. 48, dep. May 12, 1659. {CHLR A:51, ARMD 53:42}
HARRIS, ANNE (Mrs.), of Prince George's County, aet. 50, dep. Jul 23, 1747. {PGLR BB:300}
HARRIS (HARRISS), BENJAMIN, of Prince George's County, aet. 51, dep. Sep 2, 1765, mentioned his mother Rachel Harris and stated that his father (not named) died about 40 years ago. {PGLR BB#2:16-17} Aet. near 53, dep. Apr 21, 1767, mentioned his father (not named) about 40 years ago. {PGLR BB#2:118} Aet. 57, dep. Sep 20, 1771, mentioned Thomas and Mordica Coleman and their father (not named) about 46 or 47 years ago. {PGLR AA#2:431}

HARRIS, GEORGE, of Charles County, aet. 30, dep. Jun 29, 1663, stated that John Lumbroso's maid Elisabeth Wiles told him she had laid with him and said he would marry her whereby he had brought her to shame. {CHLR B:165} See "Thomas Truman Greenfield," q.v.

HARRIS, JAMES, of Kent County, aet. about 42, dep. Dec 10, 1724. {KELR JS#W:404} Aet. about 48, dep. Jul 30, 1730. {KELR JS#16:41}

HARRIS, JOHN, SR., of Prince George's County, aet. 67, dep. Aug 22, 1753 (1757?), mentioned his father John Harris, deceased. {PGLR PP:64, pt. 2}

HARRIS, JOHN, of Dorchester County, aet. about 56, dep. between Nov 13, 1770 and Aug 2, 1771, mentioned his father John Harris about 45 years ago. {DOLR 25 Old 26} Aet. about 56, dep. between Nov 12, 1771 and Dec 17, 1771, mentioned James Willson, William Willson, Joseph Willson, and Thomas Willson, all brothers, who ran the bounds of *Brotherly Kindness* around 1743. {DOLR 26 Old 34} John Harriss, aet. about 45, dep. between Aug 14, 1759 and Mar 11, 1761, mentioned his mother (not named) about 36 years ago. {DOLR 17 Old 376}

HARRIS, JOHN, of Dorchester County, aet. about 50, dep. between Aug 16, 1728 and Jan 28, 1728/9, mentioned Elizabeth Halpenny who at that time, about 9 years ago, was the widow of John Allford, deceased. {DOLR 8 Old 268}

HARRIS, JOHN, of Kent County, aet. about 76, dep. Oct 3, 1748. {KELR JS#26:161}

HARRIS (HARRISS), JOHN, of Charles County, aet. 54, dep. Apr 30, 1745. {CHLR Z#2:336}

HARRIS (HARRISS), JOHN, of Prince George's County, aet. 70, dep. Aug 5, 1760. {PGLR RR:74} John Harris, aet. 79, dep. Oct 23, 1770, mentioned John Cawood about 24 years ago. {PGLR AA#2:497}

HARRIS, JOHN, see "William Rumbold" and "Abraham Gambell" and "Isaac Nicolls," q.v.

HARRIS, OLIVER, of Charles County, aet. 76, dep. Apr 24, 1755. {CHLR E#3:132}

HARRIS (HARRISS), OLIVER, of Prince George's County, aet. 77, dep. Jan 21, 1760, mentioned John Wood about 40 years ago. {PGLR RR:39} See "Philip Bryan," q.v.

HARRIS, RACHEL, see "Benjamin Harris," q.v.

HARRIS, SAMUELL, of Charles County, aet. 40, dep. May 12, 1659. {CHLR A:51, ARMD 53:42}

HARRIS (HARRISE), SAMUELL, of Charles County, aet. 24, dep. Mar 4, 1661. {ARMD 53:191}

HARRIS, WILLIAM, of Kent County, gentleman, aet. 58, dep. 1708. {KELR JS#N:84}

HARRISON, JOSEPH, of Charles County, n.a., dep. Jul 8, 1662, stated that Katherine Bud is known in Accomacke for loose living and her husband (not named) kept cattle for a living. {CHLR A:220} See "Mathias O'Brian," q.v.

HARRISON, JOSEPH HANSON, of Charles County, aet. 41, dep. May 18, 1763. {CHLR M#3:221} Aet. 46, dep. Oct 23, 1768. {CHLR X#3:13} Aet. 50, dep. May 27, 1772. {CHLR U#3:20}
HARRISON, PETTER, of Talbot County, n.a., dep. Mar 18, 1672/3. {ARMD 54:560}
HARRISON, RICHARD (colonel), of Charles County, aet. 41, dep. Dec 13, 1757, mentioned Thomas Taylor about 27 or 28 years ago. {CHLR H#3:120}
HARRISON, WILLIAM, of Talbot County, n.a., dep. Sep 2, 1736, mentioned William Skinner, wife Hesther, and their son Philemon around 1725. {TALR 14:216}
HARRYMAN, GEORGE, SR., of Baltimore County, aet. 65 or thereabouts, dep. Sep 20, 1767. {BALR AL#A:123-124}
HARRYMAN, SAMUEL, of Baltimore County, aet. 68, dep. Sep 6, 1763. {BALR B#M:173}
HART, ARTHUR, of Dorchester County, aet. about 53, dep. between Jun 12, 1764 and Aug 6, 1765, mentioned his father Richard Hart. {DOLR 20 Old 218} Aet. about 58, dep. between Nov 14, 1769 and May 21, 1770. {DOLR 24 Old 27} See "John Harper, Sr." and "James Insley," q.v.
HART, RICHARD, of Dorchester County, aet. 53, dep. between Jun 17, 1734 and Sep 19, 1734, mentioned the survey of *Safford* about 30 years ago. {DOLR 9 Old 249} See "Arthur Hart" and "John Harper" and "Arthur Smith" and "John Harper, Sr.," q.v.
HART, WILLIAM, of Frederick County, n.a., dep. Dec 2, 1765. {ARMD 32:156-157}
HARTRUP, ELIZABETH, see "John Demall," q.v.
HARTRUP, RICHARD, see "John Demall," q.v.
HARTT, ROBERT, of Dorchester County, aet. 84, dep. between Nov 16, 1734 and Apr 10, 1735. {DOLR 9 Old 436} See "James Insley," q.v.
HARVEY, HANNAH, of Queen Anne's County, aet. about 46, dep. Feb, 1737. {QAEJ - Alexander Toulson folder}
HARVEY, JOHN, of Prince George's County, aet. 66, dep. Aug 14, 1762. {PGLR BB#2:147-148} John Harvie, aet. 60 or thereabouts, dep. Mar 1, 1756. {PGLR NN:469} See "Mark Webb," q.v.
HARVEY, MARY, see "Lucretia Ward," q.v.
HARVEY, THOMAS, of Charles County, n.a., dep. 1658. {ARMD 41:236}
HARVEY, THOMAS, of Queen Anne's County, aet. about 44, dep. Feb, 1737. { QAEJ - Alexander Toulson folder}
HARVY, THOMAS, of Kent Island, Queen Anne's County, aet. about 40, dep. Sep, 1733. {QAEJ - James Hutchens folder}
HARWOOD, JOHN, see "William Warner," q.v.
HARWOOD, REBECCAH, see "Philemon Lecompte," q.v.
HARWOOD, RICHARD, see "Robert Tyler," q.v.
HARWOOD, THOMAS (captain), of Calvert County, n.a., dep. Oct 25, 1664. {ARMD 49:293}

HARWOOD, THOMAS (major), of Prince George's County, aet. 51, dep. Dec 22, 1747. {PGLR BB:666} Aet. 64, dep. May 11, 1762. {PGLR RR:267} Aet. not given, dep. Jan 31, 1766. {PGLR TT:568}
HASELDINE (HAZELDINE), HUMPHREY, see "Daniel Pearl" and "Thomas Wilson," q.v.
HATCH, JOHN, of Charles County, aet. 45, dep. Jan 26, 1658/9. {CHLR A:35}
HATCHE, MRS., see "Elisabeth Atwickes" and "Thomas Lomax," q.v.
HATCHESON, JOHN, see "James Wilson," q.v.
HATCHESON, NATHAN, of Kent County, aet. 43, dep. 1775. {KELR DD#5:83}
HATCHINSON, VINCENT, see "Philip Davis," q.v.
HATHMAN, JOHN, of Charles County, aet. 26, dep. May 3, 1742. {CHLR O#2:380}
HATTON, JAMES, see "Edward Elliott" and "Susanna Ashcroft," q.v.
HATTON, JOSEPH, of Prince George's County, aet. 52, dep. Mar 25, 1743. {PGLR Y:657} See "Thomas Middleton," q.v.
HATTON, NATHANIEL, of Prince George's County, aet. 37, dep. Feb 2, 1761. {PGLR RR:235} Aet. 38, dep. Sep 12, 1761. {PGLR RR:180}
HATTON, THOMAS, of St. Mary's County, aet. 44, dep. Jul 23, 1744. {ARMD 23:475, CHLR Y#2:222}
HATTON, THOMAS, of St. Mary's County, His Lordship's Secretary, n.a., dep. Jul 16, 1651, stated that Thomas Motham, gentleman, one of the Clarks in the Six Clark's Office in Chancery Lane, London, England, now deceased, "did about the latter end of March last was eight years" give to Thomas Hatton the Younger his godson (this deponent's son), born Mar 14, 1642, a silver and guilt spoon of about £20 value. {ARMD 10:86}
HAWKER, THOMAS, of Charles County, n.a., dep. 1658. {ARMD 41:218}
HAWKINS, ALEXANDER SMITH, of Charles County, aet. 67, dep. Sep 20, 1758. {CHLR H#3:487} Aet. about 76, dep. Oct 31, 1766 and Nov 8, 1766. {CHLR P#3:278, 283} Aet. 76, dep. May 5, 1767. {CHLR P#3:657}
HAWKINS, HENRY, see "John Baker," q.v.
HAWKINS, JAMES, of Prince George's County, aet. 35, dep. Mar 10, 1769. {PGLR AA#2:150}
HAWKINS, JOHN, of Harford County, aet. 59, dep. May 25, 1775. {Land Commission, 1774, Harford County Genealogical Society Newsletter, Jan, 1993, p. 3}
HAWKINS, JOHN, of Harford County, aet. 69, dep. May 25, 1775. {Land Commission, 1774, Harford County Genealogical Society Newsletter, Jan, 1993, p. 3}
HAWKINS, JOHN, JR., of Prince George's County, aet. 39, dep. Jun 18, 1752. {PGLR NN:34} See "James Green," q.v.
HAWKINS, MATTHEW, of Baltimore County, aet. 75, dep. between Nov 25, 1760 and Apr 13, 1761. {BALR B#L:196}
HAWKINS, NATHAN, of Baltimore County, aet. 40, dep. May 7, 1764, mentioned his father-in-law James Boring, deceased. {BALR B#N:139}

HAWKINS, ROBERT, of Harford County, aet. about 57, mentioned his father Robert Hawkins, deceased. {Land Commission, 1774, Harford County Genealogical Society Newsletter, Jan, 1993, p. 3} **Deposition taken on May 25, 1775.**
HAWTON, THOMAS, SR., of Charles County, aet. 64, dep. between Aug 18, 1763 and Dec 6, 1763, mentioned his brother William Hawton. {CHLR M#3:504}
HAWTON, WILLIAM, see "Thomas Hawton, Sr.," q.v.
HAYS, BARTHOLOMEW, of Dorchester County, aet. about 28, dep. between Nov 11, 1755 and May 29, 1756. {DOLR 15 Old 363} Bartholomew Hayes, aet. about 33, dep. between Aug 12, 1760 and Mar 2, 1761. {DOLR 17 Old 262}
HAYS, JAMES, of Charles County, aet. 23, dep. Apr 22, 1662. {CHLR A:202, ARMD 53:205} James Hays (Hay), n.a., dep. Jul 30, 1663 and Jan 12, 1664/5. {CHLR B:169, 423}
HAYS (HAYES), JAMES, of Dorchester County, aet. 56, dep. between Mar 13, 1753 and Jun 2, 1753. {DOLR 15 Old 134} See "John Andrew," q.v.
HAYS (HAYES), JAMES, SR., of Dorchester County, aet. 66, dep. between Aug 12, 1760 and Mar 2, 1761. {DOLR 17 Old 262}
HAYS, PATRICK, of Charles County, aet. 23, dep. Mar 26, 1662. {CHLR B:5}
HAYS, THOMAS, of Charles County, aet. 55, dep. Aug 6, 1736. {CHLR T#2:224} Aet. 50, dep. Mar 29, 1738. {CHLR T#2:462} Aet. 65, dep. Jan 9, 1743/4. {CHLR O#2:700}
HAYS, WILLIAMSON, of Charles County, aet. 43, dep. Jan 22, 1755, mentioned his uncle John Briscoe. {CHLR E#3:137}
HAYNES, JOHN, of Dorchester County, aet. 62, dep. Mar 11, 1706/7. {DOLR 6 Old 119}
HAYWARD, FRANCIS, of Dorchester County, aet. 59, dep. Sep 17, 1744, stated that the boundary marker for *Sandy Neck* was about ¼ mile below William Turpin's orchard. {DOLR 12 Old 107} See "William Wall," q.v.
HAYWARD, JOHN, of Dorchester County, aet. 52, dep. between Nov 16, 1734 and Apr 10, 1735, mentioned a conversation with William Wheyland regarding Mullican's Branch about 4 or 5 years ago. {DOLR 9 Old 436}
HAYWOOD, RALPE, of St. Mary's County, n.a., dep. Aug 10, 1661. {ARMD 41:484}
HAZELDINE, ABIGAIL, see "Ann Morton," q.v.
HAZELDINE, RICHARD, see "Ann Morton," q.v.
HAZLIP, HENRY, see "Henry Haislip," q.v.
HEARD, BRIGIT, see "Walter Story," q.v.
HEARD, WILLIAM, of Charles County, n.a., dep. Jul 8, 1662 and Nov 4, 1663. {CHLR A:224, CHLR B:201} See "Walter Story" and "Mathias O'Brian," q.v.
HEARN, DANIEL, see "Richard Warfield" and "Robert Ridgely," q.v.
HEATHER, EDWARD, of Queen Anne's County, aet. 47, dep. Mar, 1746. {QAEJ - Benjamin Tasker folder}
HEATHER, THOMAS, see "William McCollister," q.v.
HEBDEN, MR., see "John Halfhead," q.v.
HEBORN, THOMAS, see "Thomas Heyborn," q.v.

HEBOURN, JAMES, see "John Hepbourn," q.v.
HEDGES, WILLIAM, of Frederick County, aet. 28, dep. Aug 31, 1765, mentioned Rev. William Williams about 5 years ago. {FRLR K:425}
HELLENA, ANDREW, of Kent County, n.a., dep. Sep 1, 1658. {ARMD 54:140}
HELMES (HELME), JOHN, of Charles County, n.a., dep. Dec 18, 1662 and Oct 13, 1663, mentioned his master John Meekes. {CHLR B:50, 179}
HEMSLEY, MARY, see "John Fendall" and "John Courts," q.v.
HEMSLEY, MRS., of Anne Arundel County, n.a., dep. Jan 28, 1715. {ARMD 25:333}
HEMSLEY, PHILEMON, see "John Fendall" and "John Courts," q.v.
HENDERSON, JACOB (reverend), of Prince George's County, aet. 58, dep. Mar 24, 1742, mentioned Col. Addison. {PGLR Y:654} Aet. 63, dep. Dec 22, 1747. {PGLR BB:666} See "Mash Benjamin Duvall," q.v.
HENEBERRY, EDWARD, of Prince George's County, aet. 46, dep. Mar 9, 1728/9, mentioned Thomas Price about 17 years ago, now deceased. {PGLR M:478} Aet. 46, dep. Jun 11, 1727, mentioned Christopher Beane and his children (not named) about 16 or 17 years ago. {PGLR Q:466}
HENNESS, SAMUEL, of Prince George's County, aet. 57, dep. Jun 11, 1764, stated that he was bound as a boy to Benjamin Brashears. {PGLR TT:371}
HENNINGTON, ELIAS, of Charles County, aet. 40, dep. Jul 5, 1729. {CHLR M#2:91}
HENRICKSON, BARTHOLOMEW, of Cecil County, n.a., dep. Jan 23, 1676, mentioned William Ward, John Coke, and Abraham Strand. {CELR 1:78}
HENRY, GARTOWN, see "John Pagon," q.v.
HENRY, JOHN, of Prince George's County, aet. 76, dep. Feb 8, 1725/6. {PGLR M:63} Aet. 80, dep. Sep 29, 1731. {PGLR Q:397} See "John King" and "James Lucas," q.v.
HENRY, ROBERT JENCKINS, of Somerset County, n.a., dep. Jan 25, 1748, stated that he often saw an Indian woman with a white child until they moved from his neighborhood; in Dec, 1747, he met a man (not named) in Dorchester County with the child; this man thought the child belonged to white people in Lancaster County, Pennsylvania and the man took the child to Kent County, Delaware to establish identity. {CMSP 1:81} See "Tabitha Holston," q.v.
HENSON, WILLIAM, of Charles County, aet. 25 or thereabouts, dep. Sep. 25, 1661 and Nov 19, 1661. {CHLR A:168, ARMD 53:159}
HEPBOURN (HEBOURN), JOHN, of Kent County, planter, aet. about 43, dep. Aug 10, 1725, mentioned his father James Hebourn when he (deponent) was 16 years old. {KELR JS#W:497}
HEPBURN, PATRICK, of Prince George's County, Justice of the Peace, n.a., dep. Feb 6, 1717. {PGLR I:596} See "Thomas Lancaster," q.v.
HEPWORTH (HOPWORTH), ESTHER, of Somerset County, n.a., dep. Nov 19, 1684, mentioned her daughter Joan Kirk [wife of John], Roger Mackeele, Edward Furlong, and Francis Martin. {ARMD 17:314}

HEPWORTH, JOHN, of Somerset County, aet. 40, dep. Nov 19, 1684, stated that about 2 years ago Edward Furlong told him of the severe abuse he had received at John Kirk's house and it was no place for him. {ARMD 17:316}

HERBERT, ALEXANDER, of Prince George's County, aet. 52, dep. between Nov 11, 1729 and Mar 26, 1730, mentioned Thomas Locker, Sr. and wife (not named) about 30 years ago. {PGLR M:556} Alexander Harbert (Herbert), aet. 70, dep. Feb 16, 1745/6, mentioned Thomas Locker, deceased. {PGLR BB:2-3}

HERBERT, CAPTAIN, see "Benjamin Adams," q.v.

HEWS, MARY, of Charles County, n.a., dep. Jul 8, 1662. {CHLR A:218} Aet. not given, dep. Jul 30, 1663. {CHLR B:143} See "John Morris," q.v.

HEYBORN (HEBORN), THOMAS, of Kent County, aet. about 55, dep. Feb 21, 1743. {KELR JS#25:34}

HICKMAN, JOSHUA, of Frederick County, aet. 27 or thereabouts, dep. Aug 20, 1759, mentioned his father William Hickman. {FRLR F:778}

HICKMAN, WILLIAM, of Frederick County, aet. 60 or thereabouts, dep. Aug 20, 1759, mentioned Cornelius Elting and Cornelius Burnoye about 12 or 13 years ago. {FRLR F:778} See "Joshua Hickman," q.v.

HICKS, HENRY, of Dorchester County, aet. 54, dep. between Aug 9, 1767 and Aug 28, 1773. {DOLR 26 Old 436}

HICKS, JOHN, of Queen Anne's County, aet. 40, dep. Oct 5, 1768. {QAEJ - Gideon Emory folder}

HICKS, JOSEPH, of Kent County, aet. about 49, dep. Sep, 1740, and aet. about 51, dep. Aug, 1743. {TAEJ - John Reynolds folders}

HICKS, LEVIN (captain), of Dorchester County, aet. 49, dep. between Jun 11, 1729 and Jul 8, 1729. {DOLR 8 Old 296}

HICKS, SARAH, see "William Pearce," q.v.

HICKS, THOMAS, of Dorchester County, aet. 57, dep. between Mar 12, 1744/5 and May 17, 1745. {DOLR 14 Old 44} Aet. about 69, dep. between Nov 9, 1756 and Jun 15, 1757, mentioned John Hodson (Secundus) a few months after the town of Vienna was laid out; also mentioned the lots on which houses had been built prior to Sep, 1708. {DOLR 15 Old 522}

HICKS, THOMAS (captain), of Dorchester County, aet. 42, dep. between Jun 11, 1729 and Jul 8, 1729. {DOLR 8 Old 296} Aet. 47, dep. between Mar 11, 1734 and Jun 6, 1735. {DOLR 9 Old 293}

HICKS, THOMAS, see "John Hodson, Jr." and "Hooper Hodson" and "Elizabeth Hodson" and "James Muir" and "James Hardy" and "James Langrall," q.v.

HIDE, EDWARD, of Dorchester County, n.a., dep. May 26, 1681, mentioned Henry Swigget. {ARMD 15:360}

HIDE, HENRY, of St. Mary's County, n.a., dep. Dec 11, 1661. {ARMD 41:575}

HIGDON, JOHN, see "William Higdon," q.v.

HIGDON, THOMAS, of Charles County, aet. 32, dep. Aug 29, 1758. {CHLR H#3:577}

HIGDON, WILLIAM, SR., of Charles County, aet. 50, dep. Aug 29, 1758, mentioned his father John Higdon about 35 or 36 years ago. {CHLR H#3:577} Aet. 58, dep. Oct 3, 1767. {CHLR P#3:666}
HIGGINBOTTOM, JOEL, of Baltimore County, aet. 47, dep. Apr 6, 1773. {BALR AL#G:448}
HIGGINS, MICHAELL, prob. of St. Mary's County, n.a., dep. May 17, 1664, mentioned Thomas Thurstone, John Holmewood and wife, Thomas Turner, Thomas Meeres, Mourice Baker, William Fuller and wife, and Sarah Marsh. {ARMD 3:494}
HIGGS, JOHN, of Charles County, aet. 33, dep. Feb 20, 1738. {CHLR T#2:534}
HIGNUT, JAMES, of Dorchester County, aet. 55, dep. between Nov 10, 1761 and May 28, 1762. {DOLR 18 Old 194}
HILL, AMEY, of Dorchester County, aet. 56, dep. between Mar 13, 1738/9 and Nov 12, 1739, stated that she was shown the bounds of *Cherry Point* by her mother (not named) about 36 years ago. {DOLR 12 Old 119}
HILL, CLEMENT, of Prince George's County, gentleman, aet. 54, dep. Mar 19, 1724/5 and Oct 3, 1724. {PGLR I:597, 625} Aet. 56, dep. Jun 22, 1727. {PGLR M:218} Aet. 57, dep. May 20, 1728, mentioned Col. John Bigger and Col. Ninian Beall. {PGLR M:291} Aet. 59, dep. Jun 20, 1729. {PGLR M:438} Aet. 60, dep. 1730. {PGLR Q:236} Aet. 63, dep. Nov 29, 1734. {PGLR T:202} Clement Hill, Sr., aet. 59, dep. Jul 22, 1729. {PGLR M:480}
HILL, DANIEL, of Dorchester County, aet. 34, 35 or 36, dep. twice between Mar 14, 1771 and Nov 13, 1771, mentioned Thomas Rowe and his boys (not named) about 26 or 27 years ago. {DOLR 25 Old 238} See "William Willson" and "Solomon Wright," q.v.
HILL, ELIZABETH, see "Augustine Boyer," q.v.
HILL, HENRY, of Prince George's County, aet. 41, dep. Feb 15, 1749/50. {PGLR PP:126} Aet. about 60, dep. Aug 1, 1768, mentioned Gabriel Parker about 42 years ago. {PGLR BB#2:300} Aet. 63, planter, dep. Jul 10, 1771, mentioned his uncle Clement Brooke about 40 years ago. {PGLR AA#2:283} See "Richard Soward," q.v.
HILL, JAMES, of Baltimore County, aet. 25, dep. Nov 3, 1766. {BALR B#P:308}
HILL, JOHN, see "Phillip Tall," q.v.
HILL, JOSEPH, of Frederick County, aet. 54, dep. Aug 21, 1776, stated that he was chain carrier for Notley Thomas about 14 years ago. {FRLR BD#2:334}
HILL, LEVIN, see "Richard Soward," q.v.
HILL, MARY, see "Richard Soward," q.v.
HILL, RICHARD, see "Phillip Tall," q.v.
HILL, SAMUEL, see "Augustine Boyer," q.v.
HILL, THOMAS, of Charles County, aet. 49, dep. May 21, 1725. {CHLR P#2:39}
HILL, WILLIAM, of Baltimore County, aet. 48, dep. Sep 15, 1750, stated that Robert Jackson had twin boys Isaac and Jacob Jackson, and Isaac was the oldest; also stated that Jonathan Massey was married to an aunt (not named) of

these children; dep. witnessed by Mary Jackson, widow of Isaac Jackson, and Jamima Jackson, widow of Jacob Jackson. {BALR TR#E:7} See "Phillip Tall" and "Thomas Wheeler," q.v.

HILLARY (HILEARY), THOMAS, of Prince George's County, aet. 43, dep. Aug 23, 1750. {PGLR:87}

HILTON, JOHN, of Charles County, aet. 23, dep. May 23, 1742. {CHLR O#2:380}

HINDES, HENRY, of Dorchester County, aet. 80 or 90, dep. between Aug 14, 1744 and Sep 22, 1744. {DOLR 12 Old 92}

HINDS, THOMAS, see "John Salter," q.v.

HINSON, JOHN, see "John Salter," q.v.

HIPKIS (HIPKISS), PETER, of Charles County, aet. 24 or thereabouts, dep. Apr 22, 1662. {CHLR A:202, 203; ARMD 53:205}

HISSETT, PHILIP, see "Richard Holmstead," q.v.

HITCH, CHRISTOPHER, of Prince George's County, aet. 66, dep. Jul 9, 1764. {PGLR TT:283}

HOBART, MOSES, of Charles County, aet. 63, dep. May 9, 1772. {CHLR T#3:616} Aet. 63, dep. Aug 4, 1772. {CHLR U#3:166}

HOBBS, JONATHAN, of Dorchester County, aet. 39, dep. between Nov 10, 1761 and May 28, 1762, mentioned his father Robert Hobbs about 15 years ago. {DOLR 18 Old 194}

HOBBS, ROBERT, of Dorchester County, aet. 40, dep. Aug 30, 1738. {DOLR 12 Old 102} Aet. 41, dep. between Jun 9, 1741 and Nov 2, 1741. {DOLR 12 Old 94} See "Jonathan Hobbs," q.v.

HODGE, CHARLES, of Prince George's County, aet. 49, dep. Mar 25, 1754. {PGLR NN:255}

HODGES, ROBERT, of Kent County, aet. about 38, dep. Mar 3, 1725/6. {KELR JS#W:544}

HODGES, WILLIAM, of Kent County, aet. about 50, dep. Oct 9, 1761. {KELR DD#1:612}

HODGKIN, THOMAS, of Prince George's County, aet. 32, dep. Jul 7, 1731. {PGLR Q:525} Aet. 48, dep. Jul 23, 1747, mentioned Capt. Richard Read some years ago. {PGLR BB:300} Aet. 49, dep. Apr 15, 1748, mentioned Thomas Brooke and his (Brooke's) daughter Rebecca Howard. {PGLR BB:662} Thomas Hodgkin, Sr., aet. 53, dep. Apr 23, 1751. {PGLR PP:132, 154} Thomas Hodgkin, aet. 54, dep. Jun 15, 1753. {PGLR NN:140} Aet. 56, dep. Mar 1, 1756. {PGLR NN:468} Aet. 56, dep. Mar 22, 1756, mentioned his father (not named) and Nathan Selby about 20 years ago. {PGLR NN:470}

HODGKIN, THOMAS, of Prince George's County, aet. 40, dep. Jun 1, 1770, mentioned Dr. Leonard Hollyday, Mrs. Thomas H. Hollyday, and Mrs. Eleanor Eversfield. {PGLR AA#2:142}

HODGKIN, THOMAS, see "Leonard Piles" and "William Deakins," q.v.

HODSKINS (HOSKIN, HODGIN), DANIEL, of Charles County, aet. 64, dep. Dec 17, 1776 (signed his name as Daniel Hodgin, but was referred to as Daniel Hodskins in other depositions). {CHLR X#3:575}

HODSON, ELIZABETH, of Dorchester County, aet. about 53, dep. between Mar 13, 1764 and Jun 4, 1767, mentioned her father Capt. Thomas Hicks and her son Thomas Ball about 2 years ago. {DOLR 21 Old 382}

HODSON, HOOPER, of Dorchester County, gentleman, aet. about 39, dep. between Mar 13, 1764 and Jun 4, 1767, stated that about 3 or 4 years ago Capt. Thomas Hicks, now deceased, told him he was 77 years old. {DOLR 21 Old 382}

HODSON, JAMES, of Dorchester County, aet. about 50, dep. between Mar 13, 1764 and Jun 4, 1767, mentioned a law suit between his father John Hodson and Robert Williams between 20 and 30 years ago. {DOLR 21 Old 382}

HODSON, JAMES, of Dorchester County, gentleman, aet. about 44, dep. between Mar 10, 1761 and Mar 10, 1762, stated that he was shown the bounded tree of *Ennalls' Inheritance* about 5 years ago by Joseph Griffith, now deceased. {DOLR 18 Old 80} Aet. about 48, dep. between Mar 13, 1764 and Jun 4, 1767, stated that he lived on *Maiden's Forest* nearly 40 years; also mentioned his father John Hodson and John Hodson (the fourth) about 23 years ago. {DOLR 21 Old 382}

HODSON, JOHN (captain), of Dorchester County, aet. 62, dep. between Nov 10, 1761 and Nov 19, 1762, mentioned Capt. Henry Trippe, now deceased. {DOLR 19 Old 34} Aet. 63, dep. between Nov 10, 1761 and Mar 14, 1765, stated that he was shown the bounds of *Smithfield* and *Salsberry Plains* about 34 or 35 years ago by Thomas Smith, now deceased; also mentioned his father John Hodson, deceased. {DOLR 20 Old 18} Aet. 64, dep. between Jun 12, 1764 and Oct 10, 1764, stated that he was shown the bounded tree of *Rocky Hock* by his uncle John Hodson (Secundus) about 50 years ago. {DOLR 19 Old 432} Aet. about 64, dep. between Mar 13, 1764 and Jun 4, 1767, stated that *Maiden's Forest* belonged to his father, John Hodson, about 50 years ago; also mentioned his uncle John Hodson and Robert Williams, now deceased. {DOLR 21 Old 382} Aet. 68, dep. between Nov 10, 1767 and Mar 17, 1769, stated that he was shown the bounded tree of *Ennalls Inheritance* about 40 years ago by his uncle John Hodson (Secundus), now deceased; also mentioned John Ennalls, brother of Col. Thomas Ennalls. {DOLR 23 Old 191} See "John Caffey" and "James Hodson," q.v.

HODSON, JOHN, JR., of Dorchester County, gentleman, aet. about 43, dep. between Mar 13, 1764 and Jun 4, 1767, mentioned Capt. Thomas Hicks about 3 or 4 years ago, now deceased. {DOLR 21 Old 382} John Hodson, aet. about 47, dep. between Nov 14, 1769 and Jul 28, 1772. {DOLR 26 Old 100} See "Thomas Hicks" and "Capt. John Hodson" and "Mary Snow," q.v.

HODSON, JOHN, SR., of Dorchester County, aet. 55, dep. Feb 16, 1708. {DOLR 6 Old 184} Aet. 76, dep. Oct 31, 1729, stated that he served on a jury about 40 years ago when Daniel Clarke swore that William Stevens was the first settler and owner of the land where John Stevens, Sr., now lives. {DOLR 12 Old 149}

HODSON, ROSANNAH, see "John Caffey," q.v.

HODSON, SECUNDUS, see "Thomas Hicks" and "Capt. John Hodson" and "Mary Snow," q.v.

HOGEN, THOMAS, of Charles County, n.a., dep. Oct 13, 1663. {CHLR B:179}

HOGGINS, PETER, of Charles County, aet. 44, dep. Apr 13, 1738. {CHLR T#2:465}

HOGGINS (HOGGIN), PETER, of Prince George's County, aet. 60, dep. Jun 22, 1752. {PGLR NN:38} Aet. 60, dep. May 18, 1753, mentioned Richard Beavain about 30 years ago, now deceased. {PGLR NN:135} Peter Hoggin, aet. 77, dep. Aug 1, 1768. {PGLR BB#2:301}

HOGMIRE, CONRAD, of Frederick County, aet. 41, dep. 1767. {FRLR L:60}

HOLDING, RICHARD, of Charles County, aet. 39, dep. Jan 20, 1726/7. {CHLR P#2:491}

HOLEAGER (HOLENGER), PHILIP, see "Michael Miller," q.v.

HOLLAND, JAMES, of Dorchester County, aet. 41, dep. Jun 2, 1740. {DOLR 12 Old 128}

HOLLAND, JAMES, of Prince George's County, aet. 47, dep. Apr 21, 1748, mentioned Philip Pindle about 15 or 16 years ago, now deceased. {PGLR BB:667}

HOLLAND, MAHITABLE, see "Aron Rawlings," q.v.

HOLLEADGER, PHILIP, of Kent County, aet. 39, dep. 1735. {JS#18:185} Aet. 62, dep. 1757. {KELR JS#28:366} See "Michael Miller," q.v.

HOLLEY, JOHN, of Prince George's County, aet. 62, dep. Jul 5, 1748, mentioned old Francis Marbury about 17 years ago, now deceased. {PGLR BB:596}

HOLLEY, THOMAS, of Prince George's County, aet. 40, dep. Jan 21, 1760. {PGLR RR:39}

HOLLINGSWORTH, CHARLES, of Queen Anne's County, aet. about 62, dep. Apr, 1723. {QAEJ - William Bishop folder}

HOLLINSWORTH, WILLIAM, see "Thomas Honey," q.v.

HOLLIS, WILLIAM, of Baltimore County, aet. 44, dep. Jun 10, 1771, mentioned his father William Hollis, deceased. {BALR AL#I:11}

HOLLON, JOHN, see "Joseph Billiter," q.v.

HOLLYDAY, HENRY, of Talbot County, n.a., dep. Jun 7, 1769, stated that he has known Francis Baker several years. {ARMD 32:326}

HOLLYDAY, LEONARD (colonel), of Prince George's County, aet. 40, dep. Jul 9, 1731, stated that he has lived on part of *Brookefield* about 16 or 17 years and mentioned Capt. Samuel Posey. {PGLR Q:523} See "Thomas Hodgkin" and "Francis Waring," q.v.

HOLLYDAY, MRS. THOMAS, see "Thomas Hodgkin," q.v.

HOLLYDAY, THOMAS, see "Francis Waring," q.v.

HOLMES, WILLIAM, alias William Condeman, of Baltimore County, n.a., dep. Sep 20, 1765. {BALR B#P:173}

HOLMEWOOD, JOHN, see "Michaell Higgins" and "John Arnold," q.v.

HOLMEWOOD, SARAH, see "John Arnold," q.v.

HOLMSTEAD, RICHARD, of Kent County, n.a., dep. Feb 5, 1719 to prove the will of Philip Hissett, deceased. {Will Book 15:285}

HOLSON, GENERAL, see "John Davis," q.v.

HOLSTON, TABITHA, of Worcester County, n.a., dep. Nov 30, 1748, stated that Indian Sarah had a white child that she said was hers; they lived in deponent's cornfield between 1740 and 1746 and then moved to Dorchester County. {CMSP 1:83} See "Robert Jenckins Henry," q.v.

HOLT, ROBERT, see "Rose Smith," q.v.

HONEY, THOMAS, of Queen Anne's County, aet. 76, dep. Apr, 1755, stated that he has been blind for many years and that he lived with William Holinsworth and wife about 40 years ago. {QAEJ - Matthew Dockery folder}

HOOD, ROBERT, see "George Geves," q.v.

HOOD, ROBIN, see "Indian Robin Hood," q.v.

HOOK, JAMES, of Frederick County, aet. 58, dep. Aug 21, 1776, stated that Elias Delashmut, Sr. showed him the bounds of *Sweed's Folly* about 10 or 12 years ago. {FRLR BD#2:334}

HOOPER, GEORGE, see "Lewis Griffith," q.v.

HOOPER, GRACE, see "Andrew Goutee," q.v.

HOOPER, HENRY, of Dorchester County, aet. 63, dep. Aug 10, 1706. {DOLR 2 Old 153; DOLR 8 Old 176}

HOOPER, JOHN ASHCOM, of Dorchester County, aet. 30, dep. between Nov 13, 1764 and Dec 22, 1764. {DOLR 20 Old 11}

HOOPER, JOSIAS, of Prince George's County, aet. 36, dep. Jun 1, 1770. {PGLR AA#2:142}

HOOPER, WILLIAM, see "Andrew Goutee," q.v.

HOOSEY, JAMES, of St. Mary's County, n.a., dep. Sep 9, 1663. {ARMD 49:52}

HOPKINS, ANNA, see "James Hopkins," q.v.

HOPKINS, DENNIS, of Kent County, aet. about 41, dep. Sep, 1740, mentioned his father (not named) 10 or 12 years ago. {TAEJ - John Reynolds (vs. Leonard) folder}

HOPKINS, ELIZABETH, see "James Hopkins," q.v.

HOPKINS, JAMES, of Kent County, aet. about 66, dep. Aug, 1743. {TAEJ - John Reynolds (vs. Hopkins) folder}

HOPKINS, JAMES, of Frederick County, n.a., on May 7, 1753 requested that these certificates be recorded: William, Earl of Glencairn, one of his Majesty's Justices of the Peace for the County of Ayr and Kingdom of Scotland, certified that before him on Mar 28, 1752 appeared Mr. Robert Montgomerie, M.A., of the Town of Kilmarnock, and John Hopkins, James Wilson, and Hugh Parker, merchants of said town, and they were deposed. Robert Montgomerie, n.a., stated that Mrs. Anna Dalsell, other ways Hopkins, now of Dumfries, widow of Robert Hopkins, late of Kilmarnock, Scotland, merchant, deceased, married the said Hopkins in Apr, 1710, by whom she had four children and no more: Matthew, born in Sep, 1711; Elizabeth, born in May, 1713; James, born in Oct,

1714; and John, born in Sep, 1715. The said Robert Hopkins died at Kilmarnock in Mar, 1719, and his children Elizabeth and John had died in infancy in the same year before their father's death. Deponent stated that he witnessed the marriage of Robert and Anna Hopkins, the death and burial of their said children, Elizabeth and John, and their eldest son Matthew went to Maryland and settled there. Deponent stated that he corresponded with him from that country since the year 1745 to his death in Maryland in Jan, 1751, and that Matthew's brother John is yet alive, having received a letter from him at London dated Mar 3, 1752. John Hopkins, n.a., and James Wilson, both of Kilmarnock, merchants, gave the same information as Robert Montgomerie, adding that James Hopkins, brother of Matthew, is now the only living son and child of Robert and Anna Hopkins and he (James) was in Kilmarnock, Scotland last October. Hugh Parker, n.a., late of Fairfax County, Virginia, and now of Kilmarnock, Scotland, merchant, stated that he was well acquainted with Matthew Hopkins, late of Maryland, merchant, deceased, and he was in that country and was with him at his habitation in Rock Creek, Potomack River, in Maryland one night for a visit in Dec, 1750, and said Matthew died about ten days thereafter. Also recorded at this time (1753) were abstracts from the parish registers of Kilmarnock concerning Robert Hopkins and his children. Robert Hopkins, son to Matthew Hopkins, merchant in Kilmarnock, and Anna Dalzeel, daughter of James Dalzeel (Delazeil), late bailiff of the Burgh of Dumfries, both their first marriages, were booked Apr 8, 1710 and after three orderly Sabbath proclamations were married at Dumfries on Apr 26, 1710 by Rev. Mr. Welch, Minister of the Gospel. Their first child was born Sep 3, 1711 and baptized Matthew on Sept 9, 1711, by Rev. William Right. Their second child was born May 8, 1713 and baptized Elizabeth on May 21, 1713. Their third child was born Dec 2, 1714 and baptized James on Dec 17, 1714. Their fourth child was born Sep 25, 1715 and baptized John on Oct 2, 1715. Signed by James Smith, Parish Clerk of Kilmarnock. Nothing was said about their deaths since the records were never place in his hands, having been lost by some accident. Anna Dalzell Hopkins, n.a., now of Dumfries, Scotland, widow and relict of Robert Hopkins, late of Kilmarnock, Scotland, merchant, deceased, dep. Apr 7, 1752, stated that she was entitled to a distributive share of her son Matthew Hopkins, her late son who died intestate in Rock Creek, Potomack River, in Maryland. She appointed her son James Hopkins, merchant, now of London, England, as her attorney to demand and receive her share from Henry Threlkeld and Mary Brown, his wife, administratrix and late the widow of Matthew Hopkins, deceased. Signed before John Graham, Provost, Chief Magistrate of the Borough of Dumfries. {FRLR E:150}

HOPKINS, JOHN, see "James Hopkins," q.v.

HOPKINS, JOSEPH, of Kent County, n.a., dep. Oct 8, 1681. {ARMD 17:62}

HOPKINS, MARY, see "Mrs. Deborah Foreman," q.v.

HOPKINS, MATTHEW, see "James Hopkins," q.v.
HOPKINS, RICHARD, of Baltimore County, aet. 54, dep. May 15, 1772. {BALR AL#I:200}
HOPKINS, ROBERT, see "James Hopkins," q.v.
HOPKINS, THOMAS, of Talbot County, gentleman, aet. 77, dep. Dec 14, 1743, stated that Richard Bayly, wife (not named) and three sons, John, Richard, and Henry, about 50 years ago came from St. Mary's County and settled at Oxford in Talbot County where they kept a tavern until his (Richard's) death; the two elder sons John and Richard Bayly never married, but he (Hopkins) was present at the marriage of the youngest son Henry and the present Henry Bayly was his (Henry's) only son. {TALR 16:79}
HOPKINS, WILLIAM, of Harford County, Quaker, n.a., dep. between Jun 17 and Jun 26, 1775. {Land Commission, 1774, Harford County Genealogical Society Newsletter, Jan, 1993, p. 3}
HOPPER, WILLIAM (colonel), of Queen Anne's County, aet. 62, dep. Oct 5, 1768. {QAEJ - Gideon Emory folder}
HOPPINGTON, TOM, see "Indian Sam Isaac," q.v.
HOPWORTH, ESTHER, see "Esther Hepworth," q.v.
HOSKINS, BENEDICT, see "Samuel Hanson," q.v.
HOSKINS, COLONEL, see "Benjamin Adams" and "John Smith," q.v.
HOSKINS, DANIEL, see "Daniel Hodgkins," q.v.
HOSKINS, THOMAS, JR., see "James Hughes," q.v.
HOUSLEY, ROBERT, of Charles County, aet. 40, dep. Aug 29, 1758. {CHLR H#3:578}
HOWARD, CORNELIUS, of Baltimore County, aet. 59, dep. Feb 16, 1767. {BALR B#P:416}
HOWARD, GIDEON, see "Jason Frizel," q.v.
HOWARD, JOHN, see "Jason Frizel" and "Thomas Brooke," q.v.
HOWARD, MATTHEW, see "George Medford," q.v.
HOWARD, REBECCA, see "Thomas Hodgkin," q.v.
HOWARD, WILLIAM, of Prince George's County, aet. 48, dep. Dec 8, 1770. {PGLR AA#2:429}
HOWELL, LEWELLEN, of Frederick County, aet. 37, dep. Nov 27, 1762, stated that the saw the bounded tree of *Charlton's Forrest* marked in 1738 or 1739. {FRLR H:334}
HOWELL, THOMAS, of Dorchester County, aet. 61, dep. between Jun 10, 1761 and Sep 8, 1761. {DOLR 18 Old 14} Aet. 61, dep. between Jun 9, 1761 and Mar 9, 1762. {DOLR 18 Old 75} Aet. 61, dep. between Jun 10, 1760 and Jul 16, 1762. {DOLR 19 Old 65} Aet. 63, dep. between Mar 8, 1763 and May 10, 1763. {DOLR 18 Old 439} Aet. 64, dep. between Nov 8, 1763 and Apr 7, 1764. {DOLR 19 Old 233}
HOWES, WILLIAM, of Charles County, aet. 53, dep. Sep 23, 1741. {CHLR O#2:288}
HOXTON, WALTER, see "Robert Mills," q.v.

HOY, DORSETT, of Prince George's County, aet. 48, dep. Nov 13, 1769. {PGLR AA#2:136-137}
HUBBARD, SAMUEL, see "Samuel Hubbart" and Joseph Thomas," q.v.
HUBBART, DANIEL, see "Nehemiah Hubbart," q.v.
HUBBART, HUMPHREY, see "Humphrey Hubbert," q.v.
HUBBART, NEHEMIAH, of Dorchester County, aet. 30, dep. between Jun 8, 1756 and Jul 15, 1756, mentioned Daniel Hubbart. {DOLR 15 Old 376} See "William Gray," q.v.
HUBBART, SAMUEL, of Dorchester County, aet. 81, dep. between Aug 11, 1772 and Dec 11, 1772, mentioned his father Humphrey Hubbart about 65 years ago. {DOLR 27 Old 348} Samuel Hubbard, aet. 73, dep. between Aug 14, 1764 and Jan 8, 1765, mentioned old Joseph Thomas. {DOLR 19 Old 440}
HUBBART, TITUS, of Dorchester County, n.a., dep. Sep 6, 1746. {DOLR 14 Old 74} Aet. 39, dep. between Aug 12, 1760 and Jun 11, 1761. {DOLR 17 Old 354}
HUBBERT, DANIEL, of Dorchester County, aet. 50, dep. between Jun 14, 1737 and Aug 7, 1737, stated that his father Humphrey Hubbert divided *Brooxes Outhold* on Hodson's Creek between him (Daniel) and his three brothers (not named) about 30 years ago. {DOLR 9 Old 482} See "William Gray" and "John Brown" and "Nehemiah Hubbart" and "Humphrey Hubbert," q.v.
HUBBERT, HUMPHREY, of Dorchester County, aet. 44, dep. between Nov 10, 1761 and Sep 25, 1762, mentioned Honner Hutton, now deceased. {DOLR 19 Old 41} Aet. 50, dep. between Jun 9, 1767 and Dec 10, 1767, stated that he was shown the bounded tree of *Williams' Choice* about 28 or 29 years ago by his father Daniel Hubbert, now deceased. {DOLR 22 Old 430} See "Daniel Hubbert" and "Samuel Hubbart" and "Joseph Thomas, Sr." and "William Gray" and "Thomas Cook," q.v.
HUBBERT, JOHN, of Dorchester County, aet. 71, dep. between Nov 13, 1764 and Apr 13, 1765. {DOLR 20 Old 257}
HUBBERT, JOSEPH, of Dorchester County, aet. 32, dep. between Mar 8, 1768 and Jul 23, 1768. {DOLR 23 Old 5}
HUBBERT, NEHEMIAH, of Dorchester County, aet. 41, dep. between Nov 9, 1763 and Aug 13, 1764, stated that he was shown the bounded tree of *Canawhy* about 19 or 20 years ago by Catherine Dagg, now deceased. {DOLR 19 Old 293} Aet. 49 or 50, dep. between Nov 12, 1771 and Apr 17, 1772, mentioned Peter Adams about 27 or 28 years ago, now deceased. {DOLR 26 Old 50} Nehemiah Hubert, aet. 39, dep. between Mar 9, 1762 and Aug 10, 1762. {DOLR 18 Old 198} See "John Brown," q.v.
HUBBERT, SAMUEL, of Dorchester County, aet. about 54, dep. between Mar 8, 1742 and May 7, 1743. {DOLR 12 Old 166} Aet. about 60, dep. between Nov 11, 1746 and May 27, 1752, mentioned Cornelia Phillips, daughter of John Ross, about 40 years ago, who later married David Macawl. {DOLR 14 Old 658} Samuel Hubert, Sr., aet. about 75, dep. between Nov 10, 1761 and Feb 17, 1762. {DOLR

18 Old 337} Samuel Hubbert, aet. about 80, dep. between Apr 20, 1768 and May 27, 1768, mentioned Cornelia Ross, a daughter of John Ross. {DOLR 22 Old 423}
HUDSON, CALEB, of Charles County, aet. 26, dep. May 11, 1772. {CHLR W#3:798}
HUDSON, JOHN, see "Charles Robson, Sr." and "William Shenton," q.v.
HUDSON, ROBERT, of Charles County, aet. 39, dep. Feb 13, 1761. {CHLR K#3:152}
HUDSON, THOMAS, of Charles County, aet. 40, dep. Jun 3, 1745. {CHLR Z#2:346} Aet. 43, dep. Aug 5, 1745. {CHLR Z#2:398}
HUDSON, THOMAS, of Baltimore County, aet. 60, dep. between Sep 20, 1768 and Mar 11, 1772. {BALR AL#D:436}
HUDSON, THOMAS, see "Elizabeth Williams," q.v.
HUFF, JOHN, see "Richard Crouch," q.v.
HUFFINGTON, JOHN, of Somerset County, aet. 55, dep. between Mar 15, 1735 and Nov 9, 1737. {DOLR 9 Old 493}
HUFFINGTON, RICHARD, of Somerset County, aet. 42, dep. between Mar 15, 1735 and Nov 9, 1737, mentioned his father Richard Huffington. {DOLR 9 Old 493}
HUFFNER, FREDERICK, of Frederick County, aet. 46, dep. Jul 24, 1762. {FRLR H:102}
HUGHES, ANDREW, see "John Richard," q.v.
HUGHES, GABRIEL, of Prince George's County, n.a., dep. Dec 5, 1763. {PGLR TT:189}
HUGHES, JAMES, of Frederick County, aet. 37 or thereabouts, dep. Jul 27, 1762, stated that he followed the carpenter business about 20 years ago and mentioned Thomas Hoskins, Jr. and Grove Tomlinson (Thomlonson) at that time. {FRLR J:65}
HUGHES, JOHN, of Baltimore County, aet. 48, dep. Apr 17, 1767. {BALR B#P:110}
HUGHES, NATHANIEL, see "Samuell Carter," q.v.
HUGHES, OWEN (esquire), of the Burrough of Bowmares in County Anglesey, Wales, aet. 70, dep. Jun 21, 1699 in His Majesty's Court held in the Chamber of the Guildhall in London, England, stated that William Jones is the heir to his uncle Richard Owen, deceased, and is the last surviving child of Col. John Owens, deceased, and he (deponent) believes that Richard and Col. John are the same person; further stated that Owen, alias Evan, Owen of Longireswald in County Anglesey, gentleman, deceased, before my time had three sons: John Owen the eldest, died without issue; Edward Owen, the second son, was father of Col. John Owen and Ellinor Owen who married Henry Jones; and, Owen Owen, the third son. William Jones, son of Henry and Ellinor, now in Maryland. {AALR PK:221-227}
HUGHES, THOMAS, see "Samuell Carter," q.v.
HULSE, WILLIAM, see "Richard Shore," q.v.

HULL, MARGARETT, of Kent County, Quaker, aet. about 65, dep. affirmed Sep 12, 1764. {KELR DD#1:597}
HULL, NATHANIEL, of Queen Anne's County, aet. about 60, dep. Sep, 1730. {QAEJ - William Stavely folder} Aet. about 60, dep. Sep, 1733. {QAEJ - James Hutchens folder}
HUMES, PATRICK, of Charles County, n.a., dep. Nov 15, 1665, stated that he is a servant of Joseph Edmonds. {CHLR B:497}
HUNDLY, ROBERT, of Charles County, aet. 44 or thereabouts, dep. Sep 25, 1661 and Nov 19, 1661. {CHLR A:169, ARMD 53:159} Robert Hundley, n.a., dep. Dec 16, 1662 and Nov 4, 1663. {CHLR B:32, 197}
HUNGERFORD, BARTON, of Charles County, aet. 44, dep. Jun 7, 1731. {CHLR Q#2:516} Aet. 51, dep. Jul 21, 1737. {CHLR T#2:390} Aet. 55, dep. Jul 24, 1742. {CHLR O#2:425} Aet. 56, dep. Sep 21, 1742. {CHLR O#2:464}
HUNGERFORD, CHARLES, see "John Locker," q.v.
HUNKYN, THOMAS, of Charles County, aet. 27, dep. Mar 5, 1682/3. {CHLR K#3:126}
HUNT, GARTER, see "Elizabeth Lamphier," q.v.
HUNT, JOHN, of Frederick County, aet. 65, dep. Jun 16, 1755, stated that in 1721 he bounded a beech tree for the beginning tree of a 3,000 acre tract taken up for William Black and William Fitch Readman. {FRLR E:782} See "Elizabeth Lamphier," q.v.
HUNT, KATHERINE, see "Edmond Wormell," q.v.
HUNT, THOMAS, see "John Kirke," q.v.
HUNTER, WILLIAM, of Prince George's County, aet. 60, dep. Oct 6, 1724. {PGLR I:600} Aet. 65, dep. Jun 8, 1725. {PGLR I:647} See "Jane Wharton," q.v.
HURDLE, RACHEL, of Charles County, aet. 47, dep. Jan 19, 1746/7, mentioned her father William Carter. {CHLR Z#2:8}
HURDLE, ROBERT, of Charles County, aet. 47, dep. Jan 19, 1746/7. {CHLR Z#2:9}
HURLEY, JOHN, of Dorchester County, aet. about 50, dep. between Mar 12, 1744/5 and May 17, 1745, mentioned his father Roger Hurley. {DOLR 14 Old 44} John Hurley the Elder, aet. about 61, dep. between Aug 12, 1755 and Aug 10, 1757, mentioned his father Roger Hurley about 40 years ago. {DOLR 15 Old 512} See "Roger Hurley, Sr.," q.v.
HURLEY, ROGER, see "John Hurley" and "John Elliot," q.v.
HURLEY, ROGER, of Dorchester County, aet. 47, dep. Mar 6, 1709/10. {DOLR 6 Old 187}
HURLEY, ROGER, SR., of Dorchester County, aet. 77, dep. between Aug 14, 1770 and Oct 15, 1770, mentioned his eldest brother John Hurley when he (Roger) was about 8 or 10 years old; also mentioned Jack's Creek was named for an old Indian named Jack who lived on the west side of Nanticoke River. {DOLR 24 Old 297} Roger Hurley the Elder, aet. over 50 years, dep. between Aug 12, 1755 and Aug 10, 1757. {DOLR 15 Old 512}
HURT, JOHN, of Kent County, aet. about 53, dep. Mar 3, 1725/6. {KELR JS#W:542}

HURT, JOHN, of Kent County, aet. about 30, dep. Aug 17, 1737. {KELR JS#22:18} John Hurt, Sr., son of John, aet. about 42, dep. Apr 2, 1745. {KELR JS#25:276}

HURT, JOHN, of Kent County, aet. about 36, dep. Jun 15, 1752, mentioned his father Morgan Hunt and uncle (not named) about 25 years ago. {KELR JS#27:145} Aet. 36, dep. Jun 12, 1753. {KELR JS#27:287} Aet. about 39, dep. Feb 27, 1755 and Aug 19, 1755. {KELR JS#28:100, 162}

HURT, MORGAN, see ""John Hurt" and "John Kenslaugh" and "Philip Davis," q.v.

HUSBANDS, RICHARD, see "Thomas Munnes" and "Elkenath Bourne" and "John Russell," q.v.

HUSON (HUGHSON), JOHN, of Charles County, aet. 70, dep. Jan 1, 1747/8. {CHLR Z#2:304} See "Samuel Ellis," q.v.

HUSSEY, GEORGE, of Prince George's County, aet. 57, dep. Sep 29, 1731. {PGLR Q:397}

HUSSEY, MICHAEL, of Queen Anne's County, aet. 52, dep. Apr, 1730. {QAEJ - Ernault Hawkins folder}

HUSSEY, THOMAS, of Charles County, aet. 27, dep. Mar 4, 1661/2, mentioned Elinor Empson, now Elenor Morris. {CHLR A:195} Aet. 26 or thereabouts, dep. Apr 22, 1662. {CHLR A:202, ARMD 53:205} Aet. not given, dep. May 12, 1663. {CHLR B:122}

HUTCHINGS, JAMES, of Queen Anne's County, aet. 55, dep. July, 1770, mentioned his uncle John Elliott. {QAEJ - Henry Carter folder} See "Elizabeth Groom," q.v.

HUTCHINGS, THOMAS, of Queen Anne's County, aet. 49, dep. July, 1770. {QAEJ - Henry Carter folder}

HUTCHINGS, THOMAS ELLIOTT, of Queen Anne's County, aet. 48, dep. July, 1770. {QAEJ - Henry Carter folder}

HUTCHINS, CHARLES, see "Benjamin Palmes," q.v.

HUTCHINS, NICHOLAS, of Baltimore County, aet. 46, dep. Apr 15, 1771, mentioned his brother Thomas Hutchins. {BALR AL#C:608}

HUTCHINS, THOMAS, see "Nicholas Hutchins," q.v.

HUTCHISON, WILLIAM, see "Francis Wheeler" and "James Green" and "Robert Cloyd," q.v.

HUTTON, GEORGE, of Dorchester County, aet. 39, dep. between Jun 11, 1740 and Mar 11, 1740. {DOLR 12 Old 97} Aet. 60, dep. between Nov 10, 1761 and Sep 25, 1762, mentioned his wife Honner Hutton about 30 years ago. {DOLR 19 Old 41}

HUTTON, HONOR, of Dorchester County, aet. 50, dep. between Jun 15, 1737 and Apr 8, 1738. {DOLR 9 Old 507} Aet. 67, dep. between Mar 10, 1752 and Mar 10, 1753. {DOLR 14 Old 712} See "Andrew McCollister" and "Humphrey Hubbert" and "George Hutton," q.v.

HUTTON, RICHARD, of Prince George's County, aet. 39, dep. Feb 1, 1768. {PGLR BB#2:291}

HUTTON, WILLIAM, of Dorchester County, aet. 38, dep. between Nov 12, 1771 and Apr 17, 1772, mentioned Thomas Hackett the Elder who lived on the other side of the Fork about 8 or 9 years ago, now deceased. {DOLR 26 Old 50}

HUXTER, DAVID, of Kent Island, Queen Anne's County, aet. about 32, dep. Sep, 1733. {QAEJ - James Hutcheson folder}

HYDE, ISAAC, of Prince George's County, n.a., dep. 1730, mentioned Capt. John Murdock. {PGLR Q:138}

HYLAND, NICHOLAS, of Cecil County, n.a., dep. May 29, 1769, stated that he has known Francis and Jeremiah Baker from their youth and they have never been guilty of any misbehavior. {ARMD 32:326}

HYNSON, ANN, of Kent County, aet. about 43, dep. Feb 2, 1656. {ARMD 54:85}

HYNSON, CHARLES, of Eastern Neck, Kent County, aet. 49, dep. 1775. {KELR DD#5:87}

HYNSON, CHARLES, of Kent County, aet. 37, dep. 1730. {JS#16:41} Aet. about 50, dep. 1742. {KELR JS#24:292}

HYNSON, CHARLES, of Kent County, gentleman, aet. 46, dep. 1708. {KELR JS#N:84}

HYNSON, CHARLES, of Kent County, aet. about 35, dep. Nov 21, 1727. {KELR JS#X:211} Aet. about 37, dep. Jul 30, 1730. {KELR JS#24:123}

HYNSON, CHARLES, of Kent County, aet. 36, dep. 1750, stated he was the son of Thomas Hynson and nephew of Charles Hynson. {KELR JS#16:41} Aet. about 36, dep. Aug 2, 1751, stated he was shown an old boundary tree of *Boonly* by his father Thomas Hynson about 16 years ago while they were fishing. {KELR JS#27:27} Aet. about 42, dep. Feb 27, 1755 and Oct 4, 1756. {KELR JS#28:97, 291}

HYNSON, NATHANIEL (colonel), of Kent County, n.a., dep. Nov 4, 1721, stated he was High Sheriff of Cecil County about 14 years ago and mentioned Thomas Kelton who was appointed Sheriff of Cecil County; also mentioned Colonel French, of New Castle [Delaware]. {ARMD 25:378}

HYNSON (HINSON), THOMAS, of Kent County, sheriff, aet. 35, dep. Nov 29, 1655, mentioned Valeruse Leo, deceased. {ARMD 54:35} Aet. 36, dep. Oct 11, 1656. {ARMD 54:73}

HYNSON, THOMAS, of Kent County, aet. about 38, dep. Mar 3, 1725/6. {KELR JS#W:542} Aet. about 44, dep. Aug 14, 1732, mentioned his uncle Robert Dunn about 10 or 12 years ago, now deceased; also mentioned *Fare Harbor* and Robert Dunn, Jr. {KELR JS#X:254}

HYNSON, THOMAS (captain), of Kent County, aet. 35, dep. Sep 22, 1740. {KELR JS#23:135}

HYNSON, THOMAS, see "William Hynson" and "Charles Hynson," q.v.

HYNSON, WILLIAM (esquire), of Kent County, aet. about 42, dep. Mar 21, 1750, mentioned his brother Thomas Hynson. {KELR JS#27:27} Aet. about 44, dep. Jun 12, 1753. {KELR JS#28:287} Aet. 52 or 53, dep. Oct 9, 1761. {KELR DD#1:241, 614}

IJAMS, RICHARD, see "Richard Jiams," q.v.

IJAMS, WILLIAM, see "William Jiams," q.v.

INCH, HANNAH, of Kent County, aet. about 44, dep. Sep 16, 1735, mentioned her uncle James Gallaway when she was 8 or 9 years old. {KELR JS#18:203}

INDIAN ABABCO, of Talbot County, an Indian King of the Choptanks, n.a., dep. Mar 5, 1683 concerning an Indian prisoner named Poh Poh Caquis. {ARMD 17:228-229}

INDIAN ABRAHAM, of Dorchester County, a Choptank Indian of Locust Neck Town, n.a., dep. Jun 29, 1742 in Annapolis. {ARMD 28:261} Aet. not given, dep. Mar 9, 1748 in Cambridge, stated that about 20 years ago Philemon Lecompte (being then a youth) agreed with the then Indian Queen Mechasusa for 100 trees suitable for staves and for which trees he gave the Queen seven yards of linen; also mentioned Mrs. Elizabeth Trippe, widow, had settled on the land and John Dawson was a tenant; deposition witnessed by Indian Hopping Sam, Indian Tom Bishop, Indian John Quash, Indian John Newnon, and Indian John Quitam. {ARMD 28:424}

INDIAN ABRAHAM ASHQUASH, see "Indian Jemmy Ashquash," q.v.

INDIAN ADONDAREECHAA, of New York, a Sinnondowanne Indian, n.a., dep. Aug 22, 1677 by a Maryland delegation in Albany. {ARMD 15:166-168}

INDIAN ADONDARIRHAA, of New York, a Sinnondowanne (Sumondowanne) or Liniceke (Sinnike), n.a., dep. Mar 10, 1681/2 by a Maryland delegation in Albany. {ARMD 17:198-199}

INDIAN AILIAGARI, of New York, a Maques or Maquess Indian, n.a., dep. Aug 6, 1677 by a Maryland delegation in Albany. {ARMD 15:164-166}

INDIAN AMUNGUS, of Somerset County, Emperor of the Assateagues, n.a., dep. Jun 16, 1668. {ARMD 15:170-171}

INDIAN ANTHONY, of Dorchester County, n.a., dep. Jul 4, 1742. {ARMD 28:264}

INDIAN APONONAUS, of Choptico, St. Mary's County, an Indian woman, n.a., dep. Jun 22, 1681. {ARMD 367-368}

INDIAN ASSENDO, of New York, a Cayouge or Cajouge Indian, n.a., dep. Aug 22, 1677 by a Maryland delegation in Albany. {ARMD 15:166-168}

INDIAN ATTAWACHRET, of New York, a Cayouge or Cajouge Indian, n.a., dep. Aug 22, 1677 by a Maryland delegation in Albany. {ARMD 15:166-168}

INDIAN BASTOBELLO, of Dorchester County, n.a., dep. Jul 12, 1742 in Annapolis. {ARMD 28:269} See "Indian Coursey," q.v.

INDIAN CANENTHARE, of New York, an Oneyde or Onneyde Indian, n.a., dep. Jul 21, 1677 by a Maryland delegation in Albany. {ARMD 15:169}

INDIAN CANIACHKOE, of New York, a Maques or Maquess Indian, n.a., dep. Aug 6, 1677 by a Maryland delegation in Albany. {ARMD 15:164-166}

INDIAN CANNONDONDAWE, of New York, a Maques or Maquess Indian, n.a., dep. Aug 6, 1677 and Mar 2, 1681/2 by a Maryland delegation in Albany. {ARMD 15:164-166, 17:200-201}

INDIAN CAPTAIN JOHN, of Dorchester County, a Broad Creek Indian, n.a., dep. Jul 12, 1742 in Annapolis. {ARMD 28:268-269} See "Indian Robin Hood" and "Indian Noscomne," q.v.

INDIAN CARACHKONDIE, of New York, an Onnondage Indian, n.a., dep. Jul 21, 1677 by a Maryland delegation in Albany. {ARMD 15:168-169}
INDIAN CARRACHYNDIA, of New York, an Oneyde or Onneyde Indian, n.a., dep. Jul 21, 1677 by a Maryland delegation in Albany. {ARMD 15:169}
INDIAN CASLENOSSACHA, of New York, a Maques or Maquess Indian, n.a., dep. Aug 6, 1677 by a Maryland delegation in Albany. {ARMD 15:164-166}
INDIAN CHINEHOPPER, see "Indian Jemmy Ashquash," q.v.
INDIAN CHOTIKE, of St. Mary's County, a Choptico Indian, n.a., dep. Aug 19, 1678. {ARMD 15:185-186}
INDIAN CHOTIKE'S WIFE (name not given), of St. Mary's County, n.a., dep. Aug 24, 1681, mentioned a Nanjatico Indian named Nenheeman and Capt. Bridges in Virginia. {ARMD 17:11}
INDIAN COURSEY, of Dorchester County, n.a., dep. Jul 12, 1742 in Annapolis, mentioned Indian Bastobello and Indian Young King, both of the Somerset County Indians, and the Indian River Doctor. {ARMD 28:267-268}
INDIAN CULPUWAAN, of New York, an Esopus Indian, n.a., dep. Jul 20, 1682 by a Maryland delegation in Albany. {ARMD 17:212-213}
INDIAN D'CANENDODO, of New York, a Sinnondowanne Indian, n.a., dep. Aug 22, 1677 by a Maryland delegation in Albany. {ARMD 15:166-168}
INDIAN DEGANEOT, of New York, a Sinnondowanne (Sumondowanne) or Liniceke (Sinneke) Indian, n.a., dep. Mar 10, 1681/2 by a Maryland delegation in Albany. {ARMD 17:198-199}
INDIAN DEGAWIADANI, of New York, an Oneyde or Onneyde Indian, n.a., dep. Sep 15, 1682 by a Maryland delegation in Albany. {ARMD 17:214-215}
INDIAN DICK, of Dorchester County, n.a., dep. Jun 29, 1742 in Annapolis. {ARMD 28:262}
INDIAN DIE DIE HOKARAN, of New York, a Sinnondowanne Indian, n.a., dep. Aug 22, 1677 by a Maryland delegation in Albany. {ARMD 15:166-168}
INDIAN DIXON COURSEY, see "Indian Jemmey Cohonk" and "Indian Robin Hood," q.v.
INDIAN DOGAWEYOO, of New York, a Cayouge or Cajouge Indian, n.a., dep. Aug 22, 1677 by a Maryland delegation in Albany. {ARMD 15:166-168}
INDIAN DOCTOR JAMES, see "John Scarborough," q.v.
INDIAN EMPEROR, see "Indian Amungus" and "Henry Moore (More)," q.v.
INDIAN ESQUIRE TOM, see "Henry Moore (More)," q.v.
INDIAN GEORGE ROCOHAUN, see "John Scarborough," q.v.
INDIAN GEORGE ROKAHOMP, see "Indian Sam Isaac," q.v.
INDIAN GEORGE TERRAKELL (TERRAQUETT), see "Indian Sam Isaac" and "Indian Jemmy Ashquash," q.v.
INDIAN HATSAWAPP, see "Indian Tequassino," q.v.
INDIAN HOPPING SAM, see "Indian Abraham," q.v.
INDIAN IAGOGHNEGICHTA, of New York, an Oneyde or Onneyde Indian, n.a., dep. Sep 15, 1682 by a Maryland delegation in Albany. {ARMD 17:214-215}

INDIAN IAQUISCOUH, of St. Mary's County, a Pottuxen Indian, n.a., dep. Jun 22, 1681, mentioned his brother (not named). {ARMD 15:368-369}

INDIAN INGOGHSENAGUITA, of New York, an Oneyde or Onneyde Indian, n.a., dep. Sep 15, 1682 by a Maryland delegation in Albany. {ARMD 17:214-215}

INDIAN JACK, see "Roger Hurley, Sr.," q.v.

INDIAN JACOB PATTASAHOOK, of Dorchester County, a Nanticoke Indian, n.a., dep. Jun 30, 1742 in Annapolis. {ARMD 28:262}

INDIAN JAMES, see "Marcus Andrews," q.v.

INDIAN JACKANAPES, alias Passanucohanse, belonging to the King of Mattawoma, of St. Mary's County, n.a., dep. Jun 30, 1681. {ARMD 15:380}

INDIAN JEMMY ASHQUASH, of Dorchester County, a Chicacoan Indian, n.a., dep. Jul 12, 1742 in Annapolis, mentioned his uncle Indian Abraham Ashquash, Indian George Terraquett (a Pocomoke Indian), Indian Mulberry, Indian Panquash, Indian Chinehopper, and Indian Oliver. {ARMD 28:269}

INDIAN JEMMY (JAMES) COHONK, of Dorchester County, n.a., dep. Jul 1, 1742 in Annapolis, mentioned Indian Panquash and Indian Dixon Coursey. {ARMD 28:263} Aet. not given, dep. Jul 12, 1742 in Annapolis, mentioned Indian Tom Hoppington, a Chicacoan Indian. {ARMD 28:266}

INDIAN JEMMY PASIMMONS, of Dorchester County, a Choptank Indian, n.a., dep. Jun 26, 1742 in Annapolis. {ARMD 28:260-261}

INDIAN JEMMY SMALHOMMONEY, of Dorchester County, an Atchawamp Indian of Great Choptank, n.a., dep. Jun 25, 1742 in Annapolis. {ARMD 28:260}

INDIAN JEREMY PEAKE, see "Indian Sam Isaac," q.v.

INDIAN JOHN NEWNON, see "Indian Abraham," q.v.

INDIAN JOHN QUASH, see "Indian Abraham," q.v.

INDIAN JOHN QUITAM, see "Indian Abraham," q.v.

INDIAN JOHN WITTONKA, see "Indian Sam Isaac," q.v.

INDIAN JOSHUA, of Dorchester County, n.a., dep. Jul 12, 1742 in Annapolis. {ARMD 28:266-267} See "Indian Patrick," q.v.

INDIAN KAIANWERE, of New York, a Sinnondowanne Indian, n.a., dep. Aug 22, 1677 by a Maryland delegation in Albany. {ARMD 15:166-168}

INDIAN KANEENDODO, of New York, a Sinnondowanne (Sumondowanne) or Liniceke (Sinnike) Indian, n.a., dep. Mar 10, 1681/2 by a Maryland delegation in Albany. {ARMD 17:198-199}

INDIAN KANEHERATT, of New York, a Cayouge or Cajouge Indian, n.a., dep. Aug 22, 1677 by a Maryland delegation in Albany. {ARMD 15:166-168}

INDIAN KESHOMAHAK, of New York, a Mahikander Indian, n.a., dep. Jul 20, 1682 by a Maryland delegation in Albany. {ARMD 17:212-213}

INDIAN KOCHKETEE A SQUAE, of New York, a Catskill Indian, n.a., dep. Jul 20, 1682 by a Maryland delegation in Albany. {ARMD 17:212-213}

INDIAN LONG TOBY, see "Rozanah Williams," q.v.

INDIAN MACHANECK, of New York, a Mahikander Indian, n.a., dep. Jul 20, 1682 by a Maryland delegation in Albany. {ARMD 17:212-213}
INDIAN MAMACACHQUA A SQUAE, of New York, an Esopus Indian, n.a., dep. Jul 20, 1682 by a Maryland delegation in Albany. {ARMD 17:212-213}
INDIAN MATEREETE, of New York, a Catskill Indian, n.a., dep. Jul 20, 1682 by a Maryland delegation in Albany. {ARMD 17:212-213}
INDIAN MESSOWAN, see "Indian Pattasahook," q.v.
INDIAN MULBERRY, of Dorchester County, a Choptank Indian of Locust Neck Town, n.a., dep. Jun 29, 1742 in Annapolis. {ARMD 28:262} See "Indian Sam Isaac" and "Indian Jemmy Ashquash," q.v.
INDIAN NANTAPASQUE, of St. Mary's County, a Choptico Indian woman, n.a., dep. Jun 22, 1681. {ARMD 15:364-365}
INDIAN NENHEEMAN, see "Indian Chotike's wife," q.v.
INDIAN NICOTAGHSEN, of Choptico, St. Mary's County, Emperor of the Pascattoway Indians, n.a., dep. Aug 19, 1678. {ARMD 15:185-186}
INDIAN NOSCOMNE, alias Captain John, of St. Mary's County, a Pottuxen Indian, n.a., dep. Jun 22, 1681. {ARMD 15:370-371}
INDIAN ODIANNE, of New York, a Maques or Maquess Indian, n.a., dep. Aug 6, 1677 and Mar 2, 1681/2 by a Maryland delegation in Albany. {ARMD 15:164-166, 17:200-201}
INDIAN OGNERAIE, of New York, a Sinnondowanne Indian, n.a., dep. Aug 22, 1677 by a Maryland delegation in Albany. {ARMD 15:166-168}
INDIAN OLIVER, see "Indian Sam Isaac" and "Indian Jemmy Ashquash," q.v.
INDIAN ONIREQUICHTARO, of New York, an Onnondage Indian, n.a., dep. Jul 21, 1677 by a Maryland delegation in Albany. {ARMD 15:168-169}
INDIAN OUQUINTIMO, of Choptico, St. Mary's County, a Pascattoway Indian, n.a., dep. Aug 19, 1678. {ARMD 15:185-186}
INDIAN PAMIRAWECHAK, of New York, an Esopus Indian, n.a., dep. Jul 20, 1682 by a Maryland delegation in Albany. {ARMD 17:212-213}
INDIAN PANQUASH, of Dorchester County, a Nanticoke Indian, n.a., dep. Jul 12, 1742 in Annapolis. {ARMD 28:268} See "Indian Jemmey Cohonk" and "Indian Sam Isaac" and "Indian Jemmy Ashquash" and "Indian Robin Hood," q.v.
INDIAN PASSANUCOHANSE, see "Indian Jackanapes," q.v.
INDIAN PATRICK, of Dorchester County, a Choptank Indian of Locust Neck Town, n.a., dep. Jun 29, 1742 in Annapolis, mentioned Joshua, a Chicacoan Indian. {ARMD 28:261}
INDIAN PATTASAHOOK, of Dorchester County, n.a., dep. Jul 12, 1742 in Annapolis, mentioned a Shuan Indian War Captain named Messowan. {ARMD 28:267}
INDIAN PAUPAKINQUAH, of St. Mary's County, a Choptico Indian, n.a., dep. Jun 22, 1681, mentioned "one Kirk's wife" and Indian Wottotawaughcomoco. {ARMD 15:371-373}

INDIAN PETER MONK, of Dorchester County, a Nanticoke Indian, n.a., dep. Jul 1, 1742 in Annapolis. {ARMD 28:262-263}
INDIAN PICHKTAY A SQUAE, of New York, a Mahikander Indian, n.a., dep. Jul 20, 1682 by a Maryland delegation in Albany. {ARMD 17:212-213}
INDIAN POH POH CAQUIS, see "Indian Ababco" and "Indian Tequassino," q.v.
INDIAN QUEEN, see "John Rowles," q.v.
INDIAN QUEEN MECHASUSA, see "Indian Abraham," q.v.
INDIAN RIVER DOCTOR, see "Indian Coursey" and "Indian Robin Hood," q.v.
INDIAN RIVER QUEEN, see "Indian Robin Hood," q.v.
INDIAN ROBERT NANDUM, of Somerset County, n.a., dep. Jul 12, 1742 in Annapolis. {ARMD 28:269}
INDIAN ROBIN HOOD, of Dorchester County, a Choptank Indian, n.a., dep. Jul 4, 1742 in Annapolis, mentioned Indian Panquash, Indian Dixon Coursey, Indian Captain John, Indian Simon, Indian River Doctor, and Indian River Queen. {ARMD 28:264-265} See "Indian Tequassino," q.v.
INDIAN ROOTEE, of New York, a Maques or Maquess Indian, n.a., dep. Aug 6, 1677 by a Maryland delegation in Albany. {ARMD 15:164-166}
INDIAN SACHENNAWS, of St. Mary's County, a Choptico Indian woman, n.a., dep. Jun 22, 1681, mentioned Col. Spencer's wife and Capt. Fendall's daughter (no names were given). {ARMD 15:365-366}
INDIAN SAGGADDIOCHQUISAX, of New York, a Maques or Maquess Indian, n.a., dep. Mar 11, 1681/2 by a Maryland delegation in Albany. {ARMD 17:200-201}
INDIAN SAM ISAAC, of Dorchester County, a Chicacoan Indian, n.a., dep. Jul 1, 1742 in Annapolis. {ARMD 28:263-264} Aet. not given, dep. Jul 12, 1742 in Annapolis, mentioned Indian Panquash, Indian George Rokahomp, Indian John Wittonka, Indian Teague Wogg, Indian George Terrakell, Indian Jeremy Peake, Indian Mulberry, and Indian Oliver. {ARMD 28:266}
INDIAN SAMUEL PANQUASH, see "Thomas Willson," q.v.
INDIAN SARAH, see "Tabitha Holston" and "John Scarborough" and "John Selby," q.v.
INDIAN SARECHTOA, of New York, n.a., an Oneyde or Onneyde Indian, dep. Jul 21, 1677 by a Maryland delegation in Albany. {ARMD 15:169}
INDIAN SENACHEDGIE, of New York, a Maques or Maquess Indian, n.a., dep. Aug 6, 1677 by a Maryland delegation in Albany. {ARMD 15:164-166}
INDIAN SIENOCHARIJ, of New York, an Onnondage Indian, n.a., dep. Jul 21, 1677 by a Maryland delegation in Albany. {ARMD 15:168-169}
INDIAN SIMON, see "Indian Robin Hood," q.v.
INDIAN SKERMER HORRNE, of New York, a Catskill Indian, n.a., dep. Jul 20, 1682 by a Maryland delegation in Albany. {ARMD 17:212-213}
INDIAN SNOTRE, of New York, a Mahikander Indian, n.a., dep. Jul 20, 1682 by a Maryland delegation in Albany. {ARMD 17:212-213}

INDIAN SOLIASSIOWA, of New York, a Cayouge or Cajouge Indian, n.a., dep. Aug 22, 1677 by a Maryland delegation in Albany. {ARMD 15:166-168}
INDIAN SONNOWDAENDOWANNE, of New York, a Cayouge or Cajouge Indian, n.a., dep. Aug 22, 1677 by a Maryland delegation in Albany. {ARMD 15:166-168}
INDIAN SWERISEE, of New York, an Oneyde or Onneyde Indian, n.a., dep. Jul 21, 1677 by a Maryland delegation in Albany. {ARMD 15:169}
INDIAN TAGANSANAGOE, of New York, a Maques or Maquess Indian, n.a., dep. Aug 6, 1677 by a Maryland delegation in Albany. {ARMD 15:164-166}
INDIAN TANONIANICHTA, of New York, an Onnondage Indian, n.a., dep. Jul 21, 1677 by a Maryland delegation in Albany. {ARMD 15:168-169}
INDIAN TARONDATGETHOO, of New York, a Cayouge or Cajouge Indian, n.a., dep. Aug 22, 1677 by a Maryland delegation in Albany. {ARMD 15:166-168}
INDIAN TEAGUE WOGG, see "Indian Sam Isaac," q.v.
INDIAN TEQUASSINO, of Talbot County, an Indian King of the Choptanks, n.a., dep. Aug 6, 1681, mentioned his son Robin Hood and 13 other Indians went over the Bay to the Western Shore; mentioned Indian King Hatsawapp; also mentioned Samuel Chew and John Watkins hunting on Maggoty Bay [Anne Arundel County]; also dep. Mar 5, 1683 concerning an Indian prisoner named Poh Poh Caquis. {ARMD 15:413-414, 17:228}
INDIAN THOMAS COURSEY, see "Thomas Willson," q.v.
INDIAN THOWEKINNIO, of New York, a Sinnondowanne Indian, n.a., dep. Aug 22, 1677 by a Maryland delegation in Albany. {ARMD 15:166-168}
INDIAN TOM BISHOP, see "Indian Abraham," q.v.
INDIAN TOM HOPPINGTON, see "Indian Jemmey Cohonk," q.v.
INDIAN TORIS, of New York, a Mahikander Indian, n.a., dep. Jul 20, 1682 by a Maryland delegation in Albany. {ARMD 17:212-213}
INDIAN VANACOKASSIMON, of Dorchester County, Emperor of the Nanticoke Indians, n.a., dep. Mar 28, 1678 (treaty). {ARMD 15:173-174}
INDIAN WASSETASS, see "Daniel Cunningham" q.v.
INDIAN WOMAN, see "Robert Jenkins Henry," q.v.
INDIAN WOTTOTAWAUGHCOMOCO, see "Indian Paupakinquah," q.v.
INDIAN WUKEPEC, of New York, a Mahikander Indian, n.a., dep. Jul 20, 1682 by a Maryland delegation in Albany. {ARMD 17:212-213}
INDIAN YOUNG KING, see "Indian Coursey," q.v.
INGLE, RICHARD, see "Ralph Crouch," q.v.
INGLISH, EDWARD, see "Michael Miller" and "Benjamin Randall," q.v.
INGRAHAM, ELINOR, of Cecil County, n.a., dep. Oct 31, 1727, mentioned the encroachment of Pennsylvanians on the lands of inhabitants on the border of this province. {ARMD 25:488}
INSLEY, BETTY, of Dorchester County, aet. 40, dep. between Aug 13, 1765 and Dec 28, 1765, mentioned her husband Noah Pearson. {DOLR 21 Old 42}

INSLEY, JAMES, of Dorchester County, aet. 55, dep. between Jun 17, 1734 and Sep 19, 1734. {DOLR 9 Old 249} Aet. 55, dep. between Mar 8, 1736 and May 14, 1737, mentioned Arthur Hart and his son Robert Hart about 17 or 18 years ago. {DOLR 9 Old 456} Aet. 60, dep. between Jun 14, 1743 and Aug 1, 1743. {DOLR 12 Old 167} See "Timothy Macnemar" and "James Ensley," q.v.

INSLEY, JOSEPH, of Dorchester County, aet. 33, dep. between Jun 12, 1764 and Aug 6, 1765, mentioned his father (not named) about 16 or 17 years ago. {DOLR 20 Old 218}

INSLEY, VOLENTINE, of Dorchester County, aet. 41, dep. between Mar 8, 1763 and Jun 13, 1763, mentioned his father (not named) and his brother William Insley. {DOLR 18 Old 374}

INSLEY, WILLIAM, see "Volentine Insley" and "William Ensley," q.v.

ISAAC, RICHARD, of Prince George's County, aet. 62, dep. Nov 18, 1740, mentioned Charles Walker, deceased. {PGLR Y:233} Aet. 65, dep. Mar 26, 1741, mentioned Charles Walker and his son Charles prior to 1721 and some time later his son Charles Walker and wife Rebecca and Joseph Walker, and Richard Walker, brother of Charles Walker, deceased, regarding *Bacon Hall* land division. {PGLR Y:266} Aet. 70, dep. Jan 26, 1748/9. {PGLR BB:628} Aet. 80, dep. Aug 11, 1758. {PGLR PP:295, pt. 2}

ISAAC, SAM, see "Indian Sam Isaac," q.v.

ISGATE, CALEB, of Talbot County, aet. 83, dep. Mar 31, 1724 (but possibly 1725 since the deposition was brought by Matthew Williams to be recorded in Queen Anne's County records on Apr 23, 1725), stated that he married Sarah Turner, widow of Robert Turner, and she told him that her son Thomas Turner was the only child of Robert Turner and that she had no other issue by him; also stated that they lived on the land of said Robert until Thomas arrived at age and they then delivered up the estate to him. {QALR IK#B:320}

JACKCOE, THOMAS, of Prince George's County, aet. 30, dep. Aug 25, 1737. {PGLR T:506}

JACKSON, ABRAHAM, see "William Hill" and "Benjamin Legoe," q.v.

JACKSON, ALEXANDER, see "Benjamin Belt, Jr.," q.v.

JACKSON, ANN, of Queen Anne's County, aet. 92, dep. Apr, 1723. {QAEJ - William Bishop folder}

JACKSON, BARNABY, of Charles County, n.a., dep. 1658. {ARMD 41:218}

JACKSON, FRANCIS, of St. Mary's County, gentleman, aet. 36, dep. Dec 14, 1664, mentioned James Jolly (innholder). {ARMD 49:385}

JACKSON, ISAAC, see "William Hill" and "Benjamin Legoe," q.v.

JACKSON, ISABELLA, see "William Hill" and "Benjamin Legoe," q.v.

JACKSON, JACOB, see "William Hill," q.v.

JACKSON, JAMIMA, see "William Hill" and "Benjamin Legoe," q.v.

JACKSON, JOHN, of Dorchester County, aet. 34, dep. between Jun 14, 1763 and Aug 16, 1763. {DOLR 19 Old 279}

JACKSON, JOHN, of Baltimore County, aet. 53, dep. Mar 4, 1763. {BALR B#L:206}

JACKSON, JOHN, see "Benjamin Belt, Jr." and "William Eversfield" and "James Brown," q.v.

JACKSON, JOSEPH, of Queen Anne's County, aet. about 32, dep. Apr, 1755. {QAEJ - Matthew Dockery folder}

JACKSON, JULIUS AUGST., of Dorchester County, aet. 35, dep. between Nov 10, 1767 and Jan 11, 1768. {DOLR 22 Old 415}

JACKSON, MARY, see "William Hill," q.v.

JACKSON, PHILIP, see "William Eversfield," q.v.

JACKSON, ROBERT, see "William Hill" and "Benjamin Legoe," q.v.

JACKSON, WILLIAM, of Queen Anne's County, aet. 60, dep. Apr, 1730. {QAEJ - Ernault Hawkins folder}

JACOB, BENJAMIN, of Prince George's County, aet. 61, dep. Jan 6, 1747/8, stated that Richard Duckett, now deceased, showed him the bounds of *Duckett's Hope* about 40 years ago. {PGLR BB:691}

JACOB, JOSEPH, of Prince George's County, n.a., dep. Nov 9, 1722, stated that he was shown the bounds of *Clark's Fancy* about 14 years ago by Clark Cheney. {PGLR I:442}

JACOB, MORDECAI, of Prince George's County, aet. 33, dep. Jan 6, 1747/8. {PGLR BB:690}

JACOBS, JOHN, see "Silvester Welch," q.v.

JACOE, THOMAS, see "Joseph Surat," q.v.

JAMES, EDWARD, of Charles County, carpenter, aet. 23, dep. Jul 8, 1662. {CHLR A:219}

JAMES, JOHN, of Prince George's County, aet. 81, dep. Aug 2, 1760, mentioned Ann Morrison. {PGLR RR:121}

JAMES, MARY, of Prince George's County, aet. 72, dep. Aug 2, 1760, mentioned Christopher Ellis about 30 years ago. {PGLR RR:121}

JAMES, OWEN, of St. Mary's County, n.a., dep. 1648. {ARMD 4:472} See "Capt. John Price," q.v.

JAMES, RICHARD, of Baltimore County, aet. 40, dep. Aug 11, 1764. {BALR B#N:309}

JAMES, THOMAS, of Charles County, n.a., dep. Jul 30, 1663, mentioned Benjamin Hammon and wife (not named). {CHLR B:160} See "John Goodman" and "Robert Soper" and "James Lucas," q.v.

JAMES, WALTER, of Baltimore County, aet. 35, dep. Aug 15, 1774. {BALR AL#L:355}

JAMESON, ANN, see "Ann Dolton," q.v.

JAMESON, BENJAMIN, of Charles County, aet. 36, dep. Jul 26, 1755. {CHLR E#3:213} Aet. 50, dep. Jul 4, 1769, mentioned Ignatius Doyne about 20 years ago. {CHLR U#3:12} Aet. 53, dep. Sep 29, 1773. {CHLR U#3:599}

JAMESON, JOSEPH, of Charles County, aet. 39, dep. Aug 7, 1755, mentioned his father Thomas Jameson. {CHLR E#3:213}

JAMESON, MARY, see "Jane Wharton," q.v.

JAMESON, THOMAS, aet. 36, dep. Aug 6, 1736. {CHLR T#2:224} Aet. 45, dep. Jan 22, 1744/5. {CHLR Z#2:344} Aet. 52, dep. Jun 9, 1750. {CHLR S#3:235} Aet. 53, dep. May 14, 1752, mentioned Abraham Lemaster's son-in-law John Dennis. {CHLR B#3:355} Aet. 55, dep. May 14, 1755, mentioned his father Thomas Jameson. {CHLR E#3:133} Aet. 56, dep. Jul 26, 1755. {CHLR E#3:389} See "Ann Dolton" and "Joseph Jameson" and "Jane Wharton," q.v.

JAMESON, THOMAS, JR., of Charles County, aet. 30, dep. Jul 26, 1755. {CHLR E#3:213} Thomas Jeamson, aet. 51, dep. Mar 25, 1775. {CHLR X#3:11} See "Jane Wharton," q.v.

JANSON, PETER, of Norway, n.a., dep. Jun 2, 1659 in St. Mary's County, stated he was born in Norway and sailed with Capt. Courtmann from Amsterdam and by reason of his ill usage left said Courtmann at Barbadoes. {ARMD 41:308}

JARBO, JOHN, see "Thomas Munnes" and "Elkenath Bourne," q.v.

JARRAT, ELIZABETH, of Dorchester County, aet. 70, dep. between Mar 8, 1757 and Apr 23, 1757. {DOLR 15 Old 478}

JARVIS, REBECCA, of Queen Anne's County, aet. about 60, dep. Sep, 1730. {QAEJ - William Stavely folder} Aet. about 50(?), dep. Sep, 1733. {QAEJ - James Hutchens folder}

JEANS, JOSEPH, see "Elizabeth Row," q.v.

JEE, JOHN, of Charles County, aet. 57, dep. Mar 15, 1757, mentioned old John Glaze, now deceased, and Joshua Guibert who married the daughter (not named) of William Boarman. {CHLR F#3:495}

JELLINGS, EDWARD, see "Edward Gillins," q.v.

JENIFER, DANIEL, of Charles County, aet. 47, dep. between Nov 8, 1774 and Feb 7, 1775. {CHLR W#3:610}

JENKERSON, WILLIAM, of Charles County, aet. 40, dep. Mar 11, 1737/8. {CHLR T#2:425}

JENKINS, ASHMAN, of Frederick County, aet. 39, dep. Nov 5, 1772. {FRLR P:430}

JENKINS, EDWARD, of Charles County, aet. 62, dep. Jan 9, 1743/4. {CHLR O#2:700}

JENKINS, GEORGE, of Charles County, aet. 35, dep. Dec 15, 1760. {CHLR K#3:150} Aet. 43, dep. Mar 21, 1769, mentioned his brother Thomas Jenkins. {CHLR Q#3:410A} Aet. 45, dep. Feb 8, 1770. {CHLR T#3:47} Aet. 51, dep. between Nov 8, 1774 and Feb 7, 1775. {CHLR W#3:607}

JENKINS, JOHN, of Charles County, aet. 32, dep. Jul 23, 1744. {CHLR Y#2:223}

JENKINS, JOHN, of Prince George's County, aet. 38, dep. Nov 9, 1761. {PGLR RR:178}

JENKINS, JOHN, see "Robert Troope" and "Edmond Linsey," q.v.

JENKINS, MARY, of Dorchester County, n.a., dep. between Aug 16, 1728 and Jan 28, 1728/9, mentioned she was a former servant of John Allford the Elder. {DOLR 8 Old 268}

JENKINS, PHILIP, of Charles County, aet. 45, dep. Apr 29, 1754. {CHLR D#3:323}

JENKINS, THOMAS, see "George Jenkins," q.v.

JENKINSON, EMANUEL, see "Seth Garrett," q.v.
JENNINGS, EDWARD, of Charles County, aet. 43, dep. Jul 12, 1743, mentioned his father Edward Jennings about 30 years ago. {CHLR O#2:662}
JENNINGS, JOSEPH, see "Thomas Beatty," q.v.
JIAMS, RICHARD, of Anne Arundel County, aet. 46, dep. 1723 in Prince George's County land case. {PGLR I:441} See "William Jiams," q.v.
JIAMS, WILLIAM, of Anne Arundel County, gentleman, aet. 49, dep. Nov 9, 1722 regarding a Prince George's County land case, mentioned his brother Richard Jiams. {PGLR I:441}
JINNIG (GILLANS), EDWARD, see "Edward Gillins," q.v.
JOANES, RICHARD, see "Elizabeth Greene," q.v.
JOANS, WILLIAM, of Talbot County, n.a., dep. Sep 21, 1669, mentioned Anthony Pecheco, servant to John Kinemant. {ARMD 54:443}
JOCE, ANNE, see "Thomas Smith," q.v.
JOCE, THOMAS, see "Thomas Smith," q.v.
JOHNINGS, GEORGE, see "Nicholas Glen," q.v.
JOHNSON, ALBERT, of Queen Anne's County, aet. about 50, dep. Mar, 1746. {QAEJ - Benjamin Tasker folder} See "Solomon Watkins," q.v.
JOHNSON, ANN, of St. Mary's County, aet. 34, dep. Apr 30, 1653, stated that she and Sarah Goulson were at the house of Robert Taylor on Dec 24th "at the travail of said Taylor's wife" whose sister Alice Griffin said that Mary Taylor "wisht she might never rise" if it were not her brother's child; mentioned were Margaret Broome, a person referred to as Cuz, a man named Cetchmey, and "that ugly pott belly Edward Brisley." {ARMD 10:280-282}
JOHNSON, ARCHIBALD, of Baltimore County, aet. 46, dep. Jan 4, 1763. {BALR B#L:498} Aet. 54, dep. Dec 19, 1769. {BALR AL#A:735}
JOHNSON, BATRIX (Mrs.), of Kent County, aet. about 36, dep. Oct, 1753, mentioned her former husband Gideon Pearce. {KELR JS#28:45}
JOHNSON, CORNELIUS, of Charles County, aet. 29, dep. Mar 11, 1677/8. {CHLR G#16:140} See "Thomas Duke, Sr." and "Richard Webster," q.v.
JOHNSON, DANIELL, of Charles County, aet. 23, dep. Oct 26, 1658, stated that Haniball Spicer and Elizabeth Spicer (now being with child) said that Goodman Courts was a very slanderous man and that William Empson was a thief from the cradle. {CHLR A:26, ARMD 53:233} Aet. not given, dep. Jul 8, 1662, mentioned Mrs. Mary Vanderduncke, now wife of Hugh O'Neale. {CHLR A:223} See "Zachary Wade," q.v.
JOHNSON, HENRY, see "Solomon Watkins," q.v.
JOHNSON, ISAAC, of Dorchester County, aet. 40, dep. between Nov 9, 1762 and May 9, 1763. {DOLR 19 Old 425}
JOHNSON, JAMES, of Charles County, aet. 45, dep. Nov 14, 1665, stated that William Burnam (Burnham) and Nathaniell Button were 2 of the 4 servants of Richard Smith, now deceased. {CHLR B:493}

JOHNSON, JAMES, of Charles County, aet. 75, dep. Mar 30, 1758, mentioned the widow Sanders who married James Parrendier, and Jane Woodward, daughter of Gerard Brown. {CHLR H#3:428}

JOHNSON, JAMES, of Charles County, aet. 50, dep. Jun 22, 1767. {CHLR P#3:504}

JOHNSON, JEAN, see "Mary Mitchel," q.v.

JOHNSON, JOHN, of Prince George's County, aet. 48, dep. Apr 9, 1753. {PGLR NN:282} See "John Anderson" and "John Kerby" and "Solomon Watkins," q.v.

JOHNSON, JOSEPH, JR., of Prince George's County, aet. 63, dep. Nov 24, 1753. {PGLR NN:283}

JOHNSON, PETER, of Cecil County, n.a., dep. Mar 21, 1746/7, mentioned the separation of Isabella Barkley from her husband Thomas Barkley because he had ruined her character. {CELR 4:485}

JOHNSON, ROBERT, of Dorchester County, aet. 38, dep. between Nov 24, 1732 and Jan 31, 1732/3, mentioned John Peples, former owner of *Range Point*. {DOLR 9 Old 98} See "Walter MacDaniel," q.v.

JOHNSON, SAMUEL, of Charles County, aet. 38, dep. Mar 4, 1731. {CHLR R#2:408} See "Mary Suit," q.v.

JOHNSON, THOMAS, of Prince George's County, aet. 50 odd years, dep. May 20, 1725. {PGLR I:675} Aet. 60, dep. Sep 29, 1731. {PGLR Q:397}

JOHNSON, THOMAS, of Prince George's County, aet. 42, dep. Aug 17, 1725. {PGLR I:678}

JOHNSON, THOMAS, of Prince George's County, aet. 24, dep. Jun 16, 1730. {PGLR Q:11}

JOHNSON, WILLIAM, of London, England, merchant, aet. 24, dep. Sep 21, 1681. {ARMD 5:295}

JOHNSON, WILLIAM, of Charles County, aet. 50, dep. May 25, 1742. {CHLR O#2:506}

JOHNSTON, ELIZABETH, see "John Greenup," q.v.

JOHNSTON, GEORGE, see "John Anderson," q.v.

JOHNSTON, JANE, see "Elizabeth Lamphier," q.v.

JOHNSTON, JOHN, of Prince George's County, aet. 56, dep. Mar 21, 1761. {PGLR RR:234}

JOHNSTON, THOMAS, of Prince George's County, aet. 60, dep. between Aug 12, 1727 and Mar 30, 1728. {PGLR M:269}

JOLLY, JAMES, see "Francis Jackson," q.v.

JONES, ABRAHAM, of Prince George's County, aet. 36, dep. Apr 22, 1755, mentioned Yate Plummer about 5 or 6 years ago. {PGLR NN:371}

JONES, ANN, of Charles County, aet. 50, dep. Feb 12, 1766, mentioned William Simpson and his daughter Elizabeth Simpson. {CHLR O#3:144}

JONES, CAPTAIN, see "James Watson," q.v.

JONES, CATHRINE, see "Elizabeth Salisbury" and "William Stokes," q.v.

JONES, EDWARD, of Prince George's County, aet. 62, dep. May 9, 1774. {PGLR CC#2:56}

JONES, ELLINOR, see "Owen Hughes" and "Mary Buence," q.v.

JONES, GEORGE, 2ND, see "William Bright," q.v.
JONES, GRIFFITH, of Talbot County, n.a., dep. Oct 1, 1692. {ARMD 8:372} See "Joshua Lamb," q.v.
JONES, HENRY, see "Owen Hughes" and "Mary Buence," q.v.
JONES, JOHN, of Charles County, aet. 51, dep. Sep 18, 1731. {CHLR R#2:46}
JONES, JOHN, of Frederick County, aet. 46, dep. Mar 7, 1752. {FRLR B:544}
JONES, JOHN, of Frederick County, aet. 35, dep. Nov 27, 1762, stated that he was shown the bounded tree of *Charlton's Forrest* in 1751 or 1752. {FRLR H:335}
JONES, JOHN, of Dorchester County, aet. 40, dep. between Mar 13, 1738/9 and Nov 12, 1739. {DOLR 12 Old 119}
JONES, JOHN, of Dorchester County, aet. 74, dep. between Aug 10, 1773 and Oct 23, 1773, mentioned old Tobias Pollard and Col. Roger Woollford around 1729. {DOLR 27 Old 38}
JONES, JOHN, of St. Mary's County, n.a., dep. Apr 24, 1749. {ARMD 28:509}
JONES, JOHN, of Kent County, aet. about 43, dep. May 22, 1732. {KELR JS#16:250} Aet. about 49, dep. Nov 13, 1738, mentioned his father Rice Jones. {KELR JS#22:292} Aet. about 53, dep. Dec 10, 1741, mentioned his brother Rice Jones. {KELR JS#23:410}
JONES, JOHN, see "Thomas Jones," q.v.
JONES, JONATHAN, of Anne Arundel County, aged about 32 and a half, dep. Jul 9, 1705, stated that "he was put to live with William Sivick as an orphan child very young not above 3 years old" and after William died he lived with John Sivick on *Paschall's Purchase* until he (Jones) was 22 years old; also mentioned Abraham Nailor's land. {Chancery Court Records PC#2:540-541, pt. 2} Aet. about 42 or thereabouts, dep. May 23, 1715, mentioned John Christian and Capt. Richard Jones. {Chancery Court Records PL#3:267}
JONES, JOSHUA, of Anne Arundel County, n.a., dep. 1680, stated that he lived with Hugh Merekin about 30 years ago. {AALR IT#5:50-51}
JONES, LEVIN, of Dorchester County, planter, aet. 50 or thereabouts, dep. Mar 27, 1776. {DOLR 28 Old 178}
JONES, LEWIS, see "Charles Thompson," q.v.
JONES, LOVE, of St. Mary's County, n.a., dep. Jun 22, 1681, stated that she saw 11 Indians in a new boat at Point Lookout going over to Nanticoke about a month ago; also mentioned Arthur Thompson. {ARMD 15:369}
JONES, MORGAN, of Dorchester County, aet. 57, dep. between Aug 10, 1773 and Oct 23, 1773. {DOLR 27 Old 38}
JONES, OWEN, of St. Mary's County, aet. 20 or thereabouts, dep. Feb 17, 1659, stated that "Richard Smyth did ship three servants aboard the ship *Leopard* entered in the Boston booke their names followeth, Joseph Bishop, Thomas Allison, Margarett Williams." {ARMD 41:387}
JONES, PHILIP, see "George Presbury," q.v.
JONES, RICE, see "John Jones," q.v.

JONES, RICHARD, of Prince George's County, aet. 22, dep. Jul 7, 1772. {PGLR BB#3:75} See "Jonathan Jones," q.v.

JONES, ROBERT, of Dorchester County, aet. 48, dep. between Nov 17, 1726 and Jul 21, 1729. {DOLR 8 Old 293} Aet. about 51, dep. between Aug 16, 1728 and Jan 28, 1728/9, mentioned John Halpenny, husband of Elizabeth Halpenny. {DOLR 8 Old 268} See "William Jones" and "James Sherwin" and "William Taylard," q.v.

JONES, SARAH, see "Richard Wroth," q.v.

JONES, THOMAS, of Anne Arundel County, n.a., dep. 1696. {ARMD 20:530}

JONES, THOMAS, of Frederick County, aet. 19 or thereabouts, dep. Mar 7, 1752, stated that he and his father John Jones carried the chain when *Mill Race* was surveyed about 5 or 6 years ago. {FRLR B:545}

JONES, THOMAS, of Dorchester County, aet. 44, dep. between Mar 12, 1771 and Apr 22, 1771. {DOLR 26 Old 42}

JONES, THOMAS, of Kent County, aet. about 38, dep. Dec 10, 1741. {KELR JS#23:410}

JONES, WILLIAM, of Charles County, aet. 39, dep. Jun 8, 1772, mentioned his father William Jones. {CHLR U#3:16}

JONES, WILLIAM, of Charles County, aet. 45, dep. May 11, 1770. {CHLR T#3:605}

JONES, WILLIAM, of Baltimore County, carpenter, aet. 46 or thereabouts, dep. Apr 3, 1769. {BALR AL#A:301-302}

JONES, WILLIAM, of Prince George's County, aet. 39, dep. Jul 7, 1772. {PGLR BB#3:75}

JONES, WILLIAM, of Dorchester County, planter, aet. 55, son of Robert, dep. Mar 27, 1776. {DOLR 28 Old 177-178}

JONES, WILLIAM, of Cecil County, aet. about 33, dep. Jul 25, 1757. {KELR JS#28:366}

JONES, WILLIAM, of Kent County, aet. about 35, dep. Jun 19, 1755 and Mar 16, 1756. {KELR JS#28:136, 223}

JONES, WILLIAM, see "Elizabeth Salisbury" and "Sarah Kennerly" and "Owen Hughes" and "Mary Buence" and "William Joans" and "Blackledge Woodland," q.v.

JORDAN, CHARITY, see "Benjamin Hallowell," q.v.

JORDAN, JOHN, see "Benjamin Hallowell," q.v.

JOSEPHS, WILLIAM, JR., of Anne Arundel County, n.a., dep. Sep 1, 1698. {ARMD 23:512-513}

JOSLIN, SARAH, of Prince George's County, n.a., dep. Mar 24, 1706/7, stated that she went to the house of John Anderson at his request and found his sister Elizabeth Wallis senseless; the next day she discovered a dead female child under the bed clothes; Mary and John Anderson and Mrs. Ann Burnham also saw it. {CMSP 1:8}

JOYCE, THOMAS, of Prince George's County, aet. 57, dep. Feb 2, 1747/8, mentioned Thomas Bennet about 30 years ago. {PGLR BB:666}

JOYNER, JOHN THOMAS, of Dorchester County, aet. 40, dep. between Aug 10, 1773 and Nov 30, 1773. {DOLR 27 Old 354}
JUMP, WILLIAM, of Talbot County, aet. about 70, dep. Nov 27, 1702, stated that about 16 years ago he was shown the bounds of *Stevens Fields* by Henry Parker, then Deputy Surveyor. {TALR 9:152}
JUNIPE (JUMPE?), THOMAS, of Queen Anne's County, aet. 47, son of William, dep. Aug, 1752. {QAEJ - Sarah Starkey folder}
JUSTICE, JOHN, JR., of Frederick County, n.a., dep. Oct 14, 1765. {FRLR K:429}
KANE, WILLIAM, of Somerset County, aet. upwards of 70, dep. Aug, 1717, stated that he and his wife (not named) are very aged and unable to support their children (not named). {Somerset Judgment Records ET#B:318}
KEDGER, ROBERT, of St. Mary's County, n.a., dep. 1648. {ARMD 4:462}
KEDRICK, ROBERT, of Prince George's County, aet. 43, dep. Mar 5, 1763. {PGLR TT:13}
KEECH, COURTS, of Charles County, aet. 59, dep. Sep 26, 1747. {CHLR Z#2:188}
KEECH, GEORGE, of Charles County, aet. 35, dep. Oct 31, 1776. {CHLR P#3:284}
KEECH, JAMES, of Charles County, aet. 30, dep. Sep 8, 1753. {CHLR D#3:430} James Keech, Jr., aet. 42, dep. between Aug 11, 1765 and Nov 11, 1765. {CHLR N#3:789}
KEED (KEEDE), WILLIAM, see "Alice Davis," q.v.
KEENE, HENRY, of Dorchester County, aet. about 52, dep. between Aug 13, 1747 and Sep 18, 1749. {DOLR 14 Old 463} See "Henry Travers," q.v.
KEENE, JAMES, of Charles County, aet. 66, dep. Jan 17, 1726/7. {CHLR P#2:417}
KEENE, JOHN, of Dorchester County, aet. 54, dep. between Aug 14, 1744 and Sep 22, 1744. {DOLR 12 Old 92}
KEENE, MARY, of Charles County, aet. 53, dep. Jan 17, 1726/7. {CHLR P#2:417}
KEENE, RICHARD, of Dorchester County, aet. 62, dep. between Nov 13, 1744 and Feb 12, 1744/5, stated that he was shown the bounds of *Carmell's Fortune* by two daughters (not named) of ---- Remball (no first name given) at Remball's Landing on Slaughter Creek. {DOLR 12 Old 256} Aet. 64, dep. between Aug 15, 1746 and Sep 1, 1746. {DOLR 14 Old 89}
KEENE, RICHARD, of Prince George's County, aet. 37, dep. Oct 4, 1726, mentioned Major Josiah Wilson, lately deceased. {PGLR M:221}
KEENE, WILLIAM, of Somerset County, n.a., dep. Feb, 1677, mentioned Capt. Thomas Walker (High Sheriff of Somerset County), Col. William Coleborne (commander-in-chief of Somerset County militia), and the murder of David Williams and his family by Indians. {ARMD 15:162}
KEENE, ZEBULON, of Dorchester County, aet. 34, dep. between Aug 20, 1735 and Feb 17, 1735/6. {DOLR 9 Old 391} Aet. 70, dep. between Mar 13, 1770 and Oct 20, 1770, mentioned his brother (not named) and an elderly Raymond Shenton (Shinton) about 20 years ago. {DOLR 26 Old 396}
KEETH, ELIZABETH, see "Mary Crosson," q.v.
KEETH, GEORGE, see "George Keyth," q.v.

KEETH, MARY, of Prince George's County, aet. 64, dep. Feb 20, 1767. {PGLR BB#2:167}
KEETING (KEETEING), THOMAS, of St. Mary's County, n.a., dep. Jun 22, 1681. {ARMD 15:370}
KELLD, JOHN, see "Nicholas Glen," q.v.
KELLEY, ALEXANDER, SR., of Harford County, aet. 55, dep. May 25, 1775. {Land Commission, 1774, Harford County Genealogical Society Newsletter, Jan, 1993, p. 3}
KELLEY, DANIEL, see "Katharine Kelley," q.v.
KELLEY, ISAAC, of Sussex County on Delaware, aet. about 53, dep. between Nov 14, 1769 and Nov 6, 1770. {DOLR 24 Old 308}
KELLEY, JAMES, of Harford County, aet. 80, dep. May 25, 1775. {Land Commission, 1774, Harford County Genealogical Society Newsletter, Jan, 1993, p. 3}
KELLEY, KATHARINE, of Kent County, aet. about 38, dep. Nov 21, 1727, stated that her father Daniel Kelley showed her the bounded tree of *Bayley's Forrest* about 28 years ago. {KELR JS#X:208}
KELLY, DANIEL, of Frederick County, aet. 40, dep. Mar 13, 1761. {FRLR G:159}
KELLY, DAVID, of Prince George's County, n.a., dep. Aug 22, 1720, stated that in Feb, 1718 he was at the plantation of William Masters when a horse bit off an ear of Nathan Masters, his 4 year old son. {PGLR I:124}
KELLY, EDMUND, see "Thomas Barnes" and "Benjamin Kirby," q.v.
KELLY, THOMAS, of Frederick County, aet. 38, dep. Apr 11, 1767. {FRLR K:1346}
KELLY, THOMAS, of Queen Anne's County, aet. 64, dep. Sep, 1730. {QAEJ - William Stavely folder}
KELTON, THOMAS, see "Nathaniel Hynson," q.v.
KEMP, THOMAS, of St. Mary's County, n.a., dep. Feb 7, 1658. {ARMD 41:240}
KEMPERSON, STEPHEN, of Queen Anne's County, aet. about 48, dep. Sep, 1730. {QAEJ - William Stavely folder} See "William Rabbitt," q.v.
KENDALL, RICHARD, see "Susannah Edger," q.v.
KENEMONT, FRANCIS, see "Joana Kenemont," q.v.
KENEMONT, JOANA, of Talbot County, widow, aet. 60, dep. Aug 19, 1728, stated that Francis Kenemont, late of Talbot County, planter, deceased, was the last child of John Kenemont and his wife Frances and was mentioned in said John's will as his unborn child. {TALR 12:445}
KENEMONT, JOHN, see "Joana Kenemont," q.v.
KENNARD, JOHN, of Kent County, aet. about 23, dep. Oct 20, 1743. {KELR JS#25:194}
KENNARD, NATHANIEL, of Kent County, aet. about 34, dep. Aug 17, 1731. {KELR JS#16:164}
KENNARD, RICHARD, of Kent County, aet. about 40, dep. Aug 17, 1731 and Sep 10, 1735. {KELR JS#16:164, JS#18:195} Aet. about 52 or 53, dep. Oct 20, 1743 and May 31, 1744. {KELR JS#25:98, 195} Aet. about 60 or 61, dep. Oct 11, 1753 and Jun 19, 1755. {KELR JS#27:291, JS#28:137}
KENNEDY, CLEMENT, of Charles County, aet. 54, dep. Mar 27, 1758. {CHLR H#3:434}

KENNERLY, JOSHUA, of Dorchester County, aet. 30, dep. Aug 16, 1712. {DOLR 6 Old 217}

KENNERLY, SARAH, of Dorchester County, Quaker, dep. May 28, 1772, concerning her knowledge of Isaac Lee, shoemaker, who lived near William Jones' plantation and died about Oct, 1766; stated that she understood Isaac Lee came to Maryland about 33 years ago having been convicted for stealing horses; her husband William Kennerly bought him as a convict servant for 14 years from James Edgell, she believes, who formerly kept store for James Gildert, merchant; Isaac was set free after 6 years service. {DOLR 26 Old 3}

KENNERLY, WILLIAM, see "Sarah Kennerly" and "Ann Vickers" and "William Murray," q.v.

KENNICK, WILLIAM, of Prince George's County, aet. 53, dep. Aug 3, 1772. {PGLR BB#3:78}

KENSLAUGH, HEALIN (HELEN), see "Paul Kenslaugh," q.v.

KENSLAUGH, JOHN, of Kent County, aet. about 49, dep. Mar 7, 1758, mentioned Morgan Hurtt (now deceased) had married the widow Brown. {KELR JS#28:427}

KENSLAUGH, PAUL, of Kent County, aet. about 25, dep. Jun 20, 1757 at the request of Healin (Helen) Kenslaugh, his sister. {KELR JS#28:324, 429} Aet. about 28, dep. Dec 18, 1761. {KELR DD#1:100}

KENT, GEORGE, of Dorchester County, n.a., dep. May 22, 1681. {ARMD 15:360}

KENTON, REBECKAH, see "Seth Garrett," q.v.

KEON, HANAH, of Baltimore County, n.a., dep. Jun 6, 1711, stated that her son Edward Williams, here present, is the lawful heir of Lodowick Williams by marriage, born in wedlock. {BALR TR#A:135} See "William Wilkinson" and "John Bevans," q.v.

KERBY, JOHN, of Talbot County, mariner, n.a., dep. May 27, 1700, stated that he was present and saw all of the servants that came into Maryland this year on the ship *Anne of Newcastle* who were bound by indenture for 5 years unto Robert Allan, commander, by patent appointed at Newcastle upon Tyne (except one servant John Johnson). {TALR 9:8}

KEYTH, GEORGE, of Charles County, aet. 67, dep. Aug 20, 1762. {CHLR M#3:108}

KEYTIN, NICHOLAS, of Charles County, n.a., dep. 1658. {ARMD 41:218}

KIBERD, JOHN, of Charles County, aet. 42, dep. Jun 22, 1772, mentioned his father Thomas Kiberd. {CHLR U#3:163}

KIBERD, THOMAS, see "John Kiberd," q.v.

KIDD, WILLIAM, of Charles County, aet. 57, dep. Nov 30, 1732. {CHLR R#2:292}

KILBOURN, RICHARD, of Anne Arundel County, n.a., dep. 1696. {ARMD 20:563}

KILLMAN, WILLIAM, see "Edward Willoughby," q.v.

KILLMON, ARROBELLA, of Dorchester County, aet. about 67, dep. between Nov 11, 1746 and May 27, 1752. {DOLR 14 Old 658}

KILLMON, WILLIAM, of Dorchester County, aet. 45, dep. between Nov 11, 1746 and May 27, 1752. {DOLR 14 Old 658} William Killman, aet. 56, dep. between Jun 8, 1758 and Dec 15, 1759. {DOLR 16 Old 212}

KILLUCK, WILLIAM, see "Peter Attwood," q.v.

KIMBLE, SAMUEL, of Baltimore County, aet. 42 or 43, dep. Dec 19, 1769. {BALR AL#A:736}

KIMBOL, JOHN, of Frederick County, aet. 63, dep. Jun 29, 1761. {FRLR G:72} John Kimball (Kimbol), aet. 64, dep. Jan 5, 1763. {FRLR H:336}

KIMBRON, JOHN, of Charles County, aet. 29, dep. Mar 8, 1669/70. {CHLR D#1:133}

KIMMEY (KIMEY), WALTER, of Dorchester County, aet. 51, dep. between Mar 14, 1769 and Apr 9, 1770, stated that he lived with Mary Cratcher, now deceased, about 28 years ago at Cratcher's Ferry. {DOLR 24 Old 9} See "Henry Kimmey" and "Walter Camey," q.v.

KIMMEY (KIMEY), HENRY, of Dorchester County, aet. about 47, dep. between Nov 12, 1745 and Feb 22, 1745/6, mentioned his father Walter Kimey, now deceased. {DOLR 14 Old 57} Aet. about 68, dep. between Aug 9, 1763 and Mar 31, 1764, stated that he was shown a bounded tree of *Lemster* about 50 years ago by John Griffith, Samuel Griffith, William Williams, and John Williams. {DOLR 19 Old 418}

KIMMEY, JOHN, see "Thomas Willson," q.v.

KINDAL, RICHARD, see "Susannah Edger" and "Richard Pearson," q.v.

KINDRED, SARAH, of Talbot County, aet. 53, dep. Aug 18, 1747, stated that she was married to her first husband Philip Morgan no more than 40 years ago next February; also, David Arey married Elizabeth Cook "some time in the foure part of the same winter" and their daughter Esther Arey was not born until a considerable time after they were married. {TALR 17:117}

KINEMANT, JOHN, see "William Joans" and "William Gary," q.v.

KING, CLEEAR, of Dorchester County, aet. 60, dep. between Mar 14, 1748 and Jun 10, 1749. {DOLR 14 Old 465}

KING GEORGE, see "Thomas Walker," q.v.

KING, JOHN, see "Sarah Emory" and "James Walters," q.v.

KING, JOHN, of Prince George's County, aet. 59, dep. Nov 9, 1759, mentioned John Henry about 38 years ago. {PGLR RR:81} Aet. 69 or thereabouts, dep. Jun 5, 1769. {PGLR BB#2:437}

KING, JOHN, of Dorchester County, aet. 59, dep. between Nov 8, 1748 and Mar 15, 1748, stated that he was shown the bounds of *Rawlings Range* or *Rollings Range* by John Taylor, surveyor, and John Rawlings about 44 or 45 years ago. {DOLR 14 Old 319} Aet. 80, dep. between Mar 14, 1769 and Apr 9, 1770, mentioned Mary Cratcher, Oliver Hackett, and John Thompson the eldest, all now deceased. {DOLR 24 Old 9}

KING, JOHN, JR., of Dorchester County, aet. 27, dep. between Mar 12, 1771 and May 4, 1771. {DOLR 25 Old 6}

KING, JOHN, SR., of Dorchester County, aet. 64, dep. between Aug 11, 1772 and Jul 29, 1773, mentioned Thomas Brannock about 30 years ago as father of the present Edmond and Henry Brannock. {DOLR 27 Old 31}

KING, ROBERT, see "Sarah Emory," q.v.

KING, SARAH, see "James Walters," q.v.

KING, SOPHIA, see "James Walters," q.v.

KING, THOMAS, of Prince George's County, aet. 45 or thereabouts, dep. Mar 25, 1754, mentioned Thomas Blandford about 20 years ago, now deceased. {PGLR NN:256-257} Aet. 48, dep. Jul 3, 1754. {PGLR NN:284} Aet. 51, dep. Aug 29, 1757, mentioned Richard Groome about 30 years ago, now deceased. {PGLR PP:69, pt. 2} Aet. 60 or thereabouts, dep. Nov 10, 1766, mentioned his father (not named) and John Dawson, William Brooke, Joseph Brooke, and James Brooke about 45 years ago. {PGLR TT:651-652} Aet. 60, dep. Feb 20, 1767, stated that he and Richard Sansbery were chain carriers for Nathan Selby about 30 years ago. {PGLR BB#2:166, 168} Aet. 61, dep. Jun 15, 1767 and May 9, 1768, mentioned his father William King, deceased. {PGLR BB#2:370-371}

KING, THOMAS, of Prince George's County, aet. 64, planter, dep. Jun 30, 1752. {PGLR NN:66}

KING, THOMAS, of Prince George's County, aet. 32, dep. Feb 23, 1760. {PGLR BB#2:146} Aet. 33, dep. Aug 14, 1762. {PGLR BB#2:147} Thomas King (near Marlbro), aet. 39, dep. Nov 7, 1767, mentioned Ephraim Gover, Jr. about 16 years ago. {PGLR BB#2:162}

KING, THOMAS, see "Michael Miller," q.v.

KING, WILLIAM, of Prince George's County, aet. 64, dep. Apr 4, 1732. {PGLR Q:575} See "Thomas King," q.v.

KING, YOUNG, see "Indian Young King," q.v.

KINNISTON, THOMAS, see "Mauris Morris," q.v.

KIRBY, BENJAMIN, of Queen Anne's County, aet. 47, dep. Apr, 1769, stated that Edmund Kelly married Ann Dailey. {QAEJ - James Hutchens folder}

KIRBY, JOHN, of Charles County, aet. 30, dep. Sep 4, 1660, mentioned the wife (not named) of John Cherman. {CHLR A:100} See "John Kerby," q.v.

KIRK, JOAN, see "Joan Lewis" and "Esther Hepworth," q.v.

KIRK, JOHN, see "William Murray" and "Charles Dickinson" and "John Hepworth," q.v.

KIRK, MRS., see "Indian Paupakinquah," q.v.

KIRKE, JOHN, of Dorchester County, aet. 60 and upwards, dep. between Jun 13, 1730 and Sep 10, 1730, mentioned *Hogg Island* having been taken up by Charles Mackeel and sold by Thomas Hunt, heir at law of said Mackeel, to Patrick Brawhaun. {DOLR 8 Old 404}

KIRKE, MARIA, see "William Murray," q.v.

KIRKHAM (KIRKAM), JAMES, of Queen Anne's County, aet. 45, dep. Sep, 1761. {QAEJ - William Webb folder}

KIRKHAM, WILLIAM, of Queen Anne's County, aet. about 51, dep. Sep, 1761.
{QAEJ - William Webb folder}
KIRKMAN, GEORGE, of Dorchester County, aet. 57, dep. between Mar 14, 1769 and Apr 9, 1770, mentioned his brother Roger Kirkman and his father George Kirkman, both deceased. {DOLR 24 Old 9}
KIRKMAN, JAMES, see "Joseph Blackwell," q.v.
KIRKMAN, ROGER, see "George Kirkman," q.v.
KIRWAN, JOHN, see "John Carwin," q.v.
KIRWAN, MATTHEW, see "Anthony Shorter," q.v.
KIRWAN, PATRICK, of Dorchester County, aet. 40, dep. between Jun 16, 1727 and Mar 17, 1727/8. {DOLR 8 Old 200}
KISTON, EDWARD, of Prince George's County, aet. 45, dep. Aug 23, 1738. {PGLR T:635}
KITTEMAN, CHRISTOPHER, see "William Winfield," q.v.
KNEEL, JOHN, of Dorchester County, aet. 43, dep. between Nov 9, 1756 and Nov 7, 1760. {DOLR 17 Old 213}
KNIGHT, MARY, see "Elizabeth Lamphier," q.v.
KNOWLEMAN (KNOWLMAN, KNOLEMAN), ANTHONY, of Kent County, aet. about 39, dep. Jul 16, 1762. {KEEJ - John Carville folder} See "Benjamin Blackleach," q.v.
KNOWLEMAN (KNOLEMAN), MARY, of Cecil County, n.a., dep. Mar 8, 1706/7, stated that William Potts had not done her justice by examining her servant [John Fichgared] in private. {CMSP 1:7, 1:9 - The Black Books} See "Benjamin Blackleach" and "Joan Dewerty," q.v.
KYLE, ELIZABETH, see "Elizabeth Lamphier," q.v.
LADAMORE, MRS., see "Joan Ridgeway," q.v.
LADD, EDWARD, of Anne Arundel County, aet. 21 or thereabouts, planter, dep. Sep 13, 1664. {ARMD 49:304, 314}
LADD, WILLIAM, see "John Trew" and "William Davis," q.v.
LAINE, RICHARD, of Dorchester County, aet. 48, dep. Mar 7, 1740. {DOLR 6 Old 69}
LAKE, HENRY, of Dorchester County, aet. 46, dep. Aug 24, 1745. {DOLR 12 Old 247} Aet. 52, dep. between Nov 13, 1750 and Feb 16, 1750. {DOLR 14 Old 527} See "Thomas Whitely" and "Daniel Foxwell," q.v.
LAKE, MARY, see "Thomas Whitely" and "Susanna Bryan," q.v.
LAKE, PASON, see "Pollard Edmondson," q.v.
LAKE, ROBERT, see "Henry Fisher," q.v.
LAMAR, JOHN, of Prince George's County, aet. 72, dep. Feb 1, 1763, mentioned old Thomas Ricketts. {PGLR TT:84} Aet. 70 odd years, dep. Jun 11, 1764. {PGLR TT:370} Aet. 78, dep. Jun 26, 1770, stated that he saw Rev. Maconkey marry John Ouchterlony and Priscilla Plummer; said John used to sell goods and his first wife was Frances Wells. {PGLR AA#2:121}
LAMASTER, ISAAC, see "Isaac Lemaster," q.v.

LAMASTER, RICHARD, of Charles County, aet. 65, dep. Jan 31, 1776. {CHLR X#3:534}

LAMB, FRANCIS, of Kent County, Quaker, aet. about 54, dep. affirmed Oct 3, 1743, mentioned his father Pearce Lamb about 28 years ago; also mentioned Edward Beck's wife Ann and cousin William Beck. {KELR JS#25:193} Aet. about 63, dep. Sep 22, 1751. {KELR JS#27:69} Aet. about 64, dep. Jun 4, 1753. {KELR JS#27:316} Aet. about 66, dep. Sep, 1755. {KEEJ - Thomas Chandler folder} See "Joshua Lamb," q.v.

LAMB, JOHN, see "John Salter," q.v.

LAMB, JOSHUA, of Kent County, Quaker, aet. about 34, dep. 1753. {KELR JS#27:316} Aet. about 45, dep. Sep 12, 1764, mentioned his brother Francis Lamb and Griffith Jones, both deceased. {KELR DD#1:598} Aet. about 55, dep. circa 1773. {KEEJ - Samuel Griffith folder}

LAMB, PEARCE, see "Francis Lamb," q.v.

LAMB ROSAMOND, of Kent County, Quaker, aet. about 48, dep. Oct 3, 1743, mentioned her parents, Edward and Ann Beck, about 28 years ago. {KELR JS#25:193} Aet. about 55, dep. Aug 11, 1750, mentioned her brother Caleb Beck and father Edward Beck in 1713. {KELR JS#26:370} See "Caleb Beck," q.v.

LAMBERT, AMY, of Charles County, n.a., dep. Mar 14, 1664/5, stated that Mary Grub said she was with child by John Grub. {CHLR B:445} Aime Lambert, aet. 30, dep. Jun 11, 1669. {CHLR D#1:120}

LAMBERT, EDMOND, of Charles County, aet. 39, dep. Jun 11, 1669/70. {CHLR D#1:120}

LAMBERT, GEORGE, of Frederick County, n.a., dep. Aug 20, 1772. {FRLR P:429}

LAMBERT, JOHN, see "John Allen," q.v.

LAMBERT, JOSEPH, see "John Salter," q.v.

LAMBETH, THOMAS, of Charles County, aet. 59, dep. May 22, 1742. {CHLR O#2:384}

LAMPHIER, ELIZABETH, of Prince George's County, aet. 63, widow of Thomas Lamphier, dep. Aug 8, 1767, stated that her father Robert Going and her mother Mary Going (daughter of Gregory Rowe), both deceased, had 4 sons and 3 daughters: (1) John Going, eldest son, left Ireland when she (deponent) was a child, returned some years later, and then went to England; he married (wife not named) at Plymouth, had children, and returned to Ireland; (2) Philip Going, second son, married Sarah Pike, who died and he married second to Mary Knight, who died and he married third to Susanna Godding; (3) James Going, third son, married Dorothy Tyeney, who died and he married second to Elizabeth Kyle; (4) Mary Going, first daughter, married James Walpoole; (5) Robert Going, last son, married Jane Johnston; (6) Sarah Going, second daughter, married Richard Franklin, an attorney; and, (7) Elizabeth Going (this deponent) lived in County Tipperary in the Kingdom of Ireland and married Thomas Lamphier (son of Thomas Lamphier and Elizabeth Kyle) at Leieskeevene. Robert Going, father of deponent, had 2 brothers and 1 sister: (1)

Richard Going married (wife not named) and lived in Bristol; (2) Mary Going, married E. White, now deceased; and, (3) James Going married (wife not named), lived in Clonmel, and had 1 son and 3 daughters: (1) Mary Going married (husband not named); (2) Rebecca Going married (husband not named); (3) Susanna Going, not married; and, (4) Richard Going married (wife not named) and was Mayor of Clonmele (when deponent left Ireland) as was his father James several times before him. Deponent's mother's sister Sarah Rowe married John Bagwell and had 1 son and 2 daughters: (1) John Bagwell was a banker and merchant in Clonmell; (2) Mary Bagwell; and, (3) Sarah Bagwell. Deponent's husband Thomas Lamphier lived at Coreigheen when they were married and his father, also named Thomas, married Elizabeth Kyle and had 4 sons and 3 daughters: (1) Elizabeth Lamphier married John Burgess and their son Henry Burgess married Elizabeth Lamphier, daughter of Thomas Lamphier, Sr.; a cloathier by trade, he came to America with his uncle Thomas Lamphier (deponent's husband) and the rest of the family; Henry Burgess died a few years ago as notified in a letter to deponent from John Patterson (her son-in-law) and he left 6 children, 3 by a former wife (none were named); (2) William Lamphier, eldest son to Thomas Lamphier, Sr., married Elizabeth Lane, sister to Ambrose Lane of Lane's Park, and said Elizabeth is since dead and said William had also married an Evans as noted in a letter to her brother Thomas Lamphier; (3) Mary Lamphier, daughter of Thomas Lamphier, Sr., married Joseph Tinson (Tenson), son of Joseph Tinson of Orchard Town near Clonmell, and after Mary died he married Garter Hunt (daughter of John Hunt of Clonag); (4) Joseph Lamphier married Elizabeth Bradshaw, daughter of Robert Bradshaw, of County Limerick; (5) Thomas Lamphier, this deponent's husband; (6) John Lamphier (not married); and, (7) Sarah Lamphier, who died of smallpox before deponent left Ireland. When this deponent, her husband, and the rest of the family left for America in 1738 the following were still alive: William Lamphier and wife; Joseph Lamphier and wife; John Burgess and wife; Joseph Tinson and second wife Garter Tinson; and, John Lamphier; also, Thomas Lamphier, Sr. and wife Elizabeth had sponsored this deponent's baptism. Thomas Lamphier, father of Thomas (deponent's husband) died in Coreigheen in August before deponent left Ireland, leaving his widow Elizabeth to care of son John Lamphier who was preparing to move to a farm called *Park Town*. Deponent's children by Thomas Lamphier are Going Lamphier (who lives in Fairfax County, Virginia), Susanna Lamphier (who married John Patterson) and Venus Lamphier, both of whom live in Maryland. {PGLR BB#2:42-44}

LAMPHIER, THOMAS (family), see "Elizabeth Lamphier," q.v.

LANCASTER, THOMAS, of Prince George's County, aet. 51, dep. Jan 6, 1747/8, mentioned Dr. Patrick Hepburn and Mr. John Gerrard about 30 years ago. {PGLR BB:690}

LANDEN, ROBERT, of Charles County, aet. 20, dep. Jul 8, 1662, stated that shortly after the demise of his master, Capt. Russell, he saw Thomas Shelton and Katherine Budd in his deceased master's bed. {CHLR A:220}
LANE, AIME, of Charles County, aet. 25, dep. Jun 11, 1669/70. {CHLR D#1:120}
LANE, AMBROSE, see "Elizabeth Lamphier," q.v.
LANE, JOHN, of Queen Anne's County, aet. 68, dep. Aug 23, 1710, stated that Rev. James Clayland married John Baynard and Elizabeth Blackwell about 33 years ago in the house of Richard Dudley in Talbot County and their son Thomas Baynard was born in wedlock. {QALR ET#A:62}
LANE, JOHN, of Queen Anne's County, aet. 82, dep. between Jun 11, 1765 and Mar 9, 1767 in Dorchester County. {DOLR 21 Old 315}
LANE, RICHARD, of Dorchester County, aet. 68, dep. between Aug 11, 1761 and Dec 5, 1761. {DOLR 18 Old 85} Aet. 69, dep. between Nov 10, 1761 and Mar 4, 1762. {DOLR 18 Old 83}
LANG, EDWARD, of New Connaught, Cecil County, n.a., dep. Nov 4, 1722, mentioned the encroachment of Pennsylvanians on his land, particularly Isaac Taylor and son (not named), Elisha Gatchell, William Brown, John Churchman, Richard Brown, and Roger Nerck. {ARMD 25:396}
LANGFITT, FRANCIS, of Dorchester County, planter, aet. about 55, dep. between Mar 13, 1764 and Jun 4, 1767. {DOLR 21 Old 382} Francis Langfit, aet. about 66, dep. between Nov 14, 1769 and Jul 28, 1772. {DOLR 26 Old 100} Aet. 67, dep. Mar 27, 1776, stated that he lived on *Bridge Neck* about 27 years ago. {DOLR 28 Old 176-177}
LANGRALL, GEORGE, see "Mary Walter," q.v.
LANGRALL, JAMES, of Dorchester County, aet. 36 or 37, dep. between Nov 14, 1752 and Jun 13, 1753, mentioned a dispute between his father (not named) and Capt. Thomas Hicks over a bounded tree on *Langrell's Chance* about 15 or 16 years ago, and stated that Michael Stogdon and John Creek who were tenants of said Hicks; also mentioned Thomas Williams about 3½ years ago, now deceased. {DOLR 14 Old 709} James Langrell, aet. 58, dep. between Nov 12, 1771 and Apr 17, 1772, mentioned Joseph Thompson about 12 or 13 years ago, now deceased. {DOLR 26 Old 50}
LANGRALL, WILLIAM, of Dorchester County, aet. about 41, dep. between Aug 12, 1755 and Aug 10, 1757. {DOLR 15 Old 512} William Langrall, Sr., aet. about 58, dep. between Aug 14, 1770 and Oct 15, 1770. {DOLR 24 Old 297}
LANGWORTH, JAMES, of St. Mary's County, aet. 20 or thereabouts, dep. Jun 19, 1650. {ARMD 10:29} Aet. not given, dep. 1659. {ARMD 41:367} See "Mary Greenway," q.v.
LANGWORTH, MARY, see "George Thorold," q.v.
LANHAM, EDWARD, see "Josiah Lanham" and "George Athey" and "Ignatius Fenwick" and "Henry Wood," q.v.

LANHAM, JOHN, of Prince George's County, aet. 65, dep. Jun 8, 1725. {PGLR I:647} John Lenham, aet. 70, dep. between Apr 17, 1729 and Jun 26, 1729. {PGLR M:445} See "Thomas Shearwood," q.v.

LANHAM, JOHN, JR., of Prince George's County, n.a., dep. Jun 11, 1727. {PGLR Q:472}

LANHAM (LANNUM), JOHN, SR., of Prince George's County, aet. 67, dep. Aug 25, 1755. {PGLR NN:392}

LANHAM, JOHN, 3RD, see "John Palmer, Jr.," q.v.

LANHAM, JOSIAH, of Prince George's County, aet. 45, dep. Nov 14, 1774, mentioned his father Edward Lanham about 30 or 40 years ago, now deceased. {PGLR CC#2:58}

LANHAM, THOMAS, of Prince George's County, aet. 68, dep. Sep 21, 1761, stated that he has known this area for about 54 or 55 years. {PGLR RR:227}

LANHAM (LANNUM), THOMAS, JR., of Prince George's County, aet. 45, dep. Aug 25, 1755. {PGLR NN:392} Thomas Lanham, aet. between 60 and 70, dep. Oct 15, 1776. {PGLR CC#2:310}

LANHAM (LANNUM), WILLIAM, JR., of Prince George's County, aet. 54, dep. Aug 25, 1755. {PGLR NN:392}

LANNUM, JOHN, see "John Lanham" and "Thomas Shearwood," q.v.

LANSDALE, RICHARD, of Prince George's County, n.a., dep. Nov 15, 1768, stated that he was chain carrier for Mark Brown, Jr. on *Richards & Johns* about 20 years ago. {PGLR BB#2:387}

LARCAN, ----, see "Jacob Giles," q.v.

LARKIN, THOMAS (captain), of Anne Arundel County, aet. 47, dep. 1684. {AALR IT#5:30}

LASHLEY, ROBERT, of Prince George's County, aet. 68, dep. Sep 22, 1772, stated that he leased the tract *Loanhead* from James Beall about 25 years ago. {PGLR BB#3:117}

LATIMER, JAMES, of Charles County, aet. 73, dep. May 1, 1773. {CHLR U#3:269}

LAURENCE, GEORGE, see "James Ringgold," q.v.

LAWRENCE, DANIELL, of Dorchester County, aet. 46, dep. Mar 1, 1706, stated that the tract called *Grangers* on Grangers Cove belonged to his master John Pollard about 21 or 22 years ago. {DOLR 6 Old 119} See "John Barns," q.v.

LAWRENCE, JAMES, of Queen Anne's County, aet. 28, dep. Sep 4, 1735. {QAEJ - John Coursey folder}

LAWRENCE, WILLIAM, see "Eliza Granger," q.v.

LAWSON, JOHN, see "John Burroughs," q.v.

LAWSON, THOMAS, of St. Mary's County, n.a., dep. Jul 21, 1681. {ARMD 15:393}

LAWSON, THOMAS, of Charles County, aet. 41, dep. May 24, 1747. {CHLR Z#2:80}

LAWSON, THOMAS, of Prince George's County, aet. 65, dep. Jan 12, 1748/9. {PGLR BB:663} Thomas Lawson, planter, aet. 66, dep. Jul 1, 1751, stated that he was overseer to Daniel Dulany, Esq., about 30 years ago. {PGLR PP:154-155} Aet. 67, dep. May 12, 1753. {PGLR NN:174}

LAWSON, THOMAS, of Prince George's County, aet. 69, dep. Sep 5, 1767, mentioned Thomas Wall about 14 years ago, now deceased. {PGLR PP:128, pt. 2}
LAWSON, THOMAS, see "Thomas Taylor," q.v.
LAYTON, MARGARET, of Dorchester County, aet. 28, dep. between Mar 10, 1752 and Mar 10, 1753. {DOLR 14 Old 712}
LAYTON, NICOLS, see "Patrick Connerly," q.v.
LAYTON, THOMAS, of Dorchester County, aet. 45, between Nov 9, 1742 and Nov 5, 1743. {DOLR 12 Old 157}
LAYTON, WILLIAM, see "George Andrew, Jr.," q.v.
LEAK, HENRY, of Dorchester County, aet. 44, dep. between Jun 14, 1743 and Aug 1, 1743, stated that he was shown the bounds of *Edenburrough* by his father (not named) about 24 or 25 years ago. {DOLR 12 Old 167}
LEAK, HENRY, of Dorchester County, aet. 72, dep. between Nov 19, 1731 and Feb 23, 1731/2. {DOLR 8 Old 453}
LEAKINS, JOHN, see "Staley Durham," q.v.
LEAKINS, THOMAS, see "Staley Durham," q.v.
LECOMPTE, ANTHONY, of Dorchester County, aet. 39, dep. between Aug 13, 1765 and Dec 21, 1765. {DOLR 21 Old 447} Aet. 42, dep. between Mar 8, 1768 and Jul 23, 1768, mentioned his father John Lecompte. {DOLR 23 Old 5} See "James Cullen" and "Robert Winsmore Lecompte," q.v.
LECOMPTE, CHARLES, of Dorchester County, aet. about 42, dep. between Mar 13, 1764 and Mar 14, 1765. {DOLR 20 Old 28}
LECOMPTE, CLARA, of Dorchester County, aet. about 42, dep. between Nov 10, 1741 and Mar 11, 1741/2, mentioned her mother (not named) and aunt Susannah Powell; also stated that the bounded tree of *Spocot* was burned by William Warner when she (Clara) was a girl. {DOLR 12 Old 154}
LECOMPTE, JOHN, of Dorchester County, aet. about 55, dep. between Nov 10, 1741 and Mar 11, 1741/2, stated that the bounds of *Spocot* began at the head of Cary's Creek on a point opposite where old John Bolton lived. {DOLR 12 Old 154} Aet. about 57, dep. between Nov 10, 1741 and Mar 10, 1747. {DOLR 14 Old 200} Aet. about 62, dep. between Mar 14, 1748 and Jun 10, 1749, mentioned the death of Frances Beckwith. {DOLR 14 Old 465}
LECOMPTE, JOHN, of Dorchester County, aet. 33, son of Nehemiah Lecompte, dep. between Mar 13, 1770 and Oct 20, 1770. {DOLR 26 Old 396}
LECOMPTE, JOHN, of Dorchester County, aet. 41, dep. Jun 9, 1703, stated that the tract called *Five Pines* is where Richard Davis and his wife Abigail lived some 20 to 24 years. {DOLR 6 Old 53}
LECOMPTE, JOHN, see "Ann Griffin" and "James Cullen" and "Robert Winsmore Lecompte" and "William Warner" and "Anthony Lecompte" and "Betsey Lecompte" and "Moses Lecompte" and "Giles Proctor," q.v.
LECOMPTE, JOSEPH, of Dorchester County, aet. 29, dep. between Nov 8, 1767 and Aug 26, 1768, mentioned his father Peter Lecompte, deceased. {DOLR 23 Old 258}

LECOMPTE, LAVINA, of Dorchester County, aet. 50, dep. between Apr 6, 1732 and Jun 3, 1732. {DOLR 9 Old 68}

LECOMPTE, MARY, of Dorchester County, aet. about 74, dep. between Nov 10, 1741 and Mar 10, 1747. {DOLR 14 Old 200}

LECOMPTE, MARY, of Dorchester County, aet. 41, dep. between Mar 8, 1757 and May 28, 1757, stated that her husband St. Leger Pattison told her to get Martin Driver and her father (not named) and two or three other people to put down a marker for *Pattison's Folly* (no date given, but prob. 14 to 15 years ago). {DOLR 15 Old 483}

LECOMPTE, MOSES, of Dorchester County, aet. 44, dep. between Apr 6, 1732 and Jun 3, 1732, stated that about 14 or 15 years ago James Pattison told him that when he first came out of Virginia the cove was called Crab Cove and it went by that name until a man named Rowland drowned while carrying lime across the cove and it was afterwards called Rowland's Cove. {DOLR 9 Old 68} Aet. 80, blind, dep. between Nov 8, 1767 and Aug 26, 1768, mentioned old John Lecompte and William Warner about 60 years ago. {DOLR 23 Old 258}

LECOMPTE, MOSES, JR., of Dorchester County, aet. 34, dep. between Mar 8, 1757 and May 28, 1757. {DOLR 15 Old 483}

LECOMPTE, NEHEMIAH, of Dorchester County, aet. 70, dep. between Nov 8, 1768 and Mar 14, 1769. {DOLR 23 Old 151} See "John Lecompte," q.v.

LECOMPTE, PETER, of Dorchester County, aet. about 46, dep. between Mar 13, 1764 and Mar 14, 1765, stated that he was shown the bounds of John Wheeler's land about 17 years ago by his father, Peter Lecompte, now deceased. {DOLR 20 Old 28} Aet. 65 or thereabouts, dep. Sep 20, 1776. {DOLR 28 Old 232} See "Joseph Lecompte," q.v.

LECOMPTE, PHILEMON, of Dorchester County, n.a., dep. between Mar 12, 1750/1 and Mar 14, 1753, mentioned Henry Trippe and William Warner about 47 years ago. {DOLR 14 Old 689} Dep. between Nov 13, 1759 and Mar 10, 1762, n.a., stated that he was shown the bounded tree of *Canterbury* about 44 or 45 years ago by Rebeccah Harwood, now deceased. {DOLR 18 Old 78} Dep. between Jun 11, 1765 and Aug 12, 1766, n.a., mentioned Edward Poole, Col. William Ennalls, and Major Tobias Pollard about 46 years ago. {DOLR 21 Old 110} See "Indian Abraham," q.v.

LECOMPTE, ROBERT WINSMORE, of Dorchester County, aet. 57, dep. between Nov 10, 1761 and Feb 26, 1762, mentioned his brother John Lecompte, now deceased, and his nephew Anthony Lecompte. {DOLR 18 Old 130} Aet. 58, dep. between Nov 9, 1762 and Jun 18, 1763. {DOLR 18 Old 437}

LECOMPTE, WILLIAM, see "John Long, Jr.," q.v.

LEE, ELIZABETH, see "Joseph Ryon," q.v.

LEE, FRANCIS, see "Spencer Martrum Waters," q.v.

LEE, GEORGE, of Queen Anne's County, aet. about 48, dep. July, 1756(?). {QAEJ - Thomas Wilson folder}

LEE, ISAAC, see "Sarah Kennerly" and "Ann Vickers," q.v.

LEE, JAMES, see "Sarah Chad" and "John Riddle," q.v.
LEE, JOHN, of Talbot County, aet. about 21 or 22, dep. Sep 5, 1692. {ARMD 8:374}
LEE, JOHN, of Anne Arundel County, n.a., dep. Mar 30, 1707. {CMSP 1:8}
LEE, JOHN, of Queen Anne's County, aet. about 22, dep. Sep 4, 1735. {QAEJ - John Coursey folder}
LEE, JOHN, see "Charles Thompson" and "George Stapleford," q.v.
LEE, MR., see "John Allison," q.v.
LEE, OLIVER, see "Kenellm Skillington," q.v.
LEE, PHILIP, of Prince George's County, n.a., dep. Dec 24, 1736. {PGLR Y:84}
LEE, RICHARD, see "Allen Quynn," q.v.
LEE, WILLIAM, of Dorchester County, aet. 63, dep. between Aug 10, 1762 and Oct 27, 1762. {DOLR 19 Old 88}
LEEDES, WILLIAM, of Talbot County, n.a., dep. 1659. {ARMD 41:273, 49:515}
LEFTWICH, ELISHA, of Charles County, aet. 40, dep. Nov 2, 1752. {CHLR B#3:211}
LEGOE, BENJAMIN, of Baltimore County, aet. 76, dep. Sep 15, 1750, stated that Robert and Isabella Jackson had a son Abraham Jackson some time ago and then twin sons Isaac Jackson (oldest) and Jacob Jackson (youngest); also stated that Isabella's sister (not named) married Jonathan Massey. {BALR TR#E:6}
LEIGH, JAMES, see "John Riddle," q.v.
LEISLER, JAMES, of St. Mary's County, n.a., dep. Oct 5, 1664. {ARMD 49:269}
LEISY, JOSEPH, of Prince George's County, aet. 65, dep. May 31, 1731. {PGLR Q:604}
LEITERT, HENRY, of Frederick County, aet. 23, dep. 1767. {FRLR L:60}
LEMARE, GOLLANT, see "William Moore," q.v.
LEMAR, INS., of Prince George's County, aet. 72, dep. Feb 1, 1763, mentioned his father (not named) and brother (not named). {PGLR TT:85}
LEMASTER (LAMASTER), ABRAHAM, of Charles County, aet. 39, dep. May 14, 1752, mentioned his father Richard Lemaster. {CHLR R#3:354} See "Richard Lemaster" and "Edward Cadell" and "Thomas Jameson," q.v.
LEMASTER (LAMASTER), ISAAC, of Charles County, aet. 50, dep. Jan 25, 1744/5. {CHLR Z#2:344}
LEMASTER (LAMASTER), ISAAC, of Charles County, aet. 65, dep. Jul 26, 1775. {CHLR E#3:389}
LEMASTER (LAMASTRE), JOHN, of Charles County, aet. 39, dep. Sep 13, 1720. {CHLR M#2:109} John Lemaster, Sr., aet. 55, dep. Aug 6, 1736. {CHLR T#2:224}
LEMASTER (LAMASTRE), RICHARD, of Charles County, aet. 51, dep. Sep 13, 1720. {CHLR M#2:109} Aet. 58, dep. Oct 14, 1728. {CHLR Q#2:95} Aet. 60, dep. Jun 14, 1732, mentioned his father Abraham Lamastre. {CHLR R#2:157} Aet. 61, dep. Apr 13, 1731. {CHLR R#2:42}
LEMON, HICKFORD, of Prince George's County, aet. 51, dep. Oct 6, 1724. {PGLR I:600} Aet. 56, dep. Nov 27, 1728. {PGLR M:347}

LENDRUM, ANDREW (reverend), of Baltimore County, St. George's Parish, n.a., dep. Feb 23, 1763. {BALR B#L:187}
LENHAM, JOHN, see "John Lanham," q.v.
LENNOX (LENOX), JAMES, of Baltimore County, aet. 60, dep. Mar 3, 1764. {BALR B#M:370} Aet. 60, dep. Nov 11, 1764. {BALR B#N:458} Aet. 64, dep. Nov 3, 1766. {BALR B#P:307} Aet. 66, dep. Oct 25, 1769. {BALR AL#B:283}
LENTON, JOSEPH, see "Capt. Battin" and "Francis Batcheler," q.v.
LENTON, URSULA, see "Humperie Haggate," q.v.
LEO, VALERUSE, see "Thomas Hinson," q.v.
LEWCRAFT, JOHN, of Charles County, aet. 60, dep. Sep 9, 1747. {CHLR Z#2:186} Aet. 90, dep. Jun 4, 1771, stated that he was overseer for Francis Goodrick about 40 years ago. {CHLR T#3:599}
LEWELLIN, JOHN, of Charles County, aet. 26, dep. Jun 29, 1680. {CHLR I#1:39} See "Edward Billiter" and "Thomas Simpson" and "John Llewellin," q.v.
LEWGER, JOHN, of St. Mary's County, n.a., dep. Sep 9, 1663. {ARMD 49:51}
LEWIS, ABRAHAM, of Dorchester County, aet. 49, dep. between Nov 14, 1749 and Jan 22, 1749/50, mentioned his brother Thomas Lewis, about 2 years ago, who said he was shown the bounded tree of *Glostershire Regulated* by old William Phillips, now deceased. {DOLR 14 Old 404}
LEWIS, ANN, see "Benony Phillips," q.v.
LEWIS, EDWARD, see "Thomas Stimson," q.v.
LEWIS, ELLINOR, of Dorchester County, aet. about 57, widow of James Smith (deceased), brother of Henry Smith and Stephen Smith, dep. between Nov 11, 1746 and Apr 14, 1748, mentioned John Clayburn, stepfather of said James Smith; also mentioned her daughter Mary Smith, now Mary Hall, and her father Joshua Morgaine (Morgan). {DOLR 14 Old 231}
LEWIS, GLODE, of Dorchester County, aet. 60, dep. Jul 27, 1704. {DOLR 6 Old 47} See "John Lewis," q.v.
LEWIS, JAMES, of Charles County, aet. 22, dep. Apr 11, 1663. {CHLR B:331}
LEWIS, JOAN, of Somerset County, aet. 28, dep. Nov 19, 1684, stated that she saw Joan Kirk severely beat Edward Furlong. {ARMD 17:315}
LEWIS, JOHN, of Dorchester County, aet. 48, dep. between Aug 10, 1773 and Oct 23, 1773. {DOLR 27 Old 38}
LEWIS, JOHN, of Dorchester County, aet. 46, dep. between Jun 12, 1728 and Jul 16, 1728. {DOLR 8 Old 245}
LEWIS, JOHN, of Dorchester County, aet. 74, dep. between Nov 14, 1749 and Jan 22, 1749/50, mentioned old John Phillips about 50 years ago and Benony Phillips about 30 years ago. {DOLR 14 Old 404} Aet. 74, dep. between Jun 12, 1750 and Jul 18, 1750, mentioned old John Meekins and his brother Richard Meekins about 20 or 30 years ago. {DOLR 14 Old 428} Aet. 75, dep. between Aug 14, 1750 and Nov 24, 1750, stated that he was shown the bounds of *Roberts Rest* with his father (not named) and by Samuel Millington about 47 years ago.

{DOLR 14 Old 546} Aet. 75, dep. between Nov 13, 1750 and Feb 16, 1750/1, stated that he was shown the bounds of *Foxton Is Defeated* and *The Old Baily* about 46 years ago by old Thomas Smith. {DOLR 14 Old 527} Aet. 78, dep. between Mar 11, 1755 and Jul 23, 1755. {DOLR 15 Old 452} John Lewes, Sr., aet. 83, dep. between Nov 13, 1759 and Jan 12, 1760. {DOLR 17 Old 112} John Lewis, aet. 84, dep. between Aug 12, 1760 and Mar 2, 1761, stated that he was shown the bounds of *Puzzle* about 40 years ago by old John Meekins. {DOLR 17 Old 262} Aet. 84, dep. between Aug 12, 1760 and Dec 6, 1760, mentioned his brother Gload Lewis about 22 years ago. {DOLR 17 Old 268} Aet. 84, dep. between Mar 10, 1761 and Jun 6, 1761, mentioned George Ferguson about 60 years ago. {DOLR 17 Old 318} Aet. 87, dep. between Nov 10, 1761 and Mar 14, 1765, mentioned Thomas Smith and Glode Lewis some 70 years ago. {DOLR 20 Old 18}

LEWIS, SAMUEL, of Prince George's County, aet. 51, dep. Apr 21, 1767. {PGLR BB#2:119}

LEWIS, THOMAS, of Queen Anne's County, aet. about 57, dep. Apr, 1723. {QAEJ - William Bishop (vs. Richard) folder} Aet. about 60, dep. May 6, 1728. {QAEJ - Christopher Wilkinson folder}

LEWIS, THOMAS, of Charles County, aet. 60, dep. May 28, 1771. {CHLR T#3:378} See "Abraham Lewis," q.v.

LEYNORD, JOHN, see "Edward Cayhaile," q.v.

LILLINGSTON, JOHN, see "John Salter," q.v.

LINDSEY, EDMUND, see "Edmond Linsey" and "Zachary Wade," q.v.

LINDSEY, ELINOR, see "Zachary Wade," q.v.

LINDSEY, WILLIAM, of Charles County, aet. 53, dep. Nov 20, 1770. {CHLR T#3:244}

LINEGAR, SARAH, of Kent County, aet. about 62, dep. Apr, 1759. {KEEJ - Thomas Harris folder}

LINSEY, EDMOND, of Charles County, n.a., dep. Sep 14, 1659, stated that at the house of James Linsey last March or April he was told by Richard Greynger that on the other side of the Potomac River they call Capt. Jenkins by the name of Capt. Grindingstone. {CHLR A:64, ARMD 53:51} Aet. 36, dep. Apr 17, 1660. {CHLR A:86} Aet. not given, dep. Jul 9, 1662, mentioned Little Browne, under sheriff of Virginia. {CHLR A:228} See "Thomas Chapman" and "Zachary Wade," q.v.

LINSEY, JAMES, of St. Mary's County, n.a., dep. Jun 10, 1649. {ARMD 3:187}

LINSEY, JAMES, of Charles County, n.a., dep. May 7, 1661. {CHLR A:131} James Lindsey, n.a., dep. Jul 30, 1663. {CHLR B:144} See "Edmond Linsey," q.v.

LINTHICOMBE, NATHAN, of Anne Arundel County, aet. 44, dep. 1680, stated that he was a servant to Joshua Merekin about 22 years ago. {AALR IT#5:49-50}

LITTLE, GUY, of Baltimore County, aet. 44, dep. Jan 4, 1763. {BALR B#L:497}

LITTLETON, EDMOND, see "William Littleton," q.v.

LITTLETON, JOHN, see "John Caffey" and "John Harper," q.v.

LITTLETON, WILLIAM, of Dorchester County, aet. 60, dep. between Mar 10, 1751 and Mar 10, 1753, stated that he was shown the bounded tree of *Atlantis* about 27 or 28 years ago by John McCollister, now deceased. {DOLR 14 Old 712} Aet. 70, dep. between Nov 9, 1762 and Aug 13, 1764, mentioned Edmond Littleton about 30 odd years ago and *Canawhy* was located near where John Dagg formerly lived. {DOLR 19 Old 293}

LITTON, SAMUEL, of Harford County, aet. 38, dep. May 25, 1775. {Land Commission, 1774, Harford County Genealogical Society Newsletter, Jan, 1993, p. 3}

LIVERS, ARNOLD, see "Helena Collard" and "Peter Brightwell," q.v.

LIVERS, MARY (Mrs.), of Charles County, aet. 55, dep. Feb 7, 1775. {CHLR W#3:606}

LLEWELLIN, JOHN, of St. Mary's County, n.a., dep. Mar 6, 1678, mentioned John Burdett, Christopher Rousby, and His Lordships' Negro Peter. {ARMD 15:227} See "John Lewellin," q.v.

LLOYD, ROBERT, of Queen Anne's County, n.a., dep. Jun 7, 1769, stated that he has known Francis Baker for 15 years during which time he had been a neighbor and a sober and honest man in business. {ARMD 32:327}

LLOYD, SOPHIA, see "Mary Moore," q.v.

LOCKER, JOHN, of Frederick County, n.a., dep. Jul 29, 1767, stated that at the house of Charles Hungerford last Feb 1st he got into a fray with Joseph Wilson who bit his (Locker's) left ear in such a way that Dr. James Doull had to cut out the piece before the damaged ear could be cured; he later received £15 in damages from Wilson. {FRLR L:42}

LOCKER, JOHN, of Prince George's County, aet. 40, dep. between Nov 11, 1729 and Mar 26, 1730, mentioned his father Thomas Locker, Sr. and Col. Thomas Addison about 16 or 17 years ago. {PGLR M:556}

LOCKER, PHILIP, of Prince George's County, aet. 42, dep. Sep 14, 1761, mentioned his mother (not named) and his father Thomas Locker, Sr. {PGLR RR:179}

LOCKER, THOMAS, see "John Locker" and "Philip Locker" and "Alexander Herbert" and "John Talbott," q.v.

LOCKETT (LOOKETT), ELESABETH, of Kent County, n.a., dep. Apr 1, 1661, stated that Thomas Bright was the father of her child and "theare wase a peace of munny brooken betwext theme and that he promised hur mariege before the child wase gott." {ARMD 54:211}

LOE, RAPHE, see "William Mitchell," q.v.

LOGSDON, RALPH, of Frederick County, aet. 36, dep. Dec 10, 1772. {FRLR P:681}

LOMAX, BENJAMIN, of Charles County, aet. 60, dep. Jun 24, 1764. {CHLR M#3:687}

LOMAX, CLEBORN, of Charles County, aet. 56, dep. Jul 16, 1728. {CHLR Q#2:167} See "Susanna MacNeale," q.v.

LOMAX, JOHN, of Charles County, aet. 34, dep. Jul 24, 1764. {CHLR M#3:687}

LOMAX, STEPHEN, of Charles County, aet. 27, dep. Jul 24, 1764. {CHLR M#3:687}

LOMAX, THOMAS, of Charles County, n.a., dep. May 1, 1659. {CHLR A:58, ARMD 53:47} Aet. not given, dep. Nov 14, 1659, stated that Mrs. Hatche thought Goodie Michel (wife of Thomas Michel) had bewitched her face. {CHLR A:69} Aet. not given, dep. Jul 28, 1663, mentioned James Smallwood, servant to Capt. Fendall. {CHLR B:134}

LONG, JOHN, of Dorchester County, aet. 80, dep. between Jun 11, 1765 and Aug 12, 1765. {DOLR 21 Old 110}

LONG, JOHN, JR., of Dorchester County, aet. 38, dep. between Jun 11, 1765 and Aug 12, 1765, mentioned William Lecompte and William Guy about 21 years ago, both now deceased, and the plantation where Edward Evens formerly lived. {DOLR 21 Old 110}

LONGMAN, STEPHEN, see "William Smith," q.v.

LOOCKERMAN, GOVERT, of Dorchester County, aet. 40, dep. Mar 13, 1721. {DOLR 8 Old 108}

LOOCKERMAN, JACOB, see "Andrew Gray," q.v.

LOOCKERMAN, THOMAS, of Dorchester County, aet. about 48, dep. between Mar 13, 1764 and Nov 10, 1764. {DOLR 19 Old 429} See "William Tucker," q.v.

LOOTON, JACOB, see "James Frisell," q.v.

LORD, ANDREW, of Dorchester County, aet. 68, dep. between Mar 14, 1769 and Apr 9, 1770, mentioned Francis Anderton's cousin John Franks. {DOLR 24 Old 9} Aet. 68, dep. between Mar 14, 1771 and Nov 13, 1771. {DOLR 25 Old 238}

LORD, JOSEPH, of Prince George's County, aet. 40, dep. Jun 16, 1730. {PGLR Q:14}

LORD, MOSES, see "Sarah Bryan" and "Henry Windows," q.v.

LORD, RUTH, of Prince George's County, aet. 41, dep. Jun 16, 1730, mentioned her father George Mills (Milles). {PGLR Q:10}

LORD, SARAH, of Dorchester County, aet. 63, dep. between Mar 18, 1726 and Jul 18, 1727. {DOLR 8 Old 201}

LOVE, CHARLES, of Charles County, n.a., dep. Sep 28, 1767. {CHLR P#3:613}

LOVE, SAMUEL, of Charles County, aet. 72, dep. Jul 24, 1758, mentioned his mother (not named) and grandmother (not named) showed him the bounded tree of *Westwood Manor* and his grandfather (not named) had purchased 100 acres of said tract from Thomas Garrard. {CHLR H#3:572} Aet. 71, dep. Aug 29, 1758. {CHLR H#3:578} Aet. 72, dep. Mar 1, 1759. {CHLR I#3:26}

LOVEJOY, JANE, of Charles County, aet. 37, dep. Sep 13, 1729, mentioned her former husband William Watson, deceased. {CHLR Q#2:345}

LOVEJOY, JOSEPH, of Prince George's County, aet. 78, dep. Jul 1, 1738. {PGLR T:605}

LOVEJOY, JOSEPH, JR., of Prince George's County, aet. 28, dep. Mar 11, 1745/6. {PGLR BB:6}

LOVINGTON, RICHARD, of Baltimore County, aet. 60, dep. Oct 22, 1767. {BALR B#Q:588}

LOVELESS, JOHN, of Charles County, aet. 65, dep. Sep 25, 1764. {CHLR N#3:167}

LOVELY, ELIZABETH (Mrs.), of Kent County, widow, n.a., dep. Sep 1, 1658. {ARMD 54:140}
LOW, WILLIAM, of Dorchester County, aet. 48, dep. between Aug 9, 1763 and Mar 31, 1764. {DOLR 19 Old 418} See "Patrick McCollister," q.v.
LOWE, COLONEL, see "Joseph Billiter," q.v.
LOWE, GEORGE, of Prince George's County, aet. 70 odd years, dep. Apr 24, 1759. {PGLR PP:315, pt. 2} Aet. 72, dep. Jul 19, 1760. {PGLR RR:121}
LOWE, HENRY, of Prince George's County, aet. 48, dep. Aug 29, 1768. {PGLR BB#2:389}
LOWE, HENRY, JR., of Prince George's County, aet. 33, dep. Aug 29, 1768. {PGLR BB#2:390}
LOWE, JACOB, see "Robert Parkinson," q.v.
LOWE, WILLIAM, SR., of Prince George's County, aet. 63, dep. Apr 24, 1759. {PGLR PP:315, pt. 2}
LOYLE, JOHN, of Charles County, aet. 20, dep. Jun 11, 1669/70. {CHLR D#1:119}
LOYON, JOHN, see "Charles Thompson," q.v.
LUCAS, BARTON, of Prince George's County, aet. 36, dep. Apr 21, 1767, mentioned Samuel Queen. {PGLR BB#2:121}
LUCAS (LUCASS), JAMES, of Prince George's County, aet. 49, dep. Feb 4, 1760. {PGLR RR:81} Aet. 56, dep. Jun 5, 1769, mentioned John Henry about 30 years ago. {PGLR BB#2:437} Aet. 56, dep. Oct 30, 1769, mentioned Joseph Story and Thomas James about 35 years ago. {PGLR AA#2:186}
LUCAS, THOMAS, SR., of Prince George's County, n.a., dep. Feb 18, 1717/8. {PGLR I:595} See "James Burns" and "William Barker" and "Basil Warring" and "John Wight" and "Lydia Harbin," q.v.
LUCKETT, ELIZABETH, see "Robert Hanson," q.v.
LUCKETT, IGNATIUS, of Charles County, aet. 45, dep. May 26, 1770, mentioned Jane Luckett and her son Thomas Hussey Luckett. {CHLR T#3:604} Aet. 46, dep. Jan 23, 1772. {CHLR T#3:618}
LUCKETT, JANE, see "Ignatius Luckett," q.v.
LUCKETT, NOTLEY, of Charles County, aet. 36, dep. Jan 23, 1772. {CHLR T#2:618}
LUCKETT, SAMUEL, of Prince George's County, aet. 44, dep. Apr 21, 1767. {PGLR BB#2:119}
LUCKETT, THOMAS, of Charles County, aet. 43, dep. Apr 25, 1767. {CHLR P#3:427}
LUCKETT, THOMAS HUSSEY, see "Ignatius Luckett" and "Robert Hanson," q.v.
LUCROFT, JOHN, of Charles County, aet. 83, dep. Jul 5, 1762. {CHLR M#3:214}
LUDFORD, ARTER, see "Philip Willocy," q.v.
LUMBROSO, JOHN (doctor), see "Joseph Dorrosell" and "John Browne" and "George Harris" and "Elizabeth Weales" and "George Bradshaw," q.v.
LUMLEY, ALEXANDER, of Anne Arundel County, n.a., dep. 1696. {ARMD 20:563}
LUN, JOHN, see "Lewis Griffin," q.v.

163

LUSBY, SAMUEL, of Prince George's County, aet. 26, dep. Aug 16, 1757. {PGLR PP:57, pt. 2}

LUX, WILLIAM (magistrate), of Elk Ridge, Anne Arundel County, n.a., dep. Dec 10, 1765. {ARMD 32:111}

LYLES, DAVID, see "William Depriest," q.v.

LYNCH, MRS., see "Ann Dolton," q.v.

LYNCH, NICHOLAS, of Kent County, aet. about 40, dep. Oct, 1753. {KELR JS#28:44}

LYNE, GEORGE, of St. Mary's County, n.a., dep. Jun 2, 1659, stated that he was a member of the company that surprised and overtook a ship called the *St. George* of Amsterdam at Barbadoes upon suspicion of piracy. {ARMD 41:308-309}

LYNES, JOHN, of London, England, master of the ship *Friends Increase* of London, aet. about 32, dep. Sep 23, 1681 in London, stated he had been in Maryland this present year. {ARMD 5:298}

LYNES, PHIL, see "John Swift," q.v.

LYON, JOHN, of Charles County, aet. 58, dep. Oct 29, 1767. {CHLR Q#3:311}

LYONS, JOHN, see "James Cannon," q.v.

LYTNER, ADAM, see "Johannes Bubenheim" and "John Skuyl" and "Henry Styls," q.v.

MACAWL, CORNELIA, see "Jane Thomas" and "Samuel Hubbert," q.v.

MACAWL, DAVID, see "Samuel Hubbert," q.v.

MACDANIEL, WALTER, of Dorchester County, aet. 47, dep. between Mar 16, 1733/4 and Jun 3, 1734, stated that he was shown the bounds of *Farginson's Forrest* about 25 years ago by Joseph Stannaway and Robert Johnson, deceased. {DOLR 9 Old 187}

MACE, EDMON, of Dorchester County, aet. 43, dep. between Mar 8, 1774 and May 2, 1774. {DOLR 27 Old 304}

MACE (MAACE), JOSIAH, of Dorchester County, aet. 62, dep. between Dec 15, 1727 and Nov 14, 1729, mentioned William Marchant and John Taylor, deceased. {DOLR 8 Old 328}

MACE, JOSIAH, of Dorchester County, aet. 28, dep. between Mar 12, 1771 and May 4, 1771. {DOLR 25 Old 6}

MACE, JOSIAS, see "Patrick Carrowan," q.v.

MACE, THOMAS, see "Joshua Busick," q.v.

MACKEEL, CHARLES, see "John Kirke," q.v.

MACKEEL, CLEER, see "Elinor Barney," q.v.

MACKEEL, THOMAS, see "Elinor Barney" and "John Mitchel," q.v.

MACKEELE, ROGER, see "Esther Hepworth," q.v.

MACKEY, ELIZABETH, see "Thomas Annis," q.v.

MACKEY, JAMES, of Charles County, n.a., dep. May 12, 1663. {CHLR B:115} See "Thomas Annis," q.v.

MACKKON, WILLIAM, of Charles County, aet. 46, dep. Jul 31, 1755. {CHLR E#3:387}
MACKLIN, RICHARD, see "John Salter," q.v.
MACKLIN, ROBERT, of Calvert County, n.a., dep. 1659. {ARMD 41:276}
MACLOUGHLIN, KENELM, see "Henry Tanner," q.v.
MACNEALE, JOHN, of Charles County, aet. 37, dep. Oct 10, 1738. {CHLR T#2:514}
MACNEALE, SUSANNA, of Charles County, aet. 40, dep. Apr 28, 1737, mentioned her former husband Cleborn Lomax. {CHLR T#2:368} Susannah McNeale, aet. 67, dep. Aug 20, 1753, mentioned her former husband Cleborn Lomax. {CHLR D#3:154}
MACNEMAR, TIMOTHY, of Dorchester County, aet. 68, dep. Aug 22, 1753. {DOLR 15 Old 74} Timothy Macknemar, aet. 55, dep. between Nov 20, 1738 and Dec 2, 1738, mentioned his father, Timothy Macknemar, about 35 or 36 years ago. {DOLR 12 Old 111} Timothy Macknimar, aet. 67, dep. between Jun 14, 1743 and Aug 1, 1743, mentioned James Insley and Phillip Wingate, commissioners, about 11 years ago. {DOLR 12 Old 167} See "George Booz," q.v.
MACONKEY, REVEREND, see "John Lamar," q.v.
MACUBINS, ZACH., of Anne Arundel County, aet. 41, dep. 1684. {AALR IT#5:32}
MADDOCK, EDWARD, of Charles County, aet. 22 or 23, dep. Mar 8, 1669/70. {CHLR D#1:133} Aet. 26, dep. Jun 14, 1670. {CHLR D#1:166}
MADDOCKE, EDWARD, of Charles County, aet. 77, dep. Feb 18, 1768. {CHLR Q#3:63}
MADDOCKE, JAMES, of Charles County, aet. 35, dep. Jan 23, 1772, mentioned his father Notley Maddocke. {CHLR T#3:617}
MADDOCKE, NOTLEY, of Charles County, aet. 57, dep. Jun 4, 1771. {CHLR T#3:600} See "James Maddocke," q.v.
MADDOX, CORNELIUS, of Charles County, aet. 42, dep. Jan 23, 1772. {CHLR T#3:618}
MADDOX, EDWARD, of Charles County, aet. 50, dep. May 14, 1744. {CHLR Y#2:397} Aet. 51, dep. Oct 1, 1744. {CHLR Y#2:189} Aet. 70, dep. Jun 28, 1761. {CHLR K#3:302} Aet. 79, dep. Jul 9, 1770. {CHLR T#3:608}
MADDOX, IGNATIUS, of Charles County, aet. 40, dep. Jun 5, 1770. {CHLR T#3:608}
MADDOX, JAMES, of Charles County, aet. 27, dep. Mar 27, 1764. {CHLR M#3:680} Aet. 30, dep. Nov 8, 1766, mentioned his father Notley Maddox. {CHLR P#3:276}
MADDOX, JOHN, of Charles County, aet. 56, dep. Oct 21, 1736. {CHLR T#2:268}
MADDOX, NOTLEY, of Charles County, aet. 52, dep. Feb 5, 1767. {CHLR P#3:270} Aet. 53, dep. Apr 25, 1767. {CHLR P#3:426} See "James Maddox," q.v.
MADDOX, WILLIAM, of Charles County, aet. 52, dep. Jan 31, 1776. {CHLR X#3:535}
MADKIN, HANNAH, of Dorchester County, aet. 60, dep. between Mar 13, 1738/9 and Nov 12, 1739. {DOLR 12 Old 119}

MADKINS, SARAH, of Dorchester County, aet. 60 or thereabouts, dep. Dec 15, 1774, mentioned her father (not named). {DOLR 28 Old 173}
MADKIN, THEODORE, of Dorchester County, aet. about 37, dep. between Nov 13, 1744 and Nov 10, 1748. {DOLR 14 Old 315}
MAGRUDER, ALEXANDER, of Prince George's County, aet. about 60, dep. Jul 7, 1732. {PGLR Q:525} Aet. about 70, dep. Aug 24, 1741, mentioned Col. Beall and Col. Thomas Greenfield about 50 years ago. {PGLR Y:361}
MAGRUDER, ALEXANDER, SR., of Prince George's County, aet. 66, dep. Aug 25, 1737. {PGLR T:506}
MAGRUDER, ALEXANDER, SR., of Prince George's County, aet. 50, dep. Feb 1, 1768. {PGLR BB#2:291} Alexander Magruder, aet. 50, dep. Jul 4, 1768. {PGLR AA#2:194}
MAGRUDER, GEORGE, of Prince George's County, aet. 48, dep. Feb 18, 1771, mentioned his brother Nathaniel Magruder. {PGLR AA#2:227} Aet. 50, dep. Oct 18, 1774, mentioned old John Sawser and old Thomas Swan and his son Thomas Swan about 30 years ago. {PGLR CC#2:25}
MAGRUDER, JAMES, JR., see "Jeremiah Magruder," q.v.
MAGRUDER, JAMES, SR., of Prince George's County, aet. 60, dep. Apr 24, 1759. {PGLR PP:315, pt. 2}
MAGRUDER, JEREMIAH, of Prince George's County, aet. 29, dep. Feb 4, 1760, mentioned a time when he and James Magruder, Jr. were boys. {PGLR RR:82}
MAGRUDER, JOHN, of Prince George's County, aet. 50, dep. Feb 4, 1760, mentioned his father (not named), uncle John Magruder, and cousin Samuel Magruder. {PGLR RR:82} See "Nathaniel Magruder" and "Mordecai Mitchell" and "Benjamin Perry," q.v.
MAGRUDER, NATHANIEL, of Prince George's County, aet. 39, dep. Nov 9, 1759, mentioned his father Ninian Magruder and brother John Magruder. {PGLR RR:80} See "George Magruder" and "Aaron Roberts" and "James Watson, Sr.," q.v.
MAGRUDER, NINIAN, see "Nathaniel Magruder" and "Benjamin Perry" and Samuel Magruder, 3rd," q.v.
MAGRUDER, SAMUEL, of Prince George's County, aet. 44, dep. May 20, 1728. {PGLR M:292}
MAGRUDER, SAMUEL (captain), of Prince George's County, aet. 43, dep. Jun 10, 1751, mentioned Samuel Magruder about 5 or 6 years ago, now deceased. {PGLR PP:123} Aet. 50, dep. Nov 9, 1759, mentioned his uncle Ninian Magruder about 30 years ago and his (Ninian's) father (not named). {PGLR RR:81}
MAGRUDER, SAMUEL, 3RD, of Frederick County, aet. 52, dep. Jun 3, 1760 and Jun 20, 1760, mentioned his father (not named) and his uncle Samuel Magruder about 33 or 34 years ago, also Charles Beall and his brother George Beall; also stated that Christian Gun was killed near the bounded tree of *Addition* (date not stated that). {FRLR F:1058} Samuel Magruder, the third, aet. 57, also listed as Samuel Magruder, aged about 57 years, dep. Aug 5, 1765. {FRLR K:1349}

Samuel Magruder, the third, of Prince George's County, aet. 52, dep. Feb 4, 1760, mentioned his father Ninian Magruder, grandfather (not named) and uncle (not named) when he (deponent) was a boy. {PGLR RR:82} Aet. 60 and upwards, dep. Sep 25, 1772. {FRLR P:432}

MAGRUDER, SAMUEL, see "Maureen Duvall, Sr." and "Samuel Magruder 3rd" and "Zachariah Magruder" and "John Magruder" and "Burgis Mitchell," q.v.

MAGRUDER, ZACHARIAH, of Prince George's County, aet. 47, dep. Feb 4, 1760, mentioned riding with his brother Samuel Magruder and father (not named) about 20 years ago. {PGLR RR:82}

MAHANY, JOHN, of Dorchester County, aet. 35, dep. Jan 15, 1744/5. {DOLR 12 Old 253}

MAHUGH, EDWARD, SR., of Prince George's County, aet. 60, dep. Mar 26, 1753. {PGLR NN:292}

MAIDWELL, THOMAS, of St. Mary's County, n.a., dep. Sep 2, 1650, stated that he was assaulted and struck on the head by John Dandy's wife while he was at work in his shop at St. Inigoes fort. {ARMD 10:31}

MAJOR, ELIZABETH, see "Thomas Brooke," q.v.

MALHAM, JOHN, of Northumberland County, Virginia, sheriff, n.a., dep. Jun 25, 1650 in St. Mary's County, stated that he captured two runaway servants, William Greenestead and Thomas Merriday, in the middle of March last and turned them over to Lt. William Lewis who took them with him to Portoback. {ARMD 10:24}

MALLONNEE, JOHN, of Baltimore County, n.a., dep. Jan 11, 1767. {BALR B#P:459}

MANAH (MANOR?), TIMOTHY, of Queen Anne's County, aet. about 60, dep. Feb, 1737. {QAEJ - Alexander Toulson folder}

MANER, JOHN, of Baltimore County, aet. 37, dep. Sep 20, 1767, mentioned his father William Maner. {BALR AL#A:122, 126}

MANER, WILLIAM, see "John Maner," q.v.

MANKIN, JAMES, of Charles County, aet. 56, dep. Jun 22, 1772. {CHLR U#3:263}

MANKIN, STEPHEN, of Charles County, aet. 44, dep. Jul 16, 1728. {CHLR Q#2:167}

MANKIN, STEPHEN, of Charles County, aet. 35, dep. Jun 4, 1771. {CHLR T#2:599}

MANKIN, WILLIAM, of Charles County, aet. 49, dep. Apr 25, 1774. {CHLR W#3:81}

MANNERS, GEORGE, of St. Mary's County, n.a., dep. Nov 19, 1649, mentioned Elias Beach (his attorney) and Henry Adams. {ARMD 4:531} See "Thomas Hamper," q.v.

MANNING, JOHN, of Charles County, aet. 56, dep. Oct 10, 1734, mentioned his father Joseph Manning. {CHLR R#2:537}

MANNING, JOHN, of Charles County, aet. 54, dep. Mar 21, 1769, mentioned his parents John and Mary Manning and his brother Joseph Manning. {CHLR

Q#3:409} Aet. 58, dep. Mar 31, 1773. {CHLR U#3:274} Aet. 60, dep. between Nov 8, 1774 and Feb 7, 1775. {CHLR W#3:610}
MANNING, JOSEPH, of Charles County, aet. 48, dep. Dec 15, 1760, mentioned his father John Manning. {CHLR K#3:150} See "John Manning," q.v.
MANNING, MARY, see "John Manning," q.v.
MANNING, THOMAS, of Dorchester County, aet. 40, dep. between Jun 9, 1761 and Mar 9, 1762. {DOLR 18 Old 75}
MANOR, TIMOTHY, see "Timothy Manah," q.v.
MANSFIELD, SAMUEL, of Kent County, aet. about 47, dep. Jul 21, 1762. {KEEJ - Christopher Bellican folder}
MANSHIP, CHARLES, see "Ann Cox," q.v.
MANWARING, RICHARD, of New Kent County, Virginia, n.a., dep. Sep 12, 1681 in St. Mary's County. {ARMD 17:22}
MANYARD, BENJAMIN, of Frederick County, aet. 26, dep. Nov 28, 1760. {FRLR G:72}
MANYARD, THOMAS, see "Jeremiah Covill" and "Solomon Turner," q.v.
MARBURY, FRANCIS, of Prince George's County, aet. 62, dep. Oct 6, 1724. {PGLR I:600} Aet. 64, dep. Mar 2, 1725. {PGLR I:645} Aet. 65, dep. Jul 1, 1726, mentioned Hillary Ball and Francis Clarboe about 20 years ago. {PGLR M:26} Aet. 67, dep. Jun 25, 1728, mentioned Major Wilson, High Sheriff of Prince George's County. {PGLR M:285} See "Luke Marbury" and "Leonard Wheeler" and "William Underwood" and "John Holley," q.v.
MARBURY, JONATHAN, of Charles County, aet. 26, dep. May 29, 1772. {CHLR U#3:21}
MARBURY, LUKE, of Prince George's County, aet. 32, dep. Mar 25, 1743, mentioned his father Francis Marbury. {PGLR Y:657} Aet. 37, dep. Jul 5, 1748, mentioned his father Francis Marbury. {PGLR BB:596}
MARBURY, MARY, see "Leonard Marbury," q.v.
MARBURY, WILLIAM, of Prince George's County, aet. 38, dep. Mar 26, 1756. {PGLR NN:480} Aet. 43, dep. Feb 2, 1761. {PGLR RR:235} Aet. 44, dep. Nov 6, 1762. {PGLR TT:125}
MARCHANT, WILLIAM, see "Josiah Mace," q.v.
MARDIN (MARDING), ANNE, see "Nicholas Phillips" and "Joan Nevill" and "Richard Smith," q.v.
MARKLE, FREDERICK, of Frederick County, n.a., dep. Aug 20, 1772. {FRLR P:429}
MARKLE, GEORGE, of Frederick County, n.a., dep. Aug 20, 1772. {FRLR P:429}
MARLBOROUGH, FRANCIS, of Prince George's County, aet. 70 odd years, dep. Aug 17, 1731. {PGLR Q:528}
MARLER, JONATHAN, of Charles County, aet. 26, dep. Nov 27, 1666. {CHLR C#1:923}
MARLOW, RALPH, of Prince George's County, aet. 63, dep. Mar 26, 1756. {PGLR NN:479} Aet. 69, dep. Feb 2, 1761. {PGLR RR:235}

MARLOW, WILLIAM, of Prince George's County, aet. 51, dep. Nov 5, 1770, stated that he was a chain carrier for William Hanson about 27 years ago; also mentioned Thomas Thompson, deceased. {PGLR AA#2:497-498}

MARMADUKE, ROBERT, of Talbot County, aet. 25, dep. Feb 18, 1672/3, mentioned his master George Robbins. {ARMD 54:553}

MARR, MACKNE, of Prince George's County, aet. 31, dep. Jul 29, 1754. {PGLR NN:373}

MARRET, ISAAC, of Dorchester County, aet. 70, dep. between Aug 14, 1750 and Dec 20, 1750. {DOLR 14 Old 497}

MARRIOT, SILVANUS, see "Richard Warfield," q.v.

MARSH, GEORGE, of Queen Anne's County, aet. 25, dep. Apr, 1769. {QAEJ - James Hutchens folder}

MARSH, JOHN, of Baltimore County, aet. 50, dep. Feb 16, 1767. {BALR B#P:419}

MARSH, JOSIAS, of Baltimore County, aet. 52, dep. Jan 15, 1766, stated that 35 years ago he was with Morris Baker who was 60 years old. {BALR B#P:80}

MARSH, RICHARD, of Baltimore County, aet. 55, dep. Jan 15, 1766, stated that 37 years ago he was with Christopher Randall (who was 40 to 50 years old), uncle of Emanuel Teal. {BALR B#P:83}

MARSH, SARAH, see "Michaell Higgins" and "John Arnold," q.v.

MARSHALL, ANNE, of Queen Anne's County, aet. about 56, dep. May 6, 1728. {QAEJ - Christopher Wilkinson folder}

MARSHALL, DUTTON, see "Solomon Wright," q.v.

MARSHALL, GARRARD, see "Edward Brawner," q.v.

MARSHALL, MARY, see "Edward Brawner," q.v.

MARSHALL, RICHARD, see "Edward Brawner," q.v.

MARSHALL, THOMAS, of Prince George's County, aet. 59, dep. Mar 15, 1774, mentioned his father William Marshall. {PGLR BB#3:400}

MARSHALL, WILLIAM, of Charles County, aet. not given, dep. Oct 1, 1662. {CHLR A:246} Aet. 75, dep. Mar 8, 1669/70. {CHLR D#1:135}

MARSHALL, WILLIAM, of Prince George's County, aet. 40, dep. 1731. {PGLR Q:374}

MARSHALL, WILLIAM, see "Thomas Marshall" and "Margaret Brent" and "Capt. John Price," q.v.

MARTAIN, ELIZABETH, of Charles County, aet. 28, dep. between Oct 1, 1772 and Nov 2, 1772. {CHLR D#1:135}

MARTEN, BARTEN, of Charles County, aet. 23, dep. Mar 23, 1764, mentioned his father John Marten. {CHLR M#3:505}

MARTEN, JOHN, of Charles County, aet. 33, dep. Jun 6, 1726, mentioned his father Michael Marten. {CHLR P#2:392} Aet. 62, dep. Jul 26, 1755, stated that Mrs. Mudd and Mrs. Green were sisters. {CHLR E#3:389} John Marten, Sr., aet. 61, dep. Aug 20, 1753. {CHLR D#3:151} John Martin, of Charles County, aet. 38, dep. Nov 9, 1730, mentioned his father Michael Martin. {CHLR Q#2:449}

MARTEN, MICHAEL, of Charles County, aet. 33, dep. Oct 15, 1733. {CHLR O#2:661} Aet. 54, dep. Nov 8, 1767, mentioned his father John Marten. {CHLR P#3:375} Aet. 59, dep. Aug 9, 1771, mentioned his father John Marten. {CHLR T#3:601} Michael Martin, of Charles County, aet. 55, dep. May 5, 1767, mentioned his father John Martin and his (John's) son-in-law Jacob Miller. {CHLR P#3:268} See "John Marten," q.v.

MARTIN, FRANCIS, see "Esther Hepworth," q.v.

MARTIN, HENRY, see "James Wilson," q.v.

MARTIN, JOHN, of Charles County, aet. 40, dep. Aug 9, 1681. {CHLR I#1:147}

MARTIN, JOHN, of Charles County, aet. 43, dep. Sep 24, 1772. {CHLR U#3:265}

MARTIN (MARTEN), JOHN, see "John Marten" and "Barten Marten" and "Michael Marten," q.v.

MARTIN, MARY, of St. Mary's County, n.a., dep. Feb 28, 1749. {ARMD 28:510}

MARTIN, MATTHEW, of Charles County, aet. 69, dep. Mar 4, 1762. {CHLR K#3:475}

MARTIN, MICHAEL, see "Michael Marten" and "John Marten," q.v.

MARTIN, SARAH, see "John McPherson," q.v.

MASLIN, THOMAS, of Kent County, Quaker, aet. 47, dep. circa 1761. {KEEJ - James Dunn folder}

MASON, ANN (ANNE), see "Richard Hargrave, Sr." and "William Stokes" and "Ann Trego" and "William Skinner," q.v.

MASON, GEORGE, see "John Gardiner" and "William Skinner," q.v.

MASON, LEMUEL, see "Richard Hargrave, Sr.," q.v.

MASON, MILES, see "William Stokes" and "Ann Trego," q.v.

MASON, SARAH, see "William Stokes" and "Ann Trego," q.v.

MASON, WILLIAM, of Prince George's County, aet. 27, dep. Nov 21, 1751, mentioned Mary Pile, wife of John Pile, deceased. {PGLR PP:157}

MASSEY, JONATHAN, see "Benjamin Legoe" and William Hill," q.v.

MASSEY, JOSEPH, of Kent County, aet. 37, son of Nicholas, dep. Apr 5, 1773. {KEEJ - Gilbert Falconar folder}

MASSEY, NICHOLAS, SR., of Queen Anne's County, aet. about 70, dep. Apr, 1723. {QAEJ - William Bishop folder} See "Joseph Massey," q.v.

MASSEY, PETER, of Kent County, aet. about 52, dep. Dec 12, 1730, stated that he lived with Daniel Toaes about 26 years ago. {KELR JS#16:58} Aet. about 60, dep. Oct 22, 1740. {KELR JS#23:106}

MASTEN, RICHARD, of Charles County, aet. 37, dep. Sep 30, 1742. {CHLR O#2:467} Aet. 39, dep. May 7, 1744. {CHLR Y#2:17}

MASTERS, NATHAN, see "David Kelly," q.v.

MASTERS, WILLIAM, of Prince George's County, aet. 29, dep. Apr 14, 1759. {PGLR PP:313, pt. 2}

MASTERS, WILLIAM, of Prince George's County, aet. 90, dep. Sep 20, 1771, stated that he has lived in this area since he was 16 years old. {PGLR AA#2:431}

MASTERS, WILLIAM, see "David Kelly," q.v.

MASTIN, FRANCIS, see "William Skinner," q.v.
MASTIN, RICHARD, of Charles County, aet. 21, dep. Jul 11, 1762, mentioned his father Richard Mastin, deceased. {CHLR M#3:224} See "Richard Masten" and "Sarah Scroggin," q.v.
MASTIN, ROBERT, of Charles County, aet. 28, dep. Jun 5, 1770. {CHLR T#3:607}
MASTIN, SARAH, of Charles County, aet. 40, dep. Apr 28, 1753. {CHLR D#3:79}
MATHENA, DAVID, of Charles County, n.a., dep. Aug 10, 1681. {ARMD 15:409}
MATSON, CHRISTIAN, of Frederick County, n.a., dep. Dec 2, 1765. {ARMD 32:156-157}
MATSON, RALPH, see "Evan Shelby," q.v.
MATTECEY, GEFFERY, of Talbot County, aet. 30, dep. Sep 19, 1671, mentioned his master Dr. Richard Tilghman. {ARMD 54:509}
MATTHEWS, HESTER, of Charles County, n.a., dep. 1658. {ARMD 41:218}
MATTHEWS, JOHN, of Baltimore County, aet. 58, dep. Dec 10, 1773. {BALR AL#I:200}
MATTHEWS, MARY, see "Elizabeth Woodward" and "Mary Moore" and "Mary Mitchel" and "Jane Wharton," q.v.
MATTHEWS, MAXIMILIAN, of Charles County, aet. 36, dep. Feb 13, 1761, mentioned his father Thomas Matthews. {CHLR K#3:152}
MATTHEWS, THOMAS, of Charles County, n.a., dep. 1658. {ARMD 41:218} See "Maximilian Matthews" and "Bartholomew Phillips," q.v.
MATTHEWS, TIMOTHY, see "Thomas Barnes," q.v.
MATTINGLY, JOHN, of Charles County, aet. 27, dep. Jun 20, 1769, mentioned his father James Mattingly. {CHLR U#3:11}
MATTINGLY, ROBERT, of Charles County, aet. 32, dep. Jun 20, 1769, mentioned Robert Thompson, son of Thomas Thompson. {CHLR U#3:11}
MAUD, DANIEL, see "Thomas Stevens," q.v.
MAUD, MAGDALEN, see "Thomas Stevens," q.v.
MAUGHAN, JOHN, see "Thomas Wilson," q.v.
MAXWELL, JAMES (captain), of Baltimore County, aet. 55, dep. Nov 3, 1766. {BALR B#P:307} Aet. 59, dep. May 8, 1770. {BALR AL#B:287}
MAXWELL, ROBERT, SR., of Kent County, aet. 71, dep. 1766. {KELR DD#2:349}
MAY, JAMES, of Dorchester County, aet. 46, dep. between Nov 13, 1764 and Apr 13, 1765. {DOLR 20 Old 257}
MAYL (MAYLE), ANTHONY, of Talbot County, n.a., dep. Sep 16, 1673. {ARMD 54:574} See "Sarah Birk," q.v.
MAYL (MAYLE), MARY, see "Sarah Birk," q.v.
MAYNARD, CHARLES, of St. Mary's County, n.a., dep. Nov 25, 1652. {ARMD 10:208}
McADOW (McADOO), JOHN, of Baltimore County, aet. 48 or thereabouts, dep. Nov 22, 1768, mentioned Thomas Bond the Elder about 15 or 16 years ago and *Meriton's Lot* on Binam's Run. {BALR AL#A:300-301}
McATEE, EDMOND, see "John McAtee" and "Thomas McAtee," q.v.

McATEE, JAMES, of Charles County, aet. 37, dep. Mar 26, 1772, mentioned his father William McAtee, deceased. {CHLR T#3:611} See "Thomas McAtee," q.v.

McATEE, JOHN, of Charles County, aet. 66, dep. Mar 26, 1772, mentioned his father Edmond McAtee, deceased. {CHLR T#3:611}

McATEE, PATRICK, see "Rosamond Ferrall," q.v.

McATEE, THOMAS, of Charles County, aet. 35 or 36, dep. Mar 21, 1772, mentioned his brother William McAtee, uncle James McAtee, and father Edmond McAtee, deceased. {CHLR T#3:611}

McATEE, WILLIAM, see "James McAtee" and "Thomas McAtee," q.v.

McBEAN, MALCOM, see "Nathaniel Halley," q.v.

McBOY, EDWARD, of Frederick County, aet. 40 or thereabouts, dep. Jul 27, 1762. {FRLR J:67}

McCALLISTER, DAVID, see "Thomas Bryan," q.v.

McCALLISTER, PATRICK, see "Patrick McCollister," q.v.

McCANLIS, ALEXANDER, of Baltimore County, aet. 70, dep. Oct 11, 1763. {BALR B#N:63}

McCANN, EDWARD, of Kent County, aet. about 58, dep. twice Aug 22, 1774, stated that John Worthington, schoolmaster, was either half-brother or brother-in-law to Daniel Mullican. {KEEJ - John Comegys folder}

McCARTY, DENNIS, see "Augustine Boyer," q.v.

McCASLEY, ABRAHAM, of Queen Anne's County, aet. 55, dep. between Jun 11, 1765 and Mar 9, 1767. {DOLR 21 Old 315} See "Patrick McCollister," q.v.

McCLOUD, ANGUISH, see "William Penson," q.v.

McCOLLISTER, ANDREW, of Dorchester County, aet. about 49, dep. between Nov 14, 1758 and Jun 13, 1759, mentioned his father Patrick McCollister, David McCollister, William Urvin, and Honor Hutton, all deceased. {DOLR 16 Old 184}

McCOLLISTER, DAVID, see "Andrew McCollister" and "Thomas Bryan," q.v.

McCOLLISTER, ELLINER, see "Patrick McCollister," q.v.

McCOLLISTER, JOHN, see "William Littleton," q.v.

McCOLLISTER, PATRICK, of Dorchester County, aet. 45, dep. between Mar 10, 1752 and Mar 10, 1753, stated that he was shown the bounded tree of *Atlantis* about 25 years ago by his mother Elliner McCollister, now deceased, on the main road near Andrew McCollister's. {DOLR 14 Old 712} Aet. 55, dep. between Nov 10, 1761 and Sep 25, 1762, stated that he was shown the bounded tree of *Brices' Range* about 40 years ago by his father Patrick McCollister and William Urvin, both now deceased. {DOLR 19 Old 41} Patrick McCallister, aet. 55, dep. between Nov 9, 1762 and Aug 13, 1764. {DOLR 19 Old 293} Patrick McCollister, aet. 57, dep. between Aug 9, 1763 and Mar 31, 1764, mentioned Thomas Williams and his sons (not named) about 16 years ago at the house where William Low now lives. {DOLR 19 Old 418} See "Charles Thompson" and "Andrew McCollister" and "William McCollister," q.v.

McCOLLISTER, WILLIAM, of Dorchester County, aet. about 45, dep. between Nov 14, 1758 and Jun 13, 1759, mentioned his father Patrick McCollister and Peter Taylor and his brother John Taylor, surveyor; also stated that David McCollister, now deceased, told him about 20 years that the uppermost bounded tree of Major Henry Ennalls' land stood near the place where a certain Thomas Heather was found dead. {DOLR 16 Old 184}

McCOMAS, DANIEL, of Baltimore County, aet. 60, dep. May 12, 1764. {BALR B#O:113}

McCONNIKEN (MACCONIKIN), JOHN, of Baltimore County, aet. 47, dep. Sep 1, 1763. {BALR B#M:92}

McDANIEL, WALTER, of Dorchester County, aet. 64, dep. Aug 24, 1745, stated that he was once a servant to Morgan Addams. {DOLR 12 Old 247}

McDONALD, ANN (Mrs.), of Charles County, aet. 60, dep. Sep 15, 1759, mentioned Ignatius Boarman and his son Gerrard Boarman who was born Nov 9, 1722. {CHLR O#3:646}

McDONALD, ARCHIBALD, of Prince George's County, aet. 35, dep. Nov 8, 1758, mentioned Capt. Joshua Beall about 6 years ago. {PGLR PP:228, pt. 2}

McDONALD, EVAN, see "Thomas Tomkins," q.v.

McDONALL, EWEN, of Prince George's County, n.a., dep. May 24, 1748, mentioned Thomas Crisap, Hendry Mundaye and his daughter Henarota Mundaye. {PGLR BB:459}

McDONALD, MILES, of Charles County, aet. 70, dep. Jul 1, 1765. {CHLR N#3:787}

McFADIEN, MARY, see "Samuel Dawson," q.v.

McGEE, ROBERT, of Baltimore County, aet. 41, dep. Jun 18, 1770. {BALR AL#B:414}

McGRAW, PHILIP, of Charles County, aet. 44, dep. Dec 15, 1760. {CHLR K#3:156}

McHON, ROBERT, of Charles County, aet. 68, dep. Sep 23, 1741. {CHLR O#2:288}

McHONEY, TIMOTHY, of Charles County, aet. 70, dep. May 22, 1733. {CHLR R#3:334}

McKEEL, EDMUND, see "John Rix," q.v.

McKEEL, JOHN, see "John Anderson," q.v.

McKENNY, GABRIEL, of Frederick County, n.a., dep. Mar 11, 1765. {FRLR K:428}

McKENSEY, KENNETT, of Charles County, aet. 46, dep. Sep 18, 1731. {CHLR R#2:46}

McLEOD, ALEXANDER, of Charles County, aet. 81, dep. Nov 14, 1766. {CHLR P#3:281}

McNEALE, SUSANNAH, see "Susanna MacNeale," q.v.

McNEW, JEREMIAH, of Prince George's County, aet. 60, dep. Oct 2, 1769. {PGLR AA#2:186}

McPHERSON, ALEXANDER, of Charles County, aet. 63, dep. Nov 8, 1774. {CHLR W#3:608} Aet. 67, dep. May 13, 1745. {CHLR Z#2:338} Aet. 77, dep. Nov 15, 1756, mentioned Ralph Gwynn about 50 years ago. {CHLR F#3:300} See "John McPherson," q.v.

McPHERSON, BARBRY, of Charles County, aet. 55, dep. Aug 6, 1762, mentioned John Ensey about 36 or 37 years ago. {CHLR M#3:5}
McPHERSON, JOHN, of Charles County, aet. 49, dep. Jul 31, 1765, mentioned his father Alexander McPherson. {CHLR N#3:720} Aet. 52, dep. Nov 8, 1766. {CHLR P#3:275} Aet. 52, dep. Feb 5, 1767, stated that Sarah Martin, daughter of Mr. Martin who owned *Martin's Supply*, married Jacob Miller. {CHLR P#3:269} Aet. 53, dep. Jun 13, 1767. {CHLR P#3:652} Aet. 62, dep. Feb 5, 1776. {CHLR X#3:628}
McPHERSON, WILLIAM, of Charles County, aet. 48, dep. Jul 26, 1755. {CHLR E#3:389} Aet. 62, dep. Jul 12, 1769, mentioned Ignatius Boarman was the father of Gerrard (aged 42) and William Boarman. {CHLR O#3:646}
MEAKS, WILLIAM, of Frederick County, n.a., dep. Dec 2, 1765. {ARMD 32:156-157}
MEANS, JAMES, of Talbot County, n.a., dep. Mar 15, 1760, stated that he heard Richard Bruff of St. Michael's River, lately deceased, say that negroes Ben and Jacob were children of his negro woman Rose and he (Richard) gave them to his daughter Rebecca Bruff. {TALR 19:185}
MEARTHERS, MARY, of Dorchester County, aet. 18, dep. Feb 26, 1772. {DOLR 25 Old 459}
MEARTHERS, ROSANNAH, of Dorchester County, aet. 40 and upwards, dep. Feb 26, 1772, mentioned Peter Ross, now deceased, and John Ross, nephew and only heir of said Peter Ross. {DOLR 25 Old 459}
MEDCALF, GEORGE, see "Benjamin Beckett," q.v.
MEDDIS, GODFREY, of Dorchester County, aet. 38, dep. between Aug 15, 1746 and Sep 1, 1746, mentioned old Edward Taylor about 4 years ago. {DOLR 14 Old 89}
MEDDIS, SARAH, of Dorchester County, aet. 33, dep. between Aug 15, 1746 and Sep 1, 1746. {DOLR 14 Old 89}
MEDDIS, THOMAS, of Dorchester County, aet. 63, dep. between Aug 11, 1772 and Jul 29, 1773. {DOLR 28 Old 31}
MEDFORD, GEORGE (captain), of Kent County, aet. 46, dep. Apr 2, 1754, mentioned Matthew Howard, deceased. {KEEJ - Edward Dingan folder} Aet. 48, dep. Sep, 1755. {KEEJ - Thomas Chandler folder}
MEDFORD, ROBERT, of Dorchester County, aet. 61, dep. between Nov 9, 1762 and Aug 13, 1764. {DOLR 19 Old 293}
MEE, GEORGE, see "William Eddey," q.v.
MEEK, ANN, of Charles County, aet. 18, dep. Nov 2, 1752, mentioned her mother Mrs. Sarah Meek. {CHLR B#3:210}
MEEK, FRANCIS, of Charles County, aet. 48, dep. Oct 20, 1741. {CHLR O#2:286} Francis Meeke, aet. 51, dep. Jul 3, 1745. {CHLR Z#2:438} See "Henry Tanner," q.v.
MEEK, FRANCIS, JR., of Charles County, aet. 27, dep. Dec 13, 1757. {CHLR H#3:124} Francis Meeke, aet. 23, dep. Nov 2, 1752, mentioned his parents

Francis and Sarah Meeke and that Sarah was a sister of John Booker. {CHLR B#3:210}
MEEK, JOHN, of Charles County, aet. 26, dep. Dec 13, 1757. {CHLR H#3:124}
MEEK, MARY, see "Henry Tanner," q.v.
MEEK, SARAH, see "Ann Meek" and "Francis Meek, Jr.," q.v.
MEEKES, JOHN, see "John Helmes," q.v.
MEEKINS, ABRAHAM, of Dorchester County, aet. 31, dep. between Mar 10, 1761 and Jun 6, 1761, mentioned his father (not named). {DOLR 17 Old 318}
MEEKINS, ELIZABETH, of Dorchester County, aet. 37, dep. between Jun 12, 1750 and Jul 18, 1750, mentioned James Gallaway (now deceased) and her husband William Gallaway. {DOLR 14 Old 428}
MEEKINS, JOHN, of Dorchester County, aet. 53 or 54, dep. between Jun 12, 1750 and Jul 18, 1750, mentioned his uncle John Meekins about 30 years ago. {DOLR 14 Old 428}
MEEKINS, JOHN, of Dorchester County, aet. 34, dep. between Mar 10, 1761 and Jun 6, 1761, mentioned his father John Meekins about 16 or 17 years ago. {DOLR 17 Old 318}
MEEKINS, JOHN, SR., of Dorchester County, aet. 54, son of Richard Meekins, deceased, dep. between Jun 12, 1728 and Jul 16, 1728. {DOLR 8 Old 245} See "John Lewis," q.v.
MEEKINS, RICHARD, of Dorchester County, aet. 51, dep. between Aug 14, 1750 and Nov 24, 1750. {DOLR 14 Old 546} Aet. 65, dep. between Mar 10, 1761 and Jun 6, 1761. {DOLR 17 Old 318} See "John Lewis," q.v.
MEEKINS, UNKLE, see "Henry Travers," q.v.
MEEKS, FRANCIS, of Kent County, planter, aet. about 50, dep. Aug 18, 1735, mentioned Michael Hackett (now deceased) and his wife Mary who were living 14 years ago. {KELR JS#18:181} Aet. about 60, dep. June, 1743. {KELR JS#24:405}
MEEKS, ROBERT, of Kent County, aet. about 54, dep. Dec 19, 1738, stated that Ann Glenn showed him the bounds of *Dineing Room* near Fairy Meadow about 30 years ago; also mentioned Isaac Bowles, master of Darby Bryan. {KELR JS#22:293}
MEERES, THOMAS, see "Michaell Higgins" and "John Arnold," q.v.
MELLVIN, CATHREN, see "Mary Boxell," q.v.
MELVILL (MELVELL), DAVID, of Dorchester County, aet. 60, dep. between Jun 9, 1741 and Nov 2, 1741, stated that the bounds of *Edmondson's Reserve* were shown to him about 36 years ago by Thomas Turner and about 12 years ago by Marsy Fountain and William Fountain, both now deceased. {DOLR 12 Old 94} Aet. 72, dep. between Mar 10, 1752 and Mar 10, 1753, stated that he and John Rawlings were shown the second bounded tree of *Atlantis* in 1701 by Thomas Turner, now deceased. {DOLR 14 Old 712} See "Thomas Bryan" and "William Payne" and "Mary Boxell" and "William Thomas" and "Elizabeth Woodward," q.v.
MELVILL, CATURN, see "William Thomas," q.v.

MERCHANT, JOSEPH, of Dorchester County, aet. 28, dep. between Dec 15, 1727 and Nov 14, 1729, stated that the bounds of *Haverdy Grace* were shown to him by Joseph Woodward, Sr., now deceased. {DOLR 8 Old 328} Aet. 32, dep. between Nov 19, 1732 and May 10, 1732/3, mentioned John Button, son of John Button, who was the owner of *Turkey Point*. {DOLR 9 Old 64}

MERCHANT, WILLIAM, of Dorchester County, aet. 70, dep. Sep 2, 1702. {DOLR 5 Old 230} See "Josiah Mace," q.v.

MEREDITH, JAMES, of Queen Anne's County, aet. about 70, dep. Apr, 1750. {QAEJ - William Bishop folder}

MEREDITH, JOHN, SR., of Queen Anne's County, aet. 75, dep. Apr, 1723. {QAEJ - William Bishop folder} See "Lewis Griffith" and "Mathew Dockery," q.v.

MEREDITH, SARAH, see "Lewis Griffith," q.v.

MEREDITH, THOMAS, of Queen Anne's County, aet. 48, dep. Mar 15, 1760. {QAEJ - Richard Tilghman Earle folder} See "Mathew Dockery," q.v.

MEREDITH, WILLIAM, of Dorchester County, aet. 63, dep. between Mar 9, 1773 and Feb 5, 1774. {DOLR 27 Old 115} See "Lewis Griffith" and "James Walters," q.v.

MEREKIN, HUGH, see "Robert Eagle" and "Mary Eagle" and "Margaret Todd" and "Nathan Linthicombe" and "David Rablin" and "Joshua Jones," q.v.

MEREKIN (MERRIKIN), JOHN (captain), of Anne Arundel County, aet. 45, dep. 1734. {AALR RD#2:135} See "Edward Smith" and "Robert Eagle" and "Mary Eagle" and "Margaret Todd," q.v.

MEREKIN, JOSHUA, see "Mary Eagle" and "Nathan Linthicombe," q.v.

MERRIATER, ARDEN, of Prince George's County, aet. 60, dep. Oct 12, 1770. {PGLR AA#2:206}

MERRIDAY, THOMAS, see "John Malham," q.v.

MERRITT, LOVERING, of Kent County, aet. 25, dep. 1740. {KELR JS#23:187} Aet. 52, dep. 1769. {KELR DD#3:194}

MERRITT, WILLIAM, of Kent County, aet. 44, dep. 1775. {KELR DD#5:90}

MERRYMAN, JOHN, see "Thomas Franklin," q.v.

MERRYMAN, SAMUEL, of Baltimore County, aet. 40, dep. between Apr 13, 1761 and Nov 22, 1762. {BALR B#L:200}

MESECK, SARAH, of Dorchester County, aet. 31, dep. between Mar 16, 1733/4 and Jul 6, 1734, mentioned her father-in-law John Robson. {DOLR 9 Old 193}

METCALFE, JOHN, of St. Mary's County, n.a., dep. Sep 9, 1663. {ARMD 49:53}

MICHAEL, ANDREW, of Frederick County, aet. 46, dep. Aug 21, 1776. {FRLR BD#2:335}

MICHELL (MICHEL), GOODIE, see "Thomas Lomax" and "Elisabeth Atwickes" and "Richard Tarlin," q.v.

MICHELL, JOANE, see "James Hay," q.v.

MICHELL (MICHEL), THOMAS, of Charles County, n.a., dep. Nov 8, 1664. {CHLR B:414} See "Thomas Lomax" and "Elisabeth Atwickes," q.v.

MIDDLETON, GEORGE, of Dorchester County, aet. 48, dep. between Mar 10, 1767 and Jun 8, 1767, mentioned his father (not named) and his uncle Major Frame. {DOLR 21 Old 443} Aet. about 51, dep. between Nov 14, 1769 and May 21, 1770. {DOLR 24 Old 27}
MIDDLETON, GEORGE, see "William Barney," q.v.
MIDDLETON, JAMES, of Prince George's County, aet. 55, dep. Nov 28, 1728. {PGLR M:346}
MIDDLETON, JOHN (captain), of Prince George's County, aet. 52, dep. Oct 5, 1725, mentioned Robert Middleton. {PGLR I:696} Aet. 55, dep. between Apr 17, 1729 and Jun 26, 1729. {PGLR M:445} See "Thomas Middleton," q.v.
MIDDLETON, ROBERT, see "John Middleton," q.v.
MIDDLETON, THOMAS, of Prince George's County, aet. 47, dep. Oct 5, 1725. {PGLR I:696} Aet. 50, dep. between Apr 17, 1729 and Jun 26, 1729, mentioned his father (not named). {PGLR M:445}
MIDDLETON, THOMAS, of Prince George's County, aet. 52, dep. Feb 2, 1761, mentioned John Middleton and Thomas Middleton about 30 or 40 years ago. {PGLR RR:235} Aet. 54, dep. Jun 28, 1762, mentioned his father Thomas Middleton and Joseph Hatton about 30 years ago, both now deceased. {PGLR RR:262} Aet. between 60 and 70, dep. Oct 15, 1776, mentioned Edward Edelen, brother of Christopher Edelen; a second deposition on the same day stated he was aged 67. {PGLR CC#2:309-310}
MIDDLETON, WILLIAM, of Charles County, aet. 57, dep. Jul 4, 1743. {CHLR O#2:616} Aet. 82, dep. Jul 1, 1765. {CHLR N#3:786} Aet. 83, dep. Apr 25, 1767. {CHLR A#3:426} Aet. 85, dep. Jun 17, 1768, mentioned Eleanor Tear and her daughter Elizabeth Tear. {CHLR Q#3:190}
MIFLIN, JOHN, of Dorchester County, Quaker, n.a., dep. between Mar 12, 1744 and Aug 5, 1745. {DOLR 12 Old 215}
MILES, HENRY, of Charles County, aet. 48, dep. Sep 28, 1764. {CHLR N#3:167}
MILES, MORRIS, of Prince George's County, aet. 50, dep. Sep 22, 1730. {PGLR Q:157} Aet. 60, dep. Jun 5, 1740. {PGLR Y:185} Aet. 70, dep. Jan 26, 1748/9. {PGLR BB:629}
MILES, WILLIAM, of Prince George's County, aet. 40, dep. Feb 22, 1753. {PGLR NN:175} Aet. 51, dep. Oct 6, 1763, mentioned his father (not named). {PGLR TT:122}
MILES, WILLIAM, SR., of Prince George's County, aet. 63, dep. Aug 25, 1737. {PGLR T:505}
MILLAR, JOHN, of Dorchester County, aet. 51, dep. between Nov 13, 1739 and Apr 4, 1740. {DOLR 12 Old 109}
MILLER, ADAM, of Prince George's County, aet. 38, dep. May 11, 1733. {PGLR T:25}
MILLER, ADAM, of Prince George's County, aet. 44, dep. Jun 16, 1730, mentioned his father George Miller. {PGLR Q:10} Aet. 73, dep. Apr 25, 1758,

mentioned his father George Miller. {PGLR PP:233-234, pt. 2} Aet. 82, dep. Nov 21, 1763. {PGLR TT:195}
MILLER, ANN, see "Michael Miller" and "Martha Miller," q.v.
MILLER, ARTHUR, see "Michael Miller," q.v.
MILLER, GEORGE, of Charles County, aet. 29 or 30, dep. Sep 13, 1681. {CHLR I#1:169}
MILLER, JACOB, of Frederick County, aet. 35, dep. 1767. {FRLR L:60} See "John Marten" and "John McPherson," q.v.
MILLER, JOHN, of Prince George's County, aet. 60, dep. between Apr 1, 1729 and Aug 29, 1729. {PGLR M:484} Aet. 63, dep. Apr 4, 1732, mentioned Roger Brooke and his sons James Brooke and Roger Brooke. {PGLR Q:575} Aet. 66, planter, dep. Aug 6, 1735, mentioned Roger Brooke about 35 years ago. {PGLR T:359} Aet. 68, dep. Dec 24, 1736. {PGLR Y:84}
MILLER, JOHN, of Charles County, aet. 32, dep. Oct 31, 1766. {CHLR P#3:284}
MILLER, MARTHA, of Kent County, n.a., dep. Feb 9, 1719/20, mentioned her husband Michael Miller and her daughter Ann Miller. {KELR JS#W:61A}
MILLER, MARY, of Charles County, aet. 60, dep. Mar 15, 1725. {CHLR P#2:298} Aet. 65, dep. Feb 14, 1728. {CHLR Q#2:347}
MILLER, MICHAEL, of Kent County, aet. 37, dep. Sep 30, 1681, mentioned Capt. Jonathan Sibrey, Thomas King, James Stavely, Philip Holeager (Holenger), William Peerce, Benjamin Randall, William Nowell, James Frisby (commissioner), and Mr. [Edward] Inglish (sheriff). {ARMD 17:59-60}
MILLER, MICHAEL, of Kent County, aet. about 45, dep. Feb 9, 1719/20, mentioned his daughter Ann Miller and his brother Arthur Miller. {KELR JS#W:61A} Aet. about 50, dep. 1726, mentioned his father Michael Miller, deceased. {KELR JS#X:41} Aet. about 51, dep. Jul 25, 1727. {KELR JS#X:89} Aet. about 54, dep. Sep, 1729. {KELR JS#X:412} Aet. about 55, dep. Jul 30, 1730. {KELR JS#16:42} Aet. about 63, dep. Apr 29, 1738. {KELR JS#22:119} See "Martha Miller," q.v.
MILLER, MICHAEL, JR., of Kent County, aet. 30, dep. 1775. {KELR DD#5:59}
MILLER, ROBERT, see "Thomas Browne," q.v.
MILLER, THOMAS, of Charles County, aet. 25, dep. Feb 12, 1668. {CHLR D#1:147}
MILLER, WILLIAM, see "Thomas Browne," q.v.
MILLINGTON, SAMUEL, of Dorchester County, aet. 41, dep. Sep 8, 1682. {DOLR 4 Old 20} See "John Lewis" and "George Stapleford" and "Lewis Griffin" and "Samuel Harper," q.v.
MILLIS, THOMAS, of Queen Anne's County, aet. 28, dep. Aug, 1762. {QAEJ - William Paca folder}
MILLS, GEORGE, see "David Traile" and "Ruth Lord," q.v.
MILLS, GOVART, SR., of Dorchester County, aet. about 40, dep. between Mar 12, 1744 and Nov 8, 1748. {DOLR 14 Old 317}
MILLS, JACOB, see "John Taylor," q.v.

MILLS, JOHN, of Dorchester County, aet. 44, dep. between Mar 13, 1738/9 and Nov 12, 1739. {DOLR 12 Old 119} Aet. 52, dep. Jul 20, 1747. {DOLR 14 Old 182} Aet. about 70, dep. between Mar 8, 1763 and May 10, 1763, mentioned his father (not named) about 50 years ago. {DOLR 18 Old 439}

MILLS, ROBERT, of Prince George's County, aet. 59 or thereabouts, dep. Mar 1, 1756. {PGLR NN:469} Aet. 60 or thereabouts, dep. Jan 15, 1756. {PGLR NN:468} Aet. 60, dep. Aug 16, 1757, mentioned Capt. Walter Hoxton about 30 years ago. {PGLR PP:56, pt. 2} Aet. 64, dep. Feb 23, 1760. {PGLR BB#2:146} Aet. 67, dep. Jun 3, 1765. {PGLR TT:453-454}

MILLS, SAMUEL, of St. Mary's County, n.a., dep. May 18, 1663. {ARMD 49:60}

MILLS, WILLIAM, of Charles County, n.a., dep. Sep 10, 1663. {ARMD 49:61}

MILLS, WILLIAM, see "Thomas Woolford," q.v.

MILSON, SAMUEL, of Talbot County, planter, aet. between 30 and 40, dep. Jun 30, 1702 in Kent County. {TALR 9:382}

MILSTEAD, CATHARINE, of Charles County, aet. 67, dep. Jul 28, 1761, mentioned her husband Francis Godfrey about 40 years ago. {CHLR K#3:302}

MILSTEAD, EDWARD, of Charles County, aet. 70, dep. Mar 15, 1725. {CHLR P#2:298} Aet. 70, dep. Feb 14, 1728/9. {CHLR T#3:538}

MILSTEAD, EDWARD, of Charles County, aet. 66, dep. Apr 13, 1761, mentioned his father Edward Milstead. {CHLR K#3:302}

MILSTEAD, THOMAS, of Charles County, aet. 24, dep. Jun 1, 1725. {CHLR P#2:44}

MINITREE, JACOB ANDREW, of Charles County, aet. 55, dep. Sep 6, 1760. {CHLR K#3:98}

MINNISH, JOHN, see "Charles Thompson," q.v.

MISHIE, WILLIAM, see "William Stokes" and "Ann Trego," q.v.

MITCHEL, JOHN, of Dorchester County, aet. about 54, dep. between Mar 13, 1764 and Nov 10, 1764, mentioned Thomas Mackeel and William Byus, commissioners about 17 years ago, and John Soward, son of John Soward. {DOLR 19 Old 429}

MITCHEL, MARY, of Dorchester County, widow, aet. 52 or 53, dep. Nov 12, 1759, stated that she has known Mary Taylor (now known as Mary Matthews) for 40 odd years; when she (Taylor) was 14, 15, or 16 years old she married Thomas Earl who ran away about 2 years later; she (Mary Earl) later ran away, was housekeeper for George Sales, of Talbot County (now deceased), and before she married him she had three children: Elizabeth Sales (now living and known as Elizabeth Conner or Cannon); Jane or Jean Sales (now living and known as Jean Johnson); and, Mary Sales (died very young); and, when Mary Earl was big with her fourth child (afterwards known as George Sales) she married George Sales, the father, about 29 or 30 years ago. {TALR 19:8}

MITCHELL, BURGIS, of Prince George's County, aet. 50, dep. Jun 10, 1751, mentioned Samuel Magruder about 5 or 6 years ago, now deceased. {PGLR PP:123}

MITCHELL, EDWARD, of Cecil County, n.a., dep. May 31, 1769, stated that he has known Francis and Jeremiah Baker from their infancy and they have behaved justly and honestly in all their dealing. {ARMD 32:326}

MITCHELL, ELIZABETH, of Prince George's County, aet. near 45, dep. Jul 17, 1763, stated that her father Hugh Ryley showed her the bounds of *Hogyard* about 30 years ago. {PGLR TT:606}

MITCHELL, HENRY (captain), of Calvert County, n.a., dep. between Jun 29, 1698 and Jul 1, 1698 in Annapolis. {ARMD 23:442}

MITCHELL, JAMES (captain), of London, England, n.a., commander of the ship *Adventure*, dep. Mar 5, 1702/3 in Annapolis. {ARMD 25:142-143} See "James Sanders," q.v.

MITCHELL, JOHN, of Prince George's County, aet. 46, dep. Nov 5, 1763. {PGLR TT:572}

MITCHELL, MARY, see "Daniel Stewart," q.v.

MITCHELL, MORDECAI, of Prince George's County, aet. 57, dep. Jul 10, 1759, mentioned the land of his mother (not named) called *Greenwood* about 36 or 37 years ago; also mentioned William Offutt and John Magruder in 1724. {PGLR RR:78-79}

MITCHELL, MORDICA, JR., of Prince George's County, aet. 39, dep. Feb 20, 1767. {PGLR BB#2:168}

MITCHELL, MORDICA MILES, of Prince George's County, aet. 16, dep. Feb 20, 1767. {PGLR BB#2:169}

MITCHELL, MORRIS, of Prince George's County, aet. 43, dep. Feb 20, 1767. {PGLR BB#2:167}

MITCHELL, THOMAS, of Charles County, aet. 66, dep. Jan 1, 1754. {CHLR D#3:236}

MITCHELL, WILLIAM, of St. Mary's County, gentleman, n.a., dep. Jan 8, 1650, mentioned the death of Raphe Beanes' servant (name not given, but a later entry indicated it was "Raphe Loe"). {ARMD 10:53, 74}

MITCHELL, ----, see "Peter Brightwell," q.v.

MOASLEY, JAMES, see "Elizabeth Ellis," q.v.

MOBBERLY, EDWARD, SR., of Prince George's County, aet. 57 or thereabouts, dep. May 23, 1774 (recorded Mar 23, 1776), mentioned Roger John Sasser about 30 years ago. {PGLR CC#2:244-245}

MOBBERLY, FRANCIS, see "Isle of Wight," q.v.

MOBBERLY, REBECCA, see "Isle of Wight," q.v.

MOBLEY, JOHN, see "Benjamin White," q.v.

MOCKBEE (MOCKIBEY), BROCK, of Prince George's County, aet. 35, dep. May 31, 1731. {PGLR Q:608} See "James Plummer," q.v.

MOCKBEE, EDWARD, of Prince George's County, aet. 48, dep. Jul 2, 1764. {PGLR TT:372}

MOCKBY, HIGGISON, of Prince George's County, aet. 17, dep. Jun 20, 1764, mentioned his uncle Thomas Mullikin. {PGLR TT:368}

MOFFETT, GEORGE, of Kent County, aet. about 50, dep. May 18, 1730. {KELR JS#16:13} Aet. about 60, dep. Sep 17, 1740, mentioned Mrs. Isabell Pearce, now deceased. {KELR JS#23:134} Aet. about 70, dep. May 12, 1746. {KELR JS#25:401}
MONG, NICHOLAS, of Frederick County, aet. 42, dep. 1767. {FRLR L:60}
MONK, PETER, see "Indian Peter Monk," q.v.
MONROE, ANDREW, see "William Boreman," q.v.
MONTECUE, WILLIAM, of Queen Anne's County, aet. 73, dep. between Jun 11, 1765 and Mar 9, 1767, mentioned Edward Richards about 52 years ago. {DOLR 21 Old 315}
MONTGOMERIE, ROBERT, see "James Hopkins," q.v.
MONTGOMERY, FRANCIS, of Charles County, aet. 36, dep. Aug 11, 1755. {CHLR E#3:501}
MONTGOMERY, FRANCIS, of Charles County, aet. 43, dep. Jan 16, 1753. {CHLR B#3:346} Aet. 45, dep. Aug 7, 1755. {CHLR E#3:495} Aet. 47, dep. Mar 15, 1757. {CHLR F#3:495}
MONTGOMERY, FRANCIS, see "Richard Montgomery," q.v.
MONTGOMERY, PETER, of Charles County, aet. 52, dep. Dec 29, 1736. {CHLR T#2:296} Aet. 60, dep. May 25, 1742. {CHLR O#2:585} Aet. 60 odd years, dep. May 23, 1745. {CHLR Z#2:342} See "Richard Montgomery," q.v.
MONTGOMERY, RICHARD, of Charles County, aet. 31, dep. Jan 16, 1753, mentioned his brother Francis Montgomery and father Peter Montgomery. {CHLR B#2:351}
MOORE, GEORGE, of Kent County, n.a., dep. May, 1771. {QAEJ - John Moore folder}
MOORE, HENNERIE, of Charles County, aet. 22, dep. Oct 26, 1658. {CHLR A:25}
MOORE (MORE), HENRY, of Charles County, aet. 33, dep. Jul 28, 1697, stated that Indian Esquire Tom [a Pomunkey Indian] told him that he believed it was the Emperor of Piscattoway that did the murder in Acquio [in Virginia] on Wigenton's wife and children (names not given). {ARMD 23:185-187}
MOORE, HENRY, of Charles County, aet. 62, dep. Jun 6, 1726. {CHLR P#2:391} Aet. 63, dep. Jan 10, 1726/7. {CHLR P#2:491} Aet. 67, dep. Jul 15, 1730. {CHLR Q#2:394}
MOORE, HENRY, of Prince George's County, aet. 64, dep. Nov 28, 1728. {PGLR M:344} Aet. 67, dep. Aug 3, 1730. {PGLR Q:68} Henry Moor, aet. 72, dep. Mar 10, 1735/6. {PGLR T:280}
MOORE (MORE), JAMES, of Prince George's County, aet. 44, dep. Jan 22, 1765. {PGLR TT:366-367} James Moore, aet. 46, dep. Jun 1, 1767, mentioned Thomas Stump, son of Thomas, about 27 or 28 years ago. {PGLR BB#2:114}
MOORE, JAMES, of Frederick County, n.a., dep. Aug 8, 1755, stated that he bounded a tree for the beginning tree of *Pile's Grove* about 20 years ago. {FRLR E:908}
MOORE, JAMES, JR., of Baltimore County, aet. 44, dep. Jan 4, 1763. {BALR B#L:499} Aet. 45, dep. May 28, 1764. {BALR B#N:143} Aet. 47, dep. Jan 11, 1767. {BALR B#P:458}

MOORE, JAMES, SR., of Prince George's County, aet. 105, dep. Jul 22, 1729. {PGLR M:480}

MOORE, JOHN, of Frederick County, aet. 60 or thereabouts, dep. Aug 14, 1772, mentioned Col. Joseph Belt and Capt. James Edmondston about 22 or 23 years ago, both now deceased. {FRLR P:683-684}

MOORE, MARY, of Dorchester County, aet. 52, dep. Nov 7, 1759, stated that she was well acquainted with Mary Earl (since Mary Matthews) and about 35 years ago she (Mary Earl) came to this deponent's father's house and delivered a baby girl (named Betty) with the assistance of this deponent's husband (not named). {TALR 19:8} See "Elizabeth Woodward," q.v.

MOORE (MOOR), MARY, of Queen Anne's County, aet. 44, dep. Oct 5, 1768, stated that her mother was sister to John and William Emory; also mentioned her sister Sophia Lloyd. {QAEJ - Gideon Emory folder}

MOORE, PATTRICK, of Talbot County, n.a., dep. Mar 18, 1672/3. {ARMD 54:560}

MOORE (MORE), PHILIP, of Prince George's County, aet. 35, dep. Nov 5, 1763. {PGLR TT:573}

MOORE, WILLIAM, of Dorchester County, aet. 56, dep. between Jun 11, 1765 and Mar 9, 1767, stated that he was shown the bounded tree of *Denton's Holme* about 4 years ago by Gollant Lemare, now deceased, whom he had known upwards of 30 years. {DOLR 21 Old 315}

MORGAINE, JOSHUA, see "Ellinor Lewis," q.v.

MORGAN, FRANCIS, of Kent County, aet. 30 or thereabouts, dep. Jan 1, 1655/6. {ARMD 54:42-43}

MORGAN, FRANCIS (captain), of York County, Virginia, n.a., dep. Nov 24, 1651 in St. Mary's County, mentioned Nicholas Cawseen and William Smoot. {ARMD 10:129}

MORGAN, HENRY, of Kent County, n.a., dep. Jan 1, 1655/6. {ARMD 54:43} See "Henry Hare" and "John Barns" and "Richard Crouch," q.v.

MORGAN, JOSEPH, of Worcester County, aet. about 46, dep. between Nov 11, 1746 and Apr 14, 1748, mentioned his father Joshua Morgan. {DOLR 14 Old 231} Joseph Morgin, of Sussex County on Delaware, aet. about 64, dep. between Jun 11, 1765 and Mar 9, 1767, mentioned Benjamin Richards about 37 years ago. {DOLR 21 Old 315}

MORGAN, JOSEPH, of Baltimore County, aet. 49, dep. Mar 22, 1764. {BALR B#N:125}

MORGAN, JOSHUA, prob. of Anne Arundel County, n.a., dep. Apr 19, 1705. {CMSP 1:3} See "Ellinor Lewis" and "Joseph Morgan," q.v.

MORGAN, PHILLIP, of St. Mary's or Calvert County, n.a., dep. Jun 17, 1656 at Patuxent, mentioned John Crabtree, deceased. {ARMD 10:453} See "Sarah Kindred," q.v.

MORRICE, RICHARD, of Charles County, aet. 24, dep. Sep 24, 1661. {CHLR A:155} Aet. 30, dep. Nov 27, 1666. {CHLR C#1:93}

MORRIS, DANIEL, see "Mary Clifton," q.v.

MORRIS, ELENOR, of Charles County, aet. 20, dep. Jul 8, 1662. {CHLR A:219} See "Thomas Hussey" and "Anne Ges," q.v.

MORRIS, JACOB, of Charles County, aet. 33, dep. Aug 6, 1765. {CHLR N#3:429}

MORRIS (MORRISS), JAMES, of Prince George's County, aet. near 56, dep. Apr 2, 1748. {PGLR BB:692}

MORRIS (MORIS), JOHN, of Charles County, aet. 30, planter, dep. Jul 8, 1662, stated that Mary Hews and Thomas Shelton said they were married and shared a bed at his house. {CHLR A:218}

MORRIS, MAURIS (MORRIS), of Prince George's County, aet. 55, dep. May 29, 1730, mentioned his master Thomas Kinniston about 33 years ago. {PGLR Q:153} Morris Morris, aet. 56, dep. Jul 7, 1731. {PGLR Q:526}

MORRIS, MORRIS, of Prince George's County, aet. 31, dep. Jun 22, 1752. {PGLR NN:38}

MORRIS, MORRIS (MAURIS), see "Mary Clifton" and "Charles Thompson" and "Mauris Morris" and "Thomas Morris," q.v.

MORRIS (MORIS), RICHARD, of Charles County, aet. 24, dep. Apr 22, 1662. {CHLR A:212} Aet. 38, dep. Nov 11, 1674. {CHLR F#1:32}

MORRIS, THOMAS, of St. Mary's County, n.a., dep. Apr 9, 1638, mentioned Zachary Mottershead, gentleman, late of St. Mary's, deceased. {ARMD 4:27}

MORRIS, THOMAS, of Charles County, aet. 43, dep. Sep 9, 1747. {CHLR Z#2:186} Aet. 44, dep. Jan 1, 1747. {CHLR Z#2:304} Aet. 60, dep. Mar 27, 1764. {CHLR M#3:505} Aet. 61, dep. Aug 6, 1765. {CHLR N#3:429} Aet. 62, dep. Jul 1, 1765. {CHLR N#3:786} Aet. 63, dep. Aug 29, 1768, mentioned Dr. Scott about 27 or 28 years ago. {PGLR BB#2:389}

MORRIS, THOMAS, of Prince George's County, aet. 44, dep. May 31, 1750, mentioned his father Morris Morris about 36 years ago. {PGLR NN:59} Aet. 48, dep. Jun 22, 1752. {PGLR NN:37}

MORRISON, ANN, see "John James," q.v.

MORRISON, COLLIN, of Charles County, aet. 50, dep. Apr 20, 1736. {CHLR T#2:197}

MORROW, ANGUISH, of Dorchester County, aet. 60, dep. Jul 12, 1708. {DOLR 6 Old 119}

MORTON, ANN, of Talbot County, widow, aet. 69, dep. May 24, 1736, mentioned Richard Hazeldine and his wife Abigail about 40 years ago. {TALR 14:159}

MOTHAM, THOMAS, see "Thomas Hatton," q.v.

MOTTERSHEAD, ZACHARY, see "Thomas Morris," q.v.

MOUNTJOY, JAMES, of St. Mary's County, n.a., dep. Jun 2, 1659, stated that he was a member of the company that surprised and overtook a ship called the *St. George* of Amsterdam at Barbadoes upon suspicion of piracy. {ARMD 41:308-309}

MOUNTSIER, THOMAS, of Queen Anne's County, aet. 34, dep. Mar, 1746. {QAEJ - Benjamin Tasker folder} See "Jacob Ford," q.v.

MOUNTSIER, THOMAS, of Queen Anne's County, aet. 35, dep. Feb, 1768, mentioned his father (not named) when he was a boy. {QAEJ - John Moore folder}

MUDD, CLEMENT, of Charles County, aet. 46, dep. Jun 8, 1772, mentioned his father John Mudd. {CHLR U#3:16}

MUDD, JOHN, SR., of Charles County, aet. 60, dep. Mar 31, 1755. {CHLR E#3:134} See "Clement Mudd," q.v.

MUDD, LUKE, of Charles County, aet. 52, dep. Jun 14, 1732. {CHLR R#2:157}

MUDD, MRS., see "William Boarman" and "John Marten" and "William Nally," q.v.

MUDD, WIDOW, see "John Smith," q.v.

MUIR, JAMES, of Dorchester County, gentleman, aet. about 38, dep. between Mar 13, 1764 and Jun 4, 1767, mentioned Major Daniel Sulivane and Capt. Thomas Hicks about 2 years ago. {DOLR 21 Old 382}

MULLIGAN (MULLICAN), DANIEL, see "James Sappington" and "John Riley" and "Edward McCann," q.v.

MULLIKIN, ANN, of Queen Anne's County, aet. 54, wife of Daniel Mullikin, dep. Apr, 1723. {QAEJ - William Bishop folder}

MULLIKIN, DANIEL, of Queen Anne's County, aet. 58, dep. Apr, 1723. {QAEJ - William Bishop folder} See "Ann Mullikin," q.v.

MULLIKIN, ELIZABETH, of Prince George's County, aet. 68, dep. Jun 20, 1764, mentioned her husband Thomas Mullikin. {PGLR TT:368} See "William Mullikin" and "John Demall," q.v.

MULLIKIN, JAMES, of Prince George's County, aet. 55, dep. Oct 2, 1724. {PGLR I:590}

MULLIKIN, JAMES, of Prince George's County, aet. near 40, dep. Dec 22, 1747, mentioned Robert Tyler, Sr., deceased. {PGLR BB:665}

MULLIKIN, JAMES, see "William Mullikin" and "Thomas Mullikin" and "John Demall" and "John Brown" and "James Duvall," q.v.

MULLIKIN, MARY, see "John Demall," q.v.

MULLIKIN, THOMAS, of Prince George's County, aet. near 32, dep. Oct 10, 1761, stated that he and his brother James Mullikin carried chains for Benjamin Hall about 12 years ago. {PGLR RR:182} See "Elizabeth Mullikin" and "Higgison Mockby," q.v.

MULLIKIN, WILLIAM, of Prince George's County, aet. 54, dep. Nov 29, 1752, mentioned his brother James Mullikin whose daughter Elizabeth married Samuel Duvall. {PGLR NN:90}

MUNDAYE, HENAROTA, see "Ewen McDonall," q.v.

MUNDAYE, HENDRY, see "Ewen McDonall," q.v.

MUNES, JOHN, of Charles County, aet. 19, dep. Jun 29, 1663. {CHLR B:164}

MUNNES, THOMAS, of St. Mary's County, seaman, n.a., dep. Feb 20, 1649, stated that he and Elkenath Bourne were employed by Richard Husbands, mariner, about 7 days ago to receive merchantable tobacco from John Jarbo for Raphe Beanes. {ARMD 10:9}

MUNT, MARY, see "Richard Sullivant," q.v.
MURFEY, JAMES, of Dorchester County, aet. 32, dep. between Aug 14, 1753 and Nov 16, 1753, mentioned his father (not named). {DOLR 15 Old 11}
MURFEY, SARAH, of Dorchester County, aet. 70, wife of William Murfey, dep. between Aug 14, 1753 and Nov 16, 1753, mentioned John Pollard, Sr., his son William Pollard, and her husband John Barns about 50 years ago. {DOLR 15 Old 11}
MURFEY, WILLIAM, see "Sarah Murfey," q.v.
MURPHY, ANN, of Frederick County, n.a., dep. Jun 23, 1757, stated that John Murphy, a 4 year old child, had about a fourth of his right ear bitten off by a horse on Jun 10, 1757; her deposition was recorded at the request of Peter Murphy. {FRLR F:271}
MURPHY, DANIEL, SR., of Charles County, aet. 69, dep. Oct 10, 1767. {CHLR Q#3:311}
MURPHY, JAMES, of Charles County, aet. 28, dep. May 9, 1772. {CHLR T#3:615}
MURPHY, JOHN, see "Ann Murphy," q.v.
MURPHY, MARY, of Kent County, widow, aet. 74, dep. circa 1750. {KEEJ - Isaac and Thomas Crown folder}
MURPHY, PETER, see "Ann Murphy," q.v.
MURPHY, SARAH, see "John Barnes," q.v.
MURPHY, THOMAS, of Dorchester County, aet. about 42, dep. between Nov 11, 1755 and May 29, 1756. {DOLR 15 Old 363}
MURPHY, TIMOTHY, of Baltimore County, aet. 50, dep. Jun 18, 1770. {BALR AL#B:415}
MURPHY, WILLIAM, see "Isaac Foxwell," q.v.
MURRAIN, ROSANNA, of Dorchester County, aet. 42, dep. between Nov 12, 1751 and May 13, 1752, mentioned a conversation between her husband (not named) and Timothy Graylis about 10 years ago. {DOLR 14 Old 604}
MURRAY (MURRY), GEORGE, of Charles County, n.a., dep. Jul 12, 1664. {CHLR B:329}
MURRAY, JAMES (captain), of Charles County, aet. 37, dep. Sep 23, 1742. {CHLR O#2:288}
MURRAY, JOSEPH, of Baltimore County, aet. 45, dep. between Nov 25, 1760 and Apr 13, 1761. {BALR B#L:197} Aet. 56, dep. Jun 15, 1772, mentioned his father Morgan Murray. {BALR AL#I:208}
MURRAY, JOSEPH, of Frederick County, aet. 50, dep. Feb 26, 1766 in Baltimore County. {BALR B#P:299}
MURRAY, MORGAN, see "Joseph Murray" and "William Barney," q.v.
MURRAY, WILLIAM, of Dorchester County, aet. 36, dep. between Nov 14, 1732 and Aug 1, 1733, mentioned Maria Kirke, now Maria Rogers; also mentioned John Kirk who was present at the laying out of the town of Cambridge. {DOLR 9 Old 355} Dr. William Murray, aet. 44, dep. between Jun 22, 1741 and Jul 13, 1741, mentioned John Foster and William Folk, about 21 years ago, two of the principal Quakers, who were then numerous, in the meeting house at Kennerly's

Mill; also mentioned Col. Thomas Ennalls, Major Henry Ennalls, and land bought by Dr. Joseph Ennalls from Thomas Foster. {DOLR 12 Old 122}

MUSCHAMP, GEORGE (esquire), of Charles County, n.a., dep. between Jun 29, 1698 and Jul 1, 1698 in Annapolis. {ARMD 23:442}

MUSCHAMP, JOHN, of Charles County, aet. 20, dep. Mar 9, 1669/70, stated that he was a servant to Capt. John Neale. {CHLR D#1:137}

MUSGRAVE, CHARLES, of Charles County, aet. 44, dep. Feb 22, 1725/6. {CHLR P#2:137} Aet. 47, dep. May 31, 1727. {CHLR P#2:486} Aet. 57, dep. Jul 21, 1737. {CHLR T#2:389}

MUSGRAVE, CUTHBERT, of Charles County, aet. 22, dep. Nov 27, 1666. {CHLR C#1:97}

MUSGROVE, BENJAMIN, of Charles County, aet. 49, dep. Aug 20, 1753. {CHLR D#3:153}

NAILOR, ABRAHAM, see "Jonathan Jones," q.v.

NAILOR, GEORGE, JR., of Prince George's County, aet. 48 dep. Sep 13, 1729. {PGLR M:519}

NAILOR, GEORGE, SR., of Prince George's County, aet. 78, dep. Jun 8, 1732. {PGLR Q:449} George Nailer, aet. 72, dep. Feb 28, 1726/7. {CHLR P#2:419}

NALLY, JOHN, of Charles County, aet. 54, dep. Oct 6, 1752. {CHLR B#3:356}

NALLY, JOHN, of Charles County, aet. 63, dep. Apr 13, 1731. {CHLR R#2:42} Aet. 74, dep. Jun 14, 1732. {CHLR R#2:157}

NALLY, WILLIAM, of Charles County, aet. 43, dep. May 14, 1752. {CHLR B#3:355} Aet. 48, dep. Jul 26, 1755, stated that Mrs. Mudd and Mrs. Green were sisters. {CHLR E#3:388}

NANDUM, ROBERT, see "Indian Robert Nandum," q.v.

NASH, THOMAS, of Charles County, aet. 62, dep. Oct 20, 1763. {CHLR M#3:355}

NAVEY, MARY, of Dorchester County, aet. 50 or thereabouts, dep. Dec 15, 1774, stated that her husband (not named) said he "came to school to Isaac Alwinkle" at the head of Peason's Creek where the schoolhouse once stood. {DOLR 28 Old 173}

NAYLOR, GEORGE, of Prince George's County, aet. 40, dep. Aug 11, 1757. {PGLR PP:28, pt. 2} Aet. 55, dep. Nov 13, 1769. {PGLR AA#2:136-137} Aet. 55, dep. Feb 18, 1771. {PGLR AA#2:226} See "George Nailor," q.v.

NAYLOR, JAMES, SR., see "William Bright," q.v.

NAYLOR, SAMUEL, of Prince George's County, aet. 56, dep. Jul 7, 1772. {PGLR BB#3:74}

NEADS, JOHN, of Charles County, n.a., dep. Dec 18, 1662. {CHLR B:51}

NEALE, ANTHONY, of Charles County, aet. 20, dep. Sep 3, 1679. {CHLR H#1:205} See "Roswell Neale," q.v.

NEALE, BENJAMIN, of Charles County, aet. 35, dep. Mar 1, 1737/8. {CHLR T#2:425}

NEALE, CHARLES, of Charles County, aet. 39, dep. Jul 23, 1744. {CHLR Y#2:223}

NEALE, EDWARD, of Charles County, aet. 38, dep. Apr 22, 1742. {CHLR O#2:379}

NEALE, ELIZABETH (Mrs.), of Charles County, aet. 66, dep. May 17, 1733, stated she was the widow of James Neale. {CHLR R#2:335}
NEALE, JAMES, see "John Muschamp" and "Elizabeth Neale," q.v.
NEALE, HENRY, of St. Mary's County, n.a., dep. Feb 14, 1661, mentioned John Tompkinson, carpenter. {ARMD 41:527}
NEALE, HENRY, of Charles County, aet. 46, dep. Mar 1, 1737/8. {CHLR T#2:427}
NEALE, HEW, of Charles County, n.a., dep. Sep 24, 1661. {CHLR A:151}
NEALE, RAPHAEL, of Charles County, aet. 49, dep. Jun 6, 1732. {CHLR R#2:155} Aet. 49, dep. May 17, 1733. {CHLR R#2:335} Aet. 59, dep. Jul 24, 1742 and Sep 21, 1742. {CHLR O#2:425, 465} Aet. 60, dep. Jul 12, 1743. {CHLR O#2:663}
NEALE, RAPHAEL, of Charles County, aet. 29, dep. between Nov 8, 1774 and Feb 7, 1775. {CHLR W#3:607}
NEALE, ROSWELL, of Charles County, aet. 59, dep. Jul 23, 1744, mentioned his father Anthony Neale. {CHLR Z#2:222}
NEALE, WILLIAM, of Prince George's County, aet. 46, planter, dep. Jun 21, 1751, mentioned John Wight's widow (not named). {PGLR PP:153} Aet. 48, dep. Apr 15, 1753. {PGLR NN:134-135}
NEEDLES (NEDELS), EDWARD, of Dorchester County, planter, aet. 46, dep. between Mar 10, 1740 and Jan 23, 1741, mentioned his sister Elizabeth Grashire. {DOLR 12 Old 89}
NEEDLES, JOHN, see "George Andrew, Jr.," q.v.
NEFF, ADAM, of Frederick County, n.a., dep. 1767. {FRLR L:60}
NEGRO BEN, see "James Means," q.v.
NEGRO JACOB, see "Francis Stockett" and "Anthony Brispo" and "James Means," q.v.
NEGRO PETER, see "John Llewellin," q.v.
NEGRO ROSE, see "James Means," q.v.
NEILL, HUGH (reverend), of Queen Anne's County, Rector of St. Paul's Parish, n.a., dep. Jun 15, 1769, stated that he has known Francis Baker since he (deponent) came into this parish 3 years ago next January, during which time Baker has maintained a good character free from drunkenness and dishonesty. {ARMD 32:327}
NELSON, ALEXANDER, of Charles County, aet. 47, dep. Mar 2, 1730/1. {CHLR Q#2:475}
NELSON (NELLSON), ARTHUR, of Prince George's County, aet. 86 or thereabouts, dep. Mar 19, 1753. {PGLR NN:172}
NELSON, ARTHUR, of Frederick County, aet. 51, dep. Aug 21, 1776, mentioned his father (not named) when he (Arthur) was a boy. {FRLR BD#2:334}
NELSON, JOHN, see "Elias Delashmet," q.v.
NELSON, RICHARD, see "William Nelson," q.v.
NELSON, WILLIAM, of Prince George's County, aet. 34, dep. Jun 6, 1735. {PGLR T:284}

NELSON, WILLIAM, of Charles County, aet. 53, dep. Sep 17, 1753, mentioned his brother Richard Nelson. {CHLR D#3:309} Aet. 58, dep. Mar 30, 1758, mentioned the widow Wise who married Timothy Dunaway. {CHLR K#3:407} Aet. 62, dep. Nov 8, 1762. {CHLR M#3:123} Aet. 64, dep. between May 15, 1764 and Aug 27, 1764. {CHLR N#3:61} Aet. 73, dep. Aug 24, 1773. {CHLR U#3:601}

NERCK, ROGER, see "Samuel Brice" and "Charles Alleyn" and "Edward Lang" and "Daniel Smith," q.v.

NESBIT, THOMAS, of Baltimore County, aet. 30, dep. Oct 11, 1763. {BALR B#N:64}

NEVETT, THOMAS, see "Charles Dickinson," q.v.

NEVILL, GOODIE, see "Thomas Baker," q.v.

NEVILL, JOAN, of Charles County, aet. 34, dep. Jul 2, 1661, stated that Anne Marding, servant to William Robisson, was with child by William Wennam and said Robisson demanded they get married. {CHLR A:142} See "Mary Row," q.v.

NEVILL, JOHN, of Charles County, aet. 35, dep. Oct 26, 1658. {CHLR A:25} Aet. 44, dep. Sep 4, 1660. {CHLR A:100} Aet. 41, dep. Jul 2, 1661. {CHLR A:142}

NEVILLE, DAVID, of Queen Anne's County, aet. about 37, dep. Aug 13, 1760. {QAEJ - John Gafford folder}

NEWMAN, ELEANOR, see "Walter Fearson," q.v.

NEWMAN, GEORGE, of Charles County, n.a., dep. Feb 11, 1662/3, mentioned William Empson, under sheriff. {CHLR B:77} See "Walter Fearson" and "Eleanor Fearson," q.v.

NEWMAN, JOHN, see "Priscilla Newman," q.v.

NEWMAN, MARY, see "Eleanor Pherson," q.v.

NEWMAN, PRISCILLA, of Charles County, aet. 35, dep. Dec 20, 1737, stated she was the widow of John Newman. {CHLR T#2:430}

NEWMAN, WILLIAM, see "Margaret Plummer," q.v.

NEWNAM (NUNAM), BENJAMIN, of Queen Anne's County, aet. about 50, dep. July, 1758; aet. 53, dep. Mar, 1762. {QAEJ - Henry Callister folders} Benjamin Nunam, aet. 51 or 52, dep. Aug 13, 1760. {QAEJ - John Gafford folder} Benjamin Newnam, aet. 56, dep. Apr, 1765. {QAEJ - William Austin folder} Aet. about 60, dep. Feb, 1769, mentioned Joanna Andrews about 30 years ago. {QAEJ - John Moore folder}

NEWNER, EDWARD, see "Edward Nooner," q.v.

NEWNON, JOHN, see "Indian Abraham," q.v.

NEWTON, RICHARD, see "Henry Woodward," q.v.

NICHOLDS, JOHN, of Charles County, aet. 40 or thereabouts, dep. 1658. {ARMD 41:50}

NICHOLLS, CHRISTOPHER, of Prince George's County, aet. 38, dep. Jul 29, 1754. {PGLR RR:201} Aet. 48, dep. Jul 10, 1759. {PGLR RR:78} Aet. 49, dep. Mar 21, 1761. {PGLR RR:234}

NICHOLLS, JOHN, of Dorchester County, aet. 60, dep. Feb 2, 1696. {DOLR 5 Old 90}

NICHOLLS, JOHN, of Prince George's County, aet. 58, dep. Jul 29, 1754, mentioned Capt. Charles Beall and the late Rev. Hugh Conn about 31 years ago. {PGLR RR:200} Aet. 72, dep. Nov 21, 1768, stated that he was shown the bounds of *Simon & Jane* about 57 years ago. {PGLR BB#2:391}

NICHOLLS, JOHN, see "John Nicholds" and "John Nicolls" and "Peter Brightwell," q.v.

NICHOLLS, SIMON, of Prince George's County, aet. 67, dep. Aug 17, 1725, called "Sr." {PGLR I:679} Aet. 70 and upwards, dep. Sep 29, 1731. {PGLR Q:396}

NICHOLLS, THOMAS, of Prince George's County, aet. 68, dep. Jul 29, 1754. {PGLR RR:201} Thomas Nicholls, Sr., aet. 76, dep. Nov 21, 1763. {PGLR TT:195}

NICHOLSON, FRANCIS, see "Kenelm Cheseldyn" and "Henry Denton," q.v.

NICHOLSON, JOSEPH (captain), of Kent County, aet. 64, dep. 1774. {KELR DD#4:367}

NICOLLS, BENJAMIN, see "Joseph Alford" and "Joseph Bowdle," q.v.

NICOLLS, ISAAC, of Dorchester County, aet. 44, dep. between Mar 15, 1728 and Jun 6, 1729. {DOLR 8 Old 291} Aet. 60, dep. between Jun 11, 1745 and Nov 15, 1745, stated that about 30 years ago he laid out *Wakefield* for John Harriss, now deceased, at the request of Matthias Alford, now deceased; also mentioned the division tree of *Britt's Hope* on Hunting Creek over 20 years ago. {DOLR 12 Old 220, 14 Old 46} Aet. 61, dep. between Jun 11, 1745 and May 23, 1746, mentioned his father John Nicolls (deceased) and grandfather John Alford (deceased); also mentioned William Edmondson, son of John Edmondson, of Talbot County. {DOLR 14 Old 50}

NICOLLS, JOHN, of Dorchester County, aet. about 42, nephew of Mathias Allford, dep. between Aug 16, 1728 and Jan 28, 1728/9. {DOLR 8 Old 268} Aet. about 51, dep. between Jun 15, 1737 and Apr 8, 1738, mentioned a conversation about 30 years ago with William Spencer, deceased. {DOLR 9 Old 507} John Nicolls, Sr., aet. about 59, dep. between Jun 11, 1745 and Nov 15, 1745, stated that *Weakefield* belonged to his grandfather (not named) about 40 years ag; also mentioned *Britt's Hope* and Solomon West about 40 years ago. {DOLR 12 Old 220} See "Isaac Nicolls" and "John Richardson" and "Thomas Andrew," q.v.

NICOLLS, JOSEPH, see "Abraham Gambell," q.v.

NICOLLS, MARK, see "Jesper Woodall," q.v.

NICOLLS, MOSES, of Dorchester County, aet. 41, dep. between Jun 11, 1745 and May 23, 1746. {DOLR 14 Old 50} Moses Nicolls, of Kent County on Delaware, aet. 47, dep. between Aug 13, 1751 and Jan 20, 1751/2. {DOLR 14 Old 577} See "Daniel Croneene," q.v.

NICOLLS, ROBERT, see "Simon Richardson" and "Philip White," q.v.

NIGHT, SARAH, of Prince George's County, aet. 61, dep. Jun 26, 1734, mentioned Capt. Charles Somerset Smith. {PGLR T:125}

NIVENTO, JEREMIAH, of Charles County, aet. 24, dep. Aug 2, 1774. {CHLR W#3:388}

NOBLE, GEORGE, of Prince George's County, n.a., dep. Nov 28, 1728. {PGLR M:346}
NOE, GEORGE, of Charles County, aet. 71, dep. between Sep 19, 1761 and Nov 23, 1761, mentioned his brother Samuel Noe and father John Noe. {CHLR K#3:407}
NOE, JOHN, see "George Noe," q.v.
NOE, SAMUEL, see "George Noe," q.v.
NOELL, BAZILL (captain), of Dorchester County, aet. 54, dep. between Nov 14, 1749 and Mar 14, 1753. {DOLR 14 Old 690}
NOONER (NEWNER), EDWARD, of Dorchester County, aet. 36, dep. between Mar 11, 1755 and Jul 23, 1755. {DOLR 15 Old 452} Edward Newner, aet. 54, dep. between Mar 9, 1773 and Feb 5, 1774, mentioned Bethewley Wallace, niece of George Stapleford. {DOLR 27 Old 115}
NORCOTT, THOMAS, of London, England, boatswain aboard the ship *Globe* commanded by Bartholomew Watts, dep. May 8, 1682 in St. Mary's County. {ARMD 7:281}
NORMAN, JOHN, of St. Mary's County, n.a., dep. Mar 2, 1643. {ARMD 4:257}
NORMAN, JOHN, of Charles County, aet. 28, dep. Apr 22, 1662. {CHLR A:201}
NORRIS, ANN, see "Daniell Norris," q.v.
NORRIS, BENJAMIN, of Baltimore County, aet. 71 or thereabouts, dep. Apr 3, 1769. {BALR AL#A:302} Aet. 71, dep. Jun 14, 1770. {BALR AL#C:276} See "John Norris," q.v.
NORRIS, CALEB, of Prince George's County, aet. 54, dep. Feb 28, 1731/2. {PGLR Q:430} Aet. 54, dep. Apr 4, 1732, mentioned his master Bartholomne Gooff. {PGLR Q:573} Aet. 61, dep. Dec 24, 1736. {PGLR Y:84}
NORRIS, DANIELL, of Kent County, aet. about 64, dep. June, 1706, stated that his eldest sister Ann Norris married William Woodroofe at Cowley in Glostershire, England; said William was the eldest brother of Thomas Woodroofe who came to Salem in West New Jersey in America and lived there 30 years before he died; Joseph Woodroofe, eldest son of said Thomas, came to visit this deponent (Norris) in Kent County, Maryland during his father's (Woodroofe's) lifetime; deponent stated he was well acquainted with the Woodroofes in London before any of them came to America; also stated that William Woodroofe had married his sister Ann Norris and their children were John, William, Francis, Thomas, Mary, and Ann, some of whom may still be alive in England; deponent knows of no one in America now alive so nearly related to deceased Thomas Woodroofe and Joseph Woodroofe (his son who died at Salem) as he this deponent is. {KELR GL#1:108, 132}
NORRIS, HENRY, see "David Davis," q.v.
NORRIS, JOHN, of Prince George's County, aet. 52, dep. Nov 5, 1731. {PGLR Q:389}
NORRIS, JOHN, of Baltimore County, aet. 57, dep. between Nov 11, 1769 and Sep 6, 1770, mentioned his father Benjamin Norris. {BALR AL#C:278}

NORRIS, JOHN, of Baltimore County, aet. 43, dep. Dec 14, 1765, mentioned his brother Thomas Norris and his grandfather John Norris of West River. {BALR B#P:178}
NORRIS, JOHN, see "Benjamin Talburt," q.v.
NORRIS, NATHANIEL, of Frederick County, aet. 22, dep. May 5, 1764, mentioned his father (not named) about 9 years ago. {FRLR J:572}
NORRIS, THOMAS, see "John Norris," q.v.
NORRIS, WILLIAM, of Frederick County, aet. 24, dep. May 5, 1764, mentioned his father (not named) about 9 years ago. {FRLR J:571}
NORRIS, WILLIAM, of Frederick County, aet. 70, dep. Mar 13, 1761. {FRLR G:160}
NORTH, GEORGE, of Dorchester County, aet. 60, dep. between Aug 8, 1749 and Nov 10, 1749. {DOLR 14 Old 392} Aet. 73, dep. between Jun 14, 1768 and Sep 3, 1768, mentioned old Stephen Ross. {DOLR 23 Old 271}
NORTH, GILBERT, of Dorchester County, aet. 41, dep. between Nov 10, 1772 and Mar 28, 1774, mentioned Richard Soward. {DOLR 27 Old 356}
NORTH, REBECCAH, see "Elizabeth Adams," q.v.
NORTH, RICHARD, of Dorchester County, aet. 51, dep. between Aug 15, 1746 and Sep 1, 1746, mentioned John Pollard and his son John about 5 years ago. {DOLR 14 Old 89}
NORTH, THOMAS, JR., of Dorchester County, aet. 30, dep. between Apr 20, 1768 and May 27, 1768, mentioned old John Clarage about 10 years ago, now deceased. {DOLR 22 Old 423}
NORTON, THOMAS, of Prince George's County, aet. 54, dep. Jun 11, 1727. {PGLR Q:472}
NOTTOOL, ARTHUR, of Calvert County, n.a., dep. Jun 21, 1664. {ARMD 49:232}
NOWELL, JAMES, JR., of Dorchester County, aet. 22, dep. Sep 8, 1705. {DOLR 6 Old 74}
NOWELL, MARGRETT, of Dorchester County, aet. 47, dep. Jun 9, 1703. {DOLR 6 Old 53}
NOWELL, WILLIAM, see "Michael Miller," q.v.
NOWLAND, SUSANNAH, of Dorchester County, aet. 53, dep. Dec 15, 1774, mentioned her father (not named). {DOLR 28 Old 173}
NURKEUM, THOMAS, see "Anthony Chilcut," q.v.
NUTTER, CHARLES, see "John Handy," q.v.
NUTTER, THOMAS, of Dorchester County, aet. about 32, dep. between Nov 11, 1746 and Apr 14, 1748. {DOLR 14 Old 231}
NUTTER, WILLIAM, see "John Handy" and "James Cannon," q.v.
NUTTHALL, JOHN, of St. Mary's County, gentleman, n.a., dep. Feb 11, 1663. {ARMD 49:142}
NUTWELL, ELEANOR, see "Thomas Prather," q.v.
NUTWELL, MARY, see "Thomas Prather," q.v.

OAKLEY, JOHN, of Charles County, aet. 40, dep. Mar 4, 1762, mentioned John Penn about 40 years ago, now deceased, and stated that he was the father of John Penn, Jr. who married the widow of Garrard O'Cain. {CHLR K#3:473}

OARD, WILLIAM, of Charles County, aet. 43, dep. Nov 1, 1736. {CHLR T#2:267} Aet. 67, dep. Feb 22, 1762. {CHLR K#3:474}

O'BRIAN (O'BRIEN), MATHIAS, of Charles County, aet. 33, dep. Feb 12, 1660/1, regarding a disturbance of the peace with mutinous and reproachful words, stated that he heard that many inhabitants were to be hanged, including Zacharie Wade, Joseph Harrison, and William Heard. {CHLR A:121} Mathias O'Brien, aet. 46, dep. Jun 1, 1669. {CHLR D#1:119}

O'BRIAN (OBRIAN), TERENCE, of Prince George's County, aet. 78, dep. Aug 22, 1757, mentioned Major Dent about 50 years ago, now deceased. {PGLR PP:64, 66, pt. 2} Turence Obrian, aet. 81, dep. Jan 21, 1760, mentioned William Durigs about 15 years ago, now deceased. {PGLR RR:40}

O'CAIN, GARRARD, see "John Oakley," q.v.

ODEL, HENRY, see "Samuel Butt," q.v.

ODELL, RIGNALD, of Prince George's County, aet. 26, dep. May 11, 1762. {PGLR RR:267} See "William Forest," q.v.

OFFUTT, NATHANIEL, of Prince George's County, aet. 45, dep. Jul 2, 1760. {PGLR RR:79}

OFFUTT, WILLIAM, see "Mordecai Mitchell" and "Thomas Drane," q.v.

OGDEN, WILLIAM, of Charles County, aet. 73, dep. Sep 24, 1757. {CHLR H#3:6}

OLIVER, BLANCH, see "Mary Clocker" and "Joseph Edlow," q.v.

OLIVER, JOHN, of Prince George's County, aet. 40, dep. Mar 19, 1724/5. {PGLR I:624} Aet. 50, dep. Sep 22, 1730. {PGLR Q:160}

OLIVER (OLLIVER), LEONARD, of Prince George's County, aet. 56, dep. Aug 3, 1772, mentioned his father William Olliver. {PGLR BB#3:78}

OLIVER, ROGER, see "Joseph Edlow," q.v.

OLIVER, WILLIAM, of Prince George's County, aet. 60, dep. Jul 1, 1738. {PGLR T:607} See "Leonard Oliver," q.v.

O'NEALE, HUGH, see "Daniell Johnson," q.v.

O'NEALE, MRS., of Charles County, n.a., dep. Jul 8, 1662, formerly Vanderduncke, now wife of Hugh O'Neale. {CHLR A:223}

OMELY, BRIAN, see "James Wilson" and "George Wilson," q.v.

ORME, AARON (ARON), of Prince George's County, aet. 58, dep. Jun 15, 1753. {PGLR NN:139-140} Aet. 62, dep. Aug 29, 1757, mentioned William Groome about 18 years ago, now deceased. {PGLR PP:69, pt. 2}

ORME (ORAM), JAMES, of Prince George's County, aet. 34, dep. Mar 1, 1756. {PGLR NN:469}

ORME, JOHN, of Prince George's County, aet. 48, dep. Mar 8, 1770. {PGLR AA#2:83}

ORME, JOHN, of Prince George's County, aet. 63, dep. Jun 15, 1753. {PGLR NN:139} John Orme, Sr., aet. 68, dep. Jul 5, 1758. {PGLR PP:276, pt. 2}

ORME, MOSES, of Prince George's County, aet. 60, dep. Jun 15, 1753. {PGLR NN:139} Aet. 72, dep. Feb 20, 1767. {PGLR BB#2:167}
ORSBERSTON, WILLIAM, of Charles County, aet. 33 or thereabouts, dep. 1658. {ARMD 41:181}
OSBORN, JAMES, of Baltimore County, aet. 58, dep. Jun 14, 1770. {BALR AL#C:276} Aged 59 on Jan 17, 1771, dep. Jun 10, 1771. {BALR AL#I:10}
OUCHTERLONY, AGNESS, see "Elizabeth Tyler," q.v.
OUCHTERLONY, MARY, see "Nathan Wells" and "Sarah Gaither," q.v.
OUCHTERLONY, JOHN, see "John Lamar" and "Nathan Wells" and "Sarah Gaither" and "Elizabeth Tyler," q.v.
OUCHTERLONY, MARY, see "Nathan Wells" and "Sarah Gaither," q.v.
OVERZEE, SYMON, see "Adam Christian," q.v.
OWEN, EDWARD, of Charles County, aet. 40, dep. Jul 12, 1743. {CHLR O#2:662} See "Owen Hughes," q.v.
OWEN (OWENS), JOHN, see "Owen Hughes" and "Mary Buence," q.v.
OWEN, OWEN (EVAN), see "Owen Hughes," q.v.
OWEN (OWENS), RICHARD, of Dorchester County, aet. 56, dep. Nov 12, 1700. {DOLR 5 Old 178} Aet. 60, dep. Sep 8, 1705. {DOLR 6 Old 74} See "Owen Hughes" and "Mary Buence," q.v.
OWEN (OWENS), ROBERT, of Dorchester County, aet. 48, dep. between Nov 9, 1742 and Nov 5, 1743. {DOLR 12 Old 157} See "Thomas Beatty" and "Roger John Sasser," q.v.
OWEN, THOMAS, of Prince George's County, aet. 64, dep. Mar 10, 1769, mentioned his father William Owen. {PGLR AA#2:152}
OWEN, WILLIAM, see "Thomas Owen" and "George Athey," q.v.
OWINES(?), DAVID, of Worcester County, aet. about 40, dep. Jul 1, ---- [sic]. {QAEJ - William Clayton folder}
PAC, JOHN, of Frederick County, n.a., dep. Dec 2, 1765. {ARMD 32:156-157}
PACA, JOHN, of Baltimore County, aet. 52, dep. May 12, 1764. {BALR B#O:114} Capt. John Paca, aet. 62, dep. Aug 15, 1774. {BALR AL#L:240}
PACHECO, ANTHONY, see "William Joans" and "William Gary," q.v.
PACKER, EDWARD, of St. Mary's County, n.a., dep. Jan 14, 1650. {ARMD 10:94}
PAGE, AQUILA, of Kent County, aet. about 29, dep. Mar 24, 1774. {KEEJ - John Comegys folder}
PAGE, RALPH, of Kent County, aet. 44, dep. 1724. {KELR JS#W:374}
PAGE, RALPH, of Kent County, aet. 56, dep. 1767. {KELR DD#2:401}
PAGET, BENJAMIN, of Charles County, aet. 31, dep. Nov 4, 1726. {CHLR P#2:401}
PAGON, JOHN, of Dorchester County, aet. 52 or 53, dep. between Nov 13, 1764 and Dec 22, 1764, mentioned "his father Roberson" [prob. the John Roberson who was mentioned in another deposition], Henry Travers (commonly called "Gartown Henry"), and Mathew Traverse, his brother James Traverse, and their father (not named). {DOLR 20 Old 11}

PAIN, EDMUND BERRY GODFREY, of Charles County, aet. 50, dep. Jan 11, 1757/8. {CHLR F#3:468} Aet. 50, dep. Dec 13, 1757. {CHLR H#3:120}
PAIN, FRANCIS, of Prince George's County, aet. 29, dep. Aug 3, 1730, stated that the daughter of John Saunders (not named) was the wife of Henry Ward. {PGLR Q:68}
PAIN, FRANCIS, of Charles County, aet. 53, dep. Sep 17, 1753. {CHLR D#3:309} Aet. 55, dep. May 22, 1755. {CHLR E#3:135} Aet. 63, dep. Sep 18, 1768. {CHLR Q#3:63} Aet. 69, dep. Jun 12, 1769. {CHLR Q#3:495} Aet. 75, dep. Oct 30, 1770. {CHLR T#3:140}
PAIN, JOHN, of Prince George's County, aet. 66, dep. Jun 6, 1735. {PGLR T:280}
PAIN, JOHN, of Charles County, aet. 75, dep. May 14, 1744. {CHLR Y#2:14}
PAIN, JOHN, of Charles County, n.a., dep. Feb 10, 1662/3. {CHLR B:69} John Paine, aet. 34, dep. Mar 11, 1669/70. {CHLR D#1:150}
PAKES, WALTER, of St. Mary's County, aet. 43, dep. Jun 8, 1653, mentioned Edward Cotten, lately deceased, and John Warren. {ARMD 10:277}
PALMER, JOHN, JR., of Prince George's County, aet. 43, dep. May 9, 1752. {PGLR NN:36} Aet. 43, dep. Jun 23, 1753, mentioned John Lanham 3rd about 13 years ago, now deceased. {PGLR NN:141}
PALMER, JOHN, SR., of Prince George's County, aet. 78, dep. May 9, 1752. {PGLR NN:36}
PALMER, ROBERT, see "Frances Shembrooke," q.v.
PALMER, SAMUEL, of Charles County, aet. 32, dep. Jan 28, 1661/2. {CHLR A:184} Samuell Palmer, aet. 33, dep. Feb 12, 1660/1, regarding a disturbance of the peace with mutinous and reproachful words, stated that he heard that many men were to be hanged, including Lt. Robert Troope and Thomas Allen. {CHLR A:121}
PALMES, BENJAMIN, of Dorchester County, n.a., dep. May 30, 1681, mentioned Thomas Harpin, Charles Hutchins, and Edward Fisher. {ARMD 15:360}
PANQUASH, SAMUEL, see "Thomas Willson," q.v.
PARKER, GABRIEL, see "Henry Hill," q.v.
PARKER, GRACE (Mrs.), of Calvert County, n.a., dep. May 31, 1664. {ARMD 49:217}
PARKER, HENRY, see "William Jump," q.v.
PARKER, HUGH, see "James Hopkins," q.v.
PARKER, PETER, of Prince George's County, aet. 60, dep. Apr 17, 1739. {PGLR Y:59}
PARKER, SAMUEL, of Charles County, aet. 24, dep. Nov 23, 1658, mentioned his bachelor brother's house (no name given) about 3 years ago. {CHLR A:31}
PARKER, WILLIAM, of Charles County, aet. 31, dep. May 17, 1755. {CHLR E#3:130}
PARKINSON, ROBERT, of Dorchester County, aet. 48, dep. between Jun 10, 1760 and Jul 16, 1752, stated that he was told by Samuel Ratcliff about 17 or 18 years ago that *Hambrook's Point* "belonged to a little girl who lived with Jacob Lowe who was Dorrington's heir." {DOLR 19 Old 65} Aet. 55, dep. between

Mar 8, 1768 and Jul 23, 1768, mentioned Jane Thomas, mother of the present Joseph Thomas. {DOLR 23 Old 5} Robert Parkeson, aet. 60, dep. between Aug 11, 1772 and Dec 11, 1772, mentioned John Soward, son of John Soward, about 26 years ago. {DOLR 27 Old 348}

PARKS, ARTHUR, of Dorchester County, aet. 46, dep. between Aug 12, 1760 and Dec 6, 1760. {DOLR 17 Old 268}

PARRAN, JOHN, see "Sarah Deaver," q.v.

PARRAN, MOSES, see "Sarah Deaver," q.v.

PARRAN, YOUNG, see "Sarah Deaver," q.v.

PARRANDIER, JOHN, of Charles County, aet. 42, dep. Jan 20, 1726/7. {CHLR P#2:492}

PARRENDIER, JAMES, see "James Johnson," q.v.

PARRIOT (PARRATT), GEORGE, of Talbot County, aet. about 55, dep. between Aug 14, 1764 and Aug 13, 1765. {DOLR 20 Old 237}

PARRISH, JOHN, of Baltimore County, n.a., Quaker, dep. Jan 11, 1767. {BALR B#P:459}

PARRISH, WILLIAM, of Baltimore County, Quaker, aet. about 92, dep. between Oct 11, 1768 and Mar 11, 1772. {BALR AL#D:437}

PARRISH, WILLIAM, JR., of Baltimore County, Quaker, aet. 45, dep. Aug 29, 1763. {BALR B#N:134}

PARSONS, FRANCIS, of Talbot County, n.a., dep. Jan 21, 1667/8. {ARMD 54:416}

PARTRIDGE, JONATHAN, of Dorchester County, aet. about 36, dep. between Aug 14, 1764 and Jan 4, 1768. {DOLR 22 Old 418}

PATE, THOMAS(?), of Queen Anne's County, aet. about 33, dep. Mar, 1746. {QAEJ - Benjamin Tasker folder}

PATTERSON, JAMES, see "John Pattison," q.v.

PATTERSON, JOHN, of Dorchester County, aet. about 85, dep. between Nov 13, 1770 and Feb 4, 1771. {DOLR 26 Old 401} See "Elizabeth Lamphier," q.v.

PATTERSON, RICHARD, of Dorchester County, aet. 47 or 48, dep. between Nov 13, 1764 and Dec 22, 1764, which listed his name as "Richard Patterson (or Chapman)." {DOLR 20 Old 11}

PATTISON, ATTHOW, see "John Pattison," q.v.

PATTISON, JACOB, of Dorchester County, aet. 50, dep. between Mar 8, 1757 and May 28, 1757. {DOLR 15 Old 483} See "Henry Travers," q.v.

PATTISON, JAMES, of Dorchester County, aet. 77, dep. between Jun 12, 1739 and Aug 13, 1739, stated that he served on a jury about 36 years ago to run out *Grass Reeden* by John Taylor, surveyor. {DOLR 12 Old 91} Aet. 78, dep. Apr 2, 1740. {DOLR 12 Old 127} Aet. 80 odd years, dep. Jan 22, 1742/3. {DOLR 14 Old 44}

PATTISON, JAMES, of Dorchester County, aet. 80, dep. between Apr 6, 1732 and Jun 3, 1732. {DOLR 9 Old 68} Aet. 92 or 93, dep. May 19, 1746. {DOLR 14 Old 75}

PATTISON, JAMES, see "Thomas Pattison" and "John Pattison" and "Richard Pattison" and "Moses Lecompte," q.v.

PATTISON, JOHN, see "Perry Pattison" and "Richard Pattison" and "Henry Travers," q.v.

PATTISON, JOHN, of Charles County, aet. 57, dep. Apr 21, 1772, stated that he was aged 30 in the first year of his marriage and mentioned his brother Perry Pattison and father John Pattison. {CHLR U#3:276}

PATTISON, JOHN, of Dorchester County, aet. 70, dep. between Nov 13, 1764 and Dec 22, 1764, mentioned James Patterson and John Roberson. {DOLR 20 Old 11}

PATTISON, JOHN, of Dorchester County, aet. 43, dep. 14, 1730. {DOLR 8 Old 422} Aet. 44, dep. between Apr 6, 1732 and Jun 3, 1732. {DOLR 9 Old 68} Aet. 53, dep. Apr 2, 1740, mentioned his grandfather (not named) about 38 years ago. {DOLR 12 Old 127} Aet. 55, dep. Jul 10, 1744, mentioned his son Atthow Pattison and stated that he (John) had a claim to *Addition to Crow's Lodge* through his wife Mary Atthow. {DOLR 12 Old 150} Aet. 71, dep. between Mar 8, 1757 and May 28, 1757, mentioned his father James Pattison. {DOLR 15 Old 483}

PATTISON, JOHN, SR., of Dorchester County, aet. 74, dep. between Aug 12, 1760 and Mar 2, 1761, mentioned his uncle John Robson about 30 years ago. {DOLR 17 Old 262}

PATTISON, PERRY, of Charles County, aet. 50, dep. Apr 15, 1772, mentioned his father John Pattison. {CHLR U#3:276} Aet. 51, dep. between Jan 8, 1772 and Mar 11, 1772. {CHLR #3:602} See "John Pattison," q.v.

PATTISON, RICHARD, of Dorchester County, aet. 40, dep. between Mar 8, 1757 and May 28, 1757, mentioned his father James Pattison and his brother John Pattison. {DOLR 15 Old 483}

PATTISON, ST. LEGER, see "Mary Lecompte," q.v.

PATTISON, THOMAS, see "Hannah Barnes" and "Mathew Gadd" and "Peter Taylor," q.v.

PATTISON, THOMAS, of Dorchester County, aet. 56, dep. Apr 2, 1740. {DOLR 12 Old 127}

PATTISON, THOMAS, of Dorchester County, aet. 60, dep. between Apr 6, 1732 and Jun 3, 1732, mentioned his brother James Pattison and his father (not named). {DOLR 9 Old 68} Aet. 64, dep. between Mar 14, 1735 and May 17, 1736. {DOLR 9 Old 393}

PATTISON, THOMAS, SR., of Dorchester County, aet. 53, dep. Jun 14, 1730. {DOLR 8 Old 422}

PAUL, CHARLES, of Dorchester County, aet. 45, dep. between Jun 14, 1743 and Aug 1, 1743. {DOLR 12 Old 167} Aet. 65, dep. between Nov 8, 1763 and Jun 11, 1764, mentioned old John Griffith. {DOLR 19 Old 237} Aet. 67, dep. between Jun 11, 1765 and Aug 15, 1765, mentioned John Cole, now deceased, who lived on Blackwater River. {DOLR 20 Old 244}

PAUL, JOHN, of Dorchester County, aet. 45, dep. between Nov 8, 1763 and Jun 11, 1764. {DOLR 19 Old 237}

PAYN, ANNE, of Dorchester County, aet. 66, dep. between Nov 10, 1772 and Mar 28, 1774. {DOLR 27 Old 356}

PAYNE, EDMUND (captain), of Charles County, n.a., dep. between Jun 29, 1698 and Jul 1, 1698 in Annapolis. {ARMD 23:442}

PAYNE, JOHN, of Charles County, aet. 76, dep. May 13, 1745. {CHLR Z#2:337}

PAYNE, WILLIAM, of Dorchester County, aet. in his 80th year, dep. between Nov 8, 1768 and Dec 10, 1768, stated that he was shown the bounded tree of *The Grove* about 50 years ago by old David Melvill, and some years later he (Payne) bought the land where "William Wright son Roger" now lives near said tract. {DOLR 23 Old 133} Aet. 80, dep. between Jun 14, 1768 and Jun 14, 1769, stated that he was shown the bounded tree of *Hope* and *Promise* about 40 years ago by John Brumwill, now deceased. {DOLR 23 Old 295} Aet. 82, dep. between Mar 12, 1771 and Jul 22, 1771. {DOLR 25 Old 73}

PEACH, JOSEPH, JR., of Prince George's County, aet. 27, dep. Aug 16, 1758. {PGLR PP:230, pt. 2}

PEACH, JOSEPH, SR., of Prince George's County, aet. upwards of 65, dep. Aug 16, 1758. {PGLR PP:230, pt. 2} Aet. near 70, dep. Jul 17, 1763, mentioned Charles Cheney about 30 years ago, now deceased. {PGLR TT:606}

PEACOCK, RICHARD, see "William Duncan," q.v.

PEACOCK, ROBERT, see "William Duncan," q.v.

PEAKE, JEREMY, see "Indian Sam Isaac," q.v.

PEARCE, DANIEL, see "George Wilson," q.v.

PEARCE, GIDEON, of Kent County, aet. 58, dep. 1736. {KELR JS#18:268} See "Mrs. Batrix Johnson," q.v.

PEARCE, ISABELL, see "George Moffett," q.v.

PEARCE, MARGARET, of Charles County, n.a., dep. Jan 26, 1658/9, stated that she heard John Ashbrooke say that if Lucie Stratton was with child she said it could belong to William Bowls, but she thought in her conscience that it was Arthur Turner's child. {CHLR A:35, ARMD 41:293}

PEARCE, WILLIAM, of Kent County, aet. 34, dep. 1750, mentioned his mother Sarah Hicks and her son John Gamble. {KELR JS#27:150}

PEARCE, WILLIAM, of Baltimore County, aet. 50, dep. Jun 6, 1763. {BALR B#N:185}

PEARCE, WILLIAM, JR., of Baltimore County, aet. 23, dep. Dec 26, 1767. {BALR B#Q:699}

PEARL, DANIEL, of Frederick County, aet. 57, dep. Apr 1, 1768, mentioned his father Robert Pearl, Meredith Davis, and Humphrey Haseldine about 22 or 23 years ago. {FRLR L:518}

PEARL, ROBERT, see "Daniel Pearl," q.v.

PEARRIE, JAMES, see "James Perrie," q.v.

PEARSON, NOAH, of Dorchester County, aet. 54, dep. between Nov 14, 1759 and Mar 9, 1759/60, stated that he was shown the bounds of *Staplefort's Desert* about 2 years ago by Edward Pritchett, Jr., now deceased. {DOLR 16 Old 146} Aet. 56, dep. between Nov 10, 1761 and Mar 4, 1762, mentioned Lewis Griffith, son of John Griffith. {DOLR 18 Old 83} Aet. 56, dep. between Nov 10, 1761 and Feb

20, 1762, mentioned his father Richard Pearson. {DOLR 18 Old 90} Noah Person, aet. 58, dep. between Aug 10, 1762 and Mar 8, 1763. {DOLR 18 Old 333} See "Betty Insley," q.v.

PEARSON, RICHARD, of Dorchester County, aet. 63, dep. between May 6, 1726 and Aug 14, 1727. {DOLR 8 Old 227} Aet. 67, dep. between Mar 15, 1731 and Apr 13, 1732. {DOLR 9 Old 63} Aet. 68, dep. between Sep 1, 1732 and Dec 9, 1732. {DOLR 9 Old 57} Aet. 71, dep. between Nov 28, 1734 and Jul 31, 1735, mentioned *Kindal's Chance* taken up by his father-in-law Richard Kindal at the head of Jacob's Creek. {DOLR 9 Old 312} See "Noah Pearson" and "Daniel Foxwell," q.v.

PEARSON, SIMON, of Baltimore County, aet. 40, dep. between Apr 11, 1704 and Aug 4, 1704. {BALR HW#2:367}

PEARSON, THOMAS, of Dorchester County, aet. about 64, dep. between Nov 10, 1741 and Feb 16, 1742. {DOLR 14 Old 54} See "Thomas Brannock, Sr.," q.v.

PEARY, JAMES, see "James Perry," q.v.

PEAYLEY(?), MARY, of Queen Anne's County, aet. 60, dep. Apr, 1723. {QAEJ - William Bishop folder}

PECK, DANIEL, of Talbot County, planter, aet. 46, dep. between Mar 11, 1755 and Jul 21, 1755, mentioned Ann Chamberlain, daughter of Samuel Chamberlain. {DOLR 15 Old 282}

PEDCOCK, JOHN, of Charles County, aet. 63, dep. Jun 12, 1769. {CHLR Q#3:496}

PEDIE, JOHN, of Charles County, aet. 47, dep. Oct 19, 1741. {CHLR O#2:282}

PEEKE, CHRISTOPHER, of Talbot County, n.a., dep. Jun 17, 1673. {ARMD 54:568}

PEERCE, WILLIAM, see "Michael Miller," q.v.

PEIRSON, RICHARD, of Dorchester County, aet. about 69, dep. between Aug 18, 1733 and Mar 15, 1733/4, mentioned James Foxon about 20 years ago. {DOLR 9 Old 155}

PEIRSON, THOMAS, of Dorchester County, aet. 60, dep. Mar 14, 1746. {DOLR 14 Old 130}

PENN, JANE, see "William Cage," q.v.

PENN, JOHN, of Charles County, aet. 42, dep. May 25, 1726. {CHLR P#2:244} Aet. 48, dep. Mar 4 1731/2, stated that he married the widow of Thomas Warring. {CHLR R#2:82} Aet. about 60, dep. Feb 17, 1742/3. {CHLR O#2:507} John Penn, Sr., aet. 59, dep. Jul 24, 1742. {CHLR O#2:426} Aet. 62, dep. Jul 23, 1744, stated that Thomas Dutton was the grandfather of Notley Dutton and said Notley was guardian of Thomas Dutton and Gerrard Dutton. {CHLR Z#2:12, 223}

PENN, JOHN, of Charles County, aet. 50, dep. Nov 1, 1746. {CHLR T#2:266}

PENN, JOHN, of Charles County, aet. 32, dep. Feb 19, 1750/1. {CHLR Z#2:143}

PENN, JOHN, see "William Cage" and "John Oakley," q.v.

PENN, JOHN, JR., see "John Oakley," q.v.

PENN, WILLIAM, of Charles County, aet. 59, dep. Mar 3, 1731/2. {CHLR R#3:84} Aet. 64, dep. Jun 18, 1736. {CHLR T#2:222}

PENN, WILLIAM, of Charles County, aet. 30, dep. Jul 23, 1744. {CHLR Y#2:223}

PENNDOK, OBEDIAH, of Charles County, aet. 33, dep. Mar 9, 1669/70. {CHLR D#1:144}
PENSON, WILLIAM, see "John Richard," q.v.
PENSON, WILLIAM, of Prince George's County, aet. 54, dep. three times between Jun 11, 1727, and Jun 15, 1731, mentioned Anguish McCloud, deceased. {PGLR Q:296, 298, 471}
PEPPER, WILLIAM, see "Frances Elbert," q.v.
PERIN, JOHN, of Frederick County, aet. 50, dep. Mar 13, 1761. {FRLR G:159}
PERRIE, HUGH, of Charles County, aet. 44, dep. Jul 18, 1749. {CHLR Z#2:527}
PERRIE (PEARRIE), JAMES, of Prince George's County, aet. 42, dep. Sep 22, 1772, mentioned his father James Pearrie about 25 years ago, now deceased. {PGLR BB#3:117} See "Benjamin Belt, Jr.," q.v.
PERRIE, JOHN, of Charles County, aet. 40, dep. Oct 19, 1742. {CHLR O#2:281}
PERRIE (PEARRIE), JOHN, of Prince George's County, aet. between 36 and 37, dep. Sep 22, 1772. {PGLR BB#3:117}
PERRIE, MARY, of Charles County, aet. 35, dep. Aug 15, 1738, mentioned her father William Thomas. {CHLR T#2:514}
PERRIGO, JOHN, of Baltimore County, aet. about 30, dep. Mar 5, 1776. {BALR WG#B:395}
PERRIGO, JOSEPH, of Baltimore County, aet. 30, dep. Mar 30, 1776. {BALR WG#B:395}
PERRY, BENJAMIN, of Prince George's County, aet. 49, dep. Nov 9, 1759, mentioned Ninian Magruder, now deceased, about 17 or 18 years ago, and his brother John Magruder. {PGLR RR:80}
PERRY, EDWARD, of Prince George's County, aet. 44, dep. Sep 13, 1760, mentioned William Ray, deceased. {PGLR RR:126}
PERRY, HUGH, of Charles County, aet. 26, dep. Aug 30, 1773, mentioned his father John Perry. {CHLR W#3:98}
PERRY, JAMES, of Prince George's County, aet. 50, dep. Sep 29, 1731. {PGLR Q:396} James Peary, Sr., aet 85, dep. Nov 21, 1763. {PGLR TT:195}
PERRY, JOHN, of Charles County, aet. 42, dep. May 24, 1771. {CHLR T#3:604} Aet. 43, dep. between Jan 8, 1772 and Mar 11, 1772. {CHLR T#3:602} See "Hugh Perry" and "Thomas Perry," q.v.
PERRY, JOHN, JR., of Prince George's County, aet. 43, dep. May 8, 1753, mentioned his father (not named). {PGLR NN:138}
PERRY, JOHN, JR., of Prince George's County, aet. 23, dep. Sep 13, 1760. {PGLR RR:126}
PERRY, JOHN, SR., see "James Drane," q.v.
PERRY, MARY, of Dorchester County, aet. 68, dep. Nov 14, 1729. {DOLR 8 Old 384} Aet. about 80, dep. Aug 22, 1744. {DOLR 12 Old 113} Aet. about 84, wife of William Perry, dep. between Mar 12, 1744 and Aug 5, 1745, mentioned the following people: old Thomas Skillington, of Talbot County, former owner of *Skillington's Right*; her husband Alexander Frazier, deceased; Thomas

Edmondson, late of Talbot County, deceased; old Kenelm Skillington, deceased, son of said Thomas Skillington; and, old John Edmondson and his son Thomas Edmondson. {DOLR 12 Old 215} See "Peter Sharpe Edmondson," q.v.

PERRY, RICHARD, see "John Richardson," q.v.

PERRY (PERY), ROBERT, of Anne Arundel County, n.a., dep. 1696. {ARMD 20:530}

PERRY, SARAH, see "Samuel Edmondson," q.v.

PERRY, THOMAS, of Charles County, aet. 43, dep. May 24, 1771, mentioned his father John Perry. {CHLR T#3:614} Aet. 45, dep. Aug 20, 1773, mentioned his father John Perry. {CHLR W#3:91}

PERRY, WILLIAM, of Dorchester County, aet. about 43, dep. between Aug 16, 1728 and Jan 28, 1728/9. {DOLR 8 Old 268} See "Peter Sharpe Edmondson" and "Mary Perry" and "James Edgell," q.v.

PERSON, NOAH, see "Noah Pearson," q.v.

PERSON, RICHARD, see "Daniel Foxwell" and "Richard Kendall Foxwell" and "Richard Pearson" and "Richard Peirson," q.v.

PERSONS, WILLIAM, of Charles County, aet. 50, dep. Jul 24, 1758. {CHLR H#3:580}

PETERKIN, DAVID, see "George Purdy" and "Charles Thompson," q.v.

PETERKIN, JAMES, of Dorchester County, aet. 28, dep. between May 17, 1740 and Jun 2, 1740, stated that he lived with Capt. Robert Wing about 7 or 8 years ago. {DOLR 12 Old 131}

PETERKIN, JAMES, of Dorchester County, aet. 77, dep. Jun 14, 1714, stated that he signed as an evidence to the will of Joseph Sargent on Jul 12, 1685, at which time Sargent called his daughter Rebecca to his side and declared she was to have all his land. {DOLR 2 Old 70}

PETERKIN, JAMES, of Dorchester County, aet. 37, dep. between Mar 14, 1748 and Jun 10, 1749. {DOLR 14 Old 465}

PETERS, SIMON, of Dorchester County, n.a., dep. Apr 16, 1672. {DOLR 4 Old 6}

PETERSON, ANDREW, of Cecil County, n.a., dep. Jan 23, 1676, mentioned William Ward, John Coke, and Abraham Strand. {CELR 1:78}

PETTE, LEWIS, see "Lewis Potee," q.v.

PETTHER, RICHARD, of Talbot County, n.a., dep. Jan 18, 1669/70. {ARMD 54:456}

PHEBUS, SAMUEL, of Dorchester County, aet. 35, dep. between Jun 14, 1743 and Aug 4, 1743. {DOLR 12 Old 164}

PHERSON, ATTWIX, see "Attwicks Fearson," q.v.

PHERSON, ELEANOR, see "Eleanor Fearson," q.v.

PHERSON, SAMUEL, see "Eleanor Fearson," q.v.

PHEYPO, MARK, of Charles County, n.a., dep. 1658. {ARMD 41:219}

PHILBERT, JOHN, of Charles County, aet. 42, dep. May 16, 1729. {CHLR Q#2:276} Aet. 48, dep. Jun 3, 1745. {CHLR Z#2:346}

PHILLIPS, BARTHOLOMEW, of St. Mary's County, n.a., dep. Jan 14, 1644. {ARMD 4:354} Bartholomewe Phillipps, of Newtowne Hundred, planter, n.a., dep. Jun 16, 1650, mentioned Thomas Mathewes of St. Inigoes, gentleman. {ARMD 10:28-29}

PHILLIPS, BENONY, of Dorchester County, aet. 20, dep. between Aug 20, 1735 and Feb 17, 1735/6, mentioned Ann Lewis about 7 years ago. {DOLR 9 Old 391} Benoni Phillips, aet. 46, dep. between Aug 11, 1761 and Sep 19, 1761. {DOLR 18 Old 17}

PHILLIPS, BENONY, of Dorchester County, aet. 49, dep. between Aug 20, 1735 and Feb 17, 1735/6, mentioned his father John Phillips about 34 or 35 years ago. {DOLR 9 Old 391} See "William Phillips" and "John Lewis" and "John Travers," q.v.

PHILLIPS, CORNELIA, see "Samuel Hubbert," q.v.

PHILLIPS, HANNAH, of Charles County, aet. 42, dep. May 25, 1726, mentioned her former husband Benoni Fanning. {CHLR P#2:245}

PHILLIPS, JAMES, of Charles County, aet. 30, dep. May 24, 1771. {CHLR T#3:604} See "Frances Shembrooke," q.v.

PHILLIPS, JOHN, of Dorchester County, aet. 38 or 39, dep. between Nov 14, 1749 and Jan 22, 1749/50, mentioned his cousin Thomas Phillips, deceased. {DOLR 14 Old 404} See "Benony Phillips" and "John Lewis," q.v.

PHILLIPS (PHILLIPS), NICHOLAS, of Charles County, aet. 21, dep. Jul 2, 1661, stated that William Wennam had laid with Anne Mardin once. {CHLR A:142}

PHILLIPS, THOMAS, see "John Phillips," q.v.

PHILLIPS, WILLIAM, of Dorchester County, aet. 45, dep. between Mar 14, 1735 and May 17, 1736. {DOLR 9 Old 393}

PHILLIPS, WILLIAM, of Dorchester County, aet. 18 or 19, dep. between Aug 20, 1735 and Feb 17, 1735/6, mentioned his father William Phillips about 4 or 5 years ago, and his (deponent's) uncle Benony Phillips. {DOLR 9 Old 391} Aet. 30, dep. between Nov 14, 1749 and Jan 22, 1749/50. {DOLR 14 Old 404}

PHILLIPS, WILLIAM, see "Abraham Lewis," q.v.

PHILPOT (PHILPOTT), BRIGIT, of Charles County, n.a., dep. Mar 14, 1664/5, stated that Mary Grub said she was with child by John Grub because no one else had anything to do with her except him and her former husband in England. {CHLR B:445}

PHILPOT (PHILPOTT), CHARLES, of Charles County, aet. 55, dep. Aug 20, 1753, mentioned his brother John Philpott and father Edward Philpott. {CHLR D#3:152}

PHILPOT (PHILPOTT), EDWARD, of Charles County, n.a., dep. Nov 8, 1664. {CHLR B:415} Aet. 70, dep. Sep 9, 1667. {CHLR C#1:239} See "John Philpot" and "Charles Philpot," q.v.

PHILPOT (PHILPOTT), JOHN, of Charles County, aet. 34, dep. May 31, 1729, mentioned his brother Edward Philpott. {CHLR P#2:487} Aet. 46, dep. Oct 10, 1738. {CHLR T#2:514} See "Charles Philpot," q.v.

PICKERING, JOHN, of Dorchester County, n.a., dep. between Jun 13, 1728 and Oct 1, 1728, stated that the bounds of *Obscurity* were shown to him by John Pollard, deceased. {DOLR 8 Old 379} Aet. 50, dep. between Nov 24, 1732 and Jan 31, 1732/3. {DOLR 9 Old 98}
PICKERING, JOHN, of Dorchester County, aet. about 39, dep. between Nov 13, 1770 and Feb 4, 1771. {DOLR 26 Old 401}
PICKETT, HEATHCOAT (HEATHCOTE), of Baltimore County, aet. 58, dep. Nov 11, 1764, stated that he was stepson of John Taylor. {BALR B#N:458, 462} Aet. 61, dep. Oct 22, 1767. {BALR B#Q:588}
PICKRELL, HENRY, see "George Elbridge," q.v.
PICKRELL, WILLIAM, see "George Elbridge," q.v.
PIERCE, WILLIAM, see "Basil Warring," q.v.
PIGGMAN, JOHN, of Prince George's County, aet. 45, dep. Jun 27, 1743. {PGLR Y:701}
PIKE, SARAH, see "Elizabeth Lamphier," q.v.
PILES (PILE), CAPTAIN, see "Edward Aprice," q.v.
PILES (PILE), FRANCIS, of Prince George's County, aet. 36, dep. between Apr 1, 1729 and Aug 29, 1729. {PGLR M:484} Aet. 47, dep. Apr 17, 1739. {PGLR Y:59} Aet. 50, dep. Jun 28, 1743, mentioned his father (not named). {PGLR Y:704} Aet. 58, dep. Nov 21, 1751, mentioned brother John Piles and his wife (not named). {PGLR PP:156} Aet. 58, dep. Mar 21, 1750/1. {PGLR NN:12} Aet. 60 or thereabouts, dep. Mar 15, 1756. {PGLR NN:469} See "Leonard Piles," q.v.
PILES, JOHN, see "Francis Piles" and "Leonard Piles" and "John Scott, Sr.," q.v.
PILES, JOSEPH, see "Thomas Simpson, Sr." and "John Scott, Sr.," q.v.
PILES (PILE), LEONARD, of Prince George's County, aet. 25, dep. between Apr 1, 1729 and Aug 28, 1729, mentioned his father Francis Piles. {PGLR M:484} Aet. 34, dep. Dec 24, 1736. {PGLR Y:84} Aet. 40, dep. Jun 28, 1743, mentioned his father (not named). {PGLR Y:703} Aet. 48, dep. Nov 21, 1751, mentioned brother John Piles and his wife (not named). {PGLR PP:156-157} Aet. 65, dep. Nov 7, 1767. {PGLR BB#2:161-162} Aet. 67, planter, dep. Nov 13, 1769, mentioned Thomas Hodgkin, schoolmaster. {PGLR AA#2:135}
PILES (PILE), RICHARD, see "Mareen Duvall," q.v.
PILES, WILLIAM, of Prince George's County, aet. 28, dep. Apr 23, 1754. {PGLR NN:253}
PINDER, EDWARD, see "Charles Thompson," q.v.
PINDER (PONDER), JAMES, of Queen Anne's County, aet. 46, dep. May 24, 1754. {QAEJ - John Gafford folder}
PINDER (PONDER), RICHARD, of Queen Anne's County, aet. 53, dep. Sep 4, 1735. {QAEJ - John Coursey folder}
PINDER (PONDER), WILLIAM, of Queen Anne's County, aet. 42, dep. Aug 13, 1760, mentioned his father (not named) and brother John. {QAEJ - John Gafford folder}

PINDER (PONDER), WILLIAM, of Queen Anne's County, aet. 45, dep. Sep 4, 1735. {QAEJ - John Coursey folder}
PINDLE, PHILIP, of Prince George's County, aet. 43, dep. May 22, 1729. {PGLR M:441} See "James Holland," q.v.
PINDLE (PINDEL), PHILIP, of Prince George's County, aet. 35, dep. Jan 6, 1747/8, mentioned his father (not named). {PGLR BB:691} Philip Pindel, aet. 42, dep. Jul 29, 1754, mentioned Humphery Beckett about a year ago, now deceased. {PGLR NN:372, 374} Phillip Pindall, aet. 46, dep. Jun 16, 1760, mentioned Thomas Crabb about 20 years ago. {PGLR RR:106} Philip Pindle, aet. 50, dep. May 11, 1762. {PGLR RR:265-266}
PINDLE, THOMAS, of Prince George's County, aet. 39, dep. May 11, 1762, stated that he "went to school to John Griffith" about 26 years ago; also mentioned old Abraham Boyd. {PGLR RR:266}
PINNER, RICHARD, see "Thomas Chapman," q.v.
PINSON, EDMOND, of Charles County, n.a., dep. Dec 18, 1662. {CHLR B:53, ARMD 53:312}
PIPER, JOHN, of Charles County, aet. 30, dep. Oct 26, 1658, stated that Haniball Spicer and Elizabeth Spicer said that Goodman Courts was a slanderous man and William Empson was a thief from his cradle. {CHLR A:25} Aet. 34, dep. Jul 9, 1662. {CHLR A:232}
PITTS (PITT), JOHN, of Talbot County, aet. 60, dep. Feb 16, 1708/9 to prove the will of William Dixon, deceased. {Will Book 12:16, pt. 2} Aet. 62, merchant, dep. Aug 23, 1710 in Queen Anne's County and "testified according to an Act of Parliament now in force concerning Quakers so called" that John Baynard and Elizabeth Blackwell lived at his house about 33 years ago when they went to the house of Richard Dudley to get married; further stated that he received a letter from Thomas Baynard, of Blackson in Somersettshire, Great Britain, wherein Thomas acknowledged the said John Baynard, deceased, to be his lawful son. {QALR ET#A:62}
PITTS, MARY, of Dorchester County, aet. 50, wife of Capt. John Pitts, dep. between Jun 22, 1741 and Jul 13, 1741, mentioned Mary Foster, wife of John Foster, both deceased, and Col. Thomas Ennalls, deceased, brother of the said Mary Foster. {DOLR 12 Old 122}
PLANT, JAMES, of Charles County, aet. 40, dep. Jul 24, 1742. {CHLR O#2:426} Aet. 60, dep. Sep 13, 1758. {CHLR K#3:97}
PLUMMER, ABIZER (ABIEZER), of Prince George's County, aet. 30, Quaker, dep. Mar 23, 1752. {PGLR NN:91} Aet. 34, Quaker, dep. Apr 25, 1754, mentioned George Plummer. {PGLR NN:255}
PLUMMER, ELIZABETH, of Prince George's County, n.a., Quaker, dep. 1730, mentioned her husband Thomas Plummer. {PGLR Q:234} See "Otho Brashears," q.v.

PLUMMER, GEORGE, of Frederick County, aet. 25 or thereabouts, dep. Jan 5, 1763, stated that he was shown the bounded tree of *Metre* or *Metere* about 7 or 8 years ago. {FRLR H:338}
PLUMMER, GEORGE, of Prince George's County, n.a., Quaker, dep. 1730, mentioned his father Thomas Plummer. {PGLR Q:235} Aet. 53, dep. Dec 22, 1747. {PGLR BB:665}
PLUMMER, GEORGE, see "Abizer Plummer," q.v.
PLUMMER, JAMES, of Prince George's County, aet. 51, Quaker, dep. Dec 22, 1747. {PGLR BB:666} Aet. 59, Quaker, dep. Apr 22, 1755 and May 12, 1755, mentioned his father Thomas Plummer about 30 years ago. {PGLR NN:371, 436} Aet. 64, dep. Sep 13, 1760, mentioned Nathaniel Wickham, Sr. and Thomas Drane about 20 years ago. {PGLR RR:125} Aet. 68, Quaker, dep. Jun 11, 1764. {PGLR TT:370} Aet. 73, Quaker, dep. Aug 15, 1769. {PGLR AA#2:83} See "Thomas Drane" and "Nathan Wells" and "Sarah Gaither," q.v.
PLUMMER, JEROME, of Prince George's County, aet. 48, Quaker, dep. Apr 21, 1748. {PGLR BB:667}
PLUMMER, MARGARET, of Charles County, aet. 40, dep. Feb 28, 1726/7, mentioned her father William Newman. {CHLR P#2:420}
PLUMMER, PRISCILLA, see "John Lamar" and "Elizabeth Tyler," q.v.
PLUMMER, SAMUEL, of Prince George's County, n.a., dep. Apr 22, 1755. {PGLR NN:371}
PLUMMER (PLUMER), THOMAS, of Prince George's County, aet. 55, Quaker, dep. between Mar 24, 1745/6 and Mar 26, 1747. {PGLR BB:196} Thomas Plummer, aet. 58, Quaker, dep. Feb 14, 1748/9, mentioned his father (not named). {PGLR BB:700-701} See "Elizabeth Plummer" and "George Plummer" and "James Plummer" and "Thomas Brereton," q.v.
PLUMMER, YATE, see "Abraham Jones," q.v.
POLK, ROBERT, see "Robert Pollock," q.v.
POLLARD, JOHN, see "Tobias Pollard" and "John Pickering" and "Daniell Lawrence" and "Richard North" and "Sarah Murfey" and "Pollard Edmondson" and "Mary Griffin" and "William Byus," q.v.
POLLARD, MR., see "Arthur Foreman," q.v.
POLLARD, TOBIAS (major), of Dorchester County, aet. 50, dep. between Jun 13, 1728 and Oct 1, 1728. {DOLR 8 Old 379} Aet. 60, dep. between Aug 17, 1729 and Dec 1, 1729, mentioned his father John Pollard. {DOLR 8 Old 378} Aet. 70, dep. between Jun 12, 1739 and Aug 13, 1739. {DOLR 12 Old 91} Major Tobias Pollard, aet. 80, dep. between Aug 15, 1746 and Sep 1, 1746. {DOLR 14 Old 89} See "Philemon Lecompte" and "John Jones" and "Pollard Edmondson," q.v.
POLLARD, WILLIAM, of Dorchester County, aet. 50, dep. between Aug 10, 1773 and Oct 23, 1773. {DOLR 27 Old 38} See "Sarah Murfey," q.v.
POLLET, THOMAS, of Dorchester County, aet. 50, dep. between Nov 9, 1773 and Nov 9, 1774, mentioned William Pollet and Joseph Conner about 30 years ago, both now deceased. {DOLR 27 Old 359}

POLLET, WILLIAM, see "Thomas Pollet," q.v.
POLLOCK, DAVID, of Dorchester County, aet. 47, dep. between Jun 11, 1751 and Oct 14, 1751, mentioned his father James Pollock about 30 years ago. {DOLR 14 Old 552}
POLLOCK, JAMES, see "David Pollock," q.v.
POLLOCK, JOSEPH, of Dorchester County, aet. 60, dep. between Aug 14, 1750 and Dec 20, 1750. {DOLR 14 Old 497}
POLLOCK (POLK), ROBERT, of Dorchester County, aet. about 35, dep. between Nov 9, 1742 and Nov 5, 1743. {DOLR 12 Old 157}
PONDER, WILLIAM, see "William Pinder," q.v.
PONNET, JOSEPH, see "Joseph Punnett," q.v.
POOLE, DAVID, of Dorchester County, aet. about 53, dep. between Mar 10, 1761 and Mar 10, 1762, mentioned Michael Caffey and William Ennalls, both now deceased. {DOLR 18 Old 80}
POOLE, EDWARD, of Dorchester County, aet. about 45, dep. between Nov 12, 1745 and Nov 11, 1747, mentioned John Chilcutt and John Griffith, both now deceased, about 25 years ago. {DOLR 14 Old 173} See "Philemon Lecompte," q.v.
POPE, FRANCIS, of Charles County, n.a., dep. Jun 4, 1658. {CHLR A:6, ARMD 53:5} Aet. not given, dep. Jul 9, 1662. {CHLR A:231} See "Thomas Abbot," q.v.
POPE, HENRY, prob. of St. Mary's or Calvert County, aet. 46, dep. affirmed Sep 25, 1657 at Patuxent. {ARMD 10:531}
POPE, NATHANIEL, see "Thomas Bradnox," q.v.
PORTER, GILES, see "Humphrey Younger," q.v.
PORTER, JOHN, see "Humphrey Younger," q.v.
POSEY, ANN, of Charles County, aet. 59, midwife, dep. Dec 19, 1766, mentioned Elizabeth Simpson, daughter of William Simpson. {CHLR O#3:143}
POSEY, BENJAMIN, see "Edward Gray" and "Francis Posey," q.v.
POSEY (POESEY), FRANCIS, of St. Mary's County, n.a., dep. Jan 11, 1650, stated that he was recently at the house where Richard Browne lately lived in St. Clemens Hundred and where George Browne then kept a store. {ARMD 10:51}
POSEY, FRANCIS, of Charles County, aet. 70, dep. May 9, 1772, mentioned his brother Benjamin Posey. {CHLR T#3:615} Aet. 73, dep. May 1, 1773. {CHLR U#3:269}
POSEY, HUMPHREY, see "Thomas Davis" and "Edward Gray," q.v.
POSEY, JOHN, of Charles County, aet. 43, dep. Mar 15, 1725. {CHLR P#2:299}
POSEY, JOHN, of Charles County, aet. 60, dep. May 24, 1771. {CHLR T#3:603}
POSEY, SAMUEL, see "Leonard Hollyday," q.v.
POSEY, THOMAS, of Charles County, aet. 45, dep. Sep 29, 1775, mentioned his father Francis Posey. {CHLR X#3:543}
POSTON, EDWARD, of Charles County, aet. 39, dep. Sep 24, 1764, mentioned his father John Poston, deceased. {CHLR N#3:63}

POSTON, JOHN, of Charles County, aet. 54, dep. Dec 27, 1731. {CHLR R#2:408} Aet. 59, dep. Jul 19, 1737. {CHLR T#3:372} John Posten, Sr., aet. 65, dep. Mar 2, 1743/4. {CHLR O#2:702} See "Edward Poston," q.v.
POSTON, WILLIAM, of Charles County, aet. 50, dep. May 1, 1769. {CHLR Q#3:498}
POTEE, LEWIS, of Baltimore County, aet. 67 or thereabouts, dep. Dec 14, 1765, mentioned Daniel Scott and Peter Potee about 28 years ago. {BALR B#P:177} Aet. 68 or thereabouts, dep. Oct 29, 1768, mentioned Daniel Scott the Elder about 24 years ago (name listed as Lewis Pette). {BALR AL#A:294} Aet. 75, dep. Aug 15, 1774, stated that he thinks John Webster died in 1716. {BALR AL#L:239}
POTEE, PETER, see "Lewis Potee," q.v.
POTTER, HENRY, see "Elizabeth Greene," q.v.
POTTER, MARY ANN, see "Mary Buence," q.v.
POTTER, WILLIAM, of Charles County, aet. 28, dep. Nov 14, 1665. {CHLR B:493}
POTTINGER, JOHN, of Prince George's County, aet. 67, dep. May 22, 1729. {PGLR M:440}
POTTS, HENRY, of Dorchester County, aet. 57, dep. Sep 7, 1725, stated that he was a servant to Walter Dickason, of Talbot County, about 40 years ago. {DOLR 8 Old 90}
POTTS, WILLIAM, see "Benjamin Blackleach" and "Joan Dewerty" and "Mary Knoleman," q.v.
POUNCE, GEORGE, of Dorchester County, aet. 74, dep. between Mar 11, 1734 and Jun 6, 1735, stated that he was shown the bounds of *Fullam* by John Dyer about 23 years ago. {DOLR 9 Old 293}
POWELL, CHARLES, of Dorchester County, aet. 48, dep. between Jun 13, 1749 and Jan 8, 1749/50. {DOLR 14 Old 394} See "William Warner," q.v.
POWELL, CLAIRE, of Dorchester County, aet. 33, dep. Sep 8, 1705. {DOLR 6 Old 74}
POWELL, HOWELL, see "Lewis Griffith" and "Kenellm Skillington," q.v.
POWELL, JOHN, see "George Beall," q.v.
POWELL, SUSANNAH, see "William Warner" and Clara Lecompte," q.v.
POWELL, THOMAS, of Talbot County, aet. about 48, dep. between Nov 14, 1758 and Jun 30, 1759. {DOLR 16 Old 220}
POWELL, WILLIAM, see "Mrs. Deborah Foreman," q.v.
POWICK, JOHN, of St. Mary's County, n.a., dep. Jan 4, 1665/6. {ARMD 49:569}
PRATHER, EDWARD, see "John Wilson," q.v.
PRATHER, JOHN, see "William Clarke," q.v.
PRATHER, THOMAS, of Prince George's County, aet. 45, dep. Mar 21, 1747/8, mentioned Eleanor Nutwell about 18 or 20 years ago and her 2 daughters Eleanor and Mary Nutwell. {PGLR BB:466-467}
PRATHER, THOMAS (colonel), of Frederick County, aet. 60 or thereabouts, dep. Oct 21, 1762. {FRLR H:195} Aet. 64 or thereabouts, dep. Apr 25, 1767, stated that he ran the first lines of *His Lordship's Manor of Conococheague* about 21

or 22 years ago; also mentioned Col. Thomas Cresap was then the Deputy Surveyor of the upper part of Prince George's County. {FRLR K:1340} Aet. 70 or thereabouts, dep. Aug 7, 1772, mentioned Evan Shelby about 25 or 26 years ago. {FRLR P:308}

PRATHER, THOMAS, see "John Banks" and "William Prather" and "Charles Walker," q.v.

PRATHER, WILLIAM, of Prince George's County, planter, aet. 60 odd years, dep. Oct 2, 1724. {PGLR I:596}

PRATHER, WILLIAM, of Prince George's County, planter, aet. 40, dep. Feb 6, 1717/8, mentioned his father-in-law John Smith and brother Thomas Prather. {PGLR I:594}

PRATHER, WILLIAM, of Prince George's County, aet. 58, dep. Sep 15, 1758. {PGLR PP:227, pt. 2}

PRATT(?), THOMAS, of Queen Anne's County, aet. 61, dep. Apr, 1723. {QAEJ - William Bishop folder}

PRESBURY, GEORGE, of Baltimore County, aet. 59, dep. Oct 25, 1769. {BALR AL#B:285} Aet. 64, dep. Aug 15, 1774, mentioned Capt. Philip Jones about 40 years ago. {BALR AL#L:248}

PRESBURY, GEORGE GOULDSMITH, of Baltimore County, aet. 29, dep. Nov 3, 1766. {BALR B#P:308} Aet. 33, dep. May 8, 1770. {BALR AL#B:290}

PRESBURY, WILLIAM, of Baltimore County, aet. 36, dep. May 8, 1770. {BALR AL#B:288}

PRESTON, DANIEL, of Baltimore County, aet. 50, dep. Dec 14, 1765. {BALR B#P:179} Aet. 51, dep. Oct 27, 1766. {BALR B#P:307} Aet. 53 or thereabouts, dep. Oct 29, 1768, mentioned Daniel Scott about 25 or 26 years ago. {BALR AL#A:292} Aet. 54, dep. Dec 19, 1769. {BALR AL#A:737} Aet. 54, dep. Oct 25, 1769. {BALR AL#B:284} Aet. 54, dep. between Nov 11, 1769 and Jun 14, 1770. {BALR AL#C:277}

PRESTON, JOHN, of Queen Anne's County, aet. 25, dep. Mar, 1753. {QAEJ - Peter Johnson folder} Aet. 40, dep. Apr, 1765. {QAEJ - William Austin folder}

PRESTON, RICHARD, see "John Smith" and "Richard Gibbs" and "Samuel Coplen" and "Samuel Styles" and "Henry Gorslett" and "Thomas Broxam," q.v.

PRESTON, THOMAS, of Baltimore County, aet. 48, dep. between Apr 11, 1704 and Aug 4, 1704. {BALR HW#2:367}

PRETTIMAN, JOHN, see "Mathias de Sousa," q.v.

PREW, WILLIAM, prob. of Charles County, n.a., dep. Dec 5, 1769. {ARMD 32:343}

PRIBBLE, JOHN, of Baltimore County, aet. 68, dep. May 12, 1764. {BALR B#O:109}

PRIBBLE, JOHN, of Baltimore County, aet. 80, dep. Apr 17, 1767. {BALR B#P:110}

PRICE, HANNAH, of Prince George's County, n.a., dep. July, 1665. {PGLR 49:492} See "William Price," q.v.

PRICE, JOHN (captain), of St. Mary's or Charles County, n.a., dep. Mar 23, 1652, mentioned Humphrey Atwixe, William Marshall, and Owen James. {ARMD 10:246}

PRICE, JOHN, of Charles County, aet. 20 or thereabouts, dep. Mar 4, 1661. {ARMD 53:190}
PRICE, JOHN, of Garrison, Baltimore County, aet. 50, dep. between Nov 25, 1760 and Apr 13, 1761. {BALR B#L:197}
PRICE, JOHN, JR., of Baltimore County, planter, aet. 67, dep. Dec 26, 1767. {BALR B#Q:700}
PRICE, JULIANA, see "Robert Hanson," q.v.
PRICE, MARY, see "Robert Hanson," q.v.
PRICE, ROBERT, see "Juliana Sympson," q.v.
PRICE, SARAH, of Queen Anne's County, aet. 44, dep. Mar, 1770. {QAEJ - Henry Carter folder}
PRICE, THOMAS, of Stafford County, Virginia, aet. 23, dep. Jun 7, 1668 in Charles County, Maryland. {CHLR C#1:274} See "Edward Heneberry," q.v.
PRICE, WILLIAM, of St. Mary's County, n.a., dep. July, 1665, mentioned his wife Hannah Price. {ARMD 49:492}
PRIGG, JOHN, see "Ezekiel Burgee," q.v.
PRIGG (PRIGGS), JOHN FREDERICK AUGUSTINE, of Prince George's County, aet. 36, dep. Nov 5, 1763. {PGLR TT:571-572} Aet. 42, dep. May 22, 1770. {PGLR AA#2:139-141}
PRITCHARD, DAVID, of Talbot County, n.a., dep. Mar 31, 1725. {TALR 13:177} See "Frances Elbert," q.v.
PRITCHARD, RICHARD, of Dorchester County, aet. about 39, dep. between Mar 15, 1727 and Jun 10, 1731. {DOLR 8 Old 430}
PRITCHETT, EDWARD, of Dorchester County, son of William, n.a., Dec 11, 1767. {DOLR 22 Old 231} See "Susanna Bryan" and "Mary Fisher" and "Daniel Foxwell" and "Zebulon Pritchett," q.v.
PRITCHETT, EDWARD, JR., see "Noah Pearson," q.v.
PRITCHETT, JOHN, see "Mary Fisher" and "Thomas Shearwood" and "Richard Edelen," q.v.
PRITCHETT, WILLIAM, of Dorchester County, aet. about 30, dep. between Nov 14, 1759 and Mar 9, 1759/60. {DOLR 16 Old 146} See "Edward Pritchett," q.v.
PRITCHETT, ZEBULON, of Dorchester County, aet. 51, dep. between Mar 15, 1731 and Apr 13, 1732, mentioned Edward Pritchett's land and stated that his father (not named) about 30 years ago showed him the bounded tree between his land and that of John Early. {DOLR 9 Old 63}
PROCTER, GILES, of Dorchester County, aet. about 39, dep. between Mar 13, 1764 and Mar 14, 1765, mentioned Samuel Wheeler, son of Charles Wheeler, deceased, and John Wheeler, son of old Charles Wheeler; also mentioned John Lecompte, deceased. {DOLR 20 Old 28}
PROCTER, WILLIAM, of Dorchester County, aet. about 43, dep. between Mar 13, 1764 and Mar 14, 1765. {DOLR 20 Old 28}
PULLUFFUS, JOSEPH, of Charles County, aet. 64, dep. Jul 6, 1742, stated that he was a servant to John Hanson, father of Col. Robert Hanson, about 40 years

ago. {CHLR O#2:423} Aet. 68, dep. Jul 23, 1745, mentioned Thomas Sanders about 24 years ago. {CHLR Z#2:394}

PULLEN, RICHARD, of Kent County, n.a., dep. Oct 8, 1681. {ARMD 17:62}

PULTON, MR., see "Mathias de Sousa," q.v.

PUNNETT (PONNET), JOSEPH, of Prince George's County, aet. 51, dep. between Nov 11, 1729 and Mar 26, 1730. {PGLR M:556} Joseph Ponnet, aet. 66, dep. Feb 16, 1745/6. {PGLR BB:2-3} Joseph Bonnet, aet. 82, dep. Sep 21, 1761. {PGLR RR:227}

PURDUM (PURDOM), JOHN, of Frederick County, aet. 28, dep. Mar 7, 1752. {FRLR B:545}

PURDY (PURDIE), GEORGE, of Dorchester County, aet. 40, dep. between May 17, 1740 and Jun 2, 1740. {DOLR 12 Old 131} George Purdie, aet. 44, dep. Oct 3, 1744, stated that he was shown the second bounded tree of *Sharp's Point* about 22 or 23 years ago by his wife (not named) and David Peterkin. {DOLR 12 Old 142}

PYSELL, HENRY, of Frederick County, aet. 44, dep. Apr 6, 1772. {FRLR P:170}

QUASH, JOHN, see "Indian Abraham," q.v.

QUATERMUS, JOHN, of Dorchester County, aet. about 52, dep. between Mar 12, 1744/5 and May 17, 1745. {DOLR 14 Old 44}

QUEEN, JOHN, of Prince George's County, aet. 40, dep. 1731, mentioned his father (not named). {PGLR Q:372}

QUEEN, MARSHAM, of Charles County, aet. 45, dep. Aug 29, 1758. {CHLR H#3:575}

QUEEN, MARSHAM, of Prince George's County, aet. 65, dep. Apr 21, 1767. {PGLR BB#2:119}

QUEEN MECHASUSA, see "Indian Abraham," q.v.

QUEEN, RICHARD, of Prince George's County, aet. 40, dep. Apr 21, 1767. {PGLR BB#2:120-121}

QUEEN, SAMUEL, see "Barton Lucas," q.v.

QUINNEY, JOYCE, see "William True," q.v.

QUINNEY, SUTTON, of Kent County, aet. about 45, dep. Oct 3, 1743, stated his uncle Edward Beck and Nicholas Barfoot showed him the bounds of *Beckworth* about 25 or 26 years ago. {KELR JS#25:192}

QUINTON, WALTER, see "John Arnett," q.v.

QUITAM, JOHN, see "Indian Abraham," q.v.

QUYNN, ALLEN, of Anne Arundel County, n.a., dep. Dec 13, 1769, stated that Richard Lee, Esq., and Richard Lee, Jr. live in Charles County. {ARMD 32:344}

RABBITT, WILLIAM, of Queen Anne's County, aet. 53, dep. Apr, 1747, stated that he once lived with his father-in-law Stephen Camperson. {QAEJ - Elizabeth Barnes folder}

RABLIN, DAVID, of Anne Arundel County, aet. 39, dep. 1680, stated that he was a servant to Mary Eagle about 22 years ago. {AALR IT#5:50}

RAMSAY, JOHN, of Anne Arundel County, n.a., dep. Mar 19, 1744/5. {ARMD 28:344}

RAMSEY, ANDREW, of Dorchester County, aet. 64, dep. between Jun 15, 1737 and Apr 8, 1738. {DOLR 9 Old 507} See "Barthulia Bradly," q.v.

RAMSEY, ROBERT, of Dorchester County, aet. 60, dep. between Apr 20, 1768 and May 27, 1768, stated that *Rosses Range* was surveyed about 40 years for ---- Ross who came here from Virginia. {DOLR 22 Old 423}

RANDALL, BENJAMIN, of Kent County, n.a., dep. Oct 8, 1681, mentioned Mr. Edward Inglish, then president of the Cecil Court, and Swithen Wells, clerk. {ARMD 17:60} See "Michael Miller," q.v.

RANDALL, CHRISTOPHER, see "Richard Marsh," q.v.

RANDALL, THOMAS, of Baltimore County, aet. 37, dep. May 7, 1764. {BALR B#N:138}

RANTON, JAMES, of Prince George's County, aet. 77, dep. May 1, 1755, mentioned John Taylor about 40 years ago. {PGLR NN:369}

RANTOR (RANTER), JAMES, of Prince George's County, aet. 74, dep. May 31, 1750. {PGLR NN:59}

RASIN, WILLIAM, of Kent County, aet. about 32, dep. Apr, 1759. {KEEJ - Thomas Harris folder}

RATCLIFF, JOHN, of Charles County, aet. 49, dep. May 18, 1763. {CHLR M#3:221}

RATCLIFF, JOSEPH, of Charles County, aet. 52, dep. Dec 13, 1757. {CHLR H#3:121}

RATCLIFF, JOSHUA, of Charles County, aet. 30, dep. Apr 13, 1731. {CHLR R#2:44}

RATCLIFFE, EMANUEL, of St. Mary's County, n.a., dep. Aug 29, 1681, mentioned James Tarleton and Thomas Courtney. {ARMD 17:51}

RATLIFFE, SAMUEL, of Dorchester County, aet. about 41, dep. between Nov 10, 1741 and Mar 11, 1741/2. {DOLR 12 Old 154} See "Robert Parkinson," q.v.

RAWDERY, JOHN, of Frederick County, aet. 25, dep. Aug 21, 1776. {FRLR BD#2:335}

RAWLES, JOHN, of Queen Anne's County, aet. 52, dep. Apr, 1747. {QAEJ - Elizabeth Barnes folder} See "John Rowles," q.v.

RAWLEY, ELIZABETH, of Dorchester County, aet. 53, dep. between Mar 13, 1732 and Jul 31, 1733. {DOLR 9 Old 137}

RAWLEY, WILLIAM, of Dorchester County, aet. 46, dep. between Apr 6, 1732 and Apr 23, 1733, mentioned the widow Frances Fisher and also stated that he was shown the bounds of *Dogwood Ridge* and *Sandy Neck* by Thomas Daniel about 27 years ago. {DOLR 9 Old 100}

RAWLINGS, ANTHONY, of Dorchester County, aet. 56, dep. between Dec 15, 1727 and Feb 14, 1727/8, mentioned William Walker who married the widow of Robert Boswell. {DOLR 8 Old 198}

RAWLINGS, ARON, of Anne Arundel County, n.a., dep. Jul 18, 1707, mentioned Capt. Silvester Welch, Mrs. Mahitable Holland, and Thomas Reading. {ARMD 25:218} See "Silvester Welch," q.v.

RAWLINGS, BERNARD JOHNSON, of Prince George's County, aet. 61, dep. Aug 29, 1763. {PGLR TT:127}
RAWLINGS, JOHN, of Frederick County, aet. 50, dep. Jun 16, 1755, mentioned John Dickerson about 20 years ago, now deceased. {FRLR E:782} See "John King" and "David Melvell," q.v.
RAWLINGS, PAUL, of Prince George's County, aet. 48, dep. Mar 15, 1747/8, stated that about 30 years ago John George showed him the bounds of Edward Truman's land and Joseph Fry was a tenant about 14 or 15 years ago. {PGLR BB:492} Paul Rawlings, Jr., aet. 54, dep. Nov 24, 1753, mentioned his father Paul Rawlings. {PGLR NN:283} Paul Rawlings, Sr., aet. 60, dep. Jun 23, 1757, stated that he went fishing with his father (not named) about 47 years ago. {PGLR PP:14, pt. 2}
RAWLINSON, CHARLES, of St. Mary's County, n.a., dep. Mar 6, 1749, mentioned Mr. and Mrs. Cuthbert Fenwick, William Smoote, and Thomas Waggate about 2 years ago. {ARMD 10:6}
RAWLS, JOHN, of Kent Island, Queen Anne's County, aet. about 54, dep. Sep, 1733. {QAEJ - James Hutchens folder}
RAWSER, ANNE, of St. Mary's County, n.a., dep. Mar 2, 1659, stated that she was bound in England to Richard Smith who assigned her indenture over to Mr. Battin [Capt. William Battin]. {ARMD 41:370}
RAY, JOSEPH, of Prince George's County, aet. 42, dep. May 31, 1731. {PGLR Q:608} Aet. 62, dep. May 8, 1753, mentioned his father William Ray about 40 years ago. {PGLR NN:137} Aet. 71, dep. Sep 13, 1760, mentioned John Demall about 40 years ago. {PGLR RR:125} Aet. 73, dep. Jun 20, 1764. {PGLR TT:368-369}
RAY, WILLIAM, see "Joseph Ray" and "Edward Perry," q.v.
READ (REED), GEORGE, of Frederick County, aet. 67, dep. Jun 20, 1760 and Nov 19, 1760. {FRLR F:1058, 1161}
READ, ELIZABETH, of Prince George's County, aet. 40, dep. Nov 11, 1740. {PGLR Y:234}
READ, JOHN, of Prince George's County, aet. 50, dep. Jul 16, 1734. {PGLR T:154}
READ, JOHN, of Prince George's County, aet. 50, dep. Apr 17, 1739. {PGLR Y:59}
READ, RICHARD, see "Thomas Hodgkin," q.v.
READ, WILLIAM, of Prince George's County, aet. 50, dep. Nov 24, 1753. {PGLR NN:283} Aet. 60, dep. Aug 29, 1763. {PGLR TT:127}
READ, WILLIAM, JR., of Anne Arundel County, aet. 26, dep. Jun 23, 1757 in Prince George's County, stated that he went fishing about 18 years ago with his grandfather John George. {PGLR PP:13, pt. 2}
READING, THOMAS, see "Aron Rawlings," q.v.
READMAN, WILLIAM FITCH, see "John Hunt," q.v.
REAGAN, JOHN, of Charles County, aet. 42, dep. Oct 28, 1726. {CHLR P#2:403}
REALY, CHARLES, see "John Realy," q.v.
REALY, JOHN, of Queen Anne's County, aet. 15, dep. Apr, 1755, mentioned his father Charles Realy. {QAEJ - Matthew Dockery folder}

RECORDS, PHILLIP, of Dorchester County, aet. 45, dep. between Nov 9, 1742 and Nov 5, 1743. {DOLR 12 Old 157} Aet. 46, dep. Aug 9, 1742. {DOLR 12 Old 260}

REDGRAVE (REDGRAVES), ELIZABETH, of Kent County, Quaker, aet. about 36, dep. Mar 13, 1753, mentioned her father James Course and her deceased husband Matthew Howard. {KELR JS#27:253} Aet. about 39, dep. circa 1755, mentioned her former husband Matthew Howard about 10 or 11 years ago. {KEEJ - Thomas Chandler folder}

REDGRAVE (REDGRAVES), JOHN, of Kent County, aet. about 36, dep. Aug 12, 1742. {KELR JS#24:118} See "Rachel Vansant," q.v.

REDICK, JOHN, of Frederick County, n.a., dep. Nov 6, 1766, mentioned his father Robert Redick. {ARMD 32:192-194}

REDICK, ROBERT, se "John Redick," q.v.

REDMAN, WILLIAM, see "William Depriest," q.v.

REED, DAVID, of Queen Anne's County, aet. 41, dep. Apr, 1765. {QAEJ - William Austin folder}

REED, GEORGE, of Prince George's County, aet. 70, dep. Nov 21, 1763. {PGLR TT:194}

REED, JAMES, see "Daniel Turpin," q.v.

REED, JOHN, of Dorchester County, aet. about 61, dep. between Nov 11, 1746 and Apr 14, 1748. {DOLR 14 Old 231} Aet. about 66, dep. between Jun 11, 1751 and Oct 14, 1751. {DOLR 14 Old 552} See "John Stevens" and "Daniel Turpin," q.v.

REED, OWEN, of Charles County, aet. 56, dep. Oct 17, 1727. {CHLR P#2:405}

REED, RICHARD, see "Thomas Truman Greenfield" and "John Clagett," q.v.

REED, THOMAS, of Charles County, aet. 84, dep. May 25, 1742. {CHLR O#2:505}

REEDER, BENJAMIN, of Charles County, aet. 46, dep. Feb 25, 1745/6. {CHLR Z#2:518} Aet. 61, dep. Dec 15, 1760. {CHLR K#3:150}

REEVES, HEZEKIAH, of Charles County, aet. 50, dep. Feb 5, 1776. {CHLR X#3:538}

REEVES, THOMAS, of Charles County, aet. 70, dep. Oct 11, 1766, stated that John Butts and wife Christian had a son Clement Butts; also stated that he knew Richard Butts, brother of John, about 50 years ago. {CHLR V#3:454} Aet. 73, dep. Dec 5, 1767, mentioned his father Ubgate Reeves. {CHLR Q#3:670}

REEVES, UBGATE, of Charles County, aet. 57, dep. Sep 29, 1726. {CHLR P#2:395} See "Thomas Reeves," q.v.

REMBALL, ----, see "Richard Keene," q.v.

RENTCH (RENCH), JOHN, of Frederick County, aet. 35, dep. Oct 21, 1762. {FRLR H:196} Aet. 40, dep. 1767. {FRLR L:60}

RENTCH (RENCH), JOSEPH, of Frederick County, aet. 45, dep. 1767. {FRLR L:60}

RENTCH (RENCH), PETER, of Frederick County, aet. 65 or thereabouts, dep. Oct 21, 1762. {FRLR H:196}

RESTON, EDWARD, of Prince George's County, aet. 46, dep. Apr 17, 1740. {PGLR Y:177}

REYNOLDS, RICHARD, see "Samuel Edmondson," q.v.
RHODES, RICHARD, JR., of Baltimore County, aet. 48, dep. between Mar 11, 1761 and Jun 22, 1762. {BALR B#M:135}
RHODES, RICHARD, SR., of Baltimore County, aet. 79, dep. between Mar 11, 1761 and Jun 22, 1762. {BALR B#M:136}
RICAND, BENJAMIN, prob. of Anne Arundel County, n.a., dep. Oct 1, 1692. {ARMD 8:375}
RICE, JOHN, see "Edward Willibee," q.v.
RICH, PETER, of Dorchester County, aet. 53, dep. Aug, 1752. {QAEJ - Sarah Starkey folder}
RICH, RICHARD, see "Ann Doughty," q.v.
RICHARD, JOHN, of Frederick County, aet. 82, dep. Jun 6, 1761, mentioned John Bradford, John Flint, and William Penson (now deceased) in 1722 or 1723 and *The Forrest* then in possession of Andrew Hughes. {FRLR G:281}
RICHARDS, BENJAMIN, see "Joseph Morgan," q.v.
RICHARDS, EDWARD, see "William Montecue," q.v.
RICHARDS, JAMES, of Baltimore County, aet. 40, dep. Jul 2, 1764. {BALR B#N:309}
RICHARDSON, ANN, of Talbot County, aet. about 52, dep. Feb, 1757. {TAEJ - Robert Larremore folder} See "Charles Symond," q.v.
RICHARDSON, ANTHONY, see "Richard Atkinson," q.v.
RICHARDSON, BENJAMIN, of Queen Anne's County, aet. about 50, dep. Apr, 1769. {QAEJ - James Hutchings folder} Aet. about 52, Quaker, dep. affirmed July, 1770. {QAEJ - Henry Carter folder}
RICHARDSON, EDWARD, of Charles County, n.a., dep. Feb 5, 1663/4 and Mar 8, 1663/4. {CHLR B:277; ARMD 53:462}
RICHARDSON, ELIZABETH, see "Richard Atkinson," q.v.
RICHARDSON, JOHN, of Dorchester County, aet. 58, dep. between Nov 10, 1767 and Aug 10, 1768, mentioned John Nicolls, Sr. about 25 or 26 years ago and John Nicolls, Jr., both now deceased. {DOLR 23 Old 1} Aet. in his 63rd year, dep. between Mar 10, 1772 and Aug 1, 1772, mentioned Richard Perry about 30 years ago, now deceased. {DOLR 26 Old 108}
RICHARDSON, JOSIAH, of Cecil County, n.a., dep. Sep 3, 1703. {CELR 1:434}
RICHARDSON, LAWRENCE, see "Charles Symond" and "Charles Smith," q.v.
RICHARDSON, MARK, see "George Clark," q.v.
RICHARDSON, SAMUEL, see "Joan Ridgeway," q.v.
RICHARDSON, SIMON (SIMOND), of St. Mary's County, n.a., dep. 1642, mentioned Robert Nicolls, John Wayvill, Edward Fleete, and John Robinson (barber). {ARMD 4:181-183}
RICHARDSON, THOMAS, of Baltimore County, aet. 69, dep. Nov 11, 1764. {BALR B#N:459}

RICHARDSON, THOMAS (captain), of Baltimore County, n.a., dep. Aug 16, 1692, mentioned Thomas Thurston, Linsey Woolsey, and the Magazine of Baltimore County. {ARMD 8:338}
RICHARDSON, THOMAS, see "Charles Symond" and "Charles Smith" and "George Clark" and "Richard Atkinson," q.v.
RICHARDSON, WILLIAM, of Talbot County, aet. about 45, dep. Jan, 1753. {TAEJ - James Lloyd folder}
RICHARDSON, WILLIAM, the Elder, of Dorchester County, aet. 64, dep. between Nov 12, 1771 and Dec 17, 1771. {DOLR 26 Old 34}
RICKETTS, NATHANIEL, of Baltimore County, aet. 49, dep. Jul 25, 1771. {BALR AL#C:575}
RICKETTS, SAMUEL, of Baltimore County, aet. 35, dep. Nov 3, 1766. {BALR B#P:308}
RICKETTS, THOMAS, of Prince George's County, aet. 70 or thereabouts, dep. Mar 13, 1756, stated that his father (not named) bought *Ridgley* about 50 years ago. {PGLR NN: See "John Lamar," q.v.
RIDDLE, JOHN, of Prince George's County, aet. 57, dep. Aug 16, 1758, mentioned James Lee (or Leigh) about 8 years ago. {PGLR PP:231, pt. 2}
RIDER, JAMES, see "James Sherwin," q.v.
RIDER, JOHN, see "William Adams," q.v.
RIDER, THOMAS, see "James Sherwin," q.v.
RIDGELY, CHARLES (colonel), of Baltimore County, aet. 67, dep. between Sep 20, 1768 and Mar 11, 1772. {BALR AL#D:435} See "Thomas Clagett," q.v.
RIDGELY, HENRY, see "James Carroll," q.v.
RIDGELY (RIDGELEY), ROBERT, of Anne Arundel County, n.a., dep. Mar 18, 1745/6, stated that he has known Daniel Hearn many years and has always took him to be an honest, quiet man. {ARMD 44:692-693}
RIDGEWAY, JOAN, of Cecil County, aet. 38, dep. Nov 14, 1699, mentioned the fornication of Mrs. Ladamore and Joseph Blackman in July, 1696, and the fornication of Mrs. Ladamore with Samuel Richardson at the house of Henry Eldesley at which time she [Ladamore] told him [Richardson] that she was with child and he promised to take care of her and her child as long as she lived. {CELR 1:181, 192}
RIDGILL, JOHN, of Charles County, aet. 47, dep. Dec 13, 1757. {CHLR H#3:121}
RIEN, DANIEL, of Dorchester County, aet. 42, dep. Jul 22, 1745. {DOLR 22 Old 259}
RIGG, THOMAS, of Charles County, aet. 48, dep. Aug 20, 1753. {CHLR D#3:153}
RIGHT, WILLIAM, see "James Hopkins," q.v.
RILEY (REILY), MARY, of Prince George's County, aet. 58, dep. Nov 11, 1740. {PGLR Y:234}
RILEY, ELIPHAS (ELIPHAZ), of Prince George's County, planter, n.a., dep. Oct 2, 1724. {PGLR I:596} Aet. 54, dep. Jun 27, 1743. {PGLR Y:702}
RILEY (RYLEY), HUGH, see "Elizabeth Mitchell," q.v.
RILEY, JOHN, of Kent County, aet. 67, dep. Mar 24, 1774, stated that 55 or 56 years ago his father (not named) told him he was sending him to school to John

Worthington who then lived on Daniel Mulligan's land. {KEEJ - John Comegys folder}
RIMMER, BENJAMIN, see "George Beall," q.v.
RINGGOLD, CHARLES, SR., of Kent County, aet. 42, dep. 1757. {KELR JS#28:426}
RINGGOLD, JAMES (major), of Kent County, n.a., dep. Nov 7, 1683, stated "George Greene, cryer of the court, made proclamation for Capt. William Laurence, one of your Lordships Justices by the title of a Mann Child about 52 yeares of age." {ARMD 17:170-171} See "Thomas Smith," q.v.
RINGGOLD, JAMES, of Eastern Neck, Kent County, aet. 30, dep. 1735. {KELR JS#18:199} Aet. 55, dep. 1761, mentioned his uncle William Ringgold, son of James Ringgold. {KELR DD#1:609} See "William Ringgold," q.v.
RINGGOLD, JOSIAS, JR., of Kent County, aet. 33, dep. 1769. {KELR DD#3:202}
RINGGOLD, MR., see "Richard Crouch," q.v.
RINGGOLD, REBECCA, see "William Ringgold," q.v.
RINGGOLD, THOMAS, see "William Ringgold," q.v.
RINGGOLD, WILLIAM, of Kent County, aet. 38, dep. Oct 9, 1761, stated that some time after his brother Thomas Ringgold's death James Ringgold, son of William, married Mary Tovey, and offered *Huntingfield* to Rebecca Ringgold. {KELR DD#1:615} Aet. 46, dep. 1769. {KELR DD#3:181} Aet. 51, dep. 1775. {KELR DD#5:133}
RINGGOLD, WILLIAM, of Kent County, aet. 66, dep. 1743. {KELR JS#24:439} Aet. about 71, dep. Apr, 1747, stated that his grandfather Thomas Ringgold purchased a tract called *Crawford* when he came out of England. {QAEJ - Elizabeth Barnes folder} See "James Ringgold," q.v.
RISDEN, EDWARD, of Prince George's County, aet. 52, dep. Apr 18, 1749. {PGLR BB:701}
RISING (RISEN), JOHN, of Charles County, aet. 40, dep. Apr 15, 1772. {CHLR U#3:276}
RISING (RISEN), PETER, of Charles County, aet. 50, dep. Sep 29, 1772. {CHLR U#3:266} See "William Rising," q.v.
RISING (RISEN), WILLIAM, of Charles County, aet. 46, dep. Apr 15, 1772, mentioned his father Peter Rising. {CHLR U#3:276}
RISTON, EDWARD, of Prince George's County, cooper, aet. 35, dep. Mar 18, 1728/9. {PGLR M:480} Aet. 70, dep. Jun 3, 1765. {PGLR TT:453} Edward Reston (Riston), aet. 74, dep. Jun 5, 1769. {PGLR BB#2:437-438}
RIVERS, ELISABETH, of Charles County, n.a., dep. Jun 29, 1663. {CHLR B:164}
RIX, JOHN, of Dorchester County, aet. 60, Jun 15, 1737 and Apr 8, 1738, stated that the boundary tree of *Sewell's Mannour* near Edward Scott's tobacco house had been cut down by Edmund McKeel. {DOLR 9 Old 507} See "Daniel Sulivane," q.v.
ROBBINS, GEORGE, see "Robert Marmaduke" and "James Smith," q.v.
ROBERSON, ELIJAH, of Charles County, aet. 21, dep. Aug 2, 1774. {CHLR W#3:387}

ROBERSON, JOHN, see "John Pagon" and "John Pattison," q.v.
ROBERSON, STEPHEN, of Charles County, aet. 25, dep. Aug 11, 1754. {CHLR D#3:366}
ROBERSON, WILLIAM, of Charles County, aet. 49, dep. Aug 2, 1774, mentioned his father John Roberson. {CHLR W#3:387}
ROBERTS, AARON, of Prince George's County, aet. 47, dep. Aug 25, 1737. {PGLR T:505} Aet. 50, dep. Aug 24, 1741, mentioned Nathaniel Magruder, deceased. {PGLR Y:361} See "James Watson," q.v.
ROBERTS, GRACE, of Dorchester County, aet. 57, dep. between Jun 12, 1750 and Jul 18, 1750, mentioned her husband Hugh Roberts, now deceased. {DOLR 14 Old 428}
ROBERTS, HUGH, see "Grace Roberts," q.v.
ROBERTS, JOHN, of Baltimore County, aet. 80, dep. Nov 11, 1764. {BALR B#N:461} See "Thomas Roberts," q.v.
ROBERTS, JONATHAN, of Queen Anne's County, aet. 35, dep. Apr, 1769. {QAEJ - James Hutchens folder}
ROBERTS, THOMAS, of Baltimore County, n.a., dep. between Nov 25, 1760 and Apr 13, 1761, mentioned his father John Christian Roberts. {BALR B#L:197}
ROBERTS, WILLIAM, of Baltimore County, aet. 57, dep. Oct 21, 1771. {BALR AL#D:276}
ROBERTSON, MATHEW, of Prince George's County, aet. 38, dep. Mar 28, 1741. {PGLR Y:267}
ROBERTSON, ROBERT, see "Abigail Tent," q.v.
ROBEY, ABSOLOM, of Charles County, aet. 22, dep. Aug 2, 1774. {CHLR W#3:381}
ROBEY, JOHN, of Charles County, aet. 40, dep. Jun 6, 1726, mentioned his father John Robey (Roby). {CHLR P#2:393} See "Richard Robey," q.v.
ROBEY, RICHARD, of Charles County, aet. 63, dep. Jul 5, 1762. {CHLR M#3:216} Aet. 65, dep. Sep 27, 1764, mentioned his father John Robey. {CHLR N#3:167}
ROBEY, THOMAS, of Charles County, aet. 74, dep. Jul 1, 1765. {CHLR N#3:787} Aet. 74, dep. Mar 24, 1767. {CHLR P#3:426}
ROBINS, ELIZABETH, see "Thomas Wills," q.v.
ROBINS, JAMES, of Charles County, aet. 47, dep. May 25, 1752. {CHLR B#3:122}
ROBINS, ROBERT, of Charles County, aet. 55, dep. Aug 9, 1681. {CHLR I#1:147} See "Thomas Wills," q.v.
ROBINSON, ----, see "Elizabeth Gootee," q.v.
ROBINSON, ANDREW, of Dorchester County, aet. 55, dep. between Jun 8, 1762 and Jan 29, 1763, mentioned his father William Robinson. {DOLR 18 Old 339} Aet. 53, dep. between Mar 8, 1763 and Jun 13, 1763, mentioned his father (not named) about 25 years ago. {DOLR 18 Old 374} Aet. 54, dep. between Jun 12, 1764 and Aug 6, 1765, mentioned his brother William Robinson about 38 years ago. {DOLR 20 Old 218} Aet. about 57, dep. between Aug 14, 1764 and Jan 4, 1768, mentioned his mother and father (not named). {DOLR 22 Old 418}. Aet. 56, planter, dep. between Jun 11, 1765 and Aug 15, 1765, stated that about 26 years

ago he came to Elliott's Island with his father William Robinson, now deceased; mentioned Henry Travers (Traverse), now called Col. Traverse, and his father Mathew Traverse; also mentioned John Elliott, great-grandfather of the present John Elliott. {DOLR 20 Old 244}

ROBINSON, CHARLES, of Prince George's County, aet. 36, dep. Mar 6, 1759, mentioned his father James Robinson. {PGLR PP:279, pt. 2}

ROBINSON, JAMES, of Baltimore County, aet. 40 or thereabouts, dep. Sep 20, 1767, mentioned William Fitch about 20 years ago. {BALR AL#A:125} See "Charles Robinson" and "John Robinson," q.v.

ROBINSON, JOHN, of Charles County, aet. 79, dep. Aug 11, 1754. {CHLR D#3:366}

ROBINSON, JOHN, of Prince George's County, aet. 28, dep. Mar 6, 1759, mentioned his father James Robinson. {PGLR PP:279, pt. 2}

ROBINSON, JOHN, see "Simon Richardson," q.v.

ROBINSON, MARY, of Dorchester County, aet. 52, dep. between Jun 8, 1762 and Jan 29, 1763. {DOLR 18 Old 339} Aet. 50, dep. between Mar 8, 1763 and Jun 13, 1763, mentioned her father-in-law William Robinson. {DOLR 18 Old 374}

ROBINSON, ROSANNAH, of Charles County, aet. 70, dep. Dec 29, 1744, stated that she was the wife of Alexander Tyer about 22 years ago. {CHLR Z#2:334}

ROBINSON, RUTH, of Dorchester County, aet. 75, dep. between Jun 8, 1762 and Jan 29, 1763, mentioned her brothers James Ensley and William Ensley. {DOLR 18 Old 339} See "John Gootee," q.v.

ROBINSON, WILLIAM, of Charles County, aet. 29, dep. Sep 4, 1660. {CHLR A:100}

ROBISSON, WILLIAM, of Charles County, n.a., dep. Jul 9, 1662. {CHLR A:230}

ROBINSON, WILLIAM, see "Andrew Robinson" and "Mary Robinson" and "William Cannon" and "John Gootee," q.v.

ROBSON, CHARLES, SR., of Dorchester County, aet. 56, dep. between Nov 19, 1732 and May 10, 1732, stated that the bounds of *Turkey Point* were proved about 11 years ago by John Hudson. {DOLR 9 Old 64}

ROBSON, FATHER, see "Henry Travers," q.v.

ROBSON, JOHN, of Dorchester County, aet. 48, dep. between Nov 13, 1744 and Feb 12, 1744/5, mentioned his father (not named) about 20 years ago. {DOLR 12 Old 256} See "John Pattison, Sr." and "William Barnes" and "Isaac Foxwell" and "Daniel Foxwell" and "Sarah Meseck," q.v.

ROCHESTER, JOHN, of Queen Anne's County, aet. about 48, dep. July, 1758. {QAEJ - Henry Callister folder}

RODGERS, JOHN, see "Samuel Beall, Sr." q.v.

RODGERS (ROGERS), JOSEPH, of Talbot County, merchant, aet. 57, dep. Feb 16, 1708/9 to prove the will of William Dixon, deceased. {Will Book 12:16, pt. 2}

ROE, EDWARD, see "Thomas Seward," q.v.

ROE, JOHN, of Tully's Neck, Queen Anne's County, aet. about 43, dep. Mar 29, 1760. {QAEJ - Earle: oversize folder}

ROE, THOMAS, see "Thomas Seward," q.v.

ROGERS, DAVID, of Dorchester County, aet. 26, dep. between Nov 13, 1764 and May 4, 1765. {DOLR 20 Old 173}

ROGERS, DAVID, of Dorchester County, aet. 23, dep. between Mar 13, 1732 and Aug 22, 1733, stated that the bounds of the Quaker's land called *Irish Hope* were shown to him about a year ago by his grandmother Evans. {DOLR 9 Old 357} See "James Wilson," q.v.

ROGERS, ELIZABETH, of Baltimore County, aet. 65, dep. Sep 1, 1763, stated that she knew Urania Shields, wife of Henry Shield. {BALR B#M:90}

ROGERS, JOHN, see "James Wilson," q.v.

ROGERS, MARIA, of Dorchester County, aet. 50, dep. between Nov 14, 1732 and Aug 1, 1733. {DOLR 9 Old 355} See "William Murray," q.v.

ROGERS, MARY, see "James Wilson," q.v.

ROGERS, MICHAEL HILL, see "William Depriest," q.v.

ROKAHOMP, GEORGE, see "Indian Sam Isaac," q.v.

ROLAND, GEORGE, of Charles County, aet. 55, dep. Oct 30, 1770. {CHLR T#3:141} Aet. 55 or 56, dep. Oct 14, 1771. {CHLR T#3:511}

ROLLINGS, PAUL, SR., of Prince George's County, aet. 71, dep. Jun 26, 1734. {PGLR T:124}

ROPER, JOHN, of Charles County, aet. 25, dep. Oct 2, 1662. {CHLR A:248}

ROPER, THOMAS, see "William Davis," q.v.

ROSS, ----, see "Robert Ramsey," q.v.

ROSS, CHARLES, of Dorchester County, aet. 33, dep. between Aug 11, 1754 and Mar 15, 1755. {DOLR 15 Old 247}

ROSS, CHARLES, of Dorchester County, aet. 53, dep. between Jun 14, 1768 and Sep 3, 1768. {DOLR 23 Old 271}

ROSS, CORNELIA, see "Samuel Hubbert," q.v.

ROSS, DAVID (doctor), of Frederick County, n.a., dep. Dec 11, 1765. {ARMD 32:112-113}

ROSS, EDWARD, of Dorchester County, aet. 47, dep. between Jun 8, 1756 and Jul 13, 1758. {DOLR 16 Old 117}

ROSS, JOHN, see "Samuel Hubbert" and "John Harrington" and "Rosannah Mearthers" and "Jane Thomas" and "Samuel Hubbert," q.v.

ROSS, PETER, see "Rosannah Mearthers," q.v.

ROSS, STEPHEN, see "George North," q.v.

ROSS, WILLIAM, of Dorchester County, aet. 54, dep. between Aug 12, 1740 and Sep 13, 1740. {DOLR 12 Old 116} Aet. 58, dep. between Nov 8, 1743 and Jan 9, 1743/4. {DOLR 12 Old 143} Aet. 70, dep. between Jun 8, 1756 and Jul 15, 1756. {DOLR 15 Old 376} See "John Harrington" and "Edward Willoughby," q.v.

ROTTEN, THOMAS, of Dorchester County, aet. 52, dep. between Aug 13, 1765 and Dec 28, 1765. {DOLR 21 Old 42} See "Thomas Wroughton" and "Thomas Wrotten" and "Daniel Foxwell," q.v.

ROTTEN, WILLIAM, see "William Harper," q.v.

ROUSBY, CHRISTOPHER, see "John Llewellin" and "Anthony Evans" and "John Burdett" and "Jane Slye," q.v.

ROUTHORN (RUTHORN), JOSEPH, of Charles County, aet. 48, dep. Jan 9, 1726/7. {CHLR P#2:420} See "Mary Routhorn," q.v.

ROUTHORN (RUTHORN), MARY, of Charles County, aet. 51, dep. Aug 13, 1734, mentioned her husband Joseph Routhorn (Ruthorn); stated she was married 33 or 34 years ago by Rev. George Thorold to John Bowling who told her he was from Lancashire, England and had a brother Roger Bowling; also stated she had a son Thomas Bowling by her husband John and said John had been dead about 24 years. {CHLR R#2:528}

ROW, ELIZABETH, of Prince George's County, aet. 85, dep. Nov 5, 1763, mentioned her husband Joseph Jeans. {PGLR TT:285}

ROW (ROE), MARY, of Charles County, n.a., dep. Jul 30, 1663, stated that Joane Nevill called Mary Dod the whore of Capt. Batten. {CHLR B:146}

ROW (ROE), RICHARD, of Charles County, n.a., dep. Jul 9, 1662. {CHLR A:229} Richard Roe, n.a., dep. May 12, 1663 and Jul 30, 1663. {CHLR B:123, 146, 151}

ROWE, GREGORY, see "Elizabeth Lamphier," q.v.

ROWE, SARAH, see "Elizabeth Lamphier," q.v.

ROWE, THOMAS, see "Daniel Hill" and "William Willson," q.v.

ROWLAND, ----, see "Moses Lecompte," q.v.

ROWLAND, GEORGE, of Charles County, aet. 44, dep. Aug 26, 1767. {CHLR P#3:654}

ROWLES, JOHN, of Queen Anne's County, aet. 51, dep. Sep, 1730, stated that about 21 years ago James Dunn told him about an Indian Queen who was married to one Brent. {QAEJ - William Stavely folder} See "John Rawles," q.v.

ROYALL, ELIJAH, of Dorchester County, aet. 44, dep. between Mar 14, 1711 and Nov 13, 1771, mentioned his father Thomas Royall (Ryall) about 26 years ago. {DOLR 25 Old 238}

ROYALL, THOMAS, of Dorchester County, aet. about 57, dep. between Mar 12, 1744 and Aug 11, 1745. {DOLR 12 Old 250} See "Elijah Royall," q.v.

RUARK, MARY, of Dorchester County, aet. 60, dep. Nov 24, 1741, mentioned her husband Timothy Ruark and the bounds of *Southamton* set about 25 years ago. {DOLR 10 Old 216}

RUARK, TIMOTHY, see "Mary Ruark," q.v.

RUDD, JAMES, of Prince George's County, aet. 28, dep. Oct 15, 1776, mentioned his grandfather Christopher Edelen. {PGLR CC#2:310}

RUMBALL, ANTHONY, see "Sarah Birk," q.v.

RUMBLEY, EDWARD, of Dorchester County, aet. about 56, dep. between Nov 14, 1769 and Nov 6, 1770. {DOLR 24 Old 308}

RUMBLY, JOHN, SR., of Dorchester County, aet. about 53, dep. between Mar 13, 1732 and Aug 22, 1733, mentioned "his father Evans" and old John Spicer about 30 years ago. {DOLR 9 Old 357}

RUMBOLD, WILLIAM, of Dorchester County, aet. 47, dep. between Nov 12, 1771 and Dec 17, 1771, mentioned William Brown Vickers was drowned and buried near the root of an oak tree said to have been the bounded tree of *Brotherly Kindness* by John Harris. {DOLR 26 Old 34}

RUMSEY, BENJAMIN, of Harford County, aet. 40, dep. Aug 12, 1775, mentioned his marriage to a daughter (not named) of Colonel Hall. {Land Commission, 1774, Harford County Genealogical Society Newsletter, Jan, 1993, p. 3}

RUMSEY, BENJAMIN, of Cecil County, n.a., dep. May 31, 1769, stated that he has known Francis and Jeremiah Baker for 6 or 7 years during which time they have behaved themselves honestly, soberly, and justly. {ARMD 32:326-327}

RUMSEY, EDWARD, of Cecil County, aet. 43, dep. Jan 29, 1745/6, mentioned John Harper, son of Thomas Harper. {CELR 4:478} See "Margaret Rumsey," q.v.

RUMSEY, JAMES, of St. Mary's County, n.a., dep. Jul 21, 1681. {ARMD 15:393}

RUMSEY, MARGARET, of Cecil County, aet. 37, wife of Edward Rumsey, dep. Jan 29, 1745/6. {CELR 4:478}

RUSH, GEORGE, of Frederick County, n.a., dep. Dec 2, 1765. {ARMD 32:155-156}

RUSH, HENRY, of Frederick County, n.a., dep. Dec 2, 1765. {ARMD 32:155-156}

RUSSELL, ABRAHAM, see "John Russell," q.v.

RUSSELL, ANDREW, see "Jesper Woodall," q.v.

RUSSELL, CHRISTOPHER, of Charles County, aet. 45, dep. Jan 26, 1658/9, stated that Arthur Turner said he could love Lucie Stratton (who bore his child) and he (Russell) accompanied him to Pickawakson to see if she would be his wife. {CHLR A:35}

RUSSELL, JOHN, of the Isle of Kent, planter, n.a., dep. Feb 24, 1649, mentioned Richard Husbands (captain of the ship *Greene Poppingay*) and John Dandy. {ARMD 3:249}

RUSSELL, JOHN, of Prince George's County, aet. 32, dep. Feb 23, 1760, mentioned his father Abraham Russell about 20 years ago. {PGLR BB#2:147} Aet. 37, dep. Aug 14, 1762, dep. Aug 14, 1762. {PGLR BB#2:147-148} Aet. 40, dep. Nov 7, 1767, mentioned his father Abraham Russell, deceased. {PGLR BB#2:161}

RUSSELL, MARY, see "Charles Thompson," q.v.

RUTTER, EDMUND, of Frederick County, n.a., dep. Aug 26, 1754, stated that Greenborne (Greenbune) Chaney, Jr. bit off part of the left ear of Thomas Walling in a fray on Aug 24, 1754. {FRLR E:524}

RUTTY, DANIEL, of Dorchester County, aet. 67, dep. Sep 7, 1725, stated that he was a servant to Walter Dickason, of Talbot County, about 40 years ag. {DOLR 8 Old 90}

RYALL, THOMAS, see "Elijah Royall" "Thomas Royall" and "William Willson," q.v.

RYDLE, JOHN, of Prince George's County, aet. 70, dep. Nov 26, 1739. {PGLR Y:107}

RYE, CHARLES, see "John Anderton," q.v.

RYE, JOHN, of Charles County, aet. 40, dep. Jan 11, 1757. {CHLR F#3:468}

RYLEY, HUGH, see "Elizabeth Mitchell," q.v.
RYLEY, PHAROAH, see "John Carrick," q.v.
RYON, JAMES, of Prince George's County, aet. 54, son of Darbey Ryon, dep. Nov 30, 1773, mentioned Abraham Wood about 21 years ago in the Town of Nottingham. {PGLR BB#3:335}
RYON, JOSEPH, of Prince George's County, aet. 40, dep. Jul 9, 1765, stated that he was overseer about 20 years ago to Mrs. Elizabeth Lee, now deceased. {PGLR TT:433} Aet. 46, dep. Nov 13, 1769. {PGLR AA#2:136}
RYON, NATHANIEL, of Prince George's County, aet. 43, dep. Nov 13, 1769. {PGLR AA#2:136-137}
SABASTINE, JOSHUA, of Charles County, aet. 33, dep. Dec 13, 1757. {CHLR H#3:124}
SADLER, JAMES, of Prince George's County, aet. 37, dep. May 12, 1753. {PGLR NN:174}
SADLER, JOSEPH, see "Barton Colins," q.v.
SALES, ELIZABETH, see "Mary Mitchel," q.v.
SALES, GEORGE, see "Elizabeth Woodward" and "Mary Mitchel," q.v.
SALES, JEAN, see "Mary Mitchel," q.v.
SALES, MARY, see "Elizabeth Woodward" and "Mary Mitchel," q.v.
SALISBURY, ELIZABETH, of Dorchester County, aet. 48, dep. May 12, 1744, mentioned riding about 13 or 14 years ago from Cambridge in company with Cathrine Jones, widow of William Jones. {DOLR 12 Old 145} Elizabeth Salsbury, aet. 65, dep. between Mar 8, 1763 and May 10, 1763, mentioned her father Edward Taylor. {DOLR 18 Old 439}
SALTER, JOHN, of Anne Arundel County, n.a., dep. Aug 3, 1659. {ARMD 41:319}
SALTER, JOHN, of Talbot County, n.a., dep. Oct 1, 1692, mentioned John Lillingston, William Cowsey, Richard Macklin, Joseph Lambert, Joseph Greene, John Hinson, Sr., Michael Earle, Richard Bennet, Thomas Hinds, John Lamb, Samuel Withers, and Thomas Smith. {ARMD 8:373}
SAMFORD, WILLIAM, of Charles County, aet. 20 or thereabouts, dep. 1658, mentioned Francis Brooks about 2 years ago. {ARMD 41:70}
SANDERS, EDWARD, of Baltimore County, aet. 63, dep. Feb 22, 1766. {BALR B#P:178}
SANDERS, EDWARD, of Charles County, aet. 34, dep. between Nov 8, 1774 and Feb 7, 1775. {CHLR W#3:610}
SANDERS, JAMES (esquire), of Anne Arundel County, one of Her Majesty's Honorable Council, n.a., dep. Mar 5, 1702/3, mentioned Capt. James Mitchell, commander of the ship *Adventure*, and Capt. Nathaniel Bostock, commander of the ship *Eagle*. {ARMD 25:141-142}
SANDERS, JOHN, of Pomfret, Charles County, aet. 56, dep. Sep 29, 1726. {CHLR P#2:396}
SANDERS, JOHN, of Charles County, aet. 37, dep. Mar 27, 1758, mentioned his first wife (not named). {CHLR H#3:430}

SANDERS, JOHN, of Charles County, aet. 44, dep. between Nov 8, 1774 and Feb 7, 1775. {CHLR W#3:609}
SANDERS, JOHN, see "John Woodyard," q.v.
SANDERS, MATHEW, of Prince George's County, aet. 60 and upwards, dep. Jun 6, 1735. {PGLR T:280}
SANDERS, MATTHEW, of Charles County, aet. 60, dep. Apr 6, 1733. {CHLR R#2:332}
SANDERS, MATTHEW, see "John Woodyard," q.v.
SANDERS, THOMAS, of Charles County, aet. 30, dep. Jul 22, 1756, mentioned his father Thomas Sanders. {CHLR F#3:123} Aet. 50, dep. between Nov 8, 1774 and Feb 7, 1775. {CHLR W#3:608}
SANDERS, THOMAS, of Prince George's County, aet. 32, dep. Sep 25, 1758. {PGLR PP:235, pt. 2}
SANDERS, THOMAS, see "Joseph Pulluffus," q.v.
SANDERS, WIDOW, see "James Johnson," q.v.
SANDERS, WILLIAM, of Charles County, aet. 50, dep. May 21, 1725. {CHLR P#2:38}
SANDFORD, ALICE, see "John Bissick," q.v.
SANDSBURY, FRANCIS, of Prince George's County, aet. 70, dep. Jul 9, 1731, stated that he has been in this country almost 53 years and he served 6 years on *The Farm*, Col. Ninian Beall's plantation. {PGLR Q:522}
SANSBERY, RICHARD, see "William Sansbery, Jr." and "Thomas King," q.v.
SANSBERY (SANDSBURY), THOMAS, of Prince George's County, aet. 70, dep. Feb 20, 1767. {PGLR BB#2:167-168} Thomas Sandsbury, Sr., aet. 74, dep. Jul 10, 1771, stated that he was employed in 1728 by Clement Brooke, now deceased, to make tobacco hogsheads. {PGLR AA#2:283}
SANSBERY, THOMAS, JR., of Prince George's County, aet. 42, dep. Feb 20, 1767. {PGLR BB#2:168}
SANSBERY, WILLIAM, of Prince George's County, aet. 61, dep. Feb 20, 1767. {PGLR BB#2:167}
SANSBERY, WILLIAM, JR., of Prince George's County, aet. 30, dep. Feb 20, 1767, mentioned his father Richard Sansbery. {PGLR BB#2:168}
SAP, HENRY, of Dorchester County, aet. 50, dep. Aug 30, 1738. {DOLR 12 Old 102}
SAPPINGTON, JAMES, of Kent County, aet. 52, dep. Mar 24, 1774, stated that over 26 years ago Daniel Mulligan married a sister (not named) of John Worthington and, they having no likelihood of having children, Mulligan sent home to England for said John Worthington who came to Maryland and was given some land by said Mulligan. {KEEJ - John Comegys folder}
SARGENT, JOSEPH, see "James Peterkin," q.v.
SARGENT, REBECCA, see "James Peterkin," q.v.
SASSER, ROGER JOHN, of Prince George's County, aet. 67, dep. Jul 1, 1738. {PGLR T:606} Roger John Saucer, aet. 82, planter, dep. Jun 6, 1751, mentioned

Richard Beaven and Rev. Robert Owen, both deceased. {PGLR PP:152, 155} See "John Sasser" and "Edward Mobberly," q.v.

SASSER, JOHN, of Prince George's County, aet. 77, dep. Mar 11, 1745/6, mentioned Thomas Tucker about 30 years ago. {PGLR BB:6}

SASSER, JOHN, of Prince George's County, aet. 70 or thereabouts, dep. May 23, 1774 (recorded Mar 23, 1776), mentioned his father (not named) and Roger John Sasser about 30 years ago. {PGLR CC#2:245}

SASSER, JOHN, see "George Magruder," q.v.

SAUNDERS, EDWARD, of Baltimore County, Quaker, aet. 66 or thereabouts, dep. Apr 3, 1769, stated that he has lived in this area for 50 years. {BALR AL#A:303}

SAUNDERS, JOHN, see "Francis Pain" and "Benjamin Carpenter," q.v.

SAUSBERG, FRANCIS, of Prince George's County, aet. 75, dep. Aug 6, 1735, mentioned Henry Culver about 30 years ago, now deceased. {PGLR T:359}

SAVAGE, THOMAS, of Dorchester County, aet. 27, dep. between Jun 9, 1752 and Mar 9, 1754, stated that he was shown the bounds of *Fisher's Discovery* about 13 years ago by Joseph Fisher. {DOLR 15 Old 66}

SAVAGE, THOMAS, of Dorchester County, aet. 29, dep. between Jun 11, 1765 and Mar 9, 1767. {DOLR 21 Old 315}

SAVORY, WILLIAM, of Kent County, aet. 64, dep. Dec 10, 1724. {KELR JS#W:404}

SAWSER, JOHN, see "George Magruder," q.v.

SCACE, WILLIAM, of Prince George's County, aet. 70, dep. Mar 19, 1746/7. {PGLR BB:198-199}

SCAGGS, RICHARD, of Prince George's County, n.a., dep. Dec 5, 1763. {PGLR TT:189}

SCALLORN, PETER, of Charles County, aet. 57, dep. Sep 30, 1745. {CHLR Z#2:466}

SCANDELL (SCANDALL), ANN, of Prince George's County, aet. 48, dep. Jul 1, 1726. {PGLR M:28} Ann Scandall, aet. 80, dep. Feb 17, 1759, mentioned her former husband Hilliary Ball about 47 years ago. {PGLR RR:232}

SCANDELL, MICHAEL, of Prince George's County, aet. 30, dep. Jul 1, 1726. {PGLR M:28}

SCARBOROUGH, JOHN, of Worcester County, n.a., dep. Nov 30, 1749, stated that he saw Indian Sarah frequently between 1740 and 1746, always with a very white child whom she said was hers; deponent thinks they moved to Dorchester County in 1746; also mentioned Indian Doctor James and Indian George Rocohaun. {CMSP 1:89}

SCARBOROUGH, MARY, of Worcester County, n.a., dep. Dec 5, 1748, stated that Indian Sarah had a white child (that she said was hers) between 1740 and 1746 and then they moved to Dorchester County. {CMSP 1:84}

SCHALES, GEORGE, of Charles County, aet. 25, dep. May 7, 1661. {CHLR A:130}

SCOTT, DANIEL, see "James Scott" and "Lewis Potee" and "Daniel Preston," q.v.

SCOTT, EDWARD, of Dorchester County, aet. 49, dep. between Aug 12, 1760 and Jun 11, 1761. {DOLR 17 Old 354} See "John Rix," q.v.
SCOTT, JAMES, of Baltimore County, n.a., dep. Jun 14, 1770, mentioned his father Daniel Scott. {BALR AL#C:277}
SCOTT (SCOT), JOHN, of Talbot County, n.a., dep. Jan 21, 1667/8. {ARMD 54:417} See "Thomas Burch, Sr.," q.v.
SCOTT, JOHN, SR., of Charles County, aet. 60 odd years, dep. Dec 12, 1719, mentioned John Piles, grandfather of Joseph Piles. {Charles County Land Commissions 1:75}
SCOTT, ROBERT, of Dorchester County, aet. 61, dep. between Mar 8, 1768 and Aug 5, 1769, mentioned Thomas Wingate (deceased), son of Phillip Wingate. {DOLR 23 Old 336}
SCOTT, THOMAS, of Prince George's County, aet. 26, dep. Jul 15, 1729, mentioned his father (not named). {PGLR M:487}
SCOTT, WILLIAM, see "Richard Weaver," q.v.
SCOTT, WILLIAM, of Prince George's County, aet. 52, dep. Nov 7, 1726. {PGLR M:153} Aet. 57, dep. Jul 15, 1729 and Aug 22, 1729. {PGLR M:487}
SCOTT, WILLIAM, of Charles County, aet. 41, dep. Sep 28, 1734, mentioned his father John Scott, Sr., deceased. {CHLR R#2:536} Aet. 45 or 46, dep. Jan 11, 1736/7. {CHLR T#2:297} Aet. 48, dep. Sep 23, 1741. {CHLR O#2:288}
SCOTT, WILLIAM, of Queen Anne's County, aet. 52, dep. Apr, 1755. {QAEJ - Matthew Dockery folder} Aet. 58, dep. Aug 13, 1760; aet. about 59, dep. Aug 20, 1761. {QAEJ - John Gafford folder} Aet. about 59, dep. Sep, 1761. {QAEJ - William Webb folder} Aet. 60, dep. Mar, 1762. {QAEJ - Henry Callister folder} Aet. 63, dep. Apr, 1765. {QAEJ - William Austin folder}
SCRIVENER, BENJAMIN, see "Thelma Smith" and "Joseph Tilly," q.v.
SCRIVENER, GRACE, see "Thelma Smith" and "Joseph Tilly," q.v.
SCROGGEN, JOHN, of Charles County, aet. 55, dep. Feb 17, 1742/3. {CHLR O#2:507}
SCROGGIN, GEORGE, of Charles County, aet. 45, dep. Dec 6, 1770, mentioned his father George Scroggin. {CHLR T#3:244}
SCROGGIN, JOHN, of Charles County, aet. 25, dep. Feb 15, 1750, mentioned his father John Scroggin. {CHLR Z#2:144}
SCROGGIN, SARAH, of Charles County, aet. 47, dep. Jul 11, 1762, mentioned her former husband Richard Mastin, deceased. {CHLR M#3:224}
SEARSON, FRANCIS, prob. of Anne Arundel County, chyrurgeon, n.a., dep. circa Sep 5, 1692. {ARMD 8:375}
SELBEE, JOHN, of Stafford County, Virginia, aet. 26, dep. Jun 7, 1668 in Charles County, Maryland. {CHLR C#1:274}
SELBY, JOHN, of Worcester County, n.a., dep. Dec 5, 1748, stated that between 1740 and 1746 Indian Sarah had a white child (no name given) that she said was hers and they moved to Dorchester County. {CMSP 1:84}
SELBY, NATHAN, see "Thomas King" and "Thomas Hodgkin," q.v.

SELBY, WILLIAM, see "William Magruder Selby," q.v.
SELBY, WILLIAM MAGRUDER, of Prince George's County, aet. 49, dep. Sep 23, 1758, mentioned his father William Selby and Major John Bradford about 30 years ago, both now deceased. {PGLR PP:238-239, pt. 2}
SELMAN, WILLIAM, see "John Bond," q.v.
SELUS (ZEALOUS), STEPHEN, of Dorchester County, aet. 55, dep. Sep 8, 1682. {DOLR 4 Old 20}
SENNET, GARRATT, of Charles County, n.a., dep. May 7, 1661. {CHLR A:130}
SENTRY, WILLIAM, of Prince George's County, aet. 73, dep. Feb 20, 1767. {PGLR BB#2:167}
SEWARD, DANIEL, of Queen Anne's County, aet. about 38, dep. Apr, 1765, stated that about 20 or 30 years ago he and his father Thomas Seward went to see Thomas Seward, this deponent's brother. {QAEJ - William Austin folder} See "William Seward," q.v.
SEWARD, FRANCIS, see "Francis Soward," q.v.
SEWARD, JOHN, of Dorchester County, aet. 33, dep. between Mar 8, 1742 and May 7, 1743. {DOLR 12 Old 166} See "Francis Soward" and "John Soward" and "Thomas Cook," q.v.
SEWARD, JOHN, of Queen Anne's County, aet. about 32, dep. Apr, 1765, stated that about 20 or 30 years ago he and his father Thomas Seward went to see Thomas Seward, Jr., this deponent's half-brother. {QAEJ - William Austin folder}
SEWARD, MARY, of Dorchester County, aet. about 68, dep. between Nov 11, 1746 and May 27, 1752. {DOLR 14 Old 658}
SEWARD, THOMAS, of Queen Anne's County, aet. about 77, dep. Apr 14, 1755, mentioned John Roe, father of Thomas and Edward Roe, about 20 or 30 years ago. {QAEJ - Matthew Dockery folder} See "Daniel Seward" and "John Seward" and "Mary Slocum," q.v.
SEWARD, WILLIAM, of Queen Anne's County, aet. about 37, dep. Apr 14, 1755, mentioned his brother Daniel Seward. {QAEJ - Matthew Dockery folder} Aet. 47, dep. Apr, 1765. {QAEJ - William Austin folder}
SEWELL, ANN, see "Richard Hargrave, Sr.," q.v.
SEWELL, CHRISTOPHER, of Baltimore County, aet. 49, dep. Oct 21, 1771. {BALR AL#D:276}
SEWELL, HENRY, see "Richard Hargrave, Sr.," q.v.
SEYMOUR, THOMAS, of Charles County, n.a., dep. 1658. {ARMD 41:73}
SHACKLADY (SHACLADY), JAMES, of St. Mary's County, n.a., dep. Mar 23, 1664/5. {ARMD 49:478}
SHANKS, JOHN, of St. Mary's County, n.a., dep. between Jun 29, 1698 and Jul 1, 1698 in Annapolis. {ARMD 23:435, 23:442}
SHAPLEIGH, PHILIP, of Northumberland County, Virginia, aet. 61, formerly Deputy Surveyor of Dorchester County in 1670, dep. between 1706 and 1709. {DOLR 2 Old 153}
SHAPLEY, ----, see "Thomas Brereton," q.v.

SHAREWOOD, THOMAS, of Prince George's County, aet. 50, dep. Apr 23, 1754. {PGLR NN:253}
SHARP, PETER, see "William Edmondson," q.v.
SHARPE, JOHN, of Dorchester County, aet. 43, dep. Nov 14, 1729. {DOLR 8 Old 384}
SHARPLESS, THOMAS, of Dorchester County, aet. 50, dep. between Mar 14, 1748 and Jun 10, 1749. {DOLR 14 Old 465}
SHAW, BENJAMIN, of Charles County, aet. 45, dep. Feb 28, 1776. {CHLR X#3:578}
SHAW, JAMES, of Dorchester County, aet. 25, dep. between Nov 12, 1771 and Apr 17, 1772. {DOLR 26 Old 50}
SHAW, JOHN, of Charles County, aet. 67, dep. Oct 25, 1731. {CHLR R#2:47} Aet. 75, dep. Mar 1, 1737. {CHLR T#2:427}
SHAW, JOHN, of Charles County, aet. 45, dep. Jul 12, 1743. {CHLR O#2:663}
SHAW, RALPH, of Charles County, aet. 50, dep. Oct 27, 1735. {CHLR T#2:101} Ralph Shaw, Sr., aet. 53, dep. Sep 5, 1738. {CHLR T#2:516} Aet. 81, dep. Aug 6, 1765. {CHLR N#3:429}
SHAW, REBECCA, see "John Adamson" and "Rebecca Beall," q.v.
SHAW, WILLIAM, of Baltimore County, aet. 38, dep. Sep 6, 1763. {BALR B#M:174}
SHAW, WILLIAM, JR., see "John Adamson," q.v.
SHAWHORN (SHAWHAWN, SHAWHAN), DARBY, of Kent County, aet. about 60, dep. Feb 26, 1733/4. {KELR JS#18:2}
SHEARWOOD, THOMAS, of Prince George's County, aet. 49, dep. Jun 19, 1755, mentioned Mathew Duly about 17 years ago, now deceased, and John Dickinson, uncle of John Lannum, now deceased. {PGLR NN:392} Aet. 70, dep. Apr 10, 1775, stated that John Pritchet showed him the bounds of *Rozier's Gift* about 30 years ago. {PGLR CC#2:179}
SHEHAWNE, THOMAS, see "William Stokes" and "Ann Trego," q.v.
SHEHEN, WILLIAM, of Prince George's County, aet. near 37, dep. Sep 10, 1763. {PGLR TT:607}
SHEIRTCLIFF, JOHN, of St. Mary's County, aet. 44, dep. Aug 5, 1662. {ARMD 41:590}
SHELBY, EVAN (captain), of Frederick County, n.a., dep. Dec 10, 1765, mentioned Joseph Flint and Ralph Matson. {ARMD 32:110} Aet. 48, dep. Aug 7, 1772, mentioned his father Evan Shelby and Joseph Chapline about 30 years ago. {FRLR P:308} See "Thomas Prather," q.v.
SHELTON, HANNAH, of Charles County, n.a., dep. Jul 30, 1663. {CHLR B:146}
SHELTON, THOMAS, of Charles County, aet. 28, dep. Jul 2, 1661. {CHLR A:140, ARMD 41:497} See "John Morris" and "Robert Landen," q.v.
SHELTON, WILLIAM, of Charles County, aet. 29, dep. Oct 19, 1741. {CHLR O#2:282}
SHEMBROOKE, FRANCES, of Kent County, n.a., dep. Jun 28, 1670, stated that James Phillips was the father of her child and that they were servants of William Bishop and Robert Palmer. {ARMD 54:292}

SHENTON, ANNE, of Dorchester County, aet. 41, wife of William Shenton, dep. between Mar 12, 1750 and Jun 10, 1751, mentioned her father-in-law Francis Harper about 15 or 16 years ago. {DOLR 14 Old 525}

SHENTON, MARY, of Dorchester County, aet. 49, dep. between Aug 14, 1750 and Nov 24, 1750. {DOLR 14 Old 546}

SHENTON, RAYMOND, of Dorchester County, aet. 52, dep. between Aug 8, 1749 and Nov 10, 1749. {DOLR 14 Old 392} See "Zebulon Keene," q.v.

SHENTON, WILLIAM, of Dorchester County, aet. 29, dep. between Nov 19, 1732 and May 10, 1732, stated that the bounds of *Turkey Point* were proved about 11 years ago by John Hudson. {DOLR 9 Old 64} Aet. 45, dep. between Aug 8, 1749 and Nov 10, 1749. {DOLR 14 Old 392} See "Anne Shenton," q.v.

SHEPPARD, JOHN, see "Richard Wroth," q.v.

SHERWIN, JAMES, of Dorchester County, aet. 46, dep. between Mar 8, 1747 and Sep 7, 1748, stated that the bounded tree of *Skillington's Right* was shown to Thomas Rider by his father James Rider when he (Sherwin) was a boy about 8 or 10 years old; also mentioned Robert Jones, of Dorchester County, deceased. {DOLR 14 Old 313} See "Jesper Woodall," q.v.

SHERWIN, JOHN, see "Jesper Woodall," q.v.

SHERWIN, ROBERT, of Dorchester County, aet. 60, dep. between Jun 14, 1729 and Jul 17, 1729, stated that the bounds of *Cleland* was surveyed about 6 or 7 years for Jonas Dawson and the bounds of said land were identified by Sherry Wansey to Edward Coxall and by Coxall to the said Robert Sherwin. {DOLR 8 Old 432} Aet. 61, dep. Nov 14, 1729. {DOLR 8 Old 384} Aet. about 78, dep. between Mar 12, 1744/5 and Aug 5, 1745, stated that he lived on *Skillington's Right* about 40 or 50 years ago and has lived near it ever since, adding that he sold it because he was stopped by William Edmondson, deceased, from going up the river further than where his numbers of perches ended. In another deposition he stated that he bought *Eason* and *Eason's Addition* about 42 years ago from old William Edmondson, deceased; also mentioned old John Fleharty at that time. {DOLR 12 Old 215, 242}

SHERWOOD, JOHN, of Talbot County, aet. about 46, dep. between Mar 13, 1764 and Oct 21, 1765, mentioned William Edmondson, William Perry, and John Sherwood about 20 years ago, all now deceased. {DOLR 20 Old 429} See "Kenellm Skillington," q.v.

SHIDECKER, GEORGE, of Frederick County, aet. 52, dep. Jul 24, 1762. {FRLR H:101}

SHIELDS, HENRY, see "Elizabeth Rogers," q.v.

SHIELDS, URANIA, see "Elizabeth Rogers," q.v.

SHIPLEY, JOHN, see "Thomas Brereton," q.v.

SHORE, RICHARD, of Prince George's County, aet. 32, dep. Aug 23, 1732, stated that William Hulse was born in St. Mary's County near the Coole Springs in King & Queen Parish, aged about 6 years, and was playing with a companion (not named) on his (Shore's) plantation when he (Hulse) was accidentally struck in the left ear by one of the plantation horses. {PGLR Q:532}

SHORT, ANN, see "Catherine Warren," q.v.

SHORT, BENJAMIN, see "Henry Bayly," q.v.

SHORT, CATHARINE, of Charles County, aet. 35, dep. Nov 20, 1735, mentioned her husband Daniel Short. {CHLR T#2:201}

SHORT, DANIEL, see "Catharine Short" and "Catherine Warren," q.v.

SHORTER, ANTHONY, of Dorchester County, aet. 37, dep. between Nov 28, 1734 and Jul 31, 1735, mentioned Matthew Kirwan about 25 years ago. {DOLR 9 Old 312} Aet. 44, dep. between Jun 14, 1743 and Aug 1, 1743. {DOLR 12 Old 167} Aet. 64, dep. between Nov 10, 1761 and Feb 20, 1762, mentioned his mother Susanna Shorter and his uncle Richard Pearson. {DOLR 18 Old 90}

SHORTER, KENDEL, see "Daniel Foxwell," q.v.

SHORTER, SUSANNA, see "Anthony Shorter" and "Daniel Foxwell," q.v.

SHRESSE, ALEXANDER, of Cecil County, n.a., dep. Jan 23, 1676, mentioned William Ward, John Coke, and Abraham Strand. {CELR 1:78}

SHUTTLEWORTH, JOSEPH, of Charles County, aet. 51, dep. Dec 5, 1764. {CHLR P#3:271}

SIBREY, JONATHAN, see "Michael Miller," q.v.

SILVERTHORNE, WILLIAM, of Calvert County (then called Patuxent County), aet. 23, dep. Aug 22, 1657, stated "that he never heard Hanna Wise nor any other person say that Mrs. Elizabeth Berry had another husband in England besides Mr. James Berry, only some rumours of late he hath heard to that purpose." {ARMD 10:519}

SILVESTER, JAMES, of Queen Anne's County, aet. 70, dep. Aug, 1752. {QAEJ - Sarah Starkey folder}

SIMES, CLEBOURN, see "William Cooksey," q.v.

SIMES, FRANCIS, of Charles County, aet. 60, dep. Oct 3, 1767. {CHLR P#3:668}

SIMES, JOHN, see "William Cooksey," q.v.

SIMES, PHILDELMUS, of Charles County, aet. 57, dep. between Aug 16, 1765 and Nov 13, 1765. {CHLR N#3:789}

SIMKIN, JOHN, of Baltimore County, aet. 45, dep. Feb 16, 1767. {BALR B#P:418}

SIMMES, ALEXIUS, of Charles County, aet. 31, dep. Aug 18, 1735. {CHLR T#2:99}

SIMMS, MARMADUKE, of Charles County, aet. 65, dep. Mar 24, 1767. {CHLR P#3:423}

SIMPSON, ALEXANDER, of Charles County, aet. 40, dep. Oct 16, 1669. {CHLR D#1:98}

SIMPSON, ELIZABETH, see "Mary Hagan" and "Ann Jones" and "Ann Posey," q.v.

SIMPSON, GILBERT, see "Gilbert Sympson," q.v.

SIMPSON, IGNATIUS, of Charles County, aet. 44, dep. Jun 5, 1752, mentioned his father Thomas Simpson, Sr. {CHLR 47:60}

SIMPSON, JAMES, of Prince George's County, aet. 50, dep. between Nov 11, 1729 and Mar 26, 1730. {PGLR M:567}

SIMPSON, THOMAS, see "William Simpson, Sr." and "James Simpson" and "Thomas Burch, Sr." and "Ignatius Simpson," q.v.

SIMPSON, THOMAS, of Charles County, aet. 48, dep. Jun 5, 1752. {CHLR B#3:60} Aet. 61, dep. Jul 5, 1762. {CHLR M#3:213} Aet. 65, dep. Jul 24, 1758, mentioned his father Thomas Simpson and Richard Lewellin, father of John Lewellin. {CHLR H#3:570}

SIMPSON, THOMAS, SR., of Charles County, aet. 61, dep. Nov 6, 1756, mentioned his brother William Simpson. {CHLR F#3:246}

SIMPSON, THOMAS, SR., of Charles County, aet. 58, dep. Dec 12, 1719, mentioned Capt. Joseph Piles about 34 years ago. {Charles County Land Commissions 1:75}

SIMPSON, WILLIAM, see "Mary Hagan" and "Ann Jones" and "Ann Posey," q.v.

SIMPSON, WILLIAM, of Charles County, aet. 35, dep. May 25, 1765, stated that William Newman married the daughter (not named) of Edward Stonestreet. {CHLR N#3:382}

SIMPSON, WILLIAM, SR., of Charles County, aet. 52, dep. Jun 5, 1752, mentioned his father Thomas Simpson, Sr. {CHLR B#3:60} Aet. 54, dep. May 29, 1752. {CHLR B#3:58} Aet. 66, dep. May 4, 1765, mentioned his brother Thomas Simpson, deceased. {CHLR N#3:382} Aet. 71, dep. Oct 1, 1771, mentioned his brother Thomas Simpson. {CHLR W#3:79} Aet. 74, dep. Oct 8, 1771, mentioned James Williams and John Baptist Boarman about 47 years ago. {CHLR W#3:613}

SIMS, ANTHONY, see "Henry Wood," q.v.

SIMS, ELANDER, of Charles County, aet. 42, dep. Sep 21, 1742. {CHLR O#2:464}

SIMS, ELIZABETH, of Charles County, aet. 35, dep. Dec 20, 1737. {CHLR T#2:431}

SIMS, FRANCIS, of Charles County, aet. 77, dep. Apr 8, 1742. {CHLR O#2:383}

SINNET, ROBERT, of Charles County, aet. 59, dep. Apr 23, 1761. {CHLR K#3:306}

SIRCOM, THOMAS, of Queen Anne's County, aet. about 58, dep. Apr, 1769. {QAEJ - James Hutchens folder}

SISSON, REUBEN, of Charles County, aet. 40, dep. May 11, 1772. {CHLR U#3:13}

SISSON, WILLIAM, of Charles County, aet. 36, dep. May 11, 1772. {CHLR U#3:14}

SIVICK, WILLIAM, see "Jonathan Jones," q.v.

SKIDMORE, EDWARD, see "Hans Hanson," q.v.

SKIDMORE, MICHAEL, see "Hans Hanson," q.v.

SKILLINGTON, KENELLM, of Talbot County, aet. 42, dep. between Mar 8, 1747 and Sep 7, 1748, mentioned his father Kenellm Skillington. about 30 years ago and that John Sherwood married the daughter (not named) of Kenellm Skillington, Sr., a short time after the bounded tree of *Skillington's Right* was shown to them by Howell Powell and Oliver Lee, both now deceased. {DOLR 14 Old 313} See "Mary Perry," q.v.

SKILLINGTON, THOMAS, see "Peter Sharpe Edmondson" and "Mary Perry," q.v.

SKINNER, CLARK, see "Thomas Coleman," q.v.
SKINNER, EDWARD, of Queen Anne's County, aet. about 63, dep. Mar, 1746. {QAEJ - Benjamin Tasker folder} Aet. 72, dep. Apr, 1755, stated that about 57 years ago he lived with George Vandeford, father of Charles, John, George, Thomas, and William Vandeford. {QAEJ - Matthew Dockery folder} Aet. about 79, dep. Aug 20, 1761. {QAEJ - John Gafford folder} Aet. 82, dep. Apr, 1765. {QAEJ - William Austin folder}
SKINNER, HESTHER, see "William Harrison," q.v.
SKINNER, JAMES, see "William Skinner," q.v.
SKINNER, PHILEMON, see "William Harrison," q.v.
SKINNER, THOMAS, of Charles County, aet. 42, dep. May 29, 1744. {CHLR Y#2:185}
SKINNER, WILLIAM, of Charles County, aet. 42, dep. Feb 25, 1745/6. {CHLR Z#2:518} Aet. 47, dep. Jul 6, 1749. {CHLR Z#2:529} Aet. 56, dep. Dec 31, 1759. {CHLR I#3:429} Aet. 67 or 68, dep. Jun 5, 1770. {CHLR T#3:606} Aet. 69, dep. Sep 29, 1773, mentioned his brother James Skinner; stated that the present Col. George Mason was a son of Col. George Mason, deceased, and Ann Mason; also stated that the wife (not named) of Francis Mastin had been formerly married to Roger Chamberlin and Thomas Brooks, both deceased. {CHLR U#3:264} See "William Harrison," q.v.
SKIRVEN, WIDOW, see "Thomas Crow," q.v.
SKUYL, JOHN, of Cecil County, n.a., dep. Jul 8, 1723, stated that John Crowman, tailor, of Cecil County, died about 2 o'clock last Saturday afternoon at the home of the widow Bayard; on Jul 5th Crowman stated he wanted Adam Lytner to have his clothes; he died and was buried on Bayard's plantation on Jul 7th. {CELR 4:20}
SLAYCOMB, GEORGE, see "Andrew Goutee," q.v.
SLADER, RICHARD, of Charles County, aet. 57, dep. Jun 22, 1767. {CHLR P#3:59}
SLATER, RICHARD, of Charles County, aet. 44, dep. Aug 18, 1763. {CHLR M#3:509}
SLATER, WILLIAM, of Baltimore County, aet. 49, dep. Mar 5, 1776. {BALR WG#B:392}
SLINEY, JOHN, of Queen Anne's County, aet. 90, dep. Apr, 1769. {QAEJ - James Hutchings folder}
SLINEY, MAURICE, see "John Smyth," q.v.
SLINEY, SARAH, of Queen Anne's County, aet. about 56, dep. Apr, 1769, mentioned her husband and her brother (no names given). {QAEJ - James Hutchens folder}
SLOCUM, MARY, of Queen Anne's County, aet. 55, dep. Apr, 1765, mentioned her father Thomas Seward about 35 years ago. {QAEJ - William Austin folder}
SLYE, GERRARD, late of St. Mary's County, now of London, England, merchant, aet. about 27, dep. Sep 23, 1681 in London, stated that he has very well known Philip Calvert, Esq., of Maryland, uncle to the now Lord Baltimore, for the past ten years. {ARMD 5:296, 299} See "Jane Slye" and "William Taylard," q.v.

SLYE, JANE, of London, England, aet. about 30, dep. Sep 23, 1681 in London, stated that she and her husband Gerrard Slye were at the home of Lord Baltimore in Maryland about May 10th last; mentioned Christopher Rousby and Samuell Groome, commander of the ship *Globe* of London. {ARMD 5:297-298}

SLYE, JOHN, of Charles County, aet. 57, dep. Dec 30, 1752. {CHLR B#3:343}

SLYE, ROBERT, of Charles County, aet. 34, dep. Sep 25, 1661. {CHLR A:157} However, a later entry on Jan 28, 1661/2 indicated Robert Sly was a merchant of St. Mary's County. {CHLR A:181}

SMALL, JOHN, of Charles County, n.a., dep. Oct 1, 1662. {CHLR A:246}

SMALL, RICHARD, of Queen Anne's County, aet. about 60, dep. Mar, 1764, stated that whilst a child he lived with his father Robert Small. {QAEJ - Robert Small folder}

SMALL, ROBERT, of Queen Anne's County, aet. about 55, dep. Mar, 1759; aet. 66, dep. Mar, 1770. {QAEJ - Henry Carter folders} See "Richard Small" and "Patrick Gordon" and "John Thurlow" and "Mary Thurlow," q.v.

SMALLWOOD, BAYNE, of Charles County, aet. 41, dep. Nov 2, 1752. {CHLR B#3:210} Aet. 59, dep. Aug 11, 1760. {CHLR K#3:4}

SMALLWOOD, BUTLER, of Charles County, aet. 38, dep. Jan 23, 1756/7. {CHLR E#3:137}

SMALLWOOD, JAMES, see "Thomas Lomax" and "Thomas Berry" and "Ledstone Smallwood" and "James Griffin," q.v.

SMALLWOOD, JAMES, of Charles County, n.a., dep. Jul 28, 1663. {CHLR B:135}

SMALLWOOD, JAMES, SR., of Charles County, aet. 48, dep. Apr 30, 1745. {CHLR Z#2:336} Aet. 45, dep. Aug 23, 1745. {CHLR Z#2:464}

SMALLWOOD, JOHN, of Charles County, aet. 40, dep. Aug 23, 1745. {CHLR Z#2:464}

SMALLWOOD, LEDSTONE, of Charles County, aet. 51, dep. Sep 5, 1738. {CHLR T#2:517} Aet. 58, dep. Nov 11, 1745, mentioned his father James Smallwood. {CHLR Z#2:468} Aet. 62, dep. Jan 6, 1748/9. {CHLR Z#2:346} Aet. 68, dep. Oct 1, 1754, mentioned his father Col. James Smallwood. {CHLR E#3:91}

SMALLWOOD, PRYOR, of Charles County, aet. 40, dep. May 30, 1721. {CHLR M#2:122}

SMART, RICHARD, see "Bartho. Ennalls," q.v.

SMITH, ARTHUR, of Charles County, aet. 39, dep. Jul 11, 1762. {CHLR M#3:223}

SMITH, ARTHUR, of Dorchester County, aet. 67, dep. between Jun 11, 1765 and Aug 15, 1765, mentioned Richard Hart, now deceased, and Jane Elliott who lived on Elliott's Island about 51 or 52 years ago. {DOLR 20 Old 244}

SMITH, CHARLES, of Baltimore County, aet. 70, dep. Sep 3, 1724, stated that he was a servant of Thomas Richardson, brother of Lawrence Richardson, about 26 years ago. {BALR IS#G:380}

SMITH, CHARLES, of Baltimore County, aet. 33, dep. May 30, 1771. {BALR AL#C:597}

SMITH, CHARLES SOMERSET, see "Sarah Night," q.v.

SMITH, DANIEL, of Cecil County, n.a., dep. Nov 4, 1722, mentioned the encroachment of Pennsylvanians on his land, particularly Isaac Taylor and son (not named), Elisha Gatchell, William Brown, John Churchman, Richard Brown, and Roger Nerck. {ARMD 25:396}

SMITH, EDWARD, of Baltimore County, dep. 1680 in Anne Arundel County, stated that about 50 years ago he heard John Merekin, grandfather of the present Joshua Merekin, had purchased part of *New Scotland* and he (deponent) knew old John quite well. {AALR IT#5:44}

SMITH, ELIAS, of Charles County, aet. 69, dep. May 25, 1745. {CHLR Z#2:341}

SMITH, ELLINOR, see "Mary Hall" and "Ellinor Lewis," q.v.

SMITH, GEORGE, of Dorchester County, n.a., dep. Feb 28, 1770. {DOLR 25 Old 5}

SMITH, HENRY, of Dorchester County, aet. 61, dep. Aug 28, 1742, mentioned his father John Smith about 40 years ago {DOLR 12 Old 125} Aet. 62, dep. between Nov 9, 1742 and Nov 5, 1743, stated that he was shown the boundary oak tree to *Dublin* by John Clayton about 40 years ago. {DOLR 12 Old 157} See "James Cannon, Sr." and "Mary Hall" and "Ellinor Lewis," q.v.

SMITH, JAMES, see "James Hopkins" and "Mary Hall" and "Ellinor Lewis," q.v.

SMITH, JAMES, of Frederick County, n.a., dep. Nov 11, 1765. {FRLR K:553}

SMITH, JAMES, of Prince George's County, aet. 29, dep. Apr 22, 1755, mentioned his father William Smith. {PGLR NN:371}

SMITH, JAMES, of Talbot County, aet. about 26, dep. Feb 18, 1672/3, mentioned Mr. and Mrs. [George] Robbins. {ARMD 54:553}

SMITH, JAMES, of Charles County, aet. 37, dep. Mar 4, 1731/2. {CHLR R#2:82}

SMITH, JAMES, of Kent County, aet. about 47, dep. Jul 16, 1762. {KEEJ - John Carville folder}

SMITH, JAMES, JR., of Charles County, aet. 36, dep. Dec 6, 1763. {CHLR M#3:503}

SMITH, JOHN, of Calvert County, n.a., servant to Richard Preston, Sr., dep. Mar 31, 1663. {ARMD 49:9-10}

SMITH, JOHN, of Dorchester County, aet. 43, dep. between Mar 8, 1774 and Nov 10, 1774, mentioned his father Thomas Smith about 14 years ago. {DOLR 27 Old 365}

SMITH, JOHN, of Charles County, aet. 81, dep. Jun 20, 1765. {CHLR P#3:272} Aet. 90, dep. Jun 8, 1772, mentioned his father Jordan Smith and stated that he owned *St. Catherine's* about 50 years ago; also stated that Col. Hoskins who married the widow Mudd claimed part of said land as his wife's thirds. {CHLR U#3:15}

SMITH, JOHN, of Charles County, aet. 24, dep. Nov 2, 1752, mentioned his father William Smith. {CHLR B#3:211}

SMITH, JOHN, of Charles County, aet. 37, dep. Dec 13, 1757, mentioned his father Thomas Smith. {CHLR H#3:121} Aet. 44, dep. May 18, 1763. {CHLR M#3:220}

SMITH, JOHN (captain), of Prince George's County, gentleman, aet. 42, dep. Jun 6, 1751, stated that some time ago he married the relict of Gunder Erickson, deceased. {PGLR PP:152}
SMITH, JOHN, see "Henry Smith" and "William Prather," q.v.
SMITH, JORDAN, see "John Smith," q.v.
SMITH, NATHAN, see "John Belt," q.v.
SMITH, NATHANIEL, of Baltimore County, aet. 44, dep. Apr 8, 1772. {BALR AL#E:402}
SMITH, NICHOLAS, of Prince George's County, aet. 55, dep. Mar 28, 1741. {PGLR Y:267}
SMITH, NICHOLAS, of Kent County, aet. about 57, dep. Apr 3, 1759. {KEEJ - Thomas Harris folder}
SMITH, RICHARD, of Charles County, aet. 23, dep. Jul 2, 1661, stated that William Wennam told him he had laid with Anne Mardin once and he had no shoes and stockings to get married in, and he was also afraid he would be excommunicated by Mr. Fitzherbert. {CHLR A:142}
SMITH, RICHARD, of Charles County, aet. 43, dep. Jun 7, 1731. {CHLR Q#2:516} Aet. 49, dep. Jul 21, 1737. {CHLR T#2:390} Aet. 50, dep. Mar 11, 1737/8. {CHLR T#2:424} Aet. 54, dep. Jul 24, 1742. {CHLR O#2:425} Aet. 55, dep. May 7, 1744. {CHLR Y#2:16} Aet. 56, dep. Sep 24, 1744. {CHLR Y#2:18} Aet. 61, dep. Jul 31, 1749. {CHLR Z#2:247} Aet. 62, dep. Feb 19, 1750/1. {CHLR Z#2:143} Aet. 64, dep. Apr 28, 1753. {CHLR D#3:79} Aet. 65, dep. Apr 29, 1754. {CHLR D#3:324} Aet. 66, dep. Feb 15, 1755. {CHLR E#3:215} Aet. 70, dep. Sep 13, 1758. {CHLR K#3:94} Aet. 73, dep. Dec 21, 1761. {CHLR K#3:477} Aet. 73, dep. Jul 28, 1761. {CHLR K#3:307}
SMITH, RICHARD, of Charles County, aet. 36, dep. Jul 11, 1762, mentioned his father Richard Smith, deceased. {CHLR M#3:223}
SMITH, RICHARD, see "Anne Rawser" and "Owen Jones" and "Thomas Clagett" and "Edward William" and "James Johnson," q.v.
SMITH, ROBERT, see "Sarah Emory," q.v.
SMITH, ROSE, of St. Mary's County, aet. 42, dep. Nov 4, 1651, stated that Robert Holt told her last September that his wife (not named, but another deposition gave her name as Dorothy) had threatened to kill him. {ARMD 10:109-110}
SMITH, SAMUEL, see "John Spry" and "Thomas Brereton," q.v.
SMITH, SAMUELL, of Charles County, aet. 24, dep. Mar 10, 1658/9. {CHLR A:43}
SMITH, STEPHEN, of Dorchester County, aet. about 54, dep. between Nov 9, 1742 and Nov 5, 1743. {DOLR 12 Old 157} Aet. about 55, dep. between Nov 11, 1746 and Apr 14, 1748. {DOLR 14 Old 231}
SMITH, STEPHEN, of Dorchester County, aet. 59, dep. Aug 28, 1742. {DOLR 12 Old 125}
SMITH, STEPHEN, see "Ellinor Lewis," q.v.
SMITH, THELMA, of Anne Arundel County, aet. 45, dep. Oct 2, 1707, stated, on behalf of the people called Quakers, that she had heard Benjamin Scrivener and

his wife Grace say that they had sold their plantation to Thomas Tench. {AALR IH#3:77}
SMITH, THOMAS, of Charles County, aet. 31, dep. Mar 9, 1679/80. {CHLR H#1:271}
SMITH, THOMAS, of Dorchester County, aet. 59, dep. between Nov 8, 1743 and Jan 9, 1743/4. {DOLR 12 Old 143} Aet. about 60, dep. between Mar 12, 1744/5 and Nov 8, 1748, stated that he was shown the bounds of *Snake Point* about 32 years ago by Anthony Taylor, Sr. {DOLR 14 Old 317}
SMITH, THOMAS, of Kent County, aet. about 36, dep. Oct 8, 1684, mentioned mortgage dispute in Nov, 1683, between Major James Ringgold and the then Mrs. Anne Tovey (relict of Samuel Tovey, deceased), now Anne Joce [wife of Thomas Joce]. {ARMD 17:289-290} Aet. about 50, dep. Sep 28, 1706. {KELR C:202}
SMITH, THOMAS, see "Anthony Evans" and "John Lewis" and "James Cannon, Sr." and "Samuel Griffin" and "John Hodson" and "John Smith" and "John Salter," q.v.
SMITH, WILLIAM, of Charles County, aet. 42, dep. Feb 25, 1729/30 and Feb 25, 1730/1. {CHLR Q#2:364, 473} Aet. 43, dep. Oct 5, 1731. {CHLR R#2:44} Aet. 44, dep. Apr 10, 1732. {CHLR R#2:159} Aet. 50, dep. Aug 15, 1738. {CHLR T#2:519} Aet. 54, dep. May 22, 1742. {CHLR O#2:384} Aet. 56, dep. May 29, 1744. {CHLR Y#2:185} Aet. 57, dep. Jun 3, 1745 and Jul 3, 1745. {CHLR Z#2:345, 400}
SMITH, WILLIAM, of Charles County, aet. 17, dep. Jul 8, 1662. {CHLR A:220}
SMITH, WILLIAM, of Dorchester County, aet. 68, dep. Jul 12, 1748. {DOLR 14 Old 312}
SMITH, WILLIAM, of Dorchester County, aet. 37, dep. between Nov 9, 1756 and Nov 7, 1760. {DOLR 17 Old 213}
SMITH, WILLIAM, of Dorchester County, aet. about 45, dep. between Mar 15, 1727 and Jun 10, 1731, stated that the bounds of *Derby* on Blackwater and the land on Hockady Creek were shown to him by John Walker about 21 years ago. {DOLR 8 Old 430} Aet. about 67, dep. between Nov 12, 1751 and May 13, 1752. {DOLR 14 Old 604}
SMITH, WILLIAM, of Dorchester County, aet. about 43, dep. between 1706 and 1709. {DOLR 2 Old 153}
SMITH, WILLIAM, of Prince George's County, aet. 55, dep. Nov 18, 1748. {PGLR BB:697}
SMITH, WILLIAM, of London, England, gentleman, aet. 33, dep. Jul 27, 1697 at His Majesty's Court held in the Chamber of the Guild Hall in London, stated that he saw Stephen Longman sign two original deeds of lease and release, and Samuell Galloway, of West River, Anne Arundel County, Maryland, requested the previous deeds be re-recorded. {AALR WH#4:11-14}
SMITH, WILLIAM, see "John Smith" and "James Smith," q.v.
SMITHERS, WILLIAM, of Queen Anne's County, aet. over 68, dep. July, 1758. {QAEJ - Henry Callister folder}
SMITHSON, THOMAS, see "Francis Dean," q.v.

SMOOT, BARTON (captain), of Charles County, aet. 43, dep. Jun 7, 1731, mentioned his grandfather William Barton. {CHLR Q#2:516} Aet. 44, dep. Mar 3, 1731/2. {CHLR R#2:84}
SMOOT, BARTON, of Charles County, aet. 36, dep. Apr 3, 1747. {CHLR Z#2:82}
SMOOT, BARTON, see "Charles Smoot" and "Thomas Smoot, Jr.," q.v.
SMOOT, CHARLES, of Charles County, aet. 58, dep. Sep 20, 1758, mentioned his brother Barton Smoot. {CHLR H#3:488}
SMOOT, EDWARD, of Charles County, aet. 38, dep. Feb 22, 1762. {CHLR K#3:473}
SMOOT, THOMAS, of Charles County, aet. 69, dep. Nov 8, 1766, mentioned his grandfather William Barton. {CHLR P#3:278} Aet. 69, dep. Feb 5, 1767. {CHLR P#3:268}
SMOOT, THOMAS, JR., of Charles County, aet. 45, dep. Sep 26, 1752. {CHLR B#3:216} Aet. 58, dep. Nov 13, 1765. {CHLR N#3:788} Aet. 60, dep. May 5, 1767, mentioned his father Capt. Barton Smoot. {CHLR P#3:656}
SMOOT (SMOOTE), WILLIAM, of Charles County, aet. 63, dep. Sep 25, 1661. {CHLR A:158} See "Charles Rawlinson" and "Francis Morgan," q.v.
SMYTH, JOHN (doctor), of Queen Anne's County, n.a., dep. Apr, 1769, stated that he was chosen as guardian of Maurice Sliney in Apr, 1744. {QAEJ - James Hutchens folder}
SMYTH, RICHARD, see "Owen Jones," q.v.
SMYTHE, THOMAS, of Kent County, aet. 44, dep. 1775. {KELR DD#5:87}
SNELSON, JOHN, see "Lewis Griffith," q.v.
SNOW, MARY, of Dorchester County, aet. 38, dep. between Mar 14, 1769 and Apr 9, 1770, mentioned her grandmother Mary Cratcher and Secundus Hodson, both deceased. {DOLR 24 Old 9}
SOLLERS, ABARILLA, see "Samuel Sollers," q.v.
SOLLERS, SAMUEL, of Baltimore County, aet. 60, dep. Feb 22, 1773, mentioned his wife Abarilla Sollers. {BALR AL#G:447}
SOLLERS, THOMAS, of Baltimore County, aet. 40, dep. Jun 4, 1771. {BALR AL#C:600}
SOPER, CHARLES, of Prince George's County, aet. 51, dep. Oct 15, 1776. {PGLR CC#2:310-311}
SOPER, ROBERT, of Prince George's County, aet. 60, dep. Oct 2, 1769, mentioned Thomas James and Joseph Story about 40 years ago, both now deceased; also mentioned the widow (not named) of Jeremiah Berry. {PGLR AA#2:185}
SOUTHERLAND, ELIZABETH, of Charles County, aet. 48, dep. Mar 12, 1742/3, stated that Mary Bryan came into this province about 20 years ago and brought her son Thomas Bryan with her. {CHLR O#2:510}
SOUTHWELL, EDWARD, of Dorchester County, aet. 34, dep. between Nov 16, 1734 and Apr 10, 1735, mentioned the wife (not named) of Lamerock Flowers about 12 or 13 years ago. {DOLR 9 Old 436}

SOWARD, FRANCIS, of Dorchester County, aet. 23, dep. between Nov 8, 1743 and Dec 17, 1743, stated that his father John Seward (Soward) showed him the bounds of *Winfield's Trouble* about 8 or 9 years ago. {DOLR 12 Old 136}
SOWARD, FRANK, see "Edmond Brannock," q.v.
SOWARD, JOHN, see "Francis Soward" and "Richard Soward" and "John Seward" and "John Mitchel" and "William Byus" and "Robert Parkinson," q.v.
SOWARD, RICHARD, of Dorchester County, aet. 23, dep. between Nov 8, 1743 and Dec 17, 1743. {DOLR 12 Old 136} Aet. 51, dep. between Aug 10, 1762 and Oct 27, 1762, mentioned Levin Hill and his father Henry Hill, and his (Levin's) daughter Mary Hill. {DOLR 19 Old 88} Aet. 53, dep. between Aug 13, 1765 and Dec 21, 1765, mentioned his father (not named) and old Joseph Thomas. {DOLR 21 Old 447} Aet. 56, dep. between Apr 20, 1768 and May 27, 1768, mentioned his brother John Soward about 30 years ago. {DOLR 22 Old 423} Aet. 57, dep. between Mar 8, 1768 and Jul 23, 1768, mentioned his father John Soward about 30 years ago. {DOLR 23 Old 5} Aet. 61, dep. between Aug 11, 1772 and Dec 11, 1772, mentioned Levin Hill, his father Henry Hill, and his (Henry's) two daughters (not named). {DOLR 27 Old 352} See "Thomas Soward" and "Gilbert North," q.v.
SOWARD, THOMAS, of Dorchester County, aet. 30, dep. between Aug 11, 1754 and Mar 15, 1755, mentioned his brother Richard Soward, widow Brawhawn, and John Stevens, grandfather of the present John Stevens. {DOLR 15 Old 247} See "Edmond Brannock," q.v.
SOWELL, JAMES, see "George Farmer," q.v.
SPARK, JOSEPH, see "Thomas Butler," q.v.
SPARKES, THOMAS, of Talbot County, n.a., dep. Sep 19, 1671, mentioned his master Dr. Richard Tilghman. {ARMD 54:508-509}
SPARROW, SOLOMON, of Anne Arundel County, n.a., dep. Aug 16, 1692. {ARMD 8:349}
SPEAKE, BOWLING, of Charles County, aet. 52, dep. Oct 17, 1727. {CHLR P#2:405} Aet. 62, dep. Jan 10, 1736/7. {CHLR T#2:292} Aet. 64, dep. Mar 29, 1738. {CHLR T#2:463} Aet. 72, dep. May 23, 1745. {CHLR Z#2:342} Aet. 77, dep. Sep 18, 1752. {CHLR B#3:346} Aet. 80, dep. Jan 16, 1753. {CHLR B#3:348} Aet. 81, dep. Aug 11, 1755. {CHLR E#3:501}
SPEAKE, JOHN, of Charles County, aet. 66, dep. Apr 29, 1729. {CHLR Q#2:275}
SPEAKE, JOHN, of Charles County, aet. 62, dep. Feb 23, 1774. {CHLR W#3:83}
SPEAKE, MARY, of Charles County, aet. 70, dep. Nov 11, 1745, mentioned her father Robert Goodrick. {CHLR Z#2:468}
SPEAKE, RICHARD, of Charles County, aet. 40, dep. Aug 15, 1738. {CHLR T#2:514}
SPEAKE, WILLIAM, of Charles County, aet. 51, dep. Sep 29, 1772, mentioned old William Godfrey died about 15 or 16 years ago. {CHLR U#3:266}
SPENCE, MARY, of Charles County, aet. 46, dep. Jun 13, 1726. {CHLR P#2:242}
SPENCER, COLONEL, see "Indian Sachennaws," q.v.

SPENCER, WILLIAM, of Dorchester County, aet. 47, dep. between Nov 10, 1732 and Jan 20, 1732/3, mentioned John Taylor, surveyor, about 26 years ago, and his father William Spencer and Thomas Turner about 28 years ago. {DOLR 9 Old 158} See "John Sulivane" and "John Nicolls" and "Andrew Gray" and "Edward Dean" and "Francis Dean" and "Joseph Bland," q.v.

SPICER, ELIZABETH, see "Daniell Johnson" and "John Piper," q.v.

SPICER, HANIBALL, see "Daniell Johnson" and "John Piper," q.v.

SPICER, JOHN, see "John Rumbly, Sr." and "Bartholomew Gibbs," q.v.

SPICER, THOMAS, of Dorchester County, aet. 45, dep. Aug 10, 1742. {DOLR 12 Old 98} Aet. 60, dep. between Aug 12, 1760 and Mar 2, 1761. {DOLR 17 Old 262}

SPORNE, NICHOLAS, of Anne Arundel County, n.a., dep. Mar 30, 1707. {CMSP 1:8}

SPOTSWOOD, ALEXANDER, see "Thomas Walker," q.v.

SPRIGG, EDWARD (colonel), of Prince George's County, aet. 50, dep. Mar 21, 1747/8. {PGLR BB:466} Aet. 52, dep. Jan 26, 1748/9, mentioned Robert Tyler about 28 or 30 years ago. {PGLR BB:629} Aet. 53, dep. Sep 17, 1750, mentioned Philip Gittings about 30 years ago. {PGLR:88} See "Joseph Brown" and "John Cooke," q.v.

SPRIGG, OSBORN, see "John Cooke," q.v.

SPRY, FRANCIS, of Queen Anne's County, aet. over 43, dep. July, 1758. {QAEJ - Henry Callister (vs. Wooleston) folder}

SPRY, JOHN, of Anne Arundel County, n.a., dep. Apr 7, 1707, mentioned a trip over the bay to Somerset County and back to South River and Richard Clarke, Thomas Wintersell and wife (not named), and Samuel Smith on Potowmack Point. {ARMD 27:114-115}

SPRY, THOMAS, of Talbot County, aet. about 50, dep. Sep, 1740, and aet. about 56, dep. Aug. 1743. {TAEJ - John Reynolds folders}

STACY, SIMON, of St. Mary's County, n.a., dep. Jul 21, 1681. {ARMD 15:393}

STAFFORD (SAFFORD), JOHN, of Dorchester County, aet. 60, dep. between Jun 14, 1743 and Aug 4, 1743. {DOLR 12 Old 164} See "Richard Woodland," q.v.

STAFFORD, RICHARD, of Charles County, aet. 45, dep. Nov 4, 1746. {CHLR P#2:401}

STAINTON, CHARLES, see "Jemima Stainton," q.v.

STAINTON, JEMIMA, of Dorchester County, aet. 27, dep. between Mar 14, 1769 and Apr 9, 1770, mentioned her husband Charles Stainton (Stanton), her grandmother Frances Hackett, Thomas Stainton (father of said Charles Stainton), Oliver Hackett (husband of said Frances Hackett), and Mary Cratcher (a reputed sister of said Frances Hackett). {DOLR 24 Old 9}

STAINTON, THOMAS, see "Jemima Stainton" and "Spencer Martrum Waters," q.v.

STANDFORD (STANFORD), CHARLES, of Dorchester County, aet. about 41, dep. between Mar 15, 1727 and Jun 10, 1731. {DOLR 8 Old 430} Charles Stanford, aet. about 48, dep. between Nov 16, 1734 and Apr 10, 1735. {DOLR

9 Old 436} Aet. 53, dep. Aug 24, 1741. {DOLR 12 Old 133} Charles Stanford, aet. 50 and upwards, dep. Jul 10, 1744, mentioned his brother John Stanford and stated that their father (not named) dwelt upon land called *Weston* that belonged to John Stevens (where Francis Bullock of Talbot County, had formerly dwelt) and he frequently passed over Blackwater River from his father's to a place called *Bear Garden* and the landing used was known as Hay Stack Landing. {DOLR 12 Old 150}

STANDFORD, CHARLES, of Kent County on Delaware, late of Dorchester County, aet. about 55, dep. between Nov 14, 1769 and Nov 6, 1770, mentioned his father Charles Standford about 20 years ago. {DOLR 24 Old 308}

STANDIFOR, SAMUEL, of Baltimore County, aet. 30, dep. between Apr 11, 1704 and Aug 4, 1704. {BALR HW#2:367}

STANDIFORD, JOHN, see "Skelton Standiford," q.v.

STANDIFORD, SKELTON, of Baltimore County, aet. 70, dep. May 10, 1771, mentioned his brother John Standiford. {BALR AL#C:604}

STANFORD, JOHN, see "Charles Standford" and "William Stanford," q.v.

STANFORD, WILLIAM, of Dorchester County, aet. 46, dep. Aug 24, 1741, mentioned his brother John Stanford. {DOLR 12 Old 133}

STANLY, JOHN, of Anne Arundel County, n.a., dep. 1696. {ARMD 20:563}

STANNAWAY, JOSEPH, see "Walter MacDaniel," q.v.

STANSBURY, DIXON, of Baltimore County, aet. 30, dep. May 10, 1771. {BALR AL#C:604}

STANSBURY, HONOUR, see "Nathan Bowen," q.v.

STANSBURY, THOMAS, of Baltimore County, aet. 50, dep. Jun 6, 1763. {BALR B#N:187}

STAPLEFORD, CHARLES, see "Samuel Harper," q.v.

STAPLEFORD, GEORGE, of Dorchester County, aet. 55, son of Raymond Stapleford, dep. between May 6, 1726 and Aug 14, 1727. {DOLR 8 Old 227} George Staplefort, aet. 57, dep. Oct 31, 1729. {DOLR 12 Old 149} George Stapleford, aet. 60, dep. between Nov 19, 1732 and May 10, 1732. {DOLR 9 Old 64} Aet. 64, dep. between Jun 16, 1735 and Dec 16, 1735, mentioned Samuel Millington about 40 years ago and his (Stapleford's) father (not named) owned *Keene's Rest* adjoining Millington; also mentioned Henry Gutrige, servant to his father, about 50 years ago; also stated that the bounds of *All Three of Us* were shown to him by John Bramble and John Lee about 50 years ago. {DOLR 9 Old 335} Aet. 70, dep. between Aug 14, 1744 and Sep 22, 1744. {DOLR 12 Old 92} See "Edward Nooner" and "Samuel Harper," q.v.

STAPLEFORD, RAYMOND, see "George Stapleford" and "Elleanor Tubman," q.v.

STAPLEFORT, ROBERT, of Dorchester County, aet. 50, dep. Feb 26, 1772. {DOLR 25 Old 459}

STARTON, GEORGE, of Kent County, n.a., dep. Oct 8, 1681. {ARMD 17:62}

STAVELY, JAMES, see "Michael Miller" and "William Comegys" and "John Greenwood," q.v.

STAVELY, JOHN, of St. Mary's County, n.a., dep. Jun 22, 1681. {ARMD 15:370} See "John Greenwood," q.v.

STEED, PETER, of Frederick County, n.a., dep. Dec 2, 1765. {ARMD 32:155-156}

STEEL, ALEXANDER, of Charles County, aet. 20, dep. Aug 2, 1774. {CHLR W#3:388}

STEEL, THOMAS, of Baltimore County, n.a., dep. Oct 11, 1763. {BALR B#N:64}

STEPHENS, EDWARD, of Dorchester County, aet. 19, dep. between Nov 8, 1748 and Mar 15, 1748/9, mentioned his father William Stephens, John Stephens, and Thomas Cook about 5 years ago. {DOLR 14 Old 319}

STEPHENS, EDWARD, of Prince George's County, aet. 65, dep. May 26, 1756. {PGLR NN:467} Aet. 70, dep. Jan 21, 1760, stated that he was a chain carrier on *Elizabeth Manor* about 30 or 40 years ago; also mentioned Col. John Fendall. {PGLR RR:38} Aet. 70, dep. Oct 4, 1762. {PGLR RR:262} Aet. 73, dep. Sep 12, 1761, stated that he has known this area for about 50 years. {PGLR RR:180}

STEPHENS, JOHN, see "Edward Stephens," q.v.

STEPHENS, WILLIAM, see "Edward Stephens," q.v.

STEVENS, BILLINDER, of Dorchester County, aet. 49, dep. between Mar 14, 1771 and Nov 13, 1771, mentioned her father Thomas Hackett about 25 or 26 years ago. {DOLR 25 Old 238}

STEVENS, EDWARD, see "William Stevens," q.v.

STEVENS, JOHN, of the North East Fork, Dorchester County, aet. 40 or upwards, dep. between Mar 14, 1771 and Nov 13, 1771, mentioned John Reed, a young boy, and son of John Reed the Elder, about 30 years ago. {DOLR 25 Old 238}

STEVENS, JOHN, of Dorchester County, aet. about 58, dep. between Mar 15, 1727 and Jun 10, 1731. {DOLR 8 Old 430} John Stevens, Sr., aet. about 70, dep. between Aug 12, 1740 and Sep 13, 1740, stated that he was shown the bounds of *Daniel's Choice* by John Winsmore about 40 years ago. {DOLR 12 Old 116} John Stevens, aet. about 72, dep. between Nov 10, 1741 and Mar 10, 1747, stated that land called *Clift* belonged to his grandfather (not named). {DOLR 14 Old 200}

STEVENS, JOHN, see "Charles Standford" and "Thomas Soward" and "James Woolford" and "John Hodson, Sr.," q.v.

STEVENS, MAGDALEN, see "Thomas Stevens," q.v.

STEVENS, THOMAS, of Talbot County, Quaker, n.a., dep. Apr 15, 1762, stated that he had met Daniel Maud about 1732 in London at the home of Daniel Maud the Elder, a merchant, and Magdalen (Stevens) Maud his wife, they being the parents of the said Daniel Maud the Younger. {DOLR 18 Old 178}

STEVENS, WALTER, of Dorchester County, aet. about 58, dep. between Nov 14, 1758 and Jun 30, 1759. {DOLR 16 Old 220} See "James Edgell," q.v.

STEVENS, WILLIAM, of Dorchester County, aet. 65, dep. between Nov 16, 1734 and Apr 10, 1735, stated that Vinson's Branch was so named for 47 years past because John Vinson lived by it. {DOLR 9 Old 436}

STEVENS, WILLIAM, of Prince George's County, aet. 53, dep. Oct 23, 1770. {PGLR AA#2:497} Aet. 54, dep. Mar 12, 1772, mentioned his father Edward Stevens, deceased. {PGLR AA#2:498}

STEVENS, WILLIAM, see "Peter Webb" and "John Hodson, Sr.," q.v.

STEVENSON, EDWARD, see "Richard Taylor," q.v.

STEVENSON, HENRY, see "Richard Taylor," q.v.

STEVENSON, RICHARD KING, of Baltimore County, aet. 50, dep. Nov 2, 1762. {BALR B#L:201}

STEWARD, JOHN, see "Robert Whitnal," q.v.

STEWART, DANIEL, of Charles County, aet. 58, dep. Apr 20, 1736. {CHLR T#2:197} Aet. 66, dep. May 14, 1744, stated that he was a servant to Mary Mitchell about 40 years ago. {CHLR Z#2:14} Aet. 85, dep. Jul 5, 1762. {CHLR M#3:217}

STEWART, JOHN, of Dorchester County, aet. 38, dep. between Jun 9, 1761 and Sep 8, 1761, stated that his father John Stewart, now deceased, was employed by the Great Choptank Parish about 14 or 15 years ago. {DOLR 18 Old 14} Aet. 41, dep. between Nov 8, 1763 and Apr 7, 1764. {DOLR 19 Old 233} See "Henry Ennalls" and "James Wallace," q.v.

STEWART, MARY, of Charles County, aet. 73 or 74, dep. Aug 6, 1761. {CHLR K#3:310}

STIMSON, SOLOMON, see "Thomas Charter," q.v.

STIMSON, THOMAS, of Prince George's County, planter, aet. 75, dep. Mar 18 and 19, 1728/9, mentioned Edward Lewis, deceased. {PGLR M:480}

STINCHCOMB, JOHN, of Baltimore County, aet. 77, dep. Jan 15, 1766, mentioned his brother-in-law Emanuel Teal. {BALR B#P:83}

STINCHICUM, NATHANIEL, prob. of Anne Arundel County, n.a., dep. Feb 21, 1704/5. {ARMD 25:185}

STITH, HENRY, see "Samuel Guitchard," q.v.

STOAKS, PETER, see "Habell Graham" and "Peter Stokes," q.v.

STOCKETT, FRANCIS, prob. of Anne Arundel County, aet. 31, dep. Oct 11, 1665, stated that he had dressed the wounds given by Negro Jacob on Mrs. Mary Utie and he believed she died of those wounds. {ARMD 49:490} See "Anthony Brispo," q.v.

STODDERT (STODDART), JAMES, of Prince George's County, aet. 57, dep. Feb 23, 1724/5. {PGLR I:626} Aet. 58, dep. Aug 9, 1725. {PGLR I:677} See "John Banks," q.v.

STOGDON, MICHAEL, see "James Langrall," q.v.

STOKES, PETER, of Dorchester County, aet. 56, dep. Jul 20, 1747. {DOLR 14 Old 182} Peter Stoaks, aet. 70, dep. between Mar 8, 1757 and Apr 29, 1757, stated that he was shown the bounds of *Ayes Addition* by Henry Trippe, son of Henry, about 30 years ago. {DOLR 15 Old 477} See "William Stokes" and "Ann Trego," q.v.

STOKES, WILLIAM, of Dorchester County, aet. 50, dep. May 12, 1744, state that he was shown the bounds of *Mulgrave* in Fishing Creek Hundred when he was about 10 years of age by his father Peter Stokes and Cathrine Jones who proposed whipping him (William) to make him remember the place, but he immediately ran past some Indian cabins to the main road and escaped. {DOLR 12 Old 145} Aet. 57, dep. Sep 11, 1749, stated that his father Peter Stokes married for his second wife Anne Mason, widow of Miles Mason, and that said Miles Mason left one young child named Sarah Mason who was brought up in said Peter Stokes' house and was later married to Thomas Shehawne by William Mishie, a magistrate. {DOLR 14 Old 375}

STONE, EDWARD, of Charles County, aet. 83, dep. Nov 1, 1762. {CHLR M#3:61}

STONE, EDWARD, of Charles County, aet. 33, dep. between Oct 1, 1772 and Nov 2, 1772, mentioned his father Edward Stone, deceased. {CHLR U#3:263}

STONE, EDWARDS, see "John Stone" and "Edward Dean," q.v.

STONE, JOHN, of Charles County, aet. 55, dep. Mar 21, 1769, mentioned his father Matthew Stone. {CHLR Q#3:440A}

STONE, JOHN, of Charles County, aet. 43, dep. between Oct 1, 1772 and Nov 2, 1772, mentioned his father Edward Stone. {CHLR U#3:263} Aet. 48, dep. Feb 23, 1774. {CHLR W#3:82}

STONE, JOHN, see "Edward Dean," q.v.

STONE, MATTHEW, of Charles County, aet. 49, dep. Feb 14, 1728. {CHLR T#2:538} Aet. 55, dep. Oct 19, 1734. {CHLR R#2:537} Aet. 64, dep. Jul 3, 1745. {CHLR Z#2:401} See "John Stone," q.v.

STONE, RICHARD, of Charles County, aet. 18, dep. Jun 6, 1660. {CHLR A:94} Aet. not given, dep. Jul 27, 1663, mentioned his father and mother (not named) when he was a child. {CHLR B:136} Aet. not given, dep. Jul 12, 1664, mentioned his brother Thomas Stone. {CHLR B:329}

STONE, THOMAS, of Charles County, aet. 47, dep. Sep 12, 1743. {CHLR O#2:667} Aet. 48, dep. Aug 5, 1745. {CHLR Z#2:398} Aet. 64, dep. Dec 15, 1760, mentioned his father William Stone. {CHLR K#3:149} Aet. 73, dep. Mar 21, 1769. {CHLR Q#3:409A} See "Richard Stone" and "Edward Dean," q.v.

STONE, WILLIAM, see "David Davis" and "Thomas Stone" and "Richard Wade," q.v.

STONE, WILLIAM, of Charles County, aet. 42, dep. between Nov 8, 1774 and Feb 7, 1775. {CHLR W#3:610}

STONE, WILLIAM, of Charles County, aet. 37, dep. May 2, 1727. {CHLR P#2:488}

STONE, WILLIAM, SR., of Charles County, aet. 60, dep. Oct 28, 1726. {CHLR P#2:403} Aet. 61, dep. Jul 23, 1728. {CHLR Q#2:166}

STONESTREET, BUTLER, of Charles County, aet. 50, dep. May 4, 1765. {CHLR N#3:382}

STONESTREET, EDWARD, of Prince George's County, aet. 50, dep. Apr 23, 1754. {PGLR NN:253} Aet. 53, dep. Aug 22, 1757. {PGLR PP:62, pt. 2}
STONESTREET, EDWARD, of Charles County, aet. 67, dep. Sep 23, 1741. {CHLR O#2:288}
STONESTREET, EDWARD, see "William Simpson," q.v.
STONESTREET, THOMAS, of Charles County, aet. 48, dep. Jun 22, 1731, mentioned his father Thomas Stonestreet, deceased. {CHLR R#2:4}
STONESTREET, THOMAS, of Prince George's County, aet. 49, dep. Jun 15, 1731. {PGLR Q:297} Aet. 57, dep. Nov 24, 1740. {PGLR Y:237} Aet. 78, dep. Sep 21, 1761, stated that he has known this area for about 50 to 60 years. {PGLR RR:227} Aet. 81, dep. Nov 5, 1763. {PGLR TT:285}
STOOKES, WILLIAM, of Dorchester County, aet. 60, dep. between Mar 8, 1757 and Apr 23, 1757. {DOLR 15 Old 478}
STORM, VANDEL, of Frederick County, aet. 58, dep. 1767. {FRLR L:60}
STORY, JOSEPH, see "Robert Soper" and "James Lucas," q.v.
STORY, WALTER, of Charles County, n.a., dep. Mar 13, 1665/6, mentioned Brigit Heard, deceased [wife of William Heard]. {ARMD 53:622}
STORY, WALTER (colonel), of Charles County, aet. 58, dep. Dec 21, 1725. {CHLR P#2:141}
STRAND, ABRAHAM, see "Bartholomew Hendrickson" and "Andrew Peterson" and "Alexander Shresse," q.v.
STRATTON, LUCIE, of Charles County, n.a., dep. Jun 4, 1658, stated she was sold by Edward Bouls to Arthur Turner to serve her term as a servant, which time has been fulfilled and she demands her corn and clothes. {CHLR A:7} See "John Ashbrooke" and "John Hatch" and "Christopher Russell" and "Edward William" and "Anne Gey" and "Walter Ges" and "Margaret Pearce" and "Robert Wilson," q.v.
STRAWBRIDGE, JOHN, of Anne Arundel County, n.a., dep. 1696. {ARMD 20:530}
STREET, FRANCIS, of Prince George's County, aet. 41, dep. Dec 10, 1764. {PGLR TT:366}
STRINGER, SAMUEL, see "William Farquhar," q.v.
STROMAT, JOHN, of Charles County, aet. 47, dep. Jan 11, 1757. {CHLR F#3:467}
STUART, GEORGE (doctor), of Prince George's County, n.a., dep. Nov 18, 1748. {PGLR BB:697}
STUMP, THOMAS, see "James Moore," q.v.
STUT, WILLIAM, of Charles County, aet. 43, dep. Jul 6, 1662. {CHLR A:219}
STYLES, SAMUEL, of Calvert County, n.a., servant to Richard Preston, Sr., dep. Mar 31, 1663. {ARMD 49:9-10}
STYLES, WILLIAM, see "Joane Warre," q.v.
STYLS, HENRY, of Cecil County, n.a., dep. Jul 8, 1723, stated that John Crowman, tailor, of Cecil County, died about 2 o'clock last Saturday afternoon at the home of the widow Bayard; on Jul 5th Crowman stated he wanted Adam

Lytner to have his clothes; he died and was buried on Bayard's plantation on Jul 7th. {CELR 4:20}

SUIT, MARY, of Charles County, aet. 37, dep. Sep 24, 1764, mentioned her father Samuel Johnson, deceased. {CHLR N#3:63}

SULIVANE, DANAIR, of Dorchester County, aet. 45, dep. between Mar 14, 1769 and Apr 9, 1770, mentioned her parents, Samuel and Mary Cratcher, both deceased. {DOLR 24 Old 9}

SULIVANE, DANIEL, of Dorchester County, aet. about 50, dep. between Mar 8, 1757 and Dec 17, 1757, stated that he was shown the bounds of *Melvill's Meadow* about 13 or 14 years ago by John Rix, now deceased. {DOLR 16 Old 170} Daniel Sulivane, Esq., aet. about 63, dep. between Nov 13, 1770 and Aug 2, 1771, mentioned Rice Willis of Kent County on Delaware now said to be deceased. {DOLR 25 Old 26} See "James Muir," q.v.

SULIVANE, FLORANCE, of Dorchester County, aet. about 44, dep. between Jun 9, 1741 and Nov 2, 1741. {DOLR 12 Old 94} Flowrence Sulivane, aet. about 49, dep. between Nov 12, 1745 and Nov 11, 1747, mentioned James Vaulx, of Dorchester County, deceased, about 2 or 3 years ago. {DOLR 14 Old 173} Florence Sulivane, aet. about 62, dep. between Jun 8, 1756 and Jul 13, 1758. {DOLR 16 Old 117}

SULIVANE, JOHN, of Dorchester County, aet. about 40, dep. between Nov 12, 1745 and Nov 11, 1747, mentioned William Spencer, now deceased, about 20 years ago. {DOLR 14 Old 173} Aet. about 55, dep. between Mar 10, 1761 and Mar 11, 1762, mentioned Peter Taylor and William Edmondson about 30 years ago, both now deceased. {DOLR 18 Old 139} Aet. about 63, dep. Mar 25, 1769. {DOLR 23 Old 347} Aet. about 65, dep. between Nov 14, 1769 and Nov 6, 1770. {DOLR 24 Old 308} Aet. about 66, dep. between Nov 13, 1770 and Aug 2, 1771. {DOLR 25 Old 26} See "Richard Webster," q.v.

SULLIVANE, DENNIS, see "John Wetherington," q.v.

SULLIVANT, RICHARD, of Kent County, aet. 25, dep. Feb 27, 1741, stated that he saw William Turner, who had escaped from Dover goal, at the house of Richard Cooper in Dorchester County; also mentioned Mary Munt, housekeeper for said Cooper. {DOLR 12 Old 236}

SUMAN, PETER, of Frederick County, aet. 35, dep. 1767. {FRLR L:60}

SUMMERS, JOHN, of Charles County, aet. 30, dep. Sep 9, 1747. {CHLR Z#2:186}

SUMMERS, JOHN, of Charles County, aet. 32, dep. Oct 15, 1742. {CHLR O#2:662} Aet. 61, dep. Nov 8, 1766. {CHLR P#3:276} Aet. 62, dep. Jun 4, 1771. {CHLR T#3:600}

SURAT, JOSEPH, of Prince George's County, aet. 70 or thereabouts, planter, dep. Mar 27, 1770, stated that Thomas Jacoe was servant to Thomas Swann about 30 years ago. {PGLR AA#2:194}

SUTE, NATHANIEL, of Charles County, aet. 66, dep. Jan 22, 1744/5. {CHLR Z#2:344}

SUTHELE, WILLIAM, of Dorchester County, aet. 40, dep. between Mar 18, 1726 and Jul 18, 1727. {DOLR 8 Old 201}
SUTTON, CHRISTOPHER, see "William Fitch," q.v.
SUTTON, JOSEPH, of Baltimore County, aet. 46, dep. Sep 20, 1767, mentioned Joseph Thomas and wife Dorcas (or Darckis) Thomas when he (deponent) was a boy about 30 years ago on Back River Neck. {BALR AL#A:124-125}
SUTTON, SAMUEL, of Baltimore County, aet. 38, dep. Dec 19, 1769. {BALR AL#A:737}
SUTTON, THOMAS, see "William Fitch," q.v.
SWANN, EDWARD, of Prince George's County, aet. 37, dep. Aug 25, 1737. {PGLR T:505} See "Samuel Swann," q.v.
SWANN, JAMES, of Charles County, aet. 52, dep. Jan 8, 1742/3. {CHLR O#2:508}
SWANN, SAMUEL, of Charles County, aet. 55, dep. Jul 22, 1731. {CHLR R#2:4}
SWANN (SWAN), SAMUEL, of Prince George's County, aet. 45, dep. Feb 18, 1771, mentioned Edward Swan, Sr. {PGLR AA#2:226-227}
SWANN (SWAN), THOMAS, JR., of Prince George's County, aet. 31, dep. Aug 25, 1737. {PGLR T:504}
SWANN (SWAN), THOMAS, SR., of Prince George's County, aet. 63, dep. Aug 25, 1737. {PGLR T:506} Thomas Swan, aet. 65, dep. Jul 1, 1738. {PGLR T:607} Thomas Swann, aet. 78, dep. Feb 22, 1753. {PGLR NN:175} Thomas Swann, Sr., aet. 80 or thereabouts, dep. Mar 15, 1756. {PGLR NN:433} See "Joseph Surat" and "William Bright" and "George Magruder," q.v.
SWEARINGEN, JOHN, of Frederick County, aet. 83, dep. Jun 8, 1776, stated that some time past Thomas Thompson showed him the bounds of William Beckwith's land. {FRLR BD#2:375-376} See "Van Swearingen," q.v.
SWEARINGEN, VAN, of Frederick County, aet. 76, dep. Apr 25, 1767, stated that he was with Peter Dent, then Deputy Surveyor of Prince George's County, in 1732 or 1733. {FRLR K:1139}
SWEARINGEN, VAN, of Frederick County, aet. 29, dep. Jun 8, 1776, mentioned his father John Swearingen. {FRLR BD#2:376}
SWEATMAN, JOSHUA, of Cecil County, n.a., dep. Sep 3, 1703. {CELR 1:434}
SWEATNAM, ELIZABETH, see "Rebecca Brooks," q.v.
SWEATNAM, WILLIAM, see "John Sweet," q.v.
SWEET, JOHN, of Queen Anne's County, aet. about 70, dep. Mar 15, 1760, mentioned his cousin William Sweatnam. {QAEJ - Richard Tilghman Earle folder}
SWIFT, JOHN, of Queen Anne's County, aet. about 69, dep. between Nov 10, 1741 and Feb 16, 1742, stated that he was shown the bounds of Phil Lynes' land called *Lynes's Park* by William Boon about 36 years ago. {DOLR 14 Old 54}
SWIFT, RALPH, of Talbot County, aet. about 53, dep. Apr, 1731. {TAEJ - Michael Fletcher folder}
SWIGGET (SWIGOTT), HENRY, of Talbot or Dorchester County, n.a., dep. Dec 17, 1670. {ARMD 51:348} See "Edward Hide," q.v.

SWINEHART, GEORGE(?), of Frederick County, aet. 39, dep. Jul 24, 1762. {FRLR H:101}

SYLLAVANE, MARY (Mrs.), of Charles County, aet. 57, dep. Jul 12, 1743, mentioned the brothers Anthony Neale and James Neale about 30 years ago. {CHLR O#2:663}

SYMMS (SIMMS), ANN, of Dorchester County, aet. 50 and upwards, dep. between Nov 14, 1758 and Jun 30, 1759. {DOLR 16 Old 220}

SYMOND, CHARLES, of Baltimore County, aet. 67, dep. Nov 12, 1736, stated that Thomas Richardson, son of Lawrance and Ann Richardson, deceased, was born in Nov, 1697. {BALR IS#IK}

SYMPSON, GILBERT, of Charles County, aet. 66, dep. Jul 1, 1765. {CHLR N#3:785}

SYMPSON, JAMES, of Charles County, aet. 45, dep. May 21, 1725. {CHLR P#2:38} Aet. 52, dep. Oct 5, 1732. {CHLR R#2:240} Aet. 56, dep. Apr 5, 1733. {CHLR R#2:332}

SYMPSON, JULIANA, of Charles County, aet. 63, dep. Nov 11, 1745, mentioned her father Robert Goodrick and her former husband Robert Price. {CHLR Z#2:469}

SYMPSON, THOMAS, of Charles County, aet. 64, dep. May 17, 1725. {CHLR P#2:36} Aet. 68, dep. Feb 24, 1728. {CHLR Q#2:346} Aet. 78, dep. Jan 11, 1736/7. {CHLR T#2:297}

SYMPSON, THOMAS, JR., of Charles County, aet. 42, dep. Jan 11, 1736/7. {CHLR T#2:297} Aet. 43, dep. Jul 19, 1737. {CHLR T#2:371}

TAHEY, JOHN, of Prince George's County, aet. 60, dep. Jul 3, 1754. {PGLR NN:284}

TAILOR, SAMUEL, see "Edward Thomson," q.v.

TALBURT (TALBERT), BENJAMIN, of Prince George's County, aet. 36, dep. Feb 16, 1745/6, mentioned his father John Talbert and Dr. John Norris, both deceased. {PGLR BB:2-3} Benjamin Taulburt, aet. 38, dep. Feb 2, 1747/8. {PGLR BB:417} Benjamin Talburt, aet. 49, dep. Apr 14, 1759. {PGLR PP:314, pt. 2}

TALBURT (TAULBURT), JOHN, see "Benjamin Talburt," q.v.

TALBOTT, JOHN, of Prince George's County, aet. 64, dep. between Nov 11, 1729 and Mar 26, 1730, mentioned old Thomas Locker some 30 years ago, now deceased. {PGLR M:556}

TALBOTT (TALBOT), JOHN, of Baltimore County, Quaker, aet. 51, dep. Aug 15, 1774. {BALR AL#L:242}

TALBOTT (TALBOT), MARGARET, of Baltimore County, Quaker, aet. 48, dep. Aug 15, 1774. {BALR AL#L:241}

TALBOTT, PAUL, of Prince George's County, aet. 52, dep. Jun 22, 1752. {PGLR NN:38}

TALFORD, WILLIAM, of Charles County, aet. 52, dep. Jul 11, 1772. {CHLR U#3:165}

TALL, DANIEL, of Dorchester County, aet. 44, dep. between Aug 10, 1773 and Oct 23, 1773. {DOLR 27 Old 38}

TALL, PHILLIP, of Dorchester County, aet. 39, dep. between Mar 13, 1738/9 and Nov 12, 1739, stated that he was shown the bounds of *Cherry Point* by John Hill about 30 years ago and later by Richard Hill and William Hill, Sr. {DOLR 12 Old 119}

TANCKS (TUNCKS), WILLIAM, of St. Mary's County, aet. 30, dep. Dec 24, 1665. {ARMD 49:541}

TANNEHILL, NINIAN, of Prince George's County, aet. 64, dep. Jun 21, 1756. {PGLR PP:15, pt. 2}

TANNEHILL, NINIAN, JR., see "John Adamson," q.v.

TANNEHILL (TANNAHILL), NINIAN, SR., of Frederick County, aet. 73, dep. Aug 5, 1765, mentioned Thomas Allison and John Allison about 37 years ago. {FRLR K:1350} See "John Adamson" and "Rebecca Beall" and "Ninian Tanyhill," q.v.

TANNEHILL, REBECCA, see "John Adamson" and "Rebecca Beall," q.v.

TANNER, HENRY, of Charles County, aet. 55, dep. Jun 19, 1713, stated that William Glover was the sole son of Giles and Elizabeth Glover and said Elizabeth later married Kenelm MacLoughlin; also stated that Francis Meek married a sister of William Glover and Mary Meek, former wife of Francis, married Richard Wade. {Chancery Court Records LP#3:15}

TANNER, HENRY, of Charles County, aet. 87, dep. May 29, 1725. {CHLR P#2:41} Aet. 89, dep. Feb 14, 1728. {CHLR T#2:538}

TANNER, HENRY, of Charles County, aet. 70 odd years, dep. Aug 20, 1719, mentioned Mathew Dike about 34 years ago. {Charles County Land Commissions 1:50}

TANYHILL (TANNYHILL), JAMES, of Prince George's County, aet. 53, dep. Feb 15, 1759. {PGLR PP:281, pt. 2} James Tannyhill, n.a., dep. Mar 23, 1771. {PGLR AA#2:430}

TANYHILL (TANIHILL), JOHN, see "George Farmer" and "Henry Bayly" and "Hezekiah Bussey," q.v.

TANYHILL (TANNIHILL), NINIAN, of Prince George's County, aet. between 72 and 73, dep. Jul 26, 1765, mentioned his father William Tanyhill. {PGLR BB#2:16} See "Thomas Beanes (Beans)," q.v.

TANYHILL (TANIHILL), WALTER, of Prince George's County, aet. 76, dep. Jun 16, 1730. {PGLR Q:9}

TANYHILL (TANIHILL), WILLIAM, of Prince George's County, aet. 73, dep. May 20, 1725. {PGLR I:677} William Tanihill (Tannihill), aet. 70, dep. Aug 27, 1730 and Sep 29, 1731. {PGLR Q:15, 161, 396} See "Ninian Tanyhill," q.v.

TANZEY, EDWARD, of Frederick County, aet. 41, dep. Aug 21, 1776, mentioned William Thomas, Sr. about 7 years ago, now deceased. {FRLR BD#2:336-337}

TARLETON, JAMES, see "Emanuel Ratcliffe," q.v.

TARLIN, MARY, of Charles County, aet. 24, dep. Feb 11, 1662/3, stated that she was bitten by Arthur Turner's bitch. {CHLR B:90, ARMD 53:338}

TARLIN (TARLINE), RICHARD, of Charles County, aet. 23, dep. Oct 23, 1660. {CHLR A:108} Richard Tarlin, aet. 25, dep. Sep 24, 1661, mentioned his wife (not named); also stated that the hen and chickens of Goodie Michell died in a strange manner and they might have been bewitched. {CHLR A:153}

TATE, ----, see "Francis Dean," q.v.

TATE(?), THOMAS, of Queen Anne's County, aet. about 33, dep. Mar, 1746, mentioned his father (not named) when he (deponent) was 10 or 11 years old. {QAEJ - Benjamin Tasker folder}

TATTMAN, WILLIAM, of Cecil County, n.a., dep. Oct 31, 1727, mentioned the encroachment of Pennsylvanians on the lands of inhabitants on the border of this province. {ARMD 25:488}

TAYLARD, WILLIAM, of St. Mary's County, n.a., dep. Jul 22, 1698, mentioned John Cood, Sr., Gerrard Sly, Henry Denton (late Clerk of the Council, deceased), and Dr. Richard Jones (who attended Mr. Denton during his sickness). {ARMD 23:470}

TAYLOR, ANN, see "John Anderton," q.v.

TAYLOR, ANTHONY, SR., see "Thomas Smith" and "Elizabeth Taylor," q.v.

TAYLOR, BRAY PLAT, of Baltimore County, aet. 66, dep. Apr 6, 1773. {BALR AL#G:449}

TAYLOR, EDWARD, of Dorchester County, aet. 66, dep. between Aug 8, 1738 and Mar 9, 1738/9. {DOLR 11 Old 244} Aet. 67, dep. between Jun 12, 1739 and Aug 13, 1739. {DOLR 12 Old 91} Aet. 67, dep. Nov 12, 1739, mentioned his father Edward Taylor and stated that the bounds of *Cherry Point* were identified about 36 years ago by Thamzen Vicars, wife of John Vicars. {DOLR 12 Old 119} See "Godfrey Meddis" and Elizabeth Salsbury," q.v.

TAYLOR, ELIZABETH, of Dorchester County, aet. about 51, dep. between Nov 10, 1741 and Mar 10, 1747. {DOLR 14 Old 200} Aet. about 55, dep. between Mar 12, 1744 and Nov 8, 1748, mentioned Anthony Taylor, Sr. {DOLR 14 Old 317}

TAYLOR, FRANCES, see "John White," q.v.

TAYLOR, ISAAC, see "Samuel Brice" and "Charles Alleyn" and "Edward Lang" and "Daniel Smith," q.v.

TAYLOR, JAMES, of Charles County, aet. 42, dep. between Aug 11, 1765 and Nov 11, 1765, mentioned his father John Taylor. {CHLR N#3:790} Aet. 54, dep. Sep 29, 1775. {CHLR X#3:543}

TAYLOR, JAMES, of Prince George's County, aet. 27, dep. Nov 15, 1763. {PGLR TT:144}

TAYLOR, JANE, see "John White," q.v.

TAYLOR, JENNY, see "Francis Dean," q.v.

TAYLOR, JOHN, of Charles County, aet. 30, dep. Jul 16, 1728. {CHLR Q#2:168}

TAYLOR, JOHN, of Dorchester County, aet. 65, dep. between Aug 13, 1765 and Dec 21, 1765. {DOLR 21 Old 447} Aet. 65, dep. between Mar 8, 1768 and Jul 23, 1768, mentioned Joseph Thomas, father of the present Joseph Thomas, about the year 1727. {DOLR 23 Old 5} John Taylor, Sr., aet. 72, dep. between Nov 8,

1774 and Jan 5, 1775, stated that he was shown the bounds of *Snake Point* about 40 years ago by Jacob Mills. {DOLR 27 Old 431}

TAYLOR, JOHN, of Dorchester County, aet. 67, dep. between Mar 14, 1735 and May 17, 1736. {DOLR 9 Old 393}

TAYLOR, JOHN, see "William McCollister" and "Josiah Mace" and "Charles Thompson" and "James Pattison" and "William Spencer" and "Thomas Taylor" and "John White" and "John King" and "Heathcoat Pickett" and "James Taylor" and "Robert Baden" and "James Ranton," q.v.

TAYLOR, JOSEPH, of Baltimore County, aet. 60, dep. May 11, 1768. {BALR AL#B:594} Aet. 66, dep. Jun 8, 1772. {BALR AL#I:201} See "Richard Taylor," q.v.

TAYLOR, MARY, see "Mary Mitchel" and "Ann Johnson," q.v.

TAYLOR, PETER, of Dorchester County, aet. 52, dep. between Jun 11, 1732 and Jan 22, 1732/3, stated that he was shown the bounds of *Bath* about 39 years ago by Thomas Pattison who had surveyed the land for his father, Major Thomas Taylor. {DOLR 9 Old 138} Peter Taylor, Sr., aet. 59, dep. Jul 30, 1739, stated that he was shown the first bounded tree of *York* by his father, Major Thomas Taylor, about 40 years ago. {DOLR 12 Old 99} See "William Green" and "William McCollister" and "John Sulivane" and "John Anderton" and "Joseph Alford," q.v.

TAYLOR, RICHARD, of Goochland County, Virginia, aet. 51, dep. Sep 8, 1739 in Baltimore County, mentioned Joseph Taylor and Henry Stevenson about 30 years ago; also mentioned his father Richard Taylor and Edward Stevenson about 22 years ago, both now deceased. {BALR HWS#1A:279}

TAYLOR, ROBERT, see "Charles Thompson" and "Ann Johnson," q.v.

TAYLOR, SAMUEL, of Prince George's County, aet. 36, dep. Aug 25, 1737. {PGLR T:504} See "John White," q.v.

TAYLOR, THOMAS, of Prince George's County, aet. 50, dep. Aug 16, 1757. {PGLR PP:57, pt. 2}

TAYLOR, THOMAS, of Prince George's County, aet. 51, dep. Nov 15, 1763, mentioned his father John Taylor, deceased, and Thomas Lawson about 5 years ago, now deceased. {PGLR TT:144}

TAYLOR, THOMAS, of Dorchester County, aet. 40, formerly Deputy Surveyor, dep. between Dec 15, 1727 and Feb 14, 1727/8. {DOLR 8 Old 198} Aet. about 42, dep. between Aug 16, 1728 and Jan 28, 1728/9, mentioned Cisley Bourk, wife of John Bourk, and Elizabeth Halpenny, sister of Cisley Bourk. {DOLR 8 Old 268} Capt. Thomas Taylor, aet. about 40, son of John Taylor, dep. between Aug 16, 1728 and Nov 13, 1728. {DOLR 8 Old 247}

TAYLOR, THOMAS, of Dorchester County, aet. 39, former Deputy Surveyor, dep. Sep 8, 1682. {DOLR 4 Old 20} Aet. 60, dep. Aug 20, 1703. {DOLR 6 Old 46}

TAYLOR, THOMAS, of Dorchester County, aet. about 34, dep. between Mar 12, 1744 and Nov 8, 1748. {DOLR 14 Old 317}

TAYLOR, THOMAS, see "Peter Taylor" and "Richard Harrison," q.v.

TAYMAN, WILLIAM, of Baltimore County, aet. 40, dep. Nov 11, 1767. {BALR B#Q:589}

TEAL, EMANUEL, see "John Stinchcomb" and "Richard Marsh," q.v.

TEAR, ELEANOR, see "William Middleton," q.v.

TEAR, ELIZABETH, see "William Middleton," q.v.

TEATE, RICHARD, of Calvert or St. Mary's County, n.a., dep. Apr 23, 1691. {ARMD 8:247}

TEMPLETON, PETER, prob. of Anne Arundel County, n.a., dep. Apr 13, 1774, stated that he was mate on the ship *Chance* which was anchored at Annapolis last March, having returned from Hampton Road. {CMSP 1:212}

TENCH, THOMAS, see "Thelma Smith" and "Joseph Tilly," q.v.

TENNALLY, PHILIP, of Prince George's County, aet. 91, dep. Aug 29, 1768, mentioned his father (not named) and Thomas Davis. {PGLR BB#2:389} See "Philip Fenerly (Fennely)," q.v.

TENNISON, JOHN, of Charles County, aet. 65, dep. Jun 14, 1732. {CHLR R#2:157}

TENT, ABIGAIL, of Prince George's County, widow, aet. 63, dep. Mar 18, 1728/9, mentioned Robert Robertson, deceased. {PGLR M:480}

TERRAKELL, GEORGE, see "Indian Sam Isaac," q.v.

THACKER, THOMAS, see "Elizabeth Thornwell," q.v.

THANLOW, JOHN, see "John Thurlow," q.v.

THARP, WILLIAM, of Talbot County, aet. 65, dep. Aug 18, 1747, stated that David and Elizabeth Arey were married no more than 40 years ago next November and their daughter Esther was born about 12 months after they were married. {TALR 17:117}

THEOBALD, CAPTAIN, see "Godshall Barnes," q.v.

THEOBALLS, CLEMENT, of Charles County, n.a., dep. Feb 10, 1662/3. {CHLR B:70}

THEOBOLD, WILLIAM, of Charles County, aet. 45, dep. Jul 6, 1742. {CHLR O#2:422}

THOLOW (THURLOW?), SAMUEL, of Queen Anne's County, aet. 70, dep. Apr, 1747. {QAEJ - Samuel Blunt folder}

THOMAS, ALLEN, of Dorchester County, aet. 29, dep. Aug 16, 1712. {DOLR 6 Old 200}

THOMAS, DORCAS, see "Joseph Sutton," q.v.

THOMAS, GEORGE, of Charles County, aet. 58, dep. Apr 10, 1732. {CHLR R#2:159} Aet. 63, dep. Aug 23, 1736. {CHLR T#2:294} Aet. 65, dep. Mar 11, 1737/8. {CHLR T#2:424}

THOMAS, HEWGH, of Charles County, aet. 24, dep. Oct 1, 1662. {CHLR A:247}

THOMAS, JAMES, of Charles County, aet. 33, dep. Dec 29, 1743. {CHLR O#2:699} Aet. 39, dep. Feb 25, 1745/6. {CHLR Z#2:518} Aet. 55, dep. Aug 2, 1765. {CHLR P#3:273} Aet. 56, dep. Mar 6, 1757. {CHLR P#3:273}

THOMAS, JANE, of Dorchester County, aet. about 71, dep. between Nov 11, 1746 and May 27, 1752, mentioned Cornelia Macawl, daughter of John Ross. {DOLR

14 Old 658} See "William Thomas" and "Thomas Cook" and "Robert Parkinson," q.v.

THOMAS, JOHN, of Charles County, aet. 47, dep. Sep 13, 1729. {CHLR Q#2:345} Aet. 54, dep. Mar 29, 1738. {CHLR T#2:462} Aet. 55, dep. Jan 1, 1738/9. {CHLR T#2:535} Capt. John Thomas, aet. 60, dep. May 26, 1743. {CHLR O#2:617}

THOMAS, JOHN, of Prince George's County, aet. 57, dep. Nov 11, 1740. {PGLR Y:234}

THOMAS, JOHN, of Frederick County, aet. 24, dep. Aug 21, 1776. {FRLR BD#2:335}

THOMAS, JOHN, see "Thomas Cook, Jr.," q.v.

THOMAS, JOSEPH, see "William Thomas" and "Robert Parkinson" and "John Taylor" and "Richard Soward" and "Robert Graves" and "Thomas Hubbart" and "Joseph Sutton," q.v.

THOMAS, JOSEPH, of Dorchester County, aet. 33, dep. Aug 16, 1712. {DOLR 6 Old 200}

THOMAS, JOSEPH, of Dorchester County, aet. about 40, dep. between Nov 11, 1746 and May 27, 1752, stated that he was shown the bounds of *Rosses Range* by his father (not named) about 10 or 12 years ago. {DOLR 14 Old 658} Aet. about 60, dep. between Aug 11, 1772 and Dec 11, 1772, mentioned his father Joseph Thomas and Samuel Hubbard about 50 years ago. {DOLR 27 Old 348}

THOMAS, JOSEPH, SR., of Dorchester County, aet. 63, dep. between Jun 14, 1737 and Aug 7, 1737, stated that he was shown the bounds of *Brooxes Outhold* by Humphrey Hubbert, Sr., about 30 years ago. {DOLR 9 Old 482}

THOMAS, KATHERINE, of Frederick County, aet. 43, dep. Aug 21, 1776, mentioned her husband and her father (names not given). {FRLR BD#2:335}

THOMAS, NOTLEY, see "Joseph Hill," q.v.

THOMAS, RICHARD, of St. Mary's County, n.a., dep. Jul 21, 1681. {ARMD 15:393}

THOMAS, ROGER, of Queen Anne's County, planter, aet. about 51, dep. Mar, 1746, mentioned his sister (not named) about 15 years ago. {QAEJ - Benjamin Tasker folder}

THOMAS, SAMUEL (colonel), of Kent County, aet. 75, dep. 1743. {KELR JS#24:440} Aet. 78, dep. 1744. {KELR JS#25:226}

THOMAS, THOMAS, of Dorchester County, aet. 46, dep. Jan 15, 1744/5. {DOLR 12 Old 253}

THOMAS, WILLIAM, of Dorchester County, tailor, aet. 30, dep. between Apr 20, 1768 and May 27, 1768. {DOLR 22 Old 423}

THOMAS, WILLIAM, of Dorchester County, aet. about 50, dep. between Nov 10, 1747 and Apr 26, 1748, mentioned his mother-in-law Cathren Mellvin, wife of David Mellvin, Sr. {DOLR 14 Old 309} Aet. about 50, dep. between Nov 11, 1746 and May 27, 1752, mentioned his mother Jane Thomas and his father Joseph Thomas about 30 years ago. {DOLR 14 Old 658}

THOMAS, WILLIAM, of Charles County, aet. 52, dep. May 3, 1729. {CHLR M#2:127} Aet. 54, dep. Mar 8, 1726/7. {CHLR P#2:484}

THOMAS, WILLIAM, see "Mary Perrie" and "Francis Cost" and "Edward Tanzey," q.v.

THOMPKINS, NEWMAN, of Charles County, aet. 29, dep. Sep 10, 1743. {CHLR O#2:666} Aet. 62, dep. Oct 29, 1774. {CHLR W#3:604}

THOMPSON, ABSALOM, of Dorchester County, aet. 60, dep. between Mar 8, 1774 and May 2, 1774. {DOLR 27 Old 304}

THOMPSON, ARTHUR, see "Love Jones," q.v.

THOMPSON, CHARLES, of Dorchester County, aet. 79, dep. between Mar 1745 and Sep 27, 1746. {DOLR 14 Old 102}

THOMPSON, CHARLES, of Dorchester County, aet. 56, dep. between Mar 15, 1735/6 and Nov 9, 1737, stated that he was shown the bounds of *Row's Lott* by John Loyon about 40 years ago. {DOLR 9 Old 493} Aet. 58, dep. between Aug 20, 1734 and Aug 25, 1735, stated that the bounds of *Rawley* were shown to him by Lewis Jones about 35 years ago. {DOLR 9 Old 337} Aet. 66, dep. Oct 3, 1744, mentioned land dispute between Mary Bruffet and David Peterkin about 36 years ago. {DOLR 12 Old 142} Aet. 67, dep. Feb 25, 1744/5, mentioned Thomas Turner, deceased, who was county ranger about 40 years ago. {DOLR 12 Old 101} Aet. 67, stated that he was shown the bounds of *Littleworth* by John Minnish about a year after the death of Edward Pinder, the father of the last Edward Pinder, and also a short time later by William Warner, father of the present William Warner. {DOLR 12 Old 117} Aet. about 67, dep. between Mar 12, 1744/5 and May 17, 1745, mentioned Thomas Wingett, Mary Russell, and Major John Taylor about 46 or 47 years ago. {DOLR 14 Old 44} Aet. 68, dep. between Jun 11, 1745 and Nov 14, 1745. {DOLR 12 Old 230, 245} Aet. 68, dep. between Mar 12, 1744/5 and Aug 11, 1745, mentioned Hugh Eccleston, John Taylor, Mauris Morris (deceased), and Robert Taylor (deceased), about 50 years ago. {DOLR 12 Old 250} Aet. about 69, dep. between Nov 12, 1745 and Mar 8, 1745/6, mentioned John Lee's land called *Rehoboth* about 40 years ago. {DOLR 14 Old 48} Aet. about 68, dep. between Nov 8, 1748 and Mar 15, 1748/9, stated that he was shown the bounds of *Rawlings Folly* about 46 years ago at the dwelling house of William Walker who lived on the same plantation where Mary Bur now lives. {DOLR 14 Old 319} Aet. about 75, dep. between Jun 11, 1751 and Oct 14, 1751. {DOLR 14 Old 552} Aet. about 77, dep. between Mar 10, 1752 and Mar 10, 1753, stated that he was shown the bounds of *Atlantis* about 45 or 46 years ago by Thomas Turner, now deceased, and later by William Bradley and Patrick McCollister, both deceased. {DOLR 14 Old 712}

THOMPSON, CHARLES, see "James Brown," q.v.

THOMPSON, CHRISTOPHER, of Prince George's County, aet. 62, dep. Aug 17, 1725. {PGLR I:677} Aet. 60, dep. between Aug 12, 1727 and Mar 30, 1728, mentioned Walter Thompson. {PGLR M:269} Aet. 65, dep. Aug 2, 1732. {PGLR Q:670} Christopher Thomson, n.a., dep. Jun 16, 1730, mentioned James Thomson about 44 years ago. {PGLR Q:15} See "William Thompson," q.v.

THOMPSON, GEORGE, of Charles County, n.a., dep. Jul 9, 1662. {ARMD 53:232}
THOMPSON, JOHN, of Baltimore County, aet. 46, dep. Aug 15, 1774. {BALR AL#L:355}
THOMPSON, JOHN, of Prince George's County, aet. 26, dep. Aug 22, 1753 (1757?), mentioned his father Thomas Thompson about 8 years ago, now deceased. {PGLR PP:65, pt. 2}
THOMPSON, JOHN, of Charles County, aet. 63, dep. Sep 29, 1726. {CHLR P#2:397}
THOMPSON, JOHN, see "John King" and "James Hardy" and "Francis Birch" and "James Green" and "William Thompson," q.v.
THOMPSON, JOSEPH, of Charles County, aet. 42, dep. May 10, 1765. {CHLR N#3:381} Aet. 53, dep. May 1, 1773, mentioned his father Thomas Thompson. {CHLR U#3:270}
THOMPSON, JOSEPH, of Dorchester County, aet. about 50, dep. between Nov 14, 1758 and Jun 13, 1759. {DOLR 16 Old 184}
THOMPSON, JOSEPH, see "Gideon Gambell" and "James Hardy" and "James Langrall," q.v.
THOMPSON, ROBERT, of Charles County, aet. 36, dep. Apr 20, 1736. {CHLR T#2:197}
THOMPSON, ROBERT, of Charles County, aet. 80, dep. May 24, 1772. {CHLR U#3:456}
THOMPSON, ROBERT, see "Robert Mattingly," q.v.
THOMPSON, THOMAS, of Charles County, aet. 48, dep. May 5, 1730. {CHLR Q#2:403} Aet. 58, dep. Mar 25, 1750. {CHLR O#2:242} See "Robert Mattingly" and "Joseph Thompson" and "John Thompson" and "William Marlow" and "John Swearingen," q.v.
THOMPSON, THOMAS, JR., of Charles County, aet. 21, dep. Apr 30, 1745. {CHLR Z#2:336}
THOMPSON, WALTER, see "William Thompson" and "Christopher Thompson," q.v.
THOMPSON, WILLIAM, of Charles County, aet. 70, dep. Nov 30, 1725. {CHLR P#2:141} Aet. 70, dep. Feb 24, 1728, stated that he has lived in this area for 40 years. {CHLR Q#2:347} Aet. 73, dep. Sep 16, 1728. {CHLR Q#2:194}
THOMPSON, WILLIAM, of Charles County, aet. 38, dep. Aug 1, 1743, mentioned his father John Thompson. {CHLR O#2:620} Aet. 52, dep. Nov 15, 1756. {CHLR F#3:299} Aet. 57, dep. Aug 6, 1762. {CHLR M#3:3} Aet. 58, dep. Aug 18, 1763. {CHLR M#3:528}
THOMPSON, WILLIAM, of Prince George's County, aet. 80, dep. between Aug 12, 1727 and Mar 30, 1728, mentioned Walter Thompson. {PGLR M:269} Aet. 80, dep. Aug 22, 1729, mentioned his brother Christopher Thompson. {PGLR M:488} Aet. 80, dep. Jun 16, 1730 at his house as he was not able to attend being sick and weak. {PGLR Q:11}
THOMPSON, WILLIAM, of Prince George's County, aet. 52, dep. Aug 22, 1753 (1757?). {PGLR PP:65, pt. 2}

THOMPSON, WILLIAM, SR., of Dorchester County, aet. 63, dep. Jan 15, 1744/5. {DOLR 12 Old 253}
THOMSON, EDWARD, of Chickacoan, Dorchester County, n.a., dep. Jan 18, 1646 in Annapolis, mentioned Samuel Tailor and Francis Gray. {ARMD 3:176}
THOMSON, JAMES, see "Christopher Thompson," q.v.
THORINGTON, FRANCIS, of Charles County, n.a., dep. Nov 5, 1662. {CHLR B:13}
THORNBURY, JOHN, see "Henry Austin," q.v.
THORNBURY, ROWLAND, see "Henry Austin," q.v.
THORNE, JOHN, of Charles County, aet. 35, dep. Jul 22, 1731, mentioned his father William Thorne. {CHLR R#2:4} John Thorn, aet. 45, dep. May 3, 1742. {CHLR O#2:380}
THORNE, WILLIAM, see "John Thorne," q.v.
THORNWELL, ELIZABETH, of Dorchester County, aet. 55, formerly wife of Thomas Thacker, dep. Mar 11, 1706/7. {DOLR 6 Old 119}
THOROLD, GEORGE, of Charles County, aet. 62, dep. Aug 13, 1734, stated that about 33 or 34 years ago he married John Bowling and Mary Langworth and their eldest son is Thomas Bowling. {CHLR R#2:529} See "Mary Routhorn," q.v.
THORPE, THOMAS, of Queen Anne's County, aet. about 36, dep. Mar, 1746. {QAEJ - Benjamin Tasker folder}
THRELKELD, HENRY, see "James Hopkins," q.v.
THRELKELD, MARY, see "James Hopkins," q.v.
THURLOW (THANLOW?), JOHN, of Queen Anne's County, aet. about 63, dep. Mar, 1764, mentioned Robert Small, father of Robert Small. {QAEJ - Robert Small folder}
THURLOW (THANLOW?), MARY, of Queen Anne's County, aet. about 60, dep. Mar, 1764, stated that she was born within 2 miles of Robert Small's plantation. {QAEJ - Robert Small folder}
THURLOW, SAMUEL, see "Samuel Tholow," q.v.
THURSTON (THURSTONE), THOMAS, see "Michaell Higgins" and "John Arnold" and "Thomas Richardson," q.v.
TILDEN, MARMADUKE, of Kent County, aet. about 47, dep. Oct 9, 1761 and Jul 16, 1762. {KEEJ - John Carville folder}
TILGHMAN, EDWARD, of Queen Anne's County, n.a., dep. Jun 5, 1769, stated that this deponent (listed only as E. Tilghman) has known Francis Baker at least 10 years during which time he has lived chiefly in this neighborhood. {ARMD 32:327} Aet. 50, dep. Apr 1, 1772, mentioned William Emory, guardian to John King Beck Downes, son of plaintiff John Downes and his wife Sophia. {QAEJ - John and Sophia Downes folder}
TILGHMAN, MATTHEW, of Talbot County, n.a., dep. Jun 7, 1769, stated that he has known Francis Baker several years. {ARMD 32:326}
TILGHMAN, RICHARD, see "Geffery Mattecey" and "Roger Weddill" and "Thomas Sparkes," q.v.

TILLY, JOSEPH, of Anne Arundel County, aet. 70, stated that in Aug, 1689, when he was deputy to Francis Downes, clerk of the court, that he entered into the book a conveyance from Benjamin Scrivener and his wife Grace to Thomas Tench. {AALR IH#3:77}

TILMAN, JOHN HANS, of Cecil County, captain (and Indian trader at the head of the bay), n.a., dep. Jul 1, 1698 in Annapolis, stated that the Susquehannahs live in this Province about 30 miles above Octerara Creek. {ARMD 23:444}

TIMMS, BENNETT, of Charles County, aet. 33, dep. Nov 8, 1774. {CHLR W#3:606}

TINSON (TENSON), JOSEPH, see "Elizabeth Lamphier," q.v.

TIPINGS(?), EDWARD, of Queen Anne's County, aet. 56, dep. Apr, 1723. {QAEJ - William Bishop folder}

TOAES, DANIEL, see "Peter Massey," q.v.

TOAT, ROBERT, of St. Mary's County, aet. about 38, dep. Sep 23, 1681 in London, England, stated that "he having lived in Maryland divers yeares together untill the eleaventh day of May last at which time he came from thence in the shippe *Globe*." {ARMD 5:298-299}

TODD, BENJAMIN, of Dorchester County, aet. 36, dep. between Jun 14, 1743 and Aug 1, 1743. {DOLR 12 Old 167} Aet. 55, dep. between Mar 8, 1763 and Jun 13, 1763. {DOLR 18 Old 374} See "William Dean," q.v.

TODD, MARGARET, of Anne Arundel County, aet. 40, dep. 1680, stated that about 25 or 30 years ago she lived with Hugh Merekin, father of the present Joshua Merekin, upon land where John Merekin, son of Joshua, now lives. {AALR IT#5:48-49}

TODD, MICHAEL, of Dorchester County, aet. 29, dep. between Jun 11, 1765 and Aug 15, 1765, mentioned John Elliott about 6 or 7 years ago, now deceased, who was the father of the present John Elliott. {DOLR 20 Old 244} See "William Dean," q.v.

TOLSON (TOULSON), BENJAMIN, of Queen Anne's County, aet. about 36, dep. Mar, 1759; aet. 48, dep. July, 1770. {QAEJ - Henry Carter folders}

TOLSON, JOHN, of Prince George's County, aet. 45, dep. Nov 5, 1763, mentioned John Abington about 30 years ago. {PGLR TT:285}

TOMKINS, THOMAS, of Frederick County, n.a., dep. Aug 8, 1755, stated that he was shown the bounded trees of *Gordon's Purchase* and *The Grove*, taken up by Joseph Chapline, by Evan McDonald near Middle Spring. {FRLR E:907}

TOMKINSON, GILS, of Charles County, n.a., dep. Nov 14, 1665, stated that he was the father of the child of his former servant (not named) and the child was not illegitimate as the woman was his lawful wife and their marriage was as good as possibly it could be made by the Protestants, he being one before that time and ever since. {ARMD 53:599}

TOMLINSON, GROVE, see "James Hughes," q.v.

TOMLINSON, HUGH, of Frederick County, aet. 70 or thereabouts, dep. Jul 27, 1762, mentioned Thomas Wilson about 23 or 24 years ago. {FRLR J:65} See "James Goare," q.v.

TOMLINSON, JOHN, of Dorchester County, planter, aet. 33, dep. between Mar 10, 1740 and Jan 23, 1741, stated that the bounds of *Wakefield* were shown to him by Jonas Dawson about 12 or 13 years ago. {DOLR 12 Old 89}

TOMPKINSON, JOHN, see "Henry Neale," q.v.

TOMS, SAMUEL, of Frederick County, n.a., dep. Mar 15, 1773, stated that he has been well acquainted with the bounds of *Toms Folly* for many years. {FRLR P:680}

TOMSON, WILLIAM, of Dorchester County, aet. 60, dep. between Nov 10, 1761 and Jan 21, 1762. {DOLR 18 Old 87}

TOSIER(?), THOMAS, of Anne Arundel County, n.a., dep. Mar 30, 1707. {CMSP 1:8}

TOURSON, SARAH, of Kent County, n.a., dep. Apr 1, 1661. {ARMD 54:211}

TOVEY, ANNE, see "Thomas Smith" and "Elizabeth Bunten," q.v.

TOVEY, MARY, see "William Ringgold," q.v.

TOVEY, SAMUEL, see "Thomas Smith" and "Jonas Greenewood," q.v.

TOWERS, MARY, see "Eleanor Brisbane," q.v.

TOWERS, THOMAS, of Queen Anne's County, aet. 63, dep. Sep, 1761. {QAEJ - William Webb folder} See "John Cooper," q.v.

TOWSON, EZEKIEL, of Baltimore County, blacksmith, aet. 31, dep. Dec 26, 1767. {BALR B#Q:699}

TOWSON, THOMAS, of Baltimore County, n.a., dep. Jan 11, 1767. {BALR B#P:459}

TRAILE, DAVID, of Prince George's County, aet. 53, dep. Jun 16, 1730, mentioned George Mills and wife (not name) about 20 years ago. {PGLR Q:10}

TRAVERS, HENRY, of Dorchester County, aet. 29, dep. May 14, 1735. {DOLR 9 Old 326} Aet. 55, dep. between Aug 12, 1760 and Mar 2, 1761, mentioned Jacob Pattison and his brother John Pattison. {DOLR 17 Old 262} Col. Henry Travers, aet. 59, dep. between Jun 11, 1765 and Aug 11, 1765, mentioned his brother William Travers, old Henry Ennalls, old Henry Keene, and his (Keene's) "father Robson and his unkle Meekins." {DOLR 21 Old 45} See "John Pagon" and "Andrew Robinson," q.v.

TRAVERS, JOHN, of Dorchester County, aet. 49, dep. between Aug 11, 1761 and Sep 19, 1761, mentioned old Mr. Benony Phillips over 30 years ago. {DOLR 18 Old 17}

TRAVERS, MATTHEW, see "Thomas Hackett," q.v.

TRAVERS, THOMAS (captain), of Dorchester County, aet. 78, dep. between Nov 13, 1764 and Dec 22, 1764. {DOLR 20 Old 11}

TRAVERS, WILLIAM, of Dorchester County, aet. 60, dep. Aug 13, 1700. {DOLR 5 Old 161} See "Henry Travers," q.v.

TRAVERSE, HENRY, see "Andrew Robinson," q.v.

TRAVERSE, JOHN, see "John Pagon," q.v.

TRAVERSE, MATHEW, see "Andrew Robinson" and "John Pagon," q.v.

TREDWAY, THOMAS, of Baltimore County, aet. 74, dep. Aug 15, 1774, stated that he had lived within 2 or 3 miles of *Elbert's Field* since 1718 and about 4 years ago he moved further away. {BALR AL#L:238}

TREGO (TREGOE), ANN, of Dorchester County, widow, aet. 61, dep. Sep 11, 1749, stated that Sarah Mason was as orphan in the house of her father Peter Stokes and was later married to Thomas Shehawne by William Mishie, and that her (Ann's) father Peter Stokes had reportedly married the mother (not named) of said Sarah Mason, who was the widow of Miles Mason. {DOLR 14 Old 375}

TREGO (TREGOE), THOMAS, of Dorchester County, aet. 40, dep. between Jun 16, 1727 and Mar 17, 1727/8. {DOLR 8 Old 200} Aet. 42, dep. between Mar 13, 1732 and Jul 31, 1733. {DOLR 9 Old 137}

TREGO (TREGOE), WILLIAM, of Dorchester County, aet. 32, dep. between Mar 13, 1753 and Jun 2, 1753. {DOLR 15 Old 134} Aet. 57, dep. between Aug 10, 1773 and Oct 23, 1773, stated that he was "at school to Isaac Allwincle" about 35 or 36 years ago. {DOLR 27 Old 38} Aet. 57, dep. Dec 15, 1774. {DOLR 28 Old 172}

TREGO (TREGOE), WILLIAM, of Dorchester County, aet. about 66, dep. between Nov 13, 1744 and Nov 10, 1748. {DOLR 14 Old 315} See "William Byus," q.v.

TREW, ANN, of Charles County, aet. 26, dep. Jun 29, 1663. {CHLR B:163}

TREW, JOHN, of Talbot County, n.a., dep. Jun 21, 1670, mentioned William Ladd's wife (not named). {ARMD 54:466}

TREW, RICHARD, of Charles County, n.a., dep. Jun 15, 1661, mentioned Gils Glover and his wife Elizabeth. {ARMD 53:127} Aet. 58, dep. Jun 29, 1663. {CHLR B:163}

TRICE, ABRAHAM, of Dorchester County, aet. 66, dep. between Jun 10, 1755 and Feb 10, 1756. {DOLR 15 Old 341}

TRICE, GEORGE, of Dorchester County, aet. 31, dep. between Jun 10, 1755 and Feb 10, 1756. {DOLR 15 Old 341}

TRIPPE, ELIZABETH, see "Indian Abraham," q.v.

TRIPPE, HENRY, see "Andrew Gray" and "Philemon Lecompte" and "Peter Stokes" and "Charles Elliot" and "William Trippe" and "John Hodson," q.v.

TRIPPE, JOHN, of Dorchester County, aet. 58, son of William Trippe, dep. between Mar 13, 1770 and Jul 21, 1770. {DOLR 24 Old 303}

TRIPPE, WILLIAM, of Dorchester County, aet. 70, dep. between Jun 8, 1758 and Dec 15, 1759, mentioned Henry Trippe about 38 years ago. {DOLR 16 Old 212} See "John Trippe," q.v.

TROOPE, ROBERT, of Charles County, n.a., dep. Sep 14, 1659, stated that Edmond Linsey was the first to call Capt. John Jenkins by the name of Capt. Grindingstone. {CHLR A:63, ARMD 53:51} Capt. Robert Troope, n.a., dep. Oct 2, 1662. {CHLR A:249} Aet. 28, dep. Nov 2, 1663. {CHLR B:200} See "Samuell Palmer" and "Daniel Gordon," q.v.

TRUE, WILLIAM of Kent County, n.a., dep. Aug 24, 1704, mentioned Mary Caulk (relict of Isaac Caulk, deceased), Francis Finch (deceased father of Mary

Caulk), and Joyce Quinney (sister of Mary Caulk) and her [Quinney's] surviving 3 children. {KELR GL#1:22, 44}

TRUMAN, BENJAMIN, of Prince George's County, aet. 47, dep. Feb 1, 1768, mentioned John Anderson about 25 or 26 years ago. {PGLR BB#2:291}

TRUMAN, EDWARD, see "Phillip Willocy" and "Paul Rawlings," q.v.

TRUMAN, HENRY, see "Phillip Willocy," q.v.

TRUMAN (TRUEMAN), THOMAS, of St. Mary's County, gentleman, n.a., dep. Aug 13, 1661. {ARMD 41:481}

TRUNDLE, MARY, of Prince George's County, aet. 50, dep. Nov 21, 1763, mentioned her former husband John Furguson who was the father of her daughter Verlinda Hall. {PGLR TT:194}

TUBB, ANN, of Charles County, aet. 60, dep. Jun 22, 1767. {CHLR P#3:503}

TUBMAN, ELLEANOR, of Dorchester County, aet. 51, daughter of Raymond Stapleford, dep. between May 6, 1726 and Aug 14, 1727. {DOLR 8 Old 227}

TUBMAN, GEORGE, of Charles County, aet. 36, dep. Jul 1, 1765. {CHLR N#3:785}

TUBMAN, RICHARD, of Charles County, aet. 63, dep. Jul 24, 1764. {CHLR M#3:687} Aet. 66, dep. Jul 1, 1765. {CHLR N#3:786}

TUBMAN, RICHARD, of Prince George's County, aet. 30, dep. between Nov 11, 1729 and Mar 26, 1730. {PGLR M:568}

TUCKER, JOHN, of Prince George's County, aet. 32, dep. Jul 1, 1738. {PGLR T:605} See "Isle of Wight," q.v.

TUCKER, THOMAS, of Prince George's County, aet. 60, dep. Jul 1, 1738. {PGLR T:605} See "Isle of Wight" and "John Sasser," q.v.

TUCKER, THOMAS, SR., of Prince George's County, aet. 60, dep. Apr 24, 1772, mentioned his father Thomas Tucker. {PGLR BB#3:81}

TUCKER, WILLIAM, of Dorchester County, aet. 40, dep. between Nov 10, 1772 and Mar 30, 1773. {DOLR 26 Old 399} Aet. 47, dep. Sep 20, 1776, mentioned Thomas Loockerman about 17 years ago, now deceased. {DOLR 28 Old 232-233}

TUELL, WILLIAM, of Prince George's County, aet. 53, dep. Jun 1, 1767, mentioned Edward Villers Harbin and William Harbin. {PGLR BB#2:114}

TUNCKS, WILLIAM, see "William Tancks," q.v.

TURBITT, WILLIAM, see "Sarah Emory," q.v.

TURNBALL, GEORGE, of Frederick County, aet. 57, dep. between Mar 29, 1759 and Jul 23, 1759, stated that Uncle Unckles ran out a line on the tract *Addition* in July, 1754, which he understood belonged to Dr. Charles Carroll. {FRLR F:763} Aet. 67, dep. Mar 14, 1768, mentioned a son (not named). {FRLR L:207} See "Uncle Unckles," q.v.

TURNER, ANNE, see "James Wilson," q.v.

TURNER, ARTHUR, of Charles County, aet. 40, dep. Apr 22, 1662. {CHLR A:211} See "Lucie Stratton" and "John Ashbrooke" and "John Hatch" and "Christopher Russell" and "Edward William" and "Anne Gey" and "Walter Ges" and "Margaret Pearce" and "Robert Wilson" and "Mary Tarlin," q.v.

TURNER, EDWARD, of Charles County, aet. 41, dep. Jun 29, 1744. {CHLR Y#2:86} Aet. 69, dep. Nov 17, 1772. {CHLR U#3:229} See "James Wilson," q.v.
TURNER, GILBERT, see "James Wilson," q.v.
TURNER, JEREMIAH, of Prince George's County, aet. 25, dep. Nov 15, 1768. {PGLR BB#2:387}
TURNER, JOSIAH, of Prince George's County, aet. 28, dep. Nov 15, 1768, mentioned his father (not named). {PGLR BB#2:387}
TURNER, JOSIAS, of Prince George's County, aet. 28, dep. Nov 15, 1758, mentioned his father Solomon Turner. {PGLR BB#2:387}
TURNER, MARY, see "James Wilson," q.v.
TURNER, ROBERT, see "Caleb Isgate," q.v.
TURNER, SAMUEL, of Charles County, aet. 60, dep. Nov 20, 1735. {CHLR T#2:201}
TURNER, SARAH, see "Caleb Isgate," q.v.
TURNER, SOLOMON, of Frederick County, aet. 46, dep. Nov 28, 1760, mentioned William Turner and Thomas Manyard (now deceased) about 10 or 11 years ago. {FRLR G:71} See "Josias Turner," q.v.
TURNER, THOMAS, see "David Melvell" and "Charles Thompson" and "David Melvell" and "Patrick McCollister" and "William Spencer" and "Michaell Higgins" and "Caleb Isgate" and "John Arnold," q.v.
TURNER, WILLIAM, see "Solomon Turner" and "Richard Sullivant" and "James Wilson," q.v.
TURPIN, DANIEL, of Dorchester County, aet. 56, dep. between Mar 14, 1771 and Nov 13, 1771, mentioned John Reed (now deceased) and his son James Reed about 35 years ago. {DOLR 25 Old 238} Aet. 58, dep. between Nov 9, 1773 and Nov 9, 1774, mentioned Thomas Wilson and James Wilson (now deceased) about 28 years ago. {DOLR 27 Old 359}
TURPIN, SOLOMON, of Dorchester County, aet. 43, dep. between Jun 11, 1751 and Oct 14, 1751, mentioned his father Solomon Turpin. {DOLR 14 Old 552} See "Abraham Covington," q.v.
TURPIN, WILLIAM, see "Francis Hayward," q.v.
TWIFORD, JOHN, of Dorchester County, aet. 58, dep. between Jun 11, 1751 and Oct 14, 1751. {DOLR 14 Old 552}
TWIFORD, WILLIAM, of Somerset County, aet. 49, dep. between Mar 15, 1735 and Nov 9, 1737. {DOLR 9 Old 493}
TWIGG, ELIZABETH, see "Caleb Beck," q.v.
TYENEY, DOROTHY, see "Elizabeth Lamphier," q.v.
TYER, ALEXANDER, see "Rosannah Robinson," q.v.
TYLER, BRAY PLAT, of Baltimore County, aet. 50, dep. Nov 12, 1768. {BALR AL#G:443}
TYLER, ELIZABETH (Mrs.), of Prince George's County, aet. 74, dep. Jun 14, 1770, stated that 37 years ago she was midwife to John Ouchterlony's wife (whose maiden name was Plummer) and delivered a daughter they named

Agness; said John came into this province as a merchant and his first wife was Frances Wells. {PGLR AA#2:120}

TYLER, ROBERT, of Prince George's County, gentleman, aet. 53, dep. Mar 19, 1724/5. {PGLR I:626} Aet. 55, dep. Oct 4, 1726 and Jun 23, 1727. {PGLR M:216, 219} Aet. 59, dep. Feb 24, 1729/30, mentioned Richard Harwood, of Anne Arundel County, deceased. {PGLR Q:233} Robert Tyler, Sr., aet. 60, dep. May 31, 1731. {PGLR Q:608} Aet. 65, dep. Feb 2, 1734/5. {PGLR T:285} See "Edward Sprigg" and "James Mullikin" and "Robert Brashears" and "Benjamin Boyd" and "Henry Bolton," q.v.

UNCKLES (UNCLES), UNCLE, of Frederick County, n.a., dep. between Mar 29, 1759 and Jul 23, 1759, stated that about 8 or 10 years ago he laid out the tract *Addition* for Dr. Charles Carroll; in June or July, 1754, he went out to run the aforesaid land for George Turnball, but could not find the bounded trees. {FRLR F:764} Uncle Uncles, n.a., dep. Mar 14, 1768. {FRLR L:206} See "George Turnball," q.v.

UNDERWOOD, RICHARD, of Kent County on Delaware, aet. about 64, dep. between Nov 11, 1746 and Apr 14, 1748. {DOLR 14 Old 231}

UNDERWOOD, WILLIAM, of Prince George's County, aet. 34, dep. Jul 5, 1748, mentioned old Francis Marbury about 17 years ago, now deceased. {PGLR BB:596}

URIE, MICHAEL, of Prince George's County, aet. 48, dep. Jun 16, 1730. {PGLR Q:14} Aet. 54, dep. Jun 8, 1732. {PGLR Y:327}

URVIN, WILLIAM, see "Andrew McCollister" and "Patrick McCollister," q.v.

UTIE, MARY, see "Francis Stockett" and "Anthony Brispo," q.v.

VANCUICK, CORNELIS, see "George Walters," q.v.

VANDEFORD, GEORGE (and sons), see "Edward Skinner," q.v.

VANDERDUNCKE, MRS., see "Daniell Johnson" and "Mrs. O'Neale," q.v.

VANHACK, JOHN, of St. Mary's County, n.a., dep. Apr 18, 1661. {ARMD 41:447}

VANIMON, NICHOLAS, of Frederick County, aet. 32, dep. Nov 27, 1762. {FRLR H:335}

VANMETER, JACOB, of Frederick County, aet. 41, dep. Jul 26, 1764, stated that he saw Joseph Chapline survey *Pell Mell* for John VanMeter about 20 years ago. {FRLR J:940}

VANMETER, JOHN, see "Joseph Chapline" and "Jacob VanMeter," q.v.

VANSANT, RACHEL, of Kent County, aet. about 42, dep. affirmed Mar 13, 1753, mentioned her father James Corse (deceased), her sister Jennett Corse, and John Redgraves (deponent's deceased former husband). {KELR JS#27:253}

VANSWEERINGEN (VANSWERENGEN), GARRET (GARRATT), gentleman, of St. Mary's City, n.a., dep. Jan 26, 1681; aet. 48 or thereabouts dep. May 12, 1684. {ARMD 5:342, 417}

VAUGHAN, ROBERT (captain), of St. Mary's County, n.a., dep. Apr 3, 1651. {ARMD 10:77} Aet. 62 or thereabouts, dep. Apr 27, 1659. {ARMD 41:395}

VAUGHAN, THOMAS, of St. Mary's County, n.a., dep. Sep 9, 1663. {ARMD 49:56}

VAUGHN, THOMAS, of Talbot County, dep. 4th day of 4th mo., 1688, mentioned land laid out on Choptank River. {TALR 5:202}

VAULX (VAUX), EBENEZAR, of Dorchester County, aet. 48, dep. between Nov 9, 1762 and May 9, 1763, stated that Henry Davis lived with him about 18 years ago. {DOLR 19 Old 425}

VAULX, JAMES, of Dorchester County, aet. about 75, dep. between Nov 10, 1741 and Feb 16, 1742. {DOLR 14 Old 54} See "Florance Sulivane" and "Sarah Vaulx," q.v.

VAULX, SARAH, of Dorchester County, aet. about 50, dep. between Nov 12, 1745 and Nov 11, 1747, mentioned her husband James Vaulx, deceased. {DOLR 14 Old 173}

VEATCH, NATHAN, see "Charles Beall," q.v.

VEITCH, JAMES, of St. Mary's County, n.a., dep. 1659. {ARMD 41:364}

VICARS, JOHN, see "Edward Taylor," q.v.

VICARS, THAMZEN, see "Edward Taylor," q.v.

VICKARS, THOMAS, JR., of Dorchester County, aet. 39, dep. between Aug 10, 1773 and Nov 24, 1773. {DOLR 27 Old 239}

VICKERS, ANN, of Dorchester County, n.a., widow, dep. Jan 1, 1767, stated that Isaac Lee, shoemaker, deceased, lived near her and died about a year ago last October; he came to this province as a convict and served William Kennerly for 14 years. {DOLR 26 Old 4}

VICKERS, WILLIAM BROWN, see "William Rumbold," q.v.

VICKERY, HEZEKIAH, see "John Andrew," q.v.

VILLETT, PETER, of Charles County, aet. 80, dep. Nov 30, 1732. {CHLR R#2:292}

VINEYARD, ABRAHAM, of Charles County, aet. 37, dep. Mar 5, 1682/3. {CHLR K#1:125}

VINSON, ANN, of Charles County, aet. 22, dep. Feb 22, 1762. {CHLR K#3:474}

VINSON, JOHN, see "William Stevens," q.v.

VIRGIN, URIAH, of Prince George's County, aet. 26, dep. Apr 23, 1754. {PGLR NN:253}

VIRMILLION, GILES, of Prince George's County, aet. 45, dep. between Nov 11, 1729 and Mar 26, 1730. {PGLR M:558} Aet. 75, dep. Aug 22, 1753 (1757?), mentioned James Green about 60 years ago and George Dixon about 40 years ago, both now deceased. {PGLR PP:64-66, pt. 2} Giles Vermillian, aet. 77, dep. Aug 5, 1760, stated that he has known of Pomonkey Branch for about 50 years. {PGLR RR:74}

WADE, MARY, see "Zachary Wade," q.v.

WADE, RICHARD, of Charles County, aet. 62, dep. May 29, 1725. {CHLR P#2:42} Aet. 64, dep. Mar 8, 1726/7. {CHLR P#2:484}

WADE, RICHARD, of Charles County, aet. 60, dep. Aug 26, 1747, mentioned his brother Zephaniah Wade, his father Robert Wade, and his uncle William Stone. {CHLR P#3:654}

WADE, RICHARD, see "Henry Tanner," q.v.

WADE, ROBERT, of Prince George's County, aet. 53, dep. Aug 22, 1757. {PGLR PP:62, pt. 2} Aet. 60, dep. Sep 7, 1761. {PGLR RR:231} Robert Wade, Sr., aet. 60, dep. Oct 4, 1762, stated that Luke Barber showed him the bounds of *Thompson's Rest* about 40 years ago; also mentioned Col. Thomas Addison, now deceased. {PGLR RR:262} Aet. 60, dep. Mar 5, 1763. {PGLR TT:13} Aet. 75, dep. Oct 15, 1776. {PGLR CC#2:310} See "Richard Wade" and "Edward Brawner," q.v.

WADE, ZACHARY (ZACHERY), of Charles County, n.a., dep. 1659 and 1663. {ARMD 41:346, 49:51} Aet. not given, dep. Oct 14, 1665, stated (as did Daniel Johnson) that Elinor Lindsey, wife of Edmund Lindsey, was very great with child and cannot come to Court at this time; a later entry stated that Zachary Wade's wife was named Mary. {ARMD 49:505, 49:515} See "Mathias O'Brian," q.v.

WADE, ZEPHANIAH, see "Richard Wade" and "Francis Wheeler," q.v.

WAGGATE, THOMAS, see "Charles Rawlinson," q.v.

WAHOPE, ARCHIBALD, of Charles County, aet. 33, dep. Apr 17, 1660. {CHLR A:86} Archibell Wahob, n.a., dep. Feb 10, 1662/3. {CHLR B:70}

WAKEFIELD, ABLE, of Charles County, aet. 28, dep. Feb 22, 1762. {CHLR K#3:480}

WAKEFIELD, JOHN, of Charles County, aet. 37, dep. Feb 17, 1742/3. {CHLR O#2:537} Aet. 39, dep. May 7, 1744. {CHLR Y#2:117} Aet. 48, dep. Apr 28, 1753, mentioned his father William Wakefield, deceased. {CHLR D#3:79} Aet. 49, dep. Feb 15, 1755. {CHLR E#3:216} See "Benjamin Douglas," q.v.

WAKEFIELD, WILLIAM, see "John Wakefield," q.v.

WALKER, ABRAHAM, of Dorchester County, aet. 60, dep. between Nov 16, 1731 and Sep 4, 1732, stated that he was a servant to Henry Beckwith about 30 years ago. {DOLR 9 Old 71} See "Daniel Bruffett," q.v.

WALKER, CHARLES, of Prince George's County, aet. 55, dep. Mar 19, 1724/5, mentioned Thomas Prather, deceased. {PGLR I:626} Aet. 60, dep. May 22, 1729. {PGLR M:440} Aet. 60, planter, dep. Mar 18, 1728/9, mentioned Thomas Box, deceased. {PGLR M:477} See "Richard Isaac" and "Henry Darnall" and "John Brightwell" and "John Brown," q.v.

WALKER, CHARLES, SR., of Prince George's County, aet. 50, dep. May 20, 1725. {PGLR I:675}

WALKER, DORMAN, of Prince George's County, aet. 66, dep. Jun 15, 1731. {PGLR Q:296, 298}

WALKER, GEORGE, of Charles County, aet. 54, dep. May 13, 1745. {CHLR Z#2:338} Aet. 69, dep. Apr 24, 1755. {CHLR E#3:131} See "Mary Ward," q.v.

WALKER, JAMES, of Charles County, aet. 40, dep. Sep 24, 1661. {CHLR A:155} Aet. 44, dep. Feb 10, 1662/3. {CHLR B:74}

WALKER, JOHN, see "William Smith," q.v.

WALKER, JOSEPH, see "Richard Isaac" and "Rebecca Walker," q.v.

WALKER, PERMAN, of Prince George's County, aet. 60, dep. Jul 1, 1726. {PGLR M:27}
WALKER, REBECCA (REBEKAH), of Prince George's County, aet. 89, dep. Nov 2, 1761, mentioned her husband (not named). {PGLR RR:182} Aet. not given, dep. Aug 8, 1767, mentioned her son Joseph Walker. {PGLR BB#2:115} See "Richard Isaac," q.v.
WALKER, RICHARD, see "Richard Isaac," q.v.
WALKER, THOMAS, of Anne Arundel County, n.a., a soldier enlisted to serve in His Majesty's Army under the command of the honorable Col. Alexander Spotswood, dep. May 3, 1740, stated that Robert Connant, Constable of Herring Creek Hundred, damned King George and all his soldiers on the night of Apr 30th last. {ARMD 28:205} See "William Keene," q.v.
WALKER, WILLIAM, see "Anthony Rawlings" and "Charles Thompson," q.v.
WALL, MARY, of Prince George's County, aet. 70, dep. Sep 5, 1767, mentioned her husband Thomas Wall, deceased. {PGLR PP:129, pt. 2}
WALL, ROBERT, of Prince George's County, aet. 59, dep. Sep 5, 1757, mentioned his father Thomas Wall about 10 years ago, now deceased. {PGLR PP:128-129, pt. 2}
WALL, THOMAS, of Prince George's County, aet. 67, dep. Jul 9, 1731, stated that he has known the bounds of *Brookefield* for 30 years, having been a chain carrier when it was surveyed; he served his time with Thomas Brooke, Esq., and has been free about 46 years. {PGLR Q:522}
WALL, THOMAS, of Prince George's County, aet. 35, dep. Nov 15, 1763, mentioned Joseph Carroll about 5 years ago, now deceased. {PGLR TT:144}
WALL, THOMAS, see "Mary Wall" and "Robert Wall," q.v.
WALL, WILLIAM, of Dorchester County, aet. 45, dep. between Mar 14, 1771 and Nov 13, 1771, mentioned his father William Wall and Francis Hayward, both deceased. {DOLR 25 Old 238} See "Thomas Wilson," q.v.
WALLACE, BETHULA, of Dorchester County, aet. 60, dep. between Nov 10, 1761 and Jan 21, 1762. {DOLR 18 Old 87} See "Edward Nooner," q.v.
WALLACE, JAMES, of Dorchester County, aet. 56, dep. between Jun 10, 1760 and Jul 16, 1762, mentioned old Mrs. Hambrook, wife of John Hambrook, and John Stewart, son of said Mrs. Hambrook. {DOLR 19 Old 65}
WALLACE, JOHN, of Dorchester County, aet. 60, dep. between Nov 12, 1771 and Apr 17, 1772. {DOLR 26 Old 50}
WALLACE, MICHAEL, prob. of Anne Arundel County, n.a., dep. Apr 14, 1774. {CMSP 1:212}
WALLACE, RICHARD, of Dorchester County, aet. 45, dep. between Nov 10, 1761 and Jan 21, 1762, mentioned Hannah Griffith and her brother George Griffith. {DOLR 18 Old 87}
WALLACE, STAPLEFORT, of Dorchester County, aet. 46 or 47, dep. between Nov 10, 1761 and Mar 4, 1762. {DOLR 18 Old 83} Aet. 46, dep. between Nov 10, 1761 and Jan 21, 1762. {DOLR 18 Old 89}

WALLER, THOMAS, of Frederick County, aet. 86 or thereabouts, dep. Apr 27, 1767, after being sworn on the Holy Evangelists of Almighty God, stated that he was with Peter Dent, then Deputy Surveyor of Prince George's County, about 26 or 28 years ago. {FRLR K:1341}
WALLING (WALLER), JAMES, JR., of Frederick County, aet. 40, dep. 1767. {FRLR L:60}
WALLING, JAMES, of Frederick County, n.a., dep. Aug 26, 1754, stated that Greenborne (Greenbune) Chaney, Jr. bit off part of the left ear of Thomas Walling in a fray on Aug 24, 1754. {FRLR E:524}
WALLING, THOMAS, of Frederick County, n.a., dep. Aug 26, 1754, stated that Greenborne (Greenbune) Chaney, Jr. bit off part of his left ear in a fray in Aug 24, 1754. {FRLR E:524} See "James Walling" and "Edmund Rutter," q.v.
WALLIS, ELIZABETH, see "Mary Anderson" and "Sarah Joslin," q.v.
WALLIS, RICHARD, of Dorchester County, aet. about 40, dep. between Nov 14, 1758 and Mar 9, 1759/60, mentioned Thomas Wallis, Sr. {DOLR 16 Old 146}
WALLIS, THOMAS, SR., see "Richard Wallis," q.v.
WALLS, ALICE, of Charles County, aet. 45, dep. Jan 1, 1738/9. {CHLR T#2:531} Else Walls, aet. 51, dep. Mar 26, 1744, mentioned her deceased husband George Walls and her deceased son George Walls who was living about 10 years ago. {CHLR Z#2:9} Alice Walls, aet. 78, dep. Oct 29, 1767, mentioned her husband George Walls, deceased. {CHLR Q#3:192}
WALLS, GEORGE, of Charles County, aet. 76, dep. Apr 13, 1738. {CHLR T#2:465} See "Alice Walls," q.v.
WALPOLE, JAMES, see "Elizabeth Lamphier," q.v.
WALTER, MARY, of Dorchester County, aet. 65, widow of Thomas Walter, dep. between Jun 11, 1765 and Aug 15, 1765, mentioned Abraham Covington and George Langrall about 35 years ago, both now deceased; also mentioned Edward Elliott, deceased, whom she lived with about 36 years ago. {DOLR 20 Old 244}
WALTERS, ALEXANDER, of Queen Anne's County, aet. 55, dep. Sep, 1771. {QAEJ - Henry Carter folder}
WALTERS, ANN, see "John Gardner," q.v.
WALTERS, GEORGE (colonel), of Bantrey in County Cork, Ireland, aet. 44 or thereabouts, dep. Feb 18, 1663 in St. Mary's County, stated he had purchased the ship *George* (burthen 80 tons) from Cornelis Van Cuick and Peter Backer on Feb 4, 1659 and he wished the bill of sale be registered in this Court. {ARMD 49:151}
WALTERS, JAMES, of Queen Anne's County, aet. 60, dep. Sep, 1766, stated that Arthur Emory was guardian to Sarah and Sophia King; also mentioned his brothers Richard and John Walters; aet. 66, dep. Apr 1, 1772, stated that he was born in 1705 and was above 33 years of age when his father Robert Walters died; also stated that William Meredith married the eldest daughter of John King. {QAEJ - John and Sophia Downes folder} See "John Gardner," q.v.

WALTERS, JOHN, see "James Walters," q.v.
WALTERS, RICHARD, see "Sarah Emory" and "James Walters," q.v.
WALTERS, ROBERT, see "Sarah Emory" and "James Walters," q.v.
WALTOM, JOHN, of Charles County, n.a., dep. Jul 8, 1662. {CHLR A:224}
WANSEY, SHERRY, see "Robert Sherwin," q.v.
WANT, MARY, see "Edward Bennett" and "Mary Fisher," q.v.
WANT, WILLIAM, see "Edward Bennett," q.v.
WAPLE, GEORGE, of Charles County, aet. 54, dep. Jan 11, 1757. {CHLR F#3:468} George Wapole, aet. 71, dep. Jun 23, 1772. {CHLR U#3:163}
WARD, ANDREW, of Charles County, n.a., dep. Jan 12, 1664/5. {CHLR B:425}
WARD, AUGUSTINE, of Charles County, aet. 60, dep. Aug 5, 1768. {CHLR Q#3:259}. Aet. 70, dep. Feb 23, 1774. {CHLR W#3:82}
WARD, CATHERINE, of Charles County, aet. 24, spinster, dep. Jan 20, 1726, mentioned her father James Ward. {CHLR P#2:491}
WARD, FRANCIS, of St. Mary's County, aet. 25, dep. Dec 11, 1661. {ARMD 41:575}
WARD, HENRY, of Charles County, aet. 50, dep. Jan 20, 1726. {CHLR P#2:491}
WARD, HENRY, of Prince George's County, aet. 54, dep. Aug 3, 1730. {PGLR Q:68} Aet. 59, dep. Jun 6, 1735. {PGLR T:282}
WARD, HENRY, see "John Ward" and "George Britt" and "John Dimpsy" and "Francis Pain," q.v.
WARD, JAMES, see "Catherine Ward," q.v.
WARD, JOHN, of Charles County, aet. 42, dep. Sep 17, 1753, mentioned his father Henry Ward. {CHLR D#3:309}
WARD, JOHN, of Charles County, aet. 75, dep. Oct 5, 1731. {CHLR R#2:331}
WARD, JOHN, of Prince George's County, aet. 65, dep. between Nov 11, 1729 and Mar 26, 1730, mentioned his father John Ward about 40 odd years ago. {PGLR M:567} Aet. 64 or 66, dep. Aug 3, 1730, mentioned his father John Ward, Sr., deceased. {PGLR Q:67}
WARD, JOHN, see "John Dimpsy" and "Lucretia Ward" and "Edward William," q.v.
WARD, LUCRETIA, of Dorchester County, n.a., dep. Nov 1, 1763, wife of John Ward, stated that she was present when Jonathan Bestpitch and Mary Harvey were married by Rev. Thomas Dell. {DOLR 19 Old 75}
WARD, MARY, of Charles County, aet. 55, dep. between Oct 1, 1772 and Nov 2, 1772, mentioned her husband George Walker about 30 years ago. {CHLR U#3:263} Aet. 56, dep. Feb 23, 1774, mentioned her husband George Walker about 35 years ago. {CHLR W#3:82}
WARD, MURPHY, of Prince George's County, aet. 46, dep. Sep 29, 1731. {PGLR Q:396} See "Bartholomew Fields," q.v.
WARD, WILLIAM, of Charles County, aet. 71 or 72, dep. Aug 7, 1738. {CHLR T#2:497} Aet. 75, dep. May 3, 1742. {CHLR O#2:381} Aet. 76, dep. May 30, 1743.

{CHLR O#2:567} See "Bartholomew Henrickson" and "Andrew Peterson" and "Alexander Shresse," q.v.

WARDEN, JOHN, of Charles County, aet. 63, dep. Mar 27, 1758. {CHLR H#3:431}

WARDEN, RICHARD, of Charles County, aet. 44, dep. Mar 27, 1758. {CHLR H#3:434}

WARDER, WILLIAM, of Charles County, aet. 57, dep. Aug 20, 1753. {CHLR D#3:153} Aet. 66, dep. Nov 8, 1762. {CHLR M#3:123} Aet. 70, dep. Aug 5, 1768. {CHLR Q#3:259}

WARE, FRANCIS, of Charles County, aet. 31, dep. Jun 6, 1726. {CHLR P#2:392} Aet. 40, dep. Oct 27, 1735. {CHLR T#2:101} Aet. 41, dep. Jul 6, 1736, mentioned George Goodrick, son of Robert Goodrick. {CHLR T#2:226} Aet. 48, dep. Mar 12, 1743, stated that Thomas Bryan was brought out of Virginia by his mother (not named) 20 years ago next April and the grandmother, Ann Eburnathy, stated that her grandson Thomas Bryan was about 2 years old the fall after that. {CHLR O#2:540}

WARE, FRANCIS (captain), of Charles County, aet. 32, dep. Aug 6, 1765. {CHLR N#3:429} Aet. 42, dep. Feb 22, 1774, mentioned his father Francis Ware, deceased. {CHLR W#3:385}

WARE, AGNES, see "Arthure Clahay," q.v.

WARE, RICHARD, see "Arthure Clahay," q.v.

WARFIELD, ALEXANDER, see "William Farquhar," q.v.

WARFIELD, RICHARD, of Prince George's County, n.a., dep. Mar 18, 1745/6, mentioned Augustine Gambol, Daniel Hearn, and Silvanus Marriot. {ARMD 44:692, CMSP 1:75}

WARFORD, ELIZABETH, of Frederick County, n.a., dep. Dec 2, 1765. {ARMD 32:156-157}

WARFORD, WILLIAM, of Frederick County, aet. 63 or thereabouts, dep. Jun 6, 1761, mentioned he kept company with Col. Bradford and Capt. Thomas Fletchall about 40 years ago. {FRLR G:280}

WARING, FRANCIS (major), of Prince George's County, aet. 37, dep. May 7, 1752. {PGLR NN:64} Major Francis Waring, aet. 42, dep. Mar 18, 1757, mentioned Col. Leonard Hollyday in 1736, Col. Thomas Greenfield and Col. Thomas Hollyday in 1701 [yet the deponent was not born until 1715?] and Richard Marsham Waring about 20 years ago. {PGLR NN:515}

WARING, RICHARD MARSHAM, see "Francis Waring," q.v.

WARING, SAMUEL (captain), of St. Mary's, n.a., dep. Mar 2, 1659 and May 31, 1664 and Apr 7, 1665. {ARMD 41:365, 49:218, 49:469} See "Philip Willocy," q.v.

WARNER, MARY, see "Elizabeth Ellis," q.v.

WARNER, RICHARD, of Queen Anne's County, aet. 50, dep. Aug 13, 1760. {QAEJ - John Gafford folder}

WARNER, SOLOMON, of Talbot County, aet. about 65, dep. Apr, 1761. {TAEJ - William Elbert folder}

WARNER, STEPHEN, see "William Warner," q.v.

WARNER, WILLIAM, of Dorchester County, aet. about 54, dep. between Nov 10, 1741 and Mar 11, 1741/2, mentioned a dispute about 40 years between his uncle Charles Powell, his aunt Susannah Powell, and his grandmother (not named). {DOLR 12 Old 154} Aet. 57, dep. Oct 3, 1744, mentioned Stephen Warner about 31 or 32 years ago. {DOLR 12 Old 142} Aet. about 75, dep. between Jun 10, 1760 and Jul 16, 1762, mentioned old John Lecompte and old John Harwood. {DOLR 19 Old 65} See "Charles Thompson" and "Clara Lecompte" and "Philemon Lecompte" and "Moses Lecompte," q.v.

WARRE, JOANE, of St. Mary's County, n.a., wife of Thomas Warre, dep. 1648, mentioned William Styles. {ARMD 4:421}

WARRE, THOMAS, see "Joane Warre," q.v.

WARREN, CATHERINE, of Charles County, aet. 53, dep. May 29, 1752, mentioned her father James Williams. {CHLR B#3:47} Aet. 53, dep. May 14, 1752, mentioned her daughter-in-law Ann Short and her husband Daniel Short about 30 years ago. {CHLR B#3:355}

WARREN, HUMPHERY, of Charles County, n.a., dep. Jul 28, 1663. {CHLR B:135}

WARREN, HUMPHREY, of Charles County, aet. 55, dep. Dec 6, 1763. {CHLR M#3:503}

WARREN, HUMPHREY, see "Margaret Warren," q.v.

WARREN, JOHN, see "Walter Pakes," q.v.

WARREN, MARGARET, of Charles County, aet. 42, dep. Dec 6, 1763, mentioned her husband Humphrey Warren. {CHLR M#3:503}

WARREN, THOMAS, of Charles County, aet. 42, dep. May 14, 1752. {CHLR B#3:354} See "William Cage," q.v.

WARRING, BASIL, of Prince George's County, aet. 43, dep. Nov 15, 1756, stated that William Pierce was tenant on *Jamaica Port Royal* about a year ago and Thomas Lucas has since died. {PGLR PP:16, pt. 2}

WARRING, ROSE, see "Richard Brightwell," q.v.

WARRING, SAMUEL, see "Phillip Willocy" and "Richard Brightwell," q.v.

WARRING, THOMAS, of Prince George's County, aet. near 50, dep. Jul 2, 1760, mentioned his father (not named) about 30 or 40 years ago. {PGLR RR:79} See "John Penn," q.v.

WATERS, JAMES, of Charles County, aet. 58, dep. Oct 18, 1763. {CHLR M#3:592}

WATERS, JOHN, of Charles County, aet. 51, dep. Oct 18, 1763. {CHLR M#3:592}

WATERS, MARGARET, of Charles County, aet. 50, dep. Jun 13, 1726. {CHLR P#2:243}

WATERS, RICHARD, of Prince George's County, aet. about 47, Quaker, dep. Jul 14, 1764, mentioned his father Samuel Waters about 35 years ago, now deceased. {PGLR TT:608}

WATERS, SAMUEL, of Prince George's County, aet. 51, Quaker, dep. Nov 14, 1757. {PGLR PP:68, pt. 2} Aet. near 55, dep. Jul 17, 1763. {PGLR TT:606}

WATERS, SAMUEL, of Prince George's County, aet. 38, Quaker, dep. Nov 15, 1768, mentioned his father (not named). {PGLR BB#2:387}

WATERS, SAMUEL, see "Richard Waters," q.v.
WATERS, SPENCER MARTRUM, of Dorchester County, aet. 39, dep. between Mar 14, 1769 and Apr 9, 1770, stated that he lived with Mary Cratcher about 15 years ago and several years before that he worked at Francis Lee's plantation and met Thomas Stainton, now deceased. {DOLR 24 Old 9}
WATERS, WILLIAM, of Prince George's County, aet. near 47, dep. Sep 10, 1763. {PGLR TT:607}
WATHEN, HUDSON, of Charles County, aet. 63, dep. Jul 24, 1758, mentioned Capt. Allen. {CHLR H#3:574} Hudson Wothen, aet. 58, dep. May 29, 1752. {CHLR B#3:58}
WATHEN, IGNATIUS, see "William Wathen," q.v.
WATHEN, WILLIAM, of Charles County, aet. 42, dep. Feb 2, 1752, mentioned his father Ignatius Wathen. {CHLR K#3:480}
WATKINS, JOHN, see "Indian Tequassino," q.v.
WATKINS, SAMUEL, of Calvert or St. Mary's County, n.a., dep. Apr 23, 1691. {ARMD 8:247}
WATKINS, SOLOMON, of Queen Anne's County, aet. about 26, dep. Mar, 1753, stated that Albert Johnson, now deceased, showed him the line that divided land between his sons Henry and John Johnson. {QAEJ - Peter Johnson folder}
WATSON (WATTSON), ABRAHAM, of St. Mary's County, n.a., dep. 1664. {ARMD 49:315, 385}
WATSON, ANDREW, of Charles County, aet. 30 or thereabouts, dep. May 1, 1659. {CHLR A:56, ARMD 53:46}
WATSON, JAMES, of Charles County, aet. 80, dep. Mar 14, 1776, mentioned the brothers George Naylor and James Naylor about 40 years ago. {CHLR Y#3:674}
WATSON, JAMES, of Prince George's County, aet. 32, dep. Sep 13, 1729, mentioned his father (not named) about 20 or 30 years ago. {PGLR M:520} Aet. 41, dep. Aug 25, 1737. {PGLR T:504} Aet. 52, dep. Jan 9, 1748/9, mentioned his father William Watson. {PGLR BB:626} James Watson, Sr., aet. 58, dep. Nov 23, 1754. {PGLR NN:207-208} Aet. 59, dep. May 12, 1755, mentioned Nathaniel Magruder about 25 years ago, now deceased. {PGLR NN:434} Aet. 75, dep. Oct 22, 1770, mentioned Aaron Roberts about 30 years ago who served his time with a Capt. Jones. {PGLR AA#2:180} Aet. 75, dep. Jun 2, 1770. {PGLR BB#3:77} Aet. 77, dep. Apr 24, 1772 and Jul 7, 1772. {PGLR BB#3:75, 81} James Watson, Sr., aet. 80, dep. Oct 18, 1774, mentioned his brother William Watson. {PGLR CC#2:25}
WATSON, JOHN, of Prince George's County, aet. 36, dep. Oct 12, 1770. {PGLR AA#2:206}
WATSON, RICHARD, see "Enock Doughty," q.v.
WATSON, ROBERT, see "Solomon Wright" and "Andrew Gray" and "Edward Dean," q.v.
WATSON, WILLIAM, see "Jane Lovejoy" and "Richard Brightwell" and "John Brightwell" and "James Watson," q.v.

WATTS, BARTHOLOMEW, of London, England, captain of the ship *Globe*, dep. May 8, 1682 in St. Mary's County. {ARMD 7:281}
WATTS, GEORGE, of St. Mary's County, n.a., dep. 1649. {ARMD 4:541}
WAYVILL, JOHN, see "Simon Richardson" and "Philip White," q.v.
WEALES (WILES), ELIZABETH, of Charles County, aet. 22, dep. Jun 29, 1663, denied she had laid with John Lumbroso and desired that he be clear from the scandal. {CHLR B:166} See "George Harris" and "John Browne," q.v.
WEATHERLY, JOHN, of Dorchester County, n.a., dep. Jun 2, 1740. {DOLR 12 Old 128}
WEAVER, RICHARD, of Prince George's County, aet. 45, dep. Jun 10, 1728 and Jun 26, 1728. {PGLR M:292, 524} Carpenter, n.a., dep. May 1, 1729, mentioned William Scott about 45 years ago. {PGLR M:443}
WEBB, MARK, of Prince George's County, aet. 59, dep. Aug 14, 1762. {PGLR BB#2:147} Aet. 65, dep. Nov 7, 1767, mentioned John Harvey about 37 or 38 years ago, now deceased. {PGLR BB#2:161}
WEBB, PETER, of Talbot County, Quaker, aet. about 59, dep. between Nov 14, 1769 and Nov 6, 1770, stated that he was shown the bounded tree of *Wiltshire* about 40 years ago by his mother Sarah Webb who had her knowledge from her brother William Stevens. {DOLR 24 Old 308}
WEBB, SARAH, see "Peter Webb," q.v.
WEBB, THOMAS, of Prince George's County, aet. 55, dep. Aug 16, 1758, mentioned John Camble about 8 or 9 years ago. {PGLR PP:231, pt. 2}
WEBSTER, ISAAC, of Baltimore County, Quaker, aet. 37 or thereabouts, dep. Oct 29, 1768, mentioned his father Isaac Webster. {BALR AL#A:298}
WEBSTER, ISAAC, of Baltimore County, Quaker, aet. 52, dep. May 20, 1772. {BALR AL#E:279} See "John Lee Webster," q.v.
WEBSTER, JOHN, see "Lewis Potee," q.v.
WEBSTER, JOHN LEE, of Baltimore County, Quaker, aet. 33, dep. Nov 22, 1768, mentioned his father Isaac Webster about 10 years ago. {BALR AL#A:301}
WEBSTER, RICHARD, of Dorchester County, aet. 50, dep. between Jun 8, 1756 and Jul 13, 1758, mentioned Cornelius Johnson, uncle of John Sulivane. {DOLR 16 Old 117} Aet. 53, dep. between Mar 10, 1761 and Mar 11, 1762, mentioned John Griffith about 27 or 28 years ago, now deceased; also mentioned John Chilcutt, now deceased, son of Anthony Chilcutt. {DOLR 18 Old 139} Aet. about 60, dep. between Mar 17, 1768 and Aug 9, 1768, mentioned George Chilcutt and John Brown about 40 years ago, both now deceased. {DOLR 22 Old 433} Aet. about 64, dep. between Nov 13, 1770 and Aug 2, 1771, mentioned John Alford about 40 or 50 years ago, now deceased. {DOLR 25 Old 26}
WEBSTER, SAMUEL, of Baltimore County, Quaker, aet. 66, dep. Aug 15, 1774. {BALR AL#L:242}
WEBSTER, WILLIAM, of Prince George's County, aet. 73, dep. Mar 10, 1769. {PGLR AA#2:150} Aet. 79, dep. Mar 15, 1774. {PGLR BB#3:400}

WEDDILL, ROGER, of Talbot County, aet. 21, dep. Sep 19, 1671, mentioned his master Dr. Richard Tilghman. {ARMD 54:510}

WEEMS, WILLIAM LOCK, of Prince George's County, aet. 40, dep. Nov 7, 1767, mentioned Benjamin Clark about 20 years ago, now deceased. {PGLR BB#2:102}

WELCH, ANTHONY, of St. Mary's County, n.a., dep. Sep 9, 1663. {ARMD 49:52}

WELCH, REVEREND, see "James Hopkins," q.v.

WELCH, SILVESTER (captain), of Anne Arundel County, n.a., dep. Jul 18, 1707, mentioned Aron Rawlings, Richard Clarke (Clark), and John Jacobs. {ARMD 25:218-219}

WELCH, WILLIAM, of Dorchester County, aet. 70, dep. Jan 15, 1744/5. {DOLR 12 Old 253}

WELLER, JACOB, of Frederick County, aet. 67, dep. Apr 6, 1772, stated that he was a member of the church known by the name of the United Brethern; also stated that he was a chain carrier when *Addition to the Blacksmith's Lott* was surveyed. {FRLR P:169-170}

WELLER, JOHN, of Frederick County, aet. 56, dep. Apr 6, 1772, stated that he was a chain carrier when *Addition to the Blacksmith's Lott* was surveyed. {FRLR P:169}

WELLS, FRANCES, see "Elizabeth Tyler" and "John Lamar" and "Nathan Wells" and "Sarah Gaither," q.v.

WELLS, GEORGE, of Prince George's County, aet. 64, dep. Nov 17, 1748. {PGLR BB:695} Aet. 71, dep. Apr 22, 1755, mentioned James Edmonston, son of Alexander Edmonston. {PGLR NN:371-372}

WELLS, HUMPHREY, JR., of Queen Anne's County, aet. about 35, dep. Mar, 1746. {QAEJ - Benjamin Tasker folder}

WELLS, JOHN, of Prince George's County, aet. 49, dep. May 11, 1762. {PGLR RR:267}

WELLS, NATHAN, SR., of Prince George's County, n.a., dep. Jul 31, 1764, stated that about 50 odd years ago John Ouchterlony came into this province a youth under the direction of Patrick Andrews, merchant, with whom he lived as storekeeper; said John married Frances Wells and had 2 daughters, Mary (married James Plummer) and Elizabeth; said John also became a merchant after Patrick Andrews declined the business. {PGLR AA#2:121}

WELLS, RICHARD, SR., of Baltimore County, aet. 66, dep. Mar 4, 1763. {BALR B#M:155} Aet. 71, dep. Oct 27, 1766. {BALR B#P:306}

WELLS, SWITHEN, see "Benjamin Randall," q.v.

WELLS, THOMAS, JR., of Prince George's County, aet. near 29, dep. Feb 3, 1747/8, mentioned his father (not named) about 20 years ago. {PGLR BB:692}

WELLS, WIDOW, see "James Edmonston" and "John Evans," q.v.

WELSH, JOHN, see "William Davis," q.v.

WELSH, MARY, of Prince George's County, aet. 68, dep. Nov 15, 1768. {PGLR BB#2:387}

WENNAM, WILLIAM, see "Richard Smith" and "Joan Nevill" and "Nicholas Phillips," q.v.
WENTWORTH, THOMAS, of Charles County, gentleman, n.a., dep. Jul 2, 1661. {CHLR A:141, ARMD 41:498}
WEST, EDWARD, of St. Mary's County, n.a., dep. Feb 11, 1661. {ARMD 41:515}
WEST, ENOCH, of Baltimore County, aet. 43, dep. May 29, 1764, mentioned his brother Robert West. {BALR B#N:128} Enock West, of Harford County, aet. 54, dep. May 25, 1775, mentioned his brother Robert West and father Robert West. {Land Commission, 1774, Harford County Genealogical Society Newsletter, Jan, 1993, p. 3}
WEST, HANNAH, of Baltimore County, n.a., widow of Robert West, dep. Mar 22, 1764. {BALR B#N:126}
WEST, JOHN, of Anne Arundel County, n.a., dep. 1696. {ARMD 20:530}
WEST, JOHN, SR., of Frederick County, aet. 64 or thereabouts, dep. Nov 11, 1765, stated that he was shown the bounded tree of *The Younger Brother* by his father (not name) about 40 years ago. {FRLR K:353}
WEST, JOSEPH, of Prince George's County, planter, aet. 62 or 63, dep. Oct 3, 1724. {PGLR I:596}
WEST, RICHARD, see "Hannah Clove," q.v.
WEST, ROBERT, of Harford County, aet. 42, dep. between Jun 17 and Jun 26, 1775, mentioned his father Robert West. {Land Commission, 1774, Harford County Genealogical Society Newsletter, Jan, 1993, p. 3} See "Joseph Morgan" and "Hannah West" and "Thomas West" and "Enoch West," q.v.
WEST, SAMUEL, of Frederick County, aet. 34, dep. Jun 5, 1764. {FRLR J:942}
WEST, SOLOMON, see "John Nicolls," q.v.
WEST, THOMAS, of Baltimore County, aet. 32, dep. May 29, 1764, mentioned Robert West (now deceased) about 23 years ago, and Robert West (son of said Robert) last year. {BALR B#N:127}
WESTERNDALL, PERCEFIELD, of Talbot County, n.a., dep. Sep 21, 1669. {ARMD 54:444}
WETHERINGTON, JOHN, of Kent County, n.a., dep. Mar 28, 1720 to prove the will of Dennis Sullivane, deceased. {Will Book 15:261}
WHARTON, HENRY, see "Jane Wharton," q.v.
WHARTON, JANE, of St. Mary's County, aet. 50, wife of Henry Wharton, gentleman, dep. Jan 16, 1738 [deposition was entered in the records of Charles County on Oct 10, 1759], stated that about Nov 10, 1698, at the home of Mrs. Jane Doyne, Thomas Jameson was married to her (Wharton's) sister Mary Matthews by Rev. William Hunter according to the rites of the Church of Rome; also stated that she (Wharton) was present at the home of Thomas Jameson in Charles County on Dec 25, 1699 when her sister (Mary Jameson) gave birth to her eldest son Thomas Jameson; also mentioned that her brother-in-law Thomas Jameson went to England several times during his marriage, stating he was heir to an estate there which he did not expect to enjoy, but he

hoped would come to some of his children; Thomas Jameson died about Nov 18, 1733. {CHLR G#3:370}
WHEAT, FRANCIS, SR., of Prince George's County, aet. 67, dep. Jul 9, 1764. {PGLR TT:283}
WHEATLEY (WHITELEY), AUGUSTUS, of Dorchester County, aet. about 48, dep. between Mar 13, 1764 and Mar 14, 1765. {DOLR 20 Old 28}
WHEATLEY, JOHN, of St. Mary's County, aet. 49, dep. Apr 18, 1654, stated that about 12 years age he and Thomas Harrison came together to this province on the same ship with Capt. Thomas Cornwallies, Esq., out of England. {ARMD 10:371}
WHEATLEY, THOMAS, of Dorchester County, aet. 32, dep. between Mar 15, 1731 and Apr 13, 1732. {DOLR 9 Old 63}
WHEELER, CHARLES, of Dorchester County, aet. 67, dep. between Jun 17, 1732 and Jun 24, 1732, stated that he was shown the bounded tree of *Hannah's Choice* by old William Willoby; also mentioned the taking up of *Swamp Square* about 28 years ago. {DOLR 9 Old 60} Charles Wheelar, aet. about 77, dep. between Nov 10, 1741 and Mar 10, 1747. {DOLR 14 Old 200} See "Giles Proctor," q.v.
WHEELER, CLEMENT, see "John Baynes," q.v.
WHEELER, FRANCIS, of Charles County, aet. 67, dep. Aug 26, 1767, stated that he was shown the bounded tree of the land he had bought from Zephaniah Wade by John Clarvo about 33 years ago. {CHLR P#3:655} Francis Wheeler, of Prince George's County, aet. 68, dep. Jul 1, 1766, mentioned John Clarvoe about 30 years ago, now deceased. {PGLR TT:612}
WHEELER, FRANCIS, of Prince George's County, gentleman, aet. 50, dep. Jul 1, 1726. {PGLR M:27} Aet. between 50 and 60, dep. Jun 25, 1728. {PGLR M:286} Aet. 55, dep. Nov 28, 1728. {PGLR M:346} Aet. between 50 and 60, dep. between Jun 11, 1729 and Nov 26, 1729. {PGLR M:522} Aet. between 50 and 60, dep. between Nov 11, 1729 and Mar 26, 1730, mentioned William Hutchison, deceased. {PGLR M:558, 561} Aet. 60, dep. 1731. {PGLR Q:372}
WHEELER, FRANCIS, see "Leonard Wheeler," q.v.
WHEELER, HENRY, of Dorchester County, aet. 40, dep. between Nov 16, 1736 and Jun 13, 1737. {DOLR 9 Old 446}
WHEELER, IGNATIUS, of Prince George's County, n.a., dep. Jun 25, 1724. {PGLR I:592}
WHEELER, JAMES, of Dorchester County, aet. 38, dep. between Nov 16, 1736 and Jun 13, 1737, stated that the bounded tree of *The Gift* was across a branch from the dwelling house of John Wheeler. {DOLR 9 Old 446}
WHEELER, JAMES, of Prince George's County, aet. 40, dep. Jul 1, 1726. {PGLR M:27} Aet. 58, dep. Mar 25, 1743. {PGLR Y:657} Aet. 72, dep. Jun 18, 1752, mentioned Hillery Baul about 47 or 48 years ago. {PGLR NN:34} Aet. 77, dep. Mar 26, 1756. {PGLR NN:479} Aet. 89, dep. Feb 17, 1759, stated that Hilliary

Ball showed him the bounds of *Brothers Delight* about 55 years ago. {PGLR RR:232}

WHEELER, JAMES, see "Henry Acton," q.v.

WHEELER, JOHN (major), of Charles County, aet. 25, dep. Oct 26, 1658 and May 1, 1659 (no age given). {CHLR A:25, 58; ARMD 53:46} Aet. not given, dep. Nov 4, 1663. {CHLR B:201} Major John Wheeler, aet. 61, dep. Oct 22, 1691, stated that William Barton and his brother (not named) were orphans of Nathan Barton. {CHLR R#1:275} See "James Wheeler" and "Peter Lecompte" and "Giles Proctor" and "Thomas Dickison," q.v.

WHEELER, JOHN, JR., of Charles County, aet. 22, dep. Sep 14, 1675. {CHLR F#1:145}

WHEELER, JOSHUA, of Dorchester County, aet. 33, dep. between Nov 9, 1762 and May 9, 1763. {DOLR 19 Old 425} Aet. 35, dep. between Nov 13, 1764 and Apr 13, 1765. {DOLR 20 Old 257}

WHEELER, LEONARD, of Charles County, aet. 52, dep. Aug 1, 1743, mentioned Francis Marbury and his wife Mary Marbury. {CHLR O#2:620} Leonard Whealor, aet. 70, dep. Feb 2, 1761. {PGLR RR:236} Leonard Wheeler, aet. 71, dep. May 17, 1762, mentioned his father Francis Wheeler about 50 or 60 years ago, now deceased. {PGLR RR:262}

WHEELER, MARY, of Charles County, aet. 40, dep. Mar 9, 1669/70. {CHLR D#1:150} See "Thomas Dickison," q.v.

WHEELER, RICHARD, of Charles County, aet. 48, dep. Apr 6, 1733. {CHLR R#2:332}

WHEELER, RICHARD, of Charles County, aet. 42, dep. Nov 20, 1766. {CHLR P#3:286}

WHEELER, SAMUEL, of Baltimore County, n.a., dep. Jan 11, 1766. {BALR B#P:300}

WHEELER, SAMUEL, of Baltimore County, aet. 55, dep. Dec 26, 1767, mentioned his father William Wheeler, deceased long ago. {BALR B#Q:700}

WHEELER (WHELER), SAMUEL, of Dorchester County, aet. 71, dep. between Mar 15, 1737 and Nov 9, 1737, stated that the bounds of *Row's Lott* were shown to him by James Anderson about 40 years ago. {DOLR 9 Old 493}

WHEELER, THOMAS, of Charles County, aet. 65, dep. Jun 6, 1726. {CHLR P#2:390}

WHEELER, THOMAS, of Dorchester County, n.a., dep. May 30, 1681, mentioned William Hill. {ARMD 15:360}

WHEELER, THOMAS, of Dorchester County, aet. 45, dep. between Jun 8, 1756 and Jul 15, 1756. {DOLR 15 Old 376}

WHEELER, THOMAS, of Prince George's County, aet. 77, dep. Apr 26, 1735, mentioned his father and brothers (not named). {PGLR T:254}

WHEELER, WILLIAM, see "Samuel Wheeler," q.v.

WHEELER, WILLIAM, JR., of Baltimore County, aet. 46, dep. Jun 6, 1763. {BALR B#N:180}

WHETSEL, GEORGE, of Frederick County, aet. 51, dep. Jul 24, 1762. {FRLR H:102}
WHEYLAND, WILLIAM, see "John Hayward," q.v.
WHISSETT(?), JOHN, of Queen Anne's County, aet. about 65, dep. Apr, 1723. {QAEJ - William Bishop folder}
WHITAKER (WHITECAR), JAMES, aet. 41 or thereabouts, dep. Nov 22, 1768, mentioned Thomas Bond the Elder about 12 to 14 years ago. {BALR AL#A:297} See "John Fichgared," q.v.
WHITAKER, PETER, of Baltimore County, aet. 70, dep. Dec 14, 1765. {BALR B#P:180}
WHITAKER, PETER, of Baltimore County, aet. 51, dep. Feb 11, 1765. {BALR B#N:180}
WHITE, ALEXANDER, of Charles County, n.a., dep. Nov 4, 1663. {CHLR B:201}
WHITE, BENJAMIN, of Prince George's County, aet. 47, dep. Mar 24, 1742. {PGLR Y:654} Aet. 51, dep. Jan 6, 1747/8, mentioned old John Mobley about 27 years ago. {PGLR BB:690} Aet. 68, dep. Oct 10, 1762, mentioned Dr. Denune about 30 years ago. {PGLR RR:264-265} Aet. 72, dep. Apr 14, 1766, stated that he was a chain carrier on *Ample Grange* about 21 or 22 years ago. {PGLR TT:570}
WHITE, EDWARD, of Dorchester County, aet. 40, dep. between Jun 8, 1756 and Jul 15, 1756. {DOLR 15 Old 376} See "Elizabeth White," q.v.
WHITE, ELIZABETH, of Dorchester County, aet. 48, dep. Jun 14, 1735, mentioned that Edward White, son of Thomas and Elizabeth White, was born Aug 3, 1713. {DOLR 9 Old 288}
WHITE, ERICK, of Baltimore County, aet. 40, dep. May 20, 1772. {BALR AL#E:277}
WHITE, JAMES, of Frederick County, aet. 42, dep. Dec 10, 1772. {FRLR P:681-682}
WHITE, JOHN, of Dorchester County, n.a., dep. Jun 1, 1681, mentioned Stephen Gary's plantation at Transquakin. {ARMD 15:361}
WHITE, JOHN, of Dorchester County, aet. 47, dep. between Nov 14, 1738 and Mar 11, 1738, mentioned Jane Taylor and Frances Taylor, two daughters of Major John Taylor. {DOLR 12 Old 112}
WHITE, JOHN, of Prince George's County, aet. 50, dep. Nov 21, 1763. {PGLR TT:195} Aet. 57, dep. Mar 27, 1770, mentioned Samuel Taylor, deceased. {PGLR AA#2:194}
WHITE, MARGARET, of Dorchester County, aet. 18, dep. between Nov 9, 1756 and Nov 7, 1760. {DOLR 17 Old 213}
WHITE, PHILIP, of St. Mary's County, n.a., dep. 1642, mentioned Robert Nicolls, John Wayvill, and Thomas Davis. {ARMD 4:181-182}
WHITE, RICHARD, of Prince George's County, aet. 33, dep. Feb 20, 1767, mentioned his father (not named). {PGLR BB#2:168}
WHITE, ROBERT, of Prince George's County, aet. 51, dep. May 11, 1733. {PGLR T:26} Aet. 83, dep. May 30, 1758, mentioned Col. Bradford about 30 odd years ago. {PGLR PP:234, pt. 2} Aet. 93, dep. Nov 21, 1763. {PGLR TT:195}

WHITE, SAMUEL, of Prince George's County, aet. 48, dep. Nov 17, 1748. {PGLR BB:695}
WHITE, THOMAS, of Dorchester County, aet. 40, dep. between Nov 9, 1756 and Nov 7, 1760. {DOLR 17 Old 213}
WHITE, THOMAS, of Philadelphia, formerly of Baltimore County, aet. 61, dep. Oct 27, 1766. {BALR B#P:305}
WHITE, THOMAS, see "Elizabeth White," q.v.
WHITE, WILLIAM, of Dorchester County, aet. 40, dep. between Mar 10, 1767 and Jun 8, 1767. {DOLR 21 Old 443}
WHITE, WILLIAM, of Charles County, aet. 36, dep. Mar 10, 1658/9. {CHLR A:43}
WHITE, WILLIAM, of Charles County, aet. 72, dep. Oct 1, 1771. {CHLR U#3:18} William White, Sr., aet. 76, dep. Mar 14, 1776. {CHLR Y#3:374}
WHITE, ZACHARIAH, of Frederick County, aet. 35 and upwards, dep. Sep 25, 1772, stated that he was in partnership with Robert Beall about 12 or 14 years ago. {FRLR P:432}
WHITELEY, AUGUSTUS, of Dorchester County, n.a., dep. Sep 6, 1746. {DOLR 14 Old 74}
WHITELEY, DAVID, of Dorchester County, aet. 25, dep. between Aug 13, 1765 and Dec 28, 1765, mentioned his father Thomas Whiteley. {DOLR 21 Old 42}
WHITELY, THOMAS, of Dorchester County, aet. 48, dep. Aug 24, 1745, stated that he was a servant to Jacob Gray about 24 years ago; also mentioned Mary Lake, now deceased, wife of Henry Lake, deceased. {DOLR 12 Old 247} See "David Whiteley," q.v.
WHITICAR, JAMES, of Baltimore County, aet. 41, dep. Oct 29, 1768. {BALR AL#A:297}
WHITLEY, THOMAS, of Dorchester County, aet. 46, dep. between Jun 14, 1743 and Aug 1, 1743. {DOLR 12 Old 167}
WHITMAN, FREDERICK, of Frederick County, aet. 38, dep. Jul 24, 1762. {FRLR H:102}
WHITMORE, HUMPHREY, of Prince George's County, aet. 44, dep. May 17, 1762, mentioned his father Humphrey Whitmore. {PGLR RR:262}
WHITNAL, ROBERT, of Frederick County, aet. 42, dep. Aug 31, 1765, stated that he carried the chain for surveyor John Steward on *Williams Project* about 12 years ago. {FRLR K:425}
WHITTIER, WILLIAM, of Charles County, aet. 57, dep. Oct 27, 1735. {CHLR T#2:101}
WHYNIARD, THOMAS, of Anne Arundel County, aet. 21 or thereabouts, dep. Sep 13, 1664. {ARMD 49:304, 314}
WICHERLY, ELIZABETH, of Charles County, aet. 40, dep. May 30, 1711. {CHLR M#2:122} Aet. 46, dep. Nov 5, 1719, mentioned her father Thomas Allison. {CHLR M#2:65}
WICHERLY, THOMAS, see "Richard Coombes," q.v.
WICKES, JOSEPH, of Kent County, aet. 54 or 55, dep. 1773. {KELR DD#4:253; KEEJ - Samuel Griffith folder}

WICKHAM, NATHANIEL, of Prince George's County, planter, aet. 61, dep. Oct 2, 1724. {PGLR I:597} Nathaniel Wickham, Sr., aet. 71, dep. Sep 22, 1730. {PGLR Q:157} Nathaniell Wickham, aet. 82, dep. Nov 26, 1739. {PGLR Y:107} Nathaniel Wikham, aet. near 91, dep. Feb 3, 1747/8, stated that he served on a jury about 47 years ago. {PGLR BB:691}

WICKHAM, NATHANIEL (colonel), of Frederick County, n.a., dep. Apr 20, 1767, stated that he surveyed *Williams Intention* in 1740. {FRLR K:1354} Aet. 72 or thereabouts, dep. Aug 24, 1768. {FRLR L:598}

WICKHAM, NATHANIEL, see "Henry Chapple" and "William Winfield," q.v.

WIGENTON, ----, see "Henry Moore (More)," q.v.

WIGHT, ANNE, see "Isle of Wight" and "John Wight," q.v.

WIGHT, ISLE OF, of Prince George's County, aet. 29, dep. Apr 15, 1753, mentioned his mother Anne Wight about 16 years ago. {PGLR NN:136} Aet. 54 or thereabouts, dep. May 23, 1774 (recorded Mar 23, 1776), mentioned Francis Mobberly, Rebecca Mobberly, John Tucker, and Thomas Tucker, about 30 years ago. {PGLR CC#2:245}

WIGHT (WIGHTT), JOHN, of Prince George's County, aet. 39, dep. Apr 15, 1753, mentioned his father John Wightt, mother Anne Wightt, and uncle James Greenfield about 20 years ago. {PGLR NN:134-135} Aet. 44, dep. Apr 25, 1758, mentioned Capt. Charles Beall about 22 years ago, now deceased. {PGLR PP:233, pt. 2} John Wight (also spelled White in another deposition), aet. near 53, dep. Apr 21, 1767, stated that Thomas Butler showed him the bounds of *Haddocks Hills* some years ago; also mentioned Thomas Lucas in 1761. {PGLR BB#2:119-121} See "William Neale," q.v.

WILCOX, JOSEPH, see "William Depriest," q.v.

WILCOXON, JOHN, of Frederick County, aet. 39, dep. Sep 7, 1757, mentioned his father John Wilcoxon, deceased. {FRLR F:777}

WILCOXON, LEWIS, see "Thomas Garton," q.v.

WILCOXON, THOMAS, of Prince George's County, aet. 37, dep. Sep 25, 1733. {PGLR T:18} Thomas Wilcoxon, Sr., aet. 57, dep. Jun 23, 1753, mentioned John Dickson about 38 years ago, now deceased. {PGLR NN:141} Thomas Wilcoxon, aet. 68, dep. Mar 5, 1763. {PGLR TT:13} Thomas Wilcoxon, Sr., aet. 69, dep. Jul 9, 1764. {PGLR TT:283}

WILCOXON, THOMAS, JR., of Prince George's County, aet. 36, dep. Sep 14, 1761. {PGLR RR:179} Aet. 39, dep. Jul 9, 1764. {PGLR TT:283}

WILDER, JOHN, of Charles County, aet. 46, dep. Oct 10, 1738. {CHLR T#2:513} Aet. 59, dep. Feb 19, 1750. {CHLR Z#2:144} Aet. 61, dep. Apr 29, 1754. {CHLR D#3:324}

WILDMAN, WILLIAM, of Stafford County, Virginia, aet. 22, dep. Jun 7, 1668 in Charles County, Maryland. {CHLR C#1:274}

WILES (WILDS), ELISABETH, see "John Browne" and "George Harris" and "Elisabeth Weales," q.v.

WILKINSON, ELIZA, of Charles County, aet. 43, dep. May 14, 1752. {CHLR B#3:354}
WILKINSON, HENRY, of Queen Anne's County, aet. about 63 or 64, dep. Mar, 1746. {QAEJ - Benjamin Tasker folder}
WILKINSON, JOHN, see "Mathew Dockery," q.v.
WILKINSON, THOMAS, see "Mathew Dockery," q.v.
WILKINSON, WILLIAM, of Baltimore County, n.a., dep. Jun 6, 1711, stated that he knew Hanah Keon, alias Dictus Keon, of North Carolina, who married Lodowick Williams, formerly of Baltimore County. {BALR TR#A:135}
WILKINSON, WILLIAM, of Baltimore County, n.a., dep. Mar 5, 1776. {BALR WG#B:394}
WILLET, CHARLES, of Charles County, aet. 23, dep. Apr 30, 1745. {CHLR Z#2:336}
WILLETT, EDWARD, of Prince George's County, n.a., dep. Mar 18, 1728/9, mentioned his parents (not named) and Col. John Bigger. {PGLR M:478} Edward Willet, aet. 63, dep. Jun 1, 1767, mentioned Edward Villers Harbin, and also John Harbin about 30 or 40 years ago. {PGLR BB#2:14}
WILLETT, GEORGE, of Charles County, aet. 24, dep. Aug 2, 1774. {CHLR W#3:387}
WILLETT, NINIAN, of Prince George's County, aet. 37, dep. Aug 23, 1738. {PGLR T:635} Ninian Willett, Sr., aet. 54, dep. Sep 15, 1755. {PGLR NN:411} Ninian Willett, aet. 48 or 58 (two different ages were given in two depositions taken on the same day), dep. Nov 9, 1759, mentioned his father (not named) and Capt. Thomas Claggett. {PGLR RR:80-81} Aet. 60, dep. Nov 9, 1761, mentioned his father Edward Willett about 33 or 34 years ago. {PGLR RR:178} Ningan Willett, aet. 68, dep. Oct 2, 1769, mentioned his father (not named). {PGLR AA#2:186} Ninian Willett, aet. 71, dep. Mar 24, 1772. {PGLR AA#2:502-503}
WILLEY, JOHN, of Dorchester County, aet. 64, dep. between Aug 14, 1744 and Sep 22, 1744. {DOLR 12 Old 92}
WILLEY, WILLIAM, of Dorchester County, aet. about 48, dep. between Aug 14, 1764 and Jan 4, 1768. {DOLR 22 Old 418}
WILLIAM, EDWARD, of Charles County, aet. 33, dep. Jan 26, 1658/9, stated that Lucie Stratton said if she was with child she would lay it upon John Ward or Richard Smith. {CHLR A:35} Aet. 34, dep. Sep 25, 1661 and Nov 19, 1661. {CHLR A:169, ARMD 53:159}
WILLIAMS, ANDREW, of Dorchester County, aet. 43, dep. Aug 30, 1738. {DOLR 12 Old 102}
WILLIAMS, DAVID, see "William Keene," q.v.
WILLIAMS, EASTER, of Charles County, aet. 36, dep. May 29, 1752, mentioned her brothers-in-law Thomas Williams and Justinian Williams. {CHLR B#3:57}
WILLIAMS, EDWARD, see "Hanah Keon" and "Edward William" and "Robert Wilson," q.v.

WILLIAMS, ELIZABETH, of Charles County, aet. 41, dep. May 11, 1772, mentioned her father Thomas Hudson. {CHLR U#3:13} See "Eleanor Fearson," q.v.
WILLIAMS, GEORGE, see "Marrin Williams," q.v.
WILLIAMS, HUGH, of Dorchester County, aet. 37, dep. between Mar 8, 1757 and Dec 17, 1757. {DOLR 16 Old 170}
WILLIAMS, JACOB, of Frederick County, aet. 28, dep. 1767. {FRLR L:59}
WILLIAMS, JAMES, see "Samuel Breshears" and "John Demall" and "William Simpson, Sr.," q.v.
WILLIAMS, JOHN, see "Henry Kimmey" and "Sarah Clark" and "William Brooke," q.v.
WILLIAMS, JOSEPH, of Anne Arundel County, aet. 42, dep. Mar 25, 1754 in Prince George's County. {PGLR NN:255} Aet. 43, dep. Nov 12, 1754. {PGLR NN:350}
WILLIAMS, JUSTINIAN, see "Easter Williams," q.v.
WILLIAMS, LODOWICK, see "William Wilkinson" and "John Bevans" and "Hannah Keon," q.v.
WILLIAMS, MARGARETT, see "Owen Jones," q.v.
WILLIAMS, MARRIN, of Charles County, aet. 63, dep. Jul 24, 1758, mentioned her husband George Williams about 28 years ago. {CHLR H#3:580}
WILLIAMS, MASON, of Charles County, aet. 63, mentioned John Woodward and wife Jane Woodward. {CHLR H#3:431}
WILLIAMS, MATTHEW, see "Caleb Isgate," q.v.
WILLIAMS, MEREDITH, see "Jacob Charles," q.v.
WILLIAMS, OLIVE, see "William Brooke," q.v.
WILLIAMS, ROBERT, see "John Hodson (captain)" and "James Hodson," q.v.
WILLIAMS, ROSEANNA, of Dorchester County, aet. 50, dep. between Nov 12, 1771 and Apr 17, 1772, mentioned her father Oliver Hackett, her uncle Thomas Hackett the Elder, and her grandfather Thomas Hackett, about 30 years ago, all now deceased. {DOLR 26 Old 50}
WILLIAMS, ROZANAH, of Dorchester County, aet. 44, dep. between Mar 14, 1769 and Apr 9, 1770, mentioned an Indian named Long Toby. {DOLR 24 Old 9}
WILLIAMS, SUSANNA, of Dorchester County, aet. 24, dep. between Aug 15, 1746 and Sep 1, 1746. {DOLR 14 Old 89}
WILLIAMS, THOMAS, of Dorchester County, aet. 28, dep. between Nov 8, 1748 and Mar 15, 1748. {DOLR 14 Old 319} Aet. 47, dep. between Nov 8, 1763 and Apr 7, 1764. {DOLR 19 Old 233}
WILLIAMS, THOMAS, of Dorchester County, aet. 49, dep. between Mar 11, 1734 and Jun 6, 1735. {DOLR 9 Old 293} Thomas Williams, Sr., aet. 63, living on the Northwest Fork of Nanticoke River, dep. Mar 8, 1747, stated that the land called *Belea* or *Balia* now belonged to young James Billings. {DOLR 14 Old 310}

WILLIAMS, THOMAS, see "Edward Dean" and "James Langrall" and "Jacob Charles" and "John Harper" and "Easter Williams" and "Mrs. Deborah Foreman," q.v.
WILLIAMS, THOMAS BOWLES, of Charles County, aet. 24, dep. Sep 24, 1757. {CHLR H#3:5}
WILLIAMS, WILLIAM, of Charles County, aet. 41, dep. May 18, 1763. {CHLR M#3:220}
WILLIAMS, WILLIAM, of Charles County, aet. 42, dep. Mar 2, 1730. {CHLR Q#2:474} Aet. 44, dep. Feb 25, 1729/30. {CHLR Q#2:364} Aet. 46, dep. Oct 5, 1731. {CHLR R#2:44}
WILLIAMS, WILLIAM, see "William Hedges" and "Joseph Chapline" and "Henry Kimmey" and "William Depriest," q.v.
WILLIBEE, EDWARD, of Dorchester County, aet. 79, dep. between Mar 14, 1748 and Jun 10, 1749, stated that he was shown the bounded trees of *Willmorth Adventure* and *Skinner's Folly* about 50 years ago by Edward Cook and John Rice. {DOLR 14 Old 465}
WILLIS, ANDREW, of Dorchester County, aet. 40, dep. between Jun 13, 1730 and Sep 10, 1730. {DOLR 8 Old 404} Aet. 43, dep. between Mar 13, 1732 and Nov 14, 1733. {DOLR 9 Old 135}
WILLIS, JOHN, see "James Woolford" and "John Edmondson" and "Rebeccah Foster" and "Thomas Church," q.v.
WILLIS, JOHN, the Elder, of Dorchester County, aet. about 67, dep. between Nov 13, 1770 and Aug 2, 1771, mentioned his father John Willis. {DOLR 25 Old 26}
WILLIS, JUDAH, of Dorchester County, aet. about 50, dep. between Nov 11, 1746 and May 27, 1752. {DOLR 14 Old 658}
WILLIS, RICE, of Kent County on Delaware, aet. 42, dep. between Jun 11, 1745 and May 23, 1746, stated that he was shown the bounded tree of *Skipton* about 26 or 27 years ago by Rice Leveness, of Dorchester County, now deceased. {DOLR 14 Old 50} See "Daniel Sulivane," q.v.
WILLIS, RICHARD (captain), of Dorchester County, aet. 49, dep. between Apr 6, 1732 and Apr 23, 1733, mentioned his mother Frances Fisher about 29 or 30 years ago. {DOLR 9 Old 100}
WILLIS, RICHARD, of Dorchester County, aet. 37, dep. between Mar 11, 1755 and Jul 23, 1755, stated that he was shown the bounded tree of *Staplefort's Lot* about 8 or 9 years ago by William Harper; also mentioned Samuel Harper, son of said William Harper, and young Daniel Foxwell. {DOLR 15 Old 452}
WILLIS, RICHARD, see "Rebeccah Foster," q.v.
WILLIS, WILLIAM, of Dorchester County, aet. about 52, dep. between Nov 11, 1746 and May 27, 1752. {DOLR 14 Old 658}
WILLMOTT, JOHN, see "Robert Willmott," q.v.
WILLMOTT, ROBERT, of Baltimore County, aet. 36, dep. Oct 31, 1763, mentioned his father John Willmott. {BALR B#N:184}

WILLOBY, ANDREW, of Dorchester County, aet. 65, dep. between Jun 11, 1745 and Oct 30, 1745. {DOLR 12 Old 233}
WILLOBY, EDWARD, of Dorchester County, aet. 62, dep. between Jun 17, 1732 and Jun 24, 1732, mentioned the bounded trees of *Hannah's Choice* marked by John Gray at the taking up of said tract. {DOLR 9 Old 60} See "Daniel Frazier" and "Edward Willibee," q.v.
WILLOBY, WILLIAM, see "Charles Wheeler," q.v.
WILLOCY (WILLOCIE), PHILLIP, of Prince George's County, aet. 68, dep. Jun 26, 1734, mentioned Col. James Haddock. {PGLR T:127} Philip Willoce, aet. 73, dep. Apr 13, 1738 in Charles County. {CHLR T#2:466} Philip Willocy (Willocee), aet. 75, dep. 1740. {PGLR Y:234} Phillip Wilocy, aet. 84, dep. Mar 15, 1747/8, stated that about 15 or 16 years ago Col. Thomas Truman Greenfield showed him the bounds of Henry Truman and Edward Truman's land. {PGLR BB:492} Philip Willocy, aet. 88, dep. Mar 26, 1753, mentioned old Samuel Warring about 50 or 60 years ago. {PGLR NN:282} Aet. 102, dep. Jun 23, 1757, stated that about 50 years ago he saw Samuel Waring, grandfather of the present Samuel Waring, who married a daughter of Arter Ludford. {PGLR PP:13, pt. 2}
WILLOUGHBY, EDWARD, of Dorchester County, aet. near 70, dep. between May 17, 1740 and Jun 2, 1740, mentioned his father William Willoughby and when he (Edward) was about 15 years old they lived about 2 miles from *Sharp* and *The Gore* at the plantation where William Ross now dwells. {DOLR 12 Old 131} Aet. 75, dep. Dec 29, 1744, stated that he was shown the bounds of *Sharp's Point* where Daniel Clark lived when he, Henry Davis, and William Killman were boys. {DOLR 12 Old 140} See "Daniel Frasher," q.v.
WILLOUGHBY, WILLIAM, of Dorchester County, aet. 86, dep. Mar 22, 1709/10. {DOLR 6 Old 221} See "Edward Willoughby," q.v.
WILLS, THOMAS, of Charles County, n.a., dep. 1658, mentioned Elizabeth Robins, wife of Robert Robins, of New Towne. {ARMD 41:50-51}
WILLSON, EDWARD, of Prince George's County, aet. 38, dep. Sep 22, 1730. {PGLR Q:156}
WILLSON, JAMES, of Dorchester County, Quaker, aet. 52, dep. between Mar 12, 1744/5 and Aug 5, 1745. {DOLR 12 Old 242}
WILLSON, JAMES, of Talbot County, aet. 37, dep. between Jun 14, 1729 and Jul 17, 1729. {DOLR 8 Old 432} James Willson, Quaker, aet. about 71, dep. between Aug 14, 1764 and Aug 13, 1765, mentioned Richard Foster, son of Richard Foster, about 60 years ago. {DOLR 20 Old 237}
WILLSON, JAMES, see "James Wilson" and "John Harris," q.v.
WILLSON, JOHN, of Prince George's County, aet. 55, dep. Nov 20, 1769. {PGLR AA#2:202}
WILLSON, JOSEPH, see "John Harris," q.v.
WILLSON, LANSLETT, of Prince George's County, aet. 35, dep. Mar 10, 1735/6, mentioned his father Thomas Wilson (Willson) about 20 years ago. {PGLR T:279}

WILLSON, THOMAS, of Dorchester County, aet. 52, dep. between Mar 14, 1769 and Apr 9, 1770, mentioned his father Thomas Willson about 35 years ago in company with Thomas Coursey, a Nanticoke Indian, and Samuel Panquash, the Principle Nanticoke Indian, and sundry other persons. {DOLR 24 Old 9} Aet. 53, dep. between Mar 14, 1771 and Nov 13, 1771, mentioned John Kimmey (Kemmey) about 30 years ago, now deceased. {DOLR 25 Old 238}
WILLSON, THOMAS, of Talbot County, Quaker, aet. 38, dep. between Mar 12, 1744/5 and Aug 5, 1745. {DOLR 12 Old 242}
WILLSON, THOMAS, see "William Willson" and "Thomas Wilson" and "John Harris," q.v.
WILLSON, WILLIAM, of Dorchester County, aet. 51, dep. between Mar 14, 1771 and Nov 13, 1771, mentioned his father Thomas Willson, Thomas Ryall, Daniel Hill, and Thomas Rowe, all deceased. {DOLR 25 Old 238}
WILLSON, WILLIAM, of Talbot County, Quaker, aet. 40, dep. between Mar 12, 1744/5 and Aug 5, 1745. {DOLR 12 Old 242}
WILLSON, WILLIAM, see "John Harris," q.v.
WILMER, ROSE (Mrs.), of Kent County, aet. 40, dep. 1762. {KELR DD#1:238}
WILMER, SIMON, of Kent County, aet. 25, dep. 1775. {KELR DD#5:133}
WILMER, SIMON, of Kent County, aet. 44 or 45, dep. May 22, 1732. {KELR JS#16:246, 250} Aet. about 49, dep. Dec 4, 1735. {KELR JS#18:199} Aet. not given, dep. Jun 21, 1740. {KELR JS#23:41}
WILMER, WILLIAM, of Kent County, aet. 35, dep. 1746. {KELR JS#25:327} Aet. 37, dep. 1748. {KELR JS#26:141} Aet. 58, dep. 1769. {KELR DD#3:195}
WILMOT, JOANE, of Charles County, n.a., dep. Nov 4, 1663. {CHLR B:203}
WILSON, ABRAHAM, of Prince George's County, aet. 32, dep. Jun 26, 1734. {PGLR T:127}
WILSON, EDWARD, of Prince George's County, aet. 50, dep. between Mar 24, 1745/6 and Mar 26, 1747, mentioned his father (not named) and Capt. Archibald Edmonston about 30 years ago. {PGLR BB:196} Aet. 55, dep. Nov 18, 1748. {PGLR BB:698}
WILSON, ELISABETH, of Charles County, n.a., dep. Jul 30, 1663. {CHLR B:143}
WILSON, GEORGE, of St. Mary's County, n.a., dep. Apr 18, 1661. {ARMD 41:447}
WILSON, GEORGE, of Kent County, aet. about 32, dep. Apr 13, 1731, mentioned his father James Wilson about 10 years ago and an inquiry by one Dawson of Talbot County about a tract belonging to Brian Omely. {KELR JS#16:127} Aet. about 43, dep. Sep 17, 1740, mentioned his father James Wilson, John Cole and father Peter Cole, and Daniel Pearce, all now deceased. {KELR JS#23:116} Aet. about 43, dep. Jan 21, 1740/1, mentioned his father James Wilson told him that one Dopson married Bryan Omely's daughter. {KELR JS#23:182}
WILSON, GEORGE, of Kent County, aet. about 34, dep. Apr 3, 1759. {KEEJ - Thomas Harris folder}
WILSON, JAMES, of Kent County, aet. about 67, dep. Apr 13, 1731, stated that one Dawson came up here from Talbot County about 30 years ago to see a tract

of land that belonged to Bryan Omely which he was about to buy of one of his sons who married one of Brian Omely's daughters. {KELR JS#16:128}

WILSON, JAMES, of Prince George's County, aet. 44, dep. Jul 29, 1754. {PGLR RR:201}

WILSON, JAMES, of Talbot County, Quaker, aet. 77, dep. affirmed in May, 1771, stated that David Rogers, of Talbot County, now deceased, by his first wife had issue John, David, and Mary Rogers, plus another son (not named) who died young, and he (Rogers) married second to a wife (not named) who survived him; some time after 1708 the widow Rogers married Henry Martin, of Talbot County; William Turner married Mary Rogers, daughter of said David; John Rogers, son of said David, died unmarried and without heirs; David Rogers, son of David, left Talbot County and died unmarried between 1719 and 1724; William Turner and wife Mary (Rogers) had children William, Edward, Gilbert, and Anne Turner; the said William Turner (Jr.) left the province many years earlier, settled in Carolina, and was living 12 months earlier *[sic]*; Gilbert and Edward died in Carolina; Anne Turner, daughter of William and Mary, married John Atkinson or Hatcheson of Queen Anne's County; David Turner died without issue. {QAEJ - John Moore folder} Aet. in his 78th year, dep. between Nov 12, 1771 and Dec 17, 1771. {DOLR 26 Old 34}

WILSON, JAMES, see "Daniel Turpin" and "James Hopkins" and "George Wilson" and "James Willson," q.v.

WILSON, JAMES, JR., of Dorchester County, Quaker, aet. about 47, dep. between Nov 14, 1769 and Nov 6, 1770. {DOLR 24 Old 308}

WILSON, JOHN, of Prince George's County, aet. 55, dep. Apr 8, 1769, mentioned William Clark, his (Clark's) father-in-law Samuel Duvall, and Edward Prather about 21 years ago, now deceased. {PGLR AA#2:201}

WILSON, JONA., of Charles County, aet. 38, dep. Jul 4, 1743. {CHLR O#2:617}

WILSON, JOSEPH, see "John Locker," q.v.

WILSON, JOSIAH, see "Richard Keene," q.v.

WILSON, LINGAN, of Prince George's County, aet. 23, dep. Jul 1, 1727. {PGLR M:221} Lingan Wilson, Sr., planter, aet. 67 or thereabouts, dep. Nov 13, 1769. {PGLR AA#2:134-135}

WILSON, MAJOR, see "Francis Marbury," q.v.

WILSON, ROBERT, of Charles County, aet. 30, dep. Jan 26, 1658/9, stated that Lucie Stratton said if she was with child she would lay it upon John Ward or Richard Smith. {CHLR A:35}

WILSON, THOMAS, of Frederick County, aet. 48, dep. Apr 1, 1768, mentioned Humphrey Hazeldine about 20 years ago. {FRLR L:519}

WILSON, THOMAS, of Dorchester County, aet. 53, dep. between Mar 14, 1771 and Nov 13, 1771, mentioned his father Thomas Wilson, William Wall, and John Maughan, all deceased. {DOLR 25 Old 238}

WILSON, THOMAS, see "Thomas Willson" and "Daniel Turpin" and "Hugh Tomlinson" and "Lanslett Willson," q.v.

WILSON, WILLIAM, of Prince George's County, aet. 38, dep. Jul 16, 1734, mentioned Ann Brown, widow of Jacob Brown. {PGLR T:155}

WILSON, WILLIAM, of Talbot County, Quaker, aet. 68, dep. between Nov 12, 1771 and Dec 17, 1771, mentioned Henry Ennalls, son of Henry Ennalls, late County Surveyor, about 35 years ago. {DOLR 26 Old 34}

WILSTEAD, THOMAS, of Prince George's County, aet. 34, dep. Apr 26, 1735. {PGLR T:253}

WINCHESTER, ISAAC, of Queen Anne's County, aet. 40, dep. Sep, 1770. {QAEJ - Henry Carter folder}

WINDOWS, HENRY, of Dorchester County, aet. 53, dep. between Nov 14, 1752 and Jun 13, 1753, stated that he was shown the bounds of *Langrell's Chance* about 20 years ago by Charles Dean, late of Somerset County, deceased, and about 16 years ago by Moses Lord, of Dorchester County, now deceased. {DOLR 14 Old 709}

WINDSOR, IGNATIUS, of Charles County, aet. 23, dep. Oct 8, 1742. {CHLR O#2:469}

WINDSOR, JARVIS, of Prince George's County, aet. 30, dep. Jul 1, 1726. {PGLR M:30}

WINDSOR (WINSER), JARVIS, of Prince George's County, aet. 73, dep. Jun 25, 1724. {PGLR I:592}

WINDSOR, THOMAS, of Charles County, aet. 44, dep. May 22, 1733. {CHLR R#2:334} Aet. 53, dep. Jan 9, 1743/4. {CHLR O#2:701} See "Henry Acton," q.v.

WINE, FRANCIS, of Charles County, aet. 30, dep. Jun 13, 1665. {CHLR B:237}

WINFIELD, WILLIAM, of Frederick County, n.a., dep. Apr 13, 1767, stated that he was a chain carrier in the survey of *Williams Intention* for Christopher Kitteman (no date was given, but 1740 was noted in Nathaniel Wickham's deposition). {FRLR K:1353}

WING, ROBERT, see "James Peterkin," q.v.

WINGATE, ANGELO, see "Robert Wingate," q.v.

WINGATE, PHILLIP, of Dorchester County, aet. 62, dep. between Jun 14, 1743 and Aug 1, 1743. {DOLR 12 Old 167} Aet. about 65, dep. between Mar 12, 1744/5 and Aug 4, 1745. {DOLR 12 Old 228} Phillip Wingate, Sr., aet. about 86, dep. between Jun 8, 1762 and Jan 29, 1763, mentioned James Ensley and William Ensley, sons of Andrew Ensley, deceased. {DOLR 18 Old 339} See "Timothy Macnemar" and "Robert Scott," q.v.

WINGATE, ROBERT, of Dorchester County, aet. 63, dep. between Mar 8, 1768 and Aug 5, 1769, mentioned his brothers Angelo Wingate and Thomas Wingate. {DOLR 23 Old 336}

WINGATE, THOMAS, see "Robert Wingate" and "Robert Scott" and "Charles Thompson," q.v.

WINN, JOHN, SR., of Charles County, aet. 65, dep. Apr 30, 1745. {CHLR Z#2:337}

WINN, TEAGAR, see "Elizabeth Greene," q.v.

WINSMORE, JOHN, see "John Stevens," q.v.

WINTER, WALTER, of Charles County, aet. 60, dep. Oct 5, 1732. {CHLR R#2:241} See "William Winter," q.v.
WINTER, WILLIAM, of Charles County, aet. 46, dep. Jan 20, 1726/7. {CHLR P#2:491}
WINTER, WILLIAM, of Charles County, aet. 46, dep. Dec 31, 1759. {CHLR I#3:428} Aet. 48, dep. Apr 13, 1761, mentioned his father Walter Winter. {CHLR K#3:298} Aet. 51, dep. between May 15, 1764 and Aug 27, 1764. {CHLR N#3:60}
WINTERS, WALTER, of Prince George's County, aet. 58, dep. between Nov 11, 1729 and Mar 26, 1730. {PGLR M:567}
WINTERSELL, THOMAS, see "John Spry," q.v.
WISE, MARY, see "Edward Brawner" and "John Franklin," q.v.
WISE, RICHARD, see "Edward Brawner," q.v.
WISE, WIDOW, see "William Nelson," q.v.
WISEMAN, JOHN, of St. Mary's County, n.a., dep. Jan 4, 1665/6. {ARMD 49:569} Aet. not given, dep. Apr 23, 1691. {ARMD 8:247}
WITHERINGTON, THOMAS, of Charles County, aet. 44, dep. Mar 9, 1775. {CHLR X#3:9}
WITHERS, SAMUEL, see "John Salter," q.v.
WITTONKA, JOHN, see "Indian Sam Isaac," q.v.
WOGG, TEAGUE, see "Indian Sam Isaac," q.v.
WOOD, ABRAHAM, of Charles County, aet. 34, dep. May 3, 1742. {CHLR O#2:381} See "James Ryon," q.v.
WOOD, HENRY, of Prince George's County, aet. 38, dep. Mar 10, 1769, mentioned Edward Lanham about 13 years ago, now deceased. {PGLR AA#2:151-152} Aet. 44, dep. Nov 14, 1774, mentioned Anthony Sims about 19 or 20 years ago. {PGLR CC#2:59}
WOOD, JAMES, see "John Wood" and "James Dunning," q.v.
WOOD, JOHN, of Charles County, n.a., dep. Jul 9, 1662, mentioned William Empson and wife (not named). {CHLR A:230}
WOOD, JOHN, of Prince George's County, aet. 43, dep. Mar 9, 1772, mentioned James Wood and John Burk about 8 or 10 years ago, both now deceased. {PGLR BB#3:79}
WOOD, JOHN, see "Oliver Harris" and "John Dunn," q.v.
WOOD, PETER, of Charles County, aet. 53, dep. Jun 5, 1752. {CHLR B#3:60}
WOOD, THOMAS, of Prince George's County, aet. 71, dep. Jul 2, 1764. {PGLR TT:372}
WOOD, THOMAS, SR., of Prince George's County, aet. 63, dep. Mar 24, 1759. {PGLR PP:275, pt. 2}
WOODALL, JESPER, of Dorchester County, aet. 39, dep. between Aug 10, 1773 and Feb 25, 1774, mentioned Mark Nicolls, Stephen Sherwin, James Sherwin, and Andrew Russell about 12 to 14 years ago, all now deceased. {DOLR 27 Old 267}

WOODALL, JOHN, of Queen Anne's County, aet. about 48, dep. Mar, 1746, stated that 5 or 6 years earlier he heard his mother mention her husband (names not given). {QAEJ - Benjamin Tasker folder} See "Juliana Browning," q.v.

WOODEN, HENRY, of Kent Island, Queen Anne's County, aet. 42, dep. Sep, 1733. {QAEJ - James Hutchens folder}

WOODLAND, BLACKLEDGE, of Kent County, n.a., dep. Oct 12, 1731, mentioned his aged father-in-law William Jones about 13 years ago. {KELR JS#16:220} Aet. about 49, dep. Mar 16, 1756, mentioned his brother Joseph Woodland about 20 years ago. {KELR JS#28:224}

WOODLAND, JOSEPH, see "Blackledge Woodland," q.v.

WOODLAND, RICHARD, of Dorchester County, aet. 27, dep. between Jun 17, 1734 and Sep 19, 1734, mentioned his father-in-law John Stafford. {DOLR 9 Old 249} Richard Woodlon, aet. 38, dep. between Mar 12, 1744/5 and Aug 4, 1745. {DOLR 12 Old 228}

WOODLAND, WILLIAM, of Dorchester County, aet. 25, dep. between Aug 12, 1760 and Dec 6, 1760. {DOLR 17 Old 268}

WOODMAN, SARAH, see "Eleanor Fearson," q.v.

WOODROOFE, ANN, see "Daniell Norris," q.v.

WOODROOFE, JOHN, see "Daniell Norris," q.v.

WOODROOFE, MARY, see "Daniell Norris," q.v.

WOODROOFE, THOMAS, see "Daniell Norris," q.v.

WOODROOFE, WILLIAM, see "Daniell Norris," q.v.

WOODS, JOHN, of Prince George's County, aet. 46, dep. Jun 8, 1732. {PGLR Y:327}

WOODWARD, BENJAMIN, see "Thomas Brannock, Sr.," q.v.

WOODWARD, ELIZABETH, of Dorchester County, aet. 50, dep. Nov 7, 1759, stated that she was well acquainted with Mary Earl, since Mary Sales, and now Mary Matthews; about 34 or 35 years ago Mary Earl came to the house of her (Elizabeth's) father David Melvill and delivered a baby girl she named Betz or Elizabeth out of wedlock; she (Elizabeth) always understood that Betty Conner was this same person; Mary further stated that the baby's father was George Sales. {TALR 19:7}

WOODWARD, HENRY, of Charles County, aet. 49, dep. Mar 27, 1758, stated his father was John Woodward and his mother (not named) was a daughter of Gerrard Brown and she married first to Richard Newton and had three sons, the eldest of whom was John Newton, and after Richard died she married John Woodward; further stated his grandmother (not named) was the widow of Gerrard Brown and after he died she married Dr. John Cornish; also stated his (Henry's) mother had been dead about 23 years and his father had been dead about 14 years. {CHLR H#3:432} Aet. 52, dep. Aug 11, 1760 and May 23, 1761. {CHLR K#3:4, 223} Aet. 53, dep. Nov 8, 1762. {CHLR M#3:123} Aet. 60, dep. Aug 5, 1768. {CHLR Q#3:258} Aet. 66, dep. between Jul 11, 1772 and Oct 6, 1772. {CHLR U#3:164}

WOODWARD, JANE, see "James Johnson" and "John Franklin" and "Mason Williams," q.v.

WOODWARD, JOHN, see "John Franklin" and "Mason Williams" and "Henry Woodward," q.v.

WOODWARD, JOSEPH, SR., see "Joseph Merchant," q.v.

WOODWARD, RICHARD, see "Christopher Carroll," q.v.

WOODWARD, WIDOW, see "Edward Wright," q.v.

WOODYARD, JOHN, of Charles County, aet. 44, dep. Nov 5, 1719, mentioned John Sanders, son of Matthew Sanders. {Charles County Land Commissions 1:67-68} Aet. 44, dep. May 31, 1721. {CHLR M#2:123} Aet. 55, dep. Oct 5, 1731. {CHLR R#2:44}

WOODYARD, RICHARD, of Charles County, aet. 43, dep. Mar 15, 1725. {CHLR P#2:298}

WOODYARD, RICHARD, of Charles County, aet. 45, dep. Apr 22, 1771. {CHLR T#3:614} Aet. 45, dep. Apr 15, 1772. {CHLR U#3:275}

WOOLCHURCH, ELIZABETH, of Talbot County, n.a., dep. Jun 17, 1673. {ARMD 54:568}

WOOLEN, THOMAS, of Dorchester County, aet. 65, dep. between Jun 14, 1743 and Aug 4, 1743. {DOLR 12 Old 164}

WOOLEY, CHARLES, of Charles County, aet. 25, dep. Jun 11, 1669/70. {CHLR D#1:119}

WOOLFORD, JAMES, of Dorchester County, aet. 50, dep. between Jun 13, 1730 and Sep 10, 1730. {DOLR 8 Old 404} Capt. James Woolford, aet. 53, dep. between Mar 13, 1732 and Nov 14, 1733, stated that the bounds of John Stevens' land called *Nothingworth* were shown to him about 23 years ago by John Willis. {DOLR 9 Old 135} James Woollford, aet. 59, dep. between Aug 12, 1740 and Sep 13, 1740, mentioned the survey of *Daniel's Choice* about 40 years ago. {DOLR 12 Old 116} Aet. about 61, dep. between Nov 10, 1741 and Mar 10, 1747. {DOLR 14 Old 200} See "John Woolford" and "Roger Woolford," q.v.

WOOLFORD, JOHN, of Dorchester County, aet. about 63, dep. between Mar 13, 1764 and Nov 16, 1764, stated that he was shown the bounded tree of *Ashbourn* about 40 years ago by his father James Woollford, now deceased. {DOLR 19 Old 434}

WOOLFORD, ROGER, of Dorchester County, aet. about 40, dep. between Mar 8, 1763 and May 10, 1763. {DOLR 18 Old 439} Aet. about 49, dep. between Mar 13, 1764 and Nov 16, 1764, mentioned his father James Woolford about 35 years ago. {DOLR 19 Old 434}

WOOLFORD, ROGER, of Dorchester County, aet. 44, dep. between Mar 12, 1771 and Apr 22, 1771, mentioned James Busick, deceased, and his son James Busick. {DOLR 26 Old 42} Aet. 46, dep. between Aug 10, 1773 and Oct 23, 1773. {DOLR 27 Old 38}

WOOLFORD, ROGER, see "John Jones," q.v.

WOOLFORD, STEVENS, of Dorchester County, aet. 41, dep. between Mar 12, 1771 and Apr 22, 1771. {DOLR 26 Old 42}

285

WOOLFORD, THOMAS, of Dorchester County, aet. about 33, dep. between Mar 13, 1732 and Nov 14, 1733. {DOLR 9 Old 135} Aet. about 46, dep. between Nov 13, 1744 and Nov 10, 1748, mentioned his father (not named) and William Mills the Elder about 30 years ago. {DOLR 14 Old 315}

WOOLLING, JOHN, of Dorchester County, aet. about 50, dep. between Aug 13, 1747 and Sep 18, 1749. {DOLR 14 Old 463}

WOOLSEY, LINSEY, see "Thomas Richardson," q.v.

WOOTTERS, RICHARD, of Queen Anne's County, aet. 82, dep. Aug, 1752. {QAEJ - Sarah Starkey folder}

WOOTTON, TURNER, of Prince George's County, aet. 52, dep. Nov 17, 1748. {PGLR BB:695} Turner Wooton, n.a., dep. Apr 18, 1749. {PGLR BB:701}

WORGAN, MATHIAS, of Charles County, n.a., dep. Feb 5, 1663/4 and Mar 8, 1663/4. {CHLR B:277, ARMD 53:461}

WORLAND, JOHN, of Charles County, aet. 50, dep. Mar 11, 1737/8. {CHLR T#2:424} Aet. 58, dep. Sep 24, 1744. {CHLR Y#2:187}

WORLEY, JOHN, see "Sarah Birk," q.v.

WORMELL, EDMOND, of St. Mary's County, gentleman, n.a., dep. Dec 3, 1651, stated that Mrs. Katherine Hunt, now deceased, made her mark on her will last July 6th. {ARMD 10:113}

WORMLEY, RALPH, see "Thomas Chapman," q.v.

WORRELL, SIMON, of Kent County, aet. 39, dep. 1769. {KELR DD#3:199}

WORTHINGTON, JOHN, see "James Sappington" and "John Riley" and "Edward McCann," q.v.

WOTHEN, HUDSON, see "Hudson Wathen," q.v.

WRIGHT, EDWARD, of Somerset County, aet. 95, dep. between Jun 16, 1733 and Feb 25, 1733/4. {DOLR 9 Old 149}

WRIGHT, EDWARD, of Dorchester County, aet. 40, dep. between Nov 13, 1739 and Apr 4, 1740, mentioned *Woodward's Content* and the bounds of the widow Woodward's land about 13 years ago. {DOLR 12 Old 109}

WRIGHT, EDWARD, see "John Carter" and "Solomon Wright," q.v.

WRIGHT, HENRY, of Dorchester County, aet. 40, dep. between Jun 11, 1751 and Oct 14, 1751. {DOLR 14 Old 552}

WRIGHT, HENRY, of Prince George's County, aet. 42, dep. Mar 11, 1745/6. {PGLR BB:6}

WRIGHT, JOHN, see "Arthur Foreman," q.v.

WRIGHT, JOSEPH, of Charles County, aet. 46, dep. May 29, 1773. {CHLR U#3:271}

WRIGHT, NATHAN, of Queen Anne's County, aet. 53, dep. Sep, 1766. {QAEJ - John and Sophia Downes folder}

WRIGHT, ROBERT NORREST, see "Barton Colins," q.v.

WRIGHT, ROGER, see "William Payne," q.v.

WRIGHT, SOLOMON, of Dorchester County, aet. 67, dep. between Mar 14, 1769 and Apr 9, 1770, stated that his father Edward Wright was commissioned about 50 years ago by the Governor and Council to survey the Indian land and he

believed "Mary Cratcher lived under the Indians by a lease." {DOLR 24 Old 9}
Solomon Wright, of Somerset County, aet. 67, dep. between Jun 14, 1768 and Jun 14, 1769, mentioned Thomas Boozman, Thomas Hackett, Daniel Hill, John Brumwell (son of Robert Brumwell), Dutton Marshall, and Robert Watson about 40 years ago, all now deceased. {DOLR 23 Old 295} See "William Eccleston," q.v.

WRIGHT, THOMAS, of Charles County, aet. 48, dep. May 29, 1729. {CHLR Q#2:277} Aet. 49, dep. Mar 2, 1730/1. {CHLR Q#2:474} Aet. 50, dep. Oct 5, 1731. {CHLR Q#2:44} Aet. 62, dep. Sep 12, 1743. {CHLR O#2:667} Aet. 64, dep. Jun 3, 1745. {CHLR Z#2:346} Aet. 65, dep. Aug 5, 1745. {CHLR Z#2:318} Aet. 71, dep. Nov 2, 1752. {CHLR B#3:212} Aet. 76, dep. Dec 13, 1757. {CHLR H#3:123}

WRIGHT, THOMAS HYNSON, of Queen Anne's County, aet. about 50, dep. Feb, 1738. {QAEJ - Alexander Toulson folder). Aet. about 50, dep. Apr, 1747. {QAEJ - Elizabeth Barnes folder}

WRIGHT, WILLIAM, see "William Payne" and "Robert Clipsham," q.v.

WRIOTHESLEY, HENRY, of Anne Arundel County, n.a., dep. 1696. {ARMD 20:563}

WROTH, RICHARD, of St. Mary's County, aet. 32 or thereabouts, dep. Apr 29, 1664, stated that about Jan, 1662, John Sheppard, mariner, sold a maid servant by the name of Sarah Jones to Thomas Bennitt. {ARMD 49:210}

WROUGHTON, THOMAS, of Dorchester County, aet. 69, dep. between Aug 12, 1760 and Dec 6, 1760. {DOLR 17 Old 268} Thomas Wrotten, n.a., dep. between Mar 9, 1773 and Feb 5, 1774, mentioned old Lewis Griffith about 20 years ago. {DOLR 27 Old 115} See "Thomas Rotten," q.v.

WYAT, JAMES, see "Rebecca Brooks," q.v.

WYATT, JOHN, of Queen Anne's County, aet. about 42, dep. July, 1758. {QAEJ - Henry Callister folder}

WYNN, JOHN, of Prince George's County, aet. 51, dep. Mar 9, 1772, mentioned Francis Green about 12 years ago, now deceased. {PGLR BB#3:79} See "Richard Blew," q.v.

YATES, CHARLES, of Charles County, n.a., dep. 1720, mentioned his father Robert Yates, deceased. {Charles County Land Commissions 1:83} Aet. 44, dep. Jun 18, 1736. {CHLR T#2:228} Aet. 52, dep. May 7, 1744. {CHLR Y#2:17}

YATES, GEORGE, see "Ninian Beall," q.v.

YATES, ROBERT (major), of Charles County, aet. 30, dep. 1720, mentioned his father Robert Yates, deceased. {Charles County Land Commissions 1:83} Major Robert Yates, aet. about 40, dep. May 19, 1725. {CHLR P#2:41} Aet. 53, dep. Feb 17, 1742/3. {CHLR O#2:507} See "Charles Yates," q.v.

YEARLY, WILLIAM, of Kent County, aet. about 65, dep. Jul 19, 1748. {KELR JS#26:144} Aet. about 70, dep. Nov 17, 1757. {KELR JS#28:392}

YOULL, THOMAS, of St. Mary's County, n.a., dep. 1649. {ARMD 4:540}

YOUNG, JACOB, of Baltimore County, planter, aet. 55, dep. Feb 26, 1766. {BALR B#P:301} Aet. 61, dep. Jun 15, 1772. {BALR AL#I:202} See "William Blankinstein," q.v.

YOUNG, JAMES, of Prince George's County, aet. 54, dep. Nov 28, 1728. {PGLR M:346} James Young, Sr., aet. 75, dep. May 31, 1750. {PGLR NN:59} Aet. 80 or thereabouts, dep. Mar 26, 1756. {PGLR NN:479}

YOUNG, JAMES, JR., of Prince George's County, aet. 44, dep. Mar 26, 1756. {PGLR NN:480} James Young, aet. 51, dep. Nov 6, 1762. {PGLR TT:125}

YOUNG, JOHN, of Queen Anne's County, aet. 53, dep. Apr, 1730. {QAEJ - Ernault Hawkins folder}

YOUNG, SAMUEL, see "George Elbridge," q.v.

YOUNG, WILLIAM, prob. of St. Mary's or Calvert County, n.a., dep. 1658. {ARMD 41:167} Aet. 31, dep. Mar 11, 1661. {ARMD 41:553}

YOUNG, WILLIAM (colonel), of Baltimore County, aet. 50, dep. Mar 3, 1764. {BALR B#M:373}

YOUNGER, HUMPHREY, of Kent County, aet. about 58, dep. Sep 10, 1735, mentioned Giles Porter and son John Porter about 30 years ago. {KELR JS#18:194}

Other books by the author:

A Closer Look at St. John's Parish Registers [Baltimore County, Maryland], 1701-1801

A Collection of Maryland Church Records

A Guide to Genealogical Research in Maryland: 5th Edition, Revised and Enlarged

Abstracts of the Ledgers and Accounts of the Bush Store and Rock Run Store, 1759-1771

Abstracts of the Orphans Court Proceedings of Harford County, 1778-1800

Abstracts of Wills, Harford County, Maryland, 1800-1805

Baltimore City [Maryland] Deaths and Burials, 1834-1840

Baltimore County, Maryland, Overseers of Roads, 1693-1793

Bastardy Cases in Baltimore County, Maryland, 1673-1783

Bastardy Cases in Harford County, Maryland, 1774-1844

Bible and Family Records of Harford County, Maryland Families: Volume V

Children of Harford County: Indentures and Guardianships, 1801-1830

Colonial Delaware Soldiers and Sailors, 1638-1776

Colonial Families of the Eastern Shore of Maryland
Volumes 5, 6, 7, 8, 9, 11, 12, 13, 14, and 16

Colonial Maryland Soldiers and Sailors, 1634-1734

Dr. John Archer's First Medical Ledger, 1767-1769, Annotated Abstracts

Early Anglican Records of Cecil County

Early Harford Countians, Individuals Living in Harford County, Maryland in Its Formative Years
Volume 1: A to K, Volume 2: L to Z, and Volume 3: Supplement

Harford County Taxpayers in 1870, 1872 and 1883

Harford County, Maryland Divorce Cases, 1827-1912: An Annotated Index

Heirs and Legatees of Harford County, Maryland, 1774-1802

Heirs and Legatees of Harford County, Maryland, 1802-1846

Inhabitants of Baltimore County, Maryland, 1763-1774

Inhabitants of Cecil County, Maryland, 1649-1774

Inhabitants of Harford County, Maryland, 1791-1800

Inhabitants of Kent County, Maryland, 1637-1787

Joseph A. Pennington & Co., Havre De Grace, Maryland Funeral Home Records:
Volume II, 1877-1882, 1893-1900

Maryland Bible Records, Volume 1: Baltimore and Harford Counties

Maryland Bible Records, Volume 2: Baltimore and Harford Counties

Maryland Bible Records, Volume 3: Carroll County

Maryland Bible Records, Volume 4: Eastern Shore

Maryland Deponents, 1634-1799

Maryland Deponents: Volume 3, 1634-1776

Maryland Public Service Records, 1775-1783: A Compendium of Men and Women of
Maryland Who Rendered Aid in Support of the American Cause against
Great Britain during the Revolutionary War

Marylanders to Carolina: Migration of Marylanders to
North Carolina and South Carolina prior to 1800

Marylanders to Kentucky, 1775-1825
Methodist Records of Baltimore City, Maryland: Volume 1, 1799-1829
Methodist Records of Baltimore City, Maryland: Volume 2, 1830-1839
Methodist Records of Baltimore City, Maryland: Volume 3, 1840-1850
(East City Station)
More Maryland Deponents, 1716-1799
More Marylanders to Carolina: Migration of Marylanders to
North Carolina and South Carolina prior to 1800
More Marylanders to Kentucky, 1778-1828
Outpensioners of Harford County, Maryland, 1856-1896
Presbyterian Records of Baltimore City, Maryland, 1765-1840
Quaker Records of Baltimore and Harford Counties, Maryland, 1801-1825
Quaker Records of Northern Maryland, 1716-1800
Quaker Records of Southern Maryland, 1658-1800
Revolutionary Patriots of Anne Arundel County, Maryland
Revolutionary Patriots of Baltimore Town and Baltimore County, 1775-1783
Revolutionary Patriots of Calvert and St. Mary's Counties, Maryland, 1775-1783
Revolutionary Patriots of Caroline County, Maryland, 1775-1783
Revolutionary Patriots of Cecil County, Maryland
Revolutionary Patriots of Charles County, Maryland, 1775-1783
Revolutionary Patriots of Delaware, 1775-1783
Revolutionary Patriots of Dorchester County, Maryland, 1775-1783
Revolutionary Patriots of Frederick County, Maryland, 1775-1783
Revolutionary Patriots of Harford County, Maryland, 1775-1783
Revolutionary Patriots of Kent and Queen Anne's Counties
Revolutionary Patriots of Lancaster County, Pennsylvania
Revolutionary Patriots of Maryland, 1775-1783: A Supplement
Revolutionary Patriots of Maryland, 1775-1783: Second Supplement
Revolutionary Patriots of Montgomery County, Maryland, 1776-1783
Revolutionary Patriots of Prince George's County, Maryland, 1775-1783
Revolutionary Patriots of Talbot County, Maryland, 1775-1783
Revolutionary Patriots of Worcester and Somerset Counties, Maryland, 1775-1783
Revolutionary Patriots of Washington County, Maryland, 1776-1783
St. George's (Old Spesutia) Parish, Harford County, Maryland:
Church and Cemetery Records, 1820-1920
St. John's and St. George's Parish Registers, 1696-1851
Survey Field Book of David and William Clark in Harford County, Maryland, 1770-1812
The Crenshaws of Kentucky, 1800-1995
The Delaware Militia in the War of 1812
Union Chapel United Methodist Church Cemetery Tombstone Inscriptions,
Wilna, Harford County, Maryland